AMERICAN CULTURE

American Culture is an anthology of primary texts from American history and culture comprising examples from advertising, autobiographies, essays, fiction, historical documents, interviews, journalism, oral histories, orations and rhetoric, poetry, political addresses, sermons, songs, and speeches. In sections covering topics such as American Indians, women's studies, geography, art, music and popular culture, and ideology, the volume brings together a cross-section of materials from 1630 to the present day.

Edited by academics who are highly experienced in the study and teaching of American studies across a wide range of institutions, the book provides:

- texts that introduce aspects of American society in a historical perspective
- primary sources and images that can be used as the basis for illustration, analysis, and discussion
- and linking texts which stress themes rather than offering a simple chronological survey.

Up-to-date and comprehensive, this new edition of *American Culture* is a perfect introduction and resource for those interested in American studies.

Anders Breidlid is Professor of International Education and former Dean of Oslo University College. He is the co-editor with Øyvind T. Gulliksen of *Aspects of American Civilization* (1983) and the author of *Resistance and Consciousness in Kenya and South Africa* (2002).

Fredrik Chr. Brøgger is Professor of American Studies at the University of Tromsø. He is the author of *Culture, Language, Text: Culture Studies within the Study of English as a Foreign Language* (1992).

Øyvind T. Gulliksen is Professor of American Literature and Culture at Telemark University College, Bø i Telemark. He has published *Twofold Identities: Norwegian–American Contributions to Midwestern Literature* (2004).

Torbjørn Sirevåg is Professor Emeritus of American Civilization at the University of Oslo and the Norwegian School of Management (BI). He is the author of *The Eclipse of the New Deal and the Fall of Vice-President Wallace, 1944* (1985). He was also Director-General of Science Policy for the Norwegian Government.

AMERICAN CULTURE

An anthology
Second edition

Edited by
Anders Breidlid, Fredrik Chr. Brøgger,
Øyvind T. Gulliksen and Torbjørn Sirevåg

Routledge
Taylor & Francis Group

LONDON AND NEW YORK

First published 1996
by Routledge

Second edition published 2008
by Routledge
2 Park Square, Milton Park, Abingdon, Oxon OX14 4RN

Simultaneously published in the USA and Canada
by Routledge
711 Third Avenue, New York, NY 10017

Routledge is an imprint of the Taylor & Francis Group, an informa business

© 1996, 2008 Anders Breidlid, Fredrik Chr. Brøgger, Øyvind T. Gulliksen and Torbjørn Sirevåg for
selection and editorial matter; individual extracts © the contributors

Typeset in Baskerville by
Keystroke, 28 High Street, Tettenhall, Wolverhampton

British Library Cataloguing in Publication Data
A catalogue record for this book is available from the British Library

Library of Congress Cataloging in Publication Data
American culture: an anthology/edited by Anders Breidlid . . . [et. al.]. — 2nd ed.
    p. cm.
Includes bibliographical references and index.
1. United States—Civilization—Sources. I. Breidlid, Anders, 1947–
E169.1.A471976 2008
973—dc22   2007013951

ISBN10: 0–415–36092–7 (hbk)
ISBN10: 0–415–36093–5 (pbk)

ISBN13: 978–0–415–36092–0 (hbk)
ISBN13: 978–0–415–36093–7 (pbk)

CONTENTS

List of illustrations   xiii
Acknowledgments   xv

Introduction   1

1 AMERICAN INDIANS   5

    Introduction   6
  1 *Thomas Jefferson*   9
    "Confidential Message to Congress" (1803)
  2 *Tecumseh*   11
    "We All Belong to One Family" (1811)
  3 *Seattle*   13
    FROM "The Dead Are Not Powerless" (1854)
  4 *Helen Hunt Jackson*   14
    FROM *A Century of Dishonor* (1881)
  5 *US Congress*   16
    FROM The General Allotment Act (1887)
  6 *John Collier*   17
    "Full Indian Democracy" (1943)
  7 *Leslie Silko*   18
    "The Man to Send Rain Clouds" (1969)
  8 *Buffy Sainte-Marie*   21
    "My Country" (1971)
  9 *Studs Terkel*   23
    "Girl of the Golden West: Ramona Bennett" (1980)
 10 *Joy Harjo*   28
    "The Woman Hanging from the Thirteenth Floor Window" (1983)

2 IMMIGRATION   31

    Introduction   32
 11 *Emma Lazarus*   35
    "The New Colossus" (1883)

CONTENTS

12 *Henry James*   36
    FROM "The Inconceivable Alien" (1883)

13 *Abraham Cahan*   37
    "The Meeting" (1896)

14 *Mary Antin*   40
    FROM *The Promised Land* (1912)

15 *Owen Wister*   42
    FROM "Shall We Let the Cuckoos Crowd Us Out of Our Nest?" (1921)

16 *Edward Bok*   43
    FROM *The Americanization of Edward Bok* (1921)

17 *Ole E. Rølvaag*   45
    FROM "The Power of Evil in High Places" (1927)

18 *Oscar Handlin*   56
    FROM *The Uprooted* (1951)

19 *Al Santoli*   58
    FROM "Mojados (Wetbacks)" (1988)

20 *Arthur M. Schlesinger, Jr.*   62
    "E Pluribus Unum?" (1992)

3 AFRICAN AMERICANS   63

    Introduction   64
21 *Moses Grandy*   66
    "The Auction Block" (pre-1860)

22 *Joseph Ingraham*   67
    "A Peep into a Slave-Mart" (pre-1860)

23 *Sojourner Truth*   67
    "Ain't I a Woman?" (1851)

24 *Abraham Lincoln*   68
    Final Emancipation Proclamation (1863)

25 *William DuBois*   70
    "This Double-Consciousness" (1903)
    FROM "Of the Faith of the Fathers" (1903)

26 *Gwendolyn Brooks*   75
    "We Real Cool" (1960)

27 *Martin Luther King, Jr.*   75
    "I Have a Dream" (1963)

28 *US Congress*   78
    The Civil Rights Act (1964)

29 *Malcolm X*   79
    FROM "The Ballot or the Bullet" (1965)
    FROM "The Black Man" (1965)

30 *Septima Clark*   82
    "Teach How Change Comes About" (pre-1987)

CONTENTS

4 WOMEN'S STUDIES   85

   Introduction   86
31 *Alexis de Tocqueville*   90
   "The Young Woman in the Character of a Wife" (1848)
32 *Seneca Falls Convention*   91
   Declaration of Sentiments and Resolutions (1848)
33 *Kate Chopin*   93
   "The Story of an Hour" (1894)
34 *Charlotte Perkins Gilman*   95
   FROM *Women and Economics* (1898)
35 *Meridel LeSueur*   96
   "Women on the Breadlines" (1932)
36 *Betty Friedan*   101
   "That Has No Name" (1963)
37 *Studs Terkel*   104
   "'Just a Housewife': Therese Carter" (1972)
38 *Marabel Morgan*   107
   "Admire Him" (1973)
39 *Merle Woo*   112
   FROM "Letter to Ma" (1980)
40 *US Supreme Court*   115
   Roe v. *Wade* (1973)

5 GOVERNMENT AND POLITICS   117

   Introduction   118
41 *Founding Fathers*   122
   FROM The Constitution of the United States (1787)
42 *James Madison*   129
   "The Union as a Safeguard against Domestic Faction and
   Insurrection" (1787)
43 *John Marshall*   134
   FROM *Marbury* v. *Madison* (1803)
44 *Thomas Jefferson*   137
   FROM "The Roots of Democracy" (1816)
45 *Andrew Jackson*   139
   FROM Proclamation to the People of South Carolina (1832)
46 *John Marshall Harlan*   141
   FROM Dissenting Opinion in *Plessy* v. *Ferguson* (1896)
47 *John F. Kennedy*   145
   First Inaugural Address (1961)
48 *Joe McGinnis*   147
   FROM *The Selling of the President* (1969)
49 *E. L. Doctorow*   149
   FROM "A Citizen Reads the Constitution" (1987)

50 *John Kenneth Galbraith*   152
    "The American Presidency: Going the Way of the Blacksmith?" (1988)

6 ECONOMY, ENTERPRISE, CLASS   155

  Introduction   156
51 *Andrew Jackson*   160
    "The Power of the Moneyed Interests" (1837)
52 *William Graham Sumner*   161
    FROM "The Forgotten Man" (1883)
53 *Andrew Carnegie*   162
    FROM *The Gospel of Wealth* (1900)
54 *Sinclair Lewis*   170
    FROM *Babbitt* (1922)
55 *Franklin D. Roosevelt*   172
    "Organized Money" (1936)
56 *Lyndon B. Johnson*   173
    FROM "The War on Poverty" (1964)
57 *Studs Terkel*   174
    FROM "Mike Lefevre" (Interview with a Steel Mill Worker, 1974)
58 *Steven VanderStaay*   176
    "Hell" (1992)
59 *Newt Gingrich*   178
    "Replacing the Welfare State with an Opportunity Society" (1995)
60 *Barbara Ehrenreich*   180
    FROM *Nickel and Dimed: On (Not) Getting By in America* (2001)

7 GEOGRAPHY, REGIONS, AND THE ENVIRONMENT   183

  Introduction   184
61 *Henry David Thoreau*   187
    "Fallen Leaves" (1862)
62 *Frederick Jackson Turner*   190
    FROM "The Significance of the Frontier in American History" (1893)
63 *F. Scott Fitzgerald*   196
    FROM "My Lost City" (1945)
64 *Christopher Isherwood*   201
    "California Is a Tragic Country" (1947)
65 *Aldo Leopold*   203
    "Thinking Like a Mountain" (1949)
66 *Peter L. Berger*   204
    "New York City 1976: A Signal of Transcendence" (1977)
67 *Joan Didion*   211
    "Marrying Absurd" (1979)
68 *Alice Walker*   213
    "The Black Writer and the Southern Experience" (1984)

CONTENTS

69 *Bill Holm*
    "Horizontal Grandeur" (1985)   216
70 *Barry Lopez*
    FROM *Arctic Dreams* (1986)   219

8 ART, FILM, MUSIC, AND POPULAR CULTURE   225

    Introduction   226
71 *Georgia O'Keeffe*   229
    To Alfred Stieglitz (1916)
72 *Bessie Smith*   230
    "Empty Bed Blues" (1928)
73 *Woody Guthrie*   231
    "This Land Is Your Land" (1944)
74 *Walt Disney*   231
    The Testimony of Walter E. Disney Before the House Committee
    on Un-American Activities (1947)
75 *Ralph Ellison*   237
    "As the Spirit Moves Mahalia" (1964)
76 *Stanley Kauffmann*   240
    "Little Big Man" (1970)
77 *Joan Didion*   242
    "Georgia O'Keeffe" (1979)
78 *Studs Terkel*   244
    FROM "Jill Robertson: Fantasia" (1982)
79 *Mikal Gilmore*   247
    FROM "Bruce Springsteen" (1987)
80 *Martin Scorsese, Paul Schrader, and Robert De Niro*   252
    FROM *"Taxi Driver"* (1992)

9 RELIGION   257

    Introduction   258
81 *John Winthrop*   261
    Letter to His Wife, Margaret (1630)
82 *Jonathan Edwards*   262
    FROM "The Christian Pilgrim" (1733)
83 *Ralph Waldo Emerson*   266
    FROM His Journals and Letters (1827–37)
84 *Anonymous*   268
    "Swing Low, Sweet Chariot" (pre-1860)
    "Go Down, Moses" (pre-1860)
85 *James Cardinal Gibbons*   269
    FROM "The Catholic Church and Labor" (1887)
86 *Will Herberg*   272
    FROM "The Three Religious Communities" (1955)

CONTENTS

87 *Flannery O'Connor*   276
    "Novelist and Believer" (1963)
88 *Martin Luther King, Jr.*   281
    "Letter from Birmingham Jail" (1963)
89 *Billy Graham*   292
    "The Unfinished Dream" (1970)
90 *Richard Rodriguez*   294
    "Credo" (1981)

10 EDUCATION   299

    Introduction   300
91 *Robert Coram*   303
    FROM "The Necessity of Compulsory Primary Education" (1791)
92 *John Dewey*   305
    "My Pedagogic Creed" (1897)
93 *Booker T. Washington*   308
    "A Harder Task Than Making Bricks Without Straw" (1901)
94 *Mary Antin*   312
    FROM *The Promised Land* (1912)
95 *US Supreme Court*   315
    The 1954 Supreme Court Decision on Segregation
96 *US Congressmen*   317
    "Protest from the South" (1956)
97 *Jonathan Kozol*   318
    FROM *Death at an Early Age: The Destruction of the Hearts and Minds
    of Negro Children in the Boston Public Schools* (1967)
98 *Studs Terkel*   322
    FROM "Public School Teacher: Rose Hoffman" (1972)
99 *Elizabeth Loza Newby*   324
    FROM "An Impossible Dream" (1977)
100 *Allan Bloom*   327
    "The Closing of the American Mind" (1987)

11 LANGUAGE AND THE MEDIA   331

    Introduction   333
101 *Noah Webster*   336
    FROM "The Reforming of Spelling" (1789)
102 *New York Herald*   339
    Review of *Uncle Tom's Cabin* (1853)
103 *Helen Keller*   341
    "Everything Has a Name" (1903)
104 *Wilfred Funk and Norman Lewis*   343
    "Thirty Days to a More Powerful Vocabulary" (1942)

CONTENTS

105 *William Labov*   345
  "The Non-Standard Vernacular of the Negro Community" (1967)
106 *Bob Woodward and Carl Bernstein*   350
  "GOP Security Aide Among 5 Arrested in Bugging Affair" (1972)
107 *Neil Postman*   353
  FROM "The Age of Show Business" (1985)
108 *Garrison Keillor*   356
  "Forebears" (1985)
109 *Amy Tan*   359
  "Mother Tongue" (1990)
110 *William Branigin*   363
  "The Checkpoint Killing" (2003)

12 FOREIGN AFFAIRS   369

  Introduction   370
111 *George Washington*   374
  FROM Farewell Address (1796)
112 *James Monroe*   376
  FROM "The Monroe Doctrine" (1823)
113 *Charles A. Beard*   378
  FROM "A Foreign Policy for America" (1940)
114 *Harry Truman*   381
  "The Truman Doctrine" (1947)
115 *George C. Marshall*   384
  "The Marshall Plan" (1947)
116 *Joseph McCarthy*   386
  FROM "The Wheeling Speech" (1950)
117 *Lyndon B. Johnson*   391
  "American Policy in Viet-Nam" (1965)
118 *George Bush*   393
  "The Launch of Attack on Iraq" (1991)
119 *E. L. Doctorow*   395
  Open Letter to the President (1991)
120 *George W. Bush*   397
  The State of the Union Address (January 29, 2002)

13 IDEOLOGY: DOMINANT BELIEFS AND VALUES   405

  Introduction   406
121 *Thomas Jefferson*   409
  A Bill for Establishing Religious Freedom in the State of Virginia
  (1779)
122 *Horace Mann*   411
  FROM "Report to the Massachusetts Board of Education" (1848)

CONTENTS

123 William James 417
FROM *Pragmatism* (1907)

124 Jane Addams 418
FROM *Twenty Years at Hull House* (1910)

125 Bruce Barton 419
FROM "Christ as a Businessman" (1925)

126 Dale Carnegie 423
FROM *How to Win Friends and Influence People* (1936)

127 Franklin D. Roosevelt 424
State of the Union Address (January 6, 1941)

128 Dwight D. Eisenhower 430
"The Military-Industrial Complex" (1961)

129 Studs Terkel 431
FROM "Jay Slabaugh, 48" (Interview with a Corporate Executive, 1980)

130 Rush H. Limbaugh, III 432
FROM *See, I Told You So* (1993)

ILLUSTRATIONS

1   Geronimo   6
2   Immigrants at Ellis Island   32
3   Martin Luther King   64
4   *Migrant Mother* by Dorothea Lange, 1936   86
5   *Declaration of Independence, 4 July, 1776* by John Trumbull   118
6   Small group of poor in Lower East Side, New York, ca. 1890, Jacob Riis   156
7   *Yosemite Valley, Thunderstorm, Yosemite National Park, 1949* by Ansel Adams   184
8   *Jack in the Pulpit* by Georgia O'Keeffe, 1930   226
9   Evangelist Billy Graham   258
10   Students at Little Rock, Alabama, 1957   300
11   Advertisement for Jordan motor cars, 1924   332
12   United Flight 175 impacting Two World Trade Center, September 11, 2001   370
13   Detail of *Peaceable Kingdom* by Edward Hicks   406

ACKNOWLEDGMENTS

We are grateful to all those who have granted us permission to reproduce the extracts listed below. While every effort has been made to trace and acknowledge ownership of copyright material used in this volume, the publisher will be glad to make suitable arrangements with any copyright holders whom it has not been possible to contact.

7   Leslie Silko
    "The Man to Send Rain Clouds" ©1969 by Leslie Marmon Silko, permission of The Wylie Agency.

8   Buffy Sainte-Marie
    "My Country," from *The Buffy Sainte-Marie Songbook* by Buffy Sainte-Marie, copyright © 1971 by Buffy Sainte-Marie. Used by permission of Grosset & Dunlap, Inc., a division of Penguin Group (USA) Inc.

9   Studs Terkel
    From "Girl of the Golden West: Ramona Bennett" in *American Dreams: Lost and Found*. Reprinted by permission of Donadio & Olson, Inc. Copyright 1980 by Studs Terkel.

10 Joy Harjo
    "The Woman Hanging from the Thirteenth Floor Window" from the book *She Had Some Horses* by Joy Harjo. Copyright © 1983, 1997 by Thunder's Mouth Press, A Division of Avalon Publishing Group, Inc.

17 Ole E. Rølvaag
    "The Power of Evil in High Places," pages from *Giants in the Earth: A Saga of the Prairie* by O. E. Rølvaag. Copyright 1927 by Harper & Row, Publishers, Inc. Renewed 1955 by Jennie Marie Berdahl Rølvaag. Reprinted by permission of HarperCollins Publishers.

18 Oscar Handlin
    From *The Uprooted* by Oscar Handlin. Copyright © 1951, 1973 by Oscar Handlin. By permission of Little, Brown and Co.

19 Al Santoli
    "Mojados (Wetbacks)," from *New Americans: An Oral History* by Al Santoli, copyright © 1988 by Al Santoli. Used by permission of the author and Viking Penguin, a division of Penguin Group (USA) Inc.

20 Arthur M. Schlesinger, Jr.
"E Pluribus Unum?" from *The Disuniting of America: Reflections on a Multicultural Society* by Arthur M. Schlesinger, Jr. Copyright © 1992, 1991 by Arthur M. Schlesinger, Jr. Used by permission of W. W. Norton & Company, Inc.

25 William DuBois
"This Double-Consciousness" and "Of the Faith of the Fathers." From *The Souls of Black Folk*. Reprinted with the permission of Simon & Schuster Adult Publishing Group from *The Souls of Black Folk* by W. E. B. DuBois. Copyright © 2005 Simon & Schuster, Inc.

26 Gwendolyn Brooks
"We Real Cool" (1960) reprinted by consent of Brooks Permissions.

27 Martin Luther King, Jr.
"I Have a Dream" (1963). Copyright 1963 Martin Luther King Jr., copyright renewed 1991 Coretta Scott King. Reprinted by arrangement with The Heirs to the Estate of Martin Luther King Jr., c/o Writers House as agent for the proprietor New York, NY

29 Malcolm X
From "The Ballot or the Bullet" Copyright © 1965, 1989 by Betty Shabazz and Pathfinder Press. Reprinted by permission.

"The Black Man" (1965) from *The Autobiography of Malcolm X* by Malcolm X and Alex Haley, copyright © 1964 by Alex Haley and Malcolm X. Copyright © 1965 by Alex Haley and Betty Shabazz. Used by permission of Random House, Inc.

"The Black Man" (1965) from *The Autobiography of Malcolm X*, published by Hutchinson. Reprinted by permission of The Random House Group.

30 Septima Clark
"Teach How Change Comes About" (pre-1987) from *Refuse to Stand Silently by* by Eliot Wigginton, copyright © 1992 by Highlander Center. Used by permission of Doubleday, a division of Random House, Inc.

35 Meridel LeSueur
"Women on the Breadlines" from *Harvest: Collected Stories*. Originally published in *The New Masses* (1932): 5–7. Reprinted with the permission of West End Press, Albuquerque, New Mexico.

36 Betty Friedan
"That Has No Name" from *The Feminine Mystique* by Betty Friedan. Copyright © 1983, 1974, 1973, 1963 by Betty Friedan. Used by permission of W. W. Norton & Company, Inc. and Victor Gollancz, a division of The Orion Publishing Group.

37 Studs Terkel
"'Just a Housewife': Therese Carter" in *Working*. Reprinted by permission of Donadio & Olson, Inc. Copyright 1972 by Studs Terkel.

38   Marabel Morgan
     "Admire Him" (1973) from *The Total Woman*. Reproduced by kind permission
     of Charles Morgan.

39   Merle Woo
     From "Letter to Ma" (1980) reproduced by kind permission of the author.

44   Thomas Jefferson
     From "The Roots of Democracy" (1816) Reprinted from Annals of America
     © 1976, 2003 Encyclopaedia Britannica, Inc.

45   Andrew Jackson
     From "The Proclamation to the People of South Carolina" (1832). Reprinted
     from Annals of America © 1976, 2003 Encyclopaedia Britannica, Inc.

48   Joe McGinnis
     From *The Selling of the President* (1969). Reproduced by kind permission of the
     Law Office of Dennis Holahan.

49   E. L. Doctorow
     From "A Citizen Reads the Constitution" (1987). Reprinted with permission
     from the February 21, 1987 issue of *The Nation*. For subscription information,
     call 1-800-333-8536. Portions of each week's Nation magazine can be accessed
     at http://www.thenation.com.

50   John Kenneth Galbraith
     "The American Presidency: Going the Way of the Blacksmith?" (1988) from
     The International Herald Tribune, December 13, 1988. Reproduced by permission
     of The Strothman Agency.

51   Andrew Jackson
     "The Power of the Moneyed Interests" (1837). Reprinted from Annals of
     America © 1976, 2003 Encyclopaedia Britannica, Inc.

53   Andrew Carnegie
     From *The Gospel of Wealth* (1900) edited by Edward C. Kirkland, Harvard
     University Press. Published originally in the *North American Review*, CXLVIII,
     June 1889, and CXLIX, December 1889.

54   Sinclair Lewis
     Excerpts from *Babbitt* by Sinclair Lewis, copyright 1922 by Harcourt, Inc. and
     renewed 1950 by Sinclair Lewis, reprinted by permission of Harcourt, Inc.

56   Lyndon B. Johnson
     From "The War on Poverty" (1964). Reprinted from Annals of America ©
     1976, 2003 Encyclopaedia Britannica, Inc.

57   Studs Terkel
     From "Mike Lefevre" (Interview with a Steel Mill Worker) in *Working*. Reprinted
     by permission of Donadio & Olson, Inc. Copyright 1972 by Studs Terkel.

58   Steven VanderStaay
      "Hell" (1992) from *Street Lives: An Oral History of the Homeless*, reproduced by kind permission of the author.

59   Newt Gingrich
      Copyright © 2006 by Newt Gingrich. All rights reserved. Reprinted by permission of the author c/o Writers Representatives LLC. From "Replacing the Welfare State with an Opportunity Society," *To Renew America* (Harper-Collins, 1995), pp. 77–9.

60   Barbara Ehrenreich
      From *Nickel and Dimed: On (Not) Getting By in America* (2001). Reprinted by permission of International Creative Management, Inc. Copyright © 2001 by Barbara Ehrenreicho.

62   Frederick Jackson Turner
      From "The Significance of the Frontier" (1893) in *Frederick Jackson Turner: Wisconsin's Historian of the Frontier*, by Martin Ridge, 1986. Reprinted with permission of the Wisconsin Historical Society. All rights reserved.

63   F. Scott Fitzgerald
      "My Lost City" by F. Scott Fitzgerald, from *The Crack-up*, copyright © 1945 by New Directions Publishing Corp. Reprinted by permission of New Directions Publishing Corp. and David Higham Associates Limited.

64   Christopher Isherwood
      "California Is a Tragic Country" (1947) in Christopher Ricks and William L. Vance, eds., *The Faber Book of America* (London: Faber and Faber, 1992), pp. 105–8. Reproduced by kind permission of Don Bachardy.

65   Aldo Leopold
      "Thinking Like a Mountain" (1949) *A Sand Country Almanac* and *Sketches Here and There* (New York: Oxford University Press, 1949). By permission of Oxford University Press, Inc.

66   Peter L. Berger
      "New York City 1976: A Signal of Transcendence" (1977) from *Facing Up to Modernity*, New York: Basic Books. Reproduced by kind permission of the author.

      "New York City 1976: A Signal of Transcendence" (1977) from *Facing Up to Modernity* by Peter L. Berger, New York: Basic Books. Reprinted by permission of Basic Books, a member of Perseus Books Group.

67   Joan Didion
      "Marrying Absurd" from *Slouching Towards Bethlehem* by Joan Didion. Copyright © 1966, 1968, renewed 1996 by Joan Didion. Reprinted by permission of Farrar, Straus and Giroux, LLC.
      "Marrying Absurd" by Joan Didion
      Copyright (c) 1967 by Joan Didion
      Originally published in *Slouching Towards Bethlehem*.
      Reprinted by permission of the author.

68   Alice Walker
"The Black Writer and the Southern Experience" from *In Search of Our Mothers' Gardens: Womanist Prose*, copyright © 1983 by Alice Walker, reprinted by permission of Harcourt, Inc. and David Higham Associates.

69   Bill Holm
"Horizontal Grandeur" from *The Music of Failure* (1985). Reproduced by kind permission of the author and Plains Press.

70   Barry Lopez
From *Arctic Dreams* (1986) Reprinted by permission of SLL/Sterling Lord Literistic, Inc. Copyright 1986 by Barry Lopez.

71   Georgia O'Keeffe
"To Alfred Stieglitz" (1916) From Jack Cowart and Juan Hamilton, Georgia O'Keeffe: Art and Letters. National Gallery of Art, Washington D.C. 1987, p. 150. Reproduced by kind permission of the repository of the letter, The Yale Collection of American Literature, Beinecke Rare Book and Manuscript Library, Yale University.

72   Bessie Smith
"Empty Bed Blues." Words and Music by J. Johnson © 1928 Record Music Publishing Co., USA, EMI United Partnership Ltd, London WC2H 0QY (Publishing) and Alfred Publishing Co., USA (Print). Administered in Europe by Faber Music Ltd. Reproduced by permission. All rights reserved.

73   Woody Guthrie
"This Land Is Your Land" (1944) © 1956 Ludlow Music, Inc., U.S.A. assigned to TRO Essex Music Ltd. Of Suite 2.07, Plaza 535 Kings Road, London SW10 0SZ. International Copyright Secured. All rights reserved. Used by permission.

75   Ralph Ellison
"As the Spirit Moves Mahalia," from *Shadow and Act* by Ralph Ellison, copyright 1953, 1964 and renewed 1981, 1992 by Ralph Ellison. Used by permission of Random House, Inc.

76   Stanley Kauffmann
Little Big Man from *Living Images* by Stanley Kauffmann. Copyright 1970–1975 by Stanley Kauffmann. Reprinted by permission of Brandt & Hochman Literary Agents, Inc.

77   Joan Didion
"Georgia O'Keeffe" by Joan Didion. Copyright © 1976 by Joan Didion. Originally published in *THE WHITE ALBUM*. Reprinted by permission of the author. Excerpt from "Georgia O'Keeffe" from THE WHITE ALBUM by Joan Didion. Copyright © 1979 by Joan Didion. Reprinted by permission of Farrar, Straus and Giroux, LLC

78   Studs Terkel
From "Jill Robertson: Fantasia" in *American Dreams: Lost and Found*. Reprinted by permission of Donadio & Olson, Inc. Copyright 1980 by Studs Terkel.

79   Mikal Gilmore
From "Bruce Springsteen" (1987) in *Rolling Stone*, 05 November 1987. Reprinted by permission of Rolling Stone LLC.

80   Martin Scorsese, Paul Schrader, and Robert De Niro
Taxi Driver (1992). From the book *Martin Scorsese: A Journey* by Mary Pat Kelly. Copyright © 1991, 1996 by Mary Pat Kelly. Appears by permission of the publisher, Thunder's Mouth Press, a division of Avalon Publishing Group, Inc.

83   Ralph Waldo Emerson
From his journals and letters (1827–1837): dated 1/15/1827 and 2/16/1827 call number *bMS Am 1280H (18)*, dated October 1836 call number *bMS Am 1280H (34)*, and dated 5/26/1837 with call number *bMS Am 1280H (35)*. By permission of the Ralph Waldo Emerson Memorial Association.

86   Will Herberg
"The Religion of Americans" (1955) from *Protestant Catholic Jew* by Will Herberg, copyright © 1955 by Will Herberg. Used by permission of Doubleday, a division of Random House, Inc.

87   Flannery O'Connor
"Novelist and Believer" from *Mystery and Manners* by Flannery O'Connor, edited by Sally and Robert Fitzgerald. Copyright © 1969 by the Estate of Mary Flannery O'Connor. Reprinted by permission of Farrar, Straus and Giroux LLC.

"Novelist and Believer" from Mystery and Manners by Flannery O'Connor, edited by Sally and Robert Fitzgerald. © 1957, 1961, 1962, 1963 by Flannery O'Connor. © 1964, 1966, 1967, 1969 by the Estate of Mary Flannery O'Connor. Reprinted by permission of the Mary Flannery O'Connor Charitable Trust, via Harold Matson Co., Inc.

88   Martin Luther King
"Letter from Birmingham Jail" (1963) Copyright 1963 Martin Luther King Jr., copyright renewed 1991 Coretta Scott King. Reprinted by arrangement with The Heirs to the Estate of Martin Luther King Jr., c/o Writers House as agent for the proprietor New York, NY.

89   Billy Graham
"The Unfinished Dream" (1970) address at the Honor America Day religious service held in Washington on July 4, 1970 as reprinted in *Christianity Today*. © Billy Graham, "The Unfinished Dream," July 4, 1970. Reproduced by permission of Billy Graham Evangelistic Association.

90   Richard Rodriguez
"Credo", from *Hunger of Memory* by Richard Rodriguez. Reprinted by permission of David R. Godine, Publisher, Inc. Copyright © 1982 by Richard Rodriguez.

91   Robert Coram
"The Necessity of Compulsory Primary Education" (1791). Reprinted by permission of the publisher from *Essays on Education in the Early Republic*, edited by Frederick Rudolph, pp. 112–27, Cambridge, Mass.: The Belknap Press of Harvard University Press, Copyright © 1965 by the President and Fellows of Harvard College.

92   John Dewey
"My Pedagogic Creed" (1897) from *The Collected Works of John Dewey, Early Works Volume 5.* © 1972 by the Board of Trustees, Southern Illinois University Press, reproduced by permission.

97   Jonathan Kozol
"The Grim Reality of Ghetto Schools" from *Death at an Early Age: The Destruction of the Hearts and Minds of Negro Children in the Boston Public Schools* by Jonathan Kozol, copyright © 1967, 1985, renewed © 1995 by Jonathan Kozol. Used by permission of Dutton Signet, a division of Penguin Group (USA) Inc. Reprinted by permission of International Creative Management, Inc. Copyright © 1967, 1985, renewed © 1995 by Jonathan Kozol.

98   Studs Terkel
From "Public School Teacher: Rose Hoffman" in *Working*. Reprinted by permission of Donadio & Olson, Inc. Copyright 1972 by Studs Terkel.

99   Elizabeth Loza Newby
"An Impossible Dream" (1977). Reprinted by permission from *Immigrant Women: Revised, Second Edition* edited by Maxine S. Seller, the State University of New York Press © 1994, State University of New York. All rights reserved.

100   Allan Bloom
"The Closing of the American Mind". Reprinted with permission of Simon & Schuster Adult Publishing Group from *The Closing of the American Mind* by Allan Bloom. Copyright © 1987 by Allan Bloom.

103   Helen Keller
"*Everything* Has a Name" From *The Story of My Life* (1903): Courtesy of the Helen Keller Archives, the American Foundation for the blind.

104   Wilfred Funk and Norman Lewis
"First Day: Give Us 15 Minutes a Day", pp. 35–37, from *30 Days to a More Powerful Vocabulary* by Wilfred Funk and Norman Lewis. © Copyright 1942 by Harper & Row, Publishers, Inc. Reprinted by permission of HarperCollins Publishers.

105   William Labov
"The Non-Standard Vernacular of the Negro Community" (1967) from Elizabeth M. Kerr and Ralpoh M. Alderman, Aspects of American English, 2. ed. (1971) Harcourt Brace Jovanovich, New York, pp. 336–342. Reproduced by kind permission of the author.

106 Bob Woodward and Carl Bernstein
"GOP Security Aide Among 5 Arrested in Bugging Affair," *The Washington Post*, June 19, 1972. © 1972, The Washington Post. Reprinted with permission.

107 Neil Postman
"The Age of Show Business" from *Amusing Ourselves to Death* by Neil Postman, copyright © 1985 by Neil Postman. Used by permission of Viking Penguin, a division of Penguin group (USA) Inc.

108 Garrison Keillor
"Forebears", pp. 74–8 and pp. 85–6 from *Lake Wobegon Days* (1985) reproduced by permission of Faber and Faber.

"Forbears", from *Lake Wobegon Days* by Garrison Keillor, copyright © 1985 by Garrison Keillor. Used by permission of Viking Penguin, a division of Penguin Group (USA) Inc.

109 Amy Tan
"Mother Language" copyright © 1990 by Amy Tan. First appeared in *The Threepenny Review*. Reprinted by permission of the author and the Sandra Dijkstra Literary Agency.

110 William Branigin
"The Checkpoint Killing" (2003) from *Embedded* by Bill Katovsky and Timothy Carlson, copyright © 2003 by Bill Katovsky, The Lyons Press, a division of The Globe Pequot Press. Reproduced with permission.

112 James Monroe
From "The Monroe Doctrine" (1823). Reprinted from Annals of America © 1976, 2003 Encyclopaedia Britannica, Inc.

113 Charles A. Beard
"A Foreign Policy for America," Alfred A. Knopf, 1940. Reproduced by kind permission of Detlev Vagts on behalf of the Estate of Charles A. Beard.

115 George C. Marshall
"The Marshall Plan" (1947). Courtesy of the George C. Marshall Research Library, Lexington, Virginia.

119 E. L. Doctorow
"Open Letter to the President" (1991). Reprinted with permission from the January 7, 1991 issue of *The Nation*. For subscription information, call 1–800–333–8536. Portions of each week's *Nation* magazine can be accessed at http://www.thenation.com.

123 William James
From *Pragmatism* (1907) from *An American Primer*, ed. Daniel Boorstin. Penguin 1985, pp. 712–15. Reproduced by kind permission of the Estate of William James.

125 Bruce Barton
From "Christ as a Businessman" (1925). Reprinted with the permission of Scribner, an imprint of Simon & Schuster Adult Publishing Group, from *The*

Man Nobody Knows by Bruce Barton. Copyright © 1925 by Bruce Barton; copyright renewed © 1953 by Bruce Barton. All rights reserved.

From "Christ as a Businessman" (1925). *The Man Nobody Knows*, 1925, in Current, Garraty and Weinberg, *Words That Made American History*, HC US 1979, pp. 379–91. Reproduced by permission of ICD International Center for the Disabled.

126   Dale Carnegie
From *How to Win Friends and Influence People.* Reprinted with permission of Simon & Schuster Adult Publishing Group. Copyright 1936 by Dale Carnegie. Copyright renewed © 1964 by Dorothy Carnegie. By permission of Blake Friedmann Literary Agency Ltd.

129   Studs Terkel
From "Jay Slabaugh, 48" (Interview with a Corporate Executive, 1980) in *American Dreams: Lost and Found.* Reprinted by permission of Donadio & Olson, Inc. Copyright 1980 by Studs Terkel.

130   Rush Limbaugh, III
From *See, I Told You So.* Reprinted with permission of Atria Books, an imprint of Simon & Schuster Adult Publishing Group, from *See, I Told You So* by Rush H. Limbaugh, III. Copyright © 1993 by Rush H. Limbaugh, III.

INTRODUCTION

This is the second edition of *American Culture*. It replaces the first edition published by the same editors in 1996. The experience of using our textbook in introductory American Studies courses for over a decade has led us to make significant changes in our new edition, even though we have kept the basic structure of the first book. First of all, every chapter now includes ten texts, provided with a revised introduction as well as study questions and topics and suggestions for further reading. New chapters entitled "Language and the Media," "Geography, Regions, and the Environment," and "Art, Film, Music, and Popular Culture" have been added. Our previous chapters on "The Structure of Government," "Parties and Politics," "Enterprise," and "Class Structure" have been combined into two. Many abbreviated texts from our first edition are now presented in complete, or near complete, form. In addition, since some texts have lost their flavor and relevance over the years, we have replaced them and added new ones. Seminal texts from American history which can be found in the most frequently used literary anthologies have been omitted from this volume.

American Culture remains an anthology of documentary texts aimed at students of American culture, particularly as a subject taught within the study of English as a second language. The study of American culture has become a truly international field, and it is our belief that students in Great Britain and the United States, as well as in other primarily English-speaking countries, may benefit from using our anthology as a textbook for their courses.

The study of English at colleges and universities outside of Britain and America usually includes three main disciplines: linguistics, literary study, and cultural studies. In many countries, university and college studies in English are now more sharply divided between linguistic studies on the one hand and literary analysis on the other. We believe that the study of cultural texts benefits greatly from an interdisciplinary approach which includes both linguistics and literary criticism. This has been the major asset of our American Studies courses. We have therefore retained the broad scope and the vision that underpinned the first edition.

Within the field of American cultural studies, there is no dearth of anthologies of scholarly essays *about* American culture, but there is a great need for a collection of primary sources *of* American culture that can be used for illustration and discussion in class – sources that students themselves analyze as cultural texts. We insist that this anthology is a textbook of essential essays which in different ways have helped to define American culture, and will continue to do so in years to come. Which of the newer texts will remain focal points of attention in the classroom remains to be seen.

1

INTRODUCTION

We have tried to find texts that are challenging and suggestive in terms of both their language and their ideological discourse, which students will be motivated to analyze from a linguistic as well as a cultural point of view. Although these documentary sources are tailored to students of English, their engaging character should also make them suited for general courses in American Studies or American Culture.

Considerable care has been taken to include most subject areas that are taught in American Culture courses, namely American Indians (chapter 1); Immigration (2); African Americans (3); Women's Studies (4); Government and Politics (5); Economy, Enterprise, Class (6); Geography, Regions, and the Environment (7); Art, Film, Music, and Popular Culture (8); Religion (9); Education (10); Language and the Media (11); Foreign Affairs (12); and Ideology: Dominant Beliefs and Values (13). Our concern with a historical perspective has furthermore produced a combination of "older" and more recent sources. At the same time, a central aim has been to furnish students with a great variety of texts. In addition to standard historical and political documents, our anthology includes essays, articles or parts of chapters, speeches, rhetoric, manifestos, autobiography, reminiscences, interviews, advertising, song lyrics, and stories. Such a variety of subjects and texts is intended to encourage multicultural and interdisciplinary approaches to the study of American culture.

As we approach our own time, the question of what texts to include becomes a very contested one. Everyone agrees that Jonathan Edwards must be represented in the context of religion but when the focus is shifted to the present day the choice becomes a delicate issue. Should we include texts from TV evangelists, even though they contain reflections of national pride and popular culture which have little to do with American religion as defined by leading American theologians? Does a text by Billy Graham lend itself to the same kind of class discussion and scrutiny as a text by Ralph W. Emerson? We have included both.

Our selection of texts for the second volume has also been guided by a particular conception of American cultural studies. The study of American culture is seen to involve both a general introduction to different aspects of American history and society and the close study of documentary texts that pertain to these subject areas. By submitting texts to analysis in class, students may themselves discover how cultural beliefs and values are embedded in the very language used in these sources, in the choice of idiom, imagery, and register. Through their examination of texts, students learn that the language of people of different groups and periods represents particular ways of looking at the world, engendered by specific social, economic, ethnic, religious, political, and/or gender-related circumstances. We hope that students of American Culture, when working with these primary texts, will understand the importance of evolving both a linguistic and a cultural competence. Multicultural, multi-topical, multi-textual, and multi-disciplinary, this anthology is intended to make students recognize that language is culture and culture is language, and that the one cannot be understood without some grasp of the other.

The four editors come to the field of American culture from different bases of study, such as history, anthropology, linguistics, and religious studies, but we all agree that the teaching and the study of American texts may use keys provided by a variety of fields, and that essentially all texts may be read (if not understood) as literary texts.

There are two major omissions in this anthology that may strike the critical reader immediately: (1) the dearth of texts of Puritan culture, and (2) the paucity of texts of imaginative literature. Although Puritan culture is essential for the understanding of a great many aspects of American life, such as its political, religious, and ideological features, we have frequently omitted texts of American Puritanism because they are amply represented in any major anthology of American literature that students are required to read, and to which they will be directed. We have, however, introduced texts by John Winthrop and Jonathan Edwards, which are not often found in other anthologies. Rather than including texts of imaginative literature in our volume, we have introduced essays in which authors of fiction reflect on such cultural features as language and on religion in the United States. We have still excluded such canonical sources as J. Hector St. John de Crèvecoeur's *Letters from an American Farmer*, since it can be found in most survey editions of American literature.

Over the last decades, the study of American culture has moved from being a search for a national character or a national identity to focus on American conflicts, within and without, as well as on attachment to the old world, which Americans – since the Puritans – have often argued they were no longer a part of. As a constructed category, identity is shaped within a cultural context given to changes and not determined once and for all. It is our conviction that the texts we have chosen help define American culture.

Scholars and teachers in the field have recently argued for more international and cross-cultural approaches to American Studies. Our second edition is based on similar reflections. It is entirely composed of American texts, yet as editors we may be just as much inspired by the Cultural Studies movement in Great Britain as by the American Studies movement in which we all were trained. Influential scholars in the field of Cultural Studies like Richard Hoggart and Raymond Williams have helped define concepts of culture and cultural history that have guided our interests in American culture far beyond narrow national concepts.

A course in American cultural studies certainly demands the reading of a general introduction to American history and society. Our anthology is first and foremost intended as a documentary companion to such a study in order to facilitate discussion in class and to turn the students' attention to the close interrelations between the studies of culture, text, and language. That is our main didactic purpose.

1

AMERICAN INDIANS

Introduction   6

 1 *Thomas Jefferson*   9
    "Confidential Message to Congress" (1803)

 2 *Tecumseh*   11
    "We All Belong to One Family" (1811)

 3 *Seattle*   13
    FROM "The Dead Are Not Powerless" (1854)

 4 *Helen Hunt Jackson*   14
    FROM *A Century of Dishonor* (1881)

 5 *US Congress*   16
    FROM The General Allotment Act (1887)

 6 *John Collier*   17
    "Full Indian Democracy" (1943)

 7 *Leslie Silko*   18
    "The Man to Send Rain Clouds" (1969)

 8 *Buffy Sainte-Marie*   21
    "My Country" (1971)

 9 *Studs Terkel*   23
    "Girl of the Golden West: Ramona Bennett" (1980)

10 *Joy Harjo*   28
    "The Woman Hanging from the Thirteenth Floor Window" (1983)

Figure 1 Portrait of Geronimo (1829–1900), American Apache chieftain, 1887
© Bettmann/CORBIS

INTRODUCTION

Although the socio-economic situation of the American Indians varies according to tribal and regional background, statistics clearly show that Indians across the nation, in cities as well as on reservations, are members of one of the most impoverished ethnic groups in the United States. In his address to a Senate sub-committee in March 1968 Robert Kennedy warned that "the first American is still the last American in terms of income, employment, health, and education. I believe his to be a national tragedy for all Americans – for we are in some ways responsible."[1]

The dismal situation of the Indians is no new phenomenon. During the nineteenth century many liberal reformers rushed to defend the Indian cause. Already in his *Notes on the State of Virginia* (1785) Thomas Jefferson admitted that it is "very much to be lamented that we have suffered so many of the Indian tribes already to extinguish."[2] Yet, in The Declaration of Independence (1776) Jefferson had included a reference to "the merciless Indian savages." Jefferson's later views, as expressed in text 1, illustrate a common attitude of guilt, paternalism, and admiration for the Indian. His confidential message to Congress (1803) concerned funding for the Lewis and Clark expedition.

We have texts related to encounters between settlers and Indians in New England from the 1630s, but these are most often reports written by settlers who described what they understood as the "superstitions," "errors," and "imperfections" of the Indians they met. Captivity stories became a well-known genre. Oral literature continued to exist on its own terms among Indian tribes. During the 1800s Indian oratory probably became the genre of Native American literature best known to the reading public. Speeches of Indian leaders contain impassioned pleas for a lost cause. The speech by Tecumseh in this chapter (text 2) was given in 1810, three years before he died in battle. It is an attempt to unite various tribes for the purpose of regaining land in the Ohio valley. Speeches by Tecumseh and Seattle do not only serve as documents of a tragic past; they are often referred to by conservationists of today. Seattle's speech (text 3) was addressed to the governor of Washington Territory in 1854. Even if his speech has a complicated (perhaps even dubious) origin, it is still a strong defence of Indian traditions.

During the 1870s Indian tribes were no longer regarded as separate nations by the American government. Military conflicts between Indians and US cavalry came to a stop as Indians had to relinquish land to a growing number of new immigrants. How the West was won from the Indians was later turned into mythic proportions by the American film industry. To the Indians, however, it was the end of a way of life. Black Elk's famous eye-witness report from what has often been called the Wounded Knee massacre of 1890 from *Black Elk Speaks* (1932) is often anthologized and therefore not used here.

In 1881 Helen Hunt Jackson published her famous study *A Century of Dishonor*, a book-length indictment of what she considered to be the government's disastrous neglect of the Indians (see text 4). A few years later (1887) Congress passed the General Allotment Act, based on the idea that transforming Indians into independent farmers would improve their situation (text 5). Whatever benign effects the Act was expected to produce, it is now regarded as at best a dubious venture.

During the 1930s John Collier, a Commissioner of Indian Affairs who had experience of social work in urban centers, became the architect responsible for the Indian New Deal (1934), a major effort of the F. D. Roosevelt administration to improve the situation of the Indians. Deploring the disastrous effects of the Allotment Act, Collier and his crew worked indefatigably to reintroduce and strengthen the tribe as a possible center of Indian life, here reflected in a memorandum Collier wrote about the topic in 1943 (text 6).

Over the last few years Indian writers have focused on their own situation, no longer as colorful victims but as keepers of a valid tradition within American culture. Among other prominent spokesmen, Vine Deloria, Jr., a Standing Rock Sioux, has analyzed the conditions of Indians from the massacre at Wounded Knee in 1890 to a new generation of activists a hundred years later. Several books on Indian history have been written and scholarly journals such as *American Indian Quarterly* are published.

In "My Country," the renowned Indian folk-singer Buffy Sainte-Marie, born in Canada, gives artistic expression to the sentiments of many Indians about their plight during the early 1970s (text 8). She was able to use popular music as an arena for her Indian songs, both traditional ballads and her own lyrics. Less militant in tone, contemporary Native American literature, including such writers as N. Scott Momaday (*House Made of Dawn*, 1969) and Louise Erdrich (*Love Medicine*, 1984), has gained general recognition over the last decades. Thus Leslie Silko's short story (text 7), set among Pueblo Indians of the southwest, captures the tension between two cultures and two religions, "resolved" in this story by what may be understood as a tacit compromise. Silko was born in 1948 on the Laguna Reservation in New Mexico.

Traditional Indian values, such as reverence for nature, strong tribal ties, and the importance of storytelling, have influenced non-Indian writers in the United States. The famous Chicago journalist Studs Terkel's interview with an Indian woman in the state of Washington (text 9) sheds light on current perceptions of the Indians' situation.

The conflict between the Indians' determination to control their own land and rivers and the attempts of private enterprise to exploit the resources on that land is still a potential powder keg. Indians themselves are sometimes in disagreement about the issues of how natural resources on reservation land should be used. In some states where gambling is illegal, casinos pop up on Indian land, which does not belong to the state in which it is situated. Some reservations profit from the gambling business, but it is not at all certain whether this is a secure and beneficial income in the long run.

Sometimes media focus on reservation land tends to take attention away from the large percentage of Native Americans now living in western and Midwestern cities, such as Chicago and Minneapolis. The contrast between country and city life is a continuing factor in Indian culture. Joy Harjo, a Creek Indian poet and musician, reflects on the plight of an urban Indian woman, torn between her present scene and her dreams of a reservation past (text 10).

Relocation (of Indians to the cities) and termination (of reservations as a federal responsibility) have been key political terms since the 1950s. The federal relocation program for the Navajos (today's largest Indian group) and the Hopi Indians is just a case in point. Politicians from states with a large Indian population, such as South Dakota, need to address Indian issues. Nixon was praised for giving a place of ancient nature worship back to Indians; Reagan was in favor of reducing or ending the situation which in his mind reduced Indians to wards of the federal government.

The growing number of American Indian Studies courses in higher education is a sign of vast improvement. Such programmes are inducive, not only to scholarly interests in the field, but to a wide and genuine community commitment.

1 Quoted in Helle H. Høyrup and Inger N. Madsen, *Red Indians: The First Americans* (Copenhagen: Munksgaard, 1974), p. 5.
2 Thomas Jefferson, Query XI: Aborigines, Original Condition and Origin," *Notes on the State of Virginia*, excerpted in *The Heath Anthology of American Literature*, Vol.1 (Lexington, Mass.: D.C. Heath and Co., 1990), p. 970.

Questions and Topics

1 What do the speeches of Tecumseh and Seattle have in common and how do they differ? How would you describe typical features of Indian oratory?

2 In Collier's opinion, how can Indian democracy be achieved? What are his arguments? Why were Americans reluctant to recognize the tribe as a legal entity?

3 What does Silko's short story tell you about the relationship between Indian religion and Catholicism? What causes the priest's conflict and how is it resolved?

4 What does Terkel's text reveal about social and educational conditions for Indians? How does the Indian woman in the interview regard the past, present, and future of American Indians?

5 What dilemma of Indian life does the woman in Harjo's poem represent? What is the difference between being "set free" and climbing "back up to claim herself"?

Suggestions for further reading

Brown, Dee, *Bury My Heart at Wounded Knee* (New York: Holt, Rinehart & Winston, 1970).

Hurtado, Albert L. and Peter Iverson, eds., *Major Problems in American Indian History* (Boston: Houghton Mifflin, 1994).

Lurie, Nancy Oestreich, *Wisconsin Indians* (Madison, Wis.: Wisconsin Historical Society Press, revised edn, 2002).

Sanders, Thomas E. and Walter W. Peek, eds., *Literature of the American Indian* (Columbus, Ohio: Glencoe Press, 1973).

Turner, Frederick, ed., *The Portable North American Indian Reader* (New York: Penguin, 1977).

1 THOMAS JEFFERSON

"Confidential Message to Congress" (1803)

Gentlemen of the Senate, and of the House of Representatives:

As the continuance of the act for establishing trading houses with the Indian tribes will be under the consideration of the legislature at its present session, I think it my duty to communicate the views which have guided me in the execution of that act, in order that you may decide on the policy of continuing it, in the present or any other form, or discontinue it altogether, if that shall, on the whole, seem most for the public good.

The Indian tribes residing within the limits of the United States have, for a considerable time, been growing more and more uneasy at the constant diminution of the territory they occupy, although effected by their own voluntary sales. And the policy has long been gaining strength with them of refusing absolutely all further sale, on any conditions; insomuch that, at this time, it hazards their friendship, and excites dangerous jealousies and perturbations in their minds to make any overture for the purchase of the smallest portions of their land.

A very few tribes only are not yet obstinately in these dispositions. In order, peaceably, to counteract this policy of theirs, and to provide an extension of territory which the rapid increase of our numbers will call for, two measures are deemed expedient. First, to encourage them to abandon hunting, to apply to the raising stock, to agriculture, and domestic manufacture, and thereby prove to themselves that less land and labor will maintain them in this better than in their former mode of living. The extensive forests necessary in the hunting life, will then become useless, and they will see advantage in exchanging them for the means of improving their farms, and of increasing their domestic comforts. Second, to multiply trading houses among them, and place within their reach those things which will contribute more to their domestic comfort than the possession of extensive, but uncultivated wilds. Experience and reflection will develop to them the wisdom of exchanging what they can spare and we want, for what we can spare and they want. In leading them to agriculture, to manufactures, and civilization; in bringing together their and our settlements, and in preparing them ultimately to participate in the benefits of our governments, I trust and believe we are acting for their greatest good.

At these trading houses we have pursued the principles of the act of Congress which directs that the commerce shall be carried on liberally, and requires only that the capital stock shall not be diminished. We, consequently, undersell private traders, foreign and domestic, drive them from the competition; and, thus, with the goodwill of the Indians, rid ourselves of a description of men who are constantly endeavoring to excite in the Indian mind suspicions, fears, and irritations toward us. A letter now enclosed shows the effect of our competition on the operations of the traders, while the Indians, perceiving the advantage of purchasing from us, are soliciting, generally, our establishment of trading houses among them. In one quarter this is particularly interesting.

The legislature, reflecting on the late occurrences on the Mississippi, must be sensible how desirable it is to possess a respectable breadth of country on that river, from our southern limit to the Illinois, at least, so that we may present as firm a front on that as on our eastern border. We possess what is below the Yazoo, and can probably acquire a certain breadth from the Illinois and Wabash to the Ohio; but, between the Ohio and Yazoo, the country all belongs to the Chickasaws, the most friendly tribe within our limits, but the most decided against the alienation of lands. The portion of their country most important for us is exactly that which they do not inhabit. Their settlements are not on the Mississippi but in the interior country. They have lately shown a desire to become agricultural; and this leads to the desire of buying implements and comforts. In the strengthening and gratifying of these wants, I see the only prospect of planting on the Mississippi itself the means of its own safety.

Duty has required me to submit these views to the judgment of the legislature; but as their disclosure might embarrass and defeat their effect, they are committed to the special confidence of the two houses.

While the extension of the public commerce among the Indian tribes may deprive of that source of profit such of our citizens as are engaged in it, it might be worthy the attention of Congress, in their care of individual as well as of the general interest, to point in another direction the enterprise of these citizens, as profitably for themselves and more usefully for the public.

The River Missouri, and the Indians inhabiting it, are not as well known as is rendered desirable by their connection with the Mississippi, and consequently with us. It is, however, understood that the country on that river is inhabited by numerous tribes, who furnish great supplies of furs and peltry to the trade of another nation, carried on in a high latitude, through an infinite number of portages and lakes shut up by ice through a long season. The commerce on that line could bear no competition with that of the Missouri, traversing a moderate climate, offering, according to the best accounts, a continued navigation from its source, and possibly with a single portage, from the western ocean, and finding to the Atlantic a choice of channels through the Illinois or Wabash, the lakes and Hudson, through the Ohio and Susquehanna, or Potomac or James rivers, and through the Tennessee and Savannah rivers.

An intelligent officer, with ten or twelve chosen men, fit for the enterprise and willing to undertake it, taken from our posts, where they may be spared without inconvenience, might explore the whole line, even to the western ocean; have conferences with the natives on the subject of commercial intercourse; get admission among them for our traders; as others are admitted, agree on convenient deposits for an interchange of articles; and return with the information acquired, in the course of two summers. Their arms and accoutrements, some instruments of observation, and light and cheap presents for the Indians would be all the apparatus they could carry, and, with an expectation of a soldier's portion of land on their return, would constitute the whole expense. Their pay would be going on, whether here or there. While other civilized nations have encountered great expense to enlarge the boundaries of knowledge by undertaking voyages of discovery and for other literary purposes, in various parts and directions, our nation seems to owe to the same object, as well as to its own interests, to explore this, the only line of easy communication across the continent, and so directly traversing our own part of it.

The interests of commerce place the principal object within the constitutional powers and care of Congress, and that it should incidentally advance the geographical knowledge of our own continent cannot be but an additional gratification. The nation claiming the territory, regarding this as a literary pursuit, which is in the habit of permitting within its dominions, would not be disposed to view it with jealousy, even if the expiring state of its interests there did not render it a matter of indifference. The appropriation of $2,500, "for the purpose of extending the external commerce of the United States," while understood and considered by the executive as giving the legislative sanction, would cover the undertaking from notice, and prevent the obstructions which interested individuals might otherwise previously prepare in its way.

2 TECUMSEH

"We All Belong to One Family" (1811)

Brothers – We all belong to one family; we are all children of the Great Spirit; we walk in the same path; slake our thirst at the same spring; and now affairs of the greatest concern lead us to smoke the pipe around the same council fire!

Brothers – We are friends; we must assist each other to bear our burdens. The blood of many of our fathers has run like water on the ground, to satisfy the avarice of the white men. We, ourselves, are threatened with a great evil; nothing will pacify them but the destruction of all the red men.

Brothers – When the white men first set foot on our grounds, they were hungry; they had no place on which to spread their blankets, or to kindle their fires. They were feeble; they could do nothing for themselves. Our fathers commiserated their distress, and shared freely with them whatever the Great Spirit had given his red children. They gave them food when hungry, medicine when sick, spread skins for them to sleep on, and gave them grounds, that they might hunt and raise corn.

Brothers – The white people are like poisonous serpents: when chilled, they are feeble, and harmless, but invigorate them with warmth, and they sting their benefactors to death.

The white people came among us feeble; and now we have made them strong, they wish to kill us, or drive us back, as they would wolves and panthers.

Brothers – The white men are not friends to the Indians: at first, they only asked for land sufficient for a wigwam; now, nothing will satisfy them but the whole of our hunting grounds, from the rising to the setting sun.

Bothers – The white men want more than our hunting grounds; they wish to kill our warriors; they would even kill our old men, women, and little ones.

Brothers – Many winters ago, there was no land; the sun did not rise and set: all was darkness. The Great Spirit made all things. He gave the white people a home beyond the great waters. He supplied these grounds with game, and gave them to his red children; and he gave them strength and courage to defend them.

Brothers – My people wish for peace; the red men all wish for peace; but where the white people are, there is no peace for them, except it be on the bosom of our mother.

Brothers – The white men despise and cheat the Indians; they abuse and insult them; they do not think the red men sufficiently good to live. The red men have borne many and great injuries; they ought to suffer them no longer. My people will not; they are determined on vengeance; they have taken up the tomahawk; they will make it fat with blood; they will drink the blood of the white people.

Brothers – My people are brave and numerous; but the white people are too strong for them alone. I wish you to take up the tomahawk with them. If we all unite, we will cause the rivers to stain the great waters with their blood.

Brothers – If you do not unite with us, they will first destroy us, and then you will fall an easy prey to them. They have destroyed many nations of red men because they were not united, because they were not friends to each other.

Brothers – The white people send runners amongst us; they wish to make us enemies, that they may sweep over and desolate our hunting grounds, like devastating winds, or rushing waters.

Brothers – Our Great Father[1] over the great waters is angry with the white people, our enemies. He will send his brave warriors against them; he will send us rifles, and whatever else we want – he is our friend, and we are his children.

Brothers – Who are the white people that we should fear them? They cannot run fast, and are good marks to shoot at: they are only men; our fathers have killed many of them; we are not squaws, and we will stain the earth red with their blood.

Brothers – The Great Spirit is angry with our enemies; he speaks in thunder, and the earth swallows up villages, and drinks up the Mississippi. The great waters will cover their lowlands; their corn cannot grow; and the Great Spirit will sweep those who escape to the hills from the earth with his terrible breath.

Brothers – We must be united; we must smoke the same pipe; we must fight each other's battles; and more than all, we must love the Great Spirit; he is for us; he will destroy our enemies, and make his red children happy.

1 I.e., King George III of England (1760–1820) (editors' note).

3 SEATTLE

FROM *"The Dead Are Not Powerless" (1854)*

Yonder sky that has wept tears of compassion upon my people for centuries untold, and which to us appears changeless and eternal, may change. Today is fair. Tomorrow it may be overcast with clouds. My words are like the stars that never change. Whatever Seattle says the great chief at Washington can rely upon with as much certainty as he can upon the return of the sun or the seasons. The White Chief says that Big Chief at Washington sends us greetings of friendship and goodwill. That is kind of him for we know he has little need of our friendship in return. His people are many. They are like the grass that covers vast prairies. My people are few. They resemble the scattering trees of a storm-swept plain. . . . I will not dwell on, nor mourn over, our untimely decay, nor reproach our paleface brothers with hastening it, as we too may have been somewhat to blame. . . .

Your God is not our God. Your God loves your people and hates mine. He folds his strong and protecting arms lovingly about the paleface and leads him by the hand as a father leads his infant son – but He has forsaken His red children – if they really are His. Our God, the Great Spirit, seems also to have forsaken us. Your God makes your people strong every day. Soon they will fill the land. Our people are ebbing away like a rapidly receding tide that will never return. The white man's God cannot love our people or He would protect them. They seem to be orphans who can look nowhere for help. How then can we be brothers? . . . We are two distinct races with separate origins and separate destinies. There is little in common between us.

To us the ashes of our ancestors are sacred and their resting place is hallowed ground. You wander far from the graves of your ancestors and seemingly without regret. Your religion was written upon tables of stone by the iron finger of your God so that you could not forget. The Red Man could never comprehend nor remember it. Our religion is the traditions of our ancestors – the dreams of our old men, given them in solemn hours of night by the Great Spirit; and the visions of our sachems; and it is written in the hearts of our people.

Your dead cease to love you and the land of their nativity as soon as they pass the portals of the tomb and wander way beyond the stars. They are soon forgotten and never return. Our dead never forget the beautiful world that gave them being. . . .

Day and night cannot dwell together. The Red Man has ever fled the approach of the White Man, as the morning mist flees before the morning sun. However, your proposition seems fair and I think that my people will accept it and will retire to the reservation you offer them. Then we will dwell apart in peace. . . . It matters little where we pass the remnant of our days. They will not be many. A few more moons; a few more winters – and not one of the descendants of the mighty hosts that once moved over this broad land or lived in happy homes, protected by the Great Spirit, will remain to mourn over the graves of a people once more powerful and hopeful than yours. But why should I mourn at the untimely fate of my people? Tribe follows tribe, and nation follows nation, like the waves of the sea. It is the order of nature, and regret is useless. Your time of decay may be distant, but it will surely come, for even the White Man whose God walked and talked with him as friend with friend, cannot be exempt from the common destiny. We may be brothers after all. We will see. . . .

Every part of this soil is sacred in the estimation of my people. Every hillside, every valley, every plain and grove, has been hallowed by some sad or happy event in days long vanished. The very dust upon which you now stand responds more lovingly to their footsteps than to yours, because it is rich with the blood of our ancestors and our bare feet are conscious of the sympathetic touch. Even the little children who lived here and rejoiced here for a brief season will love these somber solitudes and at eventide they greet shadowy returning spirits. And when the last Red Man shall have perished, and the memory of my tribe shall have become a myth among the White Men, these shores will swarm with the invisible dead of my tribe, and when your children's children think themselves alone in the field, the store, the shop, upon the highway, or in the silence of the pathless woods, they will not be alone. At night when the streets of your cities and villages are silent and you think them deserted, they will throng with the returning hosts that once filled and still love this beautiful land. The White Man will never be alone.

Let him be just and deal kindly with my people, for the dead are not powerless. Dead, did I say? There is no death, only a change of worlds.

4 HELEN HUNT JACKSON

FROM *A Century of Dishonor (1881)*

There is not among these three hundred bands of Indians [in the United States] one which has not suffered cruelly at the hands either of the Government or of white settlers. The poorer, the more insignificant, the more helpless the band, the more certain the cruelty and outrage to which they have been subjected. This is especially true of the bands on the Pacific slopes. These Indians found themselves of a sudden surrounded by and caught up in the great influx of gold-seeking settlers, as helpless creatures on a shore are caught up in a tidal wave. There was not time for the Government to make treaties; not even time for communities to make laws. The tale of the wrongs, the oppressions, the murders of the Pacific-slope Indians in the last thirty years would be a volume by itself, and is too monstrous to be believed.

It makes little difference, however, where one opens the record of the history of the Indians; every page and every year has its dark stain. The story of one tribe is the story of all, varied only by differences of time and place; but neither time nor place makes any difference in the main facts. Colorado is as greedy and unjust in 1880 as was Georgia in 1830, and Ohio in 1795; and the United States Government breaks promises now as deftly as then, and with added ingenuity from long practice.

One of its strongest supports in so doing is the wide-spread sentiment among the people of dislike to the Indian, of impatience with his presence as a "barrier to civilization," and distrust of it as a possible danger. The old tales of the frontier life, with its horrors of Indian warfare, have gradually, by two or three generations' telling, produced in the average mind something like an hereditary instinct of unquestioning and unreasoning aversion which it is almost impossible to dislodge or soften.

There are hundreds of pages of unimpeachable testimony on the side of the Indian; but it goes for nothing, is set down as sentimentalism or partisanship, tossed aside and forgotten.

President after president has appointed commission after commission to inquire into and report upon Indian affairs, and to make suggestions as to the best methods of managing them. The reports are filled with eloquent statements of wrongs done to the Indians, of perfidies on the part of the Government; they counsel, as earnestly as words can, a trial of the simple and unperplexing expedients of telling truth, keeping promises, making fair bargains, dealing justly in all ways and all things. These reports are bound up with the Government's Annual Reports, and that is the end of them. It would probably be no exaggeration to say that not one American citizen out of ten thousand ever sees them or knows that they exist, and yet any one of them, circulated throughout the country, read by the right-thinking, right-feeling men and women of this land, would be of itself a "campaign document" that would initiate a revolution which would not subside until the Indians' wrongs were, so far as is now left possible, righted.

In 1669 President Grant appointed a commission of nine men, representing the influence and philanthropy of six leading States, to visit the different Indian reservations, and to "examine all matters appertaining to Indian affairs."

In the report of this commission are such paragraphs as the following: "To assert that 'the Indian will not work' is as true as it would be to say that the white man will not work.

"Why should the Indian be expected to plant corn, fence lands, build houses, or do anything but get food from day to day, when experience has taught him that the product of his labor will be seized by the white man tomorrow? The most industrious white man would become a drone under similar circumstances. Nevertheless, many of the Indians" (the commissioners might more forcibly have said 130,000 of the Indians) "are already at work, and furnish ample refutation of the assertion that 'the Indian will not work.' There is no escape from the inexorable logic of facts.

"The history of the Government connections with the Indians is a shameful record of broken treaties and unfulfilled promises. The history of the border, white man's connection with the Indians is a sickening record of murder, outrage, robbery, and wrongs committed by the former, as the rule, and occasional savage outbreaks and unspeakably barbarous deeds of retaliation by the latter, as the exception.

"Taught by the Government that they had rights entitled to respect, when those rights have been assailed by the rapacity of the white man, the arm which should have been raised to protect them has ever been ready to sustain the aggressor.

"The testimony of some of the highest military officers of the United States is on record to the effect that, in our Indian wars, almost without exception, the first aggressions have been made by the white man, and the assertion is supported by every civilian of reputation who has studied the subject. In addition to the class of robbers and outlaws who find impunity in their nefarious pursuits on the frontiers, there is a large class of professedly reputable men who use every means in their power to bring on Indian wars for the sake of the profit to be realized from the presence of troops and the expenditures of Government funds in their midst. They proclaim death to the Indians at all times in words and publications, making no distinction between the innocent and the guilty. They irate the lowest class of men to the perpetration of the darkest deeds against their victims, and as judges and jurymen shield them from the justice due to their crimes. Every crime committed by a white man against an Indian is concealed or palliated. Every offence committed by an Indian against a white man is borne on the wings of the post or the telegraph to the remotest corner of the land, clothed with all the horrors which the reality or imagination can throw around it. Against such influences as these the people of the United States need to be warned."

5 US CONGRESS

FROM *The General Allotment Act (1887)*

An Act to provide for the allotment of lands in severalty to Indians on various reservations, and to extend the protection of the laws of the United States and the Territories over the Indians, and for other purposes.

Be it enacted by the Senate and House of Representatives of the United States of America in Congress assembled, That in all cases where any tribe or band of Indians has been, or shall hereafter be, located upon any reservation created for their use, either by treaty stipulation or by virtue of an act of Congress or Executive order setting apart the same for their use, the President of the United States be, and he hereby is, authorized, whenever in his opinion any reservation or any part thereof of such Indians is advantageous for agricultural and grazing purposes, to cause said reservation, or any part thereof, to be surveyed, or resurveyed if necessary, and to allot the lands in said reservation in severalty to any Indian located thereon in quantities as follows:

To each head of a family, one-quarter of a section;

To each single person over eighteen years of age, one-eighth of a section;

To each orphan child under eighteen years of age, one-eighth of a section; and

To each other single person under eighteen years now living, or who may be born prior to the date of the order of the President directing an allotment of the lands embraced in any reservation, one-sixteenth of a section: *Provided*, That in case there is not sufficient land in any of said reservations to allot lands to each individual of the classes above named in quantities as above provided, the lands embraced in such reservation or reservations shall be allotted to each individual of each of said classes pro rata in accordance with the provisions of this act: *And provided further*, That where the treaty or act of Congress setting apart such reservation provides for the allotment of lands in severalty in quantities in excess of those herein provided, the President, in making allotments upon such reservation, shall allot the lands to each individual Indian belonging thereon in quantity as specified in such treaty or act: *And provided further,* That when the lands allotted are only valuable for grazing purposes, an additional allotment of such grazing lands, in quantities as above provided, shall be made to each individual.

6 JOHN COLLIER

"Full Indian Democracy" (1943)

I see the broad function of Indian policy and Indian administration to be the development of Indian democracy and equality within the framework of American and world democracy. . . .

The most significant clue to achieving full Indian democracy within and as a part of American democracy, is the continued survival, through all historical change and disaster, of the Indian tribal group, both as a real entity and as a legal entity. I suspect the reason we do not always give this fact the recognition it deserves is that we do not want to recognize it. Indian "tribalism" seems to be foreign to, our American way of life. It seems to block individual development. We do not know how to deal with it. Consciously or unconsciously, we ignore it or try to eliminate it. Remove the tribe, rehabilitate the individual, and our problem is solved – so runs our instinctive thinking. . . .

We can discard everything else if we wish, and think of the tribe merely as a fact of law. At the minimum, the tribe is a legally recognized holding corporation – a holder of property and a holder of tangible rights granted by treaty or statute, by virtue of which a member enjoys valuable privileges which as a non-member he could not have. Through court decisions – many of them Supreme Court decisions – an important body of legal doctrine has grown up about the concept of the tribal entity. This fact of law is an enormously important, persistent, stubborn, living reality. . . .

Now this fact of law was greatly clarified and strengthened by the Indian Reorganization Act, which converted the tribe from a static to a dynamic concept. Congress, through the Indian Reorganization Act, invoked the tribe as a democratic operational mechanism. It reaffirmed the powers inherent in Indian tribes and set those powers to work for modern community development. In doing so, Congress recognized that most Indians were excluded from local civic government and that no human beings can prosper, or even survive, in a vacuum. If we strip the word tribe of its primitive and atavistic connotations, and consider tribes merely as primary or somewhat localized human groups, we can see that Indian tribal government, for most Indians, is the only presently feasible type of local civic self-government they can share in and use for their advancement. We can divest ourselves of the lingering fear that tribalism is a regression, and we can look upon it as a most important single step in assimilating Indians to modern democratic life. . . .

I cannot predict how long tribal government will endure. I imagine it will be variable in duration. I can imagine some tribes will remain cohesive social units for a very long time; others will more or less rapidly diffuse themselves among the rest of the population. It is not our policy to force this issue. Indians have the right of self-determination. And cultural diversity is by no means inimical to national unity, as the magnificent war effort of the Indians proves. . . .

During this transitional period (however short or long it may prove to be) the federal government is forced both by the fact of law and the fact of self-interest to continue to give a friendly guiding and protective hand to Indian advancement. As to law: there is a large body of treaties and statutes to be interpreted and enforced; Indian property must continue to be protected against unfair practices by the dominant group; Indians must be assisted in attaining self-subsistence and full citizenship. As to government self-interest: the complete withdrawal of this protection would merely substitute a more difficult problem in place of the one that is on the way to solution. It would create a permanently dispossessed and impoverished group that will either have to live on the dole or become one more sore spot in the body politic. . . .

The government's relationship to Indians is itself in a transition period. The Indian Reorganization Act made that inevitable. The Indian office is moving from guardian to advisor, from administrator to friend in court. In this transition, many powers hitherto exercised by the Indian service have been transferred to the organized tribes; many more such powers will be transferred. As Indians advance in self-government, they will begin to provide many of their own technical and social services or will depend more and more on the services ordinarily provided to American communities. I think we can agree, however, that federal advisory supervision ought not to be withdrawn until Indians have attained a fair political, economic, and cultural activity.

7 LESLIE SILKO

"The Man to Send Rain Clouds" (1969)

One

They found him under a big cottonwood tree. His Levi jacket and pants were faded light-blue so that he had been easy to find. The big cottonwood tree stood apart from a small grove of winterbare cottonwoods which grew in the wide, sandy arroyo. He had been dead for a day or more, and the sheep had wandered and scattered up and down the arroyo. Leon and his brother-in-law, Ken, gathered the sheep and left them in the pen at the sheep camp before they returned to the cottonwood tree. Leon waited under the tree while Ken drove the truck through the deep sand to the edge of the arroyo. He squinted up at the sun and unzipped his jacket – it sure was hot for this time of year. But high and northwest the blue mountains were still deep in snow. Ken came sliding below the low, crumbling bank about fifty yards down, and he was bringing the red blanket.

Before they wrapped the old man, Leon took a piece of string out of his pocket and tied a small gray feather in the old man's long white hair. Ken gave him the paint. Across the brown wrinkled forehead he drew a streak of white and along the high cheekbones he drew a strip of blue paint. He paused and watched Ken throw pinches of corn meal and pollen into the wind that fluttered the small gray feather. Then

18

Leon painted with yellow under the old man's broad nose, and finally, when he had painted green across the chin, he smiled.

"Send us rain clouds, Grandfather." They laid the bundle in the back of the pickup and covered it with a heavy tarp before they started back to the pueblo.

They turned off the highway onto the sandy pueblo road. Not long after they passed the store and post office they saw Father Paul's car coming toward them. When he recognized their faces he slowed his car and waved for them to stop. The young priest rolled down the car window.

"Did you find old Teofilo?" he asked loudly.

Leon stopped the truck. "Good morning, Father. We were just out to the sheep camp. Everything is OK now."

"Thank God for that. Teofilo is a very old man. You really shouldn't allow him to stay at the sheep camp alone."

"No, he won't do that any more now."

"Well, I'm glad you understand. I hope I'll be seeing you at Mass this week – we missed you last Sunday. See if you can get old Teofilo to come with you." The priest smiled and waved at them as they drove away.

Two

Louise and Teresa were waiting. The table was set for lunch, and the coffee was boiling on the black iron stove. Leon looked at Louise and then at Teresa.

"We found him under a cottonwood tree in the big arroyo near sheep camp. I guess he sat down to rest in the shade and never got up again." Leon walked toward the old man's bed. The red plaid shawl had been shaken and spread carefully over the bed, and a new brown flannel shirt and pair of stiff new Levis were arranged neatly beside the pillow. Louise held the screen door open while Leon and Ken carried in the red blanket. He looked small and shriveled, and after they dressed him in the new shirt and pants he seemed more shrunken.

It was noontime now because the church bells rang the Angelus. They ate the beans with hot bread, and nobody said anything until after Teresa poured the coffee.

Ken stood up and put on his jacket. "I'll see about the gravediggers. Only the top layer of soil is frozen. I think it can be ready before dark." Leon nodded his head and finished his coffee. After Ken had been gone for a while, the neighbors and clans-people came quietly to embrace Teofilo's family and to leave food on the table because the gravediggers would come to eat when they were finished.

Three

The sky in the west was full of pale-yellow light. Louise stood outside with her hands in the pockets of Leon's green army jacket that was too big for her. The funeral was over, and the old men had taken their candles and medicine bags and were gone. She waited until the body was laid into the pickup before she said anything to Leon. She touched his arm, and he noticed that her hands were still dusty from the corn meal that she had sprinkled around the old man. When she spoke, Leon could not hear her.

"What did you say? I didn't hear you."

"I said that I had been thinking about something."

"About what?"

"About the priest sprinkling holy water for Grandpa. So he won't be thirsty."

Leon stared at the new moccasins that Teofilo had made for the ceremonial dances in the summer. They were nearly hidden by the red blanket. It was getting colder, and the wind pushed gray dust down the narrow pueblo road. The sun was approaching the long mesa where it disappeared during the winter. Louise stood there shivering and watching his face. Then he zipped up his jacket and opened the truck door. "I'll see if he's there."

Four

Ken stopped the pickup at the church, and Leon got out; and then Ken drove down the hill to the graveyard where people were waiting. Leon knocked at the old carved door with its symbols of the Lamb. While he waited he looked up at the twin bells from the king of Spain with the last sunlight pouring around them in their tower.

The priest opened the door and smiled when he saw who it was. "Come in! What brings you here this evening?"

The priest walked toward the kitchen, and Leon stood with his cap in his hand, playing with the earflaps and examining the living room – the brown sofa, the green armchair, and the brass lamp that hung down from the ceiling by links of chain. The priest dragged a chair out of the kitchen and offered it to Leon.

"No thank you, Father. I only came to ask you if you would bring your holy water to the graveyard."

The priest turned away from Leon and looked out the window at the patio full of shadows and the dining-room windows of the nuns' cloister across the patio. The curtains were heavy, and the light from within faintly penetrated; it was impossible to see the nuns inside eating supper. "Why didn't you tell me he was dead? I could have brought the Last Rites anyway."

Leon smiled. "It wasn't necessary, Father."

The priest stared down at his scuffed brown loafers and the worn hem of his cassock. "For a Christian burial it was necessary."

His voice was distant, and Leon thought that his blue eyes looked tired.

"It's OK Father, we just want him to have plenty of water."

The priest sank down into the green chair and picked up a glossy missionary magazine. He turned the colored pages full of lepers and pagans without looking at them.

"You know I can't do that, Leon. There should have been the Last Rites and a funeral Mass at the very least."

Leon put on his green cap and pulled the flaps down over his ears. "It's getting late, Father. I've got to go."

When Leon opened the door Father Paul stood up and said, "Wait." He left the room and came back wearing a long brown overcoat. He followed Leon out the door and across the dim churchyard to the adobe steps in front of the church. They both stooped to fit through the low adobe entrance. And when they started down the hill to the graveyard only half of the sun was visible above the mesa.

The priest approached the grave slowly, wondering how they had managed to dig into the frozen ground; and then he remembered that this was New Mexico, and saw the pile of cold loose sand beside the hole. The people stood close to each other with little clouds of steam puffing from their faces. The priest looked at them and saw a pile of jackets, gloves, and scarves in the yellow, dry tumbleweeds that grew in the graveyard. He looked at the red blanket, not sure that Teofilo was so small, wondering if it wasn't some perverse Indian trick – something they did in March to ensure a good harvest – wondering if maybe old Teofilo was actually at sheep camp corraling the sheep for the night. But there he was, facing into a cold dry wind and squinting at the last sunlight, ready to bury a red wool blanket while the faces of his parishioners were in shadow with the last warmth of the sun on their backs.

His fingers were stiff, and it took him a long time to twist the lid off the holy water. Drops of water fell on the red blanket and soaked into dark icy spots. He sprinkled the grave and the water disappeared almost before it touched the dim, cold sand; it reminded him of something – he tried to remember what it was, because he thought if he could remember he might understand this. He sprinkled more water; he shook the container until it was empty, and the water fell through the light from sundown like August rain that fell while the sun was still shining, almost evaporating before it touched the wilted squash flowers.

The wind pulled at the priest's brown Franciscan robe and swirled away the corn meal and pollen that had been sprinkled on the blanket. They lowered the bundle into the ground, and they didn't bother to untie the stiff pieces of new rope that were tied around the ends of the blanket. The sun was gone, and over on the highway the eastbound lane was full of headlights. The priest walked away slowly. Leon watched him climb the hill, and when he had disappeared within the tall, thick walls, Leon turned to look up at the high blue mountains in the deep snow that reflected a faint red light from the west. He felt good because it was finished, and he was happy about the sprinkling of the holy water; now the old man could send them big thunderclouds for sure.

8 BUFFY SAINTE-MARIE

"My Country" (1971)

Now that your big eyes are finally opened,
Now that you're wond'ring "how must they feel?"
Meaning them that you've chased 'cross America's movie screens.
Now that you're wond'ring "how can it be real,"
That the ones you've called colorful, noble and proud
In your school propaganda – they starve in their splendor!
You've asked for my comment. I simply will render:
My country, 'tis of thy people you're dying!

Now that the long houses "breed superstition"
You force us to send our toddlers away
To your schools where they're taught to despise their traditions;
Forbid them their languages, then further say

That American history really began
When Columbus set sail out of Europe! And stress
That the nation of leeches that's conquered this land
Are the biggest and bravest and boldest and best!
And yet where in your history books is the tale
Of the genocide basic to this country's birth?
Of the preachers who lied? How the Bill of Rights failed?
How a nation of patriots returned to their earth?
And where will it tell of the liberty bell
As it rang with a thud over Kinzua mud?
And of brave Uncle Sam in Alaska this year?
My country, 'tis of thy people you're dying!

Hear how the bargain was made for the West
With her shivering children in zero degrees,
"Blankets for your land", so the treaties attest.
Oh, well, blankets for land is a bargain indeed . . .
But the blankets were those Uncle Sam had collected,
From smallpox diseased dying soldiers that day,
And the tribes were wiped out and the history books censored!
A hundred years of your statesmen have felt it's better this way,
Yet a few of the conquered have somehow survived . . .
Their blood runs the redder though genes have been paled,
From the Grand Canyon's caverns to Craven's sad hills,
The wounded, the losers, the robbed sing their tale,
From Los Angeles County to upstate New York,
The white nation fattens while others grow lean,
Oh the tricked and evicted, they know what I mean;
My country, 'tis of thy people you're dying!

The past it just crumbled: the future just threatens;
Our life blood's shut up in your chemical tanks.
And now here you come, bill of sale in your hand,
And surprise in your eyes that we're lacking in thanks,
For the blessings of civilization you've brought us,
The lessons you've taught us, the ruin you've wrought us!
Oh see what our trust in America's brought us!
My country, 'tis of thy people you're dying!

Now that the pride of the sires receive charity,
Now that we're harmless and safe behind laws,
Now that my life's to be known as your heritage,
Now that even the graves have been robbed,
Now that our own chosen way is your novelty,
Hands on our hearts, we salute you your victory,
Choke on your blue, white and scarlet hypocrisy,
Pitying the blindness that you've never seen,

That the eagles of war whose wings lent you glory,
They were never no more than carrion crows;
Pushed the wrens from their nest, stole their eggs, changed their story,
The mockingbird sings it . . . it's all that she knows,
"Ah what can I do?" say a powerless few,
With a lump in your throat and a tear in your eye,
Can't you see that their poverty's profiting you?
My country, 'tis of thy people you're dying!

9 STUDS TERKEL

"Girl of the Golden West: Ramona Bennett" (1980)

We're on the highway, heading from the Seattle airport to Tacoma.

"Do you know we're on a reservation at this moment? It was reserved forever for the members of my tribe. 'Forever' meant until some white people wanted it. I'm a member of the Puyallup tribe. It's called that by the whites because they couldn't pronounce our foreign name: Spalallapubhsh. (Laughs.) . . . .

"We were a fishing people. We had camps all the way from McNeill's Island to Salmon Bay and clear up to Rodando. In 1854, agents of the United States government met with our people and did a treaty. They promised us they only needed land to farm. They assured us that our rights as commercial fishing people would not be disturbed. Because Indian people have always been generous, we agreed to share.

"Our tribes were consolidated onto this reservation, twenty-nine thousand acres. We lost eleven thousand in the survey, so we came down to eighteen thousand. We should have known, but we're a trusting people."

We were long-house people, matriarchal, where the whole extended family lived together. We didn't have real estate problems. There was lots of space for everybody, so we didn't have to stand our long houses on end and call them skyscrapers.

The white people decided we'd make good farmers, so they separated our long-house families into forty-, eighty-, and 160-acre tracts. If we didn't improve our land, we'd lose it. They really knew it wouldn't work, but it was a way of breaking up our society. Phil Lucas, who's a beautiful Indian folk singer, says the marriage between the non-Indians and the Indians was a perfect one. The Indian measures his success by his ability to share. The white man measures his importance by how much he can take. There couldn't have been two more perfect cultures to meet, with the white people taking everything and the Indians giving everything.

They then decided that because we couldn't read or write or speak English, we should all be assigned guardians. So the lawyers and judges and police and businessmen who came out with Milwaukee Railroad and Weyerhaeuser Lumber, all these good citizens were assigned their fair share of Indians to be guardians for. They sold the land to each other, kept the money for probate fees, and had the sheriffs come out and remove any Indians still living on this land. Those Indians unwilling to be removed were put on the railroad tracks and murdered. We became landless on our own reservations.

The kids were denied access to anything traditionally theirs. They had programs called Domestic Science, where little Indian girls were taught how to wash dishes for white people, cook meals for white people, mop floors for white people. If they were very, very smart, they were taught how to be beauticians and cut white people's hair, or to be waitresses and serve white people in restaurants, to be clerk typists, maybe, and type white people's ideas. All the boys went through a program called Agricultural Science, where they were taught how to plow white people's fields and take care of white people's cows and chickens and to care for the produce that was being raised on their own land, stolen by non-Indians. If these boys were very, very smart, they were taught to be unemployed welders or unemployed sheet-metal workers. People that do the hiring are whites, and they tend to be more comfortable with people who resemble them.

We are entering a complex of buildings. One stands out from among the others; it has the appearance of a stone fortress.

This is a jail for young Indian boys. It used to be a little Indian hospital. It was the only hospital for us in the whole region. That's Alaska, Montana, Idaho, Washington, and Oregon. The good white folks saw this new modern hospital going up and right away got mad. They started lobbying to get it away from us. About eighteen years ago, the government snatched it away.

I spent eight years as chairwoman of Puyallup Tribal Council, non-stop, working to reacquire the building. Right now, it's used by Washington State as a jail for children. It's called a juvenile diagnostic center. (She nods toward a young boy on the grounds.) You just saw an Indian child. Who the hell do you think gets locked up in this country? Children, minority and white. It's a system that is so goddamn sick that it abandons and locks up its children. Didn't you see the barbed wire? (Impatient with me) I mean, didn't you see the cyclone fence? See the bars on the windows over there?

We enter one of the smaller buildings across the road. It is noninstitutional in appearance and feeling. Small, delighted children are busy at their tasks or listening quietly to one of the young women teachers. A teacher says: "Most of our students and teachers are Indian. We concentrate on traditional crafts and arts and history. We teach respect for the visions of others. We honor elders for their wisdom. We prize good humor, especially when directed at oneself. All natural things are our brothers and sisters, and will teach us if we are aware and listen. We honor persons for what they've done for their people, not what they've done for themselves."

We demanded a school building to get our kids out of the public school system, where they were being failed. It was a struggle getting this school. I've learned from the whites how to grab and how to push. When the state would not return our hospital to us, we just pushed our way on this property and occupied it.

When you read about Indians or when you see them in movies, you see John Wayne theater. You see an Indian sneaking through the bushes to kill some innocent white. (She indicates people walking by, all of whom know her. On occasion, she chats with one or two.) You'd never think those two guys are fishermen and the guy that just walked by is an accountant. So is that gal. You don't think of Indians as professionals. You think of the stereotype that everyone needs to be afraid of.

In school, I learned the same lies you learned: that Columbus discovered America, that there were no survivors at Little Big Horn, that the first baby born west of the Mississippi was born to Narcissa Whitman. All the same crap that you learned, I learned. Through those movies I learned that an Irishman who stands up for his rights is a patriot, and an Indian who stands up for his rights is a savage. I learned that the pioneers made the West a fit place for decent folks to live. I learned that white people had to take land away from the Indian people because we didn't know how to use it. It wasn't plowed, logged, and paved. It wasn't strip-mined. It had to be taken from us because we had no environmental knowledge or concerns. We were just not destructive enough to be considered *really* civilized.

What happened is we had land the whites wanted. The government ordered the Indians to move. They were moved so many times, they might as well have had handles. There were always a few patriots who'd say: "For God's sake, we were born here, we buried our dead here. Leave us alone. My God, it's a federal promise. We got a contract. I'm not makin' my grandmother move, I'm not makin' my children move. Bullshit, I'm sick of this." They pick up arms and that would be an uprising. The cavalry rides in. Since we all look alike, they'd kill the first bunch of Indians they saw. This was just tradition. Every single one of those cavalry officers had one of those damn little flags and damn little Bibles. Oh, they were very, very religious. (Laughs.) They opened fire and did a genocide.

They always teach that the only survivor at Little Big Horn was that cavalry horse. Since then, I've realized there were many survivors of Little Big Horn. (Laughs.) They were Sioux and Cheyennes and therefore didn't count, apparently. You never see a roster with all of *their* names.

When I went to school, we learned history so we won't make the same mistakes. This is what I was told. I know damn good and well that if American children in school had learned that the beautiful Cheyenne women at Sand Creek put their shawls over their babies' faces so they wouldn't see the long knives, if the American schoolchildren learned that Indian mothers held their babies close to their bodies when the Gatling guns shot and killed three hundred, there would never have been a My Lai massacre. If the history teacher had really been truthful with American children, Calley would have given an order to totally noncooperating troops. There would have been no one to fight. There would have been a national conscience. The lie has made for an American nightmare, not dream.

When I was in first grade, really tiny, I played a small child in a school play. This was during World War Two. I was born in 1938. My mother was a little dark lady. Caucasians cannot tell people of color apart. To the average white, Chinese, Filipinos, Japanese, all look the same. When my mom came to the school grounds, a little boy named Charles made slanty eyes at her and called her ugly names. I didn't understand what he was saying, but I just jumped on him and started hitting him. He was a friend of mine, and he didn't know why I was doing it. Neither did I. When the play started, my clothes were all disheveled. I was confused, hurt, and really feeling bad. When I went on that stage and looked at all those faces, I realized for the first time my mother was a different color from the others and attracted attention. Her skin had always been rich and warm, while mine looked pale and cold. My father was white. It was such a shock that someone could hate my mother for being such a warm, beautiful woman.

Much later I found out that Charles's father died in the Pacific and that his whole family was very uptight about the Japanese.

I think of Indian people who, at treaty time, offered to share with a few men from Boston. They never knew there'd be a Boeing Airplane Company or a Weyerhaeuser. They never knew there would be a statue in the harbor inviting wretched masses and that those masses would come like waves of the sea, thousands and thousands of people seeking freedom. Freedoms that those Indian people would never be afforded. With all those waves coming at us, we were just drowning in the American Dream.

The median lifespan for Indians is somewhere in the forties. That's deceptive because our infant mortality rate is four times higher than the national average. We have the magic age of nineteen, the age of drinking, violent deaths, and suicides. Our teenage suicide rate is thirty-four times higher than the national average.

Forty-five is another magic age for the Indian. That's the age of deaths from alcoholism. Our people have gone from the highest protein diet on the face of the earth – buffalo and salmon – to macaroni. If we're not alcoholics, we're popoholics. Ninety percent of us, eighteen and older, are alcoholics. It's a daily suicide: "I can't face my life, lack of future. I can't face the ugly attitudes toward me. I can't face the poverty. So I'll just drink this bottle of Ripple, and I'll kill myself for a few hours. I'll kill some brain cells. Tomorrow, when I get sober, maybe things will be different. When I get sober and things are no different, I'll drink again. I'm not so hopeless that I'll kill myself." It's an optimistic form of suicide.

I once drank very heavily. A little seventeen-year-old girl, who I considered just a child, would just get in my face and give me hell. She would say: "Don't you care about yourself? Don't you realize you're killing an Indian? Why do you want to hurt yourself?" At that point I stopped, and I can't be around people who drink. Oh, I don't mind if you drink. I don't care what non-Indian people do to themselves. But I hate to see an Indian killing himself or herself. That Indian is waiting, marking time and wasting, decade after decade. The family is broken up. They rush through our communities and gather our children. Thirty-five percent of our children have been removed from their families to boarding schools, foster homes, and institutions. A Shoshone or Sioux or Navajo woman lives in a house like mine. Substandard, no sanitation. No employment on the reservation. Inadequate education. The Mormons have a relocation – child-removal – program. Here's the routine:

A woman from the LDS [Latter Day Saints] knocks on my door. I'm gracious and I invite her in because that's our way. She says: "Oh, look at all your pretty children. Oh, what a nice family. I see that your roof leaks and your house is a little cold and you don't have sanitation. By the looks of your kitchen, you don't have much food, and I notice you have very little furniture. You don't have running water and you have an outdoor toilet. And the nearest school is sixty miles away. Wouldn't you like your children to go and live in this nice house, where they'll have their own bedrooms, wonderful people who care about them, lots of money to buy food, indoor plumbing, posturepedic mattresses and Cannon sheets, and wonderful television sets, and well-landscaped yards? And a neighborhood school, so your children won't have to spend three hours a day on a bus?" And then she says: "If you reeeeeeelly, reeeeeeally love your children, you wouldn't want them to live like this. You would want them to have all the good things they need." And that mother thinks: My God, I love my children and what a monster I am! How can I possibly keep them from this paradise?

"My mother grew up poor, like many Indians. She was taken away to boarding school, where they forbade the use of her language, her religion. But she kept her wits about her. She learned to look at things with a raised eyebrow. When she hears something that's funny, she laughs out loud. She provided me with pride, humor, and strength: you don't snivel, you don't quit, you don't back off.

"She talks to graves, talks to plants, talks to rivers. Aside from knowing the traditional things, she was busy growing things, digging clams, smoking fish, sewing. She's an excellent seamstress. At the same time, she's politically and socially sharp.

"When I was a little girl, a couple of FBI agents came to the house. I was maybe four years old. World War Two had just broken out. In a secretive way, they said: 'We'd like to talk to you about security risks. Next-door is this German family, and on the other side these Italians. We want to know if you think they're loyal.' My maiden name was Church, a very British, acceptable name. She said that the Germans were third-generation and are Americans to the core, and the Italian family had already lost a son in the Pacific. Then she said: 'If you're looking for a security risk, I suggest you investigate me, because I don't see any reason for an Indian to be fighting for a government that has stolen lands from the Indian people.' She just shouted at them to get the hell off her porch. Gee, they just back-pedaled off and went." (Laughs.)

I met a bunch of Eskimos from Alaska that the Methodists got hold of. They call it the Methodist ethic. If you work, you're good, if you don't, you're bad. I don't impose that ethic on other people. These Eskimos are now so task-oriented, they're very, very hyper. They don't know how to relax. The Methodists got hold of their heads, and they lost what they had. They're in a mad dash all the time and don't know how to sit and cogitate.

My little six-year-old will go out, just sit and talk to one of those trees or observe the birds. He can be calm and comfortable doing that. He hasn't been through the same brainwash that the rest of us have.

There's knowledge born in these little ones that ties back to the spirit world, to the Creator. Those little kids in school can tell you that the nations of fish are their brothers and sisters. They'll tell you that their life is no more important than the life of that animal or that tree or that flower. They're born knowing that. It's that our school doesn't beat it out of them.

History's important, what happened in the past is important. But I'm not satisfied with just talking about what happened in 1855 or what happened in 1903, during the murders, or 1961, when they seized our hospital. I want my children to have something good to say in 1990 about what happened in 1979. They're not gonna look in the mirror and see themselves as Indians with no future.

My little son shares the continent with 199,999,999 other folks. (Laughs.) If your government screws up and creates one more damned war, his little brown ass will get blown away, right along with all your people. All those colors (laughs) and all those attitudes. The bombs that come don't give a damn if he's got cute little braids, is a little brown boy, talks to cedar trees, and is a sweet little person.

I see the United States government as a little baby brat. If you say no, it throws something at you. If it sees something, it just grabs. Just drools all over and soils itself, and has to have others come in and clean it up. It's a 200-year-old kid. They gave us dual citizenship in 1924. How can a little teeny stupid 150-year-old government grant citizenship to a Yakima Indian who has been here for eight million years? To a Puyallup? What an insult! (Laughs.) How can a lying little trespasser that doesn't know how to act right grant anything to anybody? Why doesn't somebody get that kid in line? Eventually, some stranger will go over and grab that little kid and shake 'im up. I think the United States is just rapidly heading to be shaken around. Unfortunately, I'm living right here and I'm gonna get shaken around right along with the rest of us. (Laughs.) We're all in the same canoe.

10 JOY HARJO

"The Woman Hanging from the Thirteenth Floor Window" (1983)

She is the woman hanging from the 13th floor
window. Her hands are pressed white against the
concrete moulding of the tenement building. She
hangs from the 13th floor window in east Chicago,
with a swirl of birds over her head. They could
be a halo, or a storm of glass waiting to crush her.

She thinks she will be set free.

The woman hanging from the 13th floor window
on the east side of Chicago is not alone.
She is a woman of children, of the baby, Carlos,
and of Margaret, and of Jimmy who is the oldest.
She is her mother's daughter and her father's son.
She is several pieces between the two husbands
she has had. She is all the women of the apartment
building who stand watching her, watching themselves.

When she was young she ate wild rice on scraped down
plates in warm wood rooms. It was in the farther
north and she was the baby then. They rocked her.

She sees Lake Michigan lapping at the shores of
herself. It is a dizzy hole of water and the rich
live in tall glass houses at the edge of it. In some
places Lake Michigan speaks softly, here, it just sputters
and butts itself against the asphalt. She sees
other buildings just like hers. She sees other
women hanging from many-floored windows
counting their lives in the palms of their hands
and in the palms of their children's hands.

She is the woman hanging from the 13th floor window
on the Indian side of town. Her belly is soft from

her children's births, her worn levis swing down below
her waist, and then her feet, and then her heart.
She is dangling.

The woman hanging from the 13th floor hears voices.
They come to her in the night when the lights have gone
dim. Sometimes they are little cats mewing and scratching
at the door, sometimes they are her grandmother's voice,
and sometimes they are gigantic men of light whispering
to her to get up, to get up, to get up. That's when she wants
to have another child to hold onto in the night, to be
able to fall back into dreams.

And the woman hanging from the 13th floor window
hears other voices. Some of them scream out from below
for her to jump, they would push her over. Others cry softly
from the sidewalks, pull their children up like flowers and gather
them into their arms. They would help her, like themselves.

But she is the woman hanging from the 13th floor window,
and she knows she is hanging by her own fingers, her
own skin, her own thread of indecision.

She thinks of Carlos, of Margaret, of Jimmy.
She thinks of her father, and of her mother.
She thinks of all the women she has been, of all
the men. She thinks of the color of her skin, and
of Chicago streets, and of waterfalls and pines.
She thinks of moonlight nights, and of cool spring storms.
Her mind chatters like neon and northside bars.
She thinks of the 4 a.m. lonelinesses that have folded
her up like death, discordant, without logical and
beautiful conclusion. Her teeth break off at the edges.
She would speak.

The woman hangs from the 13th floor window crying for
the lost beauty of her own life. She sees the
sun falling west over the grey plane of Chicago.
She thinks she remembers listening to her own life
break loose, as she falls from the 13th floor
window on the east side of Chicago, or as she
climbs back up to claim herself again.

2

IMMIGRATION

Introduction	32
11 Emma Lazarus "The New Colossus" (1883)	35
12 Henry James FROM "The Inconceivable Alien" (1883)	36
13 Abraham Cahan "The Meeting" (1896)	37
14 Mary Antin FROM *The Promised Land* (1912)	40
15 Owen Wister FROM "Shall We Let the Cuckoos Crowd Us Out of Our Nest?" (1921)	42
16 Edward Bok FROM *The Americanization of Edward Bok* (1921)	43
17 Ole E. Rølvaag FROM "The Power of Evil in High Places" (1927)	45
18 Oscar Handlin FROM *The Uprooted* (1951)	56
19 Al Santoli FROM "Mojados (Wetbacks)" (1988)	58
20 Arthur M. Schlesinger, Jr. "E Pluribus Unum?" (1992)	62

Figure 2 Immigrants at Ellis Island. Photograph courtesy of Brown Brothers

INTRODUCTION

Immigration is and has always been an important theme in American history. From the 1840s until the early 1920s, when the Quota Acts began to restrict the number of newcomers, immigration was truly a mass movement. Approximately thirty million people emigrated to the United States during those years. Cultivation of the prairie and rapid industrialization were in some ways both the cause and the effect of this large-scale immigration.

The transition from the old to the new world was by no means an easy one. Immigrants were sometimes met with suspicion, prejudice and fear, particularly those from eastern and southern Europe who arrived around 1900. Often referred to as "the new immigrants," they had little or no capital, lacked industrial skills, and were often poorly educated. Since so many came at the same time and competed for low-paying jobs in new factories, they were often blamed for the problems of the fast-growing cities in which they lived, sometimes in great poverty. Their effect on American society, however, was great. At that time immigration to rural areas in the Midwest had subsided. In addition, many "new immigrants," although they came from rural districts of Europe, could not afford to go further west and remained huddled in urban immigrant ghettoes on the East Coast.

In his major study of American immigration, *The Uprooted* (1951), Oscar Handlin focused on such urban immigrants. In the historiography of American immigration Handlin's book remains a classic (see text 18), even though he is now criticized for having overemphasized the experience of a tragic uprooting. Even if he underscored the "bitter present" of the new immigrant in *The Uprooted*, Handlin later – in his essay "Immigration in American Life: A Reappraisal" (1961) – returned to the vast success of American immigrants and compared them to earlier Puritan settlers:

The story of immigration is a tale of wonderful success, the compounded biography of thousands of humble people who through their own efforts brought themselves across great distances to plant their roots and to thrive in alien soil. Its only parallel is the story of the United States which began in the huddled settlements at the edge of the wilderness and pulled itself upward to immense material and spiritual power.

Since 1886 the Statue of Liberty outside New York has been a symbol of welcome to new immigrants. Inscribed on the base of the statue is Emma Lazarus's famous poem about "the golden door," supposedly open to all immigrants in need of a better place (text 11). In 1883 novelist Henry James reflected on the entry of new immigrants to Ellis Island and concluded that "we must go . . . *more* than half-way to meet them" (see text 12). James was impressed by the sight of immigrants pushing through the doors of the Ellis Island complex and convinced that all Americans who witnessed such a scene would be for ever changed.

Immigrants were, however, not always met with such an open attitude, or with the policy of an ardent welcome. In Owen Wister's popular prose (see text 15) immigrants are seen as aliens, scornfully treated in a symbolism of negative connotations. Measured against such views, the melting-pot ideology may be understood as a blessing and an appeal to common sense. But Wister was by no means the only one to voice such opinions, even though others would not use his type of language. In fact, during the 1920s most Americans may have felt that the days of large-scale immigration were over and thus have welcomed the Quota Acts which restricted the waves of mass immigration which had continued for about the last century.

Americans varied greatly in their attitudes to how immigrants should be assimilated. Some felt that immigrants should comply completely with the already existing Anglo-American culture, which was then regarded as a given. Others felt that everyone, both the newcomers and those of older American stock, should undergo the changes of the "melting-pot" in a process of refining and blending the best elements of both the old and the new. Still others welcomed the contributions immigrants had made to a society of cultural pluralism.

The term "Melting-Pot" was first used in a popular play by that name written by Israel Zangwill (1907). The play shows how members of groups who had been fighting each other in the old country would unite in the new. But during the first two decades of the nineteenth century, when this idea was adopted and defined as a general policy, it was taken for granted that only immigrants needed to be "melted." Giving up old cultural ties in the process, the immigrant would hopefully emerge as a genuine American. On the other hand, Americans – who were not immigrants – did not have to enter the melting-pot. As a result, leaders of some immigrant groups felt the overt pressure to assimilate as a threat. The melting-pot idea was therefore often fought, sometimes desperately – but mostly with little success in the long run – by immigrant leaders who strongly identified with their mother country.

The conflict between assimilation and preservation is dramatically presented in a chapter, "The Meetings", from the novel, *Yekl* (see text 13), by the Jewish-American writer Abraham Cahan, an immigrant from Russia, who struggled to develop an American culture in Yiddish. For more than forty years he edited the *Daily Forward*, a famous Jewish-American newspaper. Cahan never felt that becoming an American meant forgetting his old country.

The Norwegian-American professor and novelist Ole E. Rølvaag felt the same way. Of all fiction produced by immigrants in the Midwest, his *The Giants in the Earth* from 1927 (in English translation) remains the classic and most widely read account of immigrant life in the Midwestern regions of the nation. The chapter chosen here (text 17) may be read as a short story about different attitudes to life on the frontier in the days of the first immigrant settlers of the 1870s. As he turns the soil into a productive farm, Per becomes the very incarnation of Turner's frontier thesis (see p. 190). He symbolizes the immigrant who gladly used his chance to cultivate a farm, the size of which he could not even have dreamt of in his old country. His wife, on the other hand, pays the terrible price of a too exuberant optimism. Her problems were undoubtedly not uncommon among early immigrants on the prairie.

The immigrants contributed to and expanded the body of American literature, sometimes in languages other than English. A vast number of immigrant letters crossed the seas; immigrants wrote diaries to record their experiences as well as an astonishing number of autobiographies. Many immigrants, like Mary Antin and Edward Bok, felt the need to define their twofold identities. Antin published her very popular *The Promised Land* in 1912 (see text 14, from her introduction), but was soon forgotten. Bok rose to become a publisher of journals. His immigrant memories, *The Americanization of Edward Bok*, won a Pulitzer Prize in 1921 (text 16). Both Antin and Bok entered the United States as immigrant children, Antin when she was 13, Bok as a 6-year-old. They came to differ in their conception of American culture; Antin felt liberated and converted to a new and better life, Bok felt that his success as an American was just as much a result of values he carried with him from his old country.

To some contemporary writers the popular ethnic revival and cultural pluralism of the 1960s and 1970s may have gone too far. Thus the historian Arthur M. Schlesinger, Jr., argues for a return to the melting-pot concept in the preface to his controversial book *The Disuniting of America: Reflections on a Multicultural Society* (1992; see text 20).

Today immigration to the United States is limited, although the old Quota Acts no longer exist. The largest groups of immigrants now come from Asian and Latin American countries. Their life in the United States has given material for a new wave of immigrant writing which unfortunately cannot be presented here. The interview with a Mexican "wetback" family (text 19) represents the voices of the more recent immigrants. Interestingly they cross a river, not an ocean.

Questions and Topics

1 Try to identify the historical context of Cahan's chapter "The Meeting" and explain the reactions of the newcomer to her husband and the American city.
2 Many immigrants dreamt of the United States as a country where "a man will find himself growing free . . . in daily contact with the newest forms of life." Compare this dream to the experience of Rølvaag's characters.

3 Compare and contrast the immigrant experiences of Antin and Bok as presented in the excerpts from their autobiographies.

4 What do you think of Handlin's metaphor of being *uprooted* as central to the immigrant experience? What other metaphors could be, or have been, used?

5 Relate the life of new immigrants from Mexico to the words that greeted earlier European immigrants on the Statue of Liberty.

Suggestions for further reading

Barkan, Elliott Robert, *And Still They Come: Immigrants and American Society 1920 to the 1990s* (Wheeling, Ill.: Harlan Davidson, 1996).

Bodnar, John, *The Transplanted: A History of Immigrants in Urban America* (Bloomington: Indiana University Press, 1985).

Gjerde, Jon, ed., *Major Problems in American Immigration and Ethnic History* (Boston: Houghton Mifflin, 1998).

Hansen, Marcus Lee, *The Immigrant in American History* (New York: Harper & Row, [1940], 1964).

Higham, John, *Send These to Me: Immigrants in Urban America* (Baltimon, Md.: Johns Hopkins University Press, [1975], revised edn, 1984).

11 EMMA LAZARUS

"The New Colossus" (1883)

Not like the brazen giant of Greek fame,
With conquering limbs astride from land to land;
Here at our sea-washed, sunset gates shall stand
A mighty woman with a torch, whose flame
Is the imprisoned lightning, and her name
Mother of Exiles. From her beacon-hand
Glows world-wide welcome; her mild eyes command
The air-bridged harbor that twin cities frame.

"Keep, ancient lands, your storied pomp!" cries she
With silent lips. "Give me your tired, your poor,
Your huddled masses yearning to breathe free,
The wretched refuse of your teeming shore.
Send these, the homeless, tempest-tost to me,
I lift my lamp beside the golden door!"

12 HENRY JAMES

FROM *"The Inconceivable Alien" (1883)*

I think indeed that the simplest account of the action of Ellis Island on the spirit of any sensitive citizen who may have happened to "look in" is that he comes back from his visit not at all the same person that he went. He has eaten of the tree of knowledge, and the taste will be for ever in his mouth. He had thought he knew before, thought he had the sense of the degree in which it is his American fate to share the sanctity of his American consciousness, the intimacy of his American patriotism, with the inconceivable alien; but the truth had never come home to him with any such force. In the lurid light projected upon it by those courts of dismay it shakes him – or I like at least to imagine it shakes him – to the depths of his being; I like to think of him, I positively *have* to think of him, as going about ever afterwards with a new look, for those who can see it, in his face, the outward sign of the new chill in his heart. So is stamped, for detection, the questionably privileged person who has had an apparition, seen a ghost in his supposedly safe old house. Let not the unwary, therefore, visit Ellis Island.

The after-sense of that acute experience, however, I myself found, was by no means to be brushed away; I felt it grow and grow, on the contrary, wherever I turned: other impressions might come and go, but this affirmed claim of the alien, however immeasurably alien, to share in one's supreme relation was everywhere the fixed element, the reminder not to be dodged. One's supreme relation, as one had always put it, was one's relation to one's country – a conception made up so largely of one's countrymen and one's countrywomen. Thus it was as if, all the while, with such a fond tradition of what these products predominantly were, the idea of the country itself underwent something of that profane overhauling through which it appears to suffer the indignity of change. Is not our instinct in this matter, in general, essentially the safe one – that of keeping the idea simple and strong and continuous, so that it shall be perfectly sound? To touch it overmuch, to pull it about, is to put it in peril of weakening; yet on this free assault upon it, this readjustment of it in *their* monstrous, presumptuous interest, the aliens, in New York, seemed perpetually to insist. The combination there of their quantity and their quality – that loud primary stage of alienism which New York most offers to sight – operates, for the native, as their note of settled possession, something they have nobody to thank for; so that unsettled possession is what we, on our side, seem reduced to – the implication of which, in its turn, is that, to recover confidence and regain lost ground, we, not they, must make the surrender and accept the orientation. We must go, in other words, *more* than halfway to meet them; which is all the difference, for us, between possession and dispossession. This sense of dispossession, to be brief about it, haunted me so, I was to feel, in the New York streets and in the packed trajectiles to which one clingingly appeals from the streets, just as one tumbles back into the streets in appalled reaction from *them*, that the art of beguiling or duping it became an art to be cultivated – though the fond alternative vision was never long to be obscured, the imagination, exasperated to envy, of the ideal, in the order in question; of the luxury of some such close and sweet and *whole* national consciousness as that of the Switzer and the Scot.

13 ABRAHAM CAHAN

"The Meeting" (1896)

A few weeks later, on a Saturday morning, Jake, with an unfolded telegram in his hand, stood in front of one of the desks at the Immigration Bureau of Ellis Island. He was freshly shaven and clipped, smartly dressed in his best clothes and ball shoes, and, in spite of the sickly expression of shamefacedness and anxiety which distorted his features, he looked younger than usual.

All the way to the island he had been in a flurry of joyous anticipation. The prospect of meeting his dear wife and child, and, incidentally, of showing off his swell attire to her, had thrown him into a fever of impatience. But on entering the big shed he had caught a distant glimpse of Gitl and Yosselé through the railing separating the detained immigrants from their visitors, and his heart had sunk at the sight of his wife's uncouth and un-American appearance. She was slovenly dressed in a brown jacket and skirt of grotesque cut, and her hair was concealed under a voluminous wig of a pitch-black hue. This she had put on just before leaving the steamer, both "in honor of the sabbath" and by way of sprucing herself up for the great event. Since Yekl had left home she had gained considerably in the measurement of her waist. The wig, however, made her seem stouter and shorter than she would have appeared without it. It also added at least five years to her looks. But she was aware neither of this nor of the fact that in New York even a Jewess of her station and orthodox breeding is accustomed to blink at the wickedness of displaying her natural hair, and that none but an elderly matron may wear a wig without being the occasional target for snowballs or stones. She was naturally dark of complexion, and the nine or ten days spent at sea had covered her face with a deep bronze, which combined with her prominent cheek bones, inky little eyes, and, above all, the smooth black wig, to lend her resemblance to a squaw.

Jake had no sooner caught sight of her than he had averted his face, as if loth to rest his eyes on her, in the presence of the surging crowd around him, before it was inevitable. He dared not even survey that crowd to see whether it contained any acquaintance of his, and he vaguely wished that her release were delayed indefinitely.

Presently the officer behind the desk took the telegram from him, and in another little while Gitl, hugging Yosselé with one arm and a bulging parcel with the other, emerged from a side door.

"Yekl!" she screamed out in a piteous high key, as if crying for mercy.

"Dot'sh alla right!" he returned in English, with a wan smile and unconscious of what he was saying. His wandering eyes and dazed mind were striving to fix themselves upon the stern functionary and the questions he bethought himself of asking before finally releasing his prisoners. The contrast between Gitl and Jake was so striking that the officer wanted to make sure – partly as a matter of official duty and partly for the fun of the thing – that the two were actually man and wife.

"*Oi* a lamentation upon me! He shaves his beard!" Gitl ejaculated to herself as she scrutinized her husband. "Yosselé, look! Here is *taté*!"

But Yosselé did not care to look at taté. Instead, he turned his frightened little eyes – precise copies of Jake's – and buried them in his mother's cheek.

When Gitl was finally discharged she made to fling herself on Jake. But he checked her by seizing both loads from her arms. He started for a distant and deserted corner of the room, bidding her follow. For a moment the boy looked stunned, then he burst out crying and fell to kicking his father's chest with might and main, his reddened little face appealingly turned to Gitl. Jake continuing his way tried to kiss his son into toleration, but the little fellow proved too nimble for him. It was in vain that Gitl, scurrying behind, kept expostulating with Yosselé: "Why, it is taté!" Taté was forced to capitulate before the march was brought to its end.

At length, when the secluded corner had been reached, and Jake and Gitl had set down their burdens, husband and wife flew into mutual embrace and fell to kissing each other. The performance had an effect of something done to order, which, it must be owned, was far from being belied by the state of their minds at the moment. Their kisses imparted the taste of mutual estrangement to both. In Jake's case the sensation was quickened by the strong steerage odors which were emitted by Gitl's person, and he involuntarily recoiled.

"You look like a *poritz*,"[1] she said shyly.

"How are you! How is mother?"

"How should she be? So, so. She sends you her love," Gitl mumbled out.

"How long was father ill?"

"Maybe a month. He cost us health enough."

He proceeded to make advances to Yosselé, she appealing to the child in his behalf. For a moment the sight of her, as they were both crouching before the boy, precipitated a wave of thrilling memories on Jake and made him feel in his own environment. Presently, however, the illusion took wing and here he was, Jake the Yankee, with this bonnetless, wigged, dowdyish little greenhorn by his side! That she was his wife, nay, that he was a married man at all, seemed incredible to him. The sturdy, thriving urchin had at first inspired him with pride; but as he now cast another side glance at Gitl's wig he lost all interest in him, and began to regard him, together with his mother, as one great obstacle dropped from heaven, as it were, in his way.

Gitl, on her part, was overcome with a feeling akin to awe. She, too, could not get herself to realize that this stylish young man – shaved and dressed as in Povodye is only some young nobleman – was Yekl, her own Yekl, who had all these three years never been absent from her mind. And while she was once more examining Jake's blue diagonal cutaway, glossy stand-up collar, the white four-in-hand necktie, coquettishly tucked away in the bosom of his starched shirt, and, above all, his patent leather shoes, she was at the same time mentally scanning the Yekl of three years before. The latter alone was hers, and she felt like crying to the image to come back to her and let her be *his* wife.

Presently, when they had got up and Jake was plying her with perfunctory questions, she chanced to recognize a certain movement of his upper lip – an old trick of his. It was as if she had suddenly discovered her own Yekl in an apparent stranger, and, with another pitiful outcry, she fell on his breast.

"Don't!" he said, with patient gentleness, pushing away her arms. "Here everything is so different."

She colored deeply.

"They don't wear wigs here," he ventured to add.

"What then?" she asked, perplexedly.

"You will see. It is quite another world."

"Shall I take it off, then? I have a nice Saturday kerchief," she faltered. "It is of silk – I bought it at Kalmen's for a bargain. It is still brand new."

"Here one does not wear even a kerchief."

"How then? Do they go about with their own hair?" she queried in ill-disguised bewilderment.

"*Vell, alla right*, put it on, quick!"

As she set about undoing her parcel, she bade him face about and screen her, so that neither he nor any stranger could see her bareheaded while she was replacing the wig by the kerchief. He obeyed. All the while the operation lasted he stood with his gaze on the floor, gnashing his teeth with disgust and shame, or hissing some Bowery oath.

"Is this better?" she asked bashfully, when her hair and part of her forehead were hidden under a kerchief of flaming blue and yellow, whose end dangled down her back.

The kerchief had a rejuvenating effect. But Jake thought that it made her look like an Italian woman of Mulberry Street on Sunday.

"*Alla right*, leave it be for the present," he said in despair, reflecting that the wig would have been the lesser evil of the two.

When they reached the city Gitl was shocked to see him lead the way to a horse car.

"*Oi* woe is me! Why, it is Sabbath!" she gasped.

He irately essayed to explain that a car, being an uncommon sort of vehicle, riding in it implied no violation of the holy day. But this she sturdily met by reference to railroads.[2] Besides, she had seen horse cars while stopping in Hamburg,[3] and knew that no orthodox Jew would use them on the seventh day. At length Jake, losing all self-control, fiercely commanded her not to make him the laughingstock of the people on the street and to get in without further ado. As to the sin of the matter he was willing to take it all upon himself. Completely dismayed by his stern manner, amid the strange, uproarious, forbidding surroundings, Gitl yielded.

As the horses started she uttered a groan of consternation and remained looking aghast and with a violently throbbing heart. If she had been a culprit on the way to the gallows she could not have been more terrified than she was now at this her first ride on the day of rest.

The conductor came up for their fares. Jake handed him a ten-cent piece, and raising two fingers, he roared out: "Two! He ain' no maur as tree years, de liddle feller!" And so great was the impression which his dashing manner and his English produced on Gitl, that for some time it relieved her mind and she even forgot to be shocked by the sight of her husband handling coin on the Sabbath.

Having thus paraded himself before his wife, Jake all at once grew kindly disposed toward her.

"You must be hungry?" he asked.

"Not at all! Where do you eat your *varimess*?"[4]

"Don't say varimess" he corrected her complaisantly; "here it is called *dinner*."

"*Dinner?*[5] And what if one becomes fatter?" she confusedly ventured an irresistible pun.

This was the way in which Gitl came to receive her first lesson in the five or six score English words and phrases which the omnivorous Jewish jargon has absorbed in the Ghettos of English-speaking countries.

1   Yiddish for nobleman.
2   Orthodox Jews are not permitted to ride in any sort of vehicle on the Sabbath.
3   German port from which immigrants embarked.
4   Yiddish for dinner.
5   Yiddish for thinner.

14 MARY ANTIN

FROM *The Promised Land (1912)*

I was born, I have lived, and I have been made over. Is it not time to write my life's story? I am just as much out of the way as if I were dead, for I am absolutely other than the person whose story I have to tell. Physical continuity with my earlier self is no disadvantage. I could speak in the third person and not feel that I was masquerading. I can analyze my subject, I can reveal anything; for *she*, not *I*, is my heroine. My life I have still to live; her life ended when mine began.

A generation is sometimes a more satisfactory unit for the study of humanity than a lifetime; and spiritual generations are as easy to demark as physical ones. Now I am the spiritual offspring of the marriage within my conscious experience of the Past and the Present. My second birth was no less a birth because there was no distinct incarnation. Surely it has happened before that one body served more than one spiritual organization. Nor am I disowning my father and mother of the flesh, for they were also partners in the generation of my second self; copartners with my entire line of ancestors. They gave me body, so that I have eyes like my father's and hair like my mother's. The spirit also they gave me, so that I reason like my father and endure like my mother. But did they set me down in a sheltered garden, where the sun should warm me, and no winter should hurt, while they fed me from their hands? No; they early let me run in the fields – perhaps because I would not be held – and eat of the wild fruits and drink of the dew. Did they teach me from books, and tell me what to believe? I soon chose my own books, and built me a world of my own.

In these discriminations *I* emerged, a new being, something that had not been before. And when I discovered my own friends, and ran home with them to convert my parents to a belief in their excellence, did I not begin to make my father and mother, as truly as they had ever made me? Did I not become the parent and they the children, in those relations of teacher and learner? And so I can say that there has been more than one birth of myself, and I can regard my earlier self as a separate being, and make it a subject of study . . .

I am not yet thirty, counting in years, and I am writing my life history. Under which of the above categories do I find my justification? I have not accomplished anything, I have not discovered anything, not even by accident, as Columbus discovered

America. My life has been unusual, but by no means unique. And this is the very core of the matter. It is because I understand my history, in its larger outlines, to be typical of many, that I consider it worth recording. My life is a concrete illustration of a multitude of statistical facts. Although I have written a genuine personal memoir, I believe that its chief interest lies in the fact that it is illustrative of scores of unwritten lives. I am only one of many whose fate it has been to live a page of modern history. We are the strands of the cable that binds the Old World to the New. As the ships that brought us link the shores of Europe and America, so our lives span the bitter sea of racial differences and misunderstandings. Before we came, the New World knew not the Old; but since we have begun to come, the Young World has taken the Old by the hand, and the two are learning to march side by side, seeking a common destiny.

Perhaps I have taken needless trouble to furnish an excuse for my autobiography. My age alone, my true age, would be reason enough for my writing. I began life in the Middle Ages, as I shall prove, and here am I still, your contemporary in the twentieth century, thrilling with your latest thought.

Had I no better excuse for writing, I still might be driven to it by my private needs. It is in one sense a matter of my personal salvation. I was at a most impressionable age when I was transplanted to the new soil. I was in that period when even normal children, undisturbed in their customary environment, begin to explore their own hearts, and endeavor to account for themselves and their world. And my zest for self-exploration seems not to have been distracted by the necessity of exploring a new outer universe. I embarked on a double voyage of discovery, and an exciting life it was! I took note of everything. I could no more keep my mind from the shifting, changing landscape than an infant can keep his eyes from the shining candle moved across his field of vision. Thus everything impressed itself on my memory, and with double associations; for I was constantly referring my new world to the old for comparison, and the old to the new for elucidation. I became a student and philosopher by force of circumstances.

Had I been brought to America a few years earlier, I might have written that in such and such a year my father emigrated, just as I would state what he did for a living, as a matter of family history. Happening when it did, the emigration became of the most vital importance to me personally. All the processes of uprooting, transportation, replanting, acclimatization, and development took place in my own soul. I felt the pang, the fear, the wonder, and the joy of it. I can never forget, for I bear the scars. But I want to forget – sometimes I long to forget. I think I have thoroughly assimilated my past – I have done its bidding – I want now to be of to-day. It is painful to be consciously of two worlds. The Wandering Jew in me seeks forgetfulness. I am not afraid to live on and on, if only I do not have to remember too much. A long past vividly remembered is like a heavy garment that clings to your limbs when you would run. And I have thought of a charm that should release me from the folds of my clinging past. I take the hint from the Ancient Mariner, who told his tale in order to be rid of it. I, too, will tell my tale, for once, and never hark back any more. I will write a bold "Finis" at the end, and shut the book with a bang!

15 OWEN WISTER

FROM *"Shall We Let the Cuckoos Crowd Us Out of Our Nest?"* (1921)

That spirit of our country which we symbolize in the figure of Uncle Sam has always been a hospitable spirit. Uncle Sam has told the whole world that the latchstring of his door hangs outside, and that if any stranger comes and pulls it, he will find a warm welcome within.

Many have pulled that string: Strangers from all sorts of shores have entered Uncle Sam's large house. He has been glad to see them all, until lately. Recently some of these newcomers have made him wonder if his hospitality is not being abused.

When a man asks you into his house, he does not expect you to complain of the food, turn his pictures to the wall, smash the windows, or tear down the staircase. Even less does he expect you to try and blow up the foundations of the house.

The Constitution of the United States was very gradually and very thoughtfully created by a rational race; a common-sense race; a race that through centuries has slowly evolved the idea of self-government, and the capacity for self-government. . . .

A cuckoo is a bird that never builds its own nest, but always lays its egg in the nest of some other bird. The bird who built the nest sits on all the eggs.

When they hatch, the young cuckoo is fed just as impartially by its stepmother as the true children are fed.

After a while, it grows and swells, and pushes the true children out to make room for itself; and the true children perish.

Our country is crowded with cuckoos, all very busy laying eggs. They meet and plot. They harangue each other. They curse the house of Uncle Sam. They ask, "Who was George Washington, anyhow?" I have heard them myself.

They tell each other that private property is highway robbery. That is merely because they haven't any, and want yours and mine without working for it. They worm their way into our schools and colleges, and ingeniously inflame the minds of our native young people, who are too immature yet to understand anything about anything. They are laying their plans to push our native young out of the nest.

These Trotzky Cuckoos, and Marx Cuckoos, and Kaiser Cuckoos, to say nothing of some cuckoos of Oriental feather, need a deal more watching than we give them. They get into the law, too, so that when some cuckoos are about to be sent back to their own countries, other cuckoos interfere and see that they don't go.

The American eagle is much larger than any cuckoo, but he is not larger than a million cuckoos. If he does not bestir himself, his eaglets some day may be pushed out of the nest.

Alien eggs are being laid in our American nests. Our native blood is a diminishing drop in the bucket of inundating aliens. Our native inheritance of Liberty, defined and assured by Law, is being mocked and undermined. Our native spirit is being diluted and polluted by organized minorities every day.

Cuckoos there are who would like to change New York's name to Moscow and call Broadway Lenine Street; other cuckoos would rename Washington, Dublin. And we have opened our doors to these birds, made them welcome!

It might actually come to pass some day that the American Eagle, simply to be able to call his soul his own, would have to deal emphatically with all cuckoos. . . . Eternal vigilance cannot watch Liberty and the movies at the same time.

16 EDWARD BOK

Editor of Ladies Home Journal. Coined term "Living room" Won Pulitzer for autobiography

FROM *The Americanization of Edward Bok (1921)*

Where America Fell Short With Me

When I came to the United States as a lad of six, the most needful lesson to me, as a boy, was the necessity for thrift. I had been taught in my home across the sea that thrift was one of the fundamentals in a successful life. My family had come from a land (the Netherlands) noted for its thrift; but we had been in the United States only a few days before realization came home strongly to my father and mother that they had brought their children to a land of waste.

Where the Dutchman saved, the American wasted. There was waste, and the most prodigal waste, on every hand. In every street-car and on every ferry-boat the floors and seats were littered with newspapers that had been read and thrown away or left behind. If I went to a grocery store to buy a peck of potatoes, and a potato rolled off the heaping measure, the groceryman, instead of picking it up, kicked it into the gutter for the wheels of his wagon to run over. The butcher's waste filled my mother's soul with dismay. If I bought a scuttle of coal at the corner grocery, the coal that missed the scuttle, instead of being shovelled up and put back into the bin, was swept into the street. My young eyes quickly saw this; in the evening I gathered up the coal thus swept away, and during the course of a week I collected a scuttleful. The first time my mother saw the garbage pail of a family almost as poor as our own, with the wife and husband constantly complaining that they could not get along, she could scarcely believe her eyes. A half pan of hominy of the preceding day's breakfast lay in the pail next to a third of a loaf of bread. In later years, when I saw, daily, a scow loaded with the garbage of Brooklyn householders being towed through New York harbor out to sea, it was an easy calculation that what was thrown away in a week's time from Brooklyn homes would feed the poor of the Netherlands. . . .

In the matter of education, America fell far short in what should be the strongest of all her institutions: the public school. A more inadequate, incompetent method of teaching, as I look back over my seven years of attendance at three different public schools, it is difficult to conceive. If there is one thing that I, as a foreign-born child, should have been carefully taught, it is the English language. The individual effort to teach this, if effort there was, and I remember none, was negligible. It was left for my father to teach me, or for me to dig it out for myself. There was absolutely no indication on the part of teacher or principal of responsibility for seeing that a foreign-born boy should acquire the English language correctly. I was taught as if I were American-born, and, of course, I was left dangling in the air, with no conception of what I was trying to do.

My father worked with me evening after evening; I plunged my young mind deep into the bewildering confusions of the language – and no one realizes the confusions of the English language as does the foreign-born – and got what I could through these joint efforts. But I gained nothing from the much-vaunted public-school system which the United States had borrowed from my own country, and then had rendered incompetent – either by a sheer disregard for the thoroughness that makes the Dutch public schools the admiration of the world, or by too close a regard for politics.

Thus, in her most important institution to the foreign-born, America fell short. And while I am ready to believe that the public school may have increased in efficiency since that day, it is, indeed, a question for the American to ponder, just how far the system is efficient for the education of the child who comes to its school without a knowledge of the first word in the English language. Without a detailed knowledge of the subject, I know enough of conditions in the average public school to-day to warrant at least the suspicion that Americans would not be particularly proud of the system, and of what it gives for which annually they pay millions of dollars in taxes.

I am aware in making this statement that I shall be met with convincing instances of intelligent effort being made with the foreign-born children in special classes. No one has a higher respect for those efforts than I have – few, other than educators, know of them better than I do, since I did not make my five-year study of the American public school system for naught. But I am not referring to the exceptional instance here and there. I merely ask of the American, interested as he is or should be in the Americanization of the strangers within his gates, how far the public school system, as a whole, urban and rural, adapts itself, with any true efficiency, to the foreign-born child. I venture to color his opinion in no wise; I simply ask that he will inquire and ascertain for himself, as he should do if he is interested in the future welfare of his country and his institutions; for what happens in America in the years to come depends, in large measure, on what is happening today in the public schools of this country. . . .

One fundamental trouble with the present desire for Americanization is that the American is anxious to Americanize two classes – if he is a reformer, the foreign-born; if he is an employer, his employees. It never occurs to him that he himself may be in need of Americanization. He seems to take it for granted that because he is American-born, he is an American in spirit and has a right understanding of American ideals. But that, by no means, always follows. There are thousands of the American-born who need Americanization just as much as do the foreign-born. There are hundreds of American cmployers who know far less of American ideals than do some of their employees. In fact, there are those actually engaged to-day in the work of Americanization, men at the top of the movement, who sadly need a better conception of true Americanism. . . .

To the American, part and parcel of his country, these particulars in which his country falls short with the foreign-born are, perhaps, not so evident; they may even seem not so very important. But to the foreign-born they seem distinct lacks; they loom large; they form serious handicaps which, in many cases, are never surmounted; they are a menace to that Americanization which is, to-day, more than ever our fondest dream, and which we now realize more keenly than before is our most vital need.

It is for this reason that I have put them down here as a concrete instance of where and how America fell short in my own Americanization, and, what is far more serious to me, where she is falling short in her Americanization of thousands of other foreign-born.

"Yet you succeeded," it will be argued.

That may be; but you, on the other hand, must admit that I did not succeed by reason of these shortcomings: it was in spite of them, by overcoming them – a result that all might not achieve.

What I Owe to America

How good an American has the process of Americanization made me? That I cannot say. Who *can* say that of himself? But when I look around me at the American-born I have come to know as my close friends, I wonder whether, after all, the foreign-born does not make in some sense a better American – whether he is not able to get a truer perspective; whether his is not the deeper desire to see America greater; whether he is not less content to let its faulty institutions be as they are; whether in seeing faults more clearly he does not make a more decided effort to have America reach those ideals or those fundamentals of his own land which he feels are in his nature, and the best of which he is anxious to graft into the character of his adopted land?

17 OLE E. RØLVAAG

FROM *"The Power of Evil in High Places"* (1927)

That summer many land seekers passed through the settlement on their way west. The arrival of a caravan was always an event of the greatest importance. How exciting they were, those little ships of the Great Plain! The prairie schooners, rigged with canvas tops which gleamed whitely in the shimmering light, first became visible as tiny specks against the eastern sky; one might almost imagine them to be sea gulls perched far, far away on an endless green meadow; but as one continued to watch, the white dots grew; they came drifting across the prairie like the day; after long waiting, they gradually floated out of the haze, distinct and clear; then, as they drew near, they proved to be veritable wagons, with horses hitched ahead, with folk and all their possessions inside, and a whole herd of cattle following behind.

The caravan would crawl slowly into the settlement and come to anchor in front of one of the sod houses; the moment it halted, people would swarm down and stretch themselves and begin to look after the teams; cattle would bellow; sheep would bleat as they ran about. Many queer races and costumes were to be seen in these caravans, and a babble of strange tongues shattered the air. Nut-brown youngsters, dressed only in a shirt and a pair of pants, would fly around between the huts, looking for other youngsters; an infant, its mother crooning softly to it, would sit securely perched in the fold of her arm; white-haired old men and women, who should have been living quietly at home, preparing for a different journey, were also to be seen in the group, running about like youngsters; the daily jogging from sky line to sky line had brightened their eyes and quickened their tongues. All were busy; each had a thousand questions to ask; every last one of them was in high spirits, though they knew no other home than the wagon and the blue skies above. . . . The Lord only could tell whence all these people had come and whither they were going! . . .

The caravan usually intended to stop only long enough for the women folk to boil coffee and get a fresh supply of water; but the starting was always delayed, for the men had so many questions to ask. Once in a while during these halts a fiddler would bring out his fiddle and play a tune or two, and then there would be dancing. Such instances were rare, but good cheer and excitement invariably accompanied these visits.

– Why not settle right here? The Spring Creek folk would ask the west-movers . . . There's plenty of good land left – nothing better to be found between here and the Pacific Ocean!

– No, not yet. They weren't quite ready to settle; these parts looked fairly crowded . . . The farther west, the better . . . They guessed they would have to go on a way, though this really looked pretty good! . . .

And so the caravans would roll onward into the green stillness of the west. How strange – they vanished faster than they had appeared! The white sails grew smaller and smaller in the glow of the afternoon, until they had dwindled to nothing; the eye might seek them out there in the waning day, and search till it grew blurred, but all in vain – they were gone, and had left no trace! . . .

Foggy weather had now been hanging over the prairie for three whole days; a warm mist of rain mizzled continuously out of the low sky. Toward evening of the third day, the fog lifted and clear sky again appeared; the setting sun burst through the cloud banks rolling up above the western horizon, and transformed them into marvellous fairy castles . . . While this was going on, over to the northeast of the Solum boys' place a lonely wagon had crept into sight; it had almost reached the creek before anyone had noticed it, for the Solum boys were visiting among the Sognings, where there were many young people. But as Beret sat out in the yard, milking, the wagon crossed her view. When she brought in the milk, she remarked in her quiet manner that they were going to have company, at which tidings the rest of the family had to run out and see who might be coming at this time of day.

There was only one wagon, with two cows following behind; on the left side walked a brown-whiskered, stooping man – he was doing the driving; close behind him came a half-grown boy, dragging his feet heavily. The wagon at last crawled up the hill and came to a stop in Per Hansa's yard, where the whole family stood waiting.

"I don't suppose there are any Norwegians in this settlement? No, that would be too much to expect," said the man in a husky, worn-out voice.

"If you're looking for Norwegians, you have found the right place, all right! We sift the people as they pass through here – keep our own, and let the others go!" . . . Per Hansa wanted to run on, for he felt in high spirits; but he checked himself, observing that the man looked as if he stood on the very brink of the grave.

– Was there any chance of putting up here for the night?

"Certainly! certainly!" cried Per Hansa, briskly, "provided you are willing to take things as they are."

The man didn't answer, but walked instead to the wagon and spoke to some one inside:

"Kari, now you must brace up and come down. Here we have found Norwegians at last!" As if fearing a contradiction, he added: "Ya, they are real Norwegians. I've talked with them."

On top of his words there came out of the wagon, first a puny boy with a hungry face, somewhat smaller than the other boy; then a girl of about the same size, but looking much older. She helped to get down another boy, about six years old, who evidently had been sleeping and looked cross and tired. That seemed to be all.

The man stepped closer to the wagon. "Aren't you coming, Kari?"

A groan sounded within the canvas. The girl grabbed hold of her father's arm. "You must untie the rope! Can't you remember *anything*?" she whispered, angrily.

"Ya, that's right! Wait a minute till I come and help you."

An irresistible curiosity took hold of Per Hansa; in two jumps he stood on the tongue of the wagon. The sight that met his eyes sent chills running down his spine. Inside sat a woman on a pile of clothes, with her back against a large immigrant chest; around her wrists and leading to the handles of the chest a strong rope was tied; her face was drawn and unnatural. Per Hansa trembled so violently that he had to catch hold of the wagon box, but inwardly he was swearing a steady stream. To him it looked as if the woman was crucified.

. . . "For God's sake, man!" . . .

The stranger paid no attention; he was pottering about and pleading: "Come down now, Kari . . . Ya, all right, I'll help you! Everything's going to be all right – I know it will! . . . Can you manage to get up?" He had untied the rope, and the woman had risen to her knees.

"O God!" she sighed, putting her hands to her head.

"Please come. That's right; I'll help you!" pleaded the man, as if he were trying to persuade a child.

She came down unsteadily. "Is this the place, Jakob?" she asked in a bewildered way. But now Beret ran up and put her arm around her; the women looked into each other's eyes and instantly a bond of understanding had been established. "You come with me!" urged Beret . . . "O God! This isn't the place, either!" wailed the woman; but she followed Beret submissively into the house.

"Well, well!" sighed the man as he began to unhitch the horses. "Life isn't easy – no, it certainly isn't." . . .

Per Hansa watched him anxiously, hardly knowing what to do. Both the boys kept close to him. Then an idea flashed through his mind: "You boys run over to Hans Olsa's and tell him not to go to bed until I come . . . No, I don't want him here. And you two stay over there tonight. Now run along!"

Turning to the man, he asked, "Aren't there any more in your party?"

"No, not now. We were five, you see, to begin with – five in all – but the others had to go on . . . Haven't they been by here yet? Well, they must be somewhere over to the westward . . . No, life isn't easy." . . . The man wandered on in his monotonous, blurred tone; he sounded all the time as if he were half sobbing.

"Where do you come from?" Per Hansa demanded, gruffly.

The man didn't give a direct answer, but continued to ramble on in the same mournful way, stretching his story out interminably . . . They had been wandering over the prairie for nearly six weeks . . . Ya, it was a hard life. When they had started from Houston County, Minnesota, there had been five wagons in all. Strange that the others hadn't turned up here. Where could they be? It seemed to him as if he had travelled far enough to reach the ends of the earth! . . . Good God, what a nightmare life was! If he had only – only known . . .!

"Did the others go away and *leave you*?" Per Hansa hadn't intended to ask that question, but it had slipped out before he realized what he was saying. He wondered if there could be anything seriously wrong . . .

"They couldn't possibly wait for us – couldn't have been expected to. Everything went wrong, you see, and I didn't know when I would be able to start again . . . Turn the horses loose, John," he said to the boy. "Take the pail and see if you can squeeze some milk out of the cows. Poor beasts, they don't give much now!" Then he turned to Per Hansa again: "I don't know what would have become of us if we hadn't reached this place tonight! We'd have been in a bad hole, that I assure you! Women folk can't bear up . . ." The man stopped and blew his nose.

Per Hansa dreaded what might be coming next. "You must have got off your course, since you are coming down from the north?"

The man shook his head helplessly. "To tell the truth, I don't know where we've been these last few days. We couldn't see the sun."

"Haven't you got a compass?"

"Compass? No! I tried to steer with a rope but the one I had wasn't long enough."

"Like hell you did!" exclaimed Per Hansa, excitedly, full of a sudden new interest.

"Ya, I tried that rope idea – hitched it to the back of the wagon, and let it drag in the wet grass. But it didn't work – I couldn't steer straight with it. The rope was so short, and kept kinking around so much, that it didn't leave any wake."

"Uh-huh!" nodded Per Hansa wisely. "You must be a seafaring man, to have tried that trick!"

"No, I'm no sailor. But fisher-folk out here have told me that it's possible to steer by a rope . . . I had to try *something*."

"Where did you cross the Sioux?"

"How do I know where I crossed it? We came to a river a long way to the east of here – that must have been the Sioux. We hunted and hunted before we could find a place shallow enough to cross . . . God! this has certainly been a wandering in the desert for me! . . . But if Kari only gets better, I won't complain – though I never dreamed that life could be so hard." . . .

"Is she – is she *sick*, that woman of yours?"

The man did not answer this question immediately; he wiped his face with the sleeve of his shirt. When he spoke again, his voice had grown even more blurred and indistinct: "Physically she seems to be as well as ever – as far as I can see. She certainly hasn't overworked since we've been travelling. I hope there's nothing wrong with her . . . But certain things are hard to bear – I suppose it's worse for the mother, too – though the Lord knows it hasn't been easy for me, either! . . . You see, we had to leave our youngest boy out there on the prairie . . ."

"*Leave* him?" . . . These were the only two words that came to Per Hansa's mind.

"Ya, there he lies, our little boy! . . . I never saw a more promising man – you know what I mean – when he grew up . . . But now – oh, well . . ."

Per Hansa felt faint in the pit of his stomach; his throat grew dry; his voice became as husky as that of the other; he came close up to him. "Tell me – how did this happen?"

The man shook his head again, in a sort of dumb despair. Then he cleared his throat and continued with great effort: "I can't tell how it happened! Fate just willed it so. Such things are not to be explained . . . The boy had been ailing for some time – we knew that, but didn't pay much attention. We had other things to think of . . . Then he began to fail fast. We were only one day's journey this side of Jackson; so we went back. That was the time when the others left us. I don't blame them much – it was uncertain when we could go on . . . The doctor we found wasn't a capable man – I realize it now. He spoke only English and couldn't understand what I was saying. He had no idea what was wrong with the boy – I could see that plainly enough . . . Ya, well – so we started again . . . It isn't any use to fight against Fate; that's an old saying, and a true one, too, I guess . . . Before long we saw that the boy wasn't going to recover. So we hurried on, day and night, trying to catch our neigh-bours . . . Well, that's about all of it. One night he was gone – just as if you had blown out a candle. Ya, let me see – that was five nights ago."

"Have you got him there in the wagon?" demanded Per Hansa, grabbing the man by the arm.

"No, no," he muttered, huskily. "We buried him out there by a big stone – no coffin or anything. But Kari took the best shirt she had and wrapped it all around him – we had to do *something*, you know . . . But," he continued suddenly straightening up, "Paul cannot lie there! As soon as I find my neighbours, I'll go and get him. Otherwise Kari . . ." The man paused between the sobs that threatened to choke him. "I have had to tie her up the last few days. She insisted on getting out and going back to Paul. I don't think she has had a wink of sleep for over a week . . . It's just as I was saying – some people can't stand things." . . .

Per Hansa leaned heavily against the wagon. "Has she gone crazy?" he asked, hoarsely.

"She isn't much worse than the rest of us. I don't believe . . . Kari is really a well-balanced woman . . . But you can imagine how it feels, to leave a child *that* way . . ."

The boy, John, had finished milking. He had put the pail down and was standing a little way off, listening to his father's story; suddenly he threw himself on the ground, sobbing as if in convulsions.

"John! John!" admonished the father. "Aren't you ashamed of yourself – a grown-up man like you! Take the milk and carry it into the house!"

"That's right!" echoed Per Hansa, pulling himself together. "We'd better all go in. There's shelter here, and plenty to eat."

Beret was bustling around the room when they entered; she had put the woman to bed, and now was tending her. "Where are the boys?" she asked.

Per Hansa told her that he had sent them to Hans Olsa's for the night. "That was hardly necessary; we could have made room here somehow," Beret's voice carried a note of keen reproach.

The man had paused at the door; now he came over to the bed, took the limp hand, and muttered: "Poor soul! . . . Why, I believe she's asleep already!"

Beret came up and pushed him gently aside. "Be careful! Don't wake her. She needs the rest."

"Ya, I don't doubt it – not I! She hasn't slept for a week, you see – the poor soul!" With a loud sniff, he turned and left the room.

When supper time came the woman seemed to be engulfed in a stupefying sleep. Beret did not join the others at the supper table, but busied herself, instead, by trying to make the woman more comfortable; she loosened her clothes, took off her shoes, and washed her face in warm water; during all this the stranger never stirred. That done, Beret began to fix up sleeping quarters for the strangers, in the barn. She carried in fresh hay and brought out all the bedding she had; she herself would take care of the woman, in case she awoke and needed attention. Beret did little talking, but she went about these arrangements with a firmness and confidence that surprised her husband.

Per Hansa came in from the barn, after helping the strangers settle themselves for the night. Beret was sitting on the edge of the bed, dressing the baby for the night; she had put And-Ongen to bed beside the distracted woman.

"Did she tell you much?" he asked in a low voice.

Beret glanced toward the other bed before she answered:

"Only that she had had to leave one of her children on the way. She wasn't able to talk connectedly."

"It's a terrible thing!" he said, looking away from his wife. "I think I'll go over to Hans Olsa's for a minute. I want to talk this matter over with him."

"Talk it over with him?" she repeated, coldly. "I don't suppose Hans Olsa knows everything!"

"No, of course not. But these people have got to be helped, and we can't do it all alone." He hesitated for a minute, as if waiting for her consent. "Well, I won't be long," he said as he went out of the door.

When he returned, an hour later, she was still sitting on the edge of the bed, with the baby asleep on her lap. They sat in silence for a long while; at last he began to undress. She waited until he was in bed, then turned the lamp low and lay down herself, but without undressing . . . The lamp shed only a faint light. It was so quiet in the room that one could hear the breathing of all the others. Beret lay there listening; though the room was still, it seemed alive to her with strange movements; she forced herself to open her eyes and look around. Noticing that Per Hansa wasn't asleep, either, she asked:

"Did you look after the boys?"

"Nothing the matter with them! They were fast asleep in Sofie's bed."

"You told them everything, at Hans Olsa's?"

"Of course!"

"What did they think of it?"

Per Hansa raised himself on his elbows and glanced at the broken creature lying in the bed back of theirs. The woman, apparently, had not stirred a muscle. "It's a bad business," he said. "We must try to get together a coffin and find the boy. We can't let him lie out there – that way." . . . As Beret made no answer, he briefly narrated the story that the man had told him. "The fellow is a good-for-nothing, stupid fool, I'm sure of that," concluded Per Hansa.

She listened to him in silence. For some time she brooded over her thoughts; then in a bitter tone she suddenly burst out: "Now you can see that this kind of a life is impossible! It's beyond human endurance."

He had not the power to read her thoughts; he did not want to know them; to-night every nerve in his body was taut with apprehension and dismay. But he tried to say, reassuringly: "Hans Olsa and I will both go with the man, as soon as the day breaks. If we only had something to make the coffin of! The few pieces of board that I've got here will hardly be enough . . . Now let's go to sleep. Be sure and call me if you need anything!"

He turned over resolutely, as if determined to sleep; but she noticed that he was a long time doing it . . . I wonder what's going through his mind? she thought. She was glad to have him awake, just the same; tonight there were strange things abroad in the room . . .

The instant the woman had climbed down from the wagon and looked into Beret's face a curtain seemed to be drawn over all the terrible experiences of the last few weeks. She entered a cozy room where things were as they should be; she felt the warm presence of folk who had dwelt here a long time. She took in the whole room at a glance – table and benches and stools; a fire was burning in a real stove; a kettle was boiling; wet clothes were hanging on a line by the stove, giving out a pleasant, familiar odor; and there actually stood two beds, made up with clean bedding! The sense of home, of people who lived in an orderly fashion, swept over her like a warm bath. A kind hand led her to one of the beds, and there she sank down. She mumbled a few words, but soon gave it up; everything about her seemed so wonderfully pleasant; she must keep quiet, so as not to disturb the dream. The hand that helped her had such a sympathetic touch; it took a rag, dipped it in lukewarm water, and wiped her face; then it loosened her clothes and even took off her shoes. But best of all, she could stretch her back again!

. . . Strange that she couldn't remember what had been going on! Had she told the woman all that she ought to know? About the makeshift coffin, and the big stone beside which they would find him? And that she would have to take a blanket with her, for the nights were chilly and Paul had very little on – only a shirt that was worn and thin? . . . No, she couldn't remember anything except that she had been able to lie down and stretch her back; the warmth of the room, and the knowledge that friendly people were near her, had overcome all her senses with a sweet languor. Her body lay as if fast asleep; but away back in the inner depths of her consciousness a wee eye peeped out, half open, and saw things . . .

She remained in the same position until three o'clock in the morning. But then the wee bit of an eye opened wider and her senses slowly began to revive; she realized that she was lying in a strange room, where a lamp burned with a dim light. Suddenly she remembered that she had arrived here last night – but Paul was not with her . . . Too bad I am so forgetful! she thought. I must hurry now before Jakob sees me, because there's no way of stopping him – he always wants to go on! . . . She was fully awake now; she sat up and buttoned her clothes, then slipped quietly out of bed.

For a moment she stood perfectly still, listening; she could hear the breathing of many people; bending suddenly over the bed, she snatched up And-Ongen. She held the child tenderly in her arms and put her cheek against the warm face . . . We must be careful now! she thought. With quiet movements she wrapped her skirt about the sleeping child; glancing around the room to see if all was well, she glided out like a shadow; she did not dare to close the door behind her, lest it should make a noise. . . . "Here is our wagon!" she murmured. "I mustn't let Jakob see me now; he doesn't understand; he only wants to get on!" . . . Clutching the child to her breast, she started on the run, taking a direction away from the house.

Beret was awakened by a voice calling to her from a great distance; it called loudly several times. What a shame they can't let me alone in peace, to get a little rest! she thought, drowsily. I was up so late last night and I need the sleep badly! . . . But the voice kept calling so persistently that after a while she sat up in bed, her mind coming back to reality; she remembered that strangers had arrived last night, that another besides herself was in deep distress. Well, she had done her best to take care of her . . . She turned her head to see how the other woman was resting.

. . . "Heaven have mercy!" . . .

Beret leaped frantically out of bed; in a second she had reached the side of the other bed, but no one was there. She did not notice that And-Ongen was gone, too. A cold draught rushing through the room told her that the door stood open; she hurried over to it. She seemed to recall dimly that some one had recently gone out. Hadn't she heard it in her sleep? Beret went through the door and stood in front of the house, but did not dare to make an outcry; she listened intently, then called in a low voice; getting no answer, she ran around the house, peering hither and thither, but the grey morning light disclosed nothing.

Running back into the house, she called her husband distractedly: "She's gone! Get up! You must hurry!"

In an instant Per Hansa was up and had tumbled into his clothes. "Run over to Hans Olsa's and tell him to come at once! Be as quick as you can! In the meanwhile I'll search down by the creek."

When they came out, the first light of day was creeping up the eastern sky, a slight fog floated along the creek; the morning air was crisp and cool. Per Hansa leaped up into the seat of the wagon and scanned the prairie in every direction. . . . What was that, over there? Wasn't it a human being standing on the top of the hill? Could she have taken that direction? . . . He jumped down from the wagon, and rushed around to the other side of the house, called to Beret, and pointed up the hill. Instantly they both started out on the run.

The woman did not seem in the least surprised at their coming. When Per Hansa had almost reached her, he stopped stone dead. What, in God's name, was she carrying in her arms? His face blanched with terror. "Come here!" he shouted. In a moment he had the child in his own arms.

And-Ongen was almost awake now and had begun to whimper; things were going on around her that she could not understand; she felt cold, and father had such a queer look on his face. Sleepily she cuddled up in the fold of his left arm, her cheek against his heart, though a hard hand which seemed to be pounding against a wall was trying to wake her up again; she would just let it go on pounding all it pleased. She had to sleep some more! . . . But now mother was here. Hurriedly she was transferred into her mother's arms and squeezed almost to a pancake. She had to gasp for breath; nevertheless she snuggled into her arms as closely as she could, for she felt, oh, so sleepy! . . . But no peace here, either! Here, too, a hand pounded against a wall. Were they tearing down the house? And-Ongen was certainly at a loss to understand all this racket in the middle of the night . . . But let 'em pound!

As Beret walked homeward, carrying the child, it seemed more precious to her than the very first time when she had held it in her arms; and she experienced a wonderful blessing. Upon this night the Lord had been with them: his mighty arm had shielded them from a fearful calamity.

The other woman was still obsessed by her own troubles; she kept on hunting up there on the hill . . . Wouldn't these people help her to find Paul? She had to find him at once – He would be cold with so little on . . . Now they had taken that blessed child away from her; but she didn't wonder – that man had a bad face. She felt afraid of him . . . But no time to think of such things now; Jakob would soon be coming? She began muttering to herself: "Oh, why can't I find the stone? What has become of it? Wasn't it somewhere here?" . . .

Per Hansa went up and spoke to her, his voice sounding hoarse and unnatural. "Come with me now! To-day Hans Olsa and I are going to find your boy." Taking her gently by the arm, he led her back to the house . . . It's very kind of him, to help find Paul, she thought, and followed willingly.

At breakfast she sat very quiet; she ate when they bade her, but never spoke. While they were making the coffin she sat looking on, wondering why they didn't hurry faster with the work. Couldn't they understand that Paul was cold? A little later a handsome woman entered the house – a woman with such a kind face, who lined the coffin inside with a white cloth . . . Now, that is fine of her; that's just what a woman with such a kind face would do! . . . She would have liked to talk to that woman; she had something very important to confide to her; but perhaps she had better not delay her in her work – the coffin had to be lined! . . .

As soon as the coffin was ready, Per Hansa and Hans Olsa, along with the stranger and his wife, left the settlement to hunt for the body of the dead boy. They took quite a stock of provisions with them. On this search they were gone four days; they crisscrossed the prairie for a long way to the east, and searched high and low; but when they returned the coffin was still empty.

After the return from the search the strangers stayed one more day with them. The morning they were to leave it looked dark and threatening, and Per Hansa wouldn't hear of their setting out; but along toward noon the sky cleared and the weather appeared more settled. The man, very anxious to be on his way, had everything loaded into the wagon, and as soon as the noon meal was over they were ready to go.

But before the man got on his way Per Hansa asked him where he intended to settle.

– Well, he wasn't positive as to the exact place. It was over somewhere toward the James River – his neighbours had told him that.

– Did he know where the James River was? Per Hansa inquired further.

– Certainly he did! How could he ask such a foolish question? The river lay off there; all he needed to do was to steer straight west. After finding the river, of course he'd have to ask. But that part of it would be quite easy . . .

Per Hansa shuddered, and asked no more questions.

The woman had been quite calm since their return. She kept away from the others, muttering to herself and pottering over insignificant things, much like a child at play; but she was docile and inoffensive, and did what anyone told her. A short while before noon that day she took a notion that she must change her clothes; she got up from what she was doing, washed, and went into the wagon. When she came back she had dressed herself in her best; in a way she looked all right, but made a bizarre appearance because she had put so much on . . . The man seemed fairly cheerful as they started; he talked a good deal, heaping many blessings upon Per Hansa . . . If he could only find his neighbours, and Kari could only forget, things would be all right in a little while. Ya, it was a hard life, but – Well, God's blessings on Per Hansa, and many thanks! And now he must be off! . . . His voice was just as husky and blurred as when he came.

The wagon started creaking; the man, short and stooping, led the way; the family piled into the wagon; the two cows jogged behind . . . They laid their course due west . . . Banks of heavy cloud were rolled up on the western horizon – huge, fantastic forms that seemed to await them in Heaven's derision – though they might have been only the last stragglers of the spell of bad weather just past.

After they had gone, Beret could find no peace in the house; her hand trembled; she felt faint and dizzy; every now and then she had to go out and look at the disappearing wagon; and when the hill finally shut off the view she took the youngest two children and went up there to watch. In a way she felt glad that these people were gone; at the same time she reproached herself for not having urged them to stay longer. Sitting now on the hilltop, a strong presentiment came over her that they should not have started to-day . . . "That's the way I've become," she thought sadly. "Here are folk in the deepest distress, and I am only glad to send them off into direr calamities! What will they do to-night if a storm comes upon them? He is all broken up – he couldn't have been much of a man at any time. And the poor wife insane from grief! Perhaps she will disappear forever this very night . . . What misery, what an unspeakable tragedy, life is for some!" . . .

Slowly, very slowly, the forlorn caravan crept off into the great, mysterious silence always hovering above the plain. To Beret, as she watched, it seemed as if the prairie were swallowing up the people, the wagon, the cows and all. At last the little caravan was merged in the very infinite itself; Beret thought she could see the wagon yet, but was not certain; it might be only a dead tuft of grass far away which the wind stirred . . .

She took the children and went home, walking with slow, dragging steps; she wanted to cry, and felt the need of it, but no tears came . . . Per Hansa and the boys were breaking prairie; to judge from the language they used in talking to the oxen, they must be hard at it. Her loneliness was so great that she felt a physical need of bringing happiness to some living thing; as soon as she got home she took her little remaining store of rice and cooked porridge for supper; the boys were very fond of that dish.

Toward evening the air grew heavy and sultry; the cloud banks, still rolling up in the western sky, had taken on a most threatening aspect; it looked as if a thunderstorm might be coming on.

After supper Per Hansa was due to meet at Hans Olsa's with the other neighbours, to lay plans for the trip to town which had to be made before harvesting set in. The boys asked leave to go, too – it was so much fun to be with the men.

When she had washed the supper dishes Beret went outdoors and sat down on the woodpile. A nameless apprehension tugged at her heart and would not leave her in peace; taking the two children as before, she again ascended the hill. The spell of the afternoon's sadness was still upon her; her constant self-reproach since then had only deepened it . . . Those poor folk were straying somewhere out there, under the towering clouds. Poor souls! The Lord pity the mother who had left a part of herself back east on the prairie! How could the good God permit creatures made in His image to fall into such tribulations? To people this desert would be as impossible as to empty the sea. For how could folk establish homes in an endless wilderness? Was it not the Evil One that had struck them with blindness? . . . Take her own case, for example: here she sat, thousands of miles from home and kindred, lost in a limitless void . . . Out yonder drifted these folk, like chips on a current . . . Must man perish because of his own foolishness? Where, then, was the guiding hand? . . . Beret was gazing at the western sky as the twilight fast gathered around her; her eyes were riveted on a certain cloud that had taken on the shape of a face, awful of mien and giantlike in proportions; the face seemed to swell out of the prairie and filled half the heavens.

She gazed a long time; now she could see the monster clearer. The face was unmistakable! There were the outlines of the nose and mouth. The eyes – deep, dark caves in the cloud – were closed. The mouth, if it were to open, would be a yawning abyss. The chin rested on the prairie . . . Black and lean the whole face, but of such gigantic, menacing proportions! Wasn't there something like a leer upon it? . . . And the terrible creature was spreading everywhere; she trembled so desperately that she had to take hold of the grass.

It was a strange emotion that Beret was harbouring at this moment; in reality she felt a certain morbid satisfaction – very much like a child that has been arguing with its parents, has turned out to be right, and, just as the tears are coming, cries, "Now, there, you see!" . . . Here was the simple solution to the whole riddle. She had known in her heart all the time that people were never led into such deep affliction unless an evil power had been turned loose among them. And hadn't she clearly felt that there were unspeakable things out yonder – that the great stillness was nothing but life asleep? . . . She sat still as death, feeling the supernatural emanations all around her. The face came closer in the dusk – didn't she feel its cold breath upon her? When that mouth opened and began to suck, terrible things would happen! . . . Without daring to look again, she snatched up the children and ran blindly home.

After a while the others returned, the boys storming boisterously into the house, the father close behind; he was evidently chasing them; by the tone of his voice, she knew he was in high spirits.

"Why, Beret," he cried gayly, as soon as he got inside, "what have you been doing to the windows – covering them up?" He was looking at her with narrow, sparkling eyes. "Beret, Beret, you're a dear girl!" he whispered. Then he came over and fondled her – he wanted to help undress her and put her to bed . . .

"No, no – not *that*!" she cried, vehemently, an intense anger surging up within her. Had he no sense whatever of decency and propriety, no feeling of shame and sin? . . . That's only one more proof, she thought, that the devil has us in his clutches!

After that time, Beret was conscious of the face whenever she was awake, but particularly along toward evening, as the twilight came on; then it drew closer to her and seemed alive. Even during the day she would often be aware of its presence; high noon might stand over the prairie, with the sun shedding a flood of light that fairly blinded the sight, but through and behind the light she would see it – huge and horrible it was, the eyes always closed, with only those empty, cavernlike sockets beneath the brows.

As she went about doing her work, now, she would frequently be seized by a faintness so great that she had to sit down . . . How was this going to end? she asked herself. Yes, how would it end? . . . Vague premonitions hovered about her like shadows. Many times she was on the point of asking her husband if he saw what she did, towering above the prairie out west; but always she seemed to be tongue-tied. . . . Well, why mention it? Couldn't he and the others see it perfectly well for themselves? How could they help it? . . . She noticed that a silence would often fall upon them when they were out-of-doors, especially in the evening. Certainly they saw it! . . . Every evening, now, whether Per Hansa was away or at home, she hung something over the windows – it helped shut out the fear . . .

At first her husband made all sorts of fun of this practice of hers; he teased her about it, as if it were a good joke, and continued to force his caresses on her, his voice low and vibrant with pent-up emotion. But as time went on he ceased laughing; the fear that possessed her had begun to affect him, too . . .

18 OSCAR HANDLIN

FROM *The Uprooted (1951)*

The Crossing

Emigration was the end of peasant life in Europe; it was also the beginning of life in America. But what a way there was yet to go before the displaced would come to rest again, what a distance between the old homes and the new! Only the fact that these harried people could not pause to measure the gulf saved them from dismay at the dizzy width of it.

Perhaps it is fortunate that, going onward, their sights are fixed backward rather than forward. From the crossroad, the man, alone or with his wife and children, turns to look upon the place of his birth. Once fixed, completely settled, he is now a wanderer. Remorseless circumstances, events beyond his control, have brought him to this last familiar spot. Passing it by, he becomes a stranger.

Sometimes, the emigrants at that moment considered the nature of the forces that had uprooted them. All the new conditions had conspired to depress the peasants into a hopeless mass, to take away their distinguishing differences and to deprive them, to an ever-greater extent, of the capacity for making willful decisions. The pressure of the changing economy had steadily narrowed every person's range of choices. Year by year, there were fewer alternatives until the critical day when only a single choice remained to be made – to emigrate or to die. Those who had the will to make that final decision departed.

That man at the crossroads knew then that this was a mass movement. Scores of his fellows in the village, hundreds in other villages, were being swept along with him. Yet he moved alone. He went as an individual. Although entire communities were uprooted at the same time, although the whole life of the Old World had been communal, the act of migration was individual. The very fact that the peasants were leaving was a sign of the disintegration of the old village ways. What happened beyond the crossroads, each would determine by himself. It was immensely significant that the first step to the New World, despite all the hazards it involved, was the outcome of a desperate individual choice.

He who turned his back upon the village at the crossroads began a long journey that his mind would forever mark as its most momentous experience. The crossing immediately subjected the emigrant to a succession of shattering shocks and decisively conditioned the life of every man that survived it. This was the initial contact with life as it was to be. For many peasants it was the first time away from home, away from the safety of the circumscribed little villages in which they had passed all their years. Now they would learn to have dealings with people essentially different from themselves. Now they would collide with unaccustomed problems, learn to understand alien ways and alien languages, manage to survive in a grossly foreign environment. . . .

Thus uprooted, they found themselves in a prolonged state of crisis – crisis in the sense that they were, and remained, unsettled. For weeks, and often for months, they were in suspense between the old and the new, literally in transit. Every adjustment was temporary and therefore in its nature bore the seeds of maladjustment, for the conditions to which the immigrants were adjusting were strange and ever changing.

As a result they reached their new homes exhausted – worn out physically by lack of rest, by poor food, by the constant strain of close, cramped quarters, worn out emotionally by the succession of new situations that had crowded in upon them. At the end was only the dead weariness of an excess of novel sensations.

Yet once arrived, the immigrants would not take time to recuperate. They would face instead the immediate, pressing necessity of finding a livelihood and of adjusting to conditions that were still more novel, unimaginably so. They would find then that the crossing had left its mark, had significantly affected their capacity to cope with the problems of the New World they faced. . . .

New Worlds, New Visions

Loneliness, separation from the community of the village, and despair at the insignificance of their own human abilities, these were the elements that, in America, colored the peasants' view of their world. From the depths of a dark pessimism, they looked up at a frustrating universe ruled by haphazard, capricious forces. Without the capacity to control or influence these forces men could but rarely gratify their hopes or wills. Their most passionate desires were doomed to failure; their lives were those of the feeble little birds which hawks attack, which lose strength from want of food, and which, at last surrendering to the savage blasts of the careless elements, flutter unnoticed to the waiting earth.

Sadness was the tone of life, and death and disaster no strangers. Outsiders would not understand the familiarity with death who had not daily met it in the close quarters of the steerage; nor would they comprehend the riotous Paddy funerals who had no insight of the release death brought. The end of life was an end to hopeless striving, to ceaseless pain, and to the endless succession of disappointments. There was a leaden grief for the ones who went; yet the tomb was only the final parting in a long series of separations that had started back at the village crossroads. . . .

In this world then, as in the Old Country, the safest way was to look back to tradition as a guide. Lacking confidence in the individual's capacity for independent inquiry, the peasants preferred to rely upon the tested knowledge of the past. It was difficult of course to apply village experience to life in America, to stretch the ancient aphorisms so they would fit new conditions. Yet that strain led not to a rejection of tradition but rather to an eager quest for a reliable interpreter. Significantly, the peasants sought to acknowledge an authority that would make that interpretation for them.

Their view of the American world led these immigrants to conservatism, and to the acceptance of tradition and authority. Those traits in turn shaped the immigrants' view of society, encouraged them to retain the peasants' regard for status and the divisions of rank. In these matters too striving was futile; it was wiser to keep each to his own station in the social order, to respect the rights of others and to exact the obligations due. For most of these people that course involved the acceptance of an inferior position. But was that not altogether realistic? The wind always blew in the face of the poor; and it was in the nature of society that some should have an abundance of possessions and others only the air they breathed.

19 AL SANTOLI

FROM *"Mojados (Wetbacks)" (1988)*

Rosa María Urbina, age thirty-five, crossed the muddy Rio Grande in 1984 with the hope that she could earn enough money as a housecleaner in El Paso to take her three children out of an orphanage. A widow, she had to place her children in an institution because the $14 a week she earned on a factory assembly line in Juárez was not enough to feed them.

Each morning she joined hundreds of other young to middle-aged women from the hillside colonias, *who walked down to the concrete riverbank and paid men called* burros *to ferry them across the river on their shoulders – and back to the squalor of Juárez in the evening. On one of these excursions, she met a handsome farm worker, José Luis, age twenty-six, with dark mestizo features. It was fate, they believe. Within months, Rosa's children joined them in a two-room apartment on the American side of the river.*

I was introduced to José and Rosa during a tour of overcrowded tenement buildings in South El Paso that house many of the city's fifty thousand illegal residents. In Mexican slang, they are called mojados, *or "wets," the river people.*

My guide, Julie Padilla, a public-health nurse from the Centro de Salud Familiar La Fe clinic, visits the Urbinas to give their two-month-old baby, José Luis, Jr., a. post-natal checkup. We walked up a dark stairwell to a dimly lit landing decorated with a colorful gold-framed mural of Our Lady of Guadalupe, the religious patron of all Mexican Catholics. There are sixteen apartments with ripped screen doors along a narrow graffiti-covered corridor. On the back fire-escape is a closet-sized communal toilet. Julie said, "There used to be one bathtub that every family on the corridor shared. But in the past year, that's been taken out. I don't know where they bathe now."

Rosa María, José, and the children have the luxury apartment. Half of the 12-foot-square room is taken up by a bed covered by a magenta Woolworth blanket. On the wall, above a calendar of the Good Shepherd, is a portrait of Pope John Paul II. A Winnie the Pooh blanket serves as a makeshift closet door. On a miniature two-tiered nightstand, alongside baby bottles and a green plant, are metal-framed elementary-school photos of the children. Their seven-year-old daughter's Honor Roll certificate is proudly displayed on a mirror above an all-purpose foldout table.

During winter months, José Luis is out of farm work. The baby is Rosa's full-time chore. They survive on $58 a month in food stamps earmarked for the baby, who is an American citizen by virtue of his birth in El Paso. And WICC, the Women, Infant and Children Care program, provides a bag of groceries each week. Although the children attend public school, José and Rosa seldom leave the apartment. They fear that border patrolmen will send them back across the river to the squalor of Juárez.

ROSA: Before I met José, I crossed back and forth across the river five days each week to my housekeeping jobs in El Paso. On weekends, I took my children out of the orphanage. Then I had to reluctantly return them to the orphanage on Sunday evenings and prepare to go back across the river.

　For a while, I traveled alone, which can be dangerous. But after I met José Luis, we crossed together. There are men who carry people across the river on their shoulders. The water is kind of rough, but that's what these men do to make a living. They charge passengers 1,500 to 2,000 pesos [$1.50 to $2.50]. The water is up to their chests, but they manage to hold us up on their shoulders so we can get to work dry.

JOSÉ: Crossing the river can be very dangerous, especially if you cross alone. There are fast water currents, and sometimes the water is quite high. If you don't know how to swim, the undercurrents can pull you right down. And in places the bottom of the river is like quicksand that can trap you. The water turns into kind of a funnel that can drag you down. Some friends of mine have died. . . .

ROSA: After José and I began living together in El Paso, I decided to bring my children across the river. The water was too high and swift to risk men carrying them on their shoulders. So I had the children taxied across on a rubber raft.

JOSÉ: Another danger for people who cross the river is crime. Packs of men hang around the riverbank like wolves. They try to steal people's knapsacks or purses. Sometimes they demand that you give your wallet or wristwatch. If you don't obey them, they will knife you. . . .

　When the *migra* catch us, they just put us in their truck and take us to their station. They ask our name, address, where we were born. They keep us in a cell maybe three or four hours. Then they put us in a bus and drive us back to Juárez.

They drop the women off very near the main bridge. The men are taken a little further away from town.

The men, like myself, who work in the fields come across the river at around 2:30 A.M. to meet the buses that take us to the fields from El Paso. The transportation is owned by the *padrone* of the farms, or by the labor-crew chiefs who hire and pay the workers. In the evenings, we ride the buses back to the river. Sometimes I work twelve hours a day and earn $20. I've learned to check around to see which farms pay the best. Some pay up to $35 a day.

Farm-labor jobs are not very steady. We just grab whatever is open at the moment. I accept anything, any time, as long as it is work. But suppose I take a job that only pays me $12 a day. It would only be enough to cover my transportation and meals in the field. I must find jobs that pay enough to feed my family.

In order to make $25, I must pick seventy-two buckets of chili peppers. That could take me four or five hours; it depends on how fast my hands are. The total amount of buckets we pick depends upon the amount contracted by the big companies in California. For a big contract, we work as long as necessary to complete the order. But the most I can earn in a day is $35.

The landlord who owns this building is very generous. He lets us owe him rent for the months that I am not working. He understands how tough our life is. We pay whatever we can, even if it's only $50. And he knows that, if the day comes where we are raided by immigration officers, we will run.

The rent for this apartment is $125 a month plus electricity. We all live and sleep in this one room. The two boys sleep on the couch. Our daughter, Miriam, sleeps with us on the bed. And the baby sleeps in a crib next to our bed. Fortunately, we have a kitchen, and a closet in this room. Living conditions in Juárez were better, but there was no work at all.

If it is possible, Rosa and I would like to become American citizens. I would have my documents, and the government wouldn't be after us. All we want is to be able to work in peace.

Our dream is to be able to give our children the best of everything. We know that, for them to have a better future and purpose in life, they need a good education. Of the three children in school now, Miriam is the fastest learner. She received an award for being an honor student, the best in her classroom.

We hope the children can finish high school and have the career of their choice. We are going to sacrifice for them, so that they can have the profession that they desire. . . .

The dreams that Rosa María and I had of living in the US and reality are not the same. We hoped to find a job and live comfortably. Now that we are here, our main purpose is to survive.

I worry about our status under the new immigration law. In the previous place where I lived, I paid the rent all the time, but the landlord threw away all of the receipts. So we have no proof that we have been living here enough years to qualify for amnesty.

On the farms where I worked, my employers or crew bosses didn't keep pay records, because I only worked temporarily at each place. And, besides, I was illegal. So what was the use? If the police showed up, we would be in trouble whether or not the employer had a record. And the employers wanted to protect themselves. They didn't pay us with checks; it was always cash.

Fortunately, the last farmer I worked for took taxes and Social Security out of our wages. He is sending me a W-2 form as proof. I am waiting for it now. But things are getting worse, because the immigration police are putting pressure on people who hire undocumented workers. If the police catch illegals on a job site, the boss can be arrested under the new law. So most places have stopped hiring illegals. For example, my last job in El Paso, I was fired because the *migra* would raid the construction site every day. We would have to stop working and run.

When the planting season begins on the farms, I hope the immigration police don't show up. They raid a farm with a truck and four or five police cars. They position themselves outside the entrance to the farm and wait for us to walk by. They ask us for identification. If we cannot show proof that we are legal, we've had it. They'll take us away.

On the farms where I work, some people are legal and others aren't. If you drive your own car, the police usually won't question you. But if you come to work in the employer's bus, they'll take you away.

ROSA: In town, we don't feel comfortable walking on the street. If the immigration officers see us, they will grab us. We are not afraid for ourselves, because we are accustomed to it. But I worry about the children. They have just begun studying in school here in El Paso. They like it very much. My sons are in the sixth and fifth grades, and Miriam is in second grade. They are learning English very quickly. My oldest boy, Lorenzo, likes social studies and mathematics; he would like to be a doctor. My other son likes the army a lot. He could probably be a good soldier.

JOSÉ: If we become citizens and the United States government asks them to spend time in the army, we would be honored if they are chosen to serve. We would be very proud of our children for doing their duty for their country.

ROSA: My daughter, Miriam, received a certificate from her teacher. You can ask her what she would like to do when she finishes school.

MIRIAM: [Big grin] I like to study English and mathematics. Some day I would like to be a teacher.

ROSA: In the buildings on this block. the majority of the people are families. In each apartment there are three or four children. This is the only area we found where the landlords don't mind renting to families with kids. The kids play outside, in the alley behind our building. Not many cars pass on this street at night, so it is pretty quiet. But other neighborhoods are more active and there is more crime on the streets.

We would like to have an ordinary life, but our problems with the *migra* are nothing new. If they catch me again and send me back to Juárez, I will just come back across the river.

20 ARTHUR M. SCHLESINGER, JR.

"E Pluribus Unum?" (1992)

America was a multiethnic country from the start. Hector St. John de Crèvecoeur emigrated from France to the American colonies in 1759, married an American woman, settled on a farm in Orange County, New York, and published his *Letters from an American Farmer* during the American Revolution. This eighteenth-century French American marveled at the astonishing diversity of the other settlers – "a mixture of English, Scotch, Irish, French, Dutch, Germans, and Swedes," a "strange mixture of blood" that you could find in no other country.

He recalled one family whose grandfather was English, whose wife was Dutch, whose son married a Frenchwoman, and whose present four sons had married women of different nationalities. "From this promiscuous breed," he wrote, "that race now called Americans have arisen." (The word *race* as used in the eighteenth and nineteenth centuries meant what we mean by nationality today; thus people spoke of "the English race," "the German race," and so on.) What, Crèvecoeur mused, were the characteristics of this suddenly emergent American race? *Letters from an American Farmer* propounded a famous question: "What then is the American, this new man?" (Twentieth-century readers must overlook eighteenth-century male obliviousness to the existence of women.)

Crèvecoeur gave his own question its classic answer: "*He* is an American, who leaving behind him all his ancient prejudices and manners, receives new ones from the new mode of life he has embraced, the new government he obeys, and the new rank he holds. The American is a new mam, who acts upon new principles. . . . *Here individuals of all nations are melted into a new race of men.*"

E pluribus unum. The United States had a brilliant solution for the inherent fragility of a multiethnic society: the creation of a brand-new national identity, carried forward by individuals who, in forsaking old loyalties and joining to make new lives, melted away ethnic differences. Those intrepid Europeans who had torn up their roots to brave the wild Atlantic *wanted* to forget a horrid past and to embrace a hopeful future. They *expected* to become Americans. Their goals were escape, deliverance, assimilation. They saw America as a transforming nation, banishing dismal memories and developing a unique national character based on common political ideals and shared experiences. The point of America was not to preserve old cultures, but to forge a new *American* culture.

3

AFRICAN AMERICANS

Introduction	64
21 *Moses Grandy* "The Auction Block" (pre-1860)	66
22 *Joseph Ingraham* "A Peep into a Slave-Mart" (pre-1860)	67
23 *Sojourner Truth* "Ain't I a Woman?" (1851)	67
24 *Abraham Lincoln* Final Emancipation Proclamation (1863)	68
25 *William DuBois* "This Double-Consciousness" (1903) FROM "Of the Faith of the Fathers" (1903)	70
26 *Gwendolyn Brooks* "We Real Cool" (1960)	75
27 *Martin Luther King, Jr.* "I Have a Dream" (1963)	75
28 *US Congress* The Civil Rights Act (1964)	78
29 *Malcolm X* FROM "The Ballot or the Bullet" (1965) FROM "The Black Man" (1965)	79
30 *Septima Clark* "Teach How Change Comes About" (pre-1987)	82

Figure 3 Martin Luther King speaking in Cleveland, July 7, 1965 © Bettmann/CORBIS

INTRODUCTION

It is impossible to conceive of black culture in the United States without a reference to the institution of slavery in the South. Human tragedies are spelled out in numerous slave narratives, such as the short account we have selected here (text 21), given by a husband upon the selling of his wife. At that time, marriages between slaves were not legally recognized. What took place in the minds of those who were offered for sale on the "slave-mart" (text 22) can only be guessed at. As James Baldwin once indicated, all blacks in the US can refer their ancestry back to a bill of sale.

In a speech given at a New York City convention in 1851 (text 23) Sojourner Truth (1797–1883) combines questions about the status of blacks and that of women. During the 1840s and 1850s abolition and other reform movements attracted many women, particularly in the northeast. Born in slavery, sold three times before she was 12, the mother of five children, Truth furnishes a voice in the struggle for the rights of black women which is unique.

Abraham Lincoln is remembered first of all as the president who freed the slaves. Although he may not have had totally humanitarian motives for issuing the Final Emancipation Proclamation in 1863 (text 24), it has since become a cornerstone in the history of legal rights for blacks. It was written into the Constitution as the thirteenth amendment and later echoed in American civil rights oratory, in Martin Luther King's speeches.

During the period of Reconstruction blacks were officially granted the right to vote and other civil rights, but their sense of freedom faded during the last decades of the nineteenth century when they found themselves victims of a strict system of segregation. It is against this historical background that we need to study the texts written by the two black leaders who emerged around 1900, Booker T. Washington and William DuBois.

Washington's "Atlanta Exposition Address" (1901) is often anthologized and therefore not included here. The second of the two excerpts (text 25) we have included from DuBois's *The Souls of Black Folk* (1903), a classic study of black culture, is an early analysis of the importance of religion and music in black culture. (See well-known blues and gospel texts in chapters 8 and 9 on religion and on mass media.) The first text presents DuBois's notion of "double-consciousness," which is now often referred to, not only by other ethnic groups in the United States but by a wide range of readers, as a valuable reflection on life in general.

In the 1950s and 1960s the black civil rights movement caught the attention of the entire nation and the whole world for its determined, but non-violent, actions for freedom and equality in American society. The role of Martin Luther King in this struggle cannot be overestimated. Dr King argued for the necessity of non-violent action as a way of forcing southern authorities to negotiate the issues at stake.

In August of 1963 King organized the massive "March on Washington for Jobs and Freedom," in which some 200,000 people participated. In his speech (text 27) to the demonstrators and, via television, to the nation he presented his visions of a future society where his children "will not be judged by the color of their skin but by the content of their character." Not only does his speech resonate with images from Jefferson's Declaration of Independence and Lincoln's Gettysburg Address, it draws heavily on traditions from within the black church at the same time. In his rhetoric he combined the words of Christian preaching with a strong sense of the political urgency of the situation. At the end of his life, King launched a campaign against poverty in the United States, a problem that concerned both the black and the white population.

The "long hot summer" of 1963 resulted in important legislation in Congress, notably the Civil Rights Act of 1964 (text 28). Its provisions included sections prohibiting discrimination in public accommodations, labor unions and voter registration. (On the desegregation of schools, see chapter 10 on education.)

Despite the legal attack upon the nation's racial caste system through the Civil Rights Act and other similar measures, many blacks were dissatisfied with the slowness of real progress, and gave vent to their frustrations by joining more militant organizations such as the Black Muslims and the Black Panthers. James Baldwin discussed these fundamental dilemmas in black culture at the time in his famous essay *The Fire Next Time* (1963). Malcolm X probably remains the symbolic figure for an alternative black vision of separatism and pride. The rhetoric of his speeches from the mid-1960s is markedly different from King's, even though both of them built on American traditions (see text 29).

To differentiate a specific African American culture may not be so easy today, and issues among blacks are different now from what they were thirty years ago. In her story, Septima Clark, a schoolteacher and administrator in South Carolina, reflects on what the tradition of King and other black leaders means to a new generation (text 30).

Black women writers, such as Alice Walker and Toni Morrison, have gained a prominent place in contemporary American literature. Belonging to an earlier generation of black writers, Gwendolyn Brooks, raised on Chicago's South Side, was the first black poet to receive the Pulitzer Prize (1950). Her poem "We Real Cool" was published in 1960 (text 26).

Questions and Topics

1 Describe and discuss the significance of DuBois's theory of "the double-consciousness" for subsequent African American Studies.
2 Discuss Du Bois's reflections on the black church in relation to Martin Luther King as a southern pastor.
3 Compare Martin Luther King's speech "I Have a Dream" with the Supreme Court decision on the "separate but equal" clause (see chapter 10 on education).
4 Malcolm X argued that he saw his country "through the eye of the victim." What does that mean and what consequences may it lead to?
5 Discuss elements of black music in Brooks's poem. You may compare her text to the blues and gospel texts you find in chapter 8 on popular culture.

Suggestions for further reading

Carson, Clayborne, David J. Garrow, Vincent Harding, Darlene Clark Hine and Toby Kleban Levine, eds., *Eyes on the Prize: America's Civil Right Years. A Reader and a Guide* (New York: Penguin, [1987], rev. edn 1991).

Franklin, John Hope *From Slavery to Freedom: A History of Negro Americans* (New York: Alfred A. Knopf, [1947], 1974).

Holt, Thomas C. and Elsa Barkley Brown, eds., *Major Problems in African-American History*, 2 vols (Boston: Houghton Mifflin, 2000).

Morrison, Toni, *Playing in the Dark: Whiteness and the Literary Imagination* (Cambridge, Mass.: Harvard University Press, 1992).

West, Cornel, *Race Matters* (Boston: Beacon Press, 1993).

21 MOSES GRANDY

"The Auction Block" (pre-1860)

I said to him, "For God's sake! Have you bought my wife?" He said he had. When I asked him what she had done, he said she had done nothing, but that her master wanted money. He drew out a pistol and said if I went near the wagon on which she was, he would shoot me. I asked for leave to shake hands with her which he refused, but said I might stand at a distance and talk with her. My heart was so full that I could say very little. . . . I have never seen or heard from her from that day to this. I loved her as I love my life.

22 JOSEPH INGRAHAM

"A Peep into a Slave-Mart" (pre-1860)

"Will you ride with me into the country?" said a young planter. "I am about purchasing a few negroes and a peep into a slave-mart may not be uninteresting to you." I readily embraced the opportunity and in a few minutes our horses were at the door.

A mile from Natchez we came to a cluster of rough wooden buildings, in the angle of two roads, in front of which several saddle-horses, either tied or held by servants, indicated a place of popular resort.

"This is the slave market," said my companion, pointing to a building in the rear; and alighting, we left our horses in charge of a neatly dressed yellow boy belonging to the establishment. Entering through a wide gate into a narrow court-yard, partially enclosed by low buildings, a scene of a novel character was at once presented. A line of negroes, commencing at the entrance with the tallest, who was not more than five feet eight or nine inches in height – for negroes are a low rather than a tall race of men – down to a little fellow about ten years of age, extended in a semicircle around the right side of the yard. There were in all about forty. Each was dressed in the usual uniform of slaves, when in market, consisting of a fashionably shaped, black fur hat, roundabout and trowsers of coarse corduroy velvet, precisely such as are worn by Irish labourers, when they first "come over the water"; good vests, strong shoes, and white cotton shirts, completed their equipment. This dress they lay aside after they are sold, or wear out as soon as may be; for the negro dislikes to retain the indication of his having recently been in the market. With their hats in their hands, which hung down by their sides, they stood perfectly still, and in close order, while some gentlemen were passing from one to another examining for the purpose of buying. With the exception of displaying their teeth when addressed, and rolling their great white eyes about the court – they were so many statues of the most glossy ebony.

As we entered the mart, one of the slave merchants – for a "lot" of slaves is usually accompanied, if not owned, by two or three individuals – approached us, saying "Good morning, gentlemen! Would you like to examine my lot of boys? I have as fine a lot as ever came into market." – We approached them, one of us as a curious spectator, the other as a purchaser; and as my friend passed along the line, with a scrutinizing eye – giving that singular look, peculiar to the buyer of slaves as he glances from head to foot over each individual – the passive subjects of his observations betrayed no other signs of curiosity than that evinced by an occasional glance. The entrance of a stranger into a mart is by no means an unimportant event to the slave, for every stranger may soon become his master and command his future destinies.

23 SOJOURNER TRUTH

"Ain't I a Woman?" (1851)

Well, children, where there is so much racket there must be something out of kilter. I think that 'twixt the negroes of the South and the women at the North, all talking about rights, the white men will be in a fix pretty soon. But what's all this here talking about?

That man over there says that women need to be helped into carriages, and lifted over ditches, and to have the best place everywhere. Nobody ever helps me into carriages, or over mud-puddles, or gives me any best place! And ain't I a woman? Look at me! Look at my arm! I have ploughed and planted, and gathered into barns, and no man could head me! And ain't I a woman? I could work as much and eat as much as a man – when I could get it – and bear the lash as well! And ain't I a woman? I have borne thirteen children, and seen them most all sold off to slavery, and when I cried out with my mother's grief, none but Jesus heard me! And ain't I a woman?

Then they talk about this thing in the head; what's this they call it? [Intellect, someone whispers.] That's it, honey. What's that got to do with women's rights or negro's rights? If my cup won't hold but a pint, and yours holds a quart, wouldn't you be mean not to let me have my little half-measure full?

Then that little man in black there, he says women can't have as much rights as men, 'cause Christ wasn't a woman! Where did your Christ come from? Where did your Christ come from? From God and a woman! Man had nothing to do with Him.

If the first woman God ever made was strong enough to turn the world upside down all alone, these women together ought to be able to turn it back, and get it right side up again! And now they is asking to do it, the men better let them.

Obliged to you for hearing me, and now old Sojourner ain't got nothing more to say.

24 ABRAHAM LINCOLN

Final Emancipation Proclamation (1863)

By the President of the United States: A Proclamation

Whereas, on the twentysecond day of September, in the year of our Lord one thousand eight hundred and sixty two, a proclamation was issued by the president of the United States, containing, among other things, the following, towit:

"That on the first day of January, in the year of our Lord one thousand eight hundred and sixty-three, all persons held as slaves within any State or designated part of a State, the people whereof shall then be in rebellion against the United States, shall be then, thenceforward, and forever free; and the Executive Government of the United States, including the military and naval authority thereof, will recognize and maintain the freedom of such persons, and will do no act or acts to repress such persons, or any of them, in any efforts they may make for their actual freedom.

"That the Executive will, on the first day of January aforesaid, by proclamation, designate the States and parts of States, if any, in which the people thereof, respectively, shall then be in rebellion against the United States; and the fact that any State, or the people thereof, shall on that day be, in good faith, represented in the Congress of the United States by members chosen thereto at elections wherein a majority of the qualified voters of such State shall have participated, shall, in the absence of strong countervailing testimony, be deemed conclusive evidence that such State, and the people thereof, are not then in rebellion against the United States."

Now, therefore I, Abraham Lincoln, President of the United States, by virtue of the power in me vested as Commander-in-Chief, of the Army and Navy of the United States in time of actual armed rebellion against authority and government of the United States, and as a fit and necessary war measure for suppressing said rebellion, do, on this first day of January, in the year of our Lord one thousand eight hundred and sixty three, and in accordance with my purpose so to do publicly proclaimed for the full period of one hundred days, from the day first above mentioned, order and designate as the States and parts of States wherein the people thereof respectively, are this day in rebellion against the United States, the following, towit:

Arkansas, Texas, Louisiana, (except the Parishes of St. Bernard, Plaquemines, Jefferson, St. Johns, St. Charles, St. James, Ascension, Assumption, Terrebonne, Lafourche, St. Mary, St. Martin, and Orleans, including the City of New-Orleans) Mississippi, Alabama, Florida, Georgia, South-Carolina, North-Carolina, and Virginia, (except the fortyeight countries designated as West Virginia, and also the counties of Berkley, Accomac, Northampton, Elizabeth-City, York, Princess Ann, and Norfolk, including the cities of Norfolk & Portsmouth); and which excepted parts are, for the present, left precisely as if this proclamation were not issued.

And by virtue of the power, and for the purpose aforesaid, I do order and declare that all persons held as slaves within said designated States, and parts of States, are, and henceforward shall be free; and that the Executive government of the United States, including the military and naval authorities thereof, will recognize and maintain the freedom of said persons.

And I hereby enjoin upon the people so declared to be free to abstain from all violence, unless in necessary self-defence; and I recommend to them that, in all cases when allowed, they labor faithfully for reasonable wages.

And I further declare and make known, that such persons of suitable condition, will be received into the armed service of the United States to garrison forts, positions, stations, and other places, and to man vessels of all sorts in said service.

And upon this act, sincerely believed to be an act of justice, warranted by the Constitution, upon military necessity, I invoke the considerate judgment of mankind, and the gracious favor of Almighty God.

In witness whereof, I have hereunto set my hand and caused the seal of the United States to be affixed.

Done at the City of Washington, this first day of January, in the year of our Lord one thousand eight hundred and sixty three, and of the Independence of the United States of America the eighty-seventh.

By the President: ABRAHAM LINCOLN

WILLIAM H. SEWARD, Secretary of State.

25 WILLIAM DUBOIS

"This Double-Consciousness" (1903)

Between me and the other world there is ever an unasked question: unasked by some through feelings of delicacy; by others through the difficulty of rightly framing it. All, nevertheless, flutter round it. They approach me in a half hesitant sort of way, eye me curiously or compassionately, and then, instead of saying directly, How does it feel to be a problem? they say, I know an excellent colored man in my town; or, I fought at Mechanicsville; or, Do not these Southern outrages make your blood boil? At these I smile, or am interested, or reduce the boiling to a simmer, as the occasion may require. To the real question, How does it feel to be a problem? I answer seldom a word.

And yet, being a problem is a strange experience, – peculiar even for one who has never been anything else, save perhaps in babyhood and in Europe. It is in the early days of rollicking boyhood that the revelation first bursts upon one, all in a day, as it were. I remember well when the shadow swept across me. I was a little thing, away up in the hills of New England, where the dark Housatonic winds between Hoosac and Taghkanic to the sea. In a wee wooden schoolhouse, something put it into the boys' and girls' heads to buy gorgeous visiting-cards – ten cents a package – and exchange. The exchange was merry, till one girl, a tall newcomer, refused my card, – refused it peremptorily, with a glance. Then it dawned upon me with a certain suddenness that I was different from the others; or like, mayhap, in heart and life and longing, but shut out from their world by a vast veil. I had thereafter no desire to tear down that veil, to creep through; I held all beyond it in common contempt, and lived above it in a region of blue sky and great wandering shadows. That sky was bluest when I could beat my mates at examination-time, or beat them at a foot-race, or even beat their stringy heads. Alas, with the years all this fine contempt began to fade; for the words I longed for, and all their dazzling opportunities, were theirs, not mine. But they should not keep these prizes, I said; some, all, I would wrest from them. Just how I would do it I could never decide: by reading law, by healing the sick, by telling the wonderful tales that swam in my head – some way. With other black boys the strife was not so fiercely sunny: their youth shrunk into tasteless sycophancy, or into silent hatred of the pale world about them and mocking distrust of everything white; or wasted itself in a bitter cry, Why did God make me an outcast and a stranger in mine own house? The shades of the prison-house closed round about us all: walls strait and stubborn to the whitest, but relentlessly narrow, tal, and unscalable to sons of night who must plod darkly on in resignation, or beat unavailing palms against the stone, or steadily, half hopelessly, watch the streak of blue above.

After the Egyptian and Indian, the Greek and Roman, the Teuton and Mongolian, the Negro is a sort of seventh son, born with a veil, and gifted with second-sight in this American world, – a world which yields him no true self-consciousness, but only lets him see himself through the revelation of the other world. It is a peculiar sensation, this double consciousness, this sense of always looking at one's self through the eyes of others, of measuring one's soul by the tape of a world that looks on in amused contempt and pity. One ever feels his twoness, – an American, a Negro; two souls, two thoughts, two unreconciled strivings; two warring ideals in one dark body, whose dogged strength alone keeps it from being torn asunder.

The history of the American Negro is the history of this strife, – this longing to attain self-conscious manhood, to merge his double self into a better and truer self. In this merging he wishes neither of the older selves to be lost. He would not Africanize America, for America has too much to teach the world and Africa. He would not bleach his Negro soul in a flood of white Americanism, for he knows that Negro blood has a message for the world. He simply wishes to make it possible for a man to be both a Negro and an American, without being cursed and spit upon by his fellows, without having the doors of Opportunity closed roughly in his face.

FROM *"Of the Faith of the Fathers"* (1903)

The Preacher is the most unique personality developed by the Negro on American soil. A leader, a politician, an orator, a "boss," an intriguer, an idealist, – all these he is, and ever, too, the centre of a group of men, now twenty, now a thousand in number. The combination of a certain adroitness with deep-seated earnestness, of tact with consummate ability, gave him his preëminence, and helps him maintain it. The type, of course, varies according to time and place, from the West Indies in the sixteenth century to New England in the nineteenth, and from the Mississippi bottoms to cities like New Orleans or New York.

The Music of Negro religion is that plaintive rhythmic melody, with its touching minor cadences, which, despite caricature and defilement, still remains the most original and beautiful expression of human life and longing yet born on American soil. Sprung from the African forests, where its counterpart can still be heard, it was adapted, changed, and intensified by the tragic soul-life of the slave, until, under the stress of law and whip, it became the one true expression of a people's sorrow, despair, and hope.

Finally the Frenzy or "Shouting," when the Spirit of the Lord passed by, and, seizing the devotee, made him mad with supernatural joy, was the last essential of Negro religion and the one more devoutly believed in than all the rest. It varied in expression from the silent rapt countenance or the low murmur and moan to the mad abandon of physical fervor, – the stamping, shrieking, and shouting, the rushing to and fro and wild waving of arms, the weeping and laughing, the vision and the trance. All this is nothing new in the world, but old as religion, as Delphi and Endor. And so firm a hold did it have on the Negro, that many generations firmly believed that without this visible manifestation of the God there could be no true communion with the Invisible.

These were the characteristics of Negro religious life as developed up to the time of Emancipation. Since under the peculiar circumstances of the black man's environment they were the one expression of his higher life, they are of deep interest to the student of his development, both socially and psychologically. Numerous are the attractive lines of inquiry that here group themselves. What did slavery mean to the African savage? What was his attitude toward the World and Life? What seemed to him good and evil, – God and Devil? Whither went his longings and strivings, and wherefore were his heart-burnings and disappointments? Answers to such questions can come only from a study of Negro religion as a development, through its gradual changes from the heathenism of the Gold Coast to the institutional Negro church of Chicago.

Moreover, the religious growth of millions of men, even though they be slaves, cannot be without potent influence upon their contemporaries. The Methodists and Baptists of America owe much of their condition to the silent but potent influence of their millions of Negro converts. Especially is this noticeable in the South, where theology and religious philosophy are on this account a long way behind the North, and where the religion of the poor whites is a plain copy of Negro thought and methods. The mass of "gospel" hymns which has swept through American churches and well-nigh ruined our sense of song consists largely of debased imitations of Negro melodies made by ears that caught the jingle but not the music, the body but not the soul, of the Jubilee songs. It is thus clear that the study of Negro religion is not only a vital part of the history of the Negro in America, but no uninteresting part of American history.

The Negro church of to-day is the social centre of Negro life in the United States, and the most characteristic expression of African character. Take a typical church in a small Virginian town: it is the "First Baptist" – a roomy brick edifice seating five hundred or more persons, tastefully finished in Georgia pine, with a carpet, a small organ, and stained-glass windows. Underneath is a large assembly room with benches. This building is the central club-house of a community of a thousand or more Negroes. Various organizations meet here, – the church proper, the Sunday-school, two or three insurance societies, women's societies, secret societies, and mass meetings of various kinds. Entertainments, suppers, and lectures are held beside the five or six regular weekly religious services. Considerable sums of money are collected and expended here, employment is found for the idle, strangers are introduced, news is disseminated and charity distributed. At the same time this social, intellectual, and economic centre is a religious centre of great power. Depravity, Sin, Redemption, Heaven, Hell, and Damnation are preached twice a Sunday with much fervor, and revivals take place every year after the crops are laid by; and few indeed of the community have the hardihood to withstand conversion. Back of this more formal religion, the Church often stands as a real conserver of morals, a strengthener of family life, and the final authority on what is Good and Right.

Thus one can see in the Negro church to-day, reproduced in microcosm, all that great world from which the Negro is cut off by color prejudice and social condition. In the great city churches the same tendency is noticeable and in many respects emphasized. A great church like the Bethel of Philadelphia has over eleven hundred members, an edifice seating fifteen hundred persons and valued at one hundred thousand dollars, an annual budget of five thousand dollars, and a government consisting of a pastor with several assisting local preachers, an executive and legislative board, financial boards and tax collectors; general church meetings for making laws; subdivided groups led by class leaders, a company of militia, and twenty-four auxiliary societies. The activity of a church like this is immense and far-reaching, and the bishops who preside over these organizations throughout the land are among the most powerful Negro rulers in the world.

Such churches are really governments of men, and consequently a little investigation reveals the curious fact that, in the South, at least, practically every

American Negro is a church member. Some, to be sure, are not regularly enrolled, and a few do not habitually attend services; but, practically, a proscribed people must have a social centre, and that centre for this people is the Negro church. The census of 1890 showed nearly twenty-four thousand Negro churches in the country, with a total enrolled membership of over two and a half millions, or ten actual church members to every twenty-eight persons, and in some Southern States one in every two persons. Besides these there is the large number who, while not enrolled as members, attend and take part in many of the activities of the church. There is an organized Negro church for every sixty black families in the nation, and in some States for every forty families, owning, on an average, a thousand dollars' worth of property each, or nearly twenty-six million dollars in all.

Such, then, is the large development of the Negro church since Emancipation. The question now is, What have been the successive steps of this social history and what are the present tendencies? First, we must realize that no such institution as the Negro church could rear itself without definite historical foundations. These foundations we can find if we remember that the social history of the Negro did not start in America. He was brought from a definite social environment, – the polygamous clan life under the headship of the chief and the potent influence of the priest. His religion was nature-worship, with profound belief in invisible surrounding influences, good and bad, and his worship was through incantation and sacrifice. The first rude change in this life was the slave ship and the West Indian sugar-fields. The plantation organization replaced the clan and tribe, and the white master replaced the chief with far greater and more despotic powers. Forced and long-continued toil became the rule of life, the old ties of blood relationship and kinship disappeared, and instead of the family appeared a new polygamy and polyandry, which, in some cases, almost reached promiscuity. It was a terrific social revolution, and yet some traces were retained of the former group life, and the chief remaining institution was the Priest or Medicine-man. He early appeared on the plantation and found his function as the healer of the sick, the interpreter of the Unknown, the comforter of the sorrowing, the supernatural avenger of wrong, and the one who rudely but picturesquely expressed the longing, disappointment, and resentment of a stolen and oppressed people. Thus, as bard, physician, judge, and priest, within the narrow limits allowed by the slave system, rose the Negro preacher, and under him the first Afro-American institution, the Negro church. This church was not at first by any means Christian nor definitely organized; rather it was an adaptation and mingling of heathen rites among the members of each plantaion, and roughly designated as Voodooism. Association with the masters, missionary effort and motives of expediency gave these rites an early veneer of Christianity, and after the lapse of many generations the Negro church became Christian. . . .

To-day the two groups of Negroes, the one in the North, the other in the South, represent these divergent ethical tendencies, the first tending toward radicalism, the other toward hypocritical compromise. It is no idle regret with which the white South mourns the loss of the old-time Negro, – the frank, honest, simple old servant who stood for the earlier religious age of submission and humility. With all his laziness and lack of many elements of true manhood, he was at least open-hearted, faithful, and sincere. To-day he is gone, but who is to blame for his going? Is it not those very persons who mourn for him? Is it not the tendency, born of Reconstruction and Reaction, to found a society on lawlessness and deception, to tamper with the moral fibre of a naturally honest and straightforward people until the whites threaten to become ungovernable tyrants and the blacks criminals and hypocrites? Deception is the natural defence of the weak against the strong, and the South used it for many years against its conquerors; to-day it must be prepared to see its black proletariat turn that same two-edged weapon against itself. And how natural this is! The death of Denmark Vesey and Nat Turner proved long since to the Negro the present hopelessness of physical defence. Political defence is becoming less and less available, and economic defence is still only partially effective. But there is a patent defence at hand, – the defence of deception and flattery, of cajoling and lying. It is the same defence which the Jews of the Middle Age used and which left its stamp on their character for centuries. Today the young Negro of the South who would succeed cannot be frank and outspoken, honest and self-assertive, but rather he is daily tempted to be silent and wary, politic and sly; he must flatter and be pleasant, endure petty insults with a smile, shut his eyes to wrong; in too many cases he sees positive personal advantage in deception and lying. His real thoughts, his real aspirations, must be guarded in whspers; he must not criticize, he must not complain. Patience, humility, and adroitness must, in these growing black youth, replace impulse, manliness, and courage. With this sacrifice there is an economic opening, and perhaps peace and some prosperity. Without this there is riot, migration, or crime. Nor is this situation peculiar to the Southern United States, – is it not rather the only method by which undeveloped races have gained the right to share modern culture? The price of culture is a Lie.

On the other hand, in the North the tendency is to emphasize the radicalism of the Negro. Driven from his birthright in the South by a situation at which every fibre of his more outspoken and assertive nature revolts, he finds himself in a land where he can scarcely earn a decent living amid the harsh competition and the color discrimination. At the same time, through schools and periodicals, discussions and lectures, he is intellectually quickened and awakened. The soul, long pent up and dwarfed, suddenly expands in new-found freedom. What wonder that every tendency is to excess, – radical complaint, radical remedies, bitter denunciation or angry silence. Some sink, some rise. The criminal and the sensualist leave the church for the gambling-hell and the brothel, and fill the slums of Chicago and Baltimore; the better classes segregate themselves from the group-life of both white and black, and form an aristocracy, cultured but pessimistic, whose bitter criticism stings while it points out no way of escape. They despise the submission and subserviency of the Southern Negroes, but offer no other means by which a poor and oppressed minority can exist side by side with its masters. Feeling deeply and keenly the tendencies and opportunities of the age in which they live, their souls are bitter at the fate which drops the Veil between; and the very fact that this bitterness is natural and justifiable only serves to intensify it and make it more maddening.

Between the two extreme types of ethical attitude which I have thus sought to make clear wavers the mass of the millions of Negroes, North and South; and their religious life and activity partake of this social conflict within their ranks. Their churches are differentiating, – now into groups of cold, fashionable devotees, in no way distinguishable from similar white groups save in color of skin; now into large social and business institutions catering to the desire for information and amusement of their members, warily avoiding unpleasant questions both within and without the black world, and preaching in effect if not in word: *Dum Divimus, vivamus.*

But back of this still broods silently the deep religious feeling of the real Negro heart, the stirring, unguided might of powerful human souls who have lost the guiding star of the past and are seeking in the great night a new religious ideal. Some day the Awakening will come, when the pent-up vigor of ten million souls shall sweep irresistibly toward the Goal, out of the Valley of the Shadow of Death, where all that makes life worth living – Liberty, Justice, and Right – is marked "For White People Only."

26 GWENDOLYN BROOKS

"We Real Cool" (1960)

THE POOL PLAYERS.
SEVEN AT THE GOLDEN SHOVEL.

> We real cool. We
> Left school. We
>
> Lurk late. We
> Strike straight. We
>
> Sing sin. We
> Thin gin. We
>
> Jazz June. We
> Die soon.

27 MARTIN LUTHER KING, JR.

"I Have a Dream" (1963)

Five score years ago, a great American, in whose symbolic shadow we stand, signed the Emancipation Proclamation. This momentous decree came as a great beacon light of hope to millions of Negro slaves who had been seared in the flames of withering injustice. It came as a joyous daybreak to end the long night of captivity.

But one hundred years later, we must face the tragic fact that the Negro is still not free. One hundred years later, the life of the Negro is still sadly crippled by the manacles of segregation and the chains of discrimination. One hundred years later, the Negro lives on a lonely island of poverty in the midst of a vast ocean of material prosperity. One hundred years later, the Negro is still languished in the corners of American society and finds himself an exile in his own land. So we have come here today to dramatize an appalling condition.

In a sense we have come to our nation's Capital to cash a check. When the archi-
tects of our republic wrote the magnificent words of the Constitution and the
Declaration of Independence, they were signing a promissory note to which every
American was to fall heir. This note was a promise that all men would be guaranteed
the unalienable rights of life, liberty, and the pursuit of happiness.

It is obvious today that America has defaulted on this promissory note insofar as
her citizens of color are concerned. Instead of honoring this sacred obligation,
America has given the Negro people a bad check; a check which has come back
marked "insufficient funds." But we refuse to believe that the bank of justice is
bankrupt. We refuse to believe that there are insufficient funds in the great vaults
of opportunity of this nation. So we have come to cash this check – a check that will
give us upon demand the riches of freedom and the security of justice. We have also
come to this hallowed spot to remind America of the fierce urgency of *now*. This is
no time to engage in the luxury of cooling off or to take the tranquilizing drug
of gradualism. *Now* is the time to make real the promises of Democracy. *Now* is the
time to rise from the dark and desolate valley of segregation to the sunlit path of racial
justice. *Now* is the time to open the doors of opportunity to all of God's children. *Now*
is the time to lift our nation from the quicksands of racial injustice to the solid rock
of brotherhood.

It would be fatal for the nation to overlook the urgency of the moment and to
underestimate the determination of the Negro. This sweltering summer of the Negro's
legitimate discontent will not pass until there is an invigorating autumn of freedom
and equality. 1963 is not an end, but a beginning. Those who hope that the Negro
needed to blow off steam and will now be content will have a rude awakening if the
nation returns to business as usual. There will be neither rest nor tranquility in
America until the Negro is granted his citizenship rights. The whirlwinds of revolt will
continue to shake the foundations of our nation until the bright day of justice emerges.

But there is something that I must say to my people who stand on the warm
threshold which leads into the palace of justice. In the process of gaining our rightful
place we must not be guilty of wrongful deeds. Let us not seek to satisfy our thirst for
freedom by drinking from the cup of bitterness and hatred. We must forever conduct
our struggle on the high plane of dignity and discipline. We must not allow our
creative protest to degenerate into physical violence. Again and again we must rise
to the majestic heights of meeting physical force with soul force. The marvelous new
militancy which has engulfed the Negro community must not lead us to a distrust of
all white people, for many of our white brothers, as evidenced by their presence here
today, have come to realize that their destiny is tied up with our destiny and their
freedom is inextricably bound to our freedom. We cannot walk alone.

And as we walk, we must make the pledge that we shall march ahead. We cannot
turn back. There are those who are asking the devotees of civil rights, "When will you
be satisfied?" We can never be satisfied as long as the Negro is the victim of the
unspeakable horrors of police brutality. We can never be satisfied as long as our bodies,
heavy with the fatigue of travel, cannot gain lodging in the motels of the highways
and the hotels of the cities. We cannot be satisfied as long as the Negro's basic mobility
is from a smaller ghetto to a larger one. We can never be satisfied as long as a Negro
in Mississippi cannot vote and a Negro in New York believes he has nothing for which

to vote. No, no, we are not satisfied, and we will not be satisfied until justice rolls down like waters and righteousness like a mighty stream.

I am not unmindful that some of you have come here out of great trials and tribulations. Some of you have come fresh from narrow jail cells. Some of you have come from areas where your quest for freedom left you battered by the storms of persecution and staggered by the winds of police brutality. You have been the veterans of creative suffering. Continue to work with the faith that unearned suffering is redemptive.

Go back to Mississippi, go back to Alabama, go back to South Carolina, go back to Georgia, back to Louisiana, go back to the slums and ghettos of our northern cities, knowing that somehow this situation can and will be changed. Let us not wallow in the valley of despair.

I say to you today, my friends, that in spite of the difficulties and frustrations of the moment I still have a dream. It is a dream deeply rooted in the American dream.

I have a dream that one day this nation will rise up and live out the true meaning of its creed: "We hold these truths to be self-evident, that all men are created equal."

I have a dream that one day on the red hills of Georgia the sons of former slaves and the sons of former slaveowners will be able to sit down together at the table of brotherhood.

I have a dream that one day even the state of Mississippi, a desert state sweltering with the heat of injustice and oppression, will be transformed into an oasis of freedom and justice.

I have a dream that my four little children will one day live in a nation where they will be not judged by the color of their skin but by the content of their character.

I have a dream today.

I have a dream that one day the state of Alabama, whose governor's lips are presently dripping with the words of interposition and nullification, will be transformed into a situation where little black boys and black girls will be able to join hands with little white boys and white girls and walk together as sisters and brothers.

I have a dream today.

I have a dream that one day every valley shall be exalted, every hill and mountain shall be made low, the rough places will be made plain, and the crooked places will be made straight, and the glory of the Lord shall be revealed, and all flesh shall see it together.

This is our hope. This is the faith with which I return to the South. With this faith we will be able to hew out of the mountain of despair a stone of hope. With this faith we will be able to transform the jangling discords of our nation into a beautiful symphony of brotherhood. With this faith we will be able to work together, to pray together, to struggle together, to go to jail together, to stand up for freedom together, knowing that we will be free one day.

This will be the day when all of God's children will be able to sing with new meaning

My county, 'tis of thee,
Sweet land of liberty,
Of thee I sing,

Land where my fathers died,
Land of the pilgrims' pride,
From every mountain-side
Let freedom ring.

And if America is to be a great nation this must become true. So let freedom ring from the prodigious hilltops of New Hampshire. Let freedom ring from the mighty mountains of New York. Let freedom ring from the heightening Alleghenies of Pennsylvania!

Let freedom ring from the snowcapped Rockies of Colorado!

Let freedom ring from the curvacious peaks of California!

But not only that; let freedom ring from Stone Mountain of Georgia!

Let freedom ring from Lookout Mountain of Tennessee!

Let freedom ring from every hill and molehill of Mississippi. From every mountainside, let freedom ring.

When we let freedom ring, when we let it ring from every village and every hamlet, from every state and every city, we will be able to speed up that day when all of God's children, black men and white men, Jews and Gentiles, Protestants and Catholics, will be able to join hands and sing in the words of the old Negro spiritual, "Free at last! free at last! thank God almighty, we are free at last!"

28 US CONGRESS

The Civil Rights Act (1964)

Title I – Voting Rights

SEC. 101 (2). No person acting under color of law shall –

(A) in determining whether any individual is qualified under State law or laws to vote in any Federal election, apply any standard, practice, or procedure different from the standards, practices, or procedures applied under such law or laws to other individuals within the same county, parish, or similar political subdivision who have been found by State officials to be qualified to vote; . . .

(C) employ any literacy test as a qualification for voting in any Federal election unless (i) such test is administered to each individual wholly in writing; (ii) a certified copy of the test and of the answers given by the individual is furnished to him within twenty-five days of the submission of his request made within the period of time during which records and papers are required to be retained and preserved pursuant to title III of the Civil Rights Act of 1960 . . .

Title II – Injunctive Relief against Discrimination in Places of Public Accommodation

SEC. 201. (a) All persons shall be entitled to the full and equal enjoyment of the goods, services, facilities, privileges, advantages, and accommodations of any place of public accommodation, as defined in this section, without discrimination or segregation on the ground of race, color, religion, or national origin.

(b) Each of the following establishments which serves the public is a place of public accommodation within the meaning of this title if its operations affect commerce, or if discrimination or segregation by it is supported by State action:

(1) any inn, motel, or other establishment which provides lodging to transient guests, other than an establishment located within a building which contains not more than five rooms for rent or hire and which is actually occupied by the proprietor of such establishment as his residence;

(2) any restaurant, cafeteria, lunch room, lunch counter, soda fountain, or other facility principally engaged in selling food for consumption on the premises . . .

(3) any motion picture house, theater, concert hall, sports arena, stadium or other place of exhibition or entertainment . . .

(d) Discrimination or segregation by an establishment is supported by State action within the meaning of this title if such discrimination or segregation (1) is carried on under color of any law, statute, ordinance, or regulation; or (2) is carried on under color of any custom or usage required or enforced by officials of the State or political subdivision thereof . . .

SEC. 202. All persons shall be entitled to be free, at any establishment or place, from discrimination or segregation of any kind on the ground of race, color, religion, or national origin, if such discrimination or segregation is or purports to be required by any law, statute, ordinance, regulation, rule, or order of a State or any agency or political subdivision thereof . . .

SEC. 206. (a) Whenever the Attorney General has reasonable cause to believe that any person or groups of persons is engaged in a pattern or practice of resistance to the full enjoyment of any of the rights secured by this title, the Attorney General may bring a civil action in the appropriate district court of the United States by filing with it a complaint . . . requesting such preventive relief, including an application for a permanent or temporary injunction, restraining order or other order against the person or persons responsible for such pattern or practice, as he deems necessary to insure the full enjoyment of the rights herein described . . .

Title VI – Nondiscrimination in Federally Assisted Programs

SEC. 601. No person in the United States shall, on the ground of race, color, or national origin, be excluded from participation in, be denied the benefits of, or be subjected to discrimination under any program or activity receiving Federal financial assistance.

29 MALCOLM X

FROM *"The Ballot or the Bullet"* (1965)

I'm not a politician, not even a student of politics; in fact, I'm not a student of much of anything. I'm not a Democrat, I'm not a Republican, and I don't even consider myself an American. If you and I were Americans, there'd be no problem. Those Hunkies that just got off the boat, they're already Americans; Polacks are already Americans; the Italian refugees are already Americans. Everything that came out of

Europe, every blue-eyed thing, is already an American. And as long as you and I have been over here, we aren't Americans yet.

Well, I am one who doesn't believe in deluding myself. I'm not going to sit at your table and watch you eat, with nothing on my plate, and call me a diner. Sitting at the table doesn't make you a diner, unless you eat some of what's on that plate. Being here in America doesn't make you an American. Why, if birth made you American, you wouldn't need any legislation, you wouldn't need any amendments to the Constitution, you wouldn't be faced with civil-rights filibustering in Washington, D.C., right now. They don't have to pass civil-rights legislation to make a Polack an American.

No, I'm not an American. I'm one of the 22 million black people who are victims of Americanism. One of the 22 million black people who are the victims of democracy, nothing but disguised hypocrisy. So, I'm not standing here speaking to you as an American, or a patriot, or a flag-saluter, or a flag-waver – no, not I. I'm speaking as a victim of this American system. And I see America through the eye of the victim. I don't see any American dream; I see an American nightmare. . . .

The political philosophy of black nationalism means that the black man should control the politics and the politicians in his own community, no more. The black man in the black community has to be re-educated into the science of politics so he will know what politics is supposed to bring him in return. Don't be throwing out any ballots. A ballot is like a bullet. You don't throw your ballots until you see a target, and if that target is not within your reach, keep your ballot in your pocket. . . .

The economic philosophy of black nationalism is pure and simple. It only means that we should control the economy of our community. Why should white people be running all the stores in our community? Why should white people be running the banks of our community? Why should the economy of our community be in the hands of the white man? Why? If a black man can't move his store into a white community, you tell me why a white man should move his store into a black community. The philosophy of black nationalism involves a re-education program in the black community in regards to economics. Our people have to be made to see that any time you take your dollar out of your community and spend it in a community where you don't live, the community where you live will get poorer and poorer, and the community where you spend your money will get richer and richer. Then you wonder why where you live is always a ghetto or a slum area.

FROM *"The Black Man" (1965)*

I felt a challenge to plan, and build, an organization that could help to cure the black man in North America of the sickness which has kept him under the white man's heel.

The black man in North America was mentally sick in his cooperative, sheeplike acceptance of the white man's culture.

The black man in North America was spiritually sick because for centuries he had accepted the white man's Christianity – which asked the black so-called Christian to expect no true Brotherhood of Man, but to endure the cruelties of the white so-called

Christians. Christianity had made black men fuzzy, nebulous, confused in their thinking. It had taught the black man to think if he had no shoes, and was hungry "we gonna get shoes and milk and honey and fish fries in Heaven."

The black man in North America was economically sick and that was evident in one simple fact: as a consumer, he got less than his share, and as a producer gave *least*. The black American today shows us the perfect parasite image – the black tick under the delusion that he is progressing because he rides on the udder of the fat, three-stomached cow that is white America. For instance, annually, the black man spends over $3 billion for automobiles, but America contains hardly any franchised black automobile dealers. For instance, forty per cent of the expensive imported Scotch whisky consumed in America goes down the throats of the status-sick black man; but the only black-owned distilleries are in bathtubs, or in the woods somewhere. Or for instance – a scandalous shame – in New York City, with over a million Negroes, there aren't twenty black-owned businesses employing over ten people. It's because black men don't own and control their own community's retail establishments that they can't stabilize their own community.

The black man in North America was sickest of all politically. He let the white man divide him into such foolishness as considering himself a black "Democrat," a black "Republican," a black "Conservative," or a black "Liberal" . . . when a ten-million black vote bloc could be the deciding balance of power in American politics, because the white man's vote is almost always evenly divided. The polls are one place where every black man could fight the black man's cause with dignity, and with the power and the tools that the white man understands, and respects, and fears, and cooperates with. Listen, let me tell you something! If a black bloc committee told Washington's worst "nigger-hater," "We represent ten million votes," why, that "nigger-hater" would leap up: "Well, how *are* you? Come on *in* here!" Why, if the Mississippi black man voted in a bloc, Eastland would pretend to be more liberal than Jacob Javits – or Eastland would not survive in his office. Why else is it that racist politicians fight to keep black men from the polls?

Whenever any group can vote in a bloc, and decide the outcome of elections, and it *fails* to do this, then that group is politically sick. Immigrants once made Tammany Hall the most powerful single force in American politics. In 1880, New York City's first Irish Catholic Mayor was elected and by 1960 America had its first Irish Catholic President. America's black man, voting as a bloc, could wield an even more powerful force.

US politics is ruled by special-interest blocs and lobbies. What group has a more urgent special interest, what group needs a bloc, a lobby, more than the black man? Labor owns one of Washington's largest non-government buildings – situated where they can literally watch the White House – and no political move is made that doesn't involve how Labor feels about it. A lobby got Big Oil its depletion allowance. The farmer, through his lobby, is the most government-subsidized special-interest group in America today, because a million farmers vote, not as Democrats, or Republicans, liberals, conservatives, but as farmers.

Doctors have the best lobby in Washington. Their special-interest influence successfully fights the Medicare program that's wanted, and needed, by millions of other people. Why, there's a Beet Growers' Lobby! A Wheat Lobby! A Cattle Lobby!

A China Lobby! Little countries no one ever heard of have their Washington lobbies, representing their special interests.

The government has departments to deal with the special-interest groups that make themselves heard and felt. A Department of Agriculture cares for the farmers' needs. There is a Department of the Interior – in which the Indians are included. Is the farmer, the doctor, the Indian, the greatest problem in America today? No – it is the black man! There ought to be a Pentagon-sized Washington department dealing with every segment of the black man's problems.

Twenty-two million black men! They have given America four hundred years of toil; they have bled and died in every battle since the Revolution; they were in America before the Pilgrims, and long before the mass immigrations – and they are still today at the bottom of everything!

Why, twenty-two million black people should tomorrow give a dollar apiece to build a skyscraper lobby building in Washington, D.C. Every morning, every legislator should receive a communication about what the black man in America expects and wants and needs. The demanding voice of the black lobby should be in the ears of every legislator who votes on any issue.

The cornerstones of this country's operation are economic and political strength and power. The black man doesn't have the economic strength – and it will take time for him to build it. But right now the American black man has the political strength and power to change his destiny overnight.

30 SEPTIMA CLARK

"Teach How Change Comes About" (pre-1987)

In one of the strangest turnabouts to occur after the turbulent sixties, Septima Clark – once fired as a public school teacher in Charleston, South Carolina – ultimately became a member of that city's school board. As the discriminated-against employee turned employer, she acquired the power once denied every black person in the South.

But in this new position, was she able to assure that the school system's classrooms also taught students about people like Dr Martin Luther King, Jr., Rosa Parks, or herself? Or were policy decisions in a public system like Charleston's more difficult to alter than when she worked within the private organizations of Highlander and the Southern Christian Leadership Conference on behalf of the Citizenship Schools?

We still have a long way to go, and I really feel determined that we've got to do a better job. We do some things, though. On 15 January, we celebrate Dr King's birthday, and I went around to school every day last January for one whole week talking about King. Then in February, it was Afro-American Month, and I went to a number of schools talking about the various blacks like Sojourner Truth. In one of the schools, they even sort of talked about me at that time. They know who I am. But we need to do more of that. And I'm not only asking them to do just that. Whenever they speak about a black in America, I think they need to find a white who does somewhat similar. The problem is it's usually all white, even now. Just recently a booklet about American government was passed around in a school board meeting so we could see if we wanted to use it in the schools, and you know there wasn't one black in that book? Not one black. I wanted to know who the black children would have to look up to in that book. I felt it was wrong to place that book in the hands of teachers. There was nothing in there that would help black children to feel that they had a right to the tree of life. And I know how important that is. I didn't feel as if I could ever do anything worthwhile when I was living in North Carolina until Mary McLeod Bethune came down and spoke. And there she was, a real black woman sitting in Roosevelt's "kitchen" cabinet, and she said, "I'm just a fly in that bowl of milk, but I'm certainly there." And that gave me a great feeling, that a black woman could be sitting in Roosevelt's cabinet. And I think this is what it would do for our children too. They need to know about such people.

They also need to know how change comes about. You have to develop them to do their own thinking and not accept unjust things but break through those things and change them. I once felt I had to accept things as they were. I rode on the bus and I sat in the section of the bus where black people were supposed to sit and I would get up and give my seat to any white man because I knew it was the law, and I did it without feeling angry. Not until I got to Highlander [*laughter*] did I learn that I should defy laws like that that are unjust.

But today, teachers say, "If I start talking to my kids about things they ought to change, I'm going to get fired." And we got that case right now. There is a young woman who has been talking to her children about standing up for their rights, and her name is on the list to be terminated: I don't want to miss that meeting Monday, because I'm going to vote on her to stay in that school. And the only reason they want to fire her is because she will speak out. And she has been an excellent teacher. They're going to try to fire her, but I'm going to fight them.

I tell teachers and students, "Stand up for your rights, regardless." You have to stand up and take the consequences. It's not going to be easy. It's not going to be pleasant. After I was fired, I went to Highlander, and for three long months I couldn't sleep. Then at the end of that time, it seemed to me as if my mind cleared up and I decided then that I must have been right. I really didn't find out for sure that I was right until Governor Edwards, in 1976, said, "You were unjustly fired," and sent me a check for the pension I was owed. And that made me realize that I was right all the time. But I had to wait until I was eighty years of age to find out. I went all those years knowing that the people thought I was wrong – even my own people. My brother said to me, "Why did you tell them that you were a member of the NAACP?"[1]

I said, "I couldn't live with myself otherwise." So you have to be strong. You have to tell the truth and take the consequences. And it's not going to be easy. It's not going to be pleasant.

Say you were one of those teachers, for example, and you said to me, "Septima, I can't talk to my white kids in class about the KKK because these kids love their parents and the parents are members of the KKK. Now I know the organization is wrong, but I'm afraid I'll hurt those kids." I would have to tell you that regardless of what happens, you are going to have to let those kids know the very truth about the KKK, because when you see the kinds of things that they have done, you will know that those things are not right. They might burn your house down. I couldn't tell you that they won't. I have had a lot of things happen to me and I had to live through it.

I've had policemen sent to my door looking for the fight. Just harassment. I've had firemen sent to my door looking for the fire. Pure harassment. I've had people call and curse me over the telephone, and I would just say, "Thank you, call again." I'd put the phone down and here would come another call. There were nights when I couldn't sleep for that kind of thing. People were even afraid of me. Thought I was a Communist.

But now that's changed. I have honorary degrees. The housing authority has named a day care center for me. A highway has been named for me. I've been on television. Not long ago I was interviewed five times in one day. I've even had visitors from Spain. So you live through the bad times. You have to have faith.

Today you don't have those unjust laws that we had to work on, but when young people look long enough, they'll see that it's more subtle things that they have to work on. I say to them, "You have to look at your administrative groups and see if any of you are sitting there helping to make the laws. What about your legislature? What about your city council? What about your county delegation? Do you see any blacks sitting there? What about your school board? Do you see any blacks? I'm the only black on our school board, and when I get off next year I wonder if there will be another one who will come on. What about stores and banks? You can find black clerks and cashiers, but what about the administrative groups? Can you find any there? What about the pollution off our coast? Do you know this is where you get your food to eat, and now this source is going to be denied you if you don't grow up and vote against things like that? And what about the inadequate health screening for our first graders? What about aides for the handicapped children? We need to have special money for handicapped kids and it's coming out in the papers every day. People are voting against those things. We need to have physical education, art, and music in first grade, and Reagan wants to cut these out. Now we've got to stand up in arms against those cuts. Don't sit down and accept them. Instead of accepting them, stand up and vote against them."

And if they get discouraged, I tell them that there were times when I felt discouraged, too, but I felt I had to go on. I could not do anything by quitting. A quitter receives nothing.

But they are going to do more. Right now I have a feeling that now that we have been able to open doors for them, they should go through those doors and get all the education that they can and then come up and be the administrators. I know I'm not going to live to see a black President, but I do hope in time to come there will be one.

So political action and education are still the keys to a better future. I really felt that the great turning point for us was the Voting Rights bill in August of '65. That had a great effect on the American people. That opened the doors for us for both political action and education. They both go together. I'll always remember when one of the fellows we were teaching in Anamanee, Alabama, went up to the bank in Camden to cash a check, and the white man took out his pen and said, "I'll make the *X*."

He said, "You don't have to make the *X* for me because I can write my own name." The white guy says, "My God, them niggers done learned to write."

1 National Association for the Advancement of Colored People, founded 1909.

4

WOMEN'S STUDIES

Introduction   86

31 *Alexis de Tocqueville*   90
    "The Young Woman in the Character of a Wife" (1848)

32 *Seneca Falls Convention*   91
    Declaration of Sentiments and Resolutions (1848)

33 *Kate Chopin*   93
    "The Story of an Hour" (1894)

34 *Charlotte Perkins Gilman*   95
    FROM *Women and Economics* (1898)

35 *Meridel LeSueur*   96
    "Women on the Breadlines" (1932)

36 *Betty Friedan*   101
    "That Has No Name" (1963)

37 *Studs Terkel*   104
    "'Just a Housewife': Therese Carter" (1972)

38 *Marabel Morgan*   107
    "Admire Him" (1973)

39 *Merle Woo*   112
    FROM "Letter to Ma" (1980)

40 *US Supreme Court*   115
    Roe v. *Wade* (1973)

Figure 4 Migrant Mother by Dorothea Lange, 1936 © CORBIS

INTRODUCTION

Since World War II an increasing number of women in the United States have gone
to college and have taken jobs outside the home. A new awareness of themselves as
workers as well as mothers inspired the upsurge of a women's liberation movement
in the 1960s. Since then members of various women's organizations have revealed
how women are – and have been – discriminated against in all walks of life. A series
of stamps issued by the United States Postal Service in 1940 may illustrate the long-
lasting invisibility of women in public life. Of the thirty-five "famous Americans" to

be included in the series only three women were found worthy of the honor, one of whom was the social reformer Jane Addams. The present women's movement has looked for ideas and inspiration in the works of earlier reformers in America, but above all it has used the Civil Rights Act of 1964 to ensure that equal opportunity for jobs is provided for them, and that they are not given less pay than males for the same work.

A large percentage of the women who joined forces to promote a feminist movement in the 1960s and 1970s had a white middle-class background.[1] In 1966 some of them helped to establish a new organization for women called NOW (the National Organization for Women). In their program they agreed to organize to put an end to what they referred to as "the silken curtain of prejudice and discrimination against women" in every "field of importance in American society." Since then working-class women and women of ethnic minorities have focused their attention on issues which had not necessarily been part of the problems voiced by the middle-class suburban wife a few years earlier. In 1973 the Supreme Court voted to delete restrictions to a woman's right to abortion, referring to the "concept of personal liberty" in the fourteenth amendment to the Constitution. In later years, however, forces within the political apparatus, largely dominated by conservative men, have again tried to limit the right to abortion.

Alexis de Tocqueville's observation of the social status of young women in the United States during the 1830s (text 31) is still a good starting point for a discussion of women's role in the history of American culture. Some would even argue for the lasting validity of his statement that whereas "an unmarried woman is less constrained there than elsewhere," a married woman on the other hand "is subjected to stricter obligations." In the media wives of leading American politicians even today often display a loyal and subservient public role that is rare in most European countries.

When women were given the right to vote in federal elections by the nineteenth amendment in 1919, suffrage had long been an issue, and some states had already granted women the right to vote, Wyoming having been the first to do so (in 1869, when Wyoming still had a territorial legislature). The declarations from the Seneca Falls Convention of 1848, the first women's right convention, modeled on the Declaration of Independence, mark the beginning of the women's suffrage movement in the United States (text 32). On the first day of the convention men were not allowed to enter, but the final resolution was also signed by men, among them Frederick Douglass, the author who had been born a slave. Although the document was often ridiculed in the press of the day by men who thought the participants to the convention were trying to overthrow "the laws of nature," the organizers such as Elizabeth Cady Stanton, Lucretia Mott, and others, ably rose to defend the resolutions passed. Before and during the Civil War women joined forces to fight slavery, as well as the abuse of alcohol. When Harriet Beecher Stowe, who wrote *Uncle Tom's Cabin* (1852), the best-selling American anti-slavery novel, visited President Lincoln during the war, he is reported to have jokingly said that she was "the little lady" who started the conflict. Beecher Stowe, as well as other women leaders of her time, brought the Protestant traditions in which they were raised to issues of social reform.

In novels and short stories from around 1900 to the 1920s Kate Chopin and Charlotte Perkins Gilman among others started to explore new definitions of women's freedom, especially in sexuality, birth control, and marriage. Kate Chopin, who lived in the South, protested against the notion of the traditional "Southern belle", as an ideal shaped by men who liked women to be presented as something untainted and passive, dolls to be admired for their grace and their lace. Her short story here (text 33) deals with the element of choice suddenly given to a woman at the most unlikely time. In addition to her fiction, Gilman also wrote essays on the issue of women's liberation and is perhaps best known for her studies of women's economic dependence (text 34). Both of these writers were almost forgotten or ignored in their own lifetime, but are widely studied today. Meridel LeSueur, a Midwestern writer born in 1900, has also found a new audience today. Her essay (text 35) is a strong comment on the severe conditions in the 1930s in an American city from a woman's point of view.

Betty Friedan's book *The Feminine Mystique*, published in 1963 (see text 36, taken from her introduction), was one of the major documents which launched the new women's movement of the 1960s and 1970s. Friedan focused on what she saw as the unsatisfactory lives of middle-class suburban housewives. She argued that women should stop playing a passive role or just helping their husbands build careers. Her account of what to her appeared as the rather depressing and tedious routines of a typical American housewife did, however, run counter to the way in which many housewives saw, and may still see, their own situation. In Studs Terkel's interview (text 37) we meet a housewife in a blue-collar community outside Chicago, who reads *Ms.* magazine, but who nevertheless thinks that "Woman's Lib puts down a housewife." Notice that the interviewer rarely enters her story.

The image of women in music, film, and the popular arts has changed over the years. The ever popular American cowboy movies, for example, usually portrayed women – if they portrayed them at all – as romantic appendages in essentially male adventures or certainly in need of the protection of a strong male hero. In popular stories and films urban women were equally depicted as secretaries or wives at the service of some male. In general, popular American culture saw the woman primarily as the romantic lover or the diligent wife who had little life of her own except in connection with a more "meaningful" male existence. Since the 1970s, however, American film producers have shown women playing active roles in the workforce and in their relationship with men. Female directors have made important films, for example Sofia Coppola's *Lost in Translation* (2003). There is, nevertheless, a sharp contrast between women role models and the more common images of young women used in the American advertising business. Duane Hanson, a modern American sculptor, has made a lifelike and unforgettable portrait of a female shopper in a supermarket, a consumer figure far from the ideals of womanhood elsewhere in the media.

Over the last decades, American colleges and universities have added Women's Studies to their curriculum and thus introduced thousands of students to a new field of study. Women writers of the past have been rediscovered and republished, to provide both an alternative sense of literary history and genuine inspiration for a new generation of readers and writers. Several female authors have gone on to deal not only with the social and economic inequality experienced by women, but with intimate and intricate emotional relations. A contemporary poet, Adrienne Rich, is especially concerned with possible new ways of expressing the full scope of female experience. In her important study *Of Women Born: Motherhood as Experience and Institution* (1976) she wanted to reexamine her womanhood and the common attitudes that women have had (and have) toward themselves, toward men, and toward their children. The letter of Merle Woo, a Korean-American writer, to her mother, may be studied as an illustration of contemporary cultural values in a mother–daughter relationship (text 39).

One should notice, however, that the best-selling book on American women during the 1970s was not produced by poets such as Adrienne Rich or Sylvia Plath. It was the enormously popular *The Total Woman* (1973), by Marabel Morgan. She started popular study groups inspired by her books on American women. Today, it may be hard to realize that the chapter from her book (excerpt 38) is written with absolutely no sense of irony.

Since the 1973 Supreme Court ruling in *Roe* v. *Wade*, women's right to abortion has been one of the most controversial issues in contemporary American life and politics (see text 40).

1 See Mary Beth Norton and Ruth M. Alexander, eds., *Major Problems in American Women's History*, 3rd edn (Boston: Houghton Mifflin Company, 2003), p. 427.

Questions and Topics

1 How did the crisis of the 1930s affect American women? How does LeSueur describe the vulnerability of city women as they fall outside the safety net of both the family and the labor force?

2 Why does the working class woman in Terkel's interview feel "put down" by the woman's liberation movement? Relate her identity and her sense of womanhood to the problems addressed by Betty Friedan.

3 Discuss the message and the genre of Merle Woo's letter to her mother. How does the issue of ethnicity intensify and broaden the female relationships here? How can the daughter "affirm" her mother and at the same see her life "in a larger framework"?

4 In what sense is the argument for legalized abortion in *Roe* v. *Wade* particularly American? Discuss legal and moral dilemmas involved.

5 Relate images of women as commonly propounded in popular culture, film, and music to definitions of female identity in the comments by Marabel Morgan.

Suggestions for further reading

Faludi, Susan, *Backlash: The Undeclared War Against American Women* (New York: Anchor Books, 1992).

Gilbert, Sandra M. and Susan Gubar, eds., *The Norton Anthology of Literature by Women: The Traditions in English* (New York: Norton, 1996).

Hoff, Joan, *Law, Gender, and Injustice: A Legal History of U.S. Women* (New York: New York University Press, 1991).

Norton, Mary Beth and Ruth M Alexander, eds., *Major Problems in American Women's History* (Boston: Houghton Mifflin Company, 3rd edn, 2003).

Yates, Gayle Graham, *What Women Want: The Ideas of the Movement* (Cambridge, Mass.: Harvard University Press, 1975).

31 ALEXIS DE TOCQUEVILLE

"The Young Woman in the Character of a Wife" (1848)

In America the independence of woman is irrecoverably lost in the bonds of matrimony. If an unmarried woman is less constrained there than elsewhere, a wife is subjected to stricter obligations. The former makes her father's house an abode of freedom and of pleasure; the latter lives in the home of her husband as if it were a cloister. Yet these two different conditions of life are perhaps not so contrary as may be supposed, and it is natural that the American women should pass through the one to arrive at the other.

Religious communities and trading nations entertain peculiarly serious notions of marriage: the former consider the regularity of woman's life as the best pledge and most certain sign of the purity of her morals; the latter regard it as the highest security for the order and prosperity of the household. The Americans are at the same time a puritanical people and a commercial nation; their religious opinions as well as their trading habits consequently lead them to require much abnegation on the part of woman and a constant sacrifice of her pleasures to her duties, which is seldom demanded of her in Europe. Thus in the United States the inexorable opinion of the public carefully circumscribes woman within the narrow circle of domestic interests and duties and forbids her to step beyond it.

Upon her entrance into the world a young American woman finds these notions firmly established; she sees the rules that are derived from them; she is not slow to perceive that she cannot depart for an instant from the established usages of her contemporaries without putting in jeopardy her peace of mind, her honor, nay, even her social existence; and she finds the energy required for such an act of submission in the firmness of her understanding and in the virile habits which her education has given her. It may be said that she has learned by the use of her independence to surrender it without a struggle and without a murmur when the time comes for making the sacrifice.

But no American woman falls into the toils of matrimony as into a snare held out to her simplicity and ignorance. She has been taught beforehand what is expected of her and voluntarily and freely enters upon this engagement. She supports her new condition with courage because she chose it. As in America paternal discipline is very relaxed and the conjugal tie very strict, a young woman does not contract the latter without considerable circumspection and apprehension. Precocious marriages are rare. American women do not marry until their understandings are exercised and ripened, whereas in other countries most women generally begin to exercise and ripen their understandings only after marriage.

I by no means suppose, however, that the great change which takes place in all the habits of women in the United States as soon as they are married ought solely to be attributed to the constraint of public opinion; it is frequently imposed upon themselves by the sole effort of their own will. When the time for choosing a husband arrives, that cold and stern reasoning power which has been educated and invigorated by the free observations of the world teaches an American woman that a spirit of levity and independence in the bonds of marriage is a constant subject of annoyance, not of pleasure; it tells her that the amusements of the girl cannot become the recreations of the wife, and that the sources of a married woman's happiness are in the home of her husband. As she clearly discerns beforehand the only road that can lead to domestic happiness, she enters upon it at once and follows it to the end without seeking to turn back.

The same strength of purpose which the young wives of America display in bending themselves at once and without repining to the austere duties of their new condition is no less manifest in all the great trials of their lives. In no country in the world are private fortunes more precarious than in the United States. It is not uncommon for the same man in the course of his life to rise and sink again through all the grades that lead from opulence to poverty. American women support these vicissitudes with calm and unquenchable energy; it would seem that their desires contract as easily as they expand with their fortunes.

The greater part of the adventurers who migrate every year to people the Western wilds belong, as I observed in the former part of this work, to the old Anglo-American race of the Northern states. Many of these men, who rush so boldly onwards in pursuit of wealth, were already in the enjoyment of a competency in their own part of the country. They take their wives along with them and make them share the countless perils and privations that always attend the commencement of these expeditions. I have often met, even on the verge of the wilderness, with young women who, after having been brought up amid all the comforts of the large towns of New England, had passed, almost without any intermediate stage, from the wealthy abode of their parents to a comfortless hovel in a forest. Fever, solitude, and a tedious life had not broken the springs of their courage. Their features were impaired and faded, but their looks were firm; they appeared to be at once sad and resolute. I do not doubt that these young American women had amassed, in the education of their early years, that inward strength which they displayed under these circumstances. The early culture of the girl may still, therefore, be traced, in the United States, under the aspect of marriage; her part is changed, her habits are different, but her character is the same.

32 SENECA FALLS CONVENTION

Declaration of Sentiments and Resolutions (1848)

When, in the course of human events, it becomes necessary for one portion of the family of man to assume among the people of the earth a position different from that which they have hitherto occupied, but one to which the laws of nature and of nature's God entitle them, a decent respect to the opinions of mankind requires that they should declare the causes that impel them to such a course.

We hold these truths to be self-evident: that all men and women are created equal; that they are endowed by their Creator with certain inalienable rights; that among these are life, liberty, and the pursuit of happiness; that to secure these rights governments are instituted, deriving their just powers from the consent of the governed. Whenever any form of government becomes destructive of these ends, it is the right of those who suffer from it to refuse allegiance to it, and to insist upon the institution of a new government, laying its foundation on such principles, and organizing its powers in such form, as to them shall seem most likely to effect their safety and happiness. Prudence, indeed, will dictate that governments long established should not be changed for light and transient causes; and accordingly all experience hath shown that mankind are more disposed to suffer, while evils are sufferable, than to right themselves by abolishing the forms to which they were accustomed. But when a long train of abuses and usurpations, pursuing invariably the same object, evinces a design to reduce them under absolute despotism, it is their duty to throw off such government, and to provide new guards for their future security. Such has been the patient sufferance of the women under this government, and such is now the necessity which constrains them to demand the equal station to which they are entitled.

The history of mankind is a history of repeated injuries and usurpations on the part of man toward woman, having in direct object the establishment of an absolute tyranny over her. To prove this, let facts be submitted to a candid world.

He has never permitted her to exercise her inalienable right to the elective franchise.

He has compelled her to submit to laws, in the formation of which she had no voice.

He has withheld from her rights which are given to the most ignorant and degraded men – both natives and foreigners.

Having deprived her of this first right of a citizen, the elective franchise, thereby leaving her without representation in the halls of legislation, he has oppressed her on all sides.

He has made her, if married, in the eye of the law, civilly dead.

He has taken from her all right in property, even to the wages she earns.

He has made her, morally, an irresponsible being, as she can commit many crimes with impunity, provided they be done in the presence of her husband. In the covenant of marriage, she is compelled to promise obedience to her husband, he becoming, to all intents and purposes, her master – the law giving him power to deprive her of her liberty, and to administer chastisement.

He has so framed the laws of divorce, as to what shall be the proper causes, and in case of separation, to whom the guardianship of the children shall be given, as to be wholly regardless of the happiness of women – the law, in all cases, going upon the false supposition of the supremacy of man, and giving all power into his hands.

After depriving her of all rights as a married woman, if single, and the owner of property, he has taxed her to support a government which recognizes her only when her property can be made profitable to it.

He has monopolized nearly all the profitable employments, and from those she is permitted to follow, she receives but a scanty remuneration. He closes against her all the avenues to wealth and distinction which he considers most honorable to himself. As a teacher of theology, medicine, or law, she is not known.

He has denied her the facilities for obtaining a thorough education, all colleges being closed against her.

He allows her in Church, as well as State, but a subordinate position, claiming Apostolic authority for her exclusion from the ministry, and, with some exceptions, from any public participation in the affairs of the Church.

He has created a false public sentiment by giving to the world a different code of morals for men and women, by which moral delinquencies which exclude women from society, are not only tolerated, but deemed of little account in man.

He has usurped the prerogative of Jehovah himself, claiming it as his right to assign for her a sphere of action, when that belongs to her conscience and to her God.

He has endeavored, in every way that he could, to destroy her confidence in her own powers, to lessen her self-respect, and to make her willing to lead a dependent and abject life.

Now, in view of this entire disfranchisement of one-half the people of this country, their social and religious degradation – in view of the unjust laws above mentioned, and because women do feel themselves aggrieved, oppressed, and fraudulently deprived of their most sacred rights, we insist that they have immediate admission to all the rights and privileges which belong to them as citizens of the United States.

In entering upon the great work before us, we anticipate no small amount of misconception, misrepresentation, and ridicule; but we shall use every instrumentality within our power to effect our object. We shall employ agents, circulate tracts, petition the State and National legislatures, and endeavor to enlist the pulpit and the press in our behalf. We hope this Convention will be followed by a series of Conventions embracing every part of the country.

33 KATE CHOPIN

"The Story of an Hour" (1894)

Knowing that Mrs. Mallard was afflicted with a heart trouble, great care was taken to break to her as gently as possible the news of her husband's death.

It was her sister Josephine who told her, in broken sentences, veiled hints that revealed in half concealing. Her husband's friend Richards was there, too, near her. It was he who had been in the newspaper office when intelligence of the railroad disaster was received, with Brently Mallard's name leading the list of "killed." He had only taken the time to assure himself of its truth by a second telegram, and had hastened to forestall any less careful, less tender friend in bearing the sad message.

She did not hear the story as many women have heard the same, with a paralyzed inability to accept its significance. She wept at once, with sudden, wild abandonment, in her sister's arms. When the storm of grief had spent itself she went away to her room alone. She would have no one follow her.

There stood, facing the open window, a comfortable, roomy armchair. Into this she sank, pressed down by a physical exhaustion that haunted her body and seemed to reach into her soul.

She could see in the open square before her house the tops of trees that were all aquiver with the new spring life. The delicious breath of rain was in the air. In the street below a peddler was crying his wares. The notes of a distant song which some one was singing reached her faintly, and countless sparrows were twittering in the eaves.

There were patches of blue sky showing here and there through the clouds that had met and piled one above the other in the west facing her window.

She sat with her head thrown back upon the cushion of the chair quite motionless, except when a sob came up into her throat and shook her, as a child who has cried itself to sleep continues to sob in its dreams.

She was young, with a fair, calm face, whose lines bespoke repression and even a certain strength. But now there was a dull stare in her eyes, whose gaze was fixed away off yonder on one of those patches of blue sky. It was not a glance of reflection, but rather indicated a suspension of intelligent thought.

There was something coming to her and she was waiting for it, fearfully. What was it? She did not know; it was too subtle and elusive to name. But she felt it, creeping out of the sky, reaching toward her through the sounds, the scents, the color that filled the air.

Now her bosom rose and fell tumultuously. She was beginning to recognize this thing that was approaching to possess her, and she was striving to beat it back with her will – as powerless as her two white slender hands would have been.

When she abandoned herself a little whispered word escaped her slightly parted lips. She said it over and over under her breath: "Free, free, free!" The vacant stare and the look of terror that had followed it went from her eyes. They stayed keen and bright. Her pulses beat fast, and the coursing blood warmed and relaxed every inch of her body.

She did not stop to ask if it were not a monstrous joy that held her. A clear and exalted perception enabled her to dismiss the suggestion as trivial.

She knew that she would weep again when she saw the kind, tender hands folded in death; the face that had never looked save with love upon her, fixed and gray and dead. But she saw beyond that bitter moment a long procession of years to come that would belong to her absolutely. And she opened and spread her arms out to them in welcome.

There would be no one to live for during those coming years; she would live for herself. There would be no powerful will bending her in that blind persistence with which men and women believe they have a right to impose a private will upon a fellow-creature. A kind intention or a cruel intention made the act seem no less a crime as she looked upon it in that brief moment of illumination.

And yet she had loved him – sometimes. Often she had not. What did it matter! What could love, the unsolved mystery, count for in face of this possession of self-assertion which she suddenly recognized as the strongest impulse of her being!

"Free! Body and soul free!" she kept whispering.

Josephine was kneeling before the closed door with her lips to the keyhole, imploring for admission. "Louise, open the door! I beg; open the door – you will make yourself ill. What are you doing, Louise? For heaven's sake open the door."

"Go away. I am not making myself ill." No; she was drinking in a very elixir of life through that open window.

Her fancy was running riot along those days ahead of her. Spring days, and summer days, and all sorts of days that would be her own. She breathed a quick prayer that life might be long. It was only yesterday she had thought with a shudder that life might be long.

She arose at length and opened the door to her sister's importunities. There was a feverish triumph in her eyes, and she carried herself unwittingly like a goddess of Victory. She clasped her sister's waist, and together they descended the stairs. Richards stood waiting for them at the bottom.

Some one was opening the front door with a latchkey. It was Brently Mallard who entered, a little travel-stained, composedly carrying his grip-sack and umbrella. He had been far from the scene of accident, and did not even know there had been one. He stood amazed at Josephine's piercing cry; at Richards' quick motion to screen him from the view of his wife.

But Richards was too late.

When the doctors came they said she had died of heart disease – of joy that kills.

34 CHARLOTTE PERKINS GILMAN

FROM *Women and Economics (1898)*

As the private home becomes a private home indeed, and no longer the woman's social and industrial horizon; as the workshops of the world – woman's sphere as well as man's – become homelike and beautiful under her influence; and as men and women move freely together in the exercise of common racial functions, – we shall have new channels for the flow of human life.

We shall not move from the isolated home to the sordid shop and back again, in a world torn and dissevered by the selfish production of one sex and the selfish consumption of the other; but we shall live in a world of men and women humanly related, as well as sexually related, working together, as they were meant to do, for the common good of all. The home will be no longer an economic entity, with its cumbrous industrial machinery huddled vulgarly behind it, but a peaceful and permanent expression of personal life as withdrawn from social contact; and that social contact will be provided for by the many common meeting places necessitated by the organization of domestic industries.

The assembling-room is as deep a need of human life as the retiring room, – not some ball-room or theatre, to which one must be invited of set purpose, but great common libraries and parlors, baths and gymnasia, work-rooms and play-rooms, to which both sexes have the same access for the same needs, and where they may mingle freely in common human expression. The kind of buildings essential to the carrying out of the organization of home industry will provide such places. There will be the separate rooms for individuals and the separate houses for families; but there will be, also, the common rooms for all. These must include a place for the children, planned and built for the happy occupancy of many children for many years, – a home such as no children have ever had. This, as well as rooms everywhere for young people and old people, in which they can be together as naturally as they can be alone, without effort, question, or remark.

Such an environment would allow of free association among us, on lines of common interest; and, in its natural, easy flow, we should develop far higher qualities than are brought out by the uneasy struggles of our present "society" to see each other without wanting to. It would make an enormous difference to woman's power of choosing the right man. Cut off from the purchasing power which is now his easiest way to compass his desires, freely seen and known in his daily work and amusements, a woman could know and judge a man as she is wholly unable to do now. Her personality developed by a free and useful life, but a personality as well as a woman, – the girl trained to economic independence, and associating freely with young men in their common work and play, would learn a new estimate of what constitutes noble manhood. . . .

This change is not a thing to prophesy and plead for. It is a change already instituted, and gaining ground among us these many years with marvellous rapidity. Neither men nor women wish the change. Neither men nor women have sought it. But the same great force of social evolution which brought us into the old relation – to our great sorrow and pain – is bringing us out, with equal difficulty and distress. The time has come when it is better for the world that women be economically independent, and therefore they are becoming so.

It is worth while for us to consider the case fully and fairly, that we may see what it is that is happening to us, and welcome with open arms the happiest change in human condition that ever came into the world. To free an entire half of humanity from an artificial position; to release vast natural forces from a strained and clumsy combination, and set them free to work smoothly and easily as they were intended to work; to introduce conditions that will change humanity from within, making for better motherhood and fatherhood, better babyhood and childhood, better food, better homes, better society, – this is to work for human improvement along natural lines. It means enormous racial advance, and that with great swiftness; for this change does not wait to create new forces, but sets free those already potentially strong, so that humanity will fly up like a released spring. And it is already happening. All we need do is to understand and help.

35 MERIDEL LeSUEUR

"Women on the Breadlines" (1932)

I am sitting in the city free employment bureau. It's the women's section. We have been sitting here now for four hours. We sit here every day, waiting for a job. There are no jobs. Most of us have had no breakfast. Some have had scant rations for over a year. Hunger makes a human being lapse into a state of lethargy, especially city hunger. Is there any place else in the world where a human being is supposed to go hungry amidst plenty without an outcry, without protest, where only the boldest steal or kill for bread, and the timid crawl the streets, hunger like the beak of a terrible bird at the vitals?

We sit looking at the floor. No one dares think of the coming winter. There are only a few more days of summer. Everyone is anxious to get work to lay up something for that long siege of bitter cold. But there is no work. Sitting in the room we all know it. That is why we don't talk much. We look at the floor dreading to see that knowledge in each other's eyes. There is a kind of humiliation in it. We look away from each other. We look at the floor. It's too terrible to see this animal terror in each other's eyes.

So we sit hour after hour, day after day, waiting for a job to come in. There are many women for a single job. A thin sharp woman sits inside a wire cage looking at a book. For four hours we have watched her looking at that book. She has a hard little eye. In the small bare room there are half a dozen women sitting on the benches waiting. Many come and go. Our faces are all familiar to each other, for we wait here every day.

This is a domestic employment bureau. Most of the women who come here are middle-aged, some have families, some have raised their families and are now alone, some have men who are out of work. Hard times and the man leaves to hunt for work. He doesn't find it. He drifts on. The woman probably doesn't hear from him for a long time. She expects it. She isn't surprised. She struggles alone to feed the many mouths. Sometimes she gets help from the charities. If she's clever she can get herself a good living from the charities, if she's naturally a lick spittle, naturally a little docile and cunning. If she's proud then she starves silently, leaving her children to find work, coming home after a day's searching to wrestle with her house, her children.

Some such story is written on the faces of all these women. There are young girls too, fresh from the country. Some are made brazen too soon by the city. There is a great exodus of girls from the farms into the city now. Thousands of farms have been vacated completely in Minnesota. The girls are trying to get work. The prettier ones can get jobs in the stores when there are any, or waiting on table, but these jobs are only for the attractive and the adroit. The others, the real peasants, have a more difficult time.

Bernice sits next to me. She is a Polish woman of thirty-five. She has been working in people's kitchens for fifteen years or more. She is large, her great body in mounds, her face brightly scrubbed. She has a peasant mind and finds it hard even yet to understand the maze of the city where trickery is worth more than brawn. Her blue eyes are not clever but slow and trusting. She suffers from loneliness and lack of talk. When you speak to her, her face lifts and brightens as if you had spoken through a great darkness, and she talks magically of little things as if the weather were magic, or tells some crazy tale of her adventures on the city streets, embellishing them in bright colors until they hang heavy and thick like embroidery. She loves the city anyhow. It's exciting to her, like a bazaar. She loves to go shopping and get a bargain, hunting out the places where stale bread and cakes can be had for a few cents. She likes walking the streets looking for men to take her to a picture show. Sometimes she goes to five picture shows in one day, or she sits through one the entire day until she knows all the dialog by heart.

She came to the city a young girl from a Wisconsin farm. The first thing that happened to her, a charlatan dentist took out all her good shining teeth and the fifty dollars she had saved working in a canning factory. After that she met men in the park who told her how to look out for herself, corrupting her peasant mind, teaching her to mistrust everyone. Sometimes now she forgets to mistrust everyone and gets taken in. They taught her to get what she could for nothing, to count her change, to go back if she found herself cheated, to demand her rights.

She lives alone in little rooms. She bought seven dollars' worth of second-hand furniture eight years ago. She rents a room for perhaps three dollars a month in an attic, sometimes in a cold house. Once the house where she stayed was condemned and everyone else moved out and she lived there all winter alone on the top floor. She spent only twenty-five dollars all winter.

She wants to get married but she sees what happens to her married friends, left with children to support, worn out before their time. So she stays single. She is virtuous. She is slightly deaf from hanging out clothes in winter. She had done people's washing and cooking for fifteen years and in that time saved thirty dollars. Now she hasn't worked steady for a year and she has spent the thirty dollars. She had dreamed of having a little house or a houseboat perhaps with a spot of ground for a few chickens. This dream she will never realize.

She has lost all her furniture now along with the dream. A married friend whose husband is gone gives her a bed for which she pays by doing a great deal of work for the woman. She comes here every day now sitting bewildered, her pudgy hands folded in her lap. She is hungry. Her great flesh has begun to hang in folds. She has been living on crackers. Sometimes a box of crackers lasts a week. She has a friend who's a baker and he sometimes steals the stale loaves and brings them to her.

A girl we have seen every day all summer went crazy yesterday at the YW. She went into hysterics, stamping her feet and screaming.

She hadn't had work for eight months. "You've got to give me something," she kept saying. The woman in charge flew into a rage that probably came from days and days of suffering on her part, because she is unable to give jobs, having none. She flew into a rage at the girl and there they were facing each other in a rage both helpless, helpless. This woman told me once that she could hardly bear the suffering she saw, hardly hear it, that she couldn't eat sometimes and had nightmares at night.

So they stood there, the two women, in a rage, the girl weeping and the woman shouting at her. In the eight months of unemployment she had gotten ragged, and the woman was shouting that she would not send her out like that. "Why don't you shine your shoes?" she kept scolding the girl, and the girl kept sobbing and sobbing because she was starving.

"We can't recommend you like that," the harassed YWCA woman said, knowing she was starving, unable to do anything. And the girls and the women sat docilely, their eyes on the ground, ashamed to look at each other, ashamed of something.

Sitting here waiting for a job, the women have been talking in low voices about the girl Ellen. They talk in low voices with not too much pity for her, unable to see through the mist of their own torment. "What happened to Ellen?" one of them asks. She knows the answer already. We all know it.

A young girl who went around with Ellen tells about seeing her last evening back of a cafe downtown, outside the kitchen door, kicking, showing her legs so that the cook came out and gave her some food and some men gathered in the alley and threw small coin on the ground for a look at her legs. And the girl says enviously that Ellen had a swell breakfast and treated her to one too, that cost two dollars.

A scrub woman whose hips are bent forward from stooping with hands gnarled like watersoaked branches clicks her tongue in disgust. No one saves their money, she says, a little money and these foolish young things buy a hat, a dollar for breakfast, a bright scarf. And they do. If you've ever been without money, or food, something very strange happens when you get a bit of money, a kind of madness. You don't care. You can't remember that you had no money before, that the money will be gone. You can remember nothing but that there is the money for which you have been suffering. Now here it is. A lust takes hold of you. You see food in the windows. In imagination you eat hugely; you taste a thousand meals. You look in windows. Colors are brighter; you buy something to dress up in. An excitement takes hold of you. You know it is suicide but you can't help it. You must have food, dainty, splendid food, and a bright hat so once again you feel blithe, rid of that ratty gnawing shame.

"I guess she'll go on the street now," a thin woman says faintly, and no one takes the trouble to comment further. Like every commodity now the body is difficult to sell and the girls say you're lucky if you get fifty cents.

It's very difficult and humiliating to sell one's body.

Perhaps it would make it clear if one were to imagine having to go out on the street to sell, say, one's overcoat. Suppose you have to sell your coat so you can have breakfast and a place to sleep, say, for fifty cents. You decide to sell your only coat. You take it off and put it on your arm. The street, that has before been just a street, now becomes a mart, something entirely different. You must approach someone now and admit you are destitute and are now selling your clothes, your most intimate possessions. Everyone will watch you talking to the stranger showing him your overcoat, what a good coat it is. People will stop and watch curiously. You will be quite naked on the street. It is even harder to try to sell one's self, more humiliating. It is even humiliating to try to sell one's labor. When there is no buyer.

The thin woman opens the wire cage. There's a job for a nursemaid, she says. The old gnarled women, like old horses, know that no one will have them walk the streets with the young so they don't move. Ellen's friend gets up and goes to the window. She is unbelievably jaunty. I know she hasn't had work since last January. But she has a flare of life in her that glows like a tiny red flame and some tenacious thing, perhaps only youth, keeps it burning bright. Her legs are thin but the runs in her old stockings are neatly mended clear down her flat shank. Two bright spots of rouge conceal her pallor. A narrow belt is drawn tightly around her thin waist, her long shoulders stoop and the blades show. She runs wild as a colt hunting pleasure, hunting sustenance.

It's one of the great mysteries of the city where women go when they are out of work and hungry. There are not many women in the bread line. There are no flop houses for women as there are for men, where a bed can be had for a quarter or less. You don't see women lying on the floor at the mission in the free flops. They obviously don't sleep in the jungle or under newspapers in the park. There is no law I suppose against their being in these places but the fact is they rarely are.

Yet there must be as many women out of jobs in cities and suffering extreme poverty as there are men. What happens to them? Where do they go? Try to get into the YW without any money or looking down at heel. Charities take care of very few and only those that are called "deserving." The lone girl is under suspicion by the virgin women who dispense charity.

I've lived in cities for many months broke, without help, too timid to get in bread lines. I've known many women to live like this until they simply faint on the street from privations, without saying a word to anyone. A woman will shut herself up in a room until it is taken away from her, and eat a cracker a day and be as quiet as a mouse so there are no social statistics concerning her.

I don't know why it is, but a woman will do this unless she has dependents, will go for weeks verging on starvation, crawling in some hole, going through the streets ashamed, sitting in libraries, parks, going for days without speaking to a living soul like some exiled beast, keeping the runs mended in her stockings, shut up in terror in her own misery, until she becomes too super-sensitive and timid to even ask for a job.

Bernice says even strange men she has met in the park have sometimes, that is in better days, given her a loan to pay her room rent. She has always paid them back.

In the afternoon the young girls, to forget the hunger and the deathly torture and fear of being jobless, try to pick up a man to take them to a ten-cent show. They never go to more expensive ones, but they can always find a man willing to spend a dime to have the company of a girl for the afternoon.

Sometimes a girl facing the night without shelter will approach a man for lodging. A woman always asks a man for help. Rarely another woman. I have known girls to sleep in men's rooms for the night on a pallet without molestation and be given breakfast in the morning.

It's no wonder these young girls refuse to marry, refuse to rear children. They are like certain savage tribes, who, when they have been conquered, refuse to breed.

Not one of them but looks forward to starvation for the coming winter. We are in a jungle and know it. We are beaten, entrapped. There is no way out. Even if there were a job, even if that thin acrid woman came and gave everyone in the room a job for a few days, a few hours, at thirty cents an hour, this would all be repeated tomorrow, the next day and the next.

Not one of these women but knows that despite years of labor there is only starvation, humiliation in front of them.

Mrs. Gray, sitting across from me, is a living spokesman for the futility of labor. She is a warning. Her hands are scarred with labor. Her body is a great puckered scar. She has given birth to six children, buried three, supported them all alive and dead, bearing them, burying them, feeding them. Bred in hunger they have been spare, susceptible to disease. For seven years she tried to save her boy's arm from amputation, diseased from tuberculosis of the bone. It is almost too suffocating to think of that long close horror of years of child-bearing, child-feeding, rearing, with the bare suffering of providing a meal and shelter.

Now she is fifty. Her children, economically insecure, are drifters. She never hears of them. She doesn't know if they are alive. She doesn't know if she is alive. Such subtleties of suffering are not for her. For her the brutality of hunger and cold. Not until these are done away with can those subtle feelings that make a human being be indulged.

She is lucky to have five dollars ahead of her. That is her security. She has a tumor that she will die of. She is thin as a worn dime with her tumor sticking out of her side. She is brittle and bitter. Her face is not the face of a human being. She has borne more than it is possible for a human being to bear. She is reduced to the least possible denominator of human feelings.

It is terrible to see her little bloodshot eyes like a beaten hound's, fearful in terror.

We cannot meet her eyes. When she looks at any of us we look away. She is like a woman drowning and we turn away. We must ignore those eyes that are surely the eyes of a person drowning, doomed. She doesn't cry out. She goes down decently. And we all look away.

The young ones know though. I don't want to marry. I don't want any children. So they all say. No children. No marriage. They arm themselves alone, keep up alone. The man is helpless now. He cannot provide. If he propagates he cannot take care of his young. The means are not in his hands. So they live alone. Get what fun they can. The life risk is too horrible now. Defeat is too clearly written on it.

So we sit in this room like cattle, waiting for a nonexistent job, willing to work to the farthest atom of energy, unable to work, unable to get food and lodging, unable to bear children – here we must sit in this shame looking at the floor, worse than beasts at a slaughter.

It is appalling to think that these women sitting so listless in the room may work as hard as it is possible for a human being to work, may labor night and day, like Mrs. Gray wash streetcars from midnight to dawn and offices in the early evening, scrub for fourteen and fifteen hours a day, sleep only five hours or so, do this their whole lives, and never earn one day of security, having always before them the pit of the future. The endless labor, the bending back, the water-soaked hands, earning never more than a week's wages, never having in their hands more life than that.

It's not the suffering of birth, death, love that the young reject, but the suffering of endless labor without dream, eating the spare bread in bitterness, being a slave without the security of a slave.

36 BETTY FRIEDAN

"That Has No Name" (1963)

The problem lay buried, unspoken, for many years in the minds of American women. It was a strange stirring, a sense of dissatisfaction, a yearning that women suffered in the middle of the twentieth century in the United States. Each suburban wife struggled with it alone. As she made the beds, shopped for groceries, matched slipcover material, ate peanut butter sandwiches with her children, chauffeured Cub Scouts and Brownies, lay beside her husband at night – she was afraid to ask even of herself the silent question – "Is this all?"

For over fifteen years there was no word of this yearning in the millions of words written about women, for women, in all the columns, books and articles by experts telling women their role was to seek fulfillment as wives and mothers. Over and over women heard in voices of tradition and of Freudian sophistication that they could desire no greater destiny than to glory in their own femininity. Experts told them how to catch a man and keep him, how to breastfeed children and handle their toilet training, how to cope with sibling rivalry and adolescent rebellion; how to buy a dishwasher, bake bread, cook gourmet snails, and build a swimming pool with their own hands; how to dress, look, and act more feminine and make marriage more exciting; how to keep their husbands from dying young and their sons from growing into delinquents. They were taught to pity the neurotic, unfeminine, unhappy women who wanted to be poets or physicists or presidents. They learned that truly feminine women do not want careers, higher education, political rights – the independence and the opportunities that the old-fashioned feminists fought for. Some women, in their forties and fifties, still remembered painfully giving up those dreams, but most of the younger women no longer even thought about them. A thousand expert voices applauded their femininity, their adjustment, their new maturity. All they had to do was devote their lives from earliest girlhood to finding a husband and bearing children.

By the end of the 1950s, the average marriage age of women in America dropped to 20, and was still dropping, into the teens. Fourteen million girls were engaged by 17. The proportion of women attending college in comparison with men dropped from 47 per cent in 1920 to 35 per cent in 1958. A century earlier, women had fought for higher education; now girls went to college to get a husband. By the mid-fifties, 60 per cent dropped out of college to marry, or because they were afraid too much education would be a marriage bar. Colleges built dormitories for "married students," but the students were almost always the husbands. A new degree was instituted for the wives – "Ph.T" (Putting Husband Through).

Then American girls began getting married in high school. And the women's magazines, deploring the unhappy statistics about these young marriages, urged that courses on marriage, and marriage counselors, be installed in the high schools. Girls started going steady at twelve and thirteen, in junior high. Manufacturers put out brassieres with false bosoms of foam rubber for little girls of ten. And an advertisement for a child's dress, sizes 3–6x, in the *New York Times* in the fall of 1960, said: "She Too Can Join the Man-Trap Set."

By the end of the fifties, the United States birthrate was overtaking India's. The birth-control movement, renamed Planned Parenthood, was asked to find a method whereby women who had been advised that a third or fourth baby would be born dead or defective might have it anyhow. Statisticians were especially astounded at the fantastic increase in the number of babies among college women. Where once they had two children, now they had four, five, six. Women who had once wanted careers were now making careers out of having babies. So rejoiced *Life* magazine in a 1956 paean to the movement of American women back to the home.

In a New York hospital, a woman had a nervous breakdown when she found she could not breastfeed her baby. In other hospitals, women dying of cancer refused a drug which research had proved might save their lives: its side effects were said to be unfeminine. "If I have only one life, let me live it as a blonde," a larger-than-life-sized picture of a pretty, vacuous woman proclaimed from newspaper, magazine, and drugstore ads. And across America, three out of every ten women dyed their hair blonde. They ate a chalk called Metrecal, instead of food, to shrink to the size of the thin young models. Department-store buyers reported that American women, since 1939, had become three and four sizes smaller. "Women are out to fit the clothes, instead of vice-versa," one buyer said.

Interior decorators were designing kitchens with mosaic murals and original paintings, for kitchens were once again the center of women's lives. Home sewing became a million-dollar industry. Many women no longer left their homes, except to shop, chauffeur their children, or attend a social engagement with their husbands. Girls were growing up in America without ever having jobs outside the home. In the late fifties, a sociological phenomenon was suddenly remarked: a third of American women now worked, but most were no longer young and very few were pursuing careers. They were married women who held part-time jobs, selling or secretarial, to put their husbands through school, their sons through college, or to help pay the mortgage. Or they were widows supporting families. Fewer and fewer women were entering professional work. The shortages in the nursing, social work, and teaching professions caused crises in almost every American city. Concerned over the Soviet Union's lead in the space race, scientists noted that America's greatest source of unused brain-power was women. But girls would not study physics: it was "unfeminine." A girl refused a science fellowship at Johns Hopkins to take a job in a real-estate office. All she wanted, she said, was what every other American girl wanted – to get married, have four children and live in a nice house in a nice suburb.

The suburban housewife – she was the dream image of the young American women and the envy, it was said, of women all over the world. The American housewife – freed by science and labor-saving appliances from the drudgery, the dangers of childbirth and the illnesses of her grandmother. She was healthy, beautiful, educated, concerned only about her husband, her children, her home. She had found true feminine fulfillment. As a housewife and mother, she was respected as a full and equal partner to man in his world. She was free to choose automobiles, clothes, appliances, supermarkets; she had everything that women ever dreamed of.

In the fifteen years after World War II, this mystique of feminine fulfillment became the cherished and self-perpetuating core of contemporary American culture. Millions of women lived their lives in the image of those pretty pictures of the American suburban housewife, kissing their husbands goodbye in front of the picture window, depositing their station-wagonsful of children at school, and smiling as they ran the new electric waxer over the spotless kitchen floor. They baked their own bread, sewed their own and their children's clothes, kept their new washing machines and dryers running all day. They changed the sheets on the beds twice a week instead of once, took the rug-hooking class in adult education, and pitied their poor frustrated mothers, who had dreamed of having a career. Their only dream was to be perfect wives and mothers; their highest ambition to have five children and a beautiful house, their only fight to get and keep their husbands. They had no thought for the unfeminine problems of the world outside the home; they wanted the men to make the major decisions. They gloried in their role as women, and wrote proudly on the census blank: "Occupation: housewife."

For over fifteen years, the words written for women, and the words women used when they talked to each other, while their husbands sat on the other side of the room and talked shop or politics or septic tanks, were about problems with their children, or how to keep their husbands happy, or improve their children's school, or cook chicken or make slipcovers. Nobody argued whether women were inferior or superior to men; they were simply different. Words like "emancipation" and "career" sounded strange and embarrassing; no one had used them for years. When a Frenchwoman named Simone de Beauvoir wrote a book called *The Second Sex*, an American critic commented that she obviously "didn't know what life was all about," and besides, she was talking about French women. The "woman problem" in America no longer existed.

If a woman had a problem in the 1950s and 1960s, she knew that something must be wrong with her marriage, or with herself. Other women were satisfied with their lives, she thought. What kind of a woman was she if she did not feel this mysterious fulfillment waxing the kitchen floor? She was so ashamed to admit her dissatisfaction that she never knew how many other women shared it. If she tried to tell her husband, he didn't understand what she was talking about. She did not really understand it herself. For over fifteen years women in America found it harder to talk about this problem than about sex. Even the psychoanalysts had no name for it. When a woman went to a psychiatrist for help, as many women did, she would say, "I'm so ashamed," or "I must be hopelessly neurotic." "I don't know what's wrong with women today," a suburban psychiatrist said uneasily. "I only know something is wrong because most of my patients happen to be women. And their problem isn't sexual." Most women with this problem did not go to see a psychoanalyst, however. "There's nothing wrong really," they kept telling themselves. "There isn't any problem."

But on an April morning in 1959, I heard a mother of four, having coffee with four other mothers in a suburban development fifteen miles from New York, say in a tone of quiet desperation, "the problem." And the others knew, without words, that she was not talking about a problem with her husband, or her children, or her home. Suddenly they realized they all shared the same problem, the problem that has no name. They began, hesitantly, to talk about it. Later, after they had picked up their children at nursery school and taken them home to nap, two of the women cried, in sheer relief, just to know they were not alone.

37 STUDS TERKEL

"'Just a Housewife': Therese Carter" (1972)

Even if it is a woman making an apple dumpling, or a man a stool,
If life goes into the pudding, good is the pudding,
  good is the stool.
Content is the woman with fresh life rippling in her,
  content is the man.

D. H. Lawrence

We're in the kitchen of the Carter home, as we were eight years ago. It is in Downers Grove Estates, an unincorporated area west of Chicago. There are one-family dwellings in this blue-collar community of skilled craftsmen – "middle class. They've all got good jobs, plumbers, electricians, truckdrivers." Her husband Bob is the foreman of an auto body repair shop. They have three children: two boys, twenty-one and fourteen, and one girl, eighteen.

It is a house Bob has, to a great extent, built himself. During my previous visit he was still working at it. Today it is finished – to his satisfaction. The room is large, remarkably tidy; all is in its place. On the wall is a small blackboard of humorous familiar comment, as well as a bulletin board of newspaper clippings and political cartoons.

On another wall is the kitchen prayer I remembered:

Bless the kitchen in which I cook
Bless each moment within this nook
Let joy and laughter share this room
With spices, skillets and my broom
Bless me and mine with love and health
And I'll not ask for greater wealth.

How would I describe myself? It'll sound terrible – just a housewife. (Laughs.) It's true. What is a housewife? You don't have to have any special talents. I don't have any.

First thing I do in the morning is come in the kitchen and have a cigarette. Then I'll put the coffee on and whatever else we're gonna have for breakfast: bacon and eggs, sausage, waffles, toast, whatever. Then I'll make one lunch for young Bob – when school's on, I'll pack more – and I get them off to work. I'll usually throw a load of clothes in the washer while I'm waiting for the next batch to get up out of bed, and carry on from there. It's nothing really.

Later I'll clean house and sew, do something. I sew a lot of dresses for Cathy and myself. I brought this sewing machine up here years ago. It belongs here. This is my room and I love it, the kitchen.

I start my dinner real early because I like to fuss. I'll bake, cook . . . There's always little interruptions, kids running in and out, take me here, take me there. After supper, I really let down. I'm not a worker after supper. I conk out. I sit and relax and read, take a bath, have my ice cream, and go to bed. (Laughs.) It's not really a full day. You think it is? You make me sound important. Keep talking. (Laughs.)

I don't think it's important because for so many years it wasn't considered. I'm doing what I'm doing and I fill my days and I'm very contented. Yet I see women all around that do a lot more than I do. Women that have to work. I feel they're worthy of much more of a title than housewife.

If anybody else would say this, I'd talk back to 'em, but I *myself* feel like it's not much. Anybody can do it. I was gone for four days and Cathy took over and managed perfectly well without me. (Laughs.) I felt great, I really did. I knew she was capable.

I'll never say I'm really a good mother until I see the way they all turn out. So far they've done fine. I had somebody tell me in the hospital I must have done a good job of raising them. I just went along from day to day and they turned out all right.

Oh – I even painted the house last year. How much does a painter get paid for painting a house? (Laughs.) What? I'm a skilled craftsman myself? I never thought about that. Artist? No. (Laughs.) I suppose if you do bake a good cake, you can be called an artist. But I never heard anybody say that. I bake bread too. Oh gosh, I've been a housewife for a long time. (Laughs.)

I never thought about what we'd be worth. I've read these things in the paper: If you were a tailor or a cook, you'd get so much an hour. I think that's a lot of boloney. I think if you're gonna be a mother or a housewife, you should do these things because you want to, not because you have to. You look around at all these career women and they're really doing things. What am I doing? Cooking and cleaning. (Laughs.) It's necessary, but it's not really great.

It's known they lead a different life than a housewife. I'm not talking about Golda Meir or anybody like that. Just even some women in the neighborhood that have to work and come home and take care of the family. I really think they deserve an awful lot of credit.

A housewife is a housewife, that's all. Low on the totem pole. I can read the paper and find that out. Someone who is a model or a movie star, these are the great ones. I don't necessarily think they are, but they're the ones you hear about. A movie star will raise this wonderful family and yet she has a career. I imagine most women would feel less worthy. Not just me.

Somebody who goes out and works for a living is more important than somebody who doesn't. What they do is very important in the business world. What I do is only important to five people. I don't like putting a housewife down, but everybody has done it for so long. It's sort of the thing you do. Deep down, I feel what I'm doing is important. But you just hate to say it, because what are you? Just a housewife? (Laughs.)

I love being a housewife. Maybe that's why I feel so guilty. I shouldn't be happy doing what I'm doing. (Laughs.) Maybe you're not supposed to be having fun. I never looked on it as a duty.

I think a lot. (Laughs.) Oh sure, I daydream. Everybody does. Some of 'em are big and some of 'em are silly. Sometimes you dream you're still a kid and you're riding your bike. Sometimes you daydream you're really someone special and people are asking you for your advice, that you're in a really big deal. (Laughs.)

I have very simple pleasures. I'm not a deep reader. I can't understand a lot of things. I've never read – oh, how do you pronounce it, Camus? I'm not musically inclined. I don't know anything about art at all. I could never converse with anybody about it. They'd have to be right, because I wouldn't know whether they're right or wrong. I go as far as Boston Pops and the Beatles. (Laughs.) I have no special talents in any direction.

I just read a new Peter De Vries book. I can't think of the name of it, that's terrible. (Suddenly) *Always Panting*. I was the first Peter De Vries fan in the world. I introduced my sister to it and that was the one big thing I've ever done in my life. (Laughs.) Now I'm reading *Grapes of Wrath*. I'm ashamed of myself. Everybody in the family has read that book and I've had it for about fifteen years. Finally I decided to read it because my daughter raved about it.

There is a paperback copy of The Savage God *by A. Alvarez nearby. I indicate it.*

I just started a little bit about Sylvia Plath and I decided I would read this book. *Ms.* magazine has an article about her. Sure I read *Ms.* I don't think it's unusual just because I live around here. I don't agree with everything in it. But I read it. I read matchbox covers too. (Laughs.)

I think Woman's Lib puts down a housewife. Even though they say if this is what a woman wants, it's perfectly all right. I feel it's said in such a snide way: "If this is all she can do and she's contented, leave her alone." It's patronizing.

I look on reading right now as strictly enjoyment and relaxation. So I won't even let myself pick up a book before ten o'clock at night. If I do, I'm afraid I might forget about everything else. During lunch time I'll look through a magazine because I can put it down and forget about it. But real enjoyable reading I'll do at night.

I'd feel guilty reading during the day. (Laughs.) In your own home. There are so many things you should be doing. If I did it, I wouldn't think the world's coming to an end, but that's the way I'm geared. That's not the time to do it, so I don't do it.

When I went to school a few years ago it was startling around here. Why would an older woman like me be wanting to go back to school? They wouldn't say it directly, but you hear things. I took some courses in college English, psychology, sociology. I enjoyed going but I didn't want to continue on and be a teacher. I still enjoyed being at home much more. Oh, I might go back if there was anything special I'd like.

I enjoy cooking. If it was a job, maybe I wouldn't like doing it. As low on the totem pole as I consider being a housewife, I love every minute of it. You will hear me gripe and groan like everybody else, but I do enjoy it.

I'll also enjoy it when the kids are all gone. I always had the feeling that I can *really* – oh, I don't know what I want to do, but whatever that would be, I can do it. I'll be on my own. I'm looking forward to it. Just a lot of things I've never taken the time to do.

I've never been to the Art Institute. Now that might be one thing I might do. (Laughs.) I've grown up in Chicago and I've never been there and I think that's terrible. Because I've never gotten on the train and gone. I can't spend all that time there yet. But pretty soon I'll be able to.

I haven't been to the Museum of Science and Industry for ten years at least. These things are nothing special to anybody else, but to me they would be. And to sit down and read one whole book in one afternoon if I felt like it. That would be something!

When the kids leave I want it to be a happy kind of time. Just to do the things I would like to do. Not traveling. Just to do what you want to do not at a certain time or a certain day. Sewing a whole dress at one time. Or cooking for just two people.

That's what makes me feel guilty. Usually when kids go off and get married the mother sits and cries. But I'm afraid I'm just gonna smile all the way through it. (Laughs.) They'll think I'm not a typical mother. I love my kids, I love 'em to pieces. But by the same token, I'll be just so happy for them and for myself and for Bob, too. I think we deserve a time together alone.

I don't look at housework as a drudgery. People will complain: "Why do I have to scrub floors?" To me, that isn't the same thing as a man standing there – it's his livelihood – putting two screws together day after day after day. It would drive anybody nuts. It would drive me wild. That poor man doesn't even get to see the finished product. I'll sit here and I'll cook a pie and I'll get to see everybody eat it. This is my offering. I think it's the greatest satisfaction in the world to know you've pleased somebody. Everybody has to feel needed. I know I'm needed. I'm doing it for them and they're doing it for me. And that's the way it is.

38 MARABEL MORGAN

"Admire Him" (1973)

Psychiatrists tell us that a man's most basic needs, outside of warm sexual love, are approval and admiration. Women need to be loved; men need to be admired. We women would do well to remember this one important difference between us and the other half.

Just the other day a woman told me, "My husband doesn't fulfill me. He never tells me his real feelings; he never expresses his love. He's about as warm as a cold fish!"

Your man, like so many American males, may be like an empty cup emotionally. He may seem void of emotions, unable to properly express his real feelings to you. Why is this? Remember that he grew up in a culture that taught him not to cry when he scratched his leg. Instead of hugging Uncle Jack, he shook hands. Grown-ups were generally unavailable to listen, so he learned to keep his feelings to himself.

We girls, on the other hand, were allowed to cry and throw temper tantrums. We were encouraged to kiss baby dolls, Aunt Susie, and the baby-sitter. We grew up full of emotions and knew basically how to express love. Then one day the fun began. Mr. Cool married Miss Passion. Is it any wonder that she felt unfulfilled because he never showed her any emotion?

Have you ever wondered why your husband doesn't just melt when you tell him how much you love him? But try saying, "I admire you," and see what happens. If you want to free him to express his thoughts and emotions, begin by filling up his empty cup with admiration. He must be filled first, for he has nothing to give until this need is met. And when his cup runs over, guess who lives in the overflow? Why, the very one who has been filling up the cup – you!

Love your husband and hold him in reverence, it says in the Bible. That means admire him. *Reverence*, according to the dictionary, means "To respect, honor, esteem, adore, praise, enjoy, and admire."

As a woman, you yearn to be loved by that man, right? He, being a man, yearns to be admired by you. And he needs it first. This irritates some women until they see that they have certain strengths that a man doesn't have. It's a great strength, not a weakness, to give for the sheer sake of giving. It is your nature to give. Calvin Coolidge once said, "No person was ever honored for what he received. Honor has been the reward for what he gave."

You are the one person your husband needs to make him feel special. He married you because he thought you were the most enchanting girl of all. The world may bestow awards on him, but above all others, he needs your admiration. He needs it to live. Without it his motivation is gone.

A young executive was literally starved for admiration from his wife. She wanted him to fulfill her before she met his needs. She explained, "Why should I give in first? Marriage is a fifty-fifty deal. I'm not about to give everything." Her husband threw himself into his business, working extra-long hours. He hoped his work would fill up that inner emptiness.

During a Total Woman class, this wife realized that she had the power to pour into him the admiration he needed. She began to admire him. Their relationship began to change. One evening he told her, "Something beautiful is happening. I don't know what it is, but it's great. You seem more alive for some reason."

Hero Worship

Try this test for a week. Starting tonight determine that you will admire your husband. By an act of your will, determine to fill up his cup, which may be bone dry. Be positive. Remember that compliments will encourage him to talk.

Admire him as he talks to you. Concentrate on what he's saying. Let him know you care. Put your magazine, down and look at him. Even if you don't care who won yesterday's football game, your attention is important to him and he needs you. Let him know he's your hero.

Don't interrupt or be preoccupied. A pilot told me, "When my wife is indifferent and doesn't respond to what I'm saying, it shatters me for two or three days. Indifference is the worst pain of all."

Another woman called me the night she was sued for divorce. When she asked her husband why, she was shocked at his reply: "You've always been completely indifferent to my life. You never cared what I did or thought."

Every marriage needs tact – that special ability to describe another person as he sees himself. Your husband needs you to see him as he sees himself. For example, take a good look at him. He happens to love his body. It's the only one he has and he lives in there. He wants you to love it too. The only way he'll ever know that you do is for you to tell him.

Perhaps this sounds very foreign to you. You may even think it vulgar. If so, your husband is probably long overdue for some badly needed praise. It is your highest privilege to assure him that he is as special as he hoped he was.

Tonight when he comes home, concentrate on his body. Look at him, really observe him. It may have been years since you actually looked at him with eyes that see. Try looking at him through another woman's eyes – his secretary's or your neighbor's. That might help bring him into focus.

Tell him you love his body. If you choke on that phrase, practice until it comes out naturally. If you haven't admired him lately, he's probably starving emotionally. He can't take too much at once, so start slowly. Give him one good compliment a day and watch him blossom right before your eyes.

Look for his admirable qualities. Even the ugliest man has certain qualities worth admiring, but we're talking about the dream man you married. Compliment that one who used to make your heart pound and make your lips stammer. Admire that one who stood far above the crowd of common men.

Pick out his most masculine characteristics and let him know they please you. His whiskers, for instance. The day he shaved for the first time was a milestone in his life. But have you ever complained with irritation, "Ouch, why don't you shave once in awhile? You're rubbing my face raw"? Instead, try telling him nicely, "Honey, your scratchy beard is too strong for my tender skin." You can compliment your husband into shaving off his weekend whiskers by reinforcing his masculine image.

Thin Arms, Full Heart

Admire him *personally*. This is what he is yearning for. When he comes home tonight would you rather have him admire your newly waxed floor, or tell you how great you look? In the same way, he'd rather hear how handsome he is than how great his corporation is.

Tomorrow morning watch your husband when he looks in the mirror. He sees an eighteen-year-old youth, with firm stomach muscles and a full head of hair. No matter what his age, he doesn't see his pouch or receding hairline. He sees what he wants to see, and wants you to see that eighteen-year-old, too. Of course, this isn't really so strange. What age girl do you see in the mirror? My own grandmother admitted to feeling that she was not much past twenty-one.

A dentist's wife told me she had blurted out one night, "Look, you're getting fat and bald. It's disgusting. Why don't you just face the truth? You're not a kid anymore." The first shot had been fired. Her husband felt devastated and to protect himself, he lashed out at her weaknesses in a brutal way that only he could do. He could not rationally answer her comment but instead struck out at her personally.

In class one day, I gave the assignment for the girls to admire their husband's body that night. One girl went right to work on her homework. Her husband was shorter than she, but quite handsome. In all their years together she had never put her admiration into words. It was a big step for her. She didn't quite know how to start, even thou it was her own husband. That evening while he was reading the paper; she sat down next to him on the sofa and began stroking his arm. After a bit, she stopped at the bicep and squeezed. He unconsciously flexed his muscle and she said, "Oh, I never knew you were so muscular!" He put down the paper, looked at her, and inquired, "What else?" He was so starved for admiration, he wanted to hear more!

The next day, she told this to her girl friend, who also decided to try it. Her husband had thin aims, but she admired his muscles anyway. Two nights later she couldn't find him at dinner time. He was out lifting his new set of weights in the garage. He wanted to build more muscles for her to admire.

By the way, admiration can also work wonders for your children. For example, one mother always nagged her son to hop out of the car to open the garage door. One afternoon she said, "Tommy, I'll bet a boy with muscles like yours could flip that garage door up in nothing flat." That's all she said, and that's all he needed. She never again had to ask him to open the door.

Your husband won't mind helping you either, if he's approached in the proper way. Instead of struggling with a jar and breaking a fingernail, ask him to loan you his strong hands for a minute. He derives pleasure from showing off his strength, even on a little old jar.

I know of only one case where this principle backfired. One wife asked her husband, one of the Miami Dolphin football players, to give her a muscular hand with the jars. Finally he asked, "Say, what's with you? You've been opening these baby food jars for five months and now all of a sudden you can't seem to manage them." So don't overdo it. Give him only the jars you really handle.

Rebuilding a Partial Man

I heard one wife say, "I feel guilty using feminine wiles on my husband. It seems dishonest. Anyway, his ego is so big, it doesn't need expanding. His body is not all that great. Why should I lie to build him up? I want to be honest, but still meet his needs."

If you're secure within yourself, you won't be afraid to give your husband credit. Instead of feeling threatened, you will feel joy in meeting his needs. As you know, you cannot express love to your husband until you really love yourself. But once you do, you can give with abandon. In fact, you can give with no thought of what you'll receive in return.

I am not advocating that you lie to give your husband a superficial ego boost; even a fool will see through flattery. But I am saying he has a deep need for sincere admiration. Look for new parts to compliment as you see him with new eyes.

Consider his weaknesses and things about which he may be self-conscious. Larry had a nasty scar on his neck as the result of an accident. His wife knew that it upset him and saw that he kept rubbing it. She said, "I really love your scar, honey. It makes you look so rugged." Her admiration made him feel relieved inside and less self-conscious.

If you haven't been communicating much lately with your husband, you may have trouble finding something to compliment. If that's your case, think back to those days when you were first convinced that he was the one. What did you love about him then?

An older couple was so estranged that the wife could not see anything to admire about her husband. She forced herself to think back, all the way to the Depression days, when he frugally kept the family together with shrewd business management. Now, nearly forty years later, she shyly mentioned how she had admired his financial leadership during that time. Those were the first appreciative words he had heard in years, and his reaction was pitiful. He looked at her with disbelieving eyes, tears welled up, and though he found no way of verbally expressing his appreciation, he was very tender that evening. The wife was amazed that such a little remark from the distant past could cause this behavior. It was a turning point in their marriage.

A marriage must not remain stagnant. You can keep yours exciting and growing, and in order to succeed, you must. At the end of a long day, your husband especially needs your compliments. One husband called his wife just before quitting time to say, "This is a partial man looking for a Total Woman; be prepared!"

Put your husband's tattered ego back together again at the end of each day. That's not using feminine wiles; that is the very nature of love. If you fulfill his needs, he won't have to escape some other way.

On the other hand, you may have a husband who does not do anything but stay home drinking beer in his underwear. The responsibility of the family may rest on your back because somewhere along the line you usurped his role. Your nagging may have taken the wind out of his sails and now he has no desire to keep working for you. If so, he needs your compliments to restart his engine, regardless of the distance or bitterness between you.

Life is made up of seemingly inconsequential things, but often it's a little thing that can turn the tide. Behind every great man is a great woman, loving him and meeting his needs. There are some exceptions to this, but very few.

Self cries, "Love me, meet my needs." Love says, "Allow me to meet your needs." Dish out some sincere compliments to your man tonight, and watch his cup fill up and overflow. What nagging cannot do, admiration will! . . .

Assignment

Man Alive

1. Accept your husband just as he is. Write out two lists – one of his faults and one of his virtues. Take a long, hard look at his faults and then throw the list away; don't ever dwell on them again. Only think about his virtues. Carry that list with you and refer to it when you are mad, sad, or glad.

2. Admire your husband every day. Refer to his virtue list if you need a place to start. Say something nice about his body today. Put his tattered ego back together with compliments.

3. Adapt to his way of life. Accept his friends, food and life-style as your own. Ask him to write the six most important changes he'd like to see take place at your house. Read the list in private, react in private, and then set out to accomplish these changes with a smile. Be a "Yes, let's!" woman some time of every day.

4. Appreciate all he does for you. Sincerely tell him "Thank you" with your attitudes, actions, and words. Give him your undivided attention, and try not to make any telephone calls after he comes home, especially after 8:00 P.M.

39 MERLE WOO

FROM *"Letter to Ma" (1980)*

January, 1980

Dear Ma,

I was depressed over Christmas, and when New Year's rolled around, do you know what one of my resolves was? Not to come by and see you as much anymore. I had to ask myself why I get so down when I'm with you, my mother, who has focused so much of her life on me, who has endured so much; one who I am proud of and respect so deeply for simply surviving.

I suppose that one of the main reasons is that when I leave your house, your pretty little round white table in the dinette where we sit while you drink tea (with only three specks of Jasmine) and I smoke and drink coffee, I am down because I believe there are chasms between us. When you say, "I support you, honey, in everything you do except . . . except . . ." I know you mean except my speaking out and writing of my anger at all those things that have caused those chasms . . . .

When I look at you, there are images: images of you as a little ten-year-old Korean girl, being sent alone from Shanghai to the United States, in steerage with only one skimpy little dress, being sick and lonely on Angel Island for three months; then growing up in a "Home" run by white missionary women. Scrubbing floors on your hands and knees, hauling coal in heavy metal buckets up three flights of stairs, tending to the younger children, putting hot bricks on your cheeks to deaden the pain from the terrible toothaches you always had. Working all your life as maid, waitress, salesclerk, office worker, mother. But throughout there is an image of you as strong and courageous, and persevering: climbing out of windows to escape from the

Home, then later, from an abusive first husband. There is so much more to these images than I can say, but I think you know what I mean. Escaping out of windows offered only temporary respites; surviving is an everyday chore. You gave me, physically, what you never had, but there was a spiritual, emotional legacy you passed down which was reinforced by society: self-contempt because of our race, our sex, our sexuality. For deeply ingrained in me, Ma, there has been that strong, compulsive force to sink into self-contempt, passivity, and despair. I am sure that my fifteen years of alcohol abuse have not been forgotten by either of us, nor my suicidal depressions.

Now, I know you are going to think that I hate and despise you for your self-hatred, for your isolation. But I don't. Because in spite of your withdrawal, in spite of your loneliness, you have not only survived, but been beside me in the worst of times when your company meant everything in the world to me. I just need more than that now, Ma. I have taken and taken from you in terms of needing you to mother me, to be by my side, and I need, now, to take from you two more things: understanding and support for who I am now and my work.

We are Asian American women and the reaction to our identity is what causes the chasms instead of connections. But do you realize, Ma, that I could never have reacted the way I have if you had not provided for me the opportunity to be free of the binds that have held you down, and to be in the process of self-affirmation? Because of your life, because of the physical security you have given me: my education, my full stomach, my clothed and starched back, my piano and dancing lessons – all those gifts you never received – I saw myself as having worth; now I begin to love myself more, see our potential, and fight for just that kind of social change that will affirm me, my race, my sex, my heritage. And while I affirm myself, Ma, I affirm you.

Today, I am satisfied to call myself either an Asian American Feminist or Yellow Feminist. The two terms are inseparable because race and sex are an integral part of me. This means that I am working with others to realize pride in culture and women and heritage (the heritage that is the exploited yellow immigrant: Daddy and you). Being a Yellow Feminist means being a community activist and a humanist. It does not mean "separatism," either by cutting myself off from non-Asians or men. It does not mean retaining the same power structure and substituting women in positions of control held by men. It does mean fighting the whites and the men who abuse us, straight-jacket us and tape our mouths; it means changing the economic class system and psychological forces (sexism, racism, and homophobia) that really hurt all of us. And I do this, not in isolation, but in the community. . . . Today, as I write to you of all these memories, I feel even more deeply hurt when I realize how many people, how so many people, because of racism and sexism, fail to see what power we sacrifice by not joining hands.

But not all white women are racist, and not all Asian American men are sexist. And we choose to trust them, love and work with them. And there are visible changes. Real tangible, positive changes. The changes I love to see are those changes within ourselves.

Your grandchildren, my children, Emily and Paul. That makes three generations. Emily loves herself. Always has. There are shades of self-doubt but much less than in you or me. She says exactly what she thinks, most of the time, either in praise or in criticism of herself or others. And at sixteen she goes after whatever she wants, usually center stage. She trusts and loves people, regardless of race or sex (but, of course, she's cautious), loves her community and works in it, speaks up against racism and sexism at school. Did you know that she got Zora Neale Hurston and Alice Walker on her reading list for a Southern Writers class when there were only white authors? That she insisted on changing a script done by an Asian American man when she saw that the depiction of the character she was playing was sexist? That she went to a California State House Conference to speak out for Third World students' needs?

And what about her little brother, Paul? Twelve years old. And remember, Ma? At one of our Saturday Night Family Dinners, how he lectured Ronnie (his uncle, yet!) about how he was a male chauvinist? Paul told me once how he knew he had to fight to be Asian American, and later he added that if it weren't for Emily and me, he wouldn't have to think about feminist stuff too. He says he can hardly enjoy a movie or TV program anymore because of the sexism. Or comic books. And he is very much aware of the different treatment he gets from adults: "You have to do everything right," he said to Emily, "and I can get away with almost anything."

Emily and Paul give us hope, Ma. Because they are proud of who they are, and they care so much about our culture and history. Emily was the first to write your biography because she knows how crucial it is to get our stories in writing.

Ma, I wish I knew the histories of the women in our family before you. I bet that would be quite a story. But that may be just as well, because I can say that *you* started something. Maybe you feel ambivalent or doubtful about it, but you did. Actually, you should be proud of what you've begun. I am. If my reaction to being a Yellow Woman is different than yours was, please know that this is not a judgment on you, a criticism or a denial of you, your worth. I have always supported you, and as the years pass, I think I begin to understand you more and more.

In the last few years, I have realized the value of Homework: I have studied the history of our people in this country. I cannot tell you how proud I am to be a Chinese/Korean American Woman. We have such a proud heritage, such a courageous tradition. I want to tell everyone about that, all the particulars that are left out in the schools. And the full awareness of being a woman makes me want to sing. And I do sing with other Asian Americans and women, Ma, anyone who will sing with me.

I feel now that I can begin to put our lives in a larger framework. Ma, a larger framework! The outlines for us are time and blood, but today there is breadth possible through making connections with others involved in community struggle. In loving ourselves for who we are – American women of color – we can make a vision for the future where we are free to fulfill our human potential. This new framework will not support repression, hatred, exploitation and isolation, but will be a human and beautiful framework, created in a community, bonded not by color, sex or class, but by love and the common goal for the liberation of mind, heart, and spirit.

Ma, today, you are as beautiful and pure to me as the picture I have of you, as a little girl, under my dresser-glass.

40 US SUPREME COURT

Roe v. Wade (1973)

We, therefore, conclude that the right of personal privacy includes the abortion decision, but that this right is not unqualified and must be considered against important state interests in regulation . . . .

The Constitution does not define "person" in so many words. Section 1 of the Fourteenth Amendment contains three references to "person." The first, in defining "citizens," speaks of "persons born or naturalized in the United States." The word also appears both in the Due Process Clause and in the Equal Protection Clause. "Person" is used in other places in the Constitution. . . . But in nearly all these instances, the use of the word is such that it has application only postnatally. None indicates, with any assurance, that it has any possible prenatal application.

All this, together with our observation, supra, that throughout the major portion of the 19th century prevailing legal abortion practices were far freer than they are today, persuades us that the word "person" as used in the Fourteenth Amendment, does not include the unborn. . . .

With respect to the State's important and legitimate interest in the health of the mother, the "compelling" point, in the light of present medical knowledge, is at approximately the end of the first trimester. This is so because of the now-established medical fact that until the end of the first trimester mortality in abortion may be less than mortality in normal childbirth. It follows that, from and after this point, a State may regulate the abortion procedure to the extent that the regulation reasonably relates to the preservation and protection of maternal health. . . .

With respect to the State's important and legitimate interest in potential life, the compelling point is at viability. This is so because the fetus then presumably has the capability of meaningful life outside the mother's womb. State regulation protective of fetal life after viability thus has both logical and biological justifications. If the State is interested in protecting fetal life after viability, it may go so far as to proscribe abortion during that period, except when it is necessary to preserve the life or health of the mother. . . .

To summarize and to repeat:

1 A state criminal abortion statute of the current Texas type, that excepts from criminality only *a life-saving* procedure on behalf of the mother, without regard to pregnancy stage and without recognition of the other interests involved, is violative of the Due Process Clause of the Fourteenth Amendment.

   a. For the stage prior to approximately the end of the first trimester, the abortion decision and its effectuation must be left to the medical judgment of the pregnant woman's attending physician.
   b. For the stage subsequent to approximately the end of the first trimester, the State, in promoting its interest in the health of the mother, may, if it chooses, regulate the abortion procedure in ways that are reasonably related to maternal health.

c. For the stage subsequent to viability, the State in promoting its interest in the potentiality of human life may, if it chooses, regulate, and even proscribe, abortion except where it is necessary, in appropriate medical judgment, for the preservation of the life or health of the mother. . . .

5
GOVERNMENT AND POLITICS

Introduction	118
41 *Founding Fathers* FROM The Constitution of the United States (1787)	122
42 *James Madison* "The Union as a Safeguard against Domestic Faction and Insurrection" (1787)	129
43 *John Marshall* FROM *Marbury* v. *Madison* (1803)	134
44 *Thomas Jefferson* FROM "The Roots of Democracy" (1816)	137
45 *Andrew Jackson* FROM Proclamation to the People of South Carolina (1832)	139
46 *John Marshall Harlan* FROM Dissenting Opinion in *Plessy* v *Ferguson* (1896)	141
47 *John F. Kennedy* First Inaugural Address (1961)	145
48 *Joe McGinnis* FROM *The Selling of the President* (1969)	147
49 *E. L. Doctorow* FROM "A Citizen Reads the Constitution" (1987)	149
50 *John Kenneth Galbraith* "The American Presidency: Going the Way of the Blacksmith?" (1988)	152

Figure 5 Detail of American signatories from *Declaration of Independence, 4 July, 1776* by John Trumbull © Bettmann/CORBIS

INTRODUCTION

With the possible exception of the Declaration of Independence (1776), no American document ranks higher in the eyes of the American people than the Constitution of the United States (drafted 1787). The Constitution is a down-to-earth document which in a practical way outlines the American republican system of government (see text 41). It is understandable that, after a period of war and upheaval, the Founding Fathers who wrote the Constitution longed for national unity.

This spirit is reflected in the Constitution itself and in the contemporary writings of James Madison, a delegate whose role at the constitutional assembly was so important that he has been called "the father of the Constitution." The main concern of Madison and most others was to prevent any one interest group or "faction" – whether a majority or a minority – from dominating the new government. They sought to do this by a system of indirect representation rather than direct democracy. The idea of federalism and the system of checks and balances reflect the same basic motive: to prevent a strong government in any form. This was a logical decision by a new nation based on colonies which had been under a strong central government in London. Along with Alexander Hamilton and John Jay, Madison wrote a series of articles, signed Publius – now known as the *Federalist Papers* – to persuade the new states to ratify the Constitution (text 42).

In 1987, two hundred years after the Founding Fathers agreed on this first written basic law that is still operative, the author E. L. Doctorow gave a talk in Philadelphia, reprinted in part in this chapter as "A Citizen Reads the Constitution" (text 49). Here he contrasts the Constitution with the eloquent and even revolutionary Declaration of Independence, examining it as an authored text. He also recounts how different generations of Americans have regarded their basic legal document.

In text 44, Thomas Jefferson gives his own view of the Constitution in a private letter of 1816, when he had retired as the third president of the United States and Madison had become the nation's fourth president. Madison had originally distinguished between a democracy which he feared and a republic which he supported. Jefferson, looking back, hails democracy rather than the republican form. His alternative vision is of a "grass-roots" or local democracy with a minimum of officialdom. Indeed, Jefferson's idea of "county republics" or "ward republics" seems very close to that form of direct democracy which Madison had believed to be so dangerous in 1787. Jefferson deplores that Americans, even at this early stage, have a tendency to look upon the Constitution as a sacred text. Nevertheless, the Jeffersonian view of a localistic, county- and state-centered community rather than a true American nation became dominant for over a century. Despite their differences, Madison helped secure the triumph of the Jeffersonian view.

When Jefferson won the presidential election in 1800 and again in 1804, Jeffersonian democracy seemed to have permanently removed from power those who believed in a strong federal government that could serve as the promoter of large industrial enterprises. But at the very moment of Jefferson's victory, the Federalists scored an important victory. In one of his last official actions, the Federalist President John Adams had named his secretary of state, John Marshall, chief justice of the Supreme Court of the United States. And Marshall aspired to make the Supreme Court the ultimate arbiter in the lawmaking process. He did so in the famous *Marbury v. Madison* case (1803) (text 43). William Marbury had also been one of Adams's late appointments – as a district judge – but Marbury's commission had not actually been delivered to him. Jefferson instructed his new secretary of state, James Madison, to withhold it. Marbury then asked the court for a *mandamus* or court order requiring him to be instated in his job. In the Supreme Court, Marshall wrote a majority opinion that said two things. First, that the president had no moral right to withhold the commission. Second, that the act on which Marbury rested his case was unconstitutional. Therefore the court was powerless to help him. In this way Marshall ingeniously introduced the system of *judicial review*: the doctrine that the US Supreme Court has the right to pass judgment on whether or not a law is constitutional. This was a challenge to the Jeffersonian doctrine that the people, not lawyers or aristocrats, should have the final say.

One of those who sympathized with Jefferson's view was Andrew Jackson, president of the United States from 1829 to 1837. Jackson went even further than Jefferson in claiming that the Supreme Court's opinions could be ignored. Neither Jefferson nor Jackson wanted a strong government in Washington, but both actually strengthened the presidency. Jefferson in 1803 had purchased an enormous tract of land west of the Mississippi and east of the Rocky Mountains – known as Louisiana – from France for $15 million. The Senate, surprised, was critical of such presidential initiative but had little choice but to accept the deal. Jackson in 1828 faced a different crisis when South Carolina declared that it had the right under the Constitution to withdraw from the federal union drawn up in 1787. In a sense, South Carolina pulled

Jeffersonian localism to its logical conclusion by declaring several acts by the national Congress to be unconstitutional and therefore not binding on South Carolina. In setting an individual state above the union, South Carolina's act of "nullification" was a preview of the conflicts that led to the Civil War. To use Madison's language, here was a "faction" or strong interest trying to dominate the rest. President Jackson, for all his sympathy with localism, refused to accept a break-up of the union. Jackson's proclamation to the South Carolinians in 1832 (text 45) shows what he thinks about the Constitution and the United States as a nation.

The Constitution has never been periodically revised and updated in the way Jefferson and his supporters believed it should be, but its many amendments have served part of that purpose. So has, above all, the interpretation of what the Constitution *means* and *permits*. For example, the three branches of government, originally designed by the Founding Fathers to be equal under the Constitution, have undergone an evolution. In the course of time, the executive branch and especially the presidency has come out as the strongest of the three. There have been attempts to change this trend. Soon after the Civil War Congress tried to make a president comply with its will. The issue was who had the power to appoint or dismiss a member of the president's Cabinet – the president or Congress. Congress believed that it, and no longer the president, should have that right, and tried to impeach (remove) President Johnson to make its point. If Congress had succeeded in its attempt to impeach Andrew Johnson in 1868, the outcome might have been a parliamentary type of government in the United States.

One of the earliest tests of the right to *judicial review* came in 1896 when the Supreme Court decided, in *Plessy* v. *Ferguson*, that a southern state could keep separate facilities for blacks and white, as long as these facilites were "equal." This notorious ruling was passed against only one dissenting vote in the court, that of Justice John Marshall Harlan (text 46). He bravely insisted on the constitutional equality of all classes and races in America and deplored the Court's acceptance of racial segregation as constitutional as long as the facilities in question – in this specific case, those of railroad coaches – were said to be "separate but equal." (Harlan's lone dissent foreshadowed the ideas half a century later of the Supreme Court decision of *Brown* v. *Board of Education*, excerpted in chapter 10 as text 95.)

What has emerged in the United States since 1896 is presidential government. The rise of what has been called the "imperial presidency" has been particularly noteworthy since the 1930s, the age of the Great Depression and Franklin D. Roosevelt's New Deal. What happened politically as a result of the so-called Watergate affair in the 1970s can be seen at least partly as an attempt by Congress to reduce the power of the modern presidency and regain some of the former prestige of the legislative branch.

In his Inaugural Address in 1961 (text 47) President John F. Kennedy – the first Catholic in the Oval Office – addressed the challenges of a changing world by promising to utilize the energy, the faith, and the devotion of a new generation. Pledging to attack the problems of the world with a youthful spirit and a flexibility unknown to the proponents of containment, Kennedy appealed both to his fellow Americans and to a global audience. Kennedy's insistent call to Americans: "ask not what your country can do for you – ask what you can do for your country"; and to his fellow citizens of the world: "ask not what Americans will do for you, but what together we can do for the freedom of man," struck a sympathetic chord in people both at home and abroad.

Many Americans lean strongly toward regarding American parties as so lacking in ideological direction that they have little choice but to "sell" their presidential candidates to the people. This is the message of Joe McGinnis's *The Selling of the President* (1969) (see text 48). McGinnis presents the presidential candidate (Nixon) as the creation of marketing experts, often referred to as "Madison Avenue" after the New York City area where important marketing firms are located.

Perhaps it is misleading to say that American presidents have become much more powerful than they used to be. This, at least, is Professor John Kenneth Galbraith's reasoning in his article "The American Presidency: Going the Way of the Black-smith?" (text 50). His controversial point is that it is the institution of the presidency, not the individual president, that has been strengthened over time. Paradoxically, because of the rising power of the presidency, the American people have occasionally boosted the power of Congress by filling it with a majority of the opposition party. As a result of the congressional election of 1994, for example, President Clinton found himself faced by a Republican-dominated Congress.

Questions and Topics

1　In his essay on the American Constitution Doctorow argues that "the voice of the Constitution is a quiet voice." Is it really?
2　What is meant by "judical review"? How did it originate and how does it function?
3　In what sense does the American system of checks and balances differ from a parliamentary system?
4　What makes John Marshall Harlan's dissent such a powerful political statement?
5　Galbraith suggests that Pentagon has "become a power unto itself". How does that influence the rhetoric of the presidents from Kennedy on?

Suggestions for further reading

Cummings, Milton C., Jr. and David Wise, *Democracy Under Pressure: An Introduction to the American Political System*, 10th edn (Belmont, Calif.: Thompson, 2003).

Hofstadter, Richard, *The Paranoid Style in American Politics and Other Essays* (New York: Knopf, 1996).

Janda, Kenneth, Jeffrey M. Berry, and Jerry Goldman, *The Challenge of Democracy: Government in America*, 8th edn (Boston, Mass.: Houghton Mifflin, 2005).

Kammen, M., *A Machine That Would Go of Itself: The Constituion in American Culture* (New York: Vintage Books, 1987).

Lind, M., *Made in Texas: George W. Bush and the Southern Takeover of American Politics* (New York: Basic Books, 2003).

41 FOUNDING FATHERS

FROM *The Constitution of the United States (1787)*

We, the People of the United States, in order to form a more perfect union, establish justice, insure domestic tranquility, provide for the common defence, promote the general welfare, and secure the blessings of liberty to ourselves and our posterity, do ordain and establish this Constitution for the United States of America.

ARTICLE I

Sec. l. All legislative powers herein granted shall be vested in a Congress of the United States, which shall consist of a Senate and House of Representatives.

Sec. 2. The House of Representatives shall be composed of members chosen every second year by the people of the several States, and the electors in each State shall have the qualifications requisite for electors of the most numerous branch of the State legislature.

No person shall be a Representative who shall not have attained to the age of twenty-five years, and been seven years a citizen of the United States, and who shall not, when elected, be an inhabitant of that State in which he shall be chosen.

Representatives and direct taxes shall be apportioned among the several States which may be included within this Union, according to their respective numbers.

When vacancies happen in the representation from any State, the executive authority thereof shall issue writs of election to fill such vacancies.

The House of Representatives shall choose their Speaker and other officers; and shall have the sole power of impeachment.

Sec. 3. The Senate of the United States shall be composed of two Senators from each State, chosen by the legislature thereof, for six years; and each Senator shall have one vote.

Immediately after they shall be assembled in consequence of the first election, they shall be divided as equally as may be into three classes. The seats of the Senators of the first class shall be vacated at the expiration of the second year, of the second class at the expiration of the fourth year, and of the third class at the expiration of the sixth year, so that one-third may be chosen every second year; and if vacancies happen by resignation, or otherwise, during the recess of the legislature of any State, the executive thereof may make temporary appointments until the next meeting of the legislature, which shall then fill such vacancies.

Sec. 7. All bills for raising revenue shall originate in the House of Representatives; but the Senate may propose or concur with amendments as on other bills.

Every bill which shall have passed the House of Representatives and the Senate, shall, before it become a law, be presented to the President of the United States; if he approve he shall sign it, but if not he shall return it, with his objections, to that house in which it shall have originated, who shall enter the objections at large on their journal, and proceed to reconsider it. If after such reconsideration two-thirds of that house shall agree to pass the bill, it shall be sent, together with the objections, to the other house, by which it shall likewise be reconsidered, and if approved by two-thirds of that house, it shall become a law. But in all such cases the votes of both houses shall be determined by yeas and nays, and the names of the persons voting for and against the bill shall be entered on the journal of each house respectively. If any bill shall not be returned by the President within ten days (Sundays excepted) after it shall have been presented to him, the same shall be a law, in like manner as if he had signed it, unless the Congress by their adjournment prevent its return, in which case it shall not be a law.

Every order, resolution, or vote to which the concurrence of the Senate and House of Representatives may be necessary (except on a question of adjournment) shall be presented to the President of the United States; and before the same shall take effect, shall be approved by him, or being disapproved by him, shall be repassed by two-thirds of the Senate and House of Representatives, according to the rules and limitations prescribed in the case of a bill.

Sec. 8. The Congress shall have power to lay and collect taxes, duties, imposts, and excises, to pay the debts and provide for the common defence and general welfare of the United States; but all duties, imposts, and excises shall be uniform throughout the United States.

ARTICLE II

Sec. 1. The executive power shall be vested in a President of the United States of America. He shall hold his office during the term of four years, and, together with the Vice President, chosen for the same term, be elected, as follows:

Each State shall appoint, in such manner as the legislature thereof may direct, a number of electors, equal to the whole number of Senators and Representatives to which the State may be entitled in the Congress.

No person except a natural-born citizen, or a citizen of the United States, at the time of the adoption of this Constitution, shall be eligible to the office of President; neither shall any person be eligible to that office who shall not have attained to the age of thirty-five years, and been fourteen years a resident within the United States.

In case of the removal of the President from office, or of his death, resignation, or inability to discharge the powers and duties of the said office, the same shall devolve on the Vice-President, and the Congress may by law provide for the case of removal, death, resignation, or inability, both of the President and Vice-President, declaring what officer shall then act as President, and such officer shall act accordingly, until the disability be removed, or a President shall be elected.

Before he enter on the execution of his office, he shall take the following oath or affirmation: "I do solemnly swear (or affirm) that I will faithfully execute the office of President of the United States, and will to the best of my ability, preserve, protect, and defend the Constitution of the United States."

Sec. 2. The President shall be Commander-in-Chief of the Army and Navy of the United States, and of the militia of the several States, when called into the actual service of the United States.

He shall have power, by and with the advice and consent of the Senate, to make treaties, provided two-thirds of the Senators present concur; and he shall nominate, and by and with the advice and consent of the Senate, shall appoint ambassadors, other public ministers and consuls, judges of the Supreme Court, and all other officers of the United States, whose appointments are not herein otherwise provided for, and which shall be established by law; but the Congress may by law vest the appointment of such inferior officers, as they think proper, in the President alone, in the courts of law, or in the heads of departments.

The President shall have power to fill up all vacancies that may happen during the recess of the Senate, by granting commissions which shall expire at the end of their next session.

Sec. 3. He shall from time to time give to the Congress information of the state of the Union, and recommend to their consideration such measures as he shall judge necessary and expedient.

Sec. 4. The President, Vice-President and all civil officers of the United States, shall be removed from office on impeachment for, and conviction of, treason, bribery, or other high crimes and misdemeanors.

ARTICLE III

Sec. 1. The judicial power of the United States, shall be vested in one Supreme Court, and in such inferior courts as the Congress may from time to time ordain and establish. The judges, both of the supreme and inferior courts, shall hold their offices during good behaviour, and shall, at stated times, receive for their services, a compensation, which shall not be diminished during their continuance in office.

Sec. 2. The judicial power shall extend to all cases, in law and equity, arising under this Constitution, the laws of the United States, and treaties made, or which shall be made, under their authority, to all cases affecting ambassadors, other public ministers and consuls; to all cases of admiralty and maritime jurisdiction; to controversies to which the United States shall be a party; to controversies between two or more States; between a State and citizens of another State; between citizens of different states, between citizens of the same State claiming lands under grants of different States, and between a State, or the citizen thereof, and foreign States, citizens or subjects.

The trial of all crimes, except in cases of impeachment, shall be by jury; and such trial shall be held in the State where the said crimes shall have been committed; but when not committed within any State, the trial shall be at such place or places as the Congress may by law have directed.

ARTICLE IV

Sec. 1. Full faith and credit shall be given in each State to the public acts, records, and judicial proceedings of every other State. And the Congress may by general laws prescribe the manner in which such acts, records, and proceedings shall be provided, and the effect thereof.

Sec. 2. The citizens of each State shall be entitled to all privileges and immunities of citizens in the several States.

A person charged in any State with treason, felony, or other crime, who shall flee from justice, and be found in another State, shall on demand of the executive authority of the State from which he fled, be delivered up, to be removed to the State having jurisdiction of the crime.

Sec. 3. New States may be admitted by the Congress into this Union; but no new States shall be formed or erected within the jurisdiction of any other State; nor any State be formed by the junction of two or more states; or parts of States, without the consent of the legislatures of the States concerned as well as of the Congress.

Amendments to the Constitution (a selection)
Articles I–X, 1791

ARTICLE I

Congress shall make no law respecting an establishment of religion, or prohibiting the free exercise thereof; or abridging the freedom of speech, or of the press; or the right of the people peaceably to assemble, and to petition the government for a redress of grievances.

ARTICLE II

A well regulated militia, being necessary to the security of a free State, the right of the people to keep and bear arms, shall not be infringed.

ARTICLE IV

The right of the people to be secure in their persons, houses, papers, and effects, against unreasonable searches and seizures, shall not be violated, and no warrants shall issue, but upon probable cause, supported by oath or affirmation, and particularly describing the place to be searched, and the persons or things to be seized.

ARTICLE V

No person shall be held to answer for a capital, or otherwise infamous crime, unless on a presentment or indictment of a grand jury, except in cases arising in the land or naval forces, or in the militia, when in actual service in time of war or public danger; nor shall any person be subject for the same offence to be twice put in jeopardy of life or limb; nor shall be compelled in any criminal case to be a witness against himself, nor be deprived of life, liberty, or property, without due process of law; nor shall private property be taken for public use, without just compensation.

ARTICLE VI

In all criminal prosecutions, the accused shall enjoy the right to a speedy and public trial, by an impartial jury of the State and district wherein the crime shall have been committed, which district shall have been previously ascertained by law, and to be informed of the nature and cause of the accusation; to be confronted with the witnesses against him; to have compulsory process for obtaining witnesses in his favor, and to have the assistance of counsel for his defence.

ARTICLE X

The powers not delegated to the United States by the Constitution, nor prohibited by it to the States, are reserved to the States respectively, or to the people.

ARTICLE XII (1804)

The electors shall meet in their respective states, and vote by ballot for President and Vice-President, one of whom, at least, shall not be an inhabitant of the same state with themselves; they shall name in their ballots the person voted for as President, and in distinct ballots the person voted for as Vice-President, and they shall make distinct lists of all persons voted for as President, and of all persons voted for as Vice-President, and of the number of votes for each, which lists they shall sign and certify, and transmit sealed to the seat of the Government of the United States, directed to the President of the Senate; The President of the Senate shall, in the presence of the Senate and House of Representatives, open all the certificates and the votes shall then be counted; The person having the greatest number of votes for President, shall be the President, if such number be a majority of the whole number of electors appointed; and if no person have such majority, then from the persons having the highest numbers not exceeding three on the list of those voted for as President, the House of Representatives shall choose immediately, by ballot, the President.

ARTICLE XIII (1865)

Sec. l. Neither slavery nor involuntary servitude, except as a punishment for crime whereof the party shall have been duly convicted, shall exist within the United States, or any place subject to their jurisdiction.

ARTICLE XIV (1868)

Sec. l. All persons born or naturalized in the United States, and subject to the jurisdiction thereof, are citizens of the United States and of the State wherein they reside. No State shall make or enforce any law which shall abridge the privileges or immunities of citizens of the United States; nor shall any State deprive any person of life, liberty, or property, without due process of law; nor deny to any person within its jurisdiction the equal protection of the laws.

Sec. 2. Representatives shall be apportioned among the several States according to their respective numbers, counting the whole number of persons in each State, excluding Indians not taxed. But when the right to vote at any election for the choice of electors for President and Vice-President of the United States, Representatives in Congress, the Executive and Judicial officers of a State, or the members of the Legislature thereof, is denied to any of the male inhabitants of such State, being twenty-one years of age, and citizens of the United States, or in any way abridged, except for participation in rebellion, or other crime, the basis of representation therein shall be reduced in the proportion which the number of such male citizens shall bear to the whole number of male citizens twenty-one years of age in such State.

ARTICLE XV (1870)

Sec. 1. The right of citizens of the United States to vote shall not be denied or abridged by the United States or by any State on account of race, color, or previous condition of servitude.

Sec. 2. The Congress shall have power to enforce this article by appropriate legislation.

ARTICLE XVII (1913)

The Senate of the United States shall be composed of two Senators from each State, elected by the people thereof, for six years; and each Senator shall have one vote. The electors in each State shall have the qualifications requisite for electors of the most numerous branch of the State legislature.

When vacancies happen in the representation of any State in the Senate, the executive authority of such State shall issue writs of election to fill such vacancies: *Provided,* That the legislature of any State may empower the executive thereof to make temporary appointments until the people fill the vacancies by election as the legislature may direct.

This amendment shall not be so construed as to affect the election or term of any Senator chosen before it becomes valid as part of the Constitution.

ARTICLE XVIII (1919)

After one year from the ratification of this article, the manufacture, sale, or transportation of intoxicating liquors within, the importation thereof into, or the exportation thereof from the United States and all territory subject to the jurisdiction thereof for beverage purposes is hereby prohibited.

The Congress and the several States shall have concurrent power to enforce this article by appropriate legislation.

ARTICLE XIX (1920)

The right of citizens of the United States to vote shall not be denied or abridged by the United States or by any States on account of sex.

The Congress shall have power to appropriate legislation to enforce the provisions of this article.

ARTICLE XXI (1933)

Sec. 1. The eighteenth article of amendment to the Constitution of the United States is hereby repealed.

Sec. 2. The transportation or importation into any State, territory or possession of the United States for delivery or use therein of intoxicating liquors, in violation of the laws thereof, is hereby prohibited.

ARTICLE XXII (1951)

Sec. 1. No person shall be elected to the office of the President more than twice, and no person who has held the office of President, or acted as President, for more than two years of a term to which some other person was elected President shall be elected to the office of the President more than once. But this Article shall not apply to any person holding the office of President when this Article was proposed by the Congress, and shall not prevent any person who may be holding the office of President or acting as President during the term within which this Article becomes operative, from holding the office of President, or acting as President, during the remainder of such term.

ARTICLE XXIV (1964)

Sec. 1. The right of citizens of the United States to vote in any primary or other election for President or Vice-President, for electors for President or Vice-President, or for Senator or Representative in Congress, shall not be denied or abridged by the United States or any State by reason of failure to pay any poll tax or other tax.

ARTICLE XXV (1967)

Sec. 1. In case of the removal of the President from office or of his death or resignation, the Vice-President shall become President.

Sec. 2. Whenever there is a vacancy in the office of the Vice-President, the President shall nominate a Vice-President who shall take office upon confirmation by a majority vote of both Houses of Congress.

ARTICLE XXVI (1971)

Sec. 1. The right of citizens of the United States, who are eighteen years of age or older, to vote shall not be denied or abridged by the United States or by any State on account of age.

42 JAMES MADISON

"The Union as a Safeguard Against Domestic Faction and Insurrection" (1787)

To the People of the State of New York

Among the numerous advantages promised by a well-constructed Union, none deserves to be more accurately developed than its tendency to break and control the violence of faction. The friend of popular governments never finds himself so much alarmed for their character and fate, as when he contemplates their propensity to this dangerous vice. He will not fail, therefore, to set a due value on any plan which, without violating the principles to which he is attached, provides a proper cure for it. The instability, injustice, and confusion introduced into the public councils, have, in truth, been the mortal diseases under which popular governments have everywhere perished; as they continue to be the favorite and fruitful topics from which the adversaries to liberty derive their most specious declamations. The valuable improvements made by the American constitutions on the popular models, both ancient and modern, cannot certainly be too much admired; but it would be an unwarrantable partiality, to contend that they have as effectually obviated the danger on this side, as was wished and expected. Complaints are everywhere heard from our most considerate and virtuous citizens, equally the friends of public and private faith, and of public and personal liberty, that our governments are too unstable, that the public good is disregarded in the conflicts of rival parties, and that measures are too often decided, not according to the rules of justice and the rights of the minor party, but by the superior force of an interested and overbearing majority. However anxiously we may wish that these complaints had no foundation, the evidence of known facts will not permit us to deny that they are in some degree true. It will be found, indeed, on a candid review of our situation, that some of the distresses under which we labor have been erroneously charged on the operation of our governments; but it will be found, at the same time, that other causes will not alone account for many of our heaviest misfortunes; and, particularly, for that prevailing and increasing distrust of public engagements, and alarm for private rights, which are echoed from one end of the continent to the other. These must be chiefly, if not wholly, effects of the unsteadiness and injustice with which a factious spirit has tainted our public administrations.

By a faction, I understand a number of citizens, whether amounting to a majority or a minority of the whole, who are united and actuated by some common impulse of passion, or of interest, adverse to the rights of other citizens, or to the permanent and aggregate interests of the community.

There are two methods of curing the mischiefs of faction: the one, by removing its causes; the other, by controlling its effects.

There are again two methods of removing the causes of faction: the one, by destroying the liberty which is essential to its existence; the other, by giving to every citizen the same opinions, the same passions, and the same interests.

It could never be more truly said than of the first remedy, that it was worse than the disease. Liberty is to faction what air is to fire, an aliment without which it instantly expires. But it could not be less folly to abolish liberty, which is essential to political life, because it nourishes faction, than it would be to wish the annihilation of air, which is essential to animal life, because it imparts to fire its destructive agency.

The second expedient is as impracticable as the first would be unwise. As long as the reason of man continues fallible, and he is at liberty to exercise it, different opinions will be formed. As long as the connection subsists between his reason and his self-love, his opinions and his passions will have a reciprocal influence on each other; and the former will be objects to which the latter will attach themselves. The diversity in the faculties of men, from which the rights of property originate, is not less an insuperable obstacle to a uniformity of interests. The protection of these faculties is the first object of government. From the protection of different and unequal faculties of acquiring property, the possession of different degrees and kinds of property immediately results; and from the influence of these on the sentiments and views of the respective proprietors, ensues a division of the society into different interests and parties.

The latent causes of faction are thus sown in the nature of man; and we see them everywhere brought into different degrees of activity, according to the different circumstances of civil society. A zeal for different opinions concerning religion, concerning government, and many other points, as well of speculation as of practice; an attachment to different leaders ambitiously contending for pre-eminence and power; or to persons of other descriptions whose fortunes have been interesting to the human passions, have, in turn, divided mankind into parties, inflamed them with mutual animosity, and rendered them much more disposed to vex and oppress each other than to co-operate for their common good. So strong is this propensity of mankind to fall into mutual animosities, that where no substantial occasion presents itself, the most frivolous and fanciful distinctions have been sufficient to kindle their unfriendly passions and excite their most violent conflicts. But the most common and durable source of factions has been the various and unequal distribution of property. Those who hold and those who are without property have ever formed distinct interests in society. Those who are creditors, and those who are debtors, fall under a like discrimination. A landed interest, a manufacturing interest, a mercantile interest, a moneyed interest, with many lesser interests, grow up of necessity in civilized nations, and divide them into different classes, actuated by different sentiments and views. The regulation of these various and interfering interests forms the principal task of modern legislation, and involves the spirit of party and faction in the necessary and ordinary operations of the government.

No man is allowed to be a judge in his own cause, because his interest would certainly bias his judgment, and, not improbably, corrupt his integrity. With equal, nay with greater reason, a body of men are unfit to be both judges and parties at the same time; yet what are many of the most important acts of legislation, but so many judicial determinations, not indeed concerning the rights of single persons, but concerning the rights of large bodies of citizens? And what are the different classes of legislators but advocates and parties to the causes which they determine? Is a law proposed concerning private debts? It is a question to which the creditors are parties on one side and the debtors on the other. Justice ought to hold the balance between them. Yet the parties are, and must be, themselves the judges; and the most numerous party, or, in other words, the most powerful faction must be expected to prevail. Shall domestic manufactures be encouraged, and in what degree, by restrictions on foreign manufactures? are questions which would be differently decided by the landed and the manufacturing classes, and probably by neither with a sole regard to justice and the public good. The apportionment of taxes on the various descriptions of property is an act which seems to require the most exact impartiality; yet there is, perhaps, no legislative act in which greater opportunity and temptation are given to a predominant party to trample on the rules of justice. Every shilling with which they overburden the inferior number, is a shilling saved to their own pockets.

It is in vain to say that enlightened statesmen will be able to adjust these clashing interests, and render them all subservient to the public good. Enlightened statesmen will not always be at the helm. Nor, in many cases, can such an adjustment be made at all without taking into view indirect and remote considerations, which will rarely prevail over the immediate interest which one party may find in disregarding the rights of another or the good of the whole.

The inference to which we are brought is that the causes of faction cannot be removed, and that relief is only to be sought in the means of controlling its effects.

If a faction consists of less than a majority, relief is supplied by the republican principle, which enables the majority to defeat its sinister views by regular vote. It may clog the administration, it may convulse the society; but it will be unable to execute and mask its violence under the forms of the Constitution. When a majority is included in a faction, the form of popular government, on the other hand, enables it to sacrifice to its ruling passion or interest both the public good and the rights of other citizens. To secure the public good and private rights against the danger of such a faction, and at the same time to preserve the spirit and the form of popular government, is then the great object to which our inquiries are directed. Let me add that it is the great desideratum by which this form of government can be rescued from the opprobrium under which it has so long labored, and be recommended to the esteem and adoption of mankind.

By what means is this object attainable? Evidently by one of two only. Either the existence of the same passion or interest in a majority at the same time must be prevented, or the majority, having such coexistent passion or interest, must be rendered, by their number and local situation, unable to concert and carry into effect schemes of oppression. If the impulse and the opportunity be suffered to coincide, we well know that neither moral nor religious motives can be relied on as an adequate control. They are not found to be such on the injustice and violence of individuals, and lose their efficacy in proportion to the number combined together, that is, in proportion as their efficacy becomes needful.

From this view of the subject it may be concluded that a pure democracy, by which I mean a society consisting of a small number of citizens, who assemble and administer the government in person, can admit of no cure for the mischiefs of faction. A common passion or interest will, in almost every case, be felt by a majority of the whole; a communication and concert result from the form of government itself; and there is nothing to check the inducements to sacrifice the weaker party or an obnoxious individual. Hence it is that such democracies have ever been spectacles of turbulence and contention; have ever been found incompatible with personal security or the rights of property; and have in general been as short in their lives as they have been violent in their deaths. Theoretic politicians, who have patronized this species of government, have erroneously supposed that by reducing mankind to a perfect equality in their political rights, they would, at the same time, be perfectly equalized and assimilated in their possessions, their opinions, and their passions.

A republic, by which I mean a government in which the scheme of representation takes place, opens a different prospect, and promises the cure for which we are seeking. Let us examine the points in which it varies from pure democracy, and we shall comprehend both the nature of the cure and the efficacy which it must derive from the Union.

The two great points of difference between a democracy and a republic are: first, the delegation of the government, in the latter, to a small number of citizens elected by the rest; secondly, the greater number of citizens, and greater sphere of country, over which the latter may be extended.

The effect of the first difference is, on the one hand, to refine and enlarge the public views, by passing them through the medium of a chosen body of citizens, whose wisdom may best discern the true interest of their country, and whose patriotism and love of justice will be least likely to sacrifice it to temporary or partial considerations. Under such a regulation, it may well happen that the public voice, pronounced by the representatives of the people, will be more consonant to the public good than if pronounced by the people themselves, convened for the purpose. On the other hand, the effect may be inverted. Men of factious tempers, of local prejudices, or of sinister designs, may, by intrigue, by corruption, or by other means, first obtain the suffrages, and then betray the interests, of the people. The question resulting is, whether small or extensive republics are more favorable to the election of proper guardians of the public weal; and it is clearly decided in favor of the latter by two obvious considerations:

In the first place, it is to be remarked that, however small the republic may be, the representatives must be raised to a certain number, in order to guard against the cabals of a few; and that, however large it may be, they must be limited to a certain number, in order to guard against the confusion of a multitude. Hence, the number of representatives in the two cases not being in proportion to that of the two constituents, and being proportionally greater in the small republic, it follows that, if the proportion of fit characters be not less in the large than in the small republic, the former will present a greater option, and consequently a greater probability of a fit choice.

In the next place, as each representative will be chosen by a greater number of citizens in the large than in the small republic, it will be more difficult for unworthy candidates to practice with success the vicious arts by which elections are too often carried; and the suffrages of the people being more free, will be more likely to centre in men who possess the most attractive merit and the most diffusive and established characters.

It must be confessed that in this, as in most other cases, there is a mean, on both sides of which inconveniences will be found to lie. By enlarging too much the number of electors, you render the representatives too little acquainted with all their local circumstances and lesser interests; as by reducing it too much, you render him unduly attached to these, and too little fit to comprehend and pursue great and national objects. The federal Constitution forms a happy combination in this respect; the great and aggregate interests being referred to the national, the local and particular to the State legislatures.

The other point of difference is, the greater number of citizens and extent of territory which may be brought within the compass of republican than of democratic government; and it is this circumstance principally which renders factious combinations less to be dreaded in the former than in the latter. The smaller the society, the fewer probably will be the distinct parties and interests composing it; the fewer the distinct parties and interests, the more frequently will a majority be found of the same party; and the smaller the number of individuals composing a majority, and the smaller the compass within which they are placed, the more easily will they concert and execute their plans of oppression. Extend the sphere, and you take in a greater variety of parties and interests; you make it less probable that a majority of the whole will have a common motive to invade the rights of other citizens; or if such a common motive exists, it will be more difficult for all who feel it to discover their own strength, and to act in unison with each other. Besides other impediments, it may be remarked that, where there is a consciousness of unjust or dishonorable purposes, communication is always checked by distrust in proportion to the number whose concurrence is necessary.

Hence, it clearly appears, that the same advantage which a republic has over a democracy, in controlling the effects of faction, is enjoyed by a large over a small republic, – is enjoyed by the Union over the States composing it. Does the advantage consist in the substitution of representatives whose enlightened views and virtuous sentiments render them superior to local prejudices and schemes of injustice? It will not be denied that the representation of the Union will be most likely to possess these requisite endowments. Does it consist in the greater security afforded by a greater variety of parties, against the event of any one party being able to outnumber and oppress the rest? In an equal degree does the increased variety of parties comprised within the Union, increase this security? Does it, in fine, consist in the greater obstacles opposed to the concert and accomplishment of the secret wishes of an unjust and interested majority? Here, again, the extent of the Union gives it the most palpable advantage.

The influence of factious leaders may kindle a flame within their particular States, but will be unable to spread a general conflagration through the other States. A religious sect may degenerate into a political faction in a part of the Confederacy; but the variety of sects dispersed over the entire face of it must secure the national councils against any danger from that source. A rage for paper money, for an abolition of debts, for an equal division of property, or for any other improper or wicked project, will be less apt to pervade the whole body of the Union than a particular member of it; in the same proportion as such a malady is more likely to taint a particular county or district, than an entire State.

In the extent and proper structure of the Union, therefore, we behold a republican remedy for the diseases most incident to republican government. And according to the degree of pleasure and pride we feel in being republicans, ought to be our zeal in cherishing the spirit and supporting the character of Federalists.

PUBLIUS.

43 JOHN MARSHALL

FROM *Marbury* v. *Madison (1803)*

It is, then, the opinion of the Court:

First, that by signing the commission of Mr. Marbury, the President of the United States appointed him a justice of peace for the County of Washington, in the District of Columbia, and that the seal of the United States, affixed thereto by the secretary of state, is conclusive testimony of the verity of the signature, and of the completion of the appointment; and that the appointment conferred on him a legal right to the office for the space of five years.

Second, that, having this legal title to the office, he has a consequent right to the commission; a refusal to deliver which is a plain violation of that right for which the laws of his country afford him a remedy.. . . .

This, then, is a plain case for a mandamus, either to deliver the commission or a copy of it from the record; and it only remains to be inquired whether it can issue from this Court.

The act to establish the judicial courts of the United States authorizes the Supreme Court "to issue writs of mandamus, in cases warranted by the principles and usages of law, to any courts appointed, or persons holding office, under the authority of the United States."

The Secretary of State, being a person holding an office under the authority of the United States, is precisely within the letter of the description; and if this Court is not authorized to issue a writ of mandamus to such an officer, it must be because the law is unconstitutional and therefore absolutely incapable of conferring the authority and assigning the duties which its words purport to confer and assign.

The constitution vests the whole judicial power of the United States in one Supreme Court and such inferior courts as Congress shall, from time to time, ordain and establish. This power is expressly extended to all cases arising under the laws of the United States and, consequently, in some form, may be exercised over the present case because the right claimed is given by a law of the United States.

In the distribution of this power it is declared that "the Supreme Court shall have original jurisdiction in all cases affecting ambassadors, other public ministers, and consuls, and those in which a state shall be a party. In all other cases, the Supreme Court shall have appellate jurisdiction." . . .

If the solicitude of the convention, respecting our peace with foreign powers, induced a provision that the supreme court should take original jurisdiction in cases which might be supposed to affect them; yet the clause would have proceeded no further than to provide for such cases, if no further restriction on the powers of congress had been intended. That they should have appellate jurisdiction in all other cases, with such exceptions as congress might make, is no restriction; unless the words be deemed exclusive of original jurisdiction.

When an instrument organizing fundamentally a judicial system, divides it into one supreme, and so many inferior courts as the legislature may ordain and establish; then enumerates its powers, and proceeds so far to distribute them, as to define the jurisdiction of the supreme court by declaring the cases in which it shall take original jurisdiction, and that in others it shall take appellate jurisdiction; the plain import of the words seems to be, that in one class of cases its jurisdiction is original, and not appellate; in the other it is appellate, and not original. If any other construction would render the clause inoperative, that is an additional reason for rejecting such other construction, and for adhering to their obvious meaning.

To enable this Court, then, to issue a mandamus, it must be shown to be an exercise of appellate jurisdiction or to be necessary to enable them to exercise appellate jurisdiction.

It has been stated at the bar that the appellate jurisdiction may be exercised in a variety of forms, and that if it be the will of the legislature that a mandamus should be used for that purpose, that will must be obeyed. This is true, yet the jurisdiction must be appellate, not original.

It is the essential criterion of appellate jurisdiction, that it revises and corrects the proceedings in a cause already instituted, and does not create that cause. Although, therefore, a mandamus may be directed to courts, yet to issue such a writ to an officer for the delivery of a paper, is in effect the same as to sustain an original action for that paper, and, therefore, seems not to belong to appellate, but to original jurisdiction. Neither is it necessary in such a case as this, to enable the court to exercise its appellate jurisdiction.

The authority, therefore, given to the Supreme Court, by the act establishing the judicial courts of the United States, to issue writs of mandamus to public officers, appears not to be warranted by the constitution; and it becomes necessary to enquire whether a jurisdiction, so conferred, can be exercised.

The question whether an act repugnant to the constitution can become the law of the land is a question deeply interesting to the United States but, happily, not of an intricacy proportioned to its interest. It seems only necessary to recognize certain principles, supposed to have been long and well established, to decide it.

That the people have an original right to establish, for their future government, such principles as, in their opinion, shall most conduce to their own happiness is the basis on which the whole American fabric has been erected. The exercise of this original right is a very great exertion; nor can it, nor ought it, to be frequently repeated. The principles, therefore, so established are deemed fundamental. And as the authority from which they proceed is supreme and can seldom act, they are designed to be permanent.

This original and supreme will organizes the government and assigns to different departments their respective powers. It may either stop here or establish certain limits not to be transcended by those departments.

The government of the United States is of the latter description. The powers of the legislature are defined and limited; and that those limits may not be mistaken, or forgotten, the constitution is written. To what purpose are powers limited, and to what purpose is that limitation committed to writing, if these limits may, at any time, be passed by those intended to be restrained? The distinction between a government with limited and unlimited powers is abolished, if those limits do not confine the persons on whom they are imposed, and if acts prohibited and acts allowed, are of equal obligation. It is a proposition too plain to be contested, that the constitution controls any legislative act repugnant to it; or, that the legislature may alter the constitution by an ordinary act.

Between these alternatives there is no middle ground. The constitution is either a superior, paramount law, unchangeable by ordinary means, or it is on a level with ordinary legislative acts, and, like other acts, is alterable when the legislature shall please to alter it.

If the former part of the alternative be true, then a legislative act contrary to the constitution is not law: if the latter part be true, then written constitutions are absurd attempts, on the part of the people, to limit a power in its own nature illimitable.

Certainly all those who have framed written constitutions contemplate them as forming the fundamental and paramount law of the nation, and consequently, the theory of every such government must be, that an act of the legislature, repugnant to the constitution, is void.

This theory is essentially attached to a written constitution and is, consequently, to be considered by this Court as one of the fundamental principles of our society. It is not, therefore, to be lost sight of in the further consideration of this subject.

If an act of the legislature repugnant to the constitution is void, does it, notwithstanding its invalidity, bind the courts and oblige them to give it effect? Or, in other words, though it be not law, does it constitute a rule as operative as if it was a law? This would be to overthrow in fact what was established in theory and would seem, at first view, an absurdity too gross to be insisted on. It shall, however, receive a more attentive consideration.

It is, emphatically, the province and duty of the Judicial Department to say what the law is. Those who apply the rule to particular cases must of necessity expound and interpret that rule. If two laws conflict with each other, the courts must decide on the operation of each. So if a law be in opposition to the constitution, if both the law and the constitution apply to a particular case, so that the court must either decide that case conformably to the law, disregarding the constitution, or conformably to the constitution, disregarding the law, the court must determine which of these conflicting rules governs the case. This is of the very essence of judicial duty. If, then, the courts are to regard the constitution, and the constitution is superior to any ordinary act of the legislature, the constitution, and not such ordinary act, must govern the case to which they both apply. . . .

The judicial power of the United States is extended to all cases arising under the constitution.

Could it be the intention of those who gave this power, to say that in using it the constitution should not be looked into? That a case arising under the constitution should be decided without examining the instrument under which it arises?

This is too extravagant to be maintained.

In some cases, then, the constitution must be looked into by the judges. And if they can open it at all, what part of it are they forbidden to read, or to obey?

There are many other parts of the constitution which serve to illustrate this subject. It is declared that "no tax or duty shall be laid on articles exported from any state." Suppose a duty on the export of cotton, of tobacco, or of flour; and a suit instituted to recover it. Ought judgment to be rendered in such a case? Ought the judges to close their eyes on the constitution, and only see the law?

The constitution declares that "no bill of attainder or ex post facto law shall be passed." If, however, such a bill should be passed, and a person should be prosecuted under it; must the court condemn to death those victims whom the constitution endeavors to preserve?

"No person," says the constitution, "shall be convicted of treason unless on the testimony of two witnesses to the same overt act, or on confession in open court." Here the language of the constitution is addressed especially to the courts. It prescribes, directly for them, a rule of evidence not to be departed from. If the legislature should change that rule, and declare one witness, or a confession out of court, sufficient for conviction, must the constitutional principle yield to the legislative act?

From these, and many other selections which might be made, it is apparent, that the framers of the constitution contemplated that instrument as a rule for the government of courts, as well as of the legislature. Why otherwise does it direct the judges to take an oath to support it? This oath certainly applies, in an especial manner, to their conduct in their official character. How immoral to impose it on them, if they were to be used as the instruments, and the knowing instruments, for violating what they swear to support!

The oath of office, too, imposed by the legislature, is completely demonstrative of the legislative opinion on this subject. It is in these words: "I do solemnly swear that I will administer justice without respect to persons, and do equal right to the poor and to the rich; and that I will faithfully and impartially discharge all the duties incumbent on me as _____, according to the best of my abilities and understanding, agreeably to the constitution, and laws of the United States." Why does a Judge swear to discharge his duties agreeably to the constitution of the United States, if that constitution forms no rule for his government? If it is closed upon him, and cannot be inspected by him?

If such be the real state of things, this is worse than solemn mockery. To prescribe, or to take this oath, becomes equally a crime.

It is also not entirely unworthy of observation that in declaring what shall be the supreme law of the land, the constitution itself is first mentioned; and not the laws of the United States generally, but those only which shall be made in pursuance of the constitution, have that rank.

Thus, the particular phraseology of the constitution of the United States confirms and strengthens the principle, supposed to be essential to all written constitutions, that a law repugnant to the constitution is void; and that courts, as well as other departments, are bound by that instrument.

The rule must be discharged.

44 THOMAS JEFFERSON

FROM *"The Roots of Democracy"* (1816)

At the birth of our republic . . . we imagined everything republican which was not monarchy. We had not yet penetrated to the mother principle, that "governments are republican only in proportion as they embody the will of their people and execute it." Hence, our first constitutions had really no leading principle in them. But experience and reflection have but more and more confirmed me in the particular importance of the equal representation then proposed. . . .

Where, then, is our republicanism to be found? Not in our Constitution certainly, but merely in the spirit of our people. That would oblige even a despot to govern us republicanly. Owing to this spirit, and to nothing in the form of our Constitution, all things have gone well. But this fact, so triumphantly misquoted by the enemies of reformation, is not the fruit of our Constitution but has prevailed in spite of it. Our functionaries have done well, because generally honest men. If any were not so, they feared to show it. . . .

The true foundation of republican government is the equal right of every citizen in his person and property and in their management. Try by this, as a tally, every provision of our Constitution and see if it hangs directly on the will of the people. Reduce your legislature to a convenient number for full but orderly discussion. Let every man who fights or pays exercise his just and equal right in their election. Submit them to approbation or rejection at short intervals. Let the executive be chosen in the same way, and for the same term, by those whose agent he is to be; and leave no screen of a council behind which to skulk from responsibility.

It has been thought that the people are not competent electors of judges learned in the law. But I do not know that this is true, and, if doubtful, we should follow principle. . . .

The organization of our county administrations may be thought more difficult. But follow principle and the knot unties itself. Divide the counties into wards of such size as that every citizen can attend, when called on, and act in person. Ascribe to them the government of their wards in all things relating to themselves exclusively. A justice chosen by themselves in each, a constable, a military company, a patrol, a school, the care of their own poor, their own portion of the public roads, the choice of one or more jurors to serve in some court, and the delivery, within their own wards, of their own votes for all elective officers of higher sphere will relieve the county administration of nearly all its business, will have it better done, and by making every citizen an acting member of the government, and in the offices nearest and most interesting to him, will attach him by his strongest feelings to the independence of his country and its republican Constitution.

The justices thus chosen by every ward would constitute the county court, would do its judiciary business, direct roads and bridges, levy county and poor rates, and administer all the matters of common interest to the whole county. These wards, called townships in New England, are the vital principle of their governments, and have proved themselves the wisest invention ever devised by the wit of man for the perfect exercise of self-government, and for its preservation.

We should thus marshal our government into: (1) the general federal republic for all concerns foreign and federal; (2) that of the state, for what relates to our own citizens exclusively; (3) the county republics, for the duties and concerns of the county; and (4) the ward republics, for the small and yet numerous and interesting concerns of the neighborhood. And in government, as well as in every other business of life, it is by division and subdivision of duties alone that all matters, great and small, can be managed to perfection. And the whole is cemented by giving to every citizen, personally, a part in the administration of the public affairs.

The sum of these amendments is: (1) general suffrage; (2) equal representation in the legislature; (3) an executive chosen by the people; (4) judges elective or amovable;

(5) justices, jurors, and sheriffs elective; (6) ward divisions; and (7) periodical amendments of the Constitution.

I have thrown out these, as loose heads of amendment, for consideration and correction; and their object is to secure self-government by the republicanism of our Constitution, as well as by the spirit of the people, and to nourish and perpetuate that spirit. I am not among those who fear the people. They, and not the rich, are our dependence for continued freedom.

And to preserve their independence, we must not let our rulers load us with perpetual debt. We must make our election between *economy and liberty*, or *profusion and servitude*. . . .

Some men look at constitutions with sanctimonious reverence and deem them, like the Ark of the Covenant, too sacred to be touched. They ascribe to the men of the preceding age a wisdom more than human and suppose what they did to be beyond amendment. I knew that age well; I belonged to it and labored with it. It deserved well of its country. It was very like the present, but without the experience of the present; and forty years of experience in government is worth a century of book reading. And this they would say themselves were they to rise from the dead. I am certainly not an advocate for frequent and untried changes in laws and constitutions. I think moderate imperfections had better be borne with because, when once known, we accommodate ourselves to them, and find practical means of correcting their ill effects.

But I know also that laws and institutions must go hand in hand with the progress of the human mind. As that becomes more developed, more enlightened, as new discoveries are made, new truths disclosed, and manners and opinions change with the change of circumstances, institutions must advance also, and keep pace with the times, We might as well require a man to wear still the coat which fitted him when a boy, as civilized society to remain ever under the regimen of their barbarous ancestors. . . .

Each generation is as independent of the one preceding as that was of all which had gone before. It has then, like them, a right to choose for itself the form of government it believes most promotive of its own happiness; consequently, to accommodate to the circumstances in which it finds itself, that received from its predecessors; and it is for the peace and good of mankind that a solemn opportunity of doing this every nineteen or twenty years should be provided by the Constitution, so that it may be handed on with periodical repairs from generation to generation, to the end of time, if anything human can so long endure.

45 ANDREW JACKSON

FROM *Proclamation to the People of South Carolina (1832)*

Here is a law of the United States, not even pretended to be unconstitutional, repealed by the authority of a small majority of the voters of a single state. Here is a provision of the Constitution which is solemnly abrogated by the same authority.

On such expositions and reasonings the ordinance grounds not only an assertion of the right to annul the laws of which it complains but to enforce it by a threat of seceding from the Union if any attempt is made to execute them.

This right to secede is deduced from the nature of the Constitution, which, they say, is a compact between sovereign states who have preserved their whole sovereignty and therefore are subject to no superior; that because they made the compact they can break it when in their opinion it has been departed from by the other states. Fallacious as this course of reasoning is, it enlists state pride and finds advocates in the honest prejudices of those who have not studied the nature of our government sufficiently to see the radical error on which it rests. . . .

The Constitution of the United States, then, forms a *government,* not a league; and whether it be formed by compact between the states or in any other manner, its character is the same. It is a government in which all the people are represented, which operates directly on the people individually, not upon the states; they retained all the power they did not grant. But each state, having expressly parted with so many powers as to constitute, jointly with the other states, a single nation, cannot, from that period, possess any right to secede, because such secession does not break a league but destroys the unity of a nation; and any injury to that unity is not only a breach which would result from the contravention of a compact but it is an offense against the whole Union.

To say that any state may at pleasure secede from the Union is to say that the United States are not a nation, because it would be a solecism to contend that any part of a nation might dissolve its connection with the other parts, to their injury or ruin, without committing any offense. Secession, like any other revolutionary act, may be morally justified by the extremity of oppression; but to call it a constitutional right is confounding the meaning of terms, and can only be done through gross error or to deceive those who are willing to assert a right, but would pause before they made a revolution or incur the penalties consequent on a failure.

Because the Union was formed by a compact, it is said the parties to that compact may, when they feel themselves aggrieved, depart from it; but it is precisely because it is a compact that they cannot. A compact is an agreement or binding obligation. It may by its terms have a sanction or penalty for its breach, or it may not. If it contains no sanction, it may be broken with no other consequence than moral guilt; if it have a sanction, then the breach incurs the designated or implied penalty. A league between independent nations generally has no sanction other than a moral one; or if it should contain a penalty, as there is no common superior it cannot be enforced. A government, on the contrary, always has a sanction, express or implied; and in our case it is both necessarily implied and expressly given. An attempt by force of arms to destroy a government is an offense, by whatever means the constitutional compact may have been formed; and such government has the right by the law of self-defense to pass acts for punishing the offender, unless that right is modified, restrained, or resumed by the constitutional act. In our system, although it is modified in the case of treason, yet authority is expressly given to pass all laws necessary to carry its powers into effect, and under this grant provision has been made for punishing acts which obstruct the due administration of the laws. . . .

Disunion by armed force is *treason.* Are you really ready to incur its guilt? If you are, on the heads of the instigators of the act be the dreadful consequences; on their heads be the dishonor, but on yours may fall the punishment. On your unhappy state will inevitably fall all the evils of the conflict you force upon the government of your

140

country. It cannot accede to the mad project of disunion, of which you would be the first victims. Its first magistrate cannot, if he would, avoid the performance of his duty. . . .

Fellow citizens of the United States, the threat of unhallowed disunion, the names of those once respected by whom it is uttered, the array of military force to support it, denote the approach of a crisis in our affairs on which the continuance of our unexampled prosperity, our political existence, and perhaps that of all free governments may depend. The conjuncture demanded a free, a full and explicit enunciation, not only of my intentions, but of my principles of action; and as the claim was asserted of a right by a state to annul the laws of the Union, and even to secede from it at pleasure, a frank exposition of my opinions in relation to the origin and form of our government and the construction I give to the instrument by which it was created seemed to be proper.

Having the fullest confidence in the justness of the legal and constitutional opinion of my duties which has been expressed, I rely with equal confidence on your undivided support in my determination to execute the laws, to preserve the Union by all constitutional means, to arrest, if possible, by moderate and firm measures the necessity of a recourse to force; and if it be the will of Heaven that the recurrence of its primeval curse on man for the shedding of a brother's blood should fall upon our land, that it be not called down by any offensive act on the part of the United States.

46 JOHN MARSHALL HARLAN

FROM *Dissenting Opinion in Plessy* v. *Ferguson (1896)*

By the Louisiana statute the validity of which is here involved, all railway companies (other than street-railroad companies) carry passengers in that state are required to have separate but equal accommodations for white and colored persons, "by providing two or more passenger coaches for each passenger train, or by dividing the passenger coaches by a partition so as to secure separate accommodations." Under this statute, no colored person is permitted to occupy a seat in a coach assigned to white persons; nor any white person to occupy a seat in a coach assigned to colored persons. The managers of the railroad are not allowed to exercise any discretion in the premises, but are required to assign each passenger to some coach or compartment set apart for the exclusive use of his race. If a passenger insists upon going into a coach or compartment not set apart for persons of his race, he is subject to be fined, or to be imprisoned in the parish jail. Penalties are prescribed for the refusal or neglect of the officers, directors, conductors, and employees of railroad companies to comply with the provisions of the act.

Only "nurses attending children of the other race" are excepted from the operation of the statute. No exception is made of colored attendants traveling with adults. A white man is not permitted to have his colored servant with him in the same coach, even if his condition of health requires the constant personal assistance of such servant. If a colored maid insists upon riding in the same coach with a white woman whom she has been employed to serve, and who may need her personal attention while traveling, she is subject to be fined or imprisoned for such an exhibition of zeal in the discharge of duty.

While there may be in Louisiana persons of different races who are not citizens of the United States, the words in the act "white and colored races" necessarily include all citizens of the United States of both races residing in that state. So that we have before us a state enactment that compels, under penalties, the separation of the two races in railroad passenger coaches, and makes it a crime for a citizen of either race to enter a coach that has been assigned to citizens of the other race.

Thus, the state regulates the use of a public highway by citizens of the United States solely upon the basis of race.

However apparent the injustice of such legislation may be, we have only to consider whether it is consistent with the constitution of the United States. . . .

In respect of civil rights, common to all citizens, the constitution of the United States does not, I think, permit any public authority to know the race of those entitled to be protected in the enjoyment of such rights. Every true man has pride of race, and under appropriate circumstances, when the rights of others, his equals before the law, are not to be affected, it is his privilege to express such pride and to take such action based upon it as to him seems proper. But I deny that any legislative body or judicial tribunal may have regard to the race of citizens when the civil rights of those citizens are involved. Indeed, such legislation as that here in question is inconsistent not only with that equality of rights which pertains to citizenship, national and state, but with the personal liberty enjoyed by every one within the United States.

The thirteenth amendment does not permit the withholding or the deprivation of any right necessarily inhering in freedom. It not only struck down the institution of slavery as previously existing in the United States, but it prevents the imposition of any burdens or disabilities that constitute badges of slavery or servitude. It decreed universal civil freedom in this country. This court has so adjudged. But, that amendment having been found inadequate to the protection of the rights of those who had been in slavery, it was followed by the fourteenth amendment, which added greatly to the dignity and glory of American citizenship, and to the security of personal liberty, by declaring that "all persons born or naturalized in the United States, and subject to the jurisdiction thereof, are citizens of the United States and of the state wherein they reside," and that "no state shall make or enforce any law which shall abridge the privileges or immunities of citizens of the United States; nor shall any state deprive any person of life, liberty or property without due process of law, nor deny to any person within its jurisdiction the equal protection of the laws." These two amendments, if enforced according to their true intent and meaning, will protect all the civil rights that pertain to freedom and citizenship. Finally, and to the end that no citizen should be denied, on account of his race, the privilege of participating in the political control of his country, it was declared by the fifteenth amendment that "the right of citizens of the United States to vote shall not be denied or abridged by the United States or by any state on account of race, color or previous condition of servitude."

These notable additions to the fundamental law were welcomed by the friends of liberty throughout the world. They removed the race line from our governmental systems. . . .

It was said in argument that the statute of Louisiana does not discriminate against either race, but prescribes a rule applicable alike to white and colored citizens. But this argument does not meet the difficulty. Every one knows that the statute in question had its origin in the purpose, not so much to exclude white persons from railroad cars occupied by blacks, as to exclude colored people from coaches occupied by or assigned to white persons. Railroad corporations of Louisiana did not make discrimination among whites in the matter of commodation for travelers. The thing to accomplish was, under the guise of giving equal accommodation for whites and blacks, to compel the latter to keep to themselves while traveling in railroad passenger coaches. No one would be so wanting in candor as to assert the contrary. The fundamental objection, therefore, to the statute, is that it interferes with the personal freedom of citizens. . . .

It is one thing for railroad carriers to furnish, or to be required by law to furnish, equal accommodations for all whom they are under a legal duty to carry. It is quite another thing for government to forbid citizens of the white and black races from traveling in the same public conveyance, and to punish officers of railroad companies for permitting persons of the two races to occupy the same passenger coach. If a state can prescribe, as a rule of civil conduct, that whites and blacks shall not travel as passengers in the same railroad coach, why may it not so regulate the use of the streets of its cities and towns as to compel white citizens to keep on one side of a street, and black citizens to keep on the other? Why may it not, upon like grounds, punish whites and blacks who ride together in street cars or in open vehicles on a public road or street? Why may it not require sheriffs to assign whites to one side of a court room, and blacks to the other? And why may it not also prohibit the commingling of the two races in the galleries of legislative halls or in public assemblages convened for the consideration of the political questions of the day? Further, if this statute of Louisiana is consistent with the personal liberty of citizens, why may not the state require the separation in railroad coaches of native and naturalized citizens of the United States, or of Protestants and Roman Catholics? . . .

The white race deems itself to be the dominant race in this country. And so it is, in prestige, in achievements, in education, in wealth, and in power. So, I doubt not, it will continue to be for all time, if it remains true to its great heritage, and holds fast to the principles of constitutional liberty. But in view of the constitution, in the eye of the law, there is in this country no superior, dominant, ruling class of citizens. There is no caste here. Our constitution is color-blind, and neither knows nor tolerates classes among citizens. In respect of civil rights, all citizens are equal before the law. The humblest is the peer of the most powerful. The law regards man as man, and takes no account of his surroundings or of his color when his civil rights as guaranteed by the supreme law of the land are involved. It is therefore to be regretted that this high tribunal, the final expositor of the fundamental law of the land, has reached the conclusion that it is competent for a state to regulate the enjoyment by citizens of their civil rights solely upon the basis of race.

In my opinion, the judgment this day rendered will, in time, prove to be quite as pernicious as the decision made by this tribunal in the Dred Scott Case.

It was adjudged in that case that the descendants of Africans who were imported into this country, and sold as slaves, were not included nor intended to be included under the word "citizens" in the constitution, and could not claim any of the rights and privileges which that instrument provided for and secured to citizens of the United States; that, at the time of the adoption of the constitution, they were "considered as a subordinate and inferior class of beings, who had been subjugated by the dominant race, and, whether emancipated or not, yet remained subject to their authority, and had no rights or privileges but such as those who held the power and the government might choose to grant them." The recent amendments of the constitution, it was supposed, had eradicated these principles from our institutions. But it seems that we have yet, in some of the states, a dominant race, – a superior class of citizens, – which assumes to regulate the enjoyment of civil rights, common to all citizens, upon the basis of race. The present decision, it may well be apprehended, will not only stimulate aggressions, more or less brutal and irritating, upon the admitted rights of colored citizens, but will encourage the belief that it is possible, by means of state enactments, to defeat the beneficent purposes which the people of the United States had in view when they adopted the recent amendments of the constitution, by one of which the blacks of this country were made citizens of the United States and of the states in which they respectively reside, and whose privileges and immunities, as citizens, the states are forbidden to abridge. Sixty millions of whites are in no danger from the presence here of eight millions of blacks. The destinies of the two races, in this country, are indissolubly linked together, and the interests of both require that the common government of all shall not permit the seeds of race hate to be planted under the sanction of law. What can more certainly arouse rce hate, what more certainly create and perpetuate a feeling of distrust between these races, than state enactments which, in fact, proceed on the ground that colored citizens are so inferior and degraded that they cannot be allowed to sit in public coaches occupied by white citizens? That, as all will admit, is the real meaning of such legislation as was enacted in Louisiana. . . .

The arbitrary separation of citizens, on the basis of race, while they are on a public highway, is a badge of servitude wholly inconsistent with the civil freedom and the equality before the law established by the constitution. It cannot be justified upon any legal grounds.

If evils will result from the commingling of the two races upon public highways established for the benefit of all, they will be infinitely less than those that will surely come from state legislation regulating the enjoyment of civil rights upon the basis of race. We boast of the freedom enjoyed by our people above all other peoples. But it is difficult to reconcile that boast with a state of the law which, practically, puts the brand of servitude and degradation upon a large class of our fellow citizens, – our equals before the law. The thin disguise of "equal" accommodations for passengers in railroad coaches will not mislead any one, nor atone for the wrong this day done. . . .

I am of opinion that the state of Louisiana is inconsistent with the personal liberty of citizens, white and black, in that state, and hostile to both the spirit and letter of the constitution of the United States. If laws of like character should be enacted in the several states of the Union, the effect would be in the highest degree mischievous. Slavery, as an institution tolerated by law, would, it is true, have disappeared from our country; but there would remain a power in the states, by sinister legislation, to interfere with the full enjoyment of the blessings of freedom, to regulate civil rights, common to all citizens, upon the basis of race, and to place in a condition of legal inferiority a large body of American citizens, now constituting a part of the political community, called the "People of the United States," for whom, and by whom through representatives, our government is administered. Such a system is inconsistent with the guaranty given by the constitution to each state of a republican form of government, and may be stricken down by congressional action, or by the courts in the discharge of their solemn duty to maintain the supreme law of the land, anything in the constitution or laws of any state to the contrary notwithstanding.

For the reason stated, I am constrained to withhold my assent from the opinion and judgment of the majority.

47 JOHN F. KENNEDY

First Inaugural Address (1961)

Vice President Johnson, Mr. Speaker, Mr. Chief Justice, President Eisenhower, Vice President Nixon, President Truman, Reverend Clergy, fellow citizens:

We observe today not a victory of party, but a celebration of freedom – symbolizing an end, as well as a beginning – signifying renewal, as well as change. For I have sworn before you and Almighty God the same solemn oath our forebears prescribed nearly a century and three-quarters ago.

The world is very different now. For man holds in his mortal hands the power to abolish all forms of human poverty and all forms of human life. And yet the same revolutionary beliefs for which our forebears fought are still at issue around the globe – the belief that the rights of man come not from the generosity of the state, but from the hand of God.

We dare not forget today that we are the heirs of that first revolution. Let the word go forth from this time and place, to friend and foe alike, that the torch has been passed to a new generation of Americans – born in this century, tempered by war, disciplined by a hard and bitter peace, proud of our ancient heritage, and unwilling to witness or permit the slow undoing of those human rights to which this nation has always been committed, and to which we are committed today at home and around the world.

Let every nation know, whether it wishes us well or ill, that we shall pay any price, bear any burden, meet any hardship, support any friend, oppose any foe, to assure the survival and the success of liberty.

This much we pledge – and more.

To those old allies whose cultural and spiritual origins we share, we pledge the loyalty of faithful friends. United there is little we cannot do in a host of cooperative ventures. Divided there is little we can do – for we dare not meet a powerful challenge at odds and split asunder.

To those new states whom we welcome to the ranks of the free, we pledge our word that one form of colonial control shall not have passed away merely to be replaced by a far more iron tyranny. We shall not always expect to find them supporting our view. But we shall always hope to find them strongly supporting their own freedom – and to remember that, in the past, those who foolishly sought power by riding the back of the tiger ended up inside.

To those people in the huts and villages of half the globe struggling to break the bonds of mass misery, we pledge our best efforts to help them help themselves, for whatever period is required – not because the Communists may be doing it, not because we seek their votes, but because it is right. If a free society cannot help the many who are poor, it cannot save the few who are rich.

To our sister republics south of our border, we offer a special pledge: to convert our good words into good deeds, in a new alliance for progress, to assist free men and free governments in casting off the chains of poverty. But this peaceful revolution of hope cannot become the prey of hostile powers. Let all our neighbors know that we shall join with them to oppose aggression or subversion anywhere in the Americas. And let every other power know that this hemisphere intends to remain the master of its own house.

To that world assembly of sovereign states, the United Nations, our last best hope in an age where the instruments of war have far outpaced the instruments of peace, we renew our pledge of support – to prevent it from becoming merely a forum for invective, to strengthen its shield of the new and the weak, and to enlarge the area in which its writ may run.

Finally, to those nations who would make themselves our adversary, we offer not a pledge but a request: that both sides begin anew the quest for peace, before the dark powers of destruction unleashed by science engulf all humanity in planned or accidental self-destruction.

We dare not tempt them with weakness. For only when our arms are sufficient beyond doubt can we be certain beyond doubt that they will never be employed.

But neither can two great and powerful groups of nations take comfort from our present course – both sides overburdened by the cost of modern weapons, both rightly alarmed by the steady spread of the deadly atom, yet both racing to alter that uncertain balance of terror that stays the hand of mankind's final war.

So let us begin anew – remembering on both sides that civility is not a sign of weakness, and sincerity is always subject to proof. Let us never negotiate out of fear, but let us never fear to negotiate.

Let both sides explore what problems unite us instead of belaboring those problems which divide us.

Let both sides, for the first time, formulate serious and precise proposals for the inspection and control of arms, and bring the absolute power to destroy other nations under the absolute control of all nations.

Let both sides seek to invoke the wonders of science instead of its terrors. Together let us explore the stars, conquer the deserts, eradicate disease, tap the ocean depths, and encourage the arts and commerce.

Let both sides unite to heed, in all corners of the earth, the command of Isaiah – to "undo the heavy burdens, and [to] let the oppressed go free."[1]

And, if a beach-head of cooperation may push back the jungle of suspicion, let both sides join in creating a new endeavor – not a new balance of power, but a new world of law – where the strong are just, and the weak secure, and the peace preserved.

All this will not be finished in the first one hundred days. Nor will it be finished in the first one thousand days; nor in the life of this Administration; nor even perhaps in our lifetime on this planet. But let us begin.

In your hands, my fellow citizens, more than mine, will rest the final success or failure of our course. Since this country was founded, each generation of Americans has been summoned to give testimony to its national loyalty. The graves of young Americans who answered the call to service surround the globe.

Now the trumpet summons us again – not as a call to bear arms, though arms we need – not as a call to battle, though embattled we are – but a call to bear the burden of a long twilight struggle, year in and year out, "rejoicing in hope; patient in tribulation,"[2] a struggle against the common enemies of man: tyranny, poverty, disease, and war itself.

Can we forge against these enemies a grand and global alliance, North and South, East and West, that can assure a more fruitful life for all mankind? Will you join in that historic effort?

In the long history of the world, only a few generations have been granted the role of defending freedom in its hour of maximum danger. I do not shrink from this responsibility – I welcome it. I do not believe that any of us would exchange places with any other people or any other generation. The energy, the faith, the devotion which we bring to this endeavor will light our country and all who serve it. And the glow from that fire can truly light the world.

And so, my fellow Americans, ask not what your country can do for you; ask what you can do for your country.

My fellow citizens of the world, ask not what America will do for you, but what together we can do for the freedom of man.

Finally, whether you are citizens of America or citizens of the world, ask of us here the same high standards of strength and sacrifice which we ask of you. With a good conscience our only sure reward, with history the final judge of our deeds, let us go forth to lead the land we love, asking His blessing and His help, but knowing that here on earth God's work must truly be our own.

1   Isaiah 58:6 (King James Version of the Holy Bible) (editors' note).
2   Romans 12:12 (King James Version of the Holy Bible) (editors' note).

48 JOE McGINNIS

FROM *The Selling of the President (1969)*

Chicago was the site of the first ten programmes that Nixon would do in states ranging from Massachusetts to Texas. The idea was to have him in the middle of a group of people, answering questions live. [Frank] Shakespeare and [Harry] Treleaven [directors of advertising in the Nixon presidential campaign] had developed the idea through the primaries and now had it sharpened to a point. Each show would run one hour. It would be live to provide suspense; there would be a studio audience [recruited by the local Republican organization] to cheer Nixon's answers and make it seem to home viewers that enthusiasm for his candidacy was all but uncontrollable;

and there would be an effort to achieve a conversational tone that would penetrate Nixon's stuffiness and drive out the displeasure he often seemed to feel when surrounded by other human beings instead of Bureau of the Budget reports. . . .

The set, now that it was finished, was impressive. There was a round blue-carpeted platform, six feet in diameter and eight inches high. Richard Nixon would stand on this and face the panel, which would be seated in a semicircle around him. Bleachers for the audience ranged out behind the panel chairs. Later, Roger Ailes [executive producer of Nixon's one-hour programmes] would think to call the whole effect "the arena concept" and bill Nixon as "the man in the arena." He got this from a Theodore Roosevelt quote which hung, framed, from a wall of his office in Philadelphia. It said something about how one man in the arena was worth ten, or a hundred, or a thousand carping critics. . . .

Three days later, Roger Ailes composed a memorandum that contained the details of his reaction to the show. He sent it to Shakespeare and Garment [directors of advertising]:

After completing the first one-hour program, I thought I would put a few general comments down on paper. . . .

I. The Look:

A. He [Nixon] looks good on his feet and shooting "in the round" gives dimension to him.
B. Standing adds to his "feel" of confidence and the viewers' "feel" of his confidence.
C. He still uses his arms a little too "predictably" and a little too often, but at this point it is better not to inhibit him.
D. He seems to be comfortable on his feet and even appears graceful and relaxed, i.e. hands on his hips or arms folded occasionally.
E. His eye contact is good with the panelists, but he should play a little more to the home audience via the head-on camera. I would like to talk to him about this.
F. We are still working on lightening up his eyes a bit, but this is not a major problem. This will be somewhat tougher in smaller studios, but don't worry, he will never look bad:
    1. I may lower the front two key spots a bit.
    2. I may try slightly whiter make-up on upper eyelids.
    3. I may lower the riser he stands on a couple of inches. . . .
I. An effort should be made to keep him in the sun occasionally to maintain a fairly constant level of healthy tan.
J. Generally, he had a very "Presidential" look and style – he smiles easily (and looks good doing it). He should continue to make lighter comments once in a while for pacing.

II. The Questions and Answers:

A. First, his opening remarks are good. He should, perhaps, be prepared with an optional cut in his closing remarks in case we get into time trouble getting off the air. I don't want to take a chance of missing the shots of the audience crowding around him at the end. Bud [Wilkinson] can specifically tell him exactly how much time he has to close.

B. In the panel briefing we should tell the panelists not to ask two-part questions. This slows down the overall pace of the show and makes it difficult for the viewer to remember and thus follow. Instead, the panelists should be instructed that they can continue a dialogue with Mr Nixon – ask two questions in a row to get the answers. . . .

On one answer from Warner Saunders [the Negro on the panel], he gave an unqualified "yes" and that was good. Whenever possible he should be that definite.

D. He still needs some memorable phrases to use in wrapping up certain points. I feel that I might be able to help in this area, but don't know if you want me to or if he would take suggestions from me on this. Maybe I could have a session with Price and Buchanan.

III. Staging:

A. The microphone cord needs to be dressed and looped to the side.

B. Bud Wilkinson felt there should be more women on the panel since over half the voters are women. Maybe combine a category, i.e. woman reporter or negro woman.

C. The panel was too large at eight. Maximum should be seven, six is still preferable to give more interaction.

D. Bud should be able to interject more often with some prepared lighter or pacing questions.

E. The family should be in the audience at every show Should I talk with them, Whitaker, or will you?

F. Political VIPs should be in the audience for every show. Nixon handles these introductions extremely well and they are good for reaction shots.

G. I am adding extenders to the zoom lens on all cameras to allow closer shooting for reactions.

IV. General:

A. The show got off to a slow start. Perhaps the opening could be made more exciting by:

    1. adding music or applause earlier. . . .

49 E. L. DOCTOROW

FROM *"A Citizen Reads the Constitution"* (1987)

Not including the amendments, it is approximately five thousand words long – about the length of a short story. It is an enigmatically dry, unemotional piece of work, tolling off in its monotone the structures and functions of government, the conditions and obligations of office, the limitations of powers, the means for redressing crimes and conducting commerce. It makes itself the supreme law of the land. It concludes with instructions on how it can amend itself, and undertakes to pay all the debts incurred by the states under its indigent parent, the Articles of Confederation.

It is no more scintillating as reading than I remember it to have been in Mrs. Brundage's seventh-grade civics class at Joseph H. Wade Junior High School. It is five thousand words but reads like fifty thousand. It lacks high rhetoric and shows not a trace of wit, as might be expected of the product of a committee of lawyers. It uses none of the tropes of literature to create empathetic states in the mind of the reader. It does not mean to persuade. It abhors metaphor as nature abhors a vacuum.

One's first reaction upon reading it is to rush for relief to an earlier American document:

> We hold these truths to be self-evident, that all men are created equal, that they are endowed by their Creator with certain unalienable Rights, that among these are Life, Liberty and the pursuit of Happiness. That to secure these rights, Governments are instituted among Men, deriving their just powers from the consent of the governed. That whenever any Form of Government becomes destructive of these ends, it is the Right of the People to alter or to abolish it, and to institute new Government.

That is the substantive diction of a single human mind – Thomas Jefferson's, as it happens – even as it speaks for all. It is engaged in the art of literary revolution, rewriting history, overthrowing divine claims to rule and genealogical hierarchies of human privilege as cruel frauds, defining human rights as universal and distributing the source and power of government to the people governed. It is the radical voice of national liberation, combative prose lifting its musketry of self-evident truths and firing away.

Surely I am not the only reader to wish that the Constitution could have been written out of something of the same spirit? Of course, I know instinctively that it could not, that statute writing in the hands of lawyers has its own demands, and those are presumably precision and clarity, which call for sentences bolted at all four corners with *wherein*s and *whereunder*s and *thereof*s and *therein*s and *notwithstanding the foregoing*s.

Still and all, an understanding of the Constitution must come of an assessment of its character as a composition, and it would serve us to explore further why it is the way it is. . . .

It is true but not sufficient to say that the Constitution reads as it does because it was written by a committee of lawyers. Something more is going on here. Every written composition has a voice, a persona, a character of presentation, whether by design of the author or not. The voice of the Constitution is a quiet voice. It does not rally us; it does not call on self-evident truths; it does not arm itself with philosophy or political principle; it does not argue, explain, condemn, excuse or justify. It is postrevolutionary. Not claiming righteousness, it is, however, suffused with rectitude. It is this way because it seeks standing in the world, the elevation of the unlawful acts of men – unlawful first because the British government has been overthrown, and second because the confederation of the states has been subverted – to the lawful standing of nationhood. All the *herein*s and *whereas*es and *thereof*s are not only legalisms;

150

they also happen to be the diction of the British Empire, the language of the deposed. Nothing has changed that much, the Constitution says, lying; we are nothing that you won't recognize.

But there is something more. The key verb of the text is *shall*, as in "All legislative powers herein granted shall be vested in a Congress of the United States which shall consist of a Senate and a House of Representatives," or "New States may be admitted by the Congress into this Union; but no new State shall be formed or erected within the jurisdiction of any other State." The Constitution does not explicitly concern itself with the grievances that brought it about. It is syntactically futuristic: it prescribes what is to come. It prophesies. Even today, living two hundred years into the prophecy, we read it and find it still ahead of us, still extending itself in time. The Constitution gives law and assumes for itself the power endlessly to give law. It ordains. In its articles and sections, one after another, it offers a ladder to heaven. It is cold, distant, remote as a voice from on high, self-authenticating.

Through most of history kings and their servitor churches did the ordaining, and always in the name of God. But here the people do it: "We the People . . . do ordain and establish this Constitution for the United States." And the word for God appears nowhere in the text. Heaven forbid! In fact, its very last stricture is that "no religious test shall ever be required as a qualification to any office or public trust under the United States."

The voice of the Constitution is the inescapably solemn self-consciousness of the people giving the law unto themselves. But since in the Judeo-Christian world of Western civilization all given law imitates God – God being the ultimate lawgiver – in affecting the transhuman voice of law, that dry monotone that disdains persuasion, the Constitution not only takes on the respectable sound of British statute, it more radically assumes the character of scripture.

The ordaining voice of the Constitution is scriptural, but in resolutely keeping the authority for its dominion in the public consent, it presents itself as the sacred text of secular humanism. . . .

Now, it is characteristic of any sacred text that it has beyond its literal instruction tremendous symbolic meaning for the people who live by it. Think of the Torah, the Koran, the Gospels. The sacred text dispenses not just social order but spiritual identity. And as the states each in its turn ratified the Constitution, usually not without vehement debate and wrangling, the public turned out in the streets of major cities for processions, festivities, with a fresh new sense of themselves and their future. . . .

Yet it is true also of sacred texts that when they create a spiritual community, they at the same time create a larger community of the excluded. The Philistines are excluded or the pagans or the unwashed. Even as the Constitution was establishing its sacred self in the general mind, it was still the work, the composition, of writers; and the writers were largely patrician, not working class. They tended to be well educated, wealthy, and not without self-interest. . . .

And so I find here in my reflections a recapitulation of the debate of American constitutional studies of the past two hundred years, in the same manner that ontogeny was once said to recapitulate phylogeny. Thus it was in the nineteenth century that historians such as George Bancroft celebrated the revolutionary nature of the Founding Fathers' work, praising them for having conceived of a republic of equal rights under law, constructed from the materials of the European Enlightenment but according to their own pragmatic Yankee design – a federalism of checks and balances that would withstand the worst buffetings of history, namely the Civil War, in the aftermath of which Bancroft happened to be writing.

Then in the early part of the twentieth century, when the worst excesses of American business were coming to light, one historian, Charles Beard, looked at old Treasury records and other documents and discovered enough to assert that the Fathers stood to gain personally from the way they put the thing together, at least their class did; that they were mostly wealthy men and lawyers; and that the celebrated system of checks and balances, instead of insuring a distribution of power and a democratic form of government, in fact could be seen as having been devised to control populist sentiment and prevent a true majoritarian politics from operating in American life at the expense of property rights. Madison had said as much, Beard claimed, in *Federalist* number 10, which he wrote to urge ratification. Beard's economic interpretation of the Constitution has ever since governed scholarly debate. At the end of the Depression a neo-Beardian, Merrill Jensen, looked again at the postrevolutionary period and came up with a thesis defending the Articles of Confederation as the true legal instrument of the Revolution, which, with modest amendments, could have effected the peace and order of the states with more democracy than a centralist government. In fact, he argued, there was no crisis under the Articles or danger of anarchy, except in the minds of the wealthy men who met in Philadelphia.

But countervailing studies appeared in the 1950s, the era of postwar conservatism, that showed Beard's research to be inadequate, asserting, for instance, that there were as many wealthy men of the framers' class who were against ratification as who were for it, or that men of power and influence tended to react according to the specific needs of their own states and localities, coastal or rural, rather than according to class.

And in the 1960s, the Kennedy years, a new argument appeared describing the Constitutional Convention above all as an exercise of democratic politics, a nationalist reform caucus that was genuinely patriotic, improvisational, and always aware that what it did must win popular approval if it was to become the law of the land.

In my citizen's self-instruction I embrace all of those interpretations. I believe all of them. I agree that something unprecedented and noble was created in Philadelphia; but that economic class self-interest was a large part of it; but that it was democratic and improvisational; but that it was, at the same time, something of a coup. I think all of those theories are true, simultaneously.

50 JOHN KENNETH GALBRAITH

"The American Presidency: Going the Way of the Blacksmith?" *(1988)*

Cambridge, Massachusetts –

Now that the US election and the ensuing discussion and recrimination are pleasantly in the past, there is satisfaction in finding one matter on which all observers are agreed: The 1988 presidential campaign set a new low in banality extending to unimaginative bad taste.

What is not commendable is the almost universal failure to see why the performance was so bad. It is that the presidency has become, by all past standards, a relatively unimportant job. Only from its past significance do its continuity, aura and interest come.

Three factors, all above dispute, have diminished the presidency. They are the exfoliation of great organizations, often referred to as bureaucracy; the fact that powerful controlling circumstances have taken over from presidential decision on foreign policy; and that they have done much the same on domestic policy.

The role of organization is the most obvious change. When Woodrow Wilson sat down at his typewriter to write a speech, as he is held to have done, one cannot doubt that he had a considerable effect on what was said.

Presidential speeches now come from a special speech-writing staff. This staff did not exist until the 1930s, when President Roosevelt, in what was thought a substantial innovation, acquired a small cadre of assistants, who were to have, it was promised, "a passion for anonymity." In the 1940 elections, the president did assemble a small group of speech writers, three or four in number, of whom I was one. When the speech was finally delivered, we listened ardently to the radio to see if any of our words had survived the presidential touch. Not many did.

The case carries on to policy. Wilson, we can safely assume, had a preeminent role in the identification and positioning of the Fourteen Points. Now each point would be the product of a task force of around 10 specialists and departmental bystanders, for a total of at least 140 persons. Only then would the president see the plan.

There is an inevitable tendency for power, in the presence of a larger organization, to pass down into the body of that organization. As the power of the president has passed down into organization, so has that of the cabinet officers. In these last years, for example, no one outside the immediate area of concern has known the name of the agriculture secretary.

Finally, there is the Pentagon. This has become a power unto itself, a power sufficiently great that neither candidate in the last election dreamed of saying anything that might seem to suggest that he was "soft on defense."

In much of his second term, President Reagan has rarely risked a press conference. This has been attributed, not wholly without reason, to an absence of acuity and knowledge. But, in fairness, more must be attributed to the fact that in many of the matters on which he would have been queried, he would have had no role at all.

As to foreign policy, the controlling circumstances to which presidential power is subservient are two. There is the specter of nuclear devastation, which neither capitalism nor communism would survive. But the reality has come to control. That reality carried Ronald Reagan from his undoubted pleasure in denouncing the evil empire to an unprecedented association with Mikhail Gorbachev. And it led to the INF Treaty, in a process that, for mutual survival, must continue.

The controlling force of circumstance has been no less compelling on other foreign policy issues. There is the determination of nations, great and small, to be free of superpower control or influence. There is also the now evident irrelevance of capitalism and communism in their developed form for much of the world.

In one of the more powerful educational exercises of all time, it was discovered that not even the most eloquent ideologue could explain the difference between capitalism and communism to the inhabitants of the Mekong Delta. So it has been, one judges, with the nomads of the mountains and deserts of Afghanistan.

It was open to past presidents to attempt intervention in Indochina, Central America, the Dominican Republic and Cuba. No more. Not even Nicaragua is available for such presidential decision. The most George Bush can hope for is another Grenada.

On domestic policy there is more scope for presidential initiative. But here, too, the great political battles of the past are in the past. The two notable revolutions of this century – that which brought the welfare state and that which gave the government macroeconomic responsibility for employment, price stability and economic growth, that is, the Keynesian revolution – were once within the sphere of presidential action. Both were accepted in the last election. Mr. Bush not only accepted the need for Keynesian deficit financing to sustain employment but, implicitly at least, went far beyond anything that Mr. Keynes would suggest.

The question remains as to why presidential contests generate so much excitement. The answer is, first of all, that thousands of press, television and radio operatives are involved and must justify moderately remunerative travel and employment in the only modern industry exempt from any question as to worker productivity. Not surprisingly, all say, even believe, that they are covering an event of decisive importance. There is also the strategic aspect of the contest. This has brought into existence a large number of political experts who are the source of nearly unlimited comment on the design for presenting and shaping the candidate's personality, guiding his commercials and disposing his money. These experts are greatly admired, perhaps compassionately so, for their public life in most cases is very brief. An electoral genius is someone who, having been on the winning side in one election, is about to lose the next.

Finally, there is, as it may be called, the Super Bowl syndrome. Those immediately participant apart, it makes no difference who wins a particular game. But that does not keep millions of people from taking a deep, even breathless interest in the outcome. So with the modern presidential election.

A desire for the job is understandable. The president continues to have a considerable ceremonial role. He enjoys a significant number of nonsalaried benefits. But the penetrating irrelevance of the modern contest is not going unnoticed. Voter turnout in November was the lowest since Calvin Coolidge defeated John W. Davis in 1924. This was at a time when, most historians will agree, the importance of the job was also at a very low ebb.

6

ECONOMY, ENTERPRISE, CLASS

Introduction	156
51 *Andrew Jackson* "The Power of the Moneyed Interests" (1837)	160
52 *William Graham Sumner* FROM "The Forgotten Man" (1883)	161
53 *Andrew Carnegie* FROM *The Gospel of Wealth* (1900)	162
54 *Sinclair Lewis* FROM *Babbitt* (1922)	170
55 *Franklin D. Roosevelt* "Organized Money" (1936)	172
56 *Lyndon B. Johnson* FROM "The War on Poverty" (1964)	173
57 *Studs Terkel* FROM "Mike Lefevre" (Interview with a Steel Mill Worker, 1974)	174
58 *Steven VanderStaay* "Hell" (1992)	176
59 *Newt Gingrich* "Replacing the Welfare State with an Opportunity Society" (1995)	178
60 *Barbara Ehrenreich* FROM *Nickel and Dimed: On (Not) Getting By in America* (2001)	180

Figure 6 Small group of poor in Lower East Side ca. 1890 – New York.
Photo by Jacob Riis © Bettmann/CORBIS

INTRODUCTION

"Capitalism," the historian Carl N. Degler once wrote, "came in the first ships."[1] Many of the colonies were established out of commercial motives. On the other hand, no matter how clever the New England Puritans were as tradesmen, their commercial instinct was usually balanced by a keen sense of religious duty. In the first decades of the nineteenth century, however, American business, secular and rapidly expanding, began to assert considerable power in its own right – so much so that the Democratic President Andrew Jackson, as he was about the leave the White House in 1837, felt urged to lash out against what he called the power of "the moneyed interests," in particular those of banks and monopolies (text 51).

A century later, during the Great Depression, President Franklin D. Roosevelt, heightened the temperature of the 1936 presidential campaign by striking out against "organized money" in a similar manner; against, in his words, "the old enemies of peace – business and financial monopoly, speculation, reckless banking, class antagonism, sectionalism, war profiteering" (text 55). Although FDR had probably done more than the American business world was ever willing to concede to safeguard American democracy and American business, he had long been the target of strong attacks from business, especially before the 1936 election. Consequently his response was predictable, but perhaps not the intensity of it. The clashes over welfare and social security in 1936 were not unlike the issues that are hotly debated in American politics today as well.

The increasingly visible social inequality that was created in the wake of the American industrial revolution and urbanization has had its champions as well as its critics. In an essay from 1883 entitled "The Forgotten Man" (excerpted in text 52), William Graham Sumner argues that destitution and dissipation should be seen not as society's responsibility but as nature's way of removing failures; similarly he sees government regulation of factories and labor conditions as a limitation of people's free choice of work place. Andrew Carnegie, well-known steel king of the Gilded Age, presents a more moderate *laissez-faire* philosophy in his book *The Gospel of Wealth*, but the influence of contemporary Social Darwinism (the idea that the fittest succeeded best in business as in life) is also strongly evident here. According to Carnegie (text 53), wealth is a burden that the rich must carry on behalf of those who are not clever or wise enough to make a fortune. In return, the rich should spend their fortunes for the benefit of mankind. In a way, this is a parallel to the late nineteenth-century colonial view that the white man had been saddled with the burden of civilizing the world's savages by means of colonization.

Carnegie's book nonetheless illustrates the fact that, at the end of the nineteenth century, the United States had become a society of two nations, a rich and a poor. The squalor of the big cities had, for instance, been amply demonstrated in both the prose and the photographs of Jacob Riis's *How the Other Half Lives: Studies among the Tenements of New York* (1890). At about the same time, the famous American sociologist Thorstein Veblen coined the phrase "conspicuous consumption" (1902). His criticism was directed at the practice of spending money lavishly on consumer goods. The issue was no longer whether America was a class society; it was instead whether this state of affairs was to be accepted as a "natural" result of the freedom of competition (as the Social Darwinists argued), or whether it was society's task to remedy such evils in order to ensure people the right to freedom (as reformers and muckraking journalists suggested). In the wake of the Wall Street Crash and the Great Depression, Franklin D. Roosevelt asserted the latter and helped develop the modern American welfare state of social security. Despite their increasing affluence during the late 1940s and the 1950s, however, the American people discovered at the outset of the 1960s (as they had in the 1890s and the 1930s) that a significant portion – one-quarter or one-fifth – of the population was poor. In his book *The Other America* (1962), a title reminiscent of Riis's work, Michael Harrington argued that the poor were caught in "a vicious circle of poverty," a poverty that had become "a culture, an institution, a way of life," and that there was "a language of the poor, a psychology of the poor, a world view of the poor."[2] Partly because it challenged traditional American conceptions of social mobility, Harrington's work caused strong political reverberations and helped trigger the "War on Poverty" that was launched by President Lyndon B. Johnson in a special message to Congress in 1964 (text 56).

The economic and social development in the United States in the twentieth century seemed to promise a new kind of classless society: a nation in which the great proportion of the population would become middle class. In the modern mass consumption society that emerged with explosive force in the 1920s in particular, the

157

economic and cultural hegemony of the middle classes became more pronounced than ever. In text 54, excerpts from Sinclair Lewis's novel *Babbitt* (1922), we see how its main character, a real estate broker named Babbitt, embraces the novelties and technological wonders of the consumer society as signs of his middle-class status and as means of asserting his increasing success.

As the white-collar service sector kept expanding and the proportion of industrial blue-collar workers in the labor force declined, many American social scientists in the latter half of the twentieth century felt that a traditional model of the class society had become outmoded and the European term "working class" itself irrelevant; they often grouped blue-collar industrial workers and white-collar non-professionals together in one class, "the lower middle class," indicative of the general American reluctance to think in terms of the traditional class divisions. Yet, as text 57 illustrates (a 1974 interview by Studs Terkel with a steel mill worker), such a grouping hides important social schisms within American society. In the interview the worker gives expression to a deep frustration with the Establishment, whether of owners, foremen, or union bosses – a strong resentment at being ignored and looked down upon in a country in which middle-class ideology reigns supreme. At the same time the interview reveals that class must be considered not merely in terms of hard facts such as income, occupation, gender, etc., but also in terms of soft criteria such as actual class identification and class consciousness. Divided loyalties characterize the steel mill worker's frame of mind; he feels a deep sense of alienation and anger while at the same time harboring middle-class aspirations for his own son. Like most cultural phenomena, class consciousness represents a mesh of conflicting and often contradictory inclinations – which is particularly noticeable in a nation in which an overwhelming majority classify themselves as belonging to the middle class.

In present-day America, where mass consumption, not least through the media, has made (upper) middle-class affluence extremely visible and insistent, it is hardly surprising that the poorest and most destitute groups have grown increasingly dejected and alienated, as may be seen from the excerpts below from Steven VanderStaay's interviews with homeless persons in 1992, here represented by a Puerto Rican woman ("Hell") (text 58). Riis's and Harrington's "two nations" (of the rich and the poor) continue to characterize the United States of the twenty-first century; some social scientists argue that the gap between the richest and the poorest, deeply connected with issues of race, ethnicity, and gender, is wider than ever before.

Despite or perhaps because of this, since the late 1960s there has been a growing disillusionment with the attempts of government programs to eradicate social inequality and destitution. At present many conservatives give voice to ideas that call to mind William Graham Sumner's discourse of the Forgotten Man, and argue that a certain unemployment rate must be tolerated in post-industrial capitalist society, thus revitalizing the Darwinist acceptance of the presence of an impoverished underclass as well as a rich overclass. References to a Silent Majority (under President Richard Nixon) or a Moral Majority (under George Bush, Sr. and Jr.) testify to the extent to which the situation of marginalized groups is not part of the main agenda of recent conservative administrations. Criticisms of the welfare state and the alleged failure of (liberal) government to deal with social inequality have been intensifying in the last few decades. A typical example is a book by Newt Gingrich, former Speaker of the

US House of Representatives (1995–99) entitled *To Renew America* (1995), in which he argues, in the words of one of his chapter headings, for "Replacing the Welfare State with an Opportunity Society" (excerpted in text 59). In his view, the welfare state is depriving all young Americans "of their God-given rights to life, liberty, and the pursuit of happiness."

However, according to a book of investigative journalism by Barbara Ehrenreich entitled *Nickel and Dimed: On (Not) Getting By in America* (2001), the above-mentioned "opportunity society" seems a long way off not only for the destitute, but for large groups of low-wage workers in the service industry, those that have often been called "the working poor" (see text 60). Working as a waitress in fast food restaurant ("Serving in Florida"), as a domestic cleaning maid ("Scrubbing in Maine"), and as a sales girl at Wal-Mart ("Selling in Minnesota") – largely non-unionized fields of work – she found that low-wage work was characterized by managerial authoritarianism, insufficient income, acute stress, and low self-esteem. As Ehrenreich ironically puts it:

> The "working poor," as they are approvingly termed, are in fact the major philanthropists of our society. They neglect their own children so that the children of others will be cared for; they live in substandard housing so that other homes will be shiny and perfect; they endure privation so that inflation will be low and stock prices high. To be a member of the working poor is to be an anonymous donor, a nameless benefactor, to everyone else.
>
> (p. 221)

1 Carl N. Degler, *Out of Our Past*, 3rd edn (New York: Harper Colophon Books, 1984), p. 2.
2 Michael Harrington, *The Other America: Poverty in the United States* (Baltimore, Md.: Penguin, 1962), pp. 21, 22, 23.

Questions and Topics

1 Compare and contrast the attitudes to business of Andrew Jackson and Franklin D. Roosevelt with those of William Graham Sumner and Andrew Carnegie.

2 Discuss in what ways the passages about Babbbit (in Sinclair Lewis's novel) and the interviews with Mike Lefevre (by Studs Terkel) and with "Hell" (by Steven VanderStaay) reflect issues of class belonging and class consciousness.

3 Social attitudes are often complex and contradictory. Analyze the interview with Mike Lefevre, steel mill worker, from this perspective.

4 What are the main arguments against the American welfare state as expressed by Newt Gingrich?

5 Discuss the depiction of low-wage waitressing in the excerpt from Barbara Ehrenreich's book *Nickel and Dimed*.

Suggestions for further reading

Bell, Daniel, *The Cultural Contradictions of Capitalism* (New York: HarperCollins, 1976, 1979)

Fussell, Paul, *Class: A Guide Through the American Status System* (New York: Simon & Schuster, 1992).

Lardner, James and David A. Smith, eds., *Inequality Matters: The Growing Economic Divide in America and Its Poisonous Consequences* (New York: The New Press, 2006).

Mills, C. Wright, *White Collar: The American Middle Classes* (London: Oxford University Press, [1951], 1956).

Potter, David M., *People of Plenty: Economic Abundance and the American Character* (Chicago: University of Chicago Press, 1954).

Warner, W. Lloyd, *Social Class in America: A Manual of Procedure for the Measurement of Social Status*, new edn with Marchia Meeker and Kenneth Ells (New York: Harper & Row, 1960).

51 ANDREW JACKSON

"The Power of the Moneyed Interests" (1837)

It is one of the serious evils of our present system of banking that it enables one class of society, and that by no means a numerous one, by its control over the currency to act injuriously upon the interests of all the others and to exercise more than its just proportion of influence in political affairs. The agricultural, the mechanical, and the laboring classes have little or no share in the direction of the great moneyed corporations; and from their habits and the nature of their pursuits, they are incapable of forming extensive combinations to act together with united force. Such concert of action may sometimes be produced in a single city or in a small district of country by means of personal communications with each other; but they have no regular or active correspondence with those who are engaged in similar pursuits in distant places. They have but little patronage to give to the press and exercise but a small share of influence over it; they have no crowd of dependents above them who hope to grow rich without labor by their countenance and favor and who are, therefore, always ready to exercise their wishes.

The planter, the farmer, the mechanic, and the laborer all know that their success depends upon their own industry and economy and that they must not expect to become suddenly rich by the fruits of their toil. Yet these classes of society form the great body of the people of the United States; they are the bone and sinew of the country; men who love liberty and desire nothing but equal rights and equal laws and who, moreover, hold the great mass of our national wealth, although it is distributed in moderate amounts among the millions of freemen who possess it. But, with overwhelming numbers and wealth on their side, they are in constant danger of losing their fair influence in the government, and with difficulty maintain their just rights against the incessant efforts daily made to encroach upon them.

The mischief springs from the power which the moneyed interest derives from a paper currency which they are able to control; from the multitude of corporations with exclusive privileges which they have succeeded in obtaining in the different states and which are employed altogether for their benefit; and unless you become more watchful in your states and check this spirit of monopoly and thirst for exclusive privileges, you will, in the end, find that the most important powers of government have been given or bartered away, and the control over your dearest interests has passed into the hands of these corporations.

The paper money system and its natural associates, monopoly and exclusive privileges, have already struck their roots deep in the soil; and it will require all your efforts to check its further growth and to eradicate the evil. The men who profit by the abuses and desire to perpetuate them will continue to besiege the halls of legislation in the general government as well as in the states and will seek, by every artifice, to mislead and deceive the public servants. It is to yourselves that you must look for safety and the means of guarding and perpetuating your free institutions. In your hands is rightfully placed the sovereignty of the country and to you everyone placed in authority is ultimately responsible. It is always in your power to see that the wishes of the people are carried into faithful execution, and their will, when once made known, must sooner or later be obeyed. And while the people remain, as I trust they ever will, uncorrupted and incorruptible and continue watchful and jealous of their rights, the government is safe, and the cause of freedom will continue to triumph over all its enemies.

But it will require steady and persevering exertions on your part to rid yourselves of the iniquities and mischiefs of the paper system and to check the spirit of monopoly and other abuses which have sprung up with it and of which it is the main support. So many interests are united to resist all reform on this subject that you must not hope the conflict will be a short one nor success easy. My humble efforts have not been spared during my administration of the government to restore the constitutional currency of gold and silver; and something, I trust, has been done toward the accomplishment of this most desirable object. But enough yet remains to require all your energy and perseverance. The power, however, is in your hands, and the remedy must and will be applied if you determine upon it.

52 WILLIAM GRAHAM SUMNER

FROM *"The Forgotten Man" (1883)*

When you see a drunkard in the gutter, you are disgusted, but you pity him. When a policeman comes and picks him up you are satisfied. You say that "society" has interfered to save the drunkard from perishing. Society is a fine word, and it saves us the trouble of thinking to say that society acts. The truth is that the policeman is paid by somebody, and when we talk about society we forget who it is that pays. It is the Forgotten Man again. It is the industrious workman going home from a hard day's work, whom you pass without noticing, who is mulcted of a percentage of his day's earnings to hire a policeman to save the drunkard from himself. All the public expenditure to prevent vice has the same effect. Vice is its own curse. If we let nature alone, she cures vice by the most frightful penalties. It may shock you to hear me say it, but when you get over the shock, it will do you good to think of it: a drunkard in the gutter is just where he ought to be. Nature is working away at him to get him out of the way, just as she sets up her processes of dissolution to remove whatever is a failure in its line. Gambling and less mentionable vices all cure themselves by the ruin and dissolution of their victims. Nine-tenths of our measures for preventing vice are really protective towards it, because they ward off the penalty. "Ward off," I say, and that is the usual way of looking at it; but is the penalty really annihilated? By no means. It is turned into police and court expenses and spread over those who have resisted vice. It is the Forgotten Man again who has been subjected to the penalty while our minds were full of the drunkards, spendthrifts, gamblers, and other victims of dissipation. Who is, then, the Forgotten Man? He is the clean, quiet, virtuous, domestic citizen, who pays his debts and his taxes and is never heard of out of his little circle. Yet who is there in the society of a civilized state who deserves to be remembered and considered by the legislator and stateman before this man?

Another class of cases is closely connected with this last. There is an apparently invincible prejudice in people's minds in favor of state regulation. All experience is against state regulation and in favor of liberty. The freer the civil institutions are, the more weak or mischievous state regulation is. The Prussian bureaucracy can do a score of things for the citizen which no governmental organ in the United States can do; and, conversely, if we want to be taken care of as Prussians and Frenchmen are, we must give up something of our personal liberty.

Now we have a great many well-intentioned people among us who believe that they are serving their country when they discuss plans for regulating the relations of employer and employee, or the sanitary regulations of dwellings, or the construction of factories, or the way to behave on Sunday, or what people ought not to eat or drink or smoke. All this is harmless enough and well enough as a basis of mutual encouragement and missionary enterprise, but it is almost always made a basis of legislation. The reformers . . . get factory acts and other acts passed regulating the relation of employers and employee and set armies of commissioners and inspectors traveling about to see to things, instead of using their efforts, if any are needed, to lead the free men to make their own conditions as to what kind of factory buildings they will work in, how many hours they will work, what they will do on Sunday and so on. The consequence is that men lose the true education in freedom which is needed to support free institutions. They are taught to rely on government officers and inspectors. The whole system of government inspectors is corrupting to free institutions. In England, the liberals used always to regard state regulation with suspicion, but since they have come into power, they plainly believe that state regulation is a good thing if *they* regulate – because, of course, they want to bring about good things. In this country each party takes turns, according as it is in or out, in supporting or denouncing the non-interference theory.

53 ANDREW CARNEGIE

FROM *The Gospel of Wealth (1900)*

The problem of our age is the proper administration of wealth, so that the ties of brotherhood may still bind together the rich and poor in harmonious relationship. The conditions of human life have not only been changed, but revolutionized, within the past few hundred years. In former days there was little difference between the dwelling, dress, food, and environment of the chief and those of his retainers. The

Indians are to-day where civilized man then was. When visiting the Sioux, I was led to the wigwam of the chief. It was just like the others in external appearance, and even within the difference was trifling between it and those of the poorest of his braves. The contrast between the palace of the millionaire and the cottage of the laborer with us to-day measures the change which has come with civilization.

This change, however, is not to be deplored, but welcomed as highly beneficial. It is well, nay, essential for the progress of the race, that the houses of some should be homes for all that is highest and best in literature and the arts, and for all the refinements of civilization, rather than that none should be so. Much better this great irregularity than universal squalor. Without wealth there can be no Maecenas. The "good old times" were not good old times. Neither master nor servant was as well situated then as today. A relapse to old conditions would be disastrous to both – not the least so to him who serves – and would sweep away civilization with it. But whether the change be for good or ill, it is upon us, beyond our power to alter, and therefore to be accepted and made the best of it. It is a waste of time to criticise the inevitable.

It is easy to see how the change has come. One illustration will serve for almost every phase of the cause. In the manufacture of products we have the whole story. It applies to all combinations of human industry, as stimulated and enlarged by the inventions of this scientific age. Formerly articles were manufactured at the domestic hearth or in small shops which formed part of the household. The master and his apprentices worked side by side, the latter living with the master, and therefore subject to the same conditions. When these apprentices rose to be masters, there was little or no change in their mode of life, and they, in turn, educated in the same routine succeeding apprentices. There was, substantially, social equality, and even political equality, for those engaged in industrial pursuits had then little or no political voice in the State.

But the inevitable result of such a mode of manufacture was crude articles at high prices. To-day the world obtains commodities of excellent quality at prices which even the generation preceding this would have deemed incredible. In the commercial world similar causes have produced similar results, and the race is benefited thereby. The poor enjoy what the rich could not before afford. What were the luxuries have become the necessaries of life. The laborer has now more comforts than the landlord had a few generations ago. The farmer has more luxuries than the landlord had, and is more richly clad and better housed. The landlord has books and pictures rarer, and appointments more artistic, than the King could then obtain.

The price we pay for this salutary change is, no doubt, great. We assemble thousands of operatives in the factory, in the mine, and in the counting-house, of whom the employer can know little or nothing, and to whom the employer is little better than a myth. All intercourse between them is at an end. Rigid Castes are formed, and, as usual, mutual ignorance breeds mutual distrust. Each Caste is without sympathy for the other, and ready to credit anything disparaging in regard to it. Under the law of competition, the employer of thousands is forced into the strictest economies, among which the rates paid to labor figure prominently, and often there is friction between the employer and the employed, between capital and labor, between rich and poor. Human society loses homogeneity.

163

The price which society pays for the law of competition, like the price it pays for cheap comforts and luxuries, is also great; but the advantages of this law are also greater still, for it is to this law that we owe our wonderful material development, which brings improved conditions in its train. But, whether the law be benign or not, we must say of it, as we say of the change in the conditions of men to which we have referred: It is here; we cannot evade it; no substitutes for it have been found; and while the law may be sometimes hard for the individual, it is best for the race, because it insures the survival of the fittest in every department. We accept and welcome therefore, as conditions to which we must accommodate ourselves, great inequality of environment, the concentration of business, industrial and commercial, in the hands of a few, and the law of competition between these, as being not only beneficial, but essential for the future progress of the race. Having accepted these, it follows that there must be great scope for the exercise of special ability in the merchant and in the manufacturer who has to conduct affairs upon a great scale. That this talent for organization and management is rare among men is proved by the fact that it invariably secures for its possessor enormous rewards, no matter where or under what laws or conditions. The experienced in affairs always rate the MAN whose services can be obtained as a partner as not only the first consideration, but such as to render the question of his capital scarcely worth considering, for such men soon create capital; while, without the special talent required, capital soon takes wings. Such men become interested in firms or corporations using millions; and estimating only simple interest to be made upon the capital invested, it is inevitable that their income must exceed their expenditures, and that they must accumulate wealth. Nor is there any middle ground which such men can occupy, because the great manufacturing or commercial concern whih does not earn at least interest upon its capital soon becomes bankrupt. It must either go forward or fall behind: to stand still is impossible. It is a condition essential for its successful operation that it should be thus far profitable, and even that, in addition to interest on capital, it should make profit. It is a law, as certain as any of the others named, that men possessed of this peculiar talent for affairs, under the free play of economic forces, must, of necessity, soon be in receipt of more revenue than can be judiciously expended upon themselves; and this law is as beneficial for the race as the others.

Objections to the foundations upon which society is based are not in order, because the condition of the race is better with these than it has been with any others which have been tried. Of the effect of any new substitutes proposed we cannot be sure. The Socialist or Anarchist who seeks to overturn present conditions is to be regarded as attacking the foundation upon which civilization itself rests, for civilization took its start from the day that the capable, industrious workman said to his incompetent and lazy fellow, "If thou dost not sow, thou shalt not reap," and thus ended primitive Communism by separating the drones from the bees. One who studies this subject will soon be brought face to face with the conclusion that upon the sacredness of property civilization itself depends – the right of the laborer to his hundred dollars in the savings bank, and equally the legal right of the millionaire to his millions. To these who propose to substitute Communism for this intense Individualism the answer, therefore, is: The race has tried that. All progress from that barbarous day to the present time has resulted from its displacement. Not evil, but good, has come to the race from the accumulation of wealth by those who have the ability and energy that produce it. But even if we admit for a moment that it might be better for the race to discard its present foundation, Individualism, – that it is a nobler ideal that man should labor, not for himself alone, but in and for a brotherhood of his fellows, and share with them all in common, realizing Swedenborg's idea of Heaven, where, as he says, the angels derive their happiness, not from laboring for self, but for each other, – even admit all this, and a sufficient answer is, This is not evolution, but revolution. It necessitates the changing of human nature itself, a work of aeons, even if it were good to change it, which we cannot know. It is not practicable in our day or in our age. Even if desirable theoretically, it belongs to another and long-succeeding sociological stratum. Our duty is with what is practicable now; with the next step possible in our day and generation. It is criminal to waste our energies in endeavoring to uproot, when all we can profitably or possibly accomplish is to bend the universal tree of humanity a little in the direction most favorable to the production of good fruit under existing circumstances. We might as well urge the destruction of the highest existing type of man because he failed to reach our ideal as favor the destruction of Individualism, Private Property, the Law of Accumulation of Wealth, and the Law of Competition; for these are the highest results of human experience, the soil in which society so far has produced the best fruit. Unequally or unjustly, perhaps, as these laws sometimes operate, and imperfect as they appear to the Idealist, they are, nevertheless, like the highest type of man, the best and most valuable of all that humanity has yet accomplished.

We start, then, with a condition of affairs under which the best interests of the race are promoted, but which inevitably gives wealth to the few. Thus far, accepting conditions as they exist, the situation can be surveyed and pronounced good. The question then arises, – and, if the foregoing be correct, it is the only question with which we have to deal, – What is the proper mode of administering wealth after the laws upon which civilization is founded have thrown it into the hands of the few? And it is of this great question that I believe I offer the true solution. It will be understood that *fortunes* are here spoken of, not moderate sums saved by many years of effort, the returns on which are required for the comfortable maintenance and education of families. This is not *wealth*, but only *competence* which it should be the aim of all to acquire.

There are but three modes in which surplus wealth can be disposed of. It can be left to the families of the decedents; or it can be bequeathed for public purposes; or, finally, it can be administered during their lives by its possessors. Under the first and second modes most of the wealth of the world that has reached the few has hitherto been applied. Let us in turn consider each of these modes. The first is the most injudicious. In monarchical countries, the estates and the greatest portion of the wealth are left to the first son, that the vanity of the parent may be gratified by the thought that his name and title are to descend to succeeding generations unimpaired. The condition of this class in Europe to-day teaches the futility of such hopes or ambitions. The successors have become impoverished through their follies or from the fall in the value of land. Even in Great Britain the strict law of entail has been found inadequate to maintain the status of an hereditary class. Its soil is rapidly passing into the hands of the stranger. Under republican institutions the division of property among the children is much fairer, but the question which forces itself upon thoughtful men in all lands is: Why should men leave great fortunes to their children? If this is done from affection, is it not misguided affection? Observation teaches that, generally speaking, it is not well for the children that they should be so burdened. Neither is it well for the state. Beyond providing for the wife and daughters moderate sources of income, and very moderate allowances indeed, if any, for the sons, men may well hesitate, for it is no longer questionable that great sums bequeathed oftener work more for the injury than for the good of the recipients. Wise men will soon conclude that, for the best interests of the members of their families and of the state, such bequests are an improper use of their means.

It is not suggested that men who have failed to educate their sons to earn a livelihood shall cast them adrift in poverty. If any man has seen fit to rear his sons with a view to their living idle lives, or, what is highly commendable, has instilled in them the sentiment that they are in a position to labor for public ends without reference to pecuniary considerations, then, of course, the duty of the parent is to see that such are provided for in *moderation*. There are instances of millionaires' sons unspoiled by wealth, who, being rich, still perform great services in the community. Such are the very salt of the earth, as valuable as, unfortunately, they are rare; still it is not the exception, but the rule, that men must regard, and, looking at the usual result of enormous sums conferred upon legatees, the thoughtful man must shortly say, "I would as soon leave to my son a curse as the almighty dollar," and admit to himself that it is not the welfare of the children, but family pride, which inspires these enormous legacies.

As to the second mode, that of leaving wealth at death for public uses, it may be said that this is only a means for the disposal of wealth, provided a man is content to wait until he is dead before it becomes of much good in the world. Knowledge of the results of legacies bequeathed is not calculated to inspire the brightest hopes of much posthumous good being accomplished. The cases are not few in which the real object sought by the testator is not attained, nor are they few in which his real wishes are thwarted. In many cases the bequests are so used as to become only monuments of his folly. It is well to remember that it requires the exercise of not less ability than that which acquired the wealth to use it so as to be really beneficial to the community. Besides this, it may fairly be said that no man is to be extolled for doing what he cannot help doing, nor is he to be thanked by the community to which he only leaves wealth at death. Men who leave vast sums in this way may fairly be thought men who would not have left it at all, had they been able to take it with them. The memories of such cannot be held in grateful remembrance, for there is no grace in their gifts. It is not to be wondered at that such bequests seem so generally to lack the blessing.

The growing disposition to tax more and more heavily large estates left at death is a cheering indication of the growth of a salutary change in public opinion. The State of Pennsylvania now takes – subject to some exceptions – one-tenth of the property left by its citizens. The budget presented in the British Parliament the other day proposes to increase the death-duties; and, most significant of all, the new tax is to be a graduated one. Of all forms of taxation, this seems the wisest. Men who continue hoarding great sums all their lives, the proper use of which for public ends would work good to the community, should be made to feel that the community, in the form of the state, cannot thus be deprived of its proper share. By taxing estates heavily at death the state marks its condemnation of the selfish millionaire's unworthy life.

It is desirable that nations should go much further in this direction. Indeed, it is difficult to set bounds to the share of a rich man's estate which should go at his death to the public through the agency of the state, and by all means such taxes should be graduated, beginning at nothing upon moderate sums to dependents, and increasing rapidly as the amounts swell, until of the millionaire's hoard, as of Shylock's, at least "The other half comes to the privy coffer of the state."

This policy would work powerfully to induce the rich man to attend to the administration of wealth during his life, which is the end that society should always have in view, as being that by far most fruitful for the people. Nor need it be feared that this policy would sap the root of enterprise and render men less anxious to accumulate, for to the class whose ambition it is to leave great fortunes and be talked about after their death, it will attract even more attention, and, indeed, be a somewhat nobler ambition to have enormous sums paid over to the state from their fortunes.

There remains, then, only one mode of using great fortunes; but in this we have the true antidote for the temporary unequal distribution of wealth, the reconciliation of the rich and the poor – a reign of harmony – another ideal, differing, indeed, from that of the Communist in requiring only the further evolution of existing conditions, not the total overthrow of our civilization. It is founded upon the present most intense individualism, and the race is projected to put it in practice by degrees whenever it pleases. Under its sway we shall have an ideal state, in which the surplus wealth of the few will become, in the best sense, the property of the many, because administered for the common good, and this wealth, passing through the hands of the few, can be made a much more potent force for the elevation of our race than if it had been distributed in small sums to the people themselves. Even the poorest can be made to see this, and to agree that great sums gathered by some of their fellow-citizens and spent for public purposes, from which the masses reap the principal benefit, are more valuable to them than if scattered among them through the course of many years in trifling amounts.

If we consider what results flow from the Cooper Institute, for instance, to the best portion of the race in New York not possessed of means, and compare these with those which would have arisen for the good of the masses from an equal sum distributed by Mr. Cooper in his lifetime in the form of wages, which is the highest form of distribution, being for work done and not for charity, we can form some estimate of the possibilities for the improvement of the race which lie embedded in the present law of the accumulation of wealth. Much of this sum, if distributed in small quantities among the people, would have been wasted in the indulgence of appetite, some of it in excess, and it may be doubted whether even the part put to the best use, that of adding to the comforts of the home, would have yielded results for the race, as a race, at all comparable to those which are flowing and are to flow from the Cooper Institute from generation to generation. Let the advocate of violent or radical change ponder well this thought.

We might even go so far as to take another instance, that of Mr. Tilden's bequest of five millions of dollars for a free library in the city of New York, but in referring to this one cannot help saying involuntarily, how much better if Mr. Tilden had devoted the last years of his own life to the proper administration of this immense sum; in which case neither legal contest nor any other cause of delay could have interfered with his aims. But let us assume that Mr. Tilden's millions finally become the means of giving to this city a noble public library, where the treasures of the world contained in books will be open to all forever, without money and without price. Considering the good of that part of the race which congregates in and around Manhattan Island, would its permanent benefit have been better promoted had these millions been allowed to circulate in small sums through the hands of the masses? Even the most strenuous advocate of Communism must entertain a doubt upon this subject. Most of those who think will probably entertain no doubt whatever.

Poor and restricted are our opportunities in this life; narrow our horizon; our best work most imperfect; but rich men should be thankful for one inestimable boon. They have it in their power during their lives to busy themselves in organizing benefactions from which the masses of their fellows will derive lasting advantage, and thus dignify their own lives. The highest life is probably to be reached, not by such imitation of the life of Christ as Count Tolstoi gives us, but, while animated by Christ's spirit, by recognizing the changed conditions of this age, and adopting modes of expressing this spirit suitable to the changed conditions under which we live; still laboring for the good of our fellows, which was the essence of his life and teaching, but laboring in a different manner.

This, then, is held to be the duty of the man of Wealth: First, to set an example of modest, unostentatious living, shunning display or extravagance; to provide moderately for the legitimate wants of those dependent upon him; and after doing so to consider all surplus revenues which come to him simply as trust funds, which he is called upon to administer, and strictly bound as a matter of duty to administer in the manner which, in his judgment, is best calculated to produce the most beneficial results for the community – the man of wealth thus becoming the mere agent and trustee for his poorer brethren, bringing to their service his superior wisdom, experience and ability to administer, doing for them better than they would or could do for themselves.

We are met here with the difficulty of determining what are moderate sums to leave to members of the family; what is modest, unostentatious living; what is the test of extravagance. There must be different standards for different conditions. The answer is that it is as impossible to name exact amounts or actions as it is to define good manners, good taste, or the rules of propriety; but, nevertheless, these are verities, well known although undefinable. Public sentiment is quick to know and to feel what offends these. So in the case of wealth. The rule in regard to good taste in the dress of men or women applies here. Whatever makes one conspicuous offends the canon. If any family be chiefly known for display, for extravagance in home, table, equipage, for enormous sums ostentatiously spent in any form upon itself, if these be its chief distinctions, we have no difficulty in estimating its nature or culture. So likewise in regard to the use or abuse of its surplus wealth, or to generous, freehanded cooperation in good public uses, or to unabated efforts to accumulate and hoard to the last, whether they administer or bequeath. The verdict rests with the best and most enlightened public sentiment. The community will surely judge and its judgments will not often be wrong.

The best uses to which surplus wealth can be put have already been indicated. Those who would administer wisely must, indeed, be wise, for one of the serious obstacles to the improvement of our race is indiscriminate charity. It were better for mankind that the millions of the rich were thrown in to the sea than so spent as to encourage the slothful, the drunken, the unworthy. Of every thousand dollars spent in so called charity to-day, it is probable that $950 is unwisely spent; so spent, indeed as to produce the very evils which it proposes to mitigate or cure. A well-known writer of philosophic books admitted the other day that he had given a quarter of a dollar to a man who approached him as he was coming to visit the house of his friend. He knew nothing of the habits of this beggar; knew not the use that would be made of this money, although he had every reason to suspect that it would be spent improperly. This man professed to be a disciple of Herbert Spencer; yet the quarter-dollar given that night will probably work more injury than all the money which its thoughtless donor will ever be able to give in true charity will do good. He only gratified his own feelings, saved himself from annoyance, – and this was probably one of the most selfish and very worst actions of his life, for in all respects he is most worthy.

In bestowing charity, the main consideration should be to help those who will help themselves; to provide part of the means by which those who desire to improve may do so; to give those who desire to use the aids by which they may rise; to assist, but rarely or never to do all. Neither the individual nor the race is improved by alms-giving. Those worthy of assistance, except in rare cases, seldom require assistance. The really valuable men of the race never do, except in cases of accident or sudden change. Every one has, of course, cases of individuals brought to his own knowledge where temporary assistance can do genuine good, and these he will not overlook. But the amount which can be wisely given by the individual for individuals is necessarily limited by his lack of knowledge of the circumstances connected with each. He is the only true reformer who is as careful and as anxious not to aid the unworthy as he is to aid the worthy, and, perhaps, even more so, for in alms-giving more injury is probably done by rewarding vice than by relieving virtue.

The rich man is thus almost restricted to following the examples of Peter Cooper, Enoch Pratt of Baltimore, Mr. Pratt of Brooklyn, Senator Stanford, and others, who know that the best means of benefiting the community is to place within its reach the ladders upon which the aspiring can rise – parks, and means of recreation, by which men are helped in body and mind; works of art, certain to give pleasure and improve the public taste, and public institutions of various kinds, which will improve the general condition of the people; – in this manner returning their surplus wealth to the mass of their fellows in the forms best calculated to do them lasting good.

Thus is the problem of Rich and Poor to be solved. The laws of accumulation will be left free; the laws of distribution free. Individualism will continue, but the millionaire will be but a trustee for the poor; intrusted for a season with a great part of the increased wealth of the community, but administering it for the community far better than it could or would have done for itself. The best minds will thus have reached a stage in the development of the race in which it is clearly seen that there is no mode of disposing of surplus wealth creditable to thoughtful and earnest men into whose hands it flows save by using it year by year for the general good. This day already dawns. But a little while, and although, without incurring the pity of their fellows, men may die sharers in great business enterprises from which their capital cannot be or has not been withdrawn, and is left chiefly at death for public uses, yet the man who dies leaving behind many millions of available wealth, which was his to administer during life, will pass away "unwept, unhonored, and unsung," no matter to what uses he leaves the dross which he cannot take with him. Of such as these the public verdict will then be: "The man who dies thus rich dies disgraced."

Such, in my opinion, is the true Gospel concerning Wealth, obedience to which is destined some day to solve the problem of the Rich and the Poor, and to bring "Peace on earth, among men Good-Will."

54 SINCLAIR LEWIS

FROM *Babbitt (1922)*

There was nothing of the giant in the aspect of the man who was beginning to awaken on the sleeping-porch of a Dutch Colonial house in that residential district of Zenith known as Floral Heights.

His name was George F. Babbitt. He was forty-six years old now, in April, 1920, and he made nothing in particular, neither butter nor shoes nor poetry, but he was nimble in the calling of selling houses for more than people could afford to pay. . . .

It was the best of nationally advertised and quantitatively produced alarm-clocks, with all modern attachments, including cathedral chime, intermittent alarm, and a phosphorescent dial. Babbitt was proud of being awakened by such a rich device. Socially it was almost as creditable as buying expensive cord tires. . . .

He creaked to his feet, groaning at the waves of pain which passed behind his eyeballs. Though he waited for their scorching recurrence, he looked blurrily out at the yard. It delighted him, as always; it was the neat yard of a successful business man of Zenith, that is, it was perfection, and made him also perfect. He regarded the corrugated iron garage. For the three-hundred-and-sixty-fifth time in a year he reflected, "No class to that tin shack. Have to build me a frame garage. But by golly it's the only thing on the place that isn't up-to-date!" While he stared he thought of a community garage for his acreage development, Glen Oriole. He stopped puffing and jiggling. His arms were akimbo. His petulant, sleep-swollen face was set in harder lines. He suddenly seemed capable, an official, a man to contrive, to direct, to get things done.

On the vigor of his idea he was carried down the hard, clean, unused-looking hall into the bathroom.

Though the house was not large it had, like all houses on Floral Heights, an altogether royal bathroom of porcelain and glazed tile and metal sleek as silver. The towel-rack was a rod of clear glass set in nickel. The tub was long enough for a Prussian Guard, and above the set bowl was a sensational exhibit of tooth-brush holder, shaving-brush holder, soap-dish, sponge-dish, and medicine-cabinet, so glittering and so ingenious that they resembled an electrical instrument-board. But the Babbitt whose god was Modern Appliances was not pleased. The air of the bathroom was thick with the smell of a heathen toothpaste. "Verona been at it again!

'Stead of sticking to Lilidol, like I've re-peat-ed-ly asked her, she's gone and gotten some confounded stinkum stuff that makes you sick!" . . .

Before he followed his wife, Babbitt stood at the westernmost window of their room. This residential settlement, Floral Heights, was on a rise; and though the center of the city was three miles away – Zenith had between three and four hundred thousand inhabitants now – he could see the top of the Second National Tower, an Indiana limestone building of thirty-five stories.

Its shining walls rose against April sky to a simple cornice like a streak of white fire. Integrity was in the tower, and decision. It bore its strength lightly as a tall soldier. As Babbitt stared, the nervousness was soothed from his face, his slack chin lifted in reverence. All he articulated was "That's one lovely sight!" but he was inspired by the rhythm of the city; his love of it renewed. He beheld the tower as a temple-spire of the religion of business, a faith passionate, exalted, surpassing common men; and as he clumped down to breakfast he whistled the ballad "Oh, by gee, by gosh, by jingo" as though it were a hymn melancholy and noble. . . .

The Lettish-Croat maid, a powerful woman, beat the dinner-gong.

The roast of beef, roasted potatoes, and string beans were excellent this evening and, after an adequate sketch of the day's progressive weather-states, his four-hundred-and-fifty-dollar fee, his lunch with Paul Riesling, and the proven merits of the new cigar-lighter, he was moved to a benign, "Sort o' thinking about buying a new car. Don't believe we'll get one till next year, but still, we might."

Verona, the older daughter, cried, "Oh, Dad, if you do, why don't you get a sedan? That would be perfectly slick! A closed car is so much more comfy than an open one."

"Well now, I don't know about that. I kind of like an open car. You get more fresh air that way."

"Oh, shoot, that's just because you never tried a sedan. Let's get one. It's got a lot more class," said Ted.

"A closed car does keep the clothes nicer," from Mrs. Babbitt; "You don't get your hair blown all to pieces," from Verona; "It's a lot sportier," from Ted; and from Tinka, the youngest, "Oh, let's have a sedan! Mary Ellen's father has got one." Ted wound up, "Oh, everybody's got a closed car now, except us!"

Babbitt faced them: "I guess you got nothing very terrible to complain about! Anyway, I don't keep a car just to enable you children to look like millionaires! And I like an open car, so you can put the top down on summer evenings and go out for a drive and get some good fresh air. Besides – A closed car costs more money."

"Aw, gee whiz, if the Doppelbraus can afford a closed car, I guess we can!" prodded Ted.

"Humph! I make eight thousand a year to his seven! But I don't blow it all in and waste it and throw it around, the way he does! Don't believe in this business of going and spending a whole lot of money to show off and –"

They went, with ardor and some thoroughness, into the matters of streamline bodies, hill-climbing power, wire wheels, chrome steel, ignition systems, and body colors. It was much more than a study of transportation. It was an aspiration for knightly rank. In the city of Zenith, in the barbarous twentieth century, a family's motor indicated its social rank as precisely as the grades of the peerage determined the rank of an English family – indeed, more precisely, considering the opinion of old county families upon newly created brewery barons and woolen-mill viscounts. The details of precedence were never officially determined. There was no court to decide whether the second son of a Pierce Arrow limousine should go in to dinner before the first son of a Buick roadster, but of their respective social importance there was no doubt; and where Babbitt as a boy had aspired to the presidency, his son Ted aspired to a Packard twin-six and an established position in the motored gentry.

55 FRANKLIN D. ROOSEVELT

"Organized Money" (1936)

For twelve years this Nation was afflicted with hear-nothing, see-nothing, do-nothing Government. The Nation looked to Government but the Government looked away. Nine mocking years with the golden calf and three long years of the scourge! Nine crazy years at the ticker and three long years in the breadlines! Nine mad years of mirage and three long years of despair! Powerful influences strive today to restore that kind of government with its doctrine that that Government is best which is most indifferent.

For nearly four years you have had an Administration which instead of twirling its thumbs has rolled up its sleeves. We will keep our sleeves rolled up.

We had to struggle with the old enemies of peace – business and financial monopoly, speculation, reckless banking, class antagonism, sectionalism, war profiteering.

They had begun to consider the Government of the United States as a mere appendage to their own affairs. We know now that Government by organized money is just as dangerous as Government by organized mob.

Never before in all our history have these forces been so united against one candidate as they stand today. They are unanimous in their hate for me – and I welcome their hatred.

I should like to have it said of my first Administration that in it the forces of selfishness and of lust for power met their match. I should like to have it said of my second Administration that in it these forces met their master.

The American people know from a four-year record that today there is only one entrance to the White House – by the front door. Since 4 March 1933, there has been only one pass-key to the White House. I have carried that key in my pocket. It is there tonight. So long as I am President, it will remain in my pocket.

Those who used to have pass-keys are not happy. Some of them are desperate. Only desperate men with their backs to the wall would descend so far below the level of decent citizenship as to foster the current pay-envelope campaign against America's working people. Only reckless men, heedless of consequences, would risk the disruption of the hope for a new peace between worker and employer by returning to the tactics of the labor spy.

Here is an amazing paradox! The very employers and politicians and publishers who talk most loudly of class antagonism and the destruction of the American system now undermine that system by this attempt to coerce the votes of the wage earners of this country. It is the 1936 version of the old threat to close down the factory or the office if a particular candidate does not win. It is an old strategy of tyrants to delude their victims into fighting their battles for them.

Every message in a pay envelope, even if it is the truth, is a command to vote according to the will of the employer. But this propaganda is worse – it is deceit.

They tell the worker his wage will be reduced by a contribution to some vague form of old-age insurance. They carefully conceal from him the fact that for every dollar of premium he pays for that insurance, the employer pays another dollar. That omission is deceit.

They carefully conceal from him the fact that under the federal law, he receives another insurance policy to help him if he loses his job, and that the premium of that policy is paid 100 percent by the employer and not one cent by the worker. They do not tell him that the insurance policy that is bought for him is far more favorable to him than any policy that any private insurance company could afford to issue. That omission is deceit.

They imply to him that he pays all the cost of both forms of insurance. They carefully conceal from him the fact that for every dollar put up by him his employer puts up three dollars – three for one. And that omission is deceit.

But they are guilty of more than deceit. When they imply that the reserves thus created against both these policies will be stolen by some future Congress, diverted to some wholly foreign purpose, they attack the integrity and honor of American Government itself. Those who suggest that, are already aliens to the spirit of American democracy. Let them emigrate and try their lot under some foreign flag in which they have more confidence.

The fraudulent nature of this attempt is well shown by the record of votes on the passage of the Social Security Act. In addition to an overwhelming majority of Democrats in both Houses, seventy-seven Republican Representatives voted for it and only eighteen against it and fifteen Republican Senators voted for it and only five against it. Where does this last-minute drive of the Republican leadership leave these Republican Representatives and Senators who helped enact this law?

I am sure the vast majority of law-abiding businessmen who are not parties to this propaganda fully appreciate the extent of the threat to honest business contained in this coercion.

I have expressed indignation at this form of campaigning and I am confident that the overwhelming majority of employers, workers and the general public share that indignation and will show it at the polls on Tuesday next.

56 LYNDON B. JOHNSON

FROM *"The War on Poverty" (1964)*

With the growth of our country has come opportunity for our people – opportunity to educate our children, to use our energies in productive work, to increase our leisure – opportunity for almost every American to hope that through work and talent he could create a better life for himself and his family.

The path forward has not been an easy one.

But we have never lost sight of our goal: an America in which every citizen shares all the opportunities of his society, in which every man has a chance to advance his welfare to the limit of his capacities.

We have come a long way toward this goal.

We still have a long way to go.

The distance which remains is the measure of the great unfinished work of our society.

To finish that work I have called for a national war on poverty. Our objective: total victory.

There are millions of Americans – one-fifth of our people – who have not shared in the abundance which has been granted to most of us, and on whom the gates of opportunity have been closed.

What does this poverty mean to those who endure it?

It means a daily struggle to secure the necessities for even a meager existence. It means that the abundance, the comforts, the opportunities they see all around them are beyond their grasp.

Worst of all, it means hopelessness for the young.

The young man or woman who grows up without a decent education, in a broken home, in a hostile and squalid environment, in ill health or in the face of racial injustice – that young man or woman is often trapped in a life of poverty.

He does not have the skills demanded by a complex society. He does not know how to acquire those skills. He faces a mounting sense of despair which drains initiative and ambition and energy. . . .

Our history has proved that each time we broaden the base of abundance, giving more people the chance to produce and consume, we create new industry, higher production, increased earnings and better income for all.

Giving new opportunity to those who have little will enrich the lives of all the rest.

Because it is right, because it is wise, and because, for the first time in our history, it is possible to conquer poverty, I submit for the consideration of the Congress and the country, the Economic Opportunity Act of 1964.

The Act does not merely expand old programs or improve what is already being done.

It charts a new course.

It strikes at the causes, not just the consequences of poverty.

It can be a milestone in our 180-year search for a better life for our people.

57 STUDS TERKEL

FROM *"Mike Lefevre" (Interview with a Steel Mill Worker, 1974)*

I'm a dying breed. A laborer. Strictly muscle work . . . pick it up, put it down, pick it up, put it down. We handle between forty and fifty thousand pounds of steel a day. (Laughs) I know this is hard to believe – from four hundred pounds to three- and four-pound pieces. It's dying.

You can't take pride any more. You remember when a guy could point to a house he built, how many logs he stacked. He built it and he was proud of it. I don't really think I could be proud if a contractor built a home for me. I would be tempted to get in there and kick the carpenter in the ass (laughs), and take the saw away from him. 'Cause I would have to be part of it, you know.

It's hard to take pride in a bridge you're never gonna cross, in a door you're never gonna open. You're mass-producing things and you never see the end result of it. (Muses) I worked for a trucker one time. And I got this tiny satisfaction when I loaded a truck. At least I could see the truck depart loaded. In a steel mill, forget it. You don't see where nothing goes.

I got chewed out by my foreman once. He said, "Mike, you're a good worker but you have a bad attitude." My attitude is that I don't get excited about my job. I do my work but I don't say whoopee-doo. The day I get excited about my job is the day I go to a head shrinker. How are you gonna get excited about pullin' steel? How are you gonna get excited when you're tired and want to sit down?

It's not just the work. Somebody built the pyramids. Somebody's going to build something. Pyramids, Empire State building – these things just don't happen. There's hard work behind it. I would like to see a building, say, the Empire State, I would like to see on one side of it a foot-wide strip from top to bottom with the name of every bricklayer, the name of every electrician, with all the names. So when a guy walked by, he could take his son and say, "See, that's me over there on the forty-fifth floor. I put the steel beam in." Picasso can point to a painting. What can I point to? A writer can point to a book. Everybody should have something to point to.

It's the not-recognition by other people. To say a woman is just a housewife is degrading, right? Okay. *Just* a housewife. It's also degrading to say *just* a laborer. The difference is that a man goes out and maybe gets smashed.

When I was single, I could quit, just split. I wandered all over the country. You worked just enough to get a poke, money in your pocket. Now I'm married and I got two kids . . . (trails off). I worked on a truck dock one time and I was single. The foreman came over and he grabbed my shoulder, kind of gave me a shove. I punched him and knocked him off the dock. I said, "Leave me alone. I'm doing my work, just stay away from me, just don't give me the with-the-hands business."

Hell, if you whip a damn mule he might kick you. Stay out of my way, that's all. Working is bad enough, don't bug me. I would rather work my ass off for eight hours a day with nobody watching me than five minutes with a guy watching me. Who you gonna sock? You can't sock General Motors, you can't sock anybody in Washington, you can't sock a system.

A mule, an old mule, that's the way I feel. Oh yeah. See. (Shows black and blue marks on arms and legs, burns). You know what I heard from more than one guy at work? "If my kid wants to work in a factory, I am going to kick the hell out of him." I want my kid to be an effete snob. Yeah, mm-hmm. (Laughs.) I want him to be able to quote Walt Whitman, to be proud of it. . . .

Oh yeah, I daydream. I fantasize about a sexy blonde in Miami who's got my union dues. (Laughs.) I think of the head of the union the way I think of the head of my company. Living it up. I think of February in Miami. Warm weather, a place to lay in. When I hear a college kid say, "I'm oppressed." I don't believe him. You know what I'd like to do for one year? Live like a college kid. Just for one year. I'd love to. Wow!

(Whispers) Wow! Sports car! Marijuana! (Laughs.) Wild, sexy broads. I'd love that, hell yes, I would.

Somebody has to do this work. If my kid ever goes to college, I just want him to have a little respect, to realize that his dad is one of those somebodies. This is why even on – (muses) yeah. I guess, sure – on the black thing . . . (Sighs heavily.) I can't really hate the colored fella that's working with me all day. The black intellectual I got no respect for. The white intellectual I got no use for. I got no use for the black militant who's gonna scream three hundred years of slavery to me while I'm busting my ass. You know what I mean? (Laughs.) I have one answer for that guy: go see Rockefeller. See Harriman. Don't bother me. We're in the same cotton field. So just don't bug me. (Laughs). . . .

This is gonna sound square, but my kid is my imprint. He's my freedom. There's a line in one of Hemingway's books. I think it's from *For Whom the Bell Tolls*. They're behind the enemy lines, somewhere in Spain, and she's pregnant. She wants to stay with him. He tells her no. He says, "if you die, I die," knowing he's gonna die. But if you go, I go. Know what I mean? The mystics call it the brass bowl. Continuum. You know what I mean? This is why I work. Every time I see a young guy walk by with a shirt and tie and dressed up real sharp, I'm lookin' at my kid, you know? That's it.

58 STEVEN VANDERSTAAY

"Hell" (1992)

Philadelphia, Pennsylvania

Tough, pleasant, opinionated, Hell limps as she walks. She wears a sweatshirt and cut-off shorts that reveal a row of livid red scars encircling her thigh. Hell is Puerto Rican and 28 years old.

I was in a couple of shelters and any shelter I was in, it was dirty. We had cockroaches the size of mice. I'm not crazy, I'm serious. I wouldn't lie. And the food . . . and violence. There's a whole lot of violence, a whole lot of it. It's like, if you don't like to fight I'd advise you don't go.

If the shelters were any better a lot of people would go to them. But they're not any good. You know, you don't get any respect. It's like you're here under martial law. And it's hard.

If you choose not to go to a shelter and you're just livin' on the street, then you have to worry about . . . well, a woman if she's by herself has to worry about being raped and beat up, and having any change she might have panhandled or whatever taken from her – you know, along with her mentality and her brain. They're gone too. Because it's just too hard. Sleepin' on the sidewalk hard.

But you still have the problem of showering, trying to keep clean. And sleeping. Because downtown you're not allowed to sleep anywhere, men or women. The cops will chase you all over the city, and you just be trying to take a nap, trying to go to sleep. You be forced to sleep places like underground with the subway system.

You get to know the route of the trains by heart 'cause you hear them all the time. And it's hard, it really is. It's real hard. You have to be strong if you're going to be homeless.

Like this girl Diane, she got busted in the head. She gets beat up by her boyfriend, her body gets taken advantage of. They call her Dirty Diane because, well, she really don't take care of her monthly thing, just lets it dribble down her leg. Maybe she do that 'cause then nobody'll bother her. I don't know. She been put in the hospital about three or four times for her mental problems. She just don't care anymore.

Hell has brown hair, round, dark eyes, and a hearty, rasping laugh.

It was my fault I dropped out, I know it was. Things wasn't right at home when I was growing up. You know, things wasn't going right. If your home life is tough you just, you lose interest in the things that are going to make you into a better person. Like your diploma; I lost interest in that and in going to college. I lost interest in my dreams.

My mom had emotional problems, some type of mental disability, and drug addiction and alcoholism on top of it. And everything that went wrong in her love life, or home life, or anything else, was my fault.

When I left home I was put into different foster homes. But they had their own children and their children were great and I wasn't shit. So I had to – I kept running away from home and everything. And nothing went right.

I was strong, that's all I had. I walked into my own world and now we're doing good. Spain [her partner] and me, we're sort of happy together most of the time. I mean like I get tired of seeing his face every day [she laughs]. I do, and he gets tired of seeing me. He hates the way I wake up in the morning. He says I wake up evil. You know, I figure I'm sleeping, it's peaceful, I don't have to think about anything – no problems, no nothing. And when I wake up, boom! There's our problems all over again. So I wake up cussing him out. 'Cause he's there. If he didn't love me he wouldn't be there.

See I work for myself. We've been homeless – I've slept in shelters with cockroaches you wouldn't believe, I've slept in the streets, the subways, all over. It's been tough, especially if you're a woman. But we have a home now because I showed a friend of mine this abandoned building that I used to rent a room in. He went downtown and he's paying back taxes on it. Since I showed him where it was he lets us stay in it. We did electrical work, put new locks on the doors, new glass in the windows. We've worked hard there.

I have a daughter, she's spunky. She failed first grade, but she's going to pass this year though. Because I did get one good foster parent when I was growing up and she's taking care of my daughter for me. My son, he's two years. About like this [she holds her hand out from her waist]. We call him "He Man." He's big. He stays with his daddy now, while I get the plumbing in my house. When we get the plumbing hooked up then he's going to come stay with me.

For food and stuff we get by panhandling. You know, where people ask people for their spare change? I do that. I do that when I can't get work. I figure it's better than begging for handouts in a dirty shelter or going out here and sticking up somebody, or robbing somebody's store. When panhandling's illegal it's tough, the cops push you along.

And I get robbed as it is; I was robbed the other day of what money and food stamps I had. That left me broke and hungry, and so I had to panhandle.

It keeps crime down, plus it keeps a little money in my pocket. It feeds me on the weekends when the soup kitchens aren't open, and it buys my cigarettes for me. And if I want a beer I buy myself a beer. I'm not robbin' nobody, 'cause I been to jail too. I spent ten months in jail when I was 16. In a woman's prison, you know. That was hard. It was; that was very hard. Most everyone downtown's been in jail at one time or another.

I don't know whose fault that is, it all depends on what they get arrested for. You know, if they get arrested for sleeping in a public area, I call it society's fault. If they get arrested for beatin' up somebody, it's their fault. If they had a bad childhood and threw away all their chances and got arrested for stealin' something, I guess it's their fault though society sure didn't make it any easier for them.

It all depends on what color you are too. The darker you are, the better chance you got of being arrested. I'm Puerto Rican, my dad's Puerto Rican and my mom's a Chicano. Puerto Ricans come in all colors. A lot of people think I'm white. They say, "What are you doing here?" They look at my man and think he's black. He's every bit Puerto Rican too.

Oh yeah, one last thing. I'm Hell; that's my name. My mother called me that.

59 NEWT GINGRICH

"Replacing the Welfare State with an Opportunity Society" (1995)

The greatest moral imperative we face is replacing the welfare state with an opportunity society. For every day that we allow the current conditions to continue, we are condemning the poor – and particularly poor children – to being deprived of their basic rights as Americans. The welfare state reduces the poor from citizens to clients. It breaks up families, minimizes work incentives, blocks people from saving and acquiring property, and overshadows dreams of a promised future with a present despair born of poverty, violence, and hopelessness.

When a welfare mother in Wisconsin can be punished for sewing her daughter's clothing and saving on food stamps so she can set aside three thousand dollars for her daughter's education, you know there is something wrong.

When a woman who sells candy out of her apartment in a public housing project cannot open a store because she would lose her subsidized rent and health care and end up paying in taxes and lost benefits all she earned in profit, you know there is something wrong.

Gary Franks, congressman from Connecticut, tells of going into grade schools and asking young children what they hope to be when they grow up. Basketball players, football players, and baseball players are the three answers, in that order. What if you can't be an athlete? he then asks. They have no answer. It is beyond the experience of these children to consider becoming a lawyer or an accountant or a businessman. The public housing children, no matter what their ethnic backgrounds, have simply no conception of the world of everyday work. Clearly something is wrong.

Charlie Rangel, the senior congressman from Harlem, asked me to imagine what it would be like to visit a first or second-grade classroom and realize that every fourth boy would be dead or in jail before he was twenty-five years old. As I think of my three nephews, Charlie's comment drives home to me the despair and rage at the heart of any black leader as he looks at the lost future of a generation of poor children. Clearly something is wrong.

The defenders of the status quo should be ashamed of themselves. The current system has trapped and ruined a whole generation while claiming to be compassionate. The burden of proof is not on the people who want to change welfare. It is on those who would defend a system that has clearly failed at incalculable human cost.

Consider the facts. Welfare spending is now [1995] $305 billion a year. Since 1965 we have spent $5 trillion on welfare – more than the cost of winning World War II. Yet despite this massive effort, conditions in most poor communities have grown measurably worse. Since 1970 the number of children living in poverty has increased by 40 percent. Since 1965 the juvenile arrest rate for violent crimes has tripled. Since 1960 the number of unmarried pregnant teenage girls has nearly doubled and teen suicide has more than tripled. As welfare spending increased since 1960, it has exactly paralleled the rise in births outside of marriage. On a graph, the two lines move together like a pair of railroad tracks. The more we spend to alleviate poverty, the more we assure that the next generation will almost certainly grow up in poverty. Clearly something is profoundly wrong.

We owe it to all young Americans in every neighborhood to save them from a system that is depriving them of their God-given rights to life, liberty, and the pursuit of happiness. There can't be true liberty while they are trapped in a welfare bureaucracy. There can't be any pursuit of happiness when they are not allowed to buy property or accumulate savings. And there can't be any reasonable right to a long life in an environment that is saturated with pimps, prostitutes, drug dealers, and violence.

Make no mistake: replacing the welfare state will not be an easy job. It will not work simply to replace one or two elements while leaving everything else intact. It will be necessary to think through the entire process before we begin.

Replacing the welfare state with an opportunity society will require eight major changes, which need to be undertaken simultaneously. Trying to change only one or two at a time will leave people trapped in the old order. We have an obligation to begin improving the lives of the poor from day one.

When people tell me I am intense on this issue, I ask them to imagine that their children were the ones dying on the evening news and then tell me how intense they would be to save their own children's lives. That is how intense we should all be.

One of the encouraging developments of the last few years has been that a lot of truly caring, intelligent people have spent a lot of time thinking about the tragedy of modern welfare systems. As a result, we now have a fairly good idea of what works and what doesn't. The eight steps we need for improving opportunities for the poor are:

1. Shifting from caretaking to caring
2. Volunteerism and spiritual renewal

3. Reasserting the values of American civilization
4. Emphasizing family and work
5. Creating tax incentives for work, investment, and entrepreneurship
6. Reestablishing savings and property ownership
7. Learning as the focus of education
8. Protection against violence and drugs

60 BARBARA EHRENREICH

FROM *Nickel and Dimed: On (Not) Getting By in America (2001)*

From "Serving in Florida"

The other problem, in addition to the less-than-nurturing management style, is that this job shows no sign of being financially viable. You might imagine, from a comfortable distance, that people who live, year in and year out, on $6 to $10 an hour have discovered some survival stratagems unknown to the middle class. But no. It's not hard to get my coworkers talking about their living situations, because housing, in almost every case, is the principal source of disruption in their lives, the first thing they fill you in on when they arrive for their shifts. After a week, I have compiled the following survey:

Gail is sharing a room in a well-known downtown flophouse for $250 a week. Her roommate, a male friend, has begun hitting on her, driving her nuts, but the rent would be impossible alone.

Claude, the Haitian cook, is desperate to get out of the tworoom apartment he shares with his girlfriend and two other, unrelated people. As far as I can determine, the other Haitian men live in similarly crowded situations.

Annette, a twenty-year-old server who is six months pregnant and abandoned by her boyfriend, lives with her mother, a postal clerk.

Marianne, who is a breakfast server, and her boyfriend are paying $170 a week for a one-person trailer.

Billy, who at $10 an hour is the wealthiest of us, lives in the trailer he owns, paying only the $400-a-month lot fee.

The other white cook, Andy, lives on his dry-docked boat, which, as far as I can tell from his loving descriptions, can't be more than twenty feet long. He offers to take me out on it once it's repaired, but the offer comes with inquiries as to my marital status, so I do not follow up on it.

Tina, another server, and her husband are paying $60 a night for a room in the Days Inn. This is because they have no car and the Days Inn is in walking distance of the Hearthside. When Marianne is tossed out of her trailer for subletting (which is against trailer park rules), she leaves her boyfriend and moves in with Tina and her husband.

Joan, who had fooled me with her numerous and tasteful outfits (hostesses wear their own clothes), lives in a van parked behind a shopping center at night and showers in Tina's motel room. The clothes are from thrift shops.[1]

It strikes me, in my middle-class solipsism, that there is gross improvidence in some of these arrangements. When Gail and I are wrapping silverware in napkins – the only task for which we are permitted to sit – she tells me she is thinking of escaping from her roommate by moving into the Days Inn herself. I am astounded: how she can even think of paying $40 to $60 a day? But if I was afraid of sounding like a social worker, I have come out just sounding like a fool. She squints at me in disbelief: "And where am I supposed to get a month's rent and a month's deposit for an apartment?" I'd been feeling pretty smug about my $500 efficiency, but of course it was made possible only by the $1,300 I had allotted myself for start-up costs when I began my low-wage life: $1,000 for the first month's rent and deposit, $100 for initial groceries and cash in my pocket, $200 stuffed away for emergencies. In poverty, as in certain propositions in physics, starting conditions are everything.

There are no secret economies that nourish the poor; on the contrary, there are a host of special costs. If you can't put up the two months' rent you need to secure an apartment, you end up paying through the nose for a room by the week. If you have only a room, with a hot plate at best, you can't save by cooking up huge lentil stews that can be frozen for the week ahead. You eat fast food or the hot dogs and Styrofoam cups of soup that can be microwaved in a convenience store. If you have no money for health insurance – and the Hearthside's niggardly plan kicks in only after three months – you go without routine care or prescription drugs and end up paying the price. Gail, for example, was doing fine, healthwise anyway, until she ran out of money for estrogen pills. She is supposed to be on the company health plan by now, but they claim to have lost her application form and to be beginning the paperwork all over again. So she spends $9 a pop for pills to control the migraines she wouldn't have, she insists, if her estrogen supplements were covered. Similarly, Marianne's boyfriend lost his job as a roofer because he missed so much time after getting a cut on his foot for which he couldn't afford the prescribed antibiotic.

My own situation, when I sit down to assess it after two weeks of work, would not be much better if this were my actual life. The seductive thing about waitressing is that you don't have to wait for payday to feel a few bills in your pocket, and my tips usually cover meals and gas, plus something left over to stuff into the kitchen drawer I use as a bank. But as the tourist business slows in the summer heat, I sometimes leave work with only $20 in tips (the gross is higher, but servers share about 15 percent of their tips with the busboys and bartenders). With wages included, this amounts to about the minimum wage of $5.15 an hour. The sum in the drawer is piling up but at the present rate of accumulation will be more than $100 short of my rent when the end of the month comes around. Nor can I see any expenses to cut. True, I haven't gone the lentil stew route yet, but that's because I don't have a large cooking pot, potholders, or a ladle to stir with (which would cost a total of about $30 at Kmart, somewhat less at a thrift store), not to mention onions, carrots, and the indispensable bay leaf. I do make my lunch almost every day – usually some slow-burning, high-protein combo like frozen chicken patties with melted cheese on top and canned pinto beans on the side. Dinner is at the Hearthside, which offers its employees a choice of BLT, fish sandwich, or hamburger for only $2. The burger lasts longest, especially if it's heaped with gutpuckering jalapenos, but by midnight my stomach is growling again.

So unless I want to start using my car as a residence, I have to find a second or an alternative job.

I start out with the beautiful, heroic idea of handling the two jobs at once, and for two days I almost do it: working the breakfast/lunch shift at Jerry's from 8:00 till 2:00, arriving at the Hearthside a few minutes late, at 2:10, and attempting to hold out until 10:00. In the few minutes I have between jobs, I pick up a spicy chicken sandwich at the Wendy's drive-through window, gobble it down in the car, and change from khaki slacks to black, from Hawaiian to rust-colored polo. There is a problem, though. When, during the 3:00–4:00 o'clock dead time, I finally sit down to wrap silver, my flesh seems to bond to the seat. I try to refuel with a purloined cup of clam chowder, as I've seen Gail and Joan do dozens of time, but Stu catches me and hisses "No eating!" although there's not a customer around to be offended by the sight of food making contact with a server's lips. So I tell Gail I'm going to quit, and she hugs me and says she might just follow me to Jerry's herself.

But the chances of this are minuscule. She has left the flophouse and her annoying roommate and is back to living in her truck. But, guess what, she reports to me excitedly later that evening, Phillip has given her permission to park overnight in the hotel parking lot, as long as she keeps out of sight, and the parking lot should be totally safe since it's patrolled by a hotel security guard! With the Hearthside offering benefits like that, how could anyone think of leaving? This must be Phillip's theory, anyway. He accepts my resignation with a shrug, his main concern being that I return my two polo shirts and aprons.

From "Scrubbing in Maine"

At least now that I'm "out" I get to ask the question I've wanted to ask all this time: How do they feel, not about Ted but about the owners [of the homes they clean], who have so much while others, like themselves, barely get by? This is the answer from Lori, who at twenty-four has a serious disk problem and an $8,000 credit card debt: "All I can think of is like, wow, I'd like to have this stuff someday. It motivates me and I don't feel the slightest resentment because, you know, it's my goal to get to where they are."

And this is the answer from Colleen, a single mother of two who is usually direct and vivacious but now looks at some spot straight ahead of her, where perhaps the ancestor who escaped from the Great Potato Famine is staring back at her, as intent as I am on what she will say: "I don't mind, really, because I guess I'm a simple person, and I don't want what they have. I mean, it's nothing to me. But what I would like is to be able to take a day off now and then . . . if I had to . . . and still be able to buy groceries the next day."

1 I could find no statistics on the number of employed people living in cars or vans, but according to a 1997 report of the National Coalition for the Homeless, "Myths and Facts about Homelessness," nearly one-fifth of all homeless people (in twenty-nine cities across the nation) are employed in full- or part-time jobs.

7

GEOGRAPHY, REGIONS, AND THE ENVIRONMENT

Introduction	184
61 *Henry David Thoreau* "Fallen Leaves" (1862)	187
62 *Frederick Jackson Turner* FROM "The Significance of the Frontier in American History" (1893)	190
63 *F. Scott Fitzgerald* FROM "My Lost City" (1945)	196
64 *Christopher Isherwood* "California Is a Tragic Country" (1947)	201
65 *Aldo Leopold* "Thinking Like a Mountain" (1949)	203
66 *Peter L. Berger* "New York City 1976: A Signal of Transcendence" (1977)	204
67 *Joan Didion* "Marrying Absurd" (1979)	211
68 *Alice Walker* "The Black Writer and the Southern Experience" (1984)	213
69 *Bill Holm* "Horizontal Grandeur" (1985)	216
70 *Barry Lopez* FROM *Arctic Dreams* (1986)	219

Figure 7 Yosemite Valley, Thunderstorm, Yosemite National Park, 1949 by Ansel Adams
© Ansel Adams Publishing Rights Trust/CORBIS

INTRODUCTION

A country the size of the United States embodies, not surprisingly, important regional differences, geographically and culturally. Early in the history of the nation, for instance, the North and the South developed in the radically different directions that ultimately led to the Civil War. Other regions have also evolved divergent cultural characteristics, for instance the Midwest, the Southwest, and the Pacific West. Some disparities, however, have not been linked to topographical location as such; from the time of the industrial revolution to the present, the socio-cultural differences between country and city were also felt to be highly divisive, involving important issues of identity such as lifestyle, morality, class, ethnicity, and religion.

An early theory of a general regional differentiation – in addition to the North–South dichotomy – was voiced by the historian Frederick Jackson Turner at the end of the nineteenth century, this time in terms of the differences between the East and the West. According to Turner's famous thesis (see text 62), the environment of the frontier served to create an essentially American spirit that was individualist, anti-social, and anti-institutional. (Compare present-day myths of the American West, the cowboy, and the self-made entrepreneur.) Interestingly, the essay was first read at the World Columbian Exhibition in Chicago in 1893, and even though the paper has been criticized, it remains one of the most crucial essays in American history of ideas. In his analysis of American geography and history, Turner – who for many years was a professor of history at the University of Wisconsin – turned away from the idea of European influence on American life to focus on the constantly moving western frontier as the basic force in shaping the American character. The spirit of optimism with which Turner imbues the frontier is, however, moderated by his observation that the frontier had disappeared by the time he published the essay – and by the fact that industrialization and urbanization had already become dominant forces that were changing the character of the nation.

These latter developments notwithstanding, an essay such as Bill Holm's from 1985 on the "horizontal grandeur" of the Midwest (text 69) testifies to the cultural mythmaking that regional differences continue to give rise to. To Holm, the openness of the prairie landscape is not merely a fact of topography; it gives rise to a particular cultural identity, a particular way of viewing the world.

In the history of American urbanization, New York City has often been regarded as the incarnation of the evils as well as the attractions of the modern metropolis. In a very unusual way, the famous American sociologist Peter L. Berger uses the language of religion to come to terms with the city of New York of 1976 (text 66). He combines the idea of New York as the symbol of modern urban life with a keen sense of the religious significance of the metaphor of the city. His reading was inspired by the bicentennial of the Declaration of Independence, a reading that now may sound as a contrast to the city images of New York imprinted in us after September 11, 2001.

Berger's affirmative version of the city of New York may be read next to F. Scott Fitzgerald's equally personal essay "My Lost City" (text 63). In his great New York novel *The Great Gatsby*, Fitzgerald had emphasized that everything was possible in New York. Driving down to Fifth Avenue, the main character admits that he "wouldn't have been surprised to see a great flock of white sheep turn the corner". After the collapse of the New York stock exchange (and his personal life), however, Fitzgerald returns to his dream city as if it was a necropolis.

This chapter contains two additional, brief characterizations of city cultures – Christopher Isherwood's essay on Los Angeles and Joan Didion's on Las Vegas (texts 64 and 67). They evoke an urbanized West with a feverish and transient lifestyle that characterizes the cityscape as well as its human relations. Their portraits may be compared with the black writer Alice Walker's vision of the rural South as she experienced it (text 68): a strongly rooted way of life which is the result of a long history "not only of silent bitterness and hate but also of neighborly kindness and sustaining love," a heritage of "a compassion for the earth, a trust in humanity beyond our knowledge of evil, and an abiding love of justice."

In the words of Perry Miller, America was historically regarded as "Nature's Nation," privileged, it seemed, among the countries of the world by its virgin lands of immense expanse and seemingly unlimited resources. Its varied geography seemed particularly suited for "nature writing," a literary genre of which Thoreau's *Walden* is the archetypal example. In this chapter we have included a short section from an essay by Thoreau describing the New England fall (text 61). Such nature writing was often accompanied by a growing concern about the exploitation of America's resources and the destruction of its natural environment, as expressed by writers such as John Muir,

Aldo Leopold, Rachel Carson, Gary Snyder, Rick Bass, and Barry Lopez. Aldo Leopold was arguably the first American writer who gave expression to a modern, scientific, ecological point of view; his essay "Thinking Like a Mountain" (text 65) has become a classic in American environmental literature. The last text of this chapter (text 70) is taken from the writings of the present-day American nature writer Barry Lopez; it is excerpted from his book *Arctic Dreams: Imagination and Desire in a Northern Landscape*, an evocation of the northernmost region of the United States (and Canada).

Questions and Topics

1 Does Turner denote any negative points about the frontier? Explain the popularity of Turner's thesis.
2 Compare F. Scott Fitzgerald's and Peter L. Berger's personal essays on New York. Explain their ideas of New York, as the city of doom and the city of bliss.
3 Are there any similarities between Christopher Isherwood's portrayal of Los Angeles and Joan Didion's view of Las Vegas? In what ways do these two pieces about the urban West project visions of a culture very different from that portrayed by Alice Walker in her essay on the southern experience?
4 Thoreau (depicting the New England fall), Bill Holm (discoursing on the Midwestern prairie landscape), and Barry Lopez (describing the North American Arctic) all display a naturalist's eye for detail and accuracy, but these three texts of nature writing each have at the same time definite thematic implications. What are they?
5 Discuss the essays of Aldo Leopold and Barry Lopez as illustrations of twentieth-century environmental/ecological thinking.

Suggestions for further reading

Buell, Lawrence, *The Environmental Imagination: Thoreau, Nature Writing, and the Formation of American Culture* (Cambridge, Mass.: Belknap Press of Harvard University Press, 1995).
Cash, W. J., *The Mind of the South* (New York: Knopf, 1941).
Gjerde, Jon, *The Minds of the West: The Ethnocultural Evolution of the Rural Middle West, 1830–1917* (Chapel Hill, NC: University of North Carolina Press, 1985).
Scheese, Don, *Nature Writing: The Pastoral Impulse in America* (New York: Twayne, 1996).
Smith, Henry Nash, *Virgin Land: The American West as Symbol and Myth* (Cambridge, Mass.: Harvard University Press, 1950).

61 HENRY DAVID THOREAU

"Fallen Leaves" (1862)

By the sixth of October the leaves generally begin to fall, in successive showers, after frost or rain; but the principal leaf-harvest, the acme of the *Fall*, is commonly about the sixteenth. Some morning at that date there is perhaps a harder frost than we have seen, and ice formed under the pump, and now, when the morning wind rises, the leaves come down in denser showers than ever. They suddenly form thick beds or carpets on the ground, in this gentle air, or even without wind, just the size and form of the tree above. Some trees, as small hickories, appear to have dropped their leaves instantaneously, as a soldier grounds arms at a signal; and those of the hickory, being bright yellow still, though withered, reflect a blaze of light from the ground where they lie. Down they have come on all sides, at the first earnest touch of autumn's wand, making a sound like rain.

Or else it is after moist and rainy weather that we notice how great a fall of leaves there has been in the night, though it may not yet be the touch that loosens the rock maple leaf. The streets are thickly strewn with the trophies, and fallen elm leaves make a dark brown pavement under our feet. After some remarkably warm Indian-summer day or days, I perceive that it is the unusual heat which, more than anything, causes the leaves to fall, there having been, perhaps, no frost nor rain for some time. The intense heat suddenly ripens and wilts them, just as it softens and ripens peaches and other fruits, and causes them to drop.

The leaves of late red maples, still bright, strew the earth, often crimson-spotted on a yellow ground, like some wild apples, – though they preserve these bright colors on the ground but a day or two, especially if it rains. On causeways I go by trees here and there all bare and smoke-like, having lost their brilliant clothing; but there it lies, nearly as bright as ever, on the ground on one side, and making nearly as regular a figure as lately on the tree. I would rather say that I first observe the trees thus flat on the ground like a permanent colored shadow, and they suggest to look for the boughs that bore them. A queen might be proud to walk where these gallant trees have spread their bright cloaks in the mud.[1] I see wagons roll over them as a shadow or a reflection, and the drivers heed them just as little as they did their shadows before.

Birds' nests, in the huckleberry and other shrubs, and in trees, are already being filled with the withered leaves. So many have fallen in the woods that a squirrel cannot run after a falling nut without being heard. Boys are raking them, in the streets, if only for the pleasure of dealing with such clean, crisp substances. Some sweep the paths scrupulously neat, and then stand to see the next breath strew them with new trophies. The swamp floor is thickly covered, and the *Lycopodium lucidulum* looks suddenly greener amid them. In dense woods they half cover pools that are three or four rods long. The other day I could hardly find a well-known spring, and even suspected that it had dried up, for it was completely concealed by freshly fallen leaves; and when I swept them aside and revealed it, it was like striking the earth, with Aaron's rod, for a new spring. Yet grounds about the edges of swamps look dry with them. At one swamp, where I was surveying, thinking to step on leafy shore from a rail, I got into the water more than a foot deep.

When I go to the river the day after the principal fall of leaves, the sixteenth, I find my boat all covered, bottom and seats, with the leaves of the golden willow under which it is moored, and I set sail with a cargo of them rustling under my feet. If I empty it, it will be full again to-morrow. I do not regard them as litter, to be swept out, but accept them as suitable straw or matting for the bottom of my carriage. When I turn up into the mouth of the Assabet, which is wooded, large fleets of leaves are floating on its surface, as if it were getting out to sea, with room to tack; but next the shore, a little farther up, they are thicker than foam, quite concealing the water for a rod in width, under and amid the alders, button-bushes, and maples, still perfectly light and dry, with fibre unrelaxed; and at a rocky bend where they are met and stopped by the morning wind, they sometimes form a broad and dense crescent quite across the river. When I turn my prow that way, and the wave which it makes strikes them, list what a pleasant rustling from these dry substances getting on one another! Often it is their undulation only which reveals the water beneath them. Also every motion of the wood turtle on the shore is betrayed by their rustling there. Or even in mid-channel, when the wind rises, I hear them blown with a rustling sound. Higher up they are slowly moving round and round in some great eddy which the river makes, as that at the "Leaning Hemlocks," where the water is deep, and the current is wearing into the bank.

Perchance, in the afternoon of such a day, when the water is perfectly calm and full of reflections. I paddle gently down the main stream, and, turning up the Assabet, reach a quiet cove, where I unexpectedly find myself surrounded by myriads of leaves, like fellow-voyagers, which seem to have the same purpose, or want of purpose, with myself. See this great fleet of scattered leaf-boats which we paddle amid, in this smooth river-bay, each one curled up on every side by the sun's skill, each nerve a stiff spruce knee, – like boats of hide, and of all patterns, – Charon's boat probably among the rest, – and some with lofty prows and poops, like the stately vessels of the ancients, scarcely moving in the sluggish current, – like the great fleets, the dense Chinese cities of boats, with which you mingle on entering some great mart, some New York or Canton, which we are all steadily approaching, together. How gently each has been deposited on the water! No violence has been used towards them yet, though, perchance, palpitating hearts were present at the launching. And painted ducks, too, the splendid wood duck among the rest, often come to sail and float amid the painted leaves, – barks of a nobler model still!

What wholesome herb drinks are to be had in the swamps now! What strong medicinal but rich scents from the decaying leaves! The rain falling on the freshly dried herbs and leaves, and filling pools and ditches into which they have dropped thus clean and rigid, will soon convert them into tea, – green, black, brown, and yellow teas, of all degrees of strength, enough to set all Nature a-gossiping. Whether we drink them or not, as yet, before their strength is drawn, these leaves, dried on great Nature's coppers, are of such various pure and delicate tints as might make the fame of Oriental teas.

How they are mixed up, of all species, oak and maple and chestnut and birch! But Nature is not cluttered with them; she is a perfect husbandman; she stores them all. Consider what a vast crop is thus annually shed on the earth! This, more than any mere grain or seed, is the great harvest of the year. The trees are now repaying the earth with interest what they have taken from it. They are discounting. They are about to add a leaf's thickness to the depth of the soil. This is the beautiful way in which Nature gets her muck, while I chaffer with this man and that, who talks to me about sulphur and the cost of carting. We are all the richer for their decay. I am more interested in this crop than in the English grass alone or in the corn. It prepares the virgin mould for future corn-fields and forests, on which the earth fattens. It keeps our homestead in good heart.

For beautiful variety no crop can be compared with this. Here is not merely the plain yellow of the grains, but nearly all the colors that we know, the brightest blue not excepted; the early blushing maple, the poison sumach blazing its sins as scarlet, the mulberry ash, the rich chrome yellow of the poplars, the brilliant red huckleberry, with which the hills' backs are painted, like those of sheep. The frost touches them, and, with the slightest breath of returning day or jarring of earth's axle, see in what showers they come floating down! The ground is all parti-colored with them. But they still live in the soil, whose fertility and bulk they increase, and in the forests that spring from it. They stoop to rise, to mount higher in coming years, by subtle chemistry, climbing by the sap in the trees; and the sapling's first fruits thus shed, transmuted at last, may adorn its crown, when, in after years, it has become the monarch of the forest.

It is pleasant to walk over the beds of these fresh, crisp, and rustling leaves. How beautifully they go to their graves! how gently lay themselves down and turn to mould! – painted of a thousand hues, and fit to make the beds of us living. So they troop to their last resting-place, light and frisky. They put on no weeds, but merrily they go scampering over the earth, selecting the spot, choosing a lot, ordering no iron fence, whispering all through the woods about it, some choosing the spot where the bodies of men are mouldering beneath, and meeting them half-way. How many flutterings before they rest quietly in their graves! They that soared so loftily, how contentedly they return to dust again, and are laid low, resigned to lie and decay at the foot of the tree, and afford nourishment to new generations of their kind, as well as to flutter on high! They teach us how to die. One wonders if the time will ever come when men, with their boasted faith in immortality, will lie down as gracefully and as ripe, – with such an Indian-summer serenity will shed their bodies, as they do their hair and nails.

When the leaves fall, the whole earth is a cemetery pleasant to walk in. I love to wander and muse over them in their graves. Here are no lying nor vain epitaphs. What though you own no lot at Mount Auburn?[2] Your lot is surely cast somewhere in this vast cemetery, which has been consecrated from of old. You need attend no auction to secure a place. There is room enough here. The loosestrife shall bloom and the huckleberry-bird sing over your bones. The woodman and hunter shall be your sextons, and the children shall tread upon the borders as much as they will. Let us walk in the cemetery of the leaves; this is your true Greenwood Cemetery.

1 Raleigh was one of Thoreau's early heroes. *Sir Walter Raleigh*, an uncollected apprentice piece, was first published in 1905 in an edition by F. B. Sanborn (editors' note).
2 A cemetery in Cambridge, Mass., where many literary men and other notables are buried. Greenwood Cemetery (end of paragraph) is Thoreau's coinage (editors' note).

62 FREDERICK JACKSON TURNER

FROM *"The Significance of the Frontier in American History"*
(1893)[1]

In a recent bulletin of the Superintendent of the Census for 1890 appear these significant words: "Up to and including 1880 the country had a frontier of settlement, but at present the unsettled area has been so broken into by isolated bodies of settlement that there can hardly be said to be a frontier line. In the discussion of its extent, its westward movement, etc., it can not, therefore, any longer have a place in the census reports." This brief official statement marks the closing of a great historic movement. Up to our own day American history has been in a large degree the history of the colonization of the Great West. The existence of an area of free land, its continuous recession, and the advance of American settlement westward, explain American development.

Behind institutions, behind constitutional forms and modifications, lie the vital forces that call these organs into life and shape them to meet changing conditions. The peculiarity of American institutions is the fact that they have been compelled to adapt themselves to the changes of an expanding people – to the changes involved in crossing a continent, in winning a wilderness, and in developing at each area of this progress out of the primitive economic and political conditions of the frontier into the complexity of city life. Said Calhoun in 1817, "We are great, and rapidly – I was about to say fearfully – growing!" So saying, he touched the distinguishing feature of American life. All peoples show development; the germ theory of politics has been sufficiently emphasized. In the case of most nations, however, the development has occurred in a limited area; and if the nation has expanded, it has met other growing peoples whom it has conquered. But in the case of the United States we have a different phenomenon. Limiting our attention to the Atlantic coast, we have the familiar phenomenon of the evolution of institutions in a limited area, such as the rise of representative government; into complex organs; the progress from primitive industrial society, without division of labor, up to manufacturing civilization. But we have in addition to this a recurrence of the process of evolution in each western area reached in the process of expansion. Thus American development has exhibited not merely advance along a single line, but a return to primitive conditions on a continually advancing frontier line, and a new development for that area. American social development has been continually beginning over again on the frontier. This perennial rebirth, this fluidity of American life, this expansion westward with its new opportunities, its continuous touch with the simplicity of primitive society, furnish the forces dominating American character. The true point of view in the history of this nation is not the Atlantic coast, it is the Great West. Even the slavery struggle, which is made so exclusive an object of attention by writers like Professor von Holst, occupies its important place in American history because of its relation to westward expansion.

In this advance, the frontier is the outer edge of the wave – the meeting point between savagery and civilization. Much has been written about the frontier from the point of view of border warfare and the chase, but as a field for the serious study of the economist and the historian it has been neglected.

The American frontier is sharply distinguished from the European frontier – a fortified boundary line running through dense populations. The most significant thing about the American frontier is, that it lies at the hither edge of free land. In the census reports it is treated as the margin of that settlement which has a density of two or more to the square mile. The term is an elastic one, and for our purposes does not need sharp definition. We shall consider the whole frontier belt including the Indian country and the outer margin of the "settled area" of the census reports. This paper will make no attempt to treat the subject exhaustively; its aim is simply to call attention to the frontier as a fertile field for investigation, and to suggest some of the problems which arise in connection with it.

In the settlement of America we have to observe how European life entered the continent, and how America modified and developed that life and reacted on Europe. Our early history is the study of European germs developing in an American environment. Too exclusive attention has been paid by institutional students to the Germanic origins, too little to the American factors. The frontier is the line of most rapid and effective Americanization. The wilderness masters the colonist. It finds him a European in dress, industries, tools, modes of travel, and thought. It takes him from the railroad car and puts him in the birch canoe. It strips off the garments of civilization and arrays him in the hunting shirt and the moccasin. It puts him in the log cabin of the Cherokee and Iroquois and runs an Indian palisade around him. Before long he has gone to planting Indian corn and plowing with a sharp stick, he shouts the war cry and takes the scalp in orthodox Indian fashion. In short, at the frontier the environment is at first too strong for the man. He must accept the conditions which it furnishes, or perish, and so he fits himself into the Indian clearings and follows the Indian trails. Little by little he transforms the wilderness, but the outcome is not the old Europe, not simply the development of Germanic germs, any more than the first phenomenon was a case of reversion to the Germanic mark. The fact is, that here is a new product that is American. At first, the frontier was the Atlantic coast. It was the frontier of Europe in a very real sense. Moving westward, the frontier became more and more American. As successive terminal moraines result from successive glaciations, so each frontier leaves its traces behind it, and when it becomes a settled area the region still partakes of the frontier characteristics. Thus the advance of the frontier has meant a steady movement away from the influence of Europe, a steady growth of independence on American lines. And to study this advance, the men who grew up under these conitions, and the political, economic, and social results of it, is to study the really American part of our history.

In the course of the seventeenth century the frontier was advanced up the Atlantic river courses, just beyond the "fall line," and the tidewater region became the settled area. In the first half of the eighteenth century another advance occurred. Traders followed the Delaware and Shawnee Indians to the Ohio as early as the end of the first quarter of the century. . . . By 1880 the settled area had been pushed into northern Michigan, Wisconsin, and Minnesota, along Dakota rivers, and in the Black Hills region, and was ascending the rivers of Kansas and Nebraska. The development of mines in Colorado had drawn isolated frontier settlements into that region, and Montana and Idaho were receiving settlers. The frontier was found in these mining camps and the ranches of the Great Plains. The superintendent of the census for 1890 reports, as previously stated, that the settlements of the West lie so scattered over the region that there can no longer be said to be a frontier line.

At the Atlantic frontier one can study the germs of processes repeated at each successive frontier. We have the complex European life sharply precipitated by the wilderness into the simplicity of primitive conditions. The first frontier had to meet its Indian question, its question of the disposition of the public domain, of the means of intercourse with older settlements, of the extension of political organization, of religious and educational activity. And the settlement of these and similar questions for one frontier served as a guide for the next. The American student needs not to go to the "prim little townships of Sleswick" for illustrations of the law of continuity and development. For example, he may study the origin of our land policies in the colonial land policy; he may see how the system grew by adapting the statutes to the customs of the successive frontiers. He may see how the mining experience in the lead regions of Wisconsin, Illinois, and Iowa was applied to the mining laws of the Sierras, and how our Indian policy has been a series of experimentations on successive frontiers. Each tier of new States has found in the older ones material for its constitutions. Each frontier has made similar contributions to American character, as will be discussed farther on.

But with all these similarities there are essential differences, due to the place element and the time element. It is evident that the farming frontier of the Mississippi Valley presents different conditions from the mining frontier of the Rocky Mountains. The frontier reached by the Pacific Railroad, surveyed into rectangles, guarded by the United States Army, and recruited by the daily immigrant ship, moves forward at a swifter pace and in a different way than the frontier reached by the birch canoe or the pack horse. The geologist traces patiently the shores of ancient seas, maps their areas, and compares the older and the newer. It would be a work worth the historian's labors to mark these various frontiers and in detail compare one with another. Not only would there result a more adequate conception of American development and characteristics, but invaluable additions would be made to the history of society. . . .

The Atlantic frontier was compounded of fisherman, fur trader, miner, cattle-raiser, and farmer. Excepting the fisherman, each type of industry was on the march toward the West, impelled by an irresistible attraction. Each passed in successive waves across the continent. Stand at Cumberland Gap and watch the procession of civilization, marching single file – the buffalo following the trail to the salt springs, the Indian, the fur trader and hunter, the cattle-raiser, the pioneer farmer – and the frontier has passed by. Stand at South Pass in the Rockies a century later and see the same procession with wider intervals between. The unequal rate of advance compels us to distinguish the frontier into the trader's frontier, the rancher's frontier, or the miner's frontier, and the farmer's frontier. When the mines and the cow pens were still near the fall line the traders' pack trains were tinkling across the Alleghanies, and the French on the Great Lakes were fortifying their posts, alarmed by the British trader's birch canoe. When the trappers scaled the Rockies, the farmer was still near the mouth of the Missouri. . . .

The farmer's advance came in distinct series of waves. In Peck's *New Guide to the West*, published in Boston in 1837, occurs this suggestive passage:

"Generally, in all the western settlements, three classes, like the waves of the ocean, have rolled one after the other. First comes the pioneer, who depends for the subsistence of his family chiefly upon the natural growth of vegetation, called the 'range,' and the proceeds of hunting. His implements of agriculture are rude, chiefly of his own make, and his efforts directed mainly to a crop of corn and a 'truck patch.' The last is a rude garden for growing cabbage, beans, corn for roasting ears, cucumbers, and potatoes. A log cabin, and, occasionally, a stable and corn-crib, and a field of a dozen acres, the timber girdled or 'deadened,' and fenced, are enough for his occupancy. It is quite immaterial whether he ever becomes the owner of the soil. He is the occupant for the time being, pays no rent, and feels as independent as the 'lord of the manor.' With a horse, cow, and one or two breeders of swine, he strikes into the woods with his family, and becomes the founder of a new county, or perhaps state. He builds his cabin, gathers around him a few other families of similar tastes and habits, and occupies till the range is somewhat subdued, and hunting a little precarious, or, which is more frequently the case, till the neighbors crowd around, roads, bridges, and fields annoy him, and he lacks elbow room. The preëmption law enables him to dispose of his cabin and cornfield to the next class of emigrants; and, to employ his own figures, he 'breaks for the high timber,' 'clears out for the New Purchase,' or migrates to Arkansas or Texas, to work the same process over.

"The next class of emigrants purchase the lands, add field to field, clear out the roads, throw rough bridges over the streams, put up hewn log houses with glass windows and brick or stone chimneys, occasionally plant orchards, build mills, school-houses, court-houses, etc., and exhibit the picture and forms of plain, frugal, civilized life.

"Another wave rolls on. The men of capital and enterprise come. The settler is ready to sell out and take the advantage of the rise in property, push farther into the interior and become, himself, a man of capital and enterprise in turn. The small village rises to a spacious town or city; substantial edifices of brick, extensive fields, orchards, gardens, colleges, and churches are seen. Broad-cloths, silks, leghorns, crepes, and all the refinements, luxuries, elegancies, frivolities, and fashions are in vogue. Thus wave after wave is rolling westward; the real Eldorado is still farther on. . . ."

Having now roughly outlined the various kinds of frontiers, and their modes of advance, chiefly from the point of view of the frontier itself, we may next inquire what were the influences on the East and on the Old World. A rapid enumeration of some of the more noteworthy effects is all that I have time for.

First, we note that the frontier promoted the formation of a composite nationality for the American people. The coast was preponderantly English, but the later tides of continental immigration flowed across to the free lands. This was the case from the early colonial days. The Scotch-Irish and the Palatine Germans, or "Pennsylvania Dutch," furnished the dominant element in the stock of the colonial frontier. With these peoples were also the freed indented servants, or redemptioners, who at the expiration of their time of service passed to the frontier. Governor Spotswood of Virginia writes in 1717, "The inhabitants of our frontiers are composed generally of such as have been transported hither as servants, and, being out of their time, settle themselves where land is to be taken up and that will produce the necessarys of life with little labour." Very generally these redemptioners were of non-English stock. In the crucible of the frontier the immigrants were Americanized, liberated, and fused into a mixed race, English in neither nationality nor characteristics. The process has gone on from the early days to our own. Burke and other writers in the middle of the eighteenth century believed that Pennsylvania was "threatened with the danger of being wholly foreign in language, manners, and perhaps even inclinations." The German and Scotch-Irish elements in the frontier of the South were only less great. In the middle of the present century the German element in Wisconsin was already so considerable that leading publicists looked to the creation of a German state out of the commonwealth by concentrating their colonization. Such examples teach us to beware of misinterpreting the fact that there is a common English speech in America into a belief that the stock is also English.

In another way the advance of the frontier decreased our dependence on England. The coast, particularly of the South, lacked diversified industries, and was dependent on England for the bulk of its supplies. In the South there was even a dependence on the Northern colonies for articles of food. Governor Glenn, of South Carolina, writes in the middle of the eighteenth century: "Our trade with New York and Philadelphia was of this sort, draining us of all the little money and bills we could gather from other places for their bread, flour, beer, hams, bacon, and other things of their produce, all which, except beer, our new townships begin to supply us with, which are settled with very industrious and thriving Germans. This no doubt diminishes the number of shipping and the appearance of our trade, but it is far from being a detriment to us. Before long the frontier created a demand for merchants. As it retreated from the coast it became less and less possible for England to bring her supplies directly to the consumer's wharfs, and carry away staple crops, and staple crops began to give way to diversified agriculture for a time. The effect of this phase of the frontier action upon the northern section is perceived when we realize how the advance of the frontier aroused seaboard cities like Boston, New York, and Baltimore, to engage in rivalry for what Washington called "the extensive and valuable trade of a rising empire."

The legislation which most developed the powers of the national government, and played the largest part in its activity, was conditioned on the frontier. Writers have discussed the subjects of tariff, land, and internal improvement, as subsidiary to the slavery question. But when American history comes to be rightly viewed it will be seen that the slavery question is an incident. In the period from the end of the first half of the present century to the close of the Civil War slavery rose to primary, but far from exclusive, importance. But this does not justify Dr. von Holst (to take an example) in treating our constitutional history in its formative period down to 1828 in a single volume, giving six volumes chiefly to the history of slavery from 1828 to 1861, under the title "Constitutional History of the United States." The growth of nationalism and the evolution of American political institutions were dependent on the advance of the frontier. Even so recent a writer as Rhodes, in his "History of the United States since the Compromise of 1850," has treated the legislation called out by the western advance as incidental to the slavery struggle.

This is a wrong perspective. . . .

It is safe to say that the legislation with regard to land, tariff, and internal improvements – the American system of the nationalizing Whig party – was conditioned on frontier ideas and needs. But it was not merely in legislative action that the frontier worked against the sectionalism of the coast. The economic and social characteristics of the frontier worked against sectionalism. The men of the frontier had closer resemblances to the Middle region than to either of the other sections. Pennsylvania had been the seed plot of frontier emigration, and, although she passed on her settlers along the Great Valley into the west of Virginia and the Carolinas, yet the industrial society of these Southern frontiersmen was always more like that of the Middle region than like that of the tide water portion of the South, which later came to spread its industrial type throughout the South.

The Middle region, entered by New York harbor, was an open door to all Europe. The tide-water part of the South represented typical Englishmen, modified by a warm climate and servile labor, and living in baronial fashion on great plantations; New England stood for a special English movement – Puritanism. The Middle region was less English than the other sections. It had a wide mixture of nationalities, a varied society, the mixed town and county system of local government, a varied economic life, many religious sects. In short, it was a region mediating between New England and the South, and the East and the West. It represented that composite nationality which the contemporary United States exhibits, that juxtaposition of non-English groups, occupying a valley or a little settlement, and presenting reflections of the map of Europe in their variety. It was democratic and nonsectional, if not national; "easy, tolerant, and contented"; rooted strongly in material prosperity. It was typical of the modern United States. It was least sectional, not only because it lay between North and South, but also because with no barriers to shut out its frontiers from its settled region, and with a system of connecting waterways, the Middle region mediated between East and West as well as between North and South. Thus it became the typically American region. Even the New Englander, who was shut out from the frontier by the Middle region, tarrying in New York or Pennsylvania on his westward march, lost the acuteness of his sectionalism on the way. . . .

But the most important effect of the frontier has been in the promotion of democracy here and in Europe. As has been indicated, the frontier is productive of individualism. Complex society is precipitated by the wilderness into a kind of primitive organization based on the family. The tendency is anti-social. It produces antipathy to control, and particularly to any direct control. The tax-gatherer is viewed as a representative of oppression. Prof. Osgood, in an able article, has pointed out that the frontier conditions prevalent in the colonies are important factors in the explanation of the American Revolution, where individual liberty was sometimes confused with absence of all effective government. The same conditions aid in explaining the difficulty of instituting a strong government in the period of the confederacy. The frontier individualism has from the beginning promoted democracy. . . .

From the conditions of frontier life came intellectual traits of profound importance. The works of travellers along each frontier from colonial days onward describe certain common traits, and these traits have, while softening down, still persisted as survivals in the place of their origin, even when a higher social organization succeeded. The result is that to the frontier the American intellect owes its striking characteristics. That coarseness and strength combined with acuteness and inquisitiveness; that practical, inventive turn of mind, quick to find expedients; that masterful grasp of material things, lacking in the artistic but powerful to effect great ends; that restless, nervous energy; that dominant individualism, working for good and for evil, and withal that buoyancy and exuberance which comes with freedom – these are traits of the frontier, or traits called out elsewhere because of the existence of the frontier. Since the days when the fleet of Columbus sailed into the waters of the New World, America has been another name for opportunity, and the people of the United States have taken their tone from the incessant expansion which has not only been open but has even been forced upon them.

He would be a rash prophet who should assert that the expansive character of American life has now entirely ceased. Movement has been its dominant fact, and, unless this training has no effect upon a people, the American energy will continually demand a wider field for its exercise. But never again will such gifts of free land offer themselves. For a moment, at the frontier, the bonds of custom are broken and unrestraint is triumphant. There is not *tabula rasa*. The stubborn American environment is there with its imperious summons to accept its conditions; the inherited ways of doing things are also there; and yet, in spite of environment, and in spite of custom, each frontier did indeed furnish a new field of opportunity, a gate of escape from the bondage of the past; and freshness, and confidence, and scorn of older society, impatience of its restraints and its ideas, and indifference to its lessons, have accompanied the frontier. What the Mediterranean Sea was to the Greeks, breaking the bond of custom, offering new experiences, calling out new institutions and activities, that, and more, the ever retreating frontier has been to the United States directly, and to the nations of Europe more remotely. And now, four centuries from the discovery of America, at the end of a hundred years of life under the Constitution, the frontier has gone, and with its going has closed the first period of American history.

1   A paper read at the meeting of the American Historical Association convened at the World Columbian Exhibition in Chicago, July 12, 1893. It first appeared in the *Proceedings of the State Historical Society of Wisconsin*, December 14, 1893.

63 F. SCOTT FITZGERALD

FROM *"My Lost City"* (1945)

There was the ferry boat moving softly from the Jersey shore at dawn – the moment crystallized into my first symbol of New York. Five years later when I was fifteen I went into the city from school to see Ina Claire *in The Quaker Girl* and Gertrude Bryan in *Little Boy Blue*. Confused by my hopeless and melancholy love for them both, I was unable to choose between them – so they blurred into one lovely entity, the girl. She was my second symbol of New York. The ferry boat stood for triumph, the girl for romance. In time I was to achieve some of both, but there was a third symbol that I have lost somewhere, and lost for ever.

I found it on a dark April afternoon after five more years.

"Oh, Bunny," I yelled. *"Bunny!"*

He did not hear me – my taxi lost him, picked him up again half a block down, the street. There were black spots of rain on the sidewalk and I saw him walking briskly through the crowd wearing a tan raincoat over his inevitable brown get-up; I noted with a shock that he was carrying a light cane.

"Bunny!" I called again, and stopped. I was still an undergraduate at Princeton while he had become a New Yorker. This was his afternoon walk, this hurry along with his stick through the gathering rain, and as I was not to meet him for an hour it seemed an intrusion to happen upon him engrossed in his private life. But the taxi kept pace with him and as I continued to watch I was impressed: he was no longer the shy little scholar of Holder Court – he walked with confidence, wrapped in his thoughts and looking straight ahead, and it was obvious that his new background was entirely sufficient to him. I knew that he had an apartment where he lived with three other men, released now from all undergraduate taboos, but there was something else that was nourishing him and I got my first impression of that new thing – the Metropolitan spirit.

Up to this time I had seen only the New York that offered itself for inspection – I was Dick Whittington up from the country gaping at the trained bears, or a youth of the Midi dazzled by the boulevards of Paris. I had come only to stare at the show, though the designers of the Woolworth Building and the Chariot Race Sign, the producers of musical comedies and problem plays, could ask for no more appreciative spectator, for I took the style and glitter of New York even above its own valuation. But I had never accepted any of the practically anonymous invitations to debutante balls that turned up in an undergraduate's mail, perhaps because I felt that no actuality could live up to my conception of New York's splendour. Moreover, she to whom I fatuously referred as "my girl" was a Middle Westerner, a fact which kept the warm centre of the world out there, so I thought of New York as essentially cynical and heartless – save for one night when she made luminous the Ritz Roof on a brief passage through.

Lately, however, I had definitely lost her and I wanted a man's world, and this sight of Bunny made me see New York as just that. . . .

When I got back to New York in 1919 I was so entangled in life that a period of mellow monasticism in Washington Square was not to be dreamed of. The thing was to make enough money in the advertising business to rent a stuffy apartment for two in the Bronx. The girl concerned had never seen New York but she was wise enough to be rather reluctant. And in a haze of anxiety and unhappiness I passed the four most impressionable months of my life.

New York had all the iridescence of the beginning of the world. The returning troops marched up Fifth Avenue and girls were instinctively drawn east and north towards them – this was the greatest nation and there was gala in the air. As I hovered ghost-like in the Plaza Red Room of a Saturday afternoon, or went to lush and liquid garden parties in the East Sixties or tippled with Princetonians in the Biltmore Bar, I was haunted always by my other life – my drab room in the Bronx, my square foot of the subway, my fixation upon the day's letter from Alabama – would it come and what would it say? – my shabby suits, my poverty, and love. While my friends were launching decently into life I had muscled my inadequate bark into midstream. The gilded youth circling around young Constance Bennett in the Club de Vingt, the classmates in the Yale-Princeton Club whooping up our first after-the-war reunion, the atmosphere of the millionaires' houses that I sometimes frequented – these things were empty for me, though I recognized them as impressive scenery and regretted that I was committed to other romance. The most hilarious luncheon table or the most moony cabaret – it was all the same; from them I returned eagerly to my home on Claremont Avenue – home because there might be a letter waiting outside the door. One by one my great dreams of New York became tainted. The remembered charm of Bunny's apartment faded with the rest when I interviewed a blowsy landlady in Greenwich Village. She told me I could bring girls to the room, and the idea filled me with dismay – why should I want to bring girls to my room? – I had a girl. I wandered through the town of 127th Street, resenting its vibrant life; or else I bought cheap theatre seats at Gray's drugstore and tried to lose myself for a few hours in my old passion for Broadway. I was a failure – mediocre at advertising work and unable to get started as a writer. Hating the city, I got roaring, weeping drunk, on my last penny and went home. . . .

Incalculable city. What ensued was only one of a thousand success stories of those gaudy days, but it plays a part in my own movie of New York. When I returned six months later the offices of editors and publishers were open to me, impresarios begged plays, the movies panted for screen material. To my bewilderment, I was adopted, not as a Middle Westerner; not even as a detached observer, but as the archetype of what New York wanted. . . .

For just a moment, before it was demonstrated that I was unable to play the role, I, who knew less of New York than any reporter of six months' standing and less of its society than any hall-room boy in a Ritz stag line, was pushed into the position not only of spokesman for the time but of the typical product of that same moment. I, or rather it was "we" now, did not know exactly what New York expected of us and found it rather confusing. Within a few months after our embarkation on the Metropolitan venture we scarcely knew any more who we were and we hadn't a notion what we were. A dive into a civic fountain, a casual brush with the law, was enough to get us into the gossip columns, and we were quoted on a variety of subjects we knew nothing about. Actually our "contacts" included half a dozen unmarried college friends and a few new literary acquaintances. I remember a lonesome Christmas when we had not one friend in the city, nor one house we could go to. Finding no nucleus to which we could cling, we became a small nucleus ourselves and gradually we fitted our disruptive personalities into the contemporary scene of New York. Or rather New York forgot us and let us stay.

This is not an account of the city's changes but of the changes in this writer's feeling for the city. . . . We felt like small children in a great bright unexplored barn. Summoned out to Griffith's studio on Long Island, we trembled in the presence of the familiar face of the *Birth of a Nation*; later I realized that behind much of the entertainment that the city poured forth into the nation there were only a lot of rather lost and lonely people. The world of the picture actors was like our own in that it was in New York and not of it. . . .

It was typical of our precarious position in New York that when our child was to be born we played safe and went home to St Paul – it seemed inappropriate to bring a baby into all that glamour and loneliness. But in a year we were back, and we began doing the same things over again and not liking them so much. We had run through a lot though we had retained an almost theatrical innocence by preferring the role of the observed to that of the observer. But innocence is no end in itself and as our minds unwillingly matured we began to see New York whole and try to save some of it for the selves we would inevitably become.

It was too late – or too soon. For us the city was inevitably linked up with Bacchic diversions, mild or fantastic. We could organize ourselves only on our return to Long Island and not always there. We had no incentive to meet the city half way. My first symbol was now a memory, for I knew that triumph is in oneself; my second one had grown commonplace – two of the actresses whom I had worshipped from afar in 1913 had dined in our house. But it filled me with a certain fear that even the third symbol had grown dim – the tranquillity of Bunny's apartment was not to be found in the ever-quickening city. Bunny himself was married, and about to become a father, other friends had gone to Europe, and the bachelors had become cadets of houses larger and more social than ours. By this time we "knew everybody" – which is to say most of those whom Ralph Barton would draw as in the orchestra on an opening night.

But we were no longer important. The flapper, upon whose activities the popularity of my first books was based had become *passé* by 1923 – anyhow in the East. . . .

It was three years before we saw New York again. As the ship glided up the river, the city burst thunderously upon us in the early dusk – the white glacier of lower New York swooping down like a strand of a bridge to rise into uptown New York, a miracle of foamy light suspended by the stars. A band started to play on deck, but the majesty of the city made the march trivial and tinkling. From that moment I knew that New York, however often I might leave it, was home.

The tempo of the city had changed sharply. The uncertainties of 1920 were drowned in a steady golden roar and many of our friends had grown wealthy. But the restlessness of New York in 1927 approached hysteria. . . .

We settled a few hours from New York and I found that every time I came to the city I was caught into a complication of events that deposited me a few days later in a somewhat exhausted state on the train for Delaware. Whole sections of the city had grown rather poisonous, but invariably I found a moment of utter peace in riding south through Central Park at dark towards where the facade of 59th Street thrusts its lights through the trees. There again was my lost city, wrapped cool in its mystery and promise. But that detachment never lasted long – as the toiler must live in the city's belly, so I was compelled to live in its disordered mind. . . .

The city was bloated, gutted, stupid with cake and circuses, and a new expression "Oh yeah?" summed up all the enthusiasm evoked by the announcement of the last super-skyscrapers. My barber retired on a half million bet in the market and I was conscious that the head waiters who bowed me, or failed to bow me, to my table were far, far wealthier than I. This was no fun – once again I had enough of New York and it was good to be safe on shipboard where the ceaseless revelry remained in the bar in transport to the fleecing rooms of France.

"What news from New York?"

"Stocks go up. A baby murdered a gangster."

"Nothing more?"

"Nothing. Radios blare in the street."

I once thought that there were no second acts in American lives, but there was certainly to be a second act to New York's boom days: We were somewhere in North Africa when, we heard a dull distant crash which echoed to the farthest wastes of the desert.

"What was that?"

"Did you hear it?"

"It was nothing."

"Do you think we ought to go home and see?"

"No – it was nothing."

In the dark autumn of two years later we saw New York again. We passed through curiously polite customs agents and then with bowed head and hat in hand I walked reverently through the echoing tomb. Among the ruins a few childish wraiths still played to keep up the pretence that they were alive, betraying by their feverish voices and hectic cheeks the thinness of the masquerade. Cocktail parties, a last hollow survival from the days of carnival, echoed to the plaints of the wounded: "Shoot me, for the love of God, someone shoot me!", and the groans and wails of the dying: "Did you see that United States Steel is down three more points?" My barber was back at work in his shop; again the head waiters bowed people to their, tables, if there were people to be bowed. From the ruins, lonely and inexplicable as the sphinx, rose the Empire State Building and, just as it had been a tradition of mine to climb to the Plaza Roof to take leave of the beautiful city, extending as far as eyes could reach, so now I went to the roof of the last and most magnificent of towers. Then I understood – everything was explained: I had discovered the crowning error of the city, its Pandora's box. Full of vaunting pride the New Yorker had climbed here and seen with dismay what he had never suspected, that the city was not the endless succession of canyons that he had supposed but that *it had limits* – from the tallest structure he saw for the first time that it faded out into the country on all sides, into an expanse of green and blue that alone was limitless. And with the awful realization that New York was a city after all and not a universe, the whole shining edifice that he had reared in his imagination came crashing to the ground. That was the rash gift of Alfred W. Smith to the citizens of New York.

Thus I take leave of my lost city. Seen from the ferry boat in the early morning, it no longer whispers of fantastic success and eternal, youth . . . [P]erhaps I am destined to return some day and find in the city new experiences that so far I have only read about. For the moment I can only cry out that I have lost my splendid mirage. Come back, come back, O glittering and white!

64 CHRISTOPHER ISHERWOOD

"California Is a Tragic Country" (1947)

California is a tragic country – like Palestine, like every Promised Land. Its short history is a fever-chart of migrations – the land rush, the gold rush, the oil rush, the movie rush, the Okie fruit-picking rush, the wartime rush to the aircraft factories – followed, in each instance, by counter-migrations of the disappointed and unsuccessful, moving sorrowfully homeward. You will find plenty of people in the Middle West and in the East who are very bitter against California in general and Los Angeles in particular. They complain that the life there is heartless, materialistic, selfish. But emigrants to Eldorado have really no right to grumble. Most of us come to the Far West with somewhat cynical intentions. Privately, we hope to get something for nothing – or, at any rate, for very little. Well, perhaps we shall. But if we don't, we have no one to blame but ourselves.

The movie industry – to take the most obvious example – is still very like a gold-mining camp slowly and painfully engaged in transforming itself into a respectable, ordered community. Inevitably, the process is violent. The anarchy of the old days, with every man for himself and winner take the jackpot, still exercises an insidious appeal. It is not easy for the writer who earns 3,000 dollars a week to make common cause with his colleague who only gets 250. The original tycoons were not monsters; they were merely adventurers, in the best and worst sense of the word. They had risked everything and won – often after an epic and ruthless struggle – and they thought themselves entitled to every cent of their winnings. Their attitude toward their employees, from stars down to stagehands, was possessive and paternalistic. Knowing nothing about art and very little about technique, they did not hesitate to interfere in every stage of film production – bluepencilling scripts, dictating casting, bothering directors and criticizing camera-angles. The spectre of the Box Office haunted them night and day. This was their own money, and they were madly afraid of losing it. "There's nothing so cowardly", a producer once told me, "as a million dollars." The paternalist is a sentimentalist at heart, and the senti-mentalist is always potentially cruel. When the studio operatives ceased to rely upon their bosses' benevolence and organized themselves into unions, the tycoon became an injured papa, hurt and enraged by their ingratitude. If the boys did not trust him – well, that was just too bad. He knew what was good for them, and to prove it he was ready to use strike-breakers and uniformed thugs masquerading as special police.

But the epoch of the tycoons is now, happily, almost over. The financier of today has learnt that it pays better to give his artists and technicians a free hand, and to concentrate his own energies on the business he really understands: the promotion and distribution of the finished product. The formation of independent units within the major studios is making possible a much greater degree of co-operation between directors, writers, actors, composers and art-directors. Without being childishly optimistic, one can foresee a time when quite a large proportion of Hollywood's films will be entertainment fit for adults, and when men and women of talent will come to the movie colony not as absurdly overpaid secretaries resigned to humouring their employers but as responsible artists free and eager to do their best. Greed is, however, only one of two disintegrating forces which threaten the immigrant's character: the other, far more terrible, is sloth. Out there, in the eternal lazy morning of the Pacific, days slip away into months, months into years; the seasons are reduced to the faintest nuance by the great central fact of the sunshine; one might pass a lifetime, it seems, between two yawns, lying bronzed and naked on the sand. The trees keep their green, the flowers perpetually bloom, beautiful girls and superb boys ride the foaming breakers. They are not always the same boys, girls, flowers and trees; but that you scarcely notice. Age and death are very discreet there; they seem as improbable as the Japanese submarines which used to lurk up and down the coast during the war and sometimes sink ships within actual sight of the land. I need not describe the de luxe, parklike cemeteries which so hospitably invite you to the final act of relaxation: Aldous Huxley has done this classically already in *After Many a Summer*. But it is worth recalling one of their advertisements, in which a charming, well-groomed elderly lady (presumably risen from the dead) assured the public: "It's better at Forest Lawn. *I speak from experience.*"

To live sanely in Los Angeles (or, I suppose, in any other large American city) you have to cultivate the art of staying awake. You must learn to resist (firmly but not tensely) the unceasing hypnotic suggestions of the radio, the billboards, the movies and the newspapers; those demon voices which are forever whispering in your ear what you should desire, what you should fear, what you should wear and eat and drink and enjoy, what you should think and do and be. They have planned a life for you – from the cradle to the grave and beyond – which it would be easy, fatally easy, to accept. The least wandering of the attention, the least relaxation of your awareness, and already the eyelids begin to droop, the eyes grow vacant, the body starts to move in obedience to the hypnotist's command. Wake up, wake up – before you sign that seven-year contract, buy that house you don't really want, marry that girl you secretly despise. Don't reach for the whisky, that won't help you. You've got to think, to discriminate, to exercise your own free will and judgment. And you must do this, I repeat, without tension, quite rationally and calmly. For if you give way to fury against the hypnotists, if you smash the radio and tear the newspapers to shreds, you will only rush to the other extreme and fossilize into defiant eccentricity. Hollywood's two polar types are the cynically drunken writer aggressively nursing a ten-year-old reputation and the theatrically self-conscious hermit who strides the boulevard in sandals, home-made shorts and a prophetic beard, muttering against the Age of the Machines.

An afternoon drive from Los Angeles will take you up into the high mountains, where eagles circle above the forests and the cold blue lakes, or out over the Mojave Desert, with its weird vegetation and immense vistas. Not very far away are Death Valley, and Yosemite, and the Sequoia Forest with its giant trees which were growing long before the Parthenon was built; they are the oldest living things in the world. One should visit such places often, and be conscious, in the midst of the city, of their surrounding presence. For this is the real nature of California and the secret of its fascination; this untamed, undomesticated, aloof, prehistoric landscape which relentlessly reminds the traveller of his human condition and the circumstances of his tenure upon the earth. "You are perfectly welcome", it tells him, "during your short visit. Everything is at your disposal. Only, I must warn you, if things go wrong, don't blame me. I accept no responsibility. I am not part of your neurosis. Don't cry to me for safety. There is no home here. There is no security in your mansions or your fortresses, your family vaults or your banks or your double beds. Understand this fact, and you will be free. Accept it, and you will be happy."

65 ALDO LEOPOLD

"Thinking Like a Mountain" (1949)

A deep chesty bawl echoes from rimrock to rimrock, rolls down the mountain, and fades into the far blackness of the night. It is an outburst of wild defiant sorrow, and of contempt for all the adversities of the world.

Every living thing (and perhaps many a dead one as well) pays heed to that call. To the deer it is the reminder of the way of all flesh, to the pine a forecast of midnight scuffles and of blood upon the snow, to the coyote a promise of gleanings to come, to the cowman a threat of red ink at the bank, to the hunter a challenge of fang against the bullet. Yet behind these obvious and immediate hopes and fears there lies a deeper meaning, known only to the mountain itself. Only the mountain has lived long enough to listen objectively to the howl of the wolf.

Those unable to decipher the hidden meaning know nevertheless that it is there, for it is felt in all wolf country, and distinguishes that country from all other land. It tingles in the spine of all who hear wolves by night, or who scan their tracks by day. Even without sight or sound of wolf, it is implicit in a hundred small events: the midnight whinny of a pack horse, the rattle of rolling rocks, the bound of a fleeing deer, the way shadows lie under the spruces. Only the ineducable tyro can fail to sense the presence or absence of wolves, or the fact that mountains have a secret about them.

My own conviction on this score dates from the day I saw a wolf die. We were eating lunch on a high rimrock, at the foot of which a turbulent river elbowed its way. We saw what we thought was a doe fording the torrent, her breast awash in white water. When she climbed the bank toward us and shook out her tail, we realized our error: it was a wolf. A half-dozen others, evidently grown pups, sprang from the willows and all joined in a welcoming mêlée of wagging tails and playful maulings. What was literally a pile of wolves writhed and tumbled in the center of an open flat at the foot of our rimrock.

In those days we had never heard of passing up a chance to kill a wolf. In a second we were pumping lead into the pack, but with more excitement than accuracy: how to aim a steep downhill shot is always confusing. When our rifles were empty, the old wolf was down, and a pup was dragging a leg into impassable slide-rocks.

We reached the old wolf in time to watch a fierce green fire dying in her eyes. I realized then, and have known ever since, that there was something new to me in those eyes – something known only to her and to the mountain. I was young then, and full of trigger-itch; I thought that because fewer wolves meant more deer, that no wolves would mean hunters' paradise. But after seeing the green fire die, I sensed that neither the wolf nor the mountain agreed with such a view.

Since then I have lived to see state after state extirpate its wolves. I have watched the face of many a newly wolfless mountain, and seen the south-facing slopes wrinkle with a maze of new deer trails. I have seen every edible bush and seedling browsed, first to anaemic desuetude, and then to death. I have seen every edible tree defoliated to the height of a saddlehorn. Such a mountain looks as if someone had given God a new pruning shears, and forbidden Him all other exercise. In the end the starved bones of the hoped for deer herd, dead of its own too-much, bleach with the bones of the dead sage, or molder under the high-lined junipers.

I now suspect that just as a deer herd lives in mortal fear of its wolves, so does a mountain live in mortal fear of its deer. And perhaps with better cause, for while a buck pulled down by wolves can be replaced in two or three years, a range pulled down by too many deer may fail of replacement in as many decades.

So also with cows. The cowman who cleans his range of wolves does not realize that he is taking over the wolf's job of trimming the herd to fit the range. He has not learned to think like a mountain. Hence we have dustbowls, and rivers washing the future into the sea.

We all strive for safety, prosperity, comfort, long life, and dullness. The deer strives with his supple legs, the cowman with trap and poison, the statesman with pen, the most of us with machines, votes, and dollars, but it all comes to the same thing: peace in our time. A measure of success in this is all well enough, and perhaps is a requisite to objective thinking, but too much safety seems to yield only danger in the long run. Perhaps this is behind Thoreau's dictum: In wildness is the salvation of the world. Perhaps this is the hidden meaning in the howl of the wolf, long known among mountains, but seldom perceived among men.

66 PETER L. BERGER

"New York City 1976: A Signal of Transcendence" (1977)

Different cities acquire great symbolic significance at different moments in human history. Paris was significant in this way in the eighteenth and nineteenth centuries, as was London (though perhaps, to a lesser degree), and Rome, over and beyond anything that was actually going on there, has retained its powerful symbolic character over many centuries. New York City undoubtedly has a comparable symbolic significance today. It is perceived as a symbol of modernity, of Western civilization, and (despite the often-repeated statement that "New York is not America") of the civilization of the United States. The curious thing is that it is widely perceived as a negative symbol, that is, as a metaphor of everything that has gone wrong with our society.

Much of the rest of the country sees New York City as one gigantic agglomeration of social ills: crime, poverty, racial hatred, mismanaged and corrupt government – not to mention dirt, pollution, and traffic congestion of virtually metaphysical dimensions. The same perceptions have been widely diffused abroad, and foreign tourists come to the city with the piquant ambivalence of apprehension and fascination that used to go with dangerous expeditions into the jungles of central Africa. (Such an attitude can be quite profitable to the tourist industry. I know of a German tourist, a middle-aged woman, who went for solitary walks in Central Park every evening, in thrilled anticipation of being sexually assaulted. She was, alas, disappointed. The worst – or best – result of her effort was that an inept mugger tried unsuccessfully to snatch her purse.) Interestingly, New York has negative symbolic value right across the political spectrum: As seen from the right, New York is the habitat of an anti-American intellectual and media establishment, bent on converting the entire nation into the decadent welfare state that the city, supposedly, has already become. Seen from the left, New York is, above all, Wall Street – the heart of the beast, headquarters of capitalist imperialism, cosmic cancer par excellence; Madison Avenue has a slightly lesser place in this particular demonological vision.

And yet, despite all this, New York City continues to be a magnet and even an object of love, sometimes fierce love. People, especially the young, continue to come in large numbers, irresistibly drawn to the city by expectations of success and excitement. And New Yorkers themselves, although they too frequently share the negative views of their own city (indeed, they relish topping each other's horror stories – "You think you had a parking problem today, well, let me tell you what happened to me this morning"), nevertheless continue to be inexplicably, perhaps dementedly, attached to the cesspool of perdition in which they reside. Such ambivalence suggests that the reality of New York is more complicated than its symbolic imagery. And so, of course, it is. From a sociological viewpoint, I could now proceed to delve into the welter of empirical facts that underlie the various perceptions of this city. My purpose here, though, is not sociological but theological.

Specifically, I propose to talk about New York City as a signal of transcendence – *not* New York in some romanticized past, *nor* New York in some utopian future, but New York *today*, a time of disillusion and of many fears, but also a time of promise and of hope. To speak of a signal of transcendence is neither to deny nor to idealize the often harsh empirical facts that make up our lives in the world. It is rather to try for a glimpse of the grace that is to be found "in, with, and under" the empirical reality of our lives. In other words, to speak of a signal of transcendence is to make an assertion about the presence of redemptive power in this world. Let me begin by telling you the most New York joke that I know. It comes, of course, from the pen of Woody Allen, and it concerns the hereafter. There are really only two questions about the hereafter, Woody Allen suggests: *How long does it stay open? And can you get there by cab from midtown Manhattan?* In a quite *non*jocular way, the rest of this chapter may be taken as *a midrash* on this text.

New York is no longer the world's largest city, but it is still the world's most potent symbol of urbanism and urbanity (two related but distinct matters). It seems to me that an exploration into its possibilities as a signal of transcendence must begin with this root fact: Here is not only a vast and vastly important city, but *the* city *par excellence*, the prototypical cosmopolis of our age. I think this is why visitors and new arrivals feel at home there so quickly. Every urban experience that they have had before has been, in a way, an anticipation of New York, and the encounter with the real thing thus has a strong note of familiarity, of deja vu (apart from the fact that the major landmarks of New York are known everywhere and serve as instant orientations for the newcomer). Wherever skyscrapers reach up toward the clouds, wherever masses of cars stream back and forth over steel-girded bridges, wherever heterogeneous crowds pour through subways, underground concourses, or cavernous lobbies encased in glass, there is a bit of New York. Conversely, the New Yorker visiting other cities finds everywhere the sights and sounds, even the smells, that remind him of home. The mystique of New York City is, above all, the mystique of modern urban life, concentrated more massively than anywhere else.

It is not accidental, I think, that the biblical imagery of redemptive fulfillment is so persistently urban. Jerusalem became the focus of religious devotion from an early period of the spiritual history of ancient Israel, and it has remained the holy city in both Jewish and Christian religious imagination ever since. And this same Jerusalem, of course, came to be transformed into an image of eschatological expectation – the Jerusalem that is to come, the heavenly city, "its radiance like a most rare jewel, like a jasper, clear as crystal." Biblical scholars disagree on the precise origins and status of the Zion tradition in the Old Testament, on the religious significance of Jerusalem at, say, the time of David and Solomon, and on the significance of the various images in the Apocalypse. Yet there is, I believe, far-reaching consensus on one simple point: The city as a sociopolitical formation marks a transition in human history from bonds based exclusively on kinship to more comprehensive human relationships. Perhaps this was not the case everywhere, but it was clearly so in the ancient Mediterranean world. Here cities – as markets, centers of political or military administration, and amphictyonic sanctuaries – served to weaken and eventually to liquidate the archaic bonds of blood, of clan and tribe. Max Weber has argued that, in this, cities are incipiently "rationalizing," that is, they constitute a social and political order based on reason, as against an older order based on magical taboos. This development reached a dramatic climax in the emergence of the Greek *polis*, but it is not fanciful to suggest that the biblical imagery of the city served as a religious legitimation of the same underlying liberation from the magic of the blood. Whatever else the city is, it is a place where different people come together and find a new unity with each other – and, in the context of the ancient world, that is a revolutionary event. But let me not get entangled here in historical controversies. Instead, let me make this proposition: The city is a signal of transcendence inasmuch as it embodies universalism and freedom.

If universalism is a root urban characteristic, then surely New York is the most universalistic of cities. And, of course, it is this quality of universalism that most impresses the newcomer and that is so often bragged about by the native. In this small space are pressed together all the races and all the nations of the world. A short subway ride separates worlds of mind-boggling human diversity – black Harlem borders on the Upper West Side, the *barrio* on the territory of East Side swingers, the Village on Little Italy, Chinatown on the financial district. And that is only in Manhattan, beyond which lie the mysterious expanses of the boroughs – places like Greenpoint, Bay Ridge, or Boro Park, each one a world of meaning and belonging almost unpenetrated by outsiders. In this city you can enter a phone booth shaped like a pagoda and make a reservation in a Czechoslovak restaurant (or, more precisely, in one of *several* Czechoslovak restaurants). You can spend weeks doing nothing else, if you have the leisure, than savoring the world's greatest concentration of museums, art galleries, musical and theatrical performances, and other cultural happenings of every conceivable kind, from the sublime to the unspeakable. When I first lived in New

York as a student, I had a job as a receptionist in a now-defunct dispensary on the Lower East Side. I still recall with pleasure my lunch hours: I would buy a bialy with lox in the old Essex Street Market, munch it while strolling through the teeming street life at the foot of the Williamsburg Bridge, and then have a quiet coffee with baklava in one of several Turkish cafes on Allen Street, surrounded by old men smoking waterpipes and playing checkers (apparently their only occupation). What I recall most of all is the exhilarating sense that here I was, in New York City, where all these things were going on and where, in principle, everything was possible.

Are these sentimental trivialities, fit only as copy for tourist promotion? I think not. For the mundane facts contain a mighty promise – the promise that God loves the human race in *all* its incredible variety, that His redemptive grace embraces *all* of humanity without any exception, and that His Kingdom will mean not the end but the glorious transfiguration of every truly human expression. The heavenly city, too, will contain every human type and condition, and in this it will necessarily resemble New York; needless to add, it will *not* resemble New York in that it will be without the degradations and deprivations that afflict human life in this aeon. Also, God's promise is one of perfect freedom. There is no such freedom short of the Kingdom of God; in this aeon, every liberty is bought at a price (often an ugly one), every liberation is incomplete, and some liberations are illusory. It is important to remember this. Nevertheless, wherever human beings are liberated from oppression or narrowness to wider horizons of life, thought, and imagination, there is a foreshadowing of the final liberation that is to come. Thus, I believe, New York City is a signal of transcendence also in the exhilaration of its freedom – and let me assure you that, in saying this, I do not forget for a moment the sordidness that may also be found here.

To some extent, the characteristics of universalism and freedom are endemic to urban life nearly everywhere, in varying degrees. The distinctiveness of New York comes from the enormous magnitude of these features. The same may be said of another characteristic which, I propose, may be taken as a signal of transcendence: *The city is a place of hope.*

If there is any New York legend that is generally known, it is that of the immigrant, and the legend, of course, has its most famous physical representation in the Statue of Liberty. This legend is, above all, a story of hope. I arrived in America a short time after World War II, very poor and very young, after a long ocean voyage that sticks in my memory as an endless bout with seasickness. The ship sailed into New York Bay in the early morning, in a dense fog, so that very little could be seen at first. Then, dramatically, the fog was pierced, and we saw first the Statue, which seemed perilously close to the ship, and then the skyline of lower Manhattan. All the passengers were assembled on the deck, and there was a hushed silence. But, curiously, what impressed me most at the time was not these majestic sights; I had, after all, expected to see them. There was something else. As the ship sailed up the Hudson toward its pier, I was fascinated by the traffic on what I later learned was the West Side Highway. All these cars seemed enormous to me. But, more than their size, it was their colors that impressed me. This was before New York taxis all came to be painted yellow; then, they came in all the colors of the rainbow, though yellow was predominant. I didn't know that these garish cars were taxis. The exuberance of color, I thought, was characteristic of ordinary American automobiles. This, then, was my first unexpected sight in New York, and it pleased me greatly. I don't think I put it quite this way to myself, but implicit in my visual pleasure was the notion that someday I, too, might be driving past the skyscrapers in a bright yellow car of surrealistic proportions, engaged (no doubt) in some business of great importance and enjoying the company of the most beautiful woman imaginable.

As immigrant stories go, mine has been lucky although I've never driven a yellow cab. Indeed, I could say that New York has kept all its promises to me. I know full well that this has not been so for all newcomers to this city. If New York has been a place of hope, it has also been a place of disappointed hope, of shattered expectations, of bitterness and despair. It has been fashionable of late to stress this negative aspect of the American dream – mistakenly so, I believe, because America has fulfilled far more expectations than it has frustrated. I would go even farther than that: The currently fashionable intellectuals, who decry the hopefulness of America, are far more in a state of "false consciousness" than the millions of immigrants who came and who continue to come to America full of hope. Nevertheless, just as it would be false to speak of the universalism and the freedom of this city without also speaking of the sordid underside of these facts, so would it be dishonest to pretend that the hopeful message emblazoned on the Statue of Liberty is an accurate description of empirical reality. Of course it is not. And yet the proclamation of hope to all those who came here across the ocean is a signal of transcendent portent. For all of us, men and women of this aeon, are on a long journey, across vast and dangerous seas, toward a city of hope.

There is more: *This is a place of useless labor.* Just compare New York with an honest-to-goodness industrial city like Detroit or Pittsburgh, or even Chicago. In these cities most people are engaged in labor that has at least an indirect relation to economic utility. Certainly there are such people in New York. The peculiarity of New York, however, is the large portion of its labor force employed in activities which only the most ingenious economic theory can interpret as a contribution to the gross national product. Leave aside the enormous number of people working in municipal government and other public services (and leave aside the timely question of how long the city will be able to afford this); you are still left with legions of people making their livelihood, or at least trying to do so, through activities which, economically speaking, are bizarre. Look at them: Promoters of Renaissance music, producers of nonverbal theater, translators of Swahili literature, purveyors of esoteric erotica, agents of nonexistent governments, revolutionaries in exile, Egyptologists, numismatic experts, scream therapists, guidance counselors for geriatric recreation, Indonesian chefs, belly dancers and teachers of belly dancing (and, for all I know, belly dancing therapists) – not to mention individuals who are on university payrolls to provide instruction in phenomenological sociology (I have frequently thought that a society that can afford me must somehow be heading for an economic crisis). Let me make a practical suggestion in this matter: Go for lunch someday to one of my favorite restaurants in New York, the Russian Tea Room on West 57th Street, in the heart of the music and ballet district. Study the customers. A few will be easy to place; these, most likely, are tourists from the Bronx. An attempt to guess the occupations of the rest should be enough to induce a nervous breakdown in any labor economist,

208

especially if he also tries to figure out how such occupations can generate enough income to pay the price of a beef Stroganoff preceded by blinis with caviar.

A Chicagoan will know what to say to all of this: These people can't be serious. Precisely! The opposite of being serious is being playful; the invincible playfulness of New York City is, I believe, in itself a signal of transcendence. *Homo ludens* is closer to redemption than *homo faber*; the clown is more of a sacramental figure than the engineer. In the heavenly Jerusalem there will be no need for psychotherapy and geriatrics, but I confidently expect that there will be an unbelievable variety of restaurants – metaphysically transfigured restaurants, to be sure, but restaurants nonetheless – and, if so, there is certain to be the Platonic prototype of the Indonesian *rijstafel*, its pure ideal, its *Ur-form*, its ultimate culmination. May I also confess to the (perhaps crypto-Muslim) expectation that there will be something like belly dancers? Anyway, I think it is good theology to expect the Kingdom of God to be a very playful affair – and in that, at the very least, it will resemble New York more than Chicago!

New Yorkers, like the inhabitants of other large cities, are supposed to be sophisticated. The word, of course, is related to sophistry – the ability to be clever with words, to be quick, to be surprised at nothing. This notion of sophistication is closely related to that of urbanity, and it is as much a source of pride for the urbanite as it is a provocation to others. Somebody once defined a true metropolis as a place where an individual can march down the street wearing a purple robe and a hat with bells on it, beating a drum and leading an elephant by the leash, and only get casual glances from passers-by. If so, then surely New York is the truest metropolis there is. To some extent, of course, this is but another expression of the aforementioned universalism. But there is more: *The city is a place of magic.* And in that, too, I would contend, it offers us a signal of transcendence.

I don't mean occultism, though there is enough of that around as well. I mean magic in a more ample sense, namely, the quality of the surreal, the intuition that reality is manipulable, unpredictable, subject to the strangest metamorphoses at any moment. If you will, I mean what Rudolf Otto called the *mysterium fascinans*. The British author Jonathan Raban, in his curious book *Soft City*, argues that modern urban life is characterized by magic, and *not* (as it is more customarily thought to be) by rationality. I think that there is much to be said for this view; Raban also maintains that New York has this magic in a particularly potent form. The magic of the city can be summed up in a sentence that sums up a recurring experience: *Anything can happen here – and it could happen right now.*

Magic always has its dark side, and it is hardly necessary to spell out the sinister possibilities of the insight that anything can happen. But it would be a mistake to limit the experience to its negative aspect. The city is a place of strangers and of strangeness, and this very fact implies a fascination of a special kind. Ordinary-looking houses contain unimaginable mysteries within. Casual encounters are transformed into revelations of shocking impact. Passions explode in the most unexpected occasions. All of this helps to account for the excitement of the city, but it also makes for a general vision of the world: Reality is not what it seems; there are realities behind the reality of everyday life; the routine fabric of our ordinary lives is not self-contained, it has holes in it, and there is no telling what wondrous things may at any moment rush in through these holes. This vision of the world is perhaps not itself religious, but it is in close proximity to the root insights of the religious attitude. The magic of the city should not, then, be identified with religious experience, but it may be said to be an antechamber of the latter. Thus, when people say that New York City is a surrealistic place, they are saying more than they intend. They are making an ontological statement about the reality of human life: Behind the empirical city lurks another city, a city of dreams and wonders. They are also making a soteriological statement, for redemption always comes into the world as a big surprise – I would even say, as a cosmic joke. Anything at all can come through the holes in the fabric of ordinary reality – a man leading an elephant by the leash, or a man riding on a donkey to inaugurate the mystery of our salvation.

Some of the above may sound as if I have become a latter-day convert to some version of secular theology (maybe a sort of North American centrist adaptation of the theology of liberation?). Let me say as strongly as I can that this is not at all the case. Indeed, the theological considerations in this chapter are directly opposite to the procedure that has been characteristic of the various expressions of secular theology. That procedure, in the final analysis, is always the same: The symbols of transcendence in the Christian tradition are reinterpreted to become symbols of the human condition, the divine becomes a metaphor of the human, the metaempirical of ordinary empirical reality. I'm suggesting here the precisely opposite procedure: The human condition itself is to be seen as the penumbra of the transcendent, the human points to the divine, the empirical is a metaphor of the metaempirical. Whatever have been the shifting contents of secular theology – philosophical, psychological, most recently political – they have served as the substratum to which the traditional symbols are reduced. I strongly reject this reductionist procedure. I suggest the precise opposite of reduction, namely, a hesitantly inductive procedure which begins with the empirical realities of human life, but which intends from the start to transcend these realities.

Nor am I proposing that these or any other signals of transcendence be taken as the substance of our faith. Rather, they are particular experiences which, for some of us, may serve as auxiliaries of faith. Contrary to what some may think, I'm not suggesting that my particular vision of New York City be incorporated in the kerygma of the church. And I'm definitely willing to remain in full Christian communion with all those who fail to understand the deeper significance of this city. If there is a polemical edge to what I have written here, it is against those who would provide a theological rationale for the antiurbanism that is rampant today in the radical wing of the ecology movement – but this was certainly not foremost in my mind.

There is a route I drive regularly, between Rutgers University in New Jersey, where I teach, and Brooklyn, where I live. It crosses from Staten Island over the Verrazano-Narrows Bridge. It has often occurred to me, especially in the evening when the light is soft and the contours of visual reality seem to lack firmness, that the entrance to heaven may well look something like this wonderful bridge, with its majestic arcs and its breathtaking vistas on both sides. I wish for all of us that we will be part of this traffic in the evening of our lives, that we will be forgiven the toll at the gate, and that we will know that, in the city on the other side of bridge, what awaits us is home. I, for one, will not be overly surprised if the gatekeeper addresses me in a Brooklyn accent.

67 JOAN DIDION

"Marrying Absurd" (1979)

To be married in Las Vegas, Clark County, Nevada, a bride must swear that she is eighteen or has parental permission and a bridegroom that he is twenty-one or has parental permission. Someone must put up five dollars for the license. (On Sundays and holidays, fifteen dollars. The Clark County Courthouse issues marriage licenses at any time of the day or night except between noon and one in the afternoon, between eight and nine in the evening, and between four and five in the morning.) Nothing else is required. The State of Nevada, alone among these United States, demands neither a premarital blood test nor a waiting period before or after the issuance of a marriage license. Driving in across the Mojave, from Los Angeles, one sees the signs way out on the desert, looming up from that moonscape of rattlesnakes and mesquite, even before the Las Vegas lights appear like a mirage on the horizon: "GETTING MARRIED? Free License Information First Strip Exit." Perhaps the Las Vegas wedding industry achieved its peak operational efficiency between 9:00 p.m. and midnight of August 26, 1965, an otherwise unremarkable Thursday which happened to be, by Presidential order, the last day on which anyone could improve his draft status merely by getting married. One hundred and seventy-one couples were pronounced man and wife in the name of Clark County and the State of Nevada that night, sixty-seven of them by a single justice of the peace, Mr. James A. Brennan. Mr. Brennan did one wedding at the Dunes and the other sixty-six in his office, and charged each couple eight dollars. One bride lent her veil to six others. "I got it down from five to three minutes," Mr. Brennan said later of his feat. "I could've married them *en masse*, but they're people, not cattle. People expect more when they get married."

What people who get married in Las Vegas actually do expect – what, in the largest sense, their "expectations" are – strikes one as a curious and self-contradictory business. Las Vegas is the most extreme and allegorical of American settlements, bizarre and beautiful in its venality and in its devotion to immediate gratification, a place the tone of which is set by mobsters and call girls and ladies' room attendants with amyl nitrite poppers in their uniform pockets. Almost everyone notes that there is no "time" in Las Vegas, no night and no day and no past and no future (no Las Vegas casino, however, has taken the obliteration of the ordinary time sense quite so far as Harold's Club in Reno, which for a while issued, at odd intervals in the day and night, mimeographed "bulletins" carrying news from the world outside); neither is there any logical sense of where one is. One is standing on a highway in the middle of a vast hostile desert looking at an eighty-foot sign which blinks "STARDUST" or "CAESAR'S PALACE." Yes, but what does that explain? This geographical implausibility reinforces the sense that what happens there has no connection with "real" life; Nevada cities like Reno and Carson are ranch towns, Western towns, places behind which there is some historical imperative. But Las Vegas seems to exist only in the eye of the beholder. All of which makes it an extraordinarily stimulating and interesting place, but an odd one in which to want to wear a candlelight satin Priscilla of Boston wedding dress with Chantilly lace insets, tapered sleeves, and a detachable modified train.

And yet the Las Vegas wedding business seems to appeal to precisely that impulse. "Sincere and Dignified Since 1954," one wedding chapel advertises. There are nineteen such wedding chapels in Las Vegas, intensely competitive, each offering better, faster, and, by implication, more sincere services than the next: Our Photos Best Anywhere, Your Wedding on A Phonograph Record, Candlelight with Your Ceremony, Honeymoon Accommodations, Free Transportation from Your Motel to Courthouse to Chapel and Return to Motel, Religious or Civil Ceremonies, Dressing Rooms, Flowers, Rings, Announcements, Witnesses Available, and Ample Parking. All of these services, like most others in Las Vegas (sauna baths, payroll-check cashing, chinchilla coats for sale or rent), are offered twenty-four hours a day, seven days a week, presumably on the premise that marriage, like craps, is a game to be played when the table seems hot.

But what strikes one most about the Strip chapels, with their wishing wells and stained-glass paper windows and their artificial bouvardia, is that so much of their business is by no means a matter of simple convenience, of late-night liaisons between show girls and baby Crosbys. Of course there is some of that. (One night about eleven o'clock in Las Vegas I watched a bride in an orange minidress and masses of flamecolored hair stumble from a Strip chapel on the arm of her bridegroom, who looked the part of the expendable nephew in movies like *Miami Syndicate*. "I gotta get the kids," the bride whimpered. "I gotta pick up the sitter, I gotta get to the midnight show." "What you gotta get," the bridegroom said, opening the door of a Cadillac Coupe de Ville and watching her crumple on the seat, "is sober.") But Las Vegas seems to offer something other than "convenience"; it is merchandising "niceness," the facsimile of proper ritual, to children who do not know how else to find it, how to make the arrangements, how to do it "right." All day and evening long on the Strip, one sees actual wedding parties, waiting under the harsh lights at a crosswalk, standing uneasily in the parking lot of the Frontier while the photographer hired by The Little Church of the West ("Wedding Place of the Stars") certifies the occasion, takes the picture: the bride in a veil and white satin pumps, the bridegroom usually in a white dinner jacket, and even an attendant or two, a sister or a best friend in hot-pink *peau de soie*, a flirtation veil, a carnation nosegay. "When I Fall in Love It Will Be Forever," the organist plays, and then a few bars of Lohengrin. The mother cries; the stepfather, awkward in his role, invites the chapel hostess to join them for a drink at the Sands. The hostess declines with a professional smile; she has already transferred her interest to the group waiting outside. One bride out, another in, and again the sign goes up on the chapel door: "One moment please – Wedding."

I sat next to one such wedding party in a Strip restaurant the last time I was in Las Vegas. The marriage had just taken place; the bride still wore her dress, the mother her corsage. A bored waiter poured out a few swallows of pink champagne ("on the house") for everyone but the bride, who was too young to be served. "You'll need something with more kick than that," the bride's father said with heavy jocularity to his new son-in-law; the ritual jokes about the wedding night had a certain Panglossian character, since the bride was clearly several months pregnant. Another round of pink champagne, this time not on the house, and the bride began to cry. "It was just as nice," she sobbed, "as I hoped and dreamed it would be."

68 ALICE WALKER

"The Black Writer and the Southern Experience" (1984)

My mother tells of an incident that happened to her in the thirties during the Depression. She and my father lived in a small Georgia town and had half a dozen children. They were sharecroppers, and food, especially flour, was almost impossible to obtain. To get flour, which was distributed by the Red Cross, one had to submit vouchers signed by a local official. On the day my mother was to go into town for flour she received a large box of clothes from one of my aunts who was living in the North. The clothes were in good condition, though well worn, and my mother needed a dress, so she immediately put on one of those from the box and wore it into town. When she reached the distribution center and presented her voucher she was confronted by a white woman who looked her up and down with marked anger and envy.

"What'd you come up here for?" the woman asked.

"For some flour," said my mother, presenting her voucher.

"Humph," said the woman, looking at her more closely and with unconcealed fury. "Anybody dressed up as good as you don't need to come here *begging* for food."

"I ain't begging," said my mother; "the government is giving away flour to those that need it, and I need it. I wouldn't be here if I didn't. And these clothes I'm wearing was given to me." But the woman had already turned to the next person in line, saying over her shoulder to the white man who was behind the counter with her, "The *gall* of niggers coming in here dressed better than me!" This thought seemed to make her angrier still, and my mother, pulling three of her small children behind her and crying from humiliation, walked sadly back into the street.

"What did you and Daddy do for flour that winter?" I asked my mother.

"Well," she said, "Aunt Mandy Aikens lived down the road from us and she got plenty of flour. We had a good stand of corn so we had plenty of meal. Aunt Mandy would swap me a bucket of flour for a bucket of meal. We got by all right."

Then she added thoughtfully, "And that old woman that turned me off so short got down so bad in the end that she was walking on two sticks." And I knew she was thinking, though she never said it: Here I am today, my eight children healthy and grown, and three of them in college and me with hardly a sick day for years. Ain't Jesus wonderful?

In this small story is revealed the condition and strength of a people. Outcasts to be used and humiliated by the larger society, the Southern black sharecropper and poor farmer clung to his own kind and to a religion that had been given to pacify him as a slave but which he soon transformed into an antidote against bitterness. Depending on one another, because they had nothing and no one else, the sharecroppers often managed to come through "all right." And when I listen to my mother tell and retell this story I find that the white woman's vindictiveness is less important than Aunt Mandy's resourceful generosity or my mother's ready stand of corn. For their lives were not about that pitiful example of Southern womanhood, but about themselves.

What the black Southern writer inherits as a natural right is a sense of *community*. Something simple but surprisingly hard, especially these days, to come by. My mother, who is a walking history of our community, tells me that when each of her children was born the midwife accepted as payment such home-grown or homemade items as a pig, a quilt, jars of canned fruits and vegetables. But there was never any question that the midwife would come when she was needed, whatever the eventual payment for her services. I consider this each time I hear of a hospital that refuses to admit a woman in labor unless she can hand over a substantial sum of money, cash.

Nor am I nostalgic, as a French philosopher once wrote, for lost poverty. I am nostalgic for the solidarity and sharing a modest existence can sometimes bring. We knew, I suppose, that we were poor. Somebody knew; perhaps the landowner who grudgingly paid my father three hundred dollars a year for twelve months' labor. But we never considered ourselves to be poor, unless, of course, we were deliberately humiliated. And because we never believed we were poor, and therefore worthless, we could depend on one another without shame. And always there were the Burial Societies, the Sick-and-Shut-in Societies, that sprang up out of spontaneous need. And no one seemed terribly upset that black sharecroppers were ignored by white insurance companies. It went without saying, in my mother's day, that birth and death required assistance from the community, and that the magnitude of these events was lost on outsiders.

As a college student I came to reject the Christianity of my parents, and it took me years to realize that though they had been force-fed a white man's palliative in the form of religion, they had made it into something at once simple and noble. True, even today, they can never successfully picture a God who is not white, and that is a major cruelty, but their lives testify to a greater comprehension of the teachings of Jesus than the lives of people who sincerely believe a God *must* have a color and that there can be such a phenomenon as a "white" church.

The richness of the black writer's experience in the South can be remarkable, though some people might not think so. Once, while in college, I told a white middle-aged Northerner that I hoped to be a poet. In the nicest possible language, which still made me as mad as I've ever been, he suggested that a "farmer's daughter" might not be the stuff of which poets are made. On one level, of course, he had a point. A shack with only a dozen or so books is an unlikely place to discover a young Keats. But, it is narrow thinking, indeed, to believe that a Keats is the only kind of poet one would want to grow up to be. One wants to write poetry that is understood by one's people, not by the Queen of England. Of course, should she be able to profit by it too, so much the better, but since that is not likely, catering to her tastes would be a waste of time.

For the black Southern writer, coming straight out of the country, as Wright did – Natchez and Jackson are still not as citified as they like to think they are – there is the world of comparisons; between town and country, between the ugly crowding and griminess of the cities and the spacious cleanliness (which actually seems impossible to dirty) of the country. A country person finds the city confining, like a too tight dress. And always, in one's memory, there remain all the rituals of one's growing up: the warmth and vividness of Sunday worship (never mind that you never quite believed) in a little church hidden from the road, and houses set so far back into the woods that at night it is impossible for strangers to find them. The daily dramas that evolve in such a private world are pure gold. But this view of a strictly private and hidden existence, with its triumphs, failures, grotesqueries, is not nearly as valuable to the socially conscious black Southern writer as his double vision is. For not only is he in a position to see his own world, and its close community ("Homecomings" on First Sundays, barbecues to raise money to send to Africa – one of the smaller ironies – the simplicity and eerie calm of a black funeral, where the beloved one is buried way in the middle of a wood with nothing to mark the spot but perhaps a wooden cross already coming apart), but also he is capable of knowing, with remarkably silent accuracy, the people who make up the larger world that surrounds and suppresses his own.

It is a credit to a writer like Ernest J. Gaines, a black writer who writes mainly about the people he grew up with in rural Louisiana, that he can write about whites and blacks exactly as he sees them and *knows* them, instead of writing of one group as a vast malignant lump and of the other as a conglomerate of perfect virtues.

In large measure, black Southern writers owe their clarity of vision to parents who refused to diminish themselves as human beings by succumbing to racism. Our parents seemed to know that an extreme negative emotion held against other human beings for reasons they do not control can be blinding. Blindness about other human beings, especially for a writer, is equivalent to death. Because of this blindness, which is, above all, racial, the works of many Southern writers have died. Much that we read today is fast expiring.

My own slight attachment to William Faulkner was rudely broken by realizing, after reading statements he made in *Faulkner in the University*, that he believed whites superior morally to blacks; that whites had a duty (which at their convenience they would assume) to "bring blacks along" politically, since blacks, in Faulkner's opinion, were "not ready" yet to function properly in a democratic society. He also thought that a black man's intelligence is directly related to the amount of white blood he has.

For the black person coming of age in the sixties, where Martin Luther King stands against the murderers of Goodman, Chaney, and Schwerner, there appears no basis for such assumptions. Nor was there any in Garvey's day, or in Du Bois's or in Douglass's or in Nat Turner's. Nor at any other period in our history, from the very founding of the country; for it was hardly incumbent upon slaves to be slaves and saints too. Unlike Tolstoy, Faulkner was not prepared to struggle to change the structure of the society he was born in. One might concede that in his fiction he did seek to examine the reasons for its decay, but unfortunately, as I have learned while trying to teach Faulkner to black students, it is not possible, from so short a range, to separate the man from his works.

One reads Faulkner knowing that his "colored" people had to come through "Mr. William's" back door, and one feels uneasy, and finally enraged that Faulkner did not burn the whole house down. When the provincial mind starts out *and continues* on a narrow and unprotesting course, "genius" itself must run on a track.

Flannery O'Connor at least had the conviction that "reality" is at best superficial and that the puzzle of humanity is less easy to solve than that of race. But Miss O'Connor was not so much of Georgia, as in it. The majority of Southern writers have been too confined by prevailing social customs to probe deeply into mysteries that the Citizens Councils insist must never be revealed.

Perhaps my Northern brothers will not believe me when I say there is a great deal of positive material I can draw from my "underprivileged" background. But they have never lived, as I have, at the end of a long road in a house that was faced by the edge of the world on one side and nobody for miles on the other. They have never experienced the magnificent quiet of a summer day when the heat is intense and one is so very thirsty, as one moves across the dusty cotton fields, that one learns forever that water is the essence of all life. In the cities it cannot be so clear to one that he is a creature of the earth, feeling the soil between the toes, smelling the dust thrown up by the rain, loving the earth so much that one longs to taste it and sometimes does.

Nor do I romanticize the Southern black country life. I can recall that I hated it, generally. The hard work in the fields, the shabby houses, the evil greedy men who worked my father to death and almost broke the courage of that strong woman, my mother. No, I am simply saying that Southern black writers, like most writers, have a heritage of love and hate, but that they also have enormous richness and beauty to draw from. And, having been placed, as Camus says, "halfway between misery and the sun," they, too, know that "though all is not well under the sun, history is not everything."

No one could wish for a more advantageous heritage than that bequeathed to the black writer in the South: a compassion for the earth, a trust in humanity beyond our knowledge of evil, and an abiding love of justice. We inherit a great responsibility as well, for we must give voice to centuries not only of silent bitterness and hate but also of neighborly kindness and sustaining love.

69 BILL HOLM

"Horizontal Grandeur" (1985)

For years I carried on a not-so-jovial argument with several friends who are north-woods types. They carted me out into the forests of northern Wisconsin or Minnesota, expected me to exclaim enthusiastically on the splendid landscape. "Looks fine," I'd say, "but there's too damn many trees, and they're all alike. If they'd cut down twenty miles or so on either side of the road, the flowers could grow, you could see the sky, and find out what the real scenery is like." Invariably, this provoked groans of disbelief that anyone could be insensitive enough to prefer dry, harsh, treeless prairies. There, a man is the tallest thing for miles around; a few lonesome cottonwoods stand with leaves shivering by a muddy creek; sky is large and readable as a Bible for the blind. The old farmers say you can see weather coming at you, not like woods, where it sneaks up and takes you by surprise.

I was raised in Minneota [a place in Minnesota], true prairie country. When settlers arrived in the 1870's they found waist-high grass studded with wild flowers; the only trees were wavy lines of cottonwoods and willows along the crooked Yellow Medicine Creek. Farmers emigrated here not for scenery, but for topsoil; 160 flat acres without trees or boulders to break plows and cramp fields was beautiful to them. They left Norway, with its picturesque but small, poor, steep farms; or Iceland, where the beautiful backyard mountains frequently covered hay fields with lava and volcanic ash. Wives, described by Ole Rolvaag in *Giants in the Earth*, were not enamored with the beauty of black topsoil, and frequently went insane from loneliness, finding nowhere to hide on these blizzardy plains. But the beauty of this landscape existed in function, rather than form, not only for immigrant farmers, but for Indians who preceded them.

Blackfeet Indians live on the Rocky Mountains' east edge in northern Montana – next to Glacier National Park. Plains were home for men and buffalo, the source of Blackfeet life; mountains were for feasting and dancing, sacred visions and ceremonies, but home only for spirits and outlaws. It puzzles tourists winding up hairpin turns, looking down three thousand feet into dense forests on the McDonald Valley floor, that Blackfeet never lived there. It did not puzzle the old farmer from Minneota who, after living and farming on prairies most of his life, vacationed in the Rockies with his children after he retired. When they reached the big stone escarpment sticking up at the prairie's edge, one of his sons asked him how he liked the view. "These are stone," the old man said; "I have stones in the north eighty. These are bigger, and harder to plow around. Let's go home."

When my mother saw the Atlantic Ocean in Virginia, she commented that though saltier, noisier, and probably somewhat larger, it was no wetter or more picturesque than Dead Coon Lake or the Yellow Medicine River and surely a good deal more trouble to cross.

There are two eyes in the human head – the eye of mystery, and the eye of harsh truth – the hidden and the open – the woods eye and the prairie eye. The prairie eye looks for distance, clarity, and light; the woods eye for closeness, complexity, and darkness. The prairie eye looks for usefulness and plainness in art and architecture; the woods eye for the baroque and ornamental. Dark old brownstones on Summit Avenue were created by a woods eye; the square white farmhouse and red barn are prairie eye's work. Sherwood Anderson wrote his stories with a prairie eye, plain and awkward, told in the voice of a man almost embarrassed to be telling them, but bullheadedly persistent to get at the meaning of the events; Faulkner, whose endless complications of motive and language take the reader miles behind the simple facts of an event, sees the world with a woods eye. One eye is not superior to the other, but they are different. To some degree, like male and female, darkness and light, they exist in all human heads, but one or the other seems dominant. The Manicheans were not entirely wrong.

I have a prairie eye. Dense woods or mountain valleys make me nervous. After once visiting Burntside Lake north of Ely for a week, I felt a fierce longing to be out. Driving home in the middle of the night, I stopped the car south of Willmar, when woods finally fell away and plains opened up. It was a clear night, lit by a brilliant moon turning blowing grasses silver. I saw for miles – endless strings of yardlights, stars fallen into the grovetops. Alone, I began singing at the top of my voice. I hope neither neighborhood cows, nor the Kandiyohi County sheriff were disturbed by this unseemly behavior from a grown man. It was simply cataracts removed from the prairie eye with a joyful rush.

Keep two facts in mind if you do not have a prairie eye: magnitude and delicacy. The prairie is endless! After the South Dakota border, it goes west for over a thousand miles, flat, dry, empty, lit by brilliant sunsets and geometric beauty. Prairies, like mountains, stagger the imagination most not in detail, but size. As a mountain is high, a prairie is wide; horizontal grandeur, not vertical. People neglect prairies as scenery because they require time and patience to comprehend. You eye a mountain, even a range, at a glance. The ocean spits and foams at its edge. You see down into the Grand Canyon. But walking the whole prairie might require months. Even in a car at 60 miles an hour it takes three days or more. Like a long symphony by Bruckner or Mahler, prairie unfolds gradually, reveals itself a mile at a time, and only when you finish crossing it do you have any idea of what you've seen. Americans don't like prairies as scenery or for national parks and preserves because they require patience and effort. We want instant gratification in scenic splendor as in most things, and simply will not look at them seriously. Prairies are to Rockies what *Paradise Lost* is to haiku. Milton is cumulative; so are prairies. Bored for days, you are suddenly struck by the magnitude of what has been working on you. It's something like knowing a woman for years before realizing that you are in love with her after all.

If prairie size moves the imagination, delicacy moves the heart. West of Minneota, the prairies quickly rise several hundred feet and form the Coteau. This land looks more like the high plains of Wyoming. Rougher and stonier than land to the east, many sections have never been plowed. Past Hendricks, along the south and west lake shores, things open up – treeless hills with grazing cattle, gullies with a few trees sliding off toward the lake. Ditches and hillsides are a jumble of flowers, grasses and thistles: purple, pink, white, yellow, blue. In deep woods, the eye misses these incredible delicate colors, washed in light and shadow by an oversized sky. In the monochromatic woods, light comes squiggling through onto a black green shadowy forest floor. My eye longs for a rose, even a sow thistle.

A woods man looks at twenty miles of prairie and sees nothing but grass, but a prairie man looks at a square foot and sees a universe; ten or twenty flowers and grasses, heights, heads, colors, shades, configurations, bearded, rough, smooth, simple, elegant. When a cloud passes over the sun, colors shift, like a child's kaleidoscope.

I stop by a roadside west of Hendricks, walk into the ditch, pick a prairie rose. This wild pink rose is far lovelier than hot-house roses wrapped in crinkly paper that teenagers buy prom dates. The dusty car fills with its smell. I ignore it for a few minutes, go on talking. When I look again, it's dry, as if pressed in an immigrant Bible for a hundred years. These prairie flowers die quickly when you take them out of their own ground. They too are immigrants who can't transplant, and wither fast in their new world.

I didn't always love prairies. On my father's farm I dreamed of traveling, living by the sea and, most of all, close to mountains. As a boy, I lay head on a stone in the cow pasture east of the house, looking up at cloud rows in the west, imagining I saw all the way to the Rockies and that white tips on the clouds were snow on mountaintops or, better yet, white hair on sleeping blue elephant spines. Living in a flat landscape drove me to indulge in mountainous metaphor, then later discover that reality lived up to it. When I finally saw the Rockies years later, they looked like pasture clouds, phantasmagorias solider than stone.

The most astonished travelers do not come from the Swiss Alps, or the California coast. Only William Carlos Williams, who lived in the industrial prairies of New Jersey, would notice the Mexico of *Desert Music*. A southwest poet with a wood's eye would have seen sequaro cactus or medieval parapets. Trust a prairie eye to find beauty and understate it truthfully, no matter how violent the apparent exaggeration. Thoreau, though a woodsman, said it right: "I can never exaggerate enough."

70 BARRY LOPEZ

FROM *Arctic Dreams (1986)*

As I moved through the Arctic I thought often about a rhythm indigenous to this land, not one imposed on it. The imposed view, however innocent, always obscures. The evidence that there is a different rhythm of life here seemed inescapably a part of the expression of the animals I encountered, though I cannot say precisely why. A coherent sense of the pervasiveness of such a rhythm is elusive.

The indigenous rhythm, or rhythms, of arctic life is important to discern for more than merely academic reasons. To understand why a region is different, to show an initial deference toward its mysteries, is to guard against a kind of provincialism that vitiates the imagination, that stifles the capacity to envision what is different.

Another reason to wonder which rhythms are innate, and what they might be, is related as well to the survival of the capacity to imagine beyond the familiar. We have long regarded animals as a kind of machinery, and the landscapes they move through as back drops, as paintings. In recent years this antiquated view has begun to change. Animals are understood as mysterious, within the context of sophisticated Western learning that takes into account such things as biochemistry and genetics. They are changeable, not fixed, entities, predictable in their behavior only to a certain extent. The world of variables they are alert to is astonishingly complex, and their responses are sometimes highly sophisticated. The closer biologists look, the more the individual animal, like the individual human being, seems a reflection of that organization of energy that quantum mechanics predicts for the particles that compose an atom.

The animal's environment, the background against which we see it, can be rendered as something like the animal itself – partly unchartable. And to try to understand the animal apart from its background, except as an imaginative exercise, is to risk the collapse of both. To be what they are they require each other . . . .

I visited Anaktuvuk Pass in 1978 with a friend, a wolf biologist who had made a temporary home there and who was warmly regarded for his tact, his penchant for listening, and his help during an epidemic of flu in the village. We spent several days watching wolves and caribou in nearby valleys and visiting at several homes. The men talked a lot about hunting. The evenings were full of stories. There were moments of silence when someone said something very true, peals of laughter when a man told a story expertly at his own expense. One afternoon we left and traveled far to the west to the headwaters of the Utukok River.

The Alaska Department of Fish and Game had a small field camp on the Utukok, at the edge of a gravel-bar landing strip. Among the biologists there were men and women studying caribou, moose, tundra grizzly, wolverine, and, now that my companion had arrived, wolves. The country around the Utukok and the headwaters of the Kokolik River is a wild and serene landscape in summer. Parts of the Western Arctic caribou herd are drifting over the hills, returning from the calving grounds. The sun is always shining, somewhere in the sky. For a week or more we had very fine, clear weather. Golden eagles circled high over the tundra, hunting. Snowy owls regarded us from a distance from their tussock perches. Short-eared owls, a gyrfalcon. Familiar faces.

A few days after we arrived, my companion and I went south six or seven miles and established a camp from which we could watch a distant wolf den. In that open, rolling country without trees, I had the feeling, sometimes, that nothing was hidden. It was during those days that I went for walks along Ilingnorak Ridge and started visiting ground-nesting birds, and developed the habit of bowing to them out of regard for what was wonderful and mysterious in their lives.

The individual animals we watched tested their surroundings, tried things they had not done before, or that possibly no animal like them had ever done before – revealing their capacity for the new. The preservation of this capacity to adapt is one of the central mysteries of evolution.

We watched wolves hunting caribou, and owls hunting lemmings. Arctic ground squirrel eating *irok*, the mountain sorrel. I thought a great deal about hunting. In 1949, Robert Flaherty told an amazing story, which Edmund Carpenter was later successful in getting published. It was about a man named Comock. In 1902, when he and his family were facing starvation, Comock decided to travel over the sea ice to an island he knew about, where he expected they would be able to find food (a small island off Cape Wolstenholme, at the northern tip of Quebec's Ungava Peninsula). On the journey across, they lost nearly all their belongings – all of Comock's knives, spears, and harpoons, all their skins, their stone lamps, and most of their dogs – when the sea ice suddenly opened one night underneath their camp. They were without hunting implements, without a stone lamp to melt water to drink, without food or extra clothing. Comock had left only one sled, several dogs, his snow knife, with which he could cut snow blocks to build a snow house, and stones to make sparks for a fire.

They ate their dogs. The dogs they kept ate the other dogs, which were killed for them. Comock got his family to the island. He fashioned, from inappropriate materials, new hunting weapons. He created shelter and warmth. He hunted successfully. He reconstructed his entire material culture, almost from scratch, by improvising and, where necessary, inventing. He survived. His family survived. His dogs survived and multiplied.

Over the years they carefully collected rare bits of driftwood and bone until Comock had enough to build the frame for an umiak. They saved bearded-seal skins, from which Comock's wife made a waterproof hull. And one summer day they sailed away, back toward Ungava Peninsula. Robert Flaherty, exploring along the coast, spotted Comock and his family and dogs approaching across the water. When they came close, Flaherty, recognizing the form of an umiak and the cut of Eskimo clothing but, seeing that the materials were strange and improvised, asked the Eskimo who he was. He said his name was Comock. "Where in the world have you come from?" asked Flaherty. "From far away, from big island, from far over there," answered Comock, pointing. Then he smiled and made a joke about how poor the umiak must appear, and his family burst into laughter.

I think of this story because at its heart is the industry and competence, the determination and inventiveness of a human family. And because it is about people who lived resolutely in the heart of every moment they found themselves in, disastrous and sublime.

During those days I spent on Ilingnorak Ridge, I did not know what I know now about hunting; but I had begun to sense the outline of what I would learn in the years ahead with Eskimos and from being introduced, by various people, to situations I could not have easily found my way to alone. The insights I felt during those days had to do with the nature of hunting, with the movement of human beings over the land, and with fear. The thoughts grew out of watching the animals.

The evidence is good that among all northern aboriginal hunting peoples, the hunter saw himself bound up in a sacred relationship with the larger animals he hunted. The relationship was full of responsibilities – to the animals, to himself, and to his family. Among the great and, at this point, perhaps tragic lapses in the study of aboriginal hunting peoples is a lack of comprehension about the role women played in hunting. We can presume, I think, that in the same way the hunter felt bound to the animals he hunted, he felt the contract incomplete and somehow even inappropriate if his wife was not part of it. In no hunting society could a man hunt successfully alone. He depended upon his wife for obvious reasons – for the preparation of food and clothing, companionship, humor, subtle encouragement – and for things we can only speculate about, things of a religious nature, bearing on the mutual obligations and courtesies with which he approached the animals he hunted.

Hunting in my experience – and by hunting I simply mean being out on the land – is a state of mind. All of one's faculties are brought to bear in an effort to become fully incorporated into the landscape. It is more than listening for animals or watching for hoofprints or a shift in the weather. It is more than an analysis of what one *senses*. To hunt means to have the land around you like clothing. To engage in a wordless dialogue with it, one so absorbing that you cease to talk with your human companions. It means to release yourself from rational images of what something "means" and to be concerned only that it "is." And then to recognize that things exist only insofar as they can be related to other things. These relationships – fresh drops of moisture on top of rocks at a river crossing and a raven's distant voice – become patterns. The patterns are always in motion. Suddenly the pattern – which includes physical hunger, a memory of your family, and memories of the valley you are walking through, these particular plants and smells – takes in the caribou. There is a caribou standing in front of you. The release of the arrow or bullet is like a word spoken out loud. It occurs at the periphery of your concentration.

The mind we know in dreaming, a nonrational, nonlinear comprehension of events in which slips in time and space are normal, is, I believe, the conscious working mind of an aboriginal hunter. It is a frame of mind that redefines patience, endurance, and expectation.

The focus of a hunter in a hunting society was not killing animals but attending to the myriad relationships he understood bound him into the world he occupied with them. He tended to those duties carefully because he perceived in them everything he understood about survival. This does not mean, certainly, that every man did this, or that good men did not starve. Or that shamans whose duty it was to intercede with the forces that empowered these relationships weren't occasionally thinking of personal gain or subterfuge. It only means that most men understood how to behave.

A fundamental difference between our culture and Eskimo culture, which can be felt even today in certain situations, is that we have irrevocably separated ourselves from the world that animals occupy. We have turned all animals and elements of the natural world into objects. We manipulate them to serve the complicated ends of our destiny. Eskimos do not grasp this separation easily, and have difficulty imagining themselves entirely removed from the world of animals. For many of them, to make this separation is analogous to cutting oneself off from light or water. It is hard to imagine how to do it.

A second difference is that, because we have objectified animals, we are able to treat them impersonally. This means not only the animals that live around us but animals that live in distant lands. For Ekimos, most relationships with animals are local and personal. The animals one encounters are part of one's community, and one has obligations to them. A most confusing aspect of Western culture for Eskimos to grasp is our depersonalization of relationships with the human and animal members of our communities. And it is compounded, rather than simplified, by their attempting to learn how to objectify animals.

Eskimos do not maintain this intimacy with nature without paying a certain price. When I have thought about the ways in which they differ from people in my own culture, I have realized that they are more afraid than we are. On a day-to-day basis, they have more fear. Not of being dumped into cold water from an umiak, not a debilitating fear. They are afraid because they accept fully what is violent and tragic in nature. It is a fear tied to their knowledge that sudden, cataclysmic events are as much a part of life, of really living, as are the moments when one pauses to look at something beautiful. A Central Eskimo shaman named Aua, queried by Knud Rasmussen about Eskimo beliefs, answered, "We do not believe. We fear."

To extend these thoughts, it is wrong to think of hunting cultures like the Eskimo's as living in perfect harmony or balance with nature. Their regard for animals and their attentiveness to nuance in the landscape were not rigorous or complete enough to approach an idealized harmony. No one knew that much. No one would say they knew that much. They faced nature with fear, with *ilira* (nervous awe) and *kappia* (apprehension). And with enthusiasm. They accepted hunting as a way of life – its violence, too, though they did not seek that out. They were unsentimental, so much so that most outsiders thought them cruel, especially in their treatment of dogs. Nor were they innocent. There is murder and warfare and tribal vendetta in their history; and today, in the same villages I walked out of to hunt, are families shattered by alcohol, drugs, and ambition. While one cannot dismiss culpability in these things, any more than one can hold to romantic notions about hunting, it is good to recall what *a struggle* it is to live with dignity and understanding, with perspicacity or grace, in circumstances far better than these. And it is helpful to imagine how the forces of life must be construed by people who live in a world where swift and fatal violence, like *ivu*, the suddenly leaping shore ice, is inherent in the land. The land, in a certain, very real way, compels the minds of the people.

A good reason to travel with Eskimo hunters in modern times is that, beyond nettlesome details – foods that are not to one's liking, a loss of intellectual conversation, a consistent lack of formal planning – in spite of these things, one feels the constant presence of people who know something about surviving. At their best they are resilient, practical, and enthusiastic. They pay close attention in realms where they feel a capacity for understanding. They have a quality of *nuannaarpoq*, of taking extravagant pleasure in being alive; and they delight in finding it in other people. Facing as we do our various Armageddons, they are a good people to know.

In the time I was in the field with Eskimos I wondered at the basis for my admiration. I admired an awareness in the men of providing for others, and the soft tone of voice they used around bloodshed. I never thought I could understand, from their point of view, that moment of preternaturally heightened awareness, and the peril inherent in taking a life; but I accepted it out of respect for their seriousness toward it. In moments when I felt perplexed, that I was dealing with an order outside my own, I discovered and put to use a part of my own culture's wisdom, the formal divisions of Western philosophy – metaphysics, epistemology, ethics, aesthetics, and logic – which pose, in order, the following questions. What is real? What can we understand? How should we behave? What is beautiful? What are the patterns we can rely upon?

As I traveled, I would say to myself, What do my companions see where I see death? Is the sunlight beautiful to them, the way it sparkles on the water? Which for the Eskimo hunter are the patterns to be trusted? The patterns, I know, could be different from ones I imagined were before us. There could be other, remarkably different insights.

THOSE days on Ilingnorak Ridge, when I saw tundra grizzly tearing up the earth looking for ground squirrels, and watched wolves hunting, and a horned lark sitting so resolutely on her nest, and caribou crossing the river and shaking off the spray like diamonds before the evening sun, I was satisfied only to watch. This was the great drift and pause of life. These were the arrangements that made the land ring with integrity. Somewhere downriver, I remembered, a scientist named Edward Sable had paused on a trek in 1947 to stare at a Folsom spear point, a perfectly fluted object of black chert resting on a sandstone ledge. People, moving over the land.

8

ART, FILM, MUSIC, AND POPULAR CULTURE

Introduction	226
71 *Georgia O'Keeffe* To Alfred Stieglitz (1916)	229
72 *Bessie Smith* "Empty Bed Blues" (1928)	230
73 *Woody Guthrie* "This Land Is Your Land" (1944)	231
74 *Walt Disney* The Testimony of Walter E. Disney Before the House Committee on Un-American Activities (1947)	231
75 *Ralph Ellison* "As the Spirit Moves Mahalia" (1964)	237
76 *Stanley Kauffmann* "Little Big Man" (1970)	240
77 *Joan Didion* "Georgia O'Keeffe" (1979)	242
78 *Studs Terkel* FROM "Jill Robertson: Fantasia" (1982)	244
79 *Mikal Gilmore* FROM "Bruce Springsteen" (1987)	247
80 *Martin Scorsese, Paul Schrader, and Robert De Niro* FROM *"Taxi Driver"* (1992)	252

Figure 8 Jack in the Pulpit by Georgia O'Keeffe, 1930. Image © Geoffrey Clements/CORBIS
Artwork © The Georgia O Keeffe Foundation / Artists Rights Society (ARS), New York

INTRODUCTION

American art, film, music, and popular culture have all had a profound effect upon cultural expressions throughout the western world. For a long time American painting, sculpture, and architecture were basically regarded as mediocre copies of European art but that is no longer the case. In the 1950s American abstract expressionism became a major school of painting and New York became one of the prime art centers in the world. Earlier on American architecture received world attention through radically new edifices conceived and constructed by Louis Sullivan (1856–1927) and Frank Lloyd Wright (1867–1959). Film originated as an American cultural form and the modern film industry is unthinkable without Hollywood, whether seen as a stronghold of film traditions which should be emulated or regarded as a place where serious film no longer stands a chance. Music and popular culture have been the major cultural exports of the United States, from the blues and jazz to rock and roll and rap music.

Georgia O'Keeffe (1887–1986) remains one of the truly original voices in American painting. Born in the Midwest, she became famous for her watercolors and oil paintings of nature, especially her close-ups of leaves and flowers. She married the American photographer Alfred Stieglitz (1864–1946), who admired her work and took several pictures of her, which he exhibited (see text 71). After his death O'Keeffe lived and worked mostly in New Mexico. She lived to be almost a hundred years old. In her essay on Georgia O'Keeffe, writer Joan Didion pays tribute to her as "a woman clean of received wisdom and open to what she sees" (text 77).

One very important reason why American culture had such a tremendous impact on people in various parts of the world in the twentieth century is the popularity of American movies, from the silent movies of the beginning of the century to the movies now being transmitted to the consumer via cable networks and satellites. Text 78, an interview with Jill Robertson, the daughter of a former Hollywood film producer, capitalizes on the make-believe world that the films and the film industry create.

The unedited recording of Walt Disney's appearance before the House Committee on Un-American Activities (text 74) is a clear token of the paranoia that led political authorities to question the loyalty of some famous artists during the Cold War. Disney's reactions and his information to the people of the committee may be read as a striking contrast to the romance and innocence displayed in all his production of films for children.

Even though most people would probably position film in the category of popular culture, a number of serious film critics insist on placing film among the "older arts." This question aside, film criticism no doubt functions as an important guide to a potential audience. In his article on "Little Big Man" (1970) (text 76), Stanley Kauffmann argues that Calder Willingham succeeded in the daring enterprise of transforming the novel *Little Big Man* into a screenplay which functions according to the principles of the film medium.

In text 80 Martin Scorsese, the film director, Paul Schrader, the scriptwriter, and Robert De Niro, the actor, give us an illuminating insight into the making of *Taxi Driver* as they discuss initial reactions to the script, the actual shooting of the movie, and the intentions and philosophy behind the movie production. They seem happy with the result as summed up by Paul Schrader: "*Taxi Driver* was as much a product of luck and timing as everything else – three sensibilities together at the right time, doing the right thing."

Film and modern advertising are close companions. Already in the beginning of the twentieth century advertising was an important part of American popular culture, dividing the population into groups based on class and income levels. For decades advertisements focused primarily on the middle class, projecting images where men were by definition businessmen and women housewives. More recently, however, the focus on class has gradually yielded to a classification of the population into different lifestyles. Yet advertisements have consistently for the last century paid little attention to religious, ethnic, and racial differences, functioning often in much the same way as the Hollywood movies.

American popular music is celebrated all over the world, in festivals, massive concerts, and music videos. But the popularity of American songs and music originated long before the days of Elvis. Bessie Smith's "Empty Bed Blues" and Woody Guthrie's "This Land Is Your Land" (texts 72 and 73) tell a different story from that of the culture of middle-class advertisements. Being the indisputable "Empress of the Blues" from 1923 until 1930 when the Depression destroyed the market for black records, Bessie Smith combined the rural blues with city-oriented lyrics, often developing themes and images that were overtly sexual, as in "Empty Bed Blues." Novelist Ralph Ellison was deeply influenced by black music and in his essay on Mahalia Jackson he explains why (text 75). The essay was written while Mahalia Jackson was still alive. She died in 1972.

Guthrie's "This Land Is Your Land" (recorded in 1944) bears the unmistakable mark of leftist protest and was a favorite of the civil rights movement of the 1960s. Guthrie's songs (e.g. "So Long, It's Been Good to Know You" and "This Land . . .") attained a large audience and influenced later stars such as Bob Dylan. Guthrie is widely regarded as America's most prominent folk singer of the twentieth century.

Even before non-British European teenagers pick up the rudiments of the English language, they become devoted listeners to American rock and folk music. Musicians such as Bob Dylan, Jimi Hendrix, Janis Joplin, and Joan Baez captivated a whole generation on both sides of the Atlantic in the 1960s, spearheading the counterculture movement of the time. It is worth noting that Bruce Springsteen, the great rocker of the 1970s and 1980s, identifies (in the interview reprinted as text 79) with many of the same ideals as the generation of the 1960s, even though the political and ideological climate has changed dramatically.

Questions and Topics

1 Look up some of Georgia O'Keeffe's watercolors or oil paintings and relate them to her own interest in nature as stated in her early letter to Stieglitz.
2 Is "the spirit" that moved Mahalia Jackson to sing her gospel songs similar to or different from the "spirit" that moved Bessie Smith to sing the blues?
3 To what extent can Bruce Springsteen's texts be read as urban poetry?
4 Write a personal essay on your favourite American film or piece of music.
5 The outsider is a recurrent character in American film and fiction. Discuss how Martin Scorsese and/or other American film producers deal with and present such characters.

Suggestions for further reading

Cowart, Jack and Juan Hamilton, eds., *Georgia O'Keeffe: Art and Letters* (Washington: National Gallery of Art, and New York: New York Graphic Society Books, 1988).

Gillett, Charlie, *The Sound of the City: The Rise of Rock and Roll*, 2nd edn (London: Da Capo Press, 1996).

Kelly, Mary Pat, *Martin Scorsese: A Journey* (London: Secker & Warburg, 1992).

Kolker, Robert Phillip, *A Cinema of Loneliness: Penn, Kubrick, Scorsese, Spielberg, Altman* (New York: Oxford University Press, 1988).

Updike, John, *Still Looking: Essays on American Art* (New York: Knopf, 2005).

71 GEORGIA O'KEEFFE

To Alfred Stieglitz (1916)

[Columbia, SC, 1 February 1916]

Mr. Stieglitz –

I like what you write me – Maybe I dont get exactly your meaning – but I like mine – like you liked your interpretation of my drawings . . . It was such a surprise to me that you saw them – and I am so glad they surprised you – that they gave you joy. I am glad I could give you once what 291 [Stieglitz's art gallery] has given me many times . . . You cant imagine how it all astonishes me.

I have been just trying to express myself – . . . I just have to say things you know – Words and I are not good friends at all except with some people – when Im close to them and can feel as well as hear their response – I have to say it someway – Last year I went color mad – but Ive almost hated to think of color since the fall went – Ive been slaving on the violin – trying to make that talk – I wish I could tell you some of the things Ive wanted to say as I felt them . . . The drawings dont count – its the life – that really counts – To say things that way may be a relief – . . . It may be interesting to see how different people react to them . . . – I am glad they said something to you. – I think so much alone – work alone – am so much alone – but for letters – that I am not always sure that Im thinking straight – Its great – I like it – The outdoors is wonderful – and Im just now having time to think things I should have thought long ago – the uncertain feeling that some of my ideas may be near insanity – adds to the fun of it – and the prospect of really talking to live human beings again – sometime in the future is great . . . – Hibernating in South Carolina is an experience that I would not advise anyone to miss – The place is of so little consequence – except for the outdoors – that one has a chance to give one's mind, time, and attention to anything one wishes.

I cant tell you how sorry I am that I cant talk to you – what Ive been thinking surprises me so – has been such fun – at times has hurt too . . . that it would be great to tell you . . . Some of the fields are green – very very green – almost unbelievably green against the dark of the pine woods – and its warm – the air feels warm and soft – and lovely . . .

I wonder if Marin's Woolworth has spring fever again this year . . . I hope it has
Sincerely
　　Georgia O'Keeffe

I put this in the envelope – stretched and laughed. Its so funny that I should write you because I want to. I wonder if many people do . . You see – I would go in and talk to you if I could – and I hate to be completely outdone by a little thing like distance.

72 BESSIE SMITH

"Empty Bed Blues" (recorded 1928)

I woke up this morning with an awful aching head,
I woke up this morning with an awful aching head,
My new man had left me just a room and an empty bed.

Bought me a coffee grinder, got the best one I could find,
Bought me a coffee grinder, got the best one I could find,
So he could grind me coffee, 'cause he had a brand new grind.

He's a deep-sea diver with a stroke that can't go wrong,
He's a deep-sea diver with a stroke that can't go wrong,
He can touch the bottom, and his wind holds out so long.

He knows how to thrill me, and he thrills me night and day,
He knows how to thrill me, and he thrills me night and day,
He's got a new way of loving, almost takes my breath away.

He's got that sweet something, and I told my galfriend Lou,
He's got that sweet something, and I told my galfriend Lou,
'Cause the way she's raving, she must have gone and tried it too.

When my bed gets empty, makes me feel awful mean and blue,
When my bed gets empty, makes me feel awful mean and blue,
'Cause my springs getting rusty, sleepin' single the way I do.

Bought him a blanket, pillow for his head at night,
Bought him a blanket, pillow for his head at night,
Then I bought him a mattress so he could lay just right.

He came home one evening with his fair head way up high,
He came home one evening with his fair head way up high,
What he had to give me made me wring my hands and cry.

He give me a lesson that I never had before,
He give me a lesson that I never had before,
When he got through teaching me, from my elbows down was sore.

He boiled my first cabbage, and he made it awful hot,
He boiled my first cabbage, and he made it awful hot,
Then he put in the bacon and it overflowed the pot.

When you get good lovin' never go and spread the news,
When you get good lovin' never go and spread the news,
They'll double-cross you and leave you with them empty bed blues.

73 WOODY GUTHRIE

"This Land Is Your Land" (1944)

This land is your land, this land is my land
From California to the New York island,
From the redwood forest to the Gulf Stream waters;
This land was made for you and me.

As I was walking that ribbon of highway
I saw above me that endless skyway;
I saw below me that golden valley;
This land was made for you and me.

I've roamed and rambled and I followed my footsteps
To the sparkling sands of her diamond deserts;
And all around me a voice was sounding;
This land was made for you and me.

One bright Sunday morning in the shadows of the steeple
By the Relief Office I seen my people;
As they stood there hungry, I stood there whistling;
This land was made for you and me.

When the sun came shining, and I was strolling,
And the wheat fields waving and the dust clouds rolling,
As the fog was lifting a voice was chanting:
This land was made for you and me.

Nobody living can ever stop me,
As I go walking that freedom highway;
Nobody living can ever make me turn back,
This land was made for you and me.

As I went walkin, I saw a sign there,
And on the sign it said, "No Trespassing,"
But on the other side it didn't say nothing,
That side was made for you and me.

74 WALT DISNEY

The Testimony of Walter E. Disney Before the House Committee on Un-American Activities (1947)

[ROBERT E.] STRIPLING [CHIEF INVESTIGATOR]: Mr. Disney, will you state your full name and present address, please?

WALTER DISNEY: Walter E. Disney, Los Angeles, California.
RES: When and where were you born, Mr. Disney?
WD: Chicago, Illinois, December 5, 1901.

RES: December 5, 1901?

WD: Yes, sir.

RES: What is your occupation?

WD: Well, I am a producer of motion-picture cartoons.

RES: Mr. Chairman, the interrogation of Mr. Disney will be done by Mr. Smith.

THE CHAIRMAN [J. PARNELL THOMAS]:   Mr. Smith.

[H. A.] SMITH: Mr. Disney, how long have you been in that business?

WD: Since 1920.

HAS: You have been in Hollywood during this time?

WD: I have been in Hollywood since 1923.

HAS: At the present time you own and operate the Walt Disney Studio at Burbank, California?

WD: Well, I am one of the owners. Part owner.

HAS: How many people are employed there, approximately?

WD: At the present time about 600.

HAS: And what is the approximate largest number of employees you have had in the studio?

WD: Well, close to 1,400 at times.

HAS: Will you tell us a little about the nature of this particular studio, the type of pictures you make, and approximately how many per year?

WD: Well, mainly cartoon films. We make about twenty short subjects, and about two features a year.

HAS: Will you talk just a little louder, Mr. Disney?

WD: Yes, sir.

HAS: How many, did you say?

WD: About twenty short subject cartoons and about two features per year.

HAS: And some of the characters in the films consist of . . .

WD: You mean such as *Mickey Mouse* and *Donald Duck* and *Snow White and the Seven Dwarfs* [1938], and things of that sort.

HAS: Where are these films distributed?

WD: All over the world.

HAS: In all countries of the world?

WD: Well, except the Russian countries.

HAS: Why aren't they distributed in Russia, Mr. Disney?

WD: Well, we can't do business with them.

HAS: What do you mean by that?

WD: Oh, well, we have sold them some films a good many years ago. They bought the *Three Little Pigs* [1933] and used it through Russia. And they looked at a lot of our pictures, and I think they ran a lot of them in Russia, but then turned them back to us and said they didn't want them, they didn't suit their purposes.

HAS: Is the dialogue in these films translated into the various foreign languages?

WD: Yes. On one film we did ten foreign versions. That was *Snow White and the Seven Dwarfs*.

HAS: Have you ever made any pictures in your studio that contained propaganda and that were propaganda films?

WD: Well, during the war we did. We made quite a few – working with different government agencies. We did one for the Treasury on taxes and I did four anti-Hitler films. And I did one on my own for air power.

HAS: From those pictures that you made, have you any opinion as to whether or not the films can be used effectively to disseminate propaganda?

WD: Yes, I think they proved that.

HAS: How do you arrive at that conclusion?

WD: Well, on the one for the Treasury on taxes, it was to let the people know that taxes were important in the war effort. As they explained to me, they had 13,000,000 new taxpayers, people who had never paid taxes, and they explained that it would be impossible to prosecute all those that were delinquent and they wanted to put this story before those people so they would get their taxes in early. I made the film, and after the film had its run the Gallup poll organization polled the public and the findings were that twenty-nine percent of the people admitted that had influenced them in getting their taxes in early and giving them a picture of what taxes will do.

HAS: Aside from those pictures you made during the war, have you made any other pictures, or do you permit pictures to be made at your studio containing propaganda?

WD: No; we never have. During the war we thought it was a different thing. It was the first time we ever allowed anything like that to go in the films. We watch so that nothing gets into the films that would be harmful in any way to any group or any country. We have large audiences of children and different groups, and we try to keep them as free from anything that would offend anybody as possible. We work hard to see that nothing of that sort creeps in.

HAS: Do you have any people in your studio at the present time that you believe are Communist or Fascist, employed there?

WD: No; at the present time I feel that everybody in my studio is one-hundred-percent American.

HAS: Have you had at any time, in your opinion, in the past, have you at any time in the past had any Communists employed at your studio?

WD: Yes; in the past I had some people that I definitely feel were Communists.

HAS: As a matter of fact, Mr. Disney, you experienced a strike at your studio, did you not?

WD: Yes.

HAS: And is it your opinion that that strike was instituted by members of the Communist Party to serve their purposes?

WD: Well, it proved itself so with time, and I definitely feel it was a Communist group trying to take over my artists and they did take them over.

CHAIRMAN: Do you say they did take them over?

WD: They did take them over.

HAS: Will you explain that to the committee, please?

WD: It came to my attention when a delegation of my boys, my artists, came to me and told me that Mr. Herbert Sorrell . . .

HAS: Is that Herbert K. Sorrell?

WD: Herbert K. Sorrell was trying to take them over. I explained to them that it was none of my concern, that I had been cautioned to not even talk with any of my boys on labor. They said it was not a matter of labor, it was just a matter of them not wanting to go with Sorrell, and they had heard that I was going to sign with Sorrell, and they said that they wanted an election to prove that Sorrell didn't have the majority, and I said that I had a right to demand an election. So when Sorrell came, I demanded an election. Sorrell wanted me to sign on a bunch of cards that he had there that he claimed were the majority, but the other side had claimed the same thing. I told Mr. Sorrell that there is only one way for me to go and that was an election and that is what the law had set up, the National Labor Relations Board was for that purpose. He laughed at me and he said that he would use the Labor Board as it suited his purposes and that he had been sucker enough to go for that Labor Board ballot and he had lost some election – I can't remember the name of the place – by one vote. He said it took him two years to get it back. He said he would strike, that that was his weapon. He said, "I have all of the tools of the trade sharpened," that I couldn't stand the ridicule or the smear of a strike. I told him that it was a matter of principle with me, that I couldn't go on working with my boys feeling that I had sold them down the river to him on his say-so, and he laughed at me and told me I was naive and foolish. He said, you can't stand this strike, I will smear you, and I will make a dust bowl out of your plant.

CHAIRMAN: What was that?

WD: He said he would make a dust bowl out of my plant if he chose to. I told him I would have to go that way, sorry, that he might be able to do all that, but I would have to stand on that. The result was that he struck. I believed at that time that Mr. Sorrell was a Communist because of all the things that I had heard and having seen his name appearing on a number of Commie front things. When he pulled the strike, the first people to smear me and put me on the unfair list were all of the Commie front organizations. I can't remember them all, they change so often, but one that is clear in my mind is the League of Women Shoppers, *The People's World*, *The Daily Worker*, and the *PM* magazine in New York. They smeared me. Nobody came near to find out what the true facts of the thing were. And I even went through the same smear in South America, through some Commie periodicals in South America, and generally throughout the world all of the Commie groups began smear campaigns against me and my pictures.

JOHN MCDOWELL: In what fashion was that smear, Mr. Disney, what type of smear?

WD: Well, they distorted everything, they lied; there was no way you could ever counteract anything that they did; they formed picket lines in front of the theaters, and, well, they called my plant a sweatshop, and that is not true, and anybody in Hollywood would prove it otherwise. They claimed things that were not true at all and there was no way you could fight it back. It was not a labor problem at all because – I mean, I have never had labor trouble, and I think that would be backed up by anybody in Hollywood.

HAS: As a matter of fact, you have how many unions operating in your plant?

CHAIRMAN: Excuse me just a minute. I would like to ask a question.

HAS: Pardon me.

CHAIRMAN: In other words, Mr. Disney, Communists out there smeared you because you wouldn't knuckle under?

WD: I wouldn't go along with their way of operating. I insisted on it going through the National Labor Relations Board. And he told me outright that he used them as it suited his purposes.

CHAIRMAN: Supposing you had given in to him, then what would have been the outcome?

WD: Well, I would never have given in to him, because it was a matter of principle with me, and I fight for principles. My boys have been there, have grown up in the business with me, and I didn't feel like I could sign them over to anybody. They were vulnerable at that time. They were not organized. It is a new industry.

CHAIRMAN: Go ahead, Mr. Smith.

HAS: How many labor unions, approximately, do you have operating in your studios at the present time?

WD: Well, we operate with around thirty-five – I think we have contacts with thirty.

HAS: At the time of this strike you didn't have any grievances or labor troubles whatsoever in your plant?

WD: No. The only real grievance was between Sorrell and the boys within my plant, they demanding an election, and they never got it.

HAS: Do you recall having had any conversations with Mr. Sorrell relative to Communism?

WD: Yes, I do.

HAS: Will you relate that conversation?

WD: Well, I didn't pull my punches on how I felt. He evidently heard that I had called them all a bunch of Communists – and I believe they are. At the meeting he leaned over and he said, "You think I am a Communist, don't you," and I told him that all I knew was what I heard and what I had seen, and he laughed and said, "Well, I used their money to finance my strike of 1937," and he said that he had gotten the money through the personal check of some actor, but he didn't name the actor. I didn't go into it any further. I just listened.

HAS: Can you name any other individuals that were active at the time of the strike that you believe in your opinion are Communists?

WD: Well, I feel that there is one artist in my plant, that came in there, he came in about 1938, and he sort of stayed in the background, he wasn't too active, but he was the real brains of this, and I believe he is a Communist. His name is David Hilberman.

HAS: How is it spelled?

WD: H-i-l-b-e-r-m-a-n, I believe. I looked into his record and I found that, number 1, that he had no religion and, number 2, that he had spent considerable time at the Moscow Art Theatre studying art direction, or something.

HAS: Any others, Mr. Disney?

WD: Well, I think Sorrell is sure tied up with them. If he isn't a Communist, he sure should be one.

HAS: Do you remember the name of William Pomerance, did he have anything to do with it?

WD: Yes, sir. He came in later. Sorrell put him in charge as business manager of cartoonists and later he went to the Screen Actors as their business agent, and in turn he put in another man by the name of Maurice Howard, the present business agent. And they are all tied up with the same outfit.

HAS: What is your opinion of Mr. Pomerance and Mr. Howard as to whether or not they are or are not Communists?

WD: In my opinion they are Communists. No one has any way of proving those things.

HAS: Were you able to produce during the strike?

WD: Yes, I did, because there was a very few, very small majority that was on the outside, and all the other unions ignored all the lines because of the setup of the thing.

HAS: What is your personal opinion of the Communist Party, Mr. Disney, as to whether or not it is a political party?

WD: Well, I don't believe it is a political party. I believe it is an un-American thing. The thing that I resent the most is that they are able to get into these unions, take them over, and represent to the world that a group of people that are in my plant, that I know are good, one-hundred-percent Americans, are trapped by this group, and they are represented to the world as supporting all of those ideologies, and it is not so, and I feel that they really ought to be smoked out and shown up for what they are, so that all of the good, free causes in this country, all the liberalisms that really are American, can go out without the taint of Communism. That is my sincere feeling on it.

HAS: Do you feel that there is a threat of Communism in the motion-picture industry?

WD: Yes, there is, and there are many reasons why they would like to take it over or get in and control it, or disrupt it, but I don't think they have gotten very far, and I think the industry is made up of good Americans, just like in my plant, good, solid Americans. My boys have been fighting it longer than I have. They are trying to get out from under it and they will in time if we can just show them up.

HAS: There are presently pending before this committee two bills relative to outlawing the Communist Party. What thoughts have you as to whether or not those bills should be passed?

WD: Well, I don't know as I qualify to speak on that. I feel if the thing can be proven un-American that it ought to be outlawed. I think in some way it should be done without interfering with the rights of the people. I think that will be done. I have that faith. Without interfering, I mean, with the good, American rights that we all have now, and we want to preserve.

HAS: Have you any suggestions to offer as to how the industry can be helped in fighting this menace?

WD: Well, I think there is a good start toward it. I know that I have been handicapped out there in fighting it, because they have been hiding behind this labor setup, they get themselves closely tied up in the labor thing, so that if you try to get rid of them they make a labor case out of it. We must keep the American labor unions clean. We have got to fight for them.

HAS: That is all of the questions I have, Mr. Chairman.

CHAIRMAN: Mr. Vail.

R. B. VAIL: No questions.

CHAIRMAN: Mr. McDowell.

J. MCDOWELL: No questions.

WD: Sir?

JM: I have no questions. You have been a good witness.

WD: Thank you.

CHAIRMAN: Mr. Disney, you are the fourth producer we have had as a witness, and each one of those four producers said, generally speaking, the same thing, and that is that the Communists have made inroads, have attempted inroads. I just want to point that out because there seems to be a very strong unanimity among the producers that have testified before us. In addition to producers, we have had actors and writers testify to the same. There is no doubt but what the movies are probably the greatest medium for entertainment in the United States and in the world. I think you, as a creator of entertainment, probably are one of the greatest examples in the profession. I want to congratulate you on the form of entertainment which you have given the American people and given the world and congratulate you for taking time out to come here and testify before this committee. He has been very helpful. Do you have any more questions, Mr. Stripling?

HAS: I am sure he does not have any more, Mr. Chairman.

RES: No; I have no more questions.

CHAIRMAN: Thank you very much, Mr. Disney.

75 RALPH ELLISON

"As the Spirit Moves Mahalia" (1964)

There are certain women singers who possess, beyond all the boundaries of our admiration for their art, an uncanny power to evoke our love. We warm with pleasure at mere mention of their names; their simplest songs sing in our hearts like the remembered voices of old dear friends, and when we are lost within the listening anonymity of darkened concert halls, they seem to seek us out unerringly. Standing regal within the bright isolation of the stage, their subtlest effects seem meant for us and us alone; privately, as across the intimate space of our own living rooms. And when we encounter the simple dignity of their immediate presence, we suddenly ponder the mystery of human greatness.

Perhaps the power springs from their dedication, their having subjected themselves successfully to the demanding discipline necessary to the mastery of their chosen art. Or perhaps it is a quality with which they are born as some are born with bright orange hair. Perhaps, though we think not, it is acquired, a technique of "presence." But whatever its source, it touches us as a rich abundance of human warmth and sympathy. Indeed, we feel that if the idea of aristocracy is more than mere class conceit, then these surely are our natural queens. For they enchant the eye as they caress the ear, and in their presence we sense the full, moony, glory of womanhood in all its mystery – maid, matron and matriarch. They are the sincere ones whose humanity dominates the artifices of the art with which they stir us, and when they sing we have some notion of our better selves. . . .

Mahalia Jackson, a large, handsome brown-skinned woman in her middle forties, who began singing in her father's church at the age of five, is a Negro of the *American Negroes*, and is, as the Spanish say, a woman of much quality. Her early experience was typical of Negro women of a certain class in the South. Born in New Orleans, she left school in the eighth grade and went to work as a nursemaid. Later she worked in the cotton fields of Louisiana and as a domestic. Her main social life was centered in the Baptist Church. She grew up with the sound of jazz in her ears, and, being an admirer of Bessie Smith, was aware of the prizes and acclaim awaiting any mistress of the blues, but in her religious views the blues and jazz are profane forms and a temptation to be resisted. She also knew something of the painful experiences which go into the forging of a true singer of the blues.

In 1927, following the classical pattern of Negro migration, Mahalia went to Chicago, where she worked as a laundress and studied beauty culture. Here, too, her social and artistic life was in the Negro community, centered in the Greater Salem Baptist Church. Here she became a member of the choir and a soloist with a quintet which toured the churches affiliated with the National Baptist Convention. Up until the forties she operated within a world of music which was confined, for the most part, to Negro communities, and it was by her ability to move such audiences as are found here that her reputation grew. It was also such audiences which, by purchasing over two million copies of her famous "Move On Up a Little Higher," brought her to national attention.

When listening to such recordings as *Sweet Little Jesus Boy, Bless This House, Mahalia Jackson*, or *In the Upper Room*, it is impossible to escape the fact that Mahalia Jackson is possessed of a profound religious conviction. Nor can we escape the awareness that no singer living has a greater ability to move us – regardless of our own religious attitudes – with the projected emotion of a song. Perhaps with the interpretive artist the distinction so often made between popular and serious art is not so great as it seems. Perhaps what counts is the personal quality of the individual artist, the depth of his experience and his sense of life. Certainly Miss Jackson possesses a quality of dignity and the ability to project a sincerity of purpose which is characteristic of only the greatest of interpretive artists.

Nor should it be assumed that her singing is simply the expression of the Negro's "natural" ability as is held by the stereotype (would that it were only true!). For although its techniques are not taught formally, Miss Jackson is the master of an art of singing which is as complex and of an even older origin than that of jazz.

It is an art which was acquired during those years when she sang in the comparative obscurity of the Negro community, and which, with the inevitable dilution, comes into our national song style usually through the singers of jazz and the blues. It is an art which depends upon the employment of the full expressive resources of the human voice – from the rough growls employed by blues singers, the intermediate sounds, half-cry, half-recitative, which are common to Eastern music; the shouts, and hollers of American Negro folk cries; the rough-edged tones; and broad vibratos, the high, shrill and grating tones which rasp one's ears like the agonized flourishes of flamenco, to the gut tones, which remind us of where the jazz trombone found its human source. It is an art which employs a broad rhythmic freedom and accents the lyric line to reinforce the emotional impact. It utilizes half-tones, glissandi, blue notes, humming and moaning. Or again, it calls upon the most lyrical, floating tones of which the voice is capable. Its diction ranges from the most precise to the near liquidation of word-meaning in the sound; a pronunciation which is almost of the academy one instant and of the broadest cotton-field dialect the next. And it is most eclectic in its use of other musical idiom; indeed, it borrows any effect which will aid in the arousing and control of emotion. Especially is it free in its use of the effect of jazz; its tempos (with the characteristic economy of Negro expression it shares a common rhythmic and harmonic base with jazz) are taken along with its intonations, and, in ensemble singing, its orchestral voicing. In Mahalia's own "Move On Up a Little Higher" there is a riff straight out of early Ellington. Most of all it is an art which swings, and in the South there are many crudely trained groups who use it naturally for the expression of religious feeling who could teach the jazz modernists quite a bit about polyrhythmics and polytonality. . . .

Indeed, many who come upon it outside the context of the Negro community tend to think of it as just another form of jazz, and the same confusion is carried over to the art of Mahalia Jackson. There is a widely held belief that she is really a blues singer who refuses, out of religious superstitions perhaps, to sing the blues; a jazz singer who coyly rejects her rightful place before a swinging band. And it *is* ironically true that just as a visitor who comes to Harlem seeking out many of the theatres and movie houses of the twenties will find them converted into churches, those who seek today for a living idea of the rich and moving art of Bessie Smith must go not to the night clubs and variety houses where those who call themselves blues singers find their existence, but must seek out Mahalia Jackson in a Negro church. And I insist upon the church and not the concert hall, because for all her concert appearances about the world she is not primarily a concert singer but a high priestess in the religious ceremony of her church. As such she is as far from the secular existentialism of the blues as Sartre is from St. John of the Cross. And it is in the setting of the church that the full timbre of her sincerity sounds most distinctly.

Certainly there was good evidence of this last July [1957] at the Newport Jazz Festival, where one of the most widely anticipated events was Miss Jackson's appearance with the Ellington Orchestra. Ellington had supplied the "Come Sunday" movement of his *Black, Brown and Beige Suite* (which with its organ-like close had contained one of Johnny Hodges's most serenely moving solos, a superb evocation of Sunday peace) with lyrics for Mahalia to sing. To make way for her, three of the original movements were abandoned along with the Hodges solo, but in their place she was given words of such banality that for all the fervor of her singing and the band's excellent performance, that Sunday sun simply would not rise. Nor does the recorded version change our opinion that this was a most unfortunate marriage and an error of taste, and the rather unformed setting of the Twenty-third Psalm which completes the side does nothing to improve things. In fact, only the sound and certain of the transitions between movements are an improvement over the old version of the suite. Originally "Come Sunday" was Ellington's moving *impression* of Sunday peace and religious quiet, but he got little of this into the words. So little, in fact, that it was impossible for Mahalia to release that vast fund of emotion with which Southern Negroes have charged the scenes and symbols of the Gospels.

Only the fortunate few who braved the Sunday morning rain to attend the Afro-American Episcopal Church services heard Mahalia at her best at Newport. Many had doubtless been absent from church or synagogue for years, but here they saw her in her proper setting and the venture into the strangeness of the Negro church was worth the visit. Here they could see, to the extent we can visualize such a thing, the world which Mahalia summons up with her voice; the spiritual reality which infuses her song. Here it could be seen that the true function of her singing is not simply to entertain, but to prepare the congregation for the minister's message, to make it receptive to the spirit and, with effects of voice and rhythm, to evoke a shared community of experience.

As she herself put it while complaining of the length of the time allowed her during a recording session, "I'm used to singing in church, where they don't stop me until the Lord comes." By which she meant, not until she had created the spiritual and emotional climate in which the Word is made manifest; not until, and as the spirit moves her, the song of Mahalia the high priestess sings within the heart of the congregation as its own voice of faith.

When in possession of the words which embody her religious convictions Mahalia can dominate even the strongest jazz beat and instill it with her own fervor. *Bless This House* contains songs set to rumba, waltz and two-step but what she does to them provides a triumphal blending of popular dance movements with religious passion. In *Sweet Little Jesus Boy*, the song "The Holy Babe" is a Negro version of an old English count-rhyme, and while enumerating the gifts of the Christian God to man, Mahalia and Mildred Falls, her pianist, create a rhythmical drive such as is expected of the entire Basie band. It is all joy and exultation and swing, but it is nonetheless religious music. Many who are moved by Mahalia and her spirit have been so impressed by the emotional release of her music that they fail to see the frame within which she moves. But even *In the Upper Room* and *Mahalia Jackson* – in which she reminds us most poignantly of Bessie Smith, and in which the common singing techniques of the spirituals and the blues are most clearly to be heard – are directed toward the after life and thus are intensely religious. For those who cannot –or will not – visit Mahalia in her proper setting, these records are the next best thing.

76 STANLEY KAUFFMANN

"Little Big Man" (1970)

Just six years ago I reviewed Thomas Berger's novel *Little Big Man* and said:

> A chief function of the tall tale is as a free-flowing conduit of history, a catch-all vehicle that, by disregarding most probabilities and some possibilities, contains a lot of historical truth.

Like Vincent McHugh's *Caleb Catlum's America* (a neglected nugget), Berger's book performed the American tall-tale magic: it summarized a chunk of basically grim history in a breezy, darn-your-eyes manner, its very style implying the one virtue that possibly counterbalances the heavy deeds done – lively, humorous grit.

Calder Willingham's adroit screenplay condenses Berger's big book and, often sensibly, rearranges matters, as it tells the story of Jack Crabb, who survives a Pawnee attack on a wagon train when he is ten, is carried off by the Cheyenne and raised by them, and whose life then fluctuates between the Cheyenne and white civilizations until the two life styles collide at the Little Bighorn in 1876. Jack is the sole white survivor, and he survives until "now" when he tells his story into a tape recorder. In the novel (1964) he was 111 when he was talking; for 1970, he had to be made 121. (The film was done just in time; even tall tales are limited in height.) The most significant change is that, in the original, Jack's Cheyenne "grandfather" goes up on a mountain at the end to die, and dies; in the film the old man can't quite make it, and has to come down again with Jack, to live. I rather liked this change, as it leads nicely into the note of Jack's own astonishing survival.

Arthur Penn directs with all his customary skill and very little of his customary artiness. This time, happily, he leaves Beauty to the eye of the beholder, and doesn't label it for us. He tells his story in a clean, vigorous manner, with a generally fine sense of where the audience should be placed to get the most out of every moment, with his humanist concerns revealed in his handling of character relationships. His weak spots are his large-scale physical conflicts; he doesn't love action enough to handle it as well as a Ford or Peckinpah or Hawks would. Ralph Nelson is a far inferior director to Penn, but the slaughter of Indians by cavalry in *Soldier Blue* was more gruesome than in *Little Big Man*.

Penn's invention falters in his battle scenes, and he also fumbles some opportunities. When Custer's cavalry rides up out of the snowy mist along the Washita to murder the Cheyenne, instead of letting them materialize out of the whiteness (as he starts to do), Penn suddenly cuts to a long shot from a hilltop to show the troops proceeding down the valley. And at the Little Bighorn, the angles and the editing don't give us a clear idea of the closing of a trap; terrain and disposition are unclear.

But there is life in the film, and the core of it is Dustin Hoffman's performance of Jack Crabb. We hear his 121-year-old voice out of the silence under the titles – there's no music until we're well along, and very little then – when we see him in his (rubber-mask) antiquity. Later, after a boy actor and an early adolescent actor have marked his growing time, Hoffman himself takes up Crabb at about the age of fifteen and carries him through his "periods" of frontier schoolboy, young Cheyenne brave, carnival man, gunfighter, boozer, storekeeper, older Cheyenne brave, hermit, and cavalry mule skinner.

Bernard Shaw said that fine art is either easy or impossible, and as Shaw meant it, Hoffman proves it yet again. He's short, he has a Feiffer profile, his voice is no great shakes, and, although he has charm, he has no great force of personality. What he has is instant credibility. It never seems to cross his mind that he is anything other than what he claims to be at the moment, so it never crosses our minds, either. His secret is not only imagination, not only the requisite vitality, but a lack of objectivity, so great as almost to be simple-minded. It's as if Hoffman were saying, "What do you mean, I'm not a Cheyenne brave? I've been one all my life." This ability to shut out objectivity – to shut out any view of one's self *playing* the part – is an essential particularly for "chameleon" actors, and it's Hoffman's ace.

In Robert Hughes's documentary film about Penn, there is a sequence showing Penn and Hoffman working on a scene from *Little Big Man*. It's a small lesson in the interweaving of two kinds of talent, and the results are in this picture.

The other noteworthy performance is by Chief Dan George as Crabb's Cheyenne "grandfather." I was prejudiced in the chief's favor because he looks a lot like my Uncle Al, dead these many years, and he fed my prejudice with his dignity and humor.

Penn's one failure with a performer is Faye Dunaway, a parson's prurient wife who later turns up as a whore. She misses no possible acting cliche. Besides, as a frontier parson's wife, she wears false eyelashes only a trifle smaller than ostrich fans.

Under the energy of the film, the ominous theme is the invincible brutality of the white man, the end of "natural" life in America. At the beginning, when Crabb's young interviewer uses the word "genocide," it irritates the old man, but the film – his story – only substantiates the term. Penn makes contradictorily sure we know his own sympathies. When Indians attack a stagecoach, the murders are supposed to be funny; when cavalrymen attack an Indian village, the murders are tragic.

The color is unobtrusive – certifying without being garish. The Panavision feels comfortable. Penn has made a tangy and, I think, unique film with American verve, about some of the grisly things that American verve has done.

77 JOAN DIDION

"Georgia O'Keeffe" (1979)

"Where I was born and where and how I have lived is unimportant," Georgia O'Keeffe told us in the book of paintings and words published in her ninetieth year on earth. She seemed to be advising us to forget the beautiful face in the Stieglitz photographs. She appeared to be dismissing the rather condescending romance that had attached to her by then, the romance of extreme good looks and advanced age and deliberate isolation. "It is what I have done with where I have been that should be of interest." I recall an August afternoon in Chicago in 1973 when I took my daughter, then seven, to see what Georgia O'Keeffe had done with where she had been. One of the vast O'Keeffe "Sky Above Clouds" canvases floated over the back stairs in the Chicago Art Institute that day, dominating what seemed to be several stories of empty light, and my daughter looked at it once, ran to the landing, and kept on looking. "Who drew it," she whispered after a while. I told her. "I need to talk to her," she said finally.

My daughter was making, that day in Chicago, an entirely unconscious but quite basic assumption about people and the work they do. She was assuming that the glory she saw in the work reflected a glory in its maker, that the painting was the painter as the poem is the poet, that every choice one made alone – every word chosen or rejected, every brush stroke laid or not laid down – betrayed one's character. *Style is character.* It seemed to me that afternoon that I had rarely seen so instinctive an application of this familiar principle, and I recall being pleased not only that my daughter responded to style as character but that it was Georgia O'Keeffe's particular style to which she responded: this was a hard woman who had imposed her 192 square feet of clouds on Chicago.

"Hardness" has not been in our century a quality much admired in women, nor in the past twenty years has it even been in official favor for men. When hardness surfaces in the very old we tend to transform it into "crustiness" or eccentricity, some tonic pepperiness to be indulged at a distance. On the evidence of her work and what she has said about it, Georgia O'Keeffe is neither "crusty" nor eccentric. She is simply hard, a straight shooter, a woman clean of received wisdom and open to what she sees. This is a woman who could early on dismiss most of her contemporaries as "dreamy", and would later single out one she liked as "a very poor painter". (And then add, apparently by way of softening the judgment: "I guess he wasn't a painter at all. He had no courage and I believe that to create one's own world in any of the arts takes courage.") This is a woman who in 1939 could advise her admirers that they were missing her point, that their appreciation of her famous flowers was merely sentimental. "When I paint a red hill," she observed coolly in the catalogue for an exhibition that year, "you say it is too bad that I don't always paint flowers. A flower touches almost everyone's heart. A red hill doesn't touch everyone's heart." This is a woman who could describe the genesis of one of her most well-known paintings – the "Cow's Skull: Red, White and Blue" owned by the Metropolitan – as an act of quite deliberate and derisive orneriness. "I thought of the city men I had been seeing in the East," she wrote. "They talked so often of writing the Great American Novel – the Great American Play – the Great American Poetry . . . So as I was painting my cow's head on blue I thought to myself, 'I'll make it an American painting. They will not think it great with the red stripes down the sides – Red, White and Blue – but they will notice it.' "

The city men. The men. They. The words crop up again and again as this astonishingly aggressive woman tells us what was on her mind when she was making her astonishingly aggressive paintings. It was those city men who stood accused of sentimentalizing her flowers: "I made you take time to look at what I saw and when you took time to really notice my flower you hung all your associations with flowers on my flower and you write about my flower as if I think and see what you think and see – and I don't."

And I don't. Imagine those words spoken, and the sound you hear is don't tread on me. "The men" believed it impossible to paint New York, so Georgia O'Keeffe painted New York. "The men" didn't think much of her bright color, so she made it brighter. The men yearned toward Europe so she went to Texas, and then New Mexico. The men talked about Cezanne, "long involved remarks about the 'plastic quality' of his form and color", and took one another's long involved remarks, in the view of this angelic rattlesnake in their midst, altogether too seriously. "I can paint one of those dismal-colored paintings like the men," the woman who regarded herself always as an outsider remembers thinking one day in 1922, and she did; a painting of a shed "all low-toned and dreary with the tree beside the door". She called this act of rancor "The Shanty" and hung it in her next show. "The men seemed to approve of it," she reported fifty-four years later, her contempt undimmed. "They seemed to think that maybe I was beginning to paint. That was my only low-toned dismal-colored painting."

Some women fight and others do not. Like so many successful guerrillas in the war between the sexes, Georgia O'Keeffe seems to have been equipped early with an immutable sense of who she was and a fairly clear understanding that she would be required to prove it. On the surface her upbringing was conventional. She was a child on the Wisconsin prairie who played with china dolls and painted watercolors with cloudy skies because sunlight was too hard to paint and, with her brother and sisters, listened every night to her mother read stories of the Wild West, of Texas, of Kit

Carson and Billy the Kid. She told adults that she wanted to be an artist and was embarrassed when they asked what kind of artist she wanted to be: she had no idea "what kind". She had no idea what artists did. She had never seen a picture that interested her, other than a pen-and-ink Maid of Athens in one of her mother's books, some Mother Goose illustrations printed on cloth, a tablet cover that showed a little girl with pink roses, and the painting of Arabs on horseback that hung in her grandmother's parlor. At thirteen, in a Dominican convent, she was mortified when the sister corrected her drawing. At Chatham Episcopal Institute in Virginia she painted lilacs and sneaked time alone to walk out to where she could see the line of the Blue Ridge Mountains on the horizon. At the Art Institute in Chicago she was shocked by the presence of live models and wanted to abandon anatomy lessons. At the Art Students League in New York one of her fellow students advised her that, since he would be a great painter and she would end up teaching painting in a girls' school, any work of hers was less important than modeling for him. Another painted over her work to show her how the Impressionists did trees. She had not before heard how the Impressionists did trees and she did not much care.

At twenty-four she left all those opinions behind and went for the first time to live in Texas, where there were no trees to paint and no one to tell her how not to paint them. In Texas there was only the horizon she craved. In Texas she had her sister Claudia with her for a while, and in the late afternoons they would walk away from town and toward the horizon and watch the evening star come out. "That evening star fascinated me," she wrote. "It was in some way very exciting to me. My sister had a gun, and as we walked she would throw bottles into the air and shoot as many as she could before they hit the ground. I had nothing but to walk into nowhere and the wide sunset space with the star. Ten watercolors were made from that star." In a way one's interest is compelled as much by the sister Claudia with the gun as by the painter Georgia with the star, but only the painter left us this shining record. Ten watercolors were made from that star.

78 STUDS TERKEL

FROM *"Jill Robertson: Fantasia"* (1982)

She is the daughter of a former Hollywood film producer.

Growing up in Hollywood was the only reality I knew. The closest I ever came to feeling glamorous was from my mother's maid, a woman named Dorothy, who used to call me Glamour. She was black. In those days, she was called coloured. When I would see my mother – or my mother's secretary, 'cause there was a hierarchy – interviewing maids or cooks, I'd think of maids and cooks represented in the movies.

I used not to like to go to school. I'd go to work with my father. I'd like to be with him because power didn't seem like work. He had four or five secretaries, and they were always pretty. I thought: How wonderful to have pretty secretaries. I used to think they'd be doing musical numbers. I could imagine them tapping along with his mail. I never saw it real.

To me, a studio head was a man who controlled everyone's lives. It was like being the principal. It was someone you were scared of, someone who knew everything, knew what you were thinking, knew where you were going, knew when you were driving on the studio lot at eighty miles an hour, knew that you had not been on the set in time. The scoldings the stars got. There was a paternalism. It was feudal. It was an archaic system designed to keep us playing: Let's pretend, let's make believe.

First of all, you invented someone, someone's image of someone. Then you'd infantilize them, keep them at a level of consciousness, so they'd be convinced that this is indeed who they are. They had doctors at the studios: "Oh, you're just fine, honey. Take this and you'll be just fine." These stars, who influenced our dreams, had no more to do with their own lives than fairies had, or elves.

I remember playing with my brother and sister. We would play Let's Make a Movie the way other kids would play cowboys and Indians. We'd cry, we'd laugh. We'd do whatever the character did. We had elaborate costumes and sets. We drowned our dolls and all the things one does. The difference was, if we didn't get it right, we'd play it again until we liked it. We even incorporated into our child play the idea of the dailies and the rushes. The repeats of film scenes to get the right angle. If the princess gets killed in a scene, she gets killed again and again and again. It's okay. She gets to live again. No one ever dies. There's no growing up. This was reality to us.

I had a feeling that out there, there were very poor people who didn't have enough to eat. But they wore wonderfully coloured rags and did musical numbers up and down the streets together. My mother did not like us to go into what was called the servants' wing of the house.

My mother was of upper-class Jewish immigrants. They lost everything in the depression. My father tried to do everything he could to revive my mother's idea of what life had been like for her father in the court of the czar. Whether her father was ever actually in the court is irrelevant. My father tried to make it classy for her. It never was good enough, never could be. She couldn't be a Boston Brahmin.

Russian-Jewish immigrants came from the *shtetls* and ghettos out to Hollywood: this combination jungle-tropical paradise crossed with a nomadic desert. In this magical place that had no relationship to any reality they had ever seen before in their lives, or that anyone else had ever seen, they decided to create their idea of an eastern aristocracy. I'm talking about the kind of homes they would never be invited to. It was, of course, overdone. It was also the baronial mansions of the dukes' homes that their parents could never have gotten into. Goldwyn, Selznick, Zukor, Lasky, Warner. Hollywood – the American Dream – is a Jewish idea.

In a sense, it's a Jewish revenge on America. It combines the Puritan ethic – there's no sex, no ultimate satisfaction – with baroque magnificence. The happy ending was the invention of Russian Jews, designed to drive Americans crazy.

It was a marvellous idea. What could make them crazy but to throw back at them their small towns? Look how happy it is here. Compare the real small towns with the small town on the MGM back lot. There's no resemblance.

The street is Elm Street. It's so green, so bright, of lawns and trees. It's a town somewhere in the centre of America. It's got the white fence and the big porch around the house. And it's got three and four generations. They're turn-of-the-century people before they learned how to yell at each other. It's the boy and girl running into each other's arms. And everybody else is singing. It's everybody sitting down to dinner and looking at each other, and everyone looks just wonderful. No one is sick. No one's mad at anyone else. It's all so simple. It's all exactly what I say it is.

Aunt Mary is a little looney and lives with us because she loves us. It's not that she's crazy and gonna wind up killing one of us one of these days. Or that she's drunk. It's simply that she'd rather live with us and take care of us. The father would be Lewis Stone. He'd have a little bit of a temper now and then. The mother is definitely Spring Byington. She's daffy, but she's never deaf. She hears everything you say and she listens. And she hugs you and her hug is soft and sweet-smelling. The daughter is Judy Garland when she believed in Aunt Em. The boy is Robert Walker before he realized he was gonna drink himself to death. And love and marriage would be innocence and tenderness. And no sex.

The dream to me was to be blond, tall, and able to disappear. I loved movies about boys running away to sea. I wanted to be the laconic, cool, tall, Aryan male. Precisely the opposite of the angry, anxious, sort of mottle-haired Jewish girl.

I wanted to be this guy who could walk away from any situation that got a little rough. Who could walk away from responsibility. The American Dream, the idea of the happy ending, is an avoidance of responsibility and commitment. If something ends happily, you don't have to worry about it tomorrow.

The idea of the movie star, the perfect-looking woman or man who has breakfast at a glass table on a terrace where there are no mosquitoes. No one ever went to the bathroom in movies. I grew up assuming that movie stars did not. I thought it was terrible to be a regular human being. Movie stars did not look awful, ever. They never threw up. They never got really sick, except in a wonderful way where they'd get a little sweaty, get sort of a gloss on the face, and then die. They didn't shrivel up or shrink away. They didn't have acne. The woman didn't have menstrual cramps. Sex, when I ran across it, in no way resembled anything I had ever seen in the movies. I didn't know how to respond.

I think the reason we're so crazy sexually in America is that all our responses are acting. We don't know how to feel. We know how it looked in the movies. We know that in the movies it's inconceivable that the bad guy will win. Therefore we don't get terribly involved in any cause. The good guy's gonna win anyway. It's a marvellous political weapon.

The Hollywood phenomenon of the forties – the Second World War – was distinct from the Vietnam War. War was fine. Sure there were bad things, but there were musicals. Comedies about soldiers. The dream was to marry someone in uniform. I believed every bit of it. I saw how the movies were made and still I believed it.

I remember seeing a carpenter in front of the house and telling my father he looked like Roy Rogers and that he ought to test him. He did. The guy couldn't act. We were always testing everyone, always seeing what raw material they would be. I'd sit in class pretending to be an executive. I'd be sitting there figuring out who could this kid play, who could that one play. I used to look at Robert Redford in class and imagine he would be a movie star. In fourth grade. You always looked at humans as property. It affected all our lives.

I hated the idea that I was bright. There was a collision between bright and pretty and seductive. I wanted to be one of those girls the guys just wanted to do one thing to. I wanted to be one of those blonde jobs. That's what they used to call them – jobs. A tall job. A slim job. Somebody you could work on.

I wanted to be Rhonda Fleming or Lana Turner. I refused to see what the inside of their lives was like. They didn't see it either. It was carefully kept from them. My God, look at the life. Getting up at five-thirty in the morning before your brain has begun to function, getting rolled out in a limousine, and having people work on your body and your face. Remember, they were very young people when they came out here. Imagine having all your waking life arranged all the time. They became machines. No wonder the sensitive ones went insane or killed themselves.

The studio had the power. The studio would hire the fan club. The head of the club was on the star's payroll. The star was usually not even aware of where the money was going, to whom, for what. The whole thing was manufactured. Fame is manufactured. Stardom is manufactured. After all these years, it still comes as a surprise to me.

79 MIKAL GILMORE

FROM *"Bruce Springsteen" (1987)*

The 1960s are often idealized as times of great innocence and wonder. Although your own work has been recorded in the Seventies and Eighties, some of your best songs seem haunted by the strife of that era. Looking back, do you see the Sixties as a period in which a great deal was at stake in American culture?

I think that in the Sixties there was a rebellion against what people felt was the dehumanization of society, where people were counted as less than people, less than human. It was almost as if there were a temper tantrum against that particular threat. In the Sixties moral lines were drawn relatively easily. "Hey, this is wrong, this is right – I'm standing *here*!" That idea busted up nearly every house in the nation. And people expected revolution. I think some people thought it was going to happen in an explosive burst of some sort of radical, joyous energy, and that all the bullshit and all the Nixons were going to be swept away, and, man, we were going to start all over again and do it right this time. Okay, that was a child-like fantasy. But a lot of those ideas were good ideas.

It's funny, but because of the naiveness of the era, it's easily trivialized and laughed at. But underneath it, I think, people were trying in some sense to redefine their own lives and the country that they lived in, in some more open and free and just fashion. And *that* was real – that desire was real. But I think that as people grew older, they found that the process of changing things actually tends to be unromantic and not very dramatic. In fact, it's very slow and very small, and if anything, it's done in inches.

The values from that time are things that I still believe in. I think that all my music – certainly the music I've done in the past five or six years – is a result of that time and those values. I don't know, it seems almost like a lost generation. How do the ideals of that time connect in some pragmatic fashion to the real world today? I don't know if anybody's answered that particular question.

One of the central events that inspired the idealism of that era – the war in Vietnam – was also the most horrific thing to happen to this society in the last twenty years. It tore us apart along political and generational lines, but it also drew a hard line across the nation and forced many of us to take a clear stand.

That's true: that *was* the last time things ever felt that morally clear. Since then – from Watergate on down – who or what the enemy is has grown more obfuscated. It's just too confusing. But you can't wait for events like Vietnam, because if you do, then maybe 55,000 men end up dying and the country is left changed forever. I mean, that experience is *still* not over. And without those particular memories, without the people who were there reminding everybody, it would've happened again already, I'm sure. Certainly, it would have happened in the past eight years if they thought they could have gotten away with it.

So what went wrong? Why is it that so few of the brave ideals of those times carried over to the social and political realities of today?

I think the problem is that people yearn for simple answers. The reason the image of the Reagan presidency is so effective is that it appeared to be very simple. I think that's also the whole reason for the canonization of Oliver North: he said all the right words and pushed all the right buttons. And people yearn for those sorts of simple answers. But the world will never ever be simple again, if it ever was. The world is nothing but complex, and if you do not learn to interpret its complexities, you're going to be on the river without a paddle.

The classic thing for me is the misinterpretation of "Born in the U.S.A." I opened the paper one day and saw where they had quizzed kids on what different songs meant, and they asked them what "Born in the U.S.A." meant. "Well, it's about my country" they answered. Well, that *is* what it's about – that's certainly one of the things it's about – but if that's as far in as you go, you're going to miss it, you know? I don't think people are being taught to think hard enough about things in general – whether it's about their own lives, politics, the situation in Nicaragua or whatever. Consequently, if you do not learn to do that – if you do not develop the skills to interpret that information – you're going to be easily manipulated, or you're going to walk around simply confused and ineffectual and powerless.

People are being dumped into this incredibly unintelligible society, and they are swimming, barely staying afloat, and then trying to catch on to whatever is going to give them a little safe ground.

I guess when I started in music I thought, "My job is pretty simple. My job is I search for the human things in myself, and I turn them into notes and words, and then in some fashion, I help people hold on to their own humanity – if I'm doing my job right."

You *can* change things – except maybe you can affect only one person, or maybe only a few people. Certainly nothing as dramatic as we expected in the Sixties. When I go onstage, my approach is "I'm going to reach just one person" – even if there's 80,000 people there. Maybe those odds aren't so great, but if that's what they are, that's okay. . . .

You keep talking about your involvement in rock & roll as a job. That's a far cry from the view that many of us had in the Sixties, when we looked upon artists – such as Bob Dylan – not so much as people performing a job but as cultural revolutionaries.

Dylan was a revolutionary. So was Elvis. I'm not that. I don't see myself as having been that. I felt that what I would be able to do, maybe, was redefine what I did in more human terms than it had been defined before, and in more everyday terms. I always saw myself as a nuts-and-bolts kind of person. I felt what I was going to accomplish I would accomplish over a long period of time, not in an enormous burst of energy or genius. To keep an even perspective on it all, I looked at it *like* a job – something that you do every day and over a long period of time.

To me, Dylan and Elvis – what they did was genius. I never really saw myself in that fashion. I'm sure there was a part of me that was afraid of having that kind of ambition or taking on those kinds of responsibilities.

"Born to Run" was certainly an ambitious record. Maybe it wasn't revolutionary, but it was certainly innovative: it redefined what an album could do in the Seventies.

Well, I was shooting for the moon, you know? I always wanted to do that too, on top of it. When I did *Born to Run*, I thought, "I'm going to make the greatest rock & roll record ever made." I guess what I'm saying is, later on my perspective changed a bit so that I felt like I could maybe redefine what doing the particular job was about. So that it does *not* have to drive you crazy or drive you to drugs or drinking, or you do not have to lose yourself in it and lose perspective of your place in the scheme of things, I guess I wanted to try and put a little more human scale on the thing. I felt that was necessary for my *own* sanity, for one thing.

Your next record, "Darkness on the Edge of Town," sounded far less hopeful than "Born to Run." Several critics attributed the sullen mood to the long stall between the records – the ten-month period in which a lawsuit prevented you from recording. What really was happening on "Darkness"?

That was a record where I spent a lot of time focusing. And what I focused on was this one idea: What do you do if your dream comes true? Where does that leave you? What do you do if that happens? And I realized part of what you have to face is the problem of isolation. You can get isolated if you've got a lot of dough or if you don't have much dough, whether you're Elvis Presley or whether you're sitting in front of the TV with a six-pack of beer. It's easy to get there. On that record it was like "Well, what I've done, does it have any greater meaning than that I've made a good album and had some luck with it?" I was trying to figure out that question, which is really one I'm still trying to figure out. . . .

On each of your records since "Darkness" – "The River," "Nebraska" and "Born in the U.S.A." – you managed to write about hard working-class realities in ways that sounded surprisingly immediate, coming from a rich, well-known pop star. Was there something about moving into fame and wealth that caused you to identify more closely with the world you were leaving behind?

I think it's probably a normal reaction. I mean, the circumstances of your life are changing, and what they are changing to is unknown to you, and you have never known closely anyone else who has had the same experience. On one hand you cannot hide in the past. You can't say, "Well, I'm the same old guy I used to be." You have to go ahead and meet that person who you're becoming and accept whatever that's about. I always wanted to live solidly in the present, always remember the past and always be planning for the future. So from *Darkness* to *The River*, I was attempting to pull myself into what I felt was going to be the adult world, so that when things became disorienting, I would be strong enough to hold my ground. Those were the records where I was trying to forge that foundation and maintain my connections and try to say, "Well, what is this going to mean? Maybe what this is all going to mean is up to me."

With the later records, that resolve seemed to have more and more political resonance. In 1979 you took part in the No Nukes benefit concert, and in November 1980 you made some scathing remarks onstage in Arizona on the evening following Ronald Reagan's election. How did events of recent years inspire your new-found political concern and awareness?

I think my response was based on an accumulation of things. I never considered myself a particularly political person. I wasn't when I was younger, and I don't think I really am now. But if you live in a situation where you have seen people's lives wasted . . . I think the thing that frightened me most was seeing all that waste. There wasn't any one specific thing that made me go in that particular direction, but it seemed like if you're a citizen, and if you're living here, then it's your turn to take out the garbage. Your tour of duty should come around.

It just seemed that people's lives are being shaped by forces they do not understand, and if you are going to begin to take a stand and fight against those things, you got to *know* the enemy – and that's getting harder to do. People are so easily affected by buzzwords; they're getting their button pushed with *God, mother, country, apple pie* – even in soda commercials. And so it's like "Where is the real thing? Where is the real America?"

What's also disturbing is the casualness with which people are getting used to being lied to. To me, Watergate felt like this big hustle was going down. And in the end it seemed to legitimize the dope dealer down on the street. "Hey, the president's doing it, so why can't I?" I guess we're pretty much left to find our way on our own these days. The sense of community that there was in the Sixties made you feel like there were a lot of people along for the ride with you. It felt like the whole country was trying to find its way. You do not have a sense that the country is trying to find its way today. And that's a shame. As a result, I think you feel more on your own in the world today. Certainly, *I* feel more isolated in it.

Maybe everybody's just got to grab hold of each other. The idea of America as a family is naive, maybe sentimental or simplistic, but it's a good idea. And if people are sick and hurting and lost, I guess that it falls on everybody to address those problems in some fashion. Because injustice, and the price of that injustice, falls on everyone's heads. The economic injustice falls on everybody's head and steals everyone's freedom. Your wife can't walk down the street at night. People keep guns in their homes. They live with a greater sense of apprehension, anxiety and fear than they would in a more just and open society. It's not an accident, and it's not simply that there are "bad" people out there. It's an inbred part of the way that we are all living: it's a product of what we have accepted, what we have acceded to. And whether we mean it or not, our silence has spoken for us in some fashion. But the challenge is still there: eight years of Reagan is not going to change that.

That seemed part of what "Nebraska" was about: a reaction to the Reagan years. Was that how you intended people to see that record?

In a funny way, I always considered it my most personal record, because it felt to me, in its tone, the most what my childhood felt like. Later on, a bunch of people wrote about it as a response to the Reagan era, and it obviously had that connection.

I think people live from the inside out. Your initial connection is to your friends and your wife and your family. From there your connection may be to your immediate community. And then if you have the energy and the strength, then you say, "Well, how do I connect up to the guy in the next state or, ultimately, to people in the world?" I think that whatever the political implications of my work have been, they've just come out of personal insight. I don't really have a particular political theory or ideology. It came from observations, like, okay, this man is being wasted. Why is this man being wasted? This person has lost himself. Why is that? And just trying to take it from there. How does my life interconnect and intertwine with my friends and everybody else? I don't know the answers yet. I'm a guitar player – that's what I do.

But millions of people see you as more than a guitar player. In fact, many see you as nothing less than an inspiring moral leader. But there's a certain irony to being a modern-day hero for the masses. Back in the Sixties nobody ever spoke of the Beatles or the Rolling Stones or Dylan as being overexposed. Yet these days, any pop artist who has a major, sustained impact on a mass audience runs the risk of seeming either overly promoted by the media or too familiar to his audience. In recent years, performers like you, Michael Jackson, Prince and Madonna have all faced this dilemma. Do you ever feel that you're running the danger of overexposure?

Well, what does that mean? What is "overexposed"? It really has no meaning, you know? It's kind of a newspaper thing. I just ignore it, to be honest with you. I make the best records I can make. I try to work on them and put them out when it feels right and they feel like they're ready. That's what it is – not whether I'm overexposed or underexposed or not exposed. It's like "Hey, put the record on. Is it good? Do you like it? Is it rockin' ya? Is it speaking to you? Am I talking to you?" And the rest is what society does to sell newspapers or magazines. You gotta fill 'em up every month. You have an entire counterlife that is attached to your own real life by the slimmest of threads. In the past year, if you believe what was in the newspapers about me, I'd be living in two houses that I've never seen, been riding in cars that I've never had [*laughs*]. This is just what happens. It's, like, uncontrollable: the media monster has to be fed.

So all that sort of stuff, if you believe that it has anything really to do with you, you know, you're gonna go nuts. In the end, people will like my records and feel they were true or feel they weren't. They'll look at the body of work I've done and pull out whatever meaning it has for them. And that's what stands. The rest is transient. It's here today and gone tomorrow. It's meaningless. Whether Michael Jackson is sleeping in a tank or not, what does it mean to you? It's just a laugh for some people; that's all it really is. And I feel like, hey, if it's a laugh for you, then have one on me. Because when you reach for and achieve fame, one of the byproducts of fame is you will be trivialized, and you will be embarrassed. You will be, I guarantee it. I look at that as a part of my job. And I ain't seen nothing compared to, you know, if you look at Elvis's life or even Michael J's. I've had it pretty easy, but I know a little bit of what it's about. These things are gonna happen, and if you don't have a strong enough sense of who you are and what you're doing, they'll kick you in the ass and knock you down and have a good time doing it. That's the nature of our society, and it's one of the roles that people like me play in society. Okay, that's fine, but my feeling is simple: my work is my defense. Simple as that. I've done things I never thought I'd be able to do, I've been places I never thought I'd be. I've written music that is better than I thought I could write. I did stuff that I didn't think I had in me.

You've also come to mean a lot to an awful lot of people.

That's a good thing, but you can take it too far. I do not believe that the essence of the rock & roll idea was to exalt the cult of personality. That is a sidetrack, a dead-end street. That is not the thing to do. And I've been as guilty of it as anybody in my own life. When I jumped over that wall to meet Elvis that night [at Graceland], I didn't know who I was gonna meet. And the guard who stopped me at the door did me the biggest favor of my life. I had misunderstood. It was innocent, and I was having a ball, but it wasn't right. In the end, you cannot live inside that dream. You cannot live within the dream of Elvis Presley or within the dream of the Beatles. It's like John Lennon said: "The dream is over." You can live with that dream in your heart, but you cannot live inside that dream, because it's a perversion, you know? What the best of art says is, it says, "Take this" – this movie or painting or photograph or record – "take what you see in this, and then go find your place in the world. This is a tool: go out and find your place in the world."

I think I made the mistake earlier on of trying to live within that dream, within that rock & roll dream. It's a seductive choice, it's a seductive opportunity. The real world, after all, is frightening. In the end, I realized that rock & roll wasn't just about finding fame and wealth. Instead, for me, it was about finding your place in the world, figuring out where you belong.

It's a tricky balance to do it correctly. You got to be able to hold a lot of contradictory ideas in your mind at one time without letting them drive you nuts. I feel like to do my job right, when I walk out onstage I've got to feel like it's the most important thing in the world. Also I got to feel like, well, it's only rock & roll. Somehow you got to believe both of those things.

80 MARTIN SCORSESE, PAUL SCHRADER, AND ROBERT DE NIRO

FROM *"Taxi Driver"* (1992)

PAUL SCHRADER: The script of *Taxi Driver is* the genuine thing. It came from the gut, and while it banged around town everyone who read it realized it was authentic, the real item. After a number of years enough people said somebody should make it so that finally someone *did*.

In 1973 I had been through a particularly rough time, living more or less in my car in Los Angeles, riding around all night, drinking heavily, going to porno movies because they were open all night, and crashing some place during the day. Then, finally, I went to the emergency room in serious pain, and it turned out I had an ulcer. While I was in the hospital, talking to the nurse, I realized I hadn't spoken to anyone in two or three weeks. It really hit me, an image that I was like a taxi driver, floating around in this metal coffin in the city, seemingly in the middle of people, but *absolutely, totally alone.*

The taxicab was a metaphor for loneliness, and once I had that, it was just a matter of creating a plot: the girl he wants but can't have, and the one he can have but doesn't want. He tries to kill the surrogate father of the first and fails, so he kills the surrogate father of the other. I think it took ten days, it may have been twelve – I just wrote continuously. I was staying at an old girlfriend's house, where the heat and gas were all turned off, and I just wrote. When I stopped, I slept on the couch, then I woke up and I went back to typing. As you get older it takes more work. Hovering in the back of my mind is a fondness for those days when it was so painful it just had to come out.

I didn't really write it the way people write scripts today – you know, with a market in mind. I wrote it because it was something that I wanted to write and it was the first thing I wrote. It jumped out of my head.

Right after writing it, I left town for about six months. I came back to Los Angeles after I was feeling a little stronger emotionally and decided to go at it again. I was a freelance critic at the time. I had written a review of *Sisters* and interviewed Brian De Palma at his place at the beach. That afternoon, we were playing chess – we were about evenly matched – and somehow the fact that I had written a script came up. So I gave it to him and he liked it a lot and wanted to do it. De Palma showed the script to the producers, Michael and Julia Phillips, who were three houses down the beach, and he showed it to Marty, who was in town after finishing *Mean Streets*. Michael and Julia told me they wanted to do it but that Marty was a better director for it. So Julia and I went and saw a rough cut of *Mean Streets*, and I agreed. In fact, I thought Marty and Bob De Niro would be the ideal combination, so we aligned ourselves – De Niro, the Phillipses and myself – but we were not powerful enough to get the film made. Then there was a hiatus of a couple of years, and in the intervening time, each of us had successes of our own. I sold my script, *The Yakuza*, for a lot of money. Marty did *Alice*, the Phillipses did *The Sting*, and De Niro did *The Godfather, Part II*.

At that time I remember describing *Taxi Driver*'s Travis as sort of a young man who wandered from the snowy waste of the midwest into an overheated New York cathedral. My own background was anti-Catholic in the style of the Reformation and the Glorious Revolution. The town I was raised in was about one-third Dutch Calvinist and one-third Catholic, and the other third were trying to figure out why they were there, and sort of keeping peace. Well, both cultures, Catholic and Calvinist, are infused with the sense of guilt, redemption by blood, and moral purpose – all acts are moral acts, all acts have consequence. It's impossible to act amorally. There's a kind of divine eye in the sky that ensures your acts are morally judged. So you know once you're raised in that kind of environment, you don't shake that, you shake a lot of things, but the sense of moral responsibility, guilt, and redemption you carry with you forever. So Scorsese and I shared that. I came from essentially a rural, midwestern Protestant and Dutch background, and he is urban and Italian Catholic, so in a way it's a very felicitous joining. The bedrock is the same.

Taxi Driver was as much a product of luck and timing as everything else – three sensibilities together at the right time, doing the right thing. It was still a low-budget, long-shot movie, but that's how it got made. At one point, we could have financed the film with Jeff Bridges, but we elected to hold out and wait until we could finance it with De Niro. It was just a matter of luck and timing. Marty was fully ready to make the film; De Niro was ready to make it. And the nation was ready to see it. You can't plan or scheme for that kind of luck. It just sort of happens – the right film at the right time.

MARTIN SCORSESE: *Taxi Driver* was, I think, the first script I'd worked on that had direct movement from beginning to end. The *Taxi Driver* screenplay seemed very close to me. It was as if I wrote it, that's how strongly I feel about it. Even though the character is from the Midwest, Bob De Niro and I both felt the same way.

Paul wrote *Taxi Driver* out of his own gut and his own heart in two-and-a-half terrible weeks. I felt close to the character by way of Dostoevski. I had always wanted to do a movie of *Notes from the Underground*. I mentioned that to Paul and he said, "Well this is what I have – *Taxi Driver*," and I said, "Great, this is it." Then Paul said, "What about De Niro? He was great in *Mean Streets*." And it turned out that Bob had a feeling for people like Travis.

Taxi Driver was almost like a commission, in a sense. Bob was the actor, I was the director, and Paul wrote the script. The three of us – Schrader, Bob and I – just came together. It was exactly what we wanted, it was one of the strangest things.

Everything was storyboarded. Even the close-ups because we had to shoot so fast. It would have to be, "Get this shot." Then, "Okay, got it." Then, "Go on, okay, next." That's the way it had to go. But we really felt strongly about the picture. It was the only script that really fell into my lap. I don't like to give scripts to people to write and two months later they come back and it's completely finished. There's very little input that can take place at that point. Thematically, you can change things, you can do things, but visualization is hard then. Schrader's scripts afford me the possibility of going back and then revisualizing.

Schrader usually has shorter scenes and has a better concept of the visual. Maybe not the visual that's going to wind up in my movie version of what he's writing, but at least he has a point of view. Other writers usually take a totally literary point of view, mainly dialogue and long descriptions of scenes. Then you've got to really do the whole thing. And very often, you just wind up shooting dialogue on certain pictures. It's not necessarily *bad*. It's just that they take a *literary* approach, and I prefer a film approach, and Schrader had a film approach.

ROBERT DE NIRO: I once told Marty we should put together a movie of outtakes. For example, there were outtakes from *Taxi Driver* I would include. When we were shooting that movie there's this terrible bloody scene and, ironically, funny things happened. That whole slaughter scene in the hallway at the end of the movie took us about four or five takes to shoot. Things went wrong technically. There were a lot of special effects and with those things something always goes wrong. You have this sort of very serious, dramatic kind of carnage going on, and all of a sudden, somebody drops something or machinery breaks down. It just blows the whole thing and it turns out to be funny. Oddly enough, in that sort of scene, I guess because it's so gruesome, everybody's ready to laugh. There was a lot of laughing and joking during the shooting between takes. I remember that. It was a lighter period, even though the material was very heavy.

MARTIN SCORSESE: I had a basic idea that caused me to be precise. Whenever I shot Travis Bickle, when he was alone in the car, or whenever people were talking to him, and that person is in the frame, then the camera was over their shoulder. He was in everybody else's light, but he was alone. Nobody was in his frame. As much as possible, I tried to stick with that. That is a big problem, because Travis is in everybody else's frame. There would be a certain look in his eyes, a certain close-up of his face, shot with a certain lens. Subtle – not too wide, not to destroy it, not to nudge the audience into, "Hey, this guy's a whacko." Not that sort of thing. But rather to let it sneak up on the audience, like Travis does, and move the camera the way he sees things – all from his point of view. Only one scene is from another point of view: The scene that was improvised was Keitel dancing with Jodie Foster.

I think Bob's range is quite extraordinary. Harry Ufland – who, at the time, was both my agent and Bob's – came by the set one day and Bob had a suit on. He was in between takes, checking out a suit for the wardrobe for *Last Tycoon*. Harry didn't recognize him. For twenty minutes Bob wasn't Travis anymore, he was Monroe Stahr. It's amazing.

9

RELIGION

Introduction		258
81	*John Winthrop* Letter to His Wife, Margaret (1630)	261
82	*Jonathan Edwards* FROM "The Christian Pilgrim" (1733)	262
83	*Ralph Waldo Emerson* FROM His Journals and Letters (1827–37)	266
84	*Anonymous* "Swing Low, Sweet Chariot" (pre-1860) "Go Down, Moses" (pre-1860)	268
85	*James Cardinal Gibbons* FROM "The Catholic Church and Labor" (1887)	269
86	*Will Herberg* FROM "The Three Religious Communities" (1955)	272
87	*Flannery O'Connor* "Novelist and Believer" (1963)	276
88	Martin Luther King, Jr. "Letter from Birmingham Jail" (1963)	281
89	*Billy Graham* "The Unfinished Dream" (1970)	292
90	*Richard Rodriguez* "Credo" (1981)	294

Figure 9 Evangelist Billy Graham preaching to an audience of 21,000 at the Upper Midwest Crusade, 1973 © Bettmann/CORBIS

INTRODUCTION

The Pilgrims and the Puritans who fled the old world to seek refuge in the Promised Land considered religion to be the basis of society. They viewed America as a Christian frontier and felt that the Church of England's break with Rome was not radical enough, wanting to cleanse the English church of Popish influence. The Puritans did not restrict religion to ritual practice in the church but emphasized the importance of bringing religion into rural and urban life. In their efforts to establish a *new* England they often referred to passages in the Old Testament. In a sermon, John Winthrop (1588–1649), the first governor of the Massachusetts Bay Colony, compared the beginning of his Puritan settlement to the idea of the city on a hill, the New Jerusalem. Considering how close they were to death and starvation, we should not read the American Puritans as if they wished to establish a leading nation. Instead, they were a band of true outcasts who asked for God's blessing on their small Puritan community in the wilderness. Winthrop is best known for his sermon and his diary, but he also wrote letters back to his wife in England during the time they were separated by the ocean. His letter to her of September 1630 (text 81), about four months after the Puritans sailed from England, reveals the intensity of his love and his religion.

How the early Puritans in New England may have influenced later American society and culture is a much debated issue. Several of the more conservative Christian groups in the United States today proudly refer to the Puritans as models, but their thinking is often far from Puritan thinking and they may never have read a Puritan text. People who disclaim the Puritans often blame them for the worst kind of dour prudishness, forgetting that education was a very important issue to the Puritans. True, they sometimes harshly consolidated their own group and showed little tolerance of people of different religious views. At the same time, their profound criticism of the Church of England may have inspired religious freedom on a broader scale in the new country.

Jonathan Edwards (1703–58) ranks among America's greatest theologians, combining the Puritan doctrine of man's sinfullness and God's omnipotence with a belief in man's rationality. Well versed in the new sciences and the works of Locke and Newton, Edwards joined his reading of science with what he considered to be the truths of Puritanism. His reputation as a late yet unyielding Puritan remains intact. Playing a significant role in the Great Awakening, the religious revival that swept through the colonies in the eighteenth century, Edwards wanted to stir people out of their complacency. In his essay "The Christian Pilgrim" (text 82), Edwards uses images familiar to readers of John Bunyan's *Pilgrim's Progress* (1684) in a very apt description of the brevity of life.

Edwards's invocation of religion as experience provides a link to Ralph Waldo Emerson (1803–82), who started out as a Unitarian minister, but soon broke with the church. During the age of Romanticism and the coming of Transcendentalism, the new doctrines of faith in man, exaltation of the individual, and worship of nature were incompatible with Edwards's position, and his spiritual influence (which had been strong long after his death) thus declined. Transcendentalism as a moral philosophy reached its peak in the years between 1830 and the Civil War and appealed particularly to those who were weary of the harsh God of traditional Puritanism. Ralph Waldo Emerson, who believed in the absolute goodness of man, and Henry David Thoreau, who believed in nature's unspotted innocence (if not goodness), were the two most prominent proponents of Transcendentalism. In his essay "Nature," Emerson emphasized the religiosity of life lived out of doors: "We have crept out of our close and crowded houses into the night and morning, and we see what majestic beauties daily wrap us in their bosom." In our excerpts from his diary (text 83), Emerson meditates on his religion from the time he started his ministry until he renounced Unitarianism in 1838, from which time he proclaimed his faith in the soul as the source of religious creativity.

The optimism of Transcendentalism faded somewhat after the horrors of the Civil War and the social crises and labor struggles of the late nineteenth century. The Catholic Church, whose recruitment was primarily from the urban workers, could not ignore the social problems of that class and involved itself in the battle for social justice. In a noteworthy memorial to Cardinal Simeoni (text 85), Archbishop James Cardinal Gibbons (1834–1921) defends the most important labor organization of its day, the Catholic-dominated Knights of Labor, insisting on the right of labor association and the necessity of righting injustices inflicted on workers. Having grown up in a family of Irish immigrants, Gibbons became a priest in Baltimore, and at the age of 43 he became archbishop there. He was a unifying force in American Catholicism at the time. Later both Flannery O'Connor (text 87) and Richard Rodriguez (text 90) reflected on other aspects of the Catholic faith in American culture.

The term "Social Gospel" was introduced by some Protestant ministers of the late nineteenth century who reinterpreted the Bible to respond to the growing inequality in the United States, stressing the social aspects of Christianity at the expense of its spiritual and moral aspects. In the twentieth century, according to Arnold Toynbee, western civilization went through a process of secularization that was welcomed even by some theologians, for example Harvey Cox in his American bestseller *The Secular City* (1965). Even so, regular weekly church attendance among adult Americans is still astonishingly high, particularly compared to that in most European countries. Religion is thus still a very essential part of American life.

It is worth noting what the reputed American sociologist Peter L. Berger said when asked whether he agreed with critics who argued that "Americans are very superficial in their religious perceptions." Berger answered: "Definitely not. I think there's more religious vitality in this country than in any other Western country . . . People are more committed, more interested . . . than Europeans are."[1]

Will Herberg's essay "The Religion of Americans" (text 86) clarified many religious issues when it was first published in the 1950s, and in many ways it still gives a sound presentation of what Eisenhower once referred to as "our three great faiths [Protestantism, Catholicism, Judaism]."

Religion is also an integral part of the black experience of the United States. Scholars discuss whether the traditional negro spirituals ("Go Down, Moses" and "Swing Low, Sweet Chariot" are included have as text 84) marked an escape from the harsh realities of pre-Civil War racial oppression, or whether they indeed voiced a subdued but real protest and hope for better days in the future. Political and religious protest is evident in Martin Luther King's famous Letter to fellow clergymen who had called his demonstrations in Birmingham, Alabama, "untimely" (text 88).

The first amendment to the Constitution proclaims that there shall be no state religion in the United States. This does not mean that religion and politics are entirely separate; in fact they are often linked and even mixed, by both political and religious leaders. Billy Graham's speech (text 89) exhibits a curious mixture of national pride and religious zeal, sometimes referred to as American Civil Religion. Graham's speech probably appears very moderate and even timid to most observers who now are used to the more aggressive rhetoric of TV evangelists. Increasingly the religious right's power is an issue in American politics.

1 *The US News and World Report*, April 11, 1977.

Questions and Topics

1 Discuss typical features of Puritanism in Winthrop's letter to his wife.
2 In what terms does Edwards describe the brevity of life, and what effects may these have on a modern reader? Relate his religious views to those presented in the essay by Flannery O'Connor.
3 Relate the two gospel songs to the history of African Americans.

> 4 How does Martin Luther King combine religious and political views in his "Letter from Birmingham Jail"? How does his text differ from Billy Graham's?
> 5 Discuss how accurate Herberg's use of the term "the three great faiths" is for an analysis of American religion today.

Suggestions for further reading

Ahlstrom, Sydney E., *Theology in America: The Major Protestant Voices from Puritanism to Neo-Orthodoxy* (Indianapolis, Ind.: Bobbs-Merrill Company, 1967).

Allitt, Patrick, ed., *Major Problems in American Religious History* (Boston: Houghton Mifflin, 2000).

Clebsch, William A., *American Religious Thought: A History* (Chicago: University of Chicago Press, 1973).

Ivory, Luther D., *Toward a Theology of Radical Involvement: The Theological Legacy of Martin Luther King Jr.* (Nashville, Tenn.: Abingdon Press, 1997).

McNamara, Patrick H., *Religion: American Style* (New York: Harper & Row, 1974).

81 JOHN WINTHROP

Letter to His Wife, Margaret (1630)

September 9, 1630
My dear wife,

The blessing of God all-sufficient be upon thee and all my dear ones with thee forever.

I praise the good Lord, though we see much morality, sickness, and trouble, yet (such is His mercy) myself and children with most of my family, are yet living, and in health, and enjoy prosperity enough, if the afflictions of our brethren did not hold under the comfort of it. The Lady Arbella is dead, and good Mr. Higginson, my servant, old Waters of Neyland, and many others. Thus the Lord is pleased still to humble us; yet he mixes so many mercies with His corrections, as we are persuaded He will not cast us off, but, in His due time, will do us good, according to the measure of our afflictions. He stays but till He hath purged our corruptions, and healed the hardness and error of our hearts, and stripped us of our vain confidence in this arm of flesh, that He may have us rely wholly upon Himself.

The French ship, so long expected, and given for lost, is now come safe to us, about a fortnight since, having been twelve weeks at sea; and yet her passengers (being but a few) all safe and well but one, and her goats but six living of eighteen. So as now we are somewhat refreshed with such goods and provisions as she brought, though much thereof hath received damage by wet. I praise God, we have many occasions of comfort here, and do hope, that our days of affliction will soon have an end, and that the Lord will do us more good in the end than we could have expected, that will abundantly recompense for all the troubles we have endured. Yet we may not look at great things here. It is enough that we shall have Heaven, though we should pass through Hell to it. We here enjoy God and Jesus Christ. Is not this enough? What would we have more? I thank God; I like so well to be here, as I do not repent my coming, and if I were to come again, I would not have altered my course, though I had foreseen all these afflictions. I never fared better in my life, never slept better, never had more content of mind, which comes merely of the Lord's good hand; for we have not the like means of these comforts here, which we had in England. But the Lord is all-sufficient, blessed be His holy name. If He please, He can still uphold us in this estate; but if He shall see good to make us partakers with others in more affliction, His will be done. He is our God, and may dispose of us as He sees good.

I am sorry to part with thee so soon, seeing we meet so seldom, and my much business hath made me too oft forget Mondays and Fridays.[1] I long for the time, when I may see thy sweet face again, and the faces of my dear children. But I must break off, and desire to thee to commend me kindly to all my good friends, and excuse my not writing at this time. If God please once to settle me, I shall make amends. I will name now but such as are nearest to thee: my brother and sister Gostlin, Mr Leigh, etc., Castleins, my neighbor Cole and his good wife, with the rest of my good neighbors, tenants, and servants. The good Lord bless thee, and all our children and family. So I kiss my sweet wife and my dear children, and rest.

Thy faithful husband
Jo. Winthrop

1 They had agreed to join in prayer on each side of the Atlantic every Monday and Friday (editors' note).

82 JONATHAN EDWARDS

FROM *"The Christian Pilgrim"* (1733)

SECTION II

Why the Christian's life is a journey, or pilgrimage?

1. THIS world is not our abiding place. Our continuance here is but very short. Man's days on the earth, are as a shadow. It was never designed by God that this world should be our home. Neither did God give us these temporal accommodations for that end. If God has given us ample estates, and children, or other pleasant friends, it is with no such design, that we should be furnished here, as for a settled abode, but with a design that we should use them for the present, and then leave them in a very little time. When we are called to any secular business, or charged with the care of a family, [and] if we improve our lives to any other purpose than as a journey toward heaven, all our labor will be lost. If we spend our lives in the pursuit of a temporal happiness; as riches, or sensual pleasures; credit and esteem from men; delight in our children, and the prospect of seeing them well brought up and well settled, etc. – All these things will be of little significancy to us. Death will blow up all our hopes, and will put an end to these enjoyments. "The places that have known us, will know us

no more": and "the eye that has seen us, shall see us no more." We must be taken away forever from all these things; and it is uncertain when: it may be soon after we are put into the possession of them. And then, where will be all our worldly employments and enjoyments, when we are laid in the silent grave! "So man lieth down, and riseth not again, till the heavens be no more." Job 14:12.

2. The future world was designed to be our settled and everlasting abode. There it was intended that we should be fixed; and there alone is a lasting habitation and a lasting inheritance. The present state is short and transitory, but our state in the other world is everlasting. And as we are there at first, so we must be without change. Our state in the future world, therefore, being eternal, is of so much greater importance than our state here, that all our concerns in this world should be wholly subordinated to it.

3. Heaven is that place alone where our highest end and highest good is to be obtained. God hath made us for himself. "Of him, and through him, and to him are all things." Therefore, then do we attain to our highest end, when we are brought to God: but that is by being brought to heaven, for that is God's throne, the place of his special presence. There is but a very imperfect union with God to be had in this world, a very imperfect knowledge of him in the midst of much darkness: a very imperfect conformity to God, mingled with abundance of estrangement. Here we can serve and glorify God, but in a very imperfect manner: our service being mingled with sin, which dishonors God. – But when we get to heaven, (if ever that be,) we shall be brought to a perfect union with God and have more clear views of him. There we shall be fully conformed to God, without any remaining sin: for "we shall see him as he is." There we shall serve God perfectly and glorify him in an exalted manner, even to the utmost of the powers and capacity of our nature. Then we shall perfectly give up ourselves to God: our hearts will be pure and holy offerings, presented in a flame of divine love.

God is the highest good of the reasonable creature, and the enjoyment of him is the only happiness with which our souls can be satisfied. – To go to heaven fully to enjoy God, is *infinitely* better than the most pleasant accommodations here. Fathers and mothers, husbands, wives, children, or the company of earthly friends, are but shadows; but the enjoyment of God is the substance. These are but scattered beams, but God is the sun. These are but streams; but God is the fountain. These are but drops; but God is the ocean. – Therefore it becomes us to spend this life only as a journey towards heaven, as it becomes us to make the seeking of our highest end and proper good, the whole work of our lives; to which we should subordinate all other concerns of life. Why should we labor for, or set our hearts on anything else, but that which is our proper end, and true happiness?

4. Our present state, and all that belongs to it, is designed by him that made all things, to be wholly in order to another world. – This world was made for a place of preparation for another. Man's mortal life was given him, that he might be prepared for his fixed state. And all that God has here given us, is given to this purpose. The sun shines, the rain falls upon us, and the earth yields her increase to us for this end. Civil, ecclesiastical, and family affairs, and all our personal concerns, are designed and ordered in subordination to a future world, by the maker and disposer of all things. To this therefore they ought to be subordinated by us.

Instruction afforded by the consideration, that life is a journey or pilgrimage,
towards heaven.

1. THIS doctrine may teach us moderation in our mourning for the loss of such dear friends, who, while they lived, improved their lives to right purposes. If they lived a holy life, then their lives were a journey towards heaven. And why should we be immoderate in mourning, when they are got to their journey's end? Death, though it appears to us with a frightful aspect, is to them a great blessing. Their end is happy, and better than their beginning. "*The day of their death, is better than the day of their birth.*" Eccles. 7:1. While they lived, they desired heaven, and chose it above this world or any of its enjoyments. For this they earnestly longed, and why should we grieve that they have obtained it? – Now they have got to their Father's house. They find more comfort a thousand times, now [that] they are got home, than they did in their journey. In this world they underwent much labour and toil; it was a wilderness they passed through. There were many difficulties in the way; mountains and rough places. It was laborious and fatiguing to travel the road; and they had many wearisome days and nights: but now they have got to their everlasting rest. "And I heard a voice from heaven, saying unto me, Write, blessed are the dead which die in the Lord from henceforth: yea, saith the Spirit, that they may rest from their labors; and their works do follow them." Rev. 14:13. They look back upon the difficulties, and sorrows, and dangers of life, rejoicing that they have surmounted them all.

We are ready to look upon death as their calamity, and to mourn that those who were so dear to us should be in the dark grave; that they are there transformed to corruption and worms; taken away from their dear children and enjoyments, etc. as though they were in awful circumstances. But this is owing to our infirmity. They are in a happy condition, inconceivably blessed. They do not mourn, but rejoice with exceeding joy: their mouths are filled with joyful songs, and they drink at rivers of pleasure. They find no mixture of grief that they have changed their earthly enjoyments, and the company of mortals, for heaven. Their life here, though in the best circumstances, was attended with much that was adverse and afflictive: but now there is an end to all adversity. "They shall hunger no more nor thirst any more; neither shall the sun light on them, nor any heat. For the Lamb which is in the midst of the throne, shall feed them and shall lead them unto living fountains of waters: and God shall wipe away all tears from their eyes." Rev. 7:16, 17.

It is true, we shall see them no more in this world, yet we ought to consider that we are travelling towards the same place; and why should we break our hearts that they have got there before us? We are following after them, and hope as soon as we get to our journey's end, to be with them again, in better circumstances. A degree of mourning for near relations when departed is not inconsistent with Christianity, but very agreeable to it; for as long as we are flesh and blood, we have animal propensities and affections. But we have just reason that our mourning should be mingled with joy. "But I would not have you to be ignorant, brethren, concerning them that are asleep, that ye sorrow not, even as others that have no hope:" 1 Thes. 4:13. *i.e.* that they should not sorrow as the Heathen, who had no knowledge of a future happiness.

This appears by the following verse; *"for if we believe that Jesus died and rose again, even so them also which sleep in Jesus, will God bring with him."*

2. If our lives ought to be only a journey towards heaven, how ill do they improve their lives, that spend them in traveling towards hell? – Some men spend their whole lives, from their infancy to their dying day, in going down the broad way to destruction. They not only draw nearer to hell as to time, but they every day grow more ripe for destruction; they are more assimilated to the inhabitants of the infernal world. While others press forward in the straight and narrow way to life and laboriously travel up the hill toward Zion, against the inclinations and tendency of the flesh, these run with a swift career down to eternal death. This is the employment of every day, with all wicked men; and the whole day is spent in it. As soon as ever they awake in the morning, they set out anew in the way to hell and spend every waking moment in it. They begin in early days. "The wicked are estranged from the womb, they go astray as soon as they are born, speaking lies." Psa. 58:3. They hold on it with perseverance. Many of them who live to be old, are never weary in it; though they live to be an hundred years old, they will not cease traveling in the way to hell, till they arrive there. And all the concerns of life are subordinated to this employment. A wicked man is a servant of sin; his powers and faculties are employed in the service of sin and in fitness for hell. And all his possessions are so used by him as to be subservient to the same purpose. Men spend their time in treasuring up wrath against the day of wrath. Thus do all unclean persons, who live in lascivious practices in secret: all malicious persons, all profane persons that neglect the duties of religion. Thus do all unjust persons; and those who are fraudulent and oppressive in their dealings. Thus do all backbiters and revilers, [and] all covetous persons that set their hearts chiefly on the riches of this world. Thus do tavern-haunters, and frequenters of evil company, and many other kinds that might be mentioned. Thus the ulk of mankind are hastening onward in the broad way to destruction, which is, as it were, filled up with the multitude that are going in it with one accord. And they are every day going to hell out of this broad way by thousands. Multitudes are continually flowing down into the great lake of fire and brimstone, as some mighty river constantly disembogues its water into the ocean.

3. Hence when persons are converted they do but begin their work and set out in the way they have to go. – They never till then do anything at that work in which their whole lives ought to be spent. Persons before conversion never take a step that way. Then does a man first set out on his journey, when he is brought home to Christ, and so far is he from having done his work, that his care and labor in his Christian work and business, is then but begun, in which he must spend the remaining part of his life.

Those persons do ill, who when they are converted, and have obtained a hope of their being in a good condition, do not strive as earnestly as they did before, while they were under awakenings. They ought, henceforward, as long as they live, to be as earnest and laborious, as watchful and careful as ever; yea, they should increase more and more. It is no just excuse that now they have obtained conversion. Should not we be as diligent as that we ourselves may be that we may serve and glorify God, as that we ourselves may be happy? And if we have obtained grace, yet we ought to strive as much that we may obtain the other degrees that are before, as we did to obtain that small degree that is behind. The apostle tells us that he forgot what was behind and reached forth towards what was before. Phil. 3:13.

Yea, those who are converted have now a further reason to strive for grace. For they have seen something of its excellency. A man who has once tasted the blessings of Canaan, has more reason to press towards it than he had before. And they who are converted, should strive to "make their calling and election sure." All those who are converted are not sure of it, and those who are sure, do not know that they shall be always so, and still, seeking and serving God with the utmost diligence, is the way to have assurance and to have it maintained.

83 RALPH WALDO EMERSON

FROM *His Journals and Letters (1827–37)*

January 15, 1827. And what is the amount of all that is called religion in the world? Who is he that has seen God of whom so much is known or where is one that has risen from the dead? Satisfy me beyond the possibility of doubt of the certainty of all that is told me concerning the other world and I will fulfil the conditions on which my salvation is suspended. The believer tells me he has an evidence historical & internal which make the presumption so strong that it is almost a certainty that it rests on the highest of probabilities. Yes; but change that imperfect to perfect evidence & I too will be a Christian. But now it must be admitted I am not certain that any of these things are true. The nature of God may be different from what he is represented. I never beheld him. I do not know that he exists. This good which invites me now is visible & specific. I will at least embrace it this time by way of experiment, & if it is wrong certainly God can in some manner signify his will in future. Moreover I will guard against evil consequences resulting to others by the vigilance with which I conceal it.

February 16, 1827. My weight is lb. $141^{1/2}$.

October, 1836. And what is God? We cannot say but we see clearly enough. We cannot say, because he is the unspeakable, the immeasureable, the perfect – but we see plain enough in what direction it lies. First we see plainly that the All is in Man, that as the proverb says, "God comes to see us without bell." That is, as there is no screen or ceiling between our heads & the infinity of space, so is there no bar or wall in the Soul where man the effect ceases & God the cause begins. The walls are taken away; we lie open on one side to all the deeps of spiritual nature, to all the attributes of God. Justice we see & know; that is of God. Truth we see & know, that is of God. Love, Freedom, Power, these are of God. For all these & much more there is a general nature in which they inhere or of which they are phases and this is Spirit. It is essentially vital. The love that is in me, the justice, the truth can never die & that is all of me that will not die. All the rest of me is so much death, my ignorance, my vice, my corporeal pleasure. But I am nothing else than a capacity for justice, truth, love, freedom, power. I can inhale, imbibe them forevermore. They shall be so much to me that I am nothing, they all. Then shall God be all in all. Herein is my Immortality. . . .

October 31, 1836. Last night at 11 o'clock, a son was born to me. Blessed child! a lovely wonder to me, and which makes the Universe look friendly to me. How remote from my knowledge, how alien, yet how kind does it make the Cause of Causes appear! The stimulated curiosity of the father sees the graces & instincts which exist, indeed, in every babe, but unnoticed in others; the right to see all, know all, to examine nearly, distinguishes this relation, & endears this sweet child. Otherwise I see nothing in it of mine; I am no conscious party to any feature, any function, any perfection I behold in it. I seem to be merely a brute occasion of its being & nowise attaining to the dignity even of a second cause no more than I taught it to suck the breast. Please God, that "he, like a tree of generous kind, By living waters set," may draw endless nourishment from the fountains of Wisdom & Virtue! [He died in 1842, 5 years old.]

May 26, 1837. Who shall define to me an Individual? I behold with awe & delight many illustrations of the One Universal Mind. I see my being imbedded in it. As a plant in the earth so I grow in God. I am only a form of him. He is the soul of me. I can even with a mountainous aspiring say, *I am God*, by transferring my *Me* out of the flimsy & unclean precincts of my body, my fortunes, my private will, & meekly retiring upon the holy austerities of the Just & the Loving – upon the secret fountains of Nature. That thin & difficult ether, I also can breathe. The mortal lungs & nostrils burst & shrivel, but the soul itself needeth no organs, it is all element & all organ. Yet why not always so? How came the Individual thus armed & impassioned to parricide, thus murderously inclined ever to traverse & kill the divine life. Ah wicked Manichee! Into that dim problem I cannot enter. A believer in Unity, a seer of Unity, I yet behold two. Whilst I feel myself in sympathy with Nature & rejoice with greatly beating heart in the course of Justice & Benevolence overpowering me, I yet find little access to this Me of Me. I fear what shall befal; I am not enough a party to the Great Order to be tranquil. I hope & I fear. I do not see. At one time, I am a Doer. A divine life, I create scenes & persons around & for me & unfold my thought by a perpetual successive projection. At least I so say, I so feel. But presently I return to the habitual attitude of suffering.

I behold; I bask in beauty; I await; I wonder; Where is my Godhead now? This is the Male & Female principle in nature. One man, male & female created he him. Hard as it is to describe God, it is harder to describe the Individual.

A certain wandering light comes to me which I instantly perceive to be the Cause of Causes. It transcends all proving. It is itself the ground of being; and I see that it is not one & I another, but this is the life of my life. That is one fact then; that in certain moments I have known that I existed directly from God, and am, as it were, his organ. And in my ultimate consciousness Am He. Then, secondly, the contradictory fact is familiar, that I am a surprised spectator & learner of all my life. This is the habitual posture of the mind – beholding. But whenever the day dawns, the great day of truth on the soul, it comes with awful invitation to me to accept it, to blend with its aurora.

Cannot I conceive the Universe without a Contradiction?

84 ANONYMOUS

"Swing Low, Sweet Chariot" (pre-1860)

    Swing low, sweet chariot,
    Comin' for to carry me home.

I looked over Jordan and what did I see,
Comin' for to carry me home?
A band of angels comin' aftah me,
Comin' for to carry me home.

If you git there before I do,
Comin' for to carry me home,
Tell all my frien's I'm a-comin', too,
Comin' for to carry me home.

The brightes' day that ever I saw,
Comin' for to carry me home,
When Jesus washed my sins away,
Comin' for to carry me home.

I'm sometimes up an' sometimes down,
Comin' for to carry me home,
But still my soul feel heavenly-boun',
Comin' for to carry me home.

"Go Down, Moses" (pre-1860)

When Israel was in Egypt's land,
    Let my people go;
Oppressed so hard dey could not stand,
    Let my people go.

        Go down, Moses,
           Way down in Egypt land,
        Tell ole Pha-roh,
           Let my people go.

Thus saith the Lord, bold Moses said,
    Let my people go;
If not I'll smite your first-born dead,
    Let my people go.
      Go down, Moses, etc.

No more shall dey in bondage toil,
    Let my people go;
Let dem come out wid Egypt's spoil,
    Let my people go.
      Go down, Moses, etc.

85 JAMES CARDINAL GIBBONS

FROM *"The Catholic Church and Labor"* (1887)

To His Eminence Cardinal Simeoni, Prefect of the Sacred Congregation of the Propaganda:

YOUR EMINENCE:

In submitting to the Holy See the conclusions which after several months of attentive observation and reflection, seem to me to sum up the truth concerning the association of the Knights of Labor, I feel profoundly convinced of the vast importance of the consequences attaching to this question, which forms but a link in the great chain of the social problems of our day, and especially of our country. . . .

1. In the first place, in the constitution, laws and official declarations of the Knights of Labor, there can clearly be found assertions and rules which we would not approve; but we have not found in them those elements so clearly pointed out by the Holy See, which places them among condemned associations. . . .

2. That there exists among us, as in the other countries of the world, grave and threatening social evils, public injustices, which call for strong resistance and legal remedy, is a fact which no one dares to deny, and the truth of which has been already acknowledged by the Congress and the President of the United States. Without entering into the sad details of these wrongs, – which does not seem necessary here, – it may suffice to mention only that monopolies on the part of both individuals and of corporations, have already called forth not only the complaints of our working classes but also the opposition of our public men and legislators; that the efforts of these monopolists, not always without success, to control legislation to their own profit, cause serious apprehension among the disinterested friends of liberty; that the heartless avarice which, through greed of gain, pitilessly grinds not only the men, but particularly the women and children in various employments, make it clear to all who love humanity and justice that it is not only the right of the laboring classes to protect themselves, but the duty of the whole people to aid them in finding a remedy against the dangers with which both civilization and the social order are menaced by avarice, oppression and corruption.

It would be vain to deny either the existence of the evils, the right of legitimate resistance, or the necessity of a remedy. At most doubt might be raised about the legitimacy of the form of resistance and the remedy employed by the Knights of Labor. This then ought to be the next point of our examination.

3. It can hardly be doubted that for the attainment of any public end, association – the organization of all interested persons – is the most efficacious means, a means altogether natural and just. This is so evident, and besides so conformable to the genius of our country, of our essentially popular social conditions, that it is unnecessary to insist upon it. It is almost the only means to invite public attention, to give force to the most legitimate resistance, to add weight to the most just demands. . . .

4. Let us now consider the objections made against this sort of organization.

(a) It is objected that in these organizations Catholics are mixed with Protestants, to the peril of their faith. Naturally, yes, they are mixed with Protestants in the workers' associations, precisely as they are at their work; for in a mixed people like ours, the separation of religions in social affairs is not possible. But to suppose that the faith of our Catholics suffers thereby is not to know the Catholic workers of America who are not like the workingmen of so many European countries – misguided and perverted children, looking on their Mother the Church as a hostile stepmother – but they are intelligent, well instructed and devoted children ready to give their blood, as they continually give their means (although small and hard-earned) for her support and protection. And in fact it is not in the present case that Catholics are mixed with Protestants, but rather that Protestants are admitted to the advantages of an association, two-thirds of whose members and the principal officers are Catholics; and in a country like ours their exclusion would be simply impossible.

(b) But it is said, could there not be substituted for such an organization confraternities which would unite the workingmen under the direction of the priests and the direct influence of religion? I answer frankly that I do not believe that either possible or necessary in our country. I sincerely admire the efforts of this sort which are made in countries where the workers are led astray by the enemies of religion; but thanks be to God, that is not our condition. We find that in our country the present and explicit influence of the clergy would not be advisable where our citizens, without distinction of religious belief, come together in regard to their industrial interests alone. Without going so far, we have abundant means for making our working people faithful Catholics, and simple good sense advises us not to go to extremes.

(c) Again, it is objected that the liberty of such an organization exposes Catholics to the evil influences of the most dangerous associates, even of atheists, communists and anarchists. That is true; but it is one of the trials of faith which our brave American Catholics are accustomed to meet almost daily, and which they know how to disregard with good sense and firmness. The press of our country tells us and the president of the Knights of Labor has related to us, how these violent and aggressive elements have endeavored to seize authority in their councils, or to inject their poison into the principles of the association; but they also verify with what determination these evil spirits have been repulsed and defeated. The presence among our citizens of this destructive element, which has come for the most part from certain nations of Europe, is assuredly for us an occasion of lively regrets and careful precautions; it is an inevitable fact, however, but one which the union between the Church and her children in our country renders comparatively free from danger. In truth, the only grave danger would come from an alienation between the Church and her children, which nothing would more certainly occasion than imprudent condemnations.

(d) An especially weighty charge is drawn from the outbursts of violence, even to bloodshed, which have characterized several of the strikes inaugurated by labor organizations. Concerning this, three things are to be remarked: first, strikes are not an invention of the Knights of Labor, but a means almost everywhere and always resorted to by employees in our land and elsewhere to protest against what they consider unjust and to demand their right; secondly in such a struggle of the poor and indignant multitudes against hard and obstinate monopoly, anger and violence are often as inevitable as they are regrettable; thirdly, the laws and chief authorities of the Knights of Labor, far from encouraging violence or the occasions of it, exercise a powerful influence to hinder it, and to keep strikes within the limits of good order and legitimate action. A careful examination of the acts of violence which have marked the struggle between capital and labor during the past year, leaves us convinced that it would be unjust to attribute them to the association of the Knights of Labor. This was but one of several associations of workers that took part in the strikes, and their chief officers, according to disinterested witnesses, used every possible effort to appease the anger of the crowds and to prevent the excesses which, in my judgment, could not justly be attributed to them. Doubtless among the Knights of Labor as among thousands of other workingmen, there are violent, or even wicked and criminal men, who have committed inexcusable deeds of violence, and have urged their associates to do the same; but to attribute this to the organization, it seems to me, would be as unreasonable as to attribute to the Church the follies and crimes of her children against which she protests. . . .

5. Whoever meditates upon the ways in which divine Providence is guiding contemporary history cannot fail to remark how important is the part which the power of the people takes therein at present and must take in the future. We behold, with profound sadness, the efforts of the prince of darkness to make this power dangerous to the social weal by withdrawing the masses of the people from the influence of religion, and impelling them towards the ruinous paths of license and anarchy. Until now our country presents a picture of altogether different character – that of a popular power regulated by love of good order, by respect for religion, by obedience to the authority of the laws, not a democracy of license and violence, but that true democracy which aims at the general prosperity through the means of sound principles and good social order.

In order to preserve so desirable a state of things it is absolutely necessary that religion should continue to hold the affections, and thus rule the conduct of the multitudes. As Cardinal Manning has so well written, "In the future era the Church has no longer to deal with princes and parliaments, but with the masses, with the people. Whether we will or no this is our work; we need a new spirit, a new direction of our life and activity." To lose influence over the people would be to lose the future altogether; and it is by the heart, far more than by the understanding, that we must hold and guide this immense power, so mighty either for good or for evil. Among all the glorious titles of the Church which her history has merited for her, there is not one which at present gives her so great influence as that of *Friend of the People*. Assuredly, in our democratic country, it is this title which wins for the Catholic Church not only the enthusiastic devotedness of the millions of her children, but also the respect and admiration of all our citizens, whatever be their religious belief. It is the power of precisely this title which renders persecution almost an impossibility, and which draws toward our holy Church the great heart of the American people.

And since it is acknowledged by all that the great questions of the future are not those of war, of commerce or finance, but the social questions, the questions which concern the improvement of the condition of the great masses of the people, and especially of the working people, it is evidently of supreme importance that the Church should always be found on the side of humanity, of justice toward the multitudes who compose the body of the human family.

86 WILL HERBERG

FROM *"The Three Religious Communities" (1955)*

The three religious communities – Protestant, Catholic, Jewish – are America. Together, they embrace almost the entire population of this country. In the scheme of things defined by the American Way of Life, they constitute the three faces of American religion, the three "pools" or "melting pots" in and through which the American people is emerging as a national entity after a century of mass immigration. In one sense these three communities stand on the same level, recognized as equi-legitimate subdivisions of the American people. In another sense, however, they are markedly different – in their historical background, their social and cultural structure, their place in the totality of American life. . . .

I

American Catholics still labor under the heavy weight of the bitter memory of non-acceptance in a society over-whelmingly and self-consciously Protestant. Hardly a century has passed since Catholics in America were brutally attacked by mobs, excluded from more desirable employment, and made to feel in every way that they were unwanted aliens. Despised as foreigners of low-grade stock, detested and denounced as "minions of Rome," they early developed the minority defensiveness that led them to withdraw into their own "ghetto" with a rankling sense of grievance and to divide the world into "we" and "they." This was, for a time, the case even with the Irish, who of all Catholic immigrants found their place in American society soonest. . . .

Partly in the interest of corporate survival in a hostile world, though basically in line with the demands and teachings of the church, Catholics in America have built up a vast and complex system of parallel institutions, the most important and pervasive of which are the church schools operating at every academic level. Though initiated under other circumstances, these parallel institutions soon fell in rather neatly with the emerging religio-communal pattern of American life. At the same time, the development of these institutions no doubt helped accentuate that tradition of Catholic "separatism" which has recently come under the criticism of Catholics themselves. . . .

The fear of Catholic domination of the United States would seem to be hardly borne out by statistics. In the period from 1926 to 1950 church membership in this country increased 59.8 per cent, as against a 28.6 per cent increase in population. The Catholic Church grew 53.9 per cent, but in the same period Protestantism increased 63.7 per cent. Moreover, Protestant proselytism seemed to be more intensive and successful than Catholic. Most of the Protestant margin of increase, however, was accounted for by the expansion of the Baptists, especially the Southern Baptists. The churches affiliated with the National Council grew only 47 per cent, falling short of the total increase as well as of the comparable Roman Catholic growth. In those parts of the country where Protestants and Catholics come into more direct contact, particularly in the urban centers, the Catholic Church has been making considerable headway.

But it is not this numerical growth, such as it is, that so deeply disquiets the Protestant consciousness, for, after all, the Protestant–Catholic balance has remained pretty steady in the past thirty years. Neither is it entirely the mounting intellectual prestige that American Catholicism has been acquiring from the work of a number of artists, philosophers, and writers, mostly European. What seems to be really disturbing many American Protestants is the sudden realization that Protestantism is no longer identical with America, that Protestantism has, in fact, become merely one of three communions (or communities) with equal status and equal legitimacy in the American scheme of things. This sudden realization, shocking enough when one considers the historical origins of American life and culture, appears to have driven Protestantism into an essentially defensive posture, in which it feels itself a mere minority threatened with Catholic domination. . . .

It would be gravely misleading, however, to leave the impression that this attitude is universal among Protestants or that there are no Protestant voices urging other counsels. There is, in the first place, a striking difference in outlook between the older and the younger generations of Protestants in America. The older generation, still thinking of America as the Protestant nation of their youth, cannot help feeling bitter and resentful at what must appear to them to be menacing encroachments of Catholics in American life; the younger generation, accustomed to America as a three-religion country, cannot understand what the excitement is all about: "After all, we're all Americans . . ."

Minority consciousness is, of course, particularly strong among American Jews, and it is among American Jews that the "philosophy" and strategy of minority-group defensiveness has been most elaborately developed. "Defense" activities play a major part in American Jewish community life: the "defense" is against "defamation" (anti-Semitism) on the one hand, and against the intrusion of the "church" into education and public life on the other.

It is not difficult to understand why an extreme secularism and "separationism" should appeal to so many American Jews as a defensive necessity. At bottom, this attitude may be traced to the conviction, widely held though rarely articulated, that because the Western Jew achieved emancipation with the secularization of society, he can preserve his free and equal status only so long as culture and society remains secular. Let but religion gain a significant place in the everyday life of the community, and the Jew, because he is outside the bounds of the dominant religion, will once again be relegated to the margins of society, displaced, disfranchised culturally if not politically, shorn of rights and opportunities. The intrusion of religion into education and public life, the weakening of the "wall of separation" between religion and the state, is feared as only too likely to result in situations in which Jews would find themselves at a disadvantage – greater isolation, higher "visibility," an accentuation of minority status. The most elementary defensive strategy would thus seem to dictate keeping religion out of education and public life at all costs.

The defensive necessities of Jewish minority interests do not, in the case of most Jews, seem to imply any particular tension with Protestants, especially the more "liberal" Protestants in the big cities where Jews are to be found; suspicion and tension emerge, however, more obviously in Jewish–Catholic relations. A recent survey indicated that more than three times as many Jews felt themselves "interfered with" by Catholics as by Protestants, almost twice as many Jews felt they were "looked down upon" by Catholics as by Protestants, and three times as many Jews confessed to harboring "ill feeling" toward Catholics as toward Protestants. Catholicism represents, to many Jews, a much more aggressive form of religion than Protestantism (most Jews never come into contact with the militant fundamentalism of rural and small-town America); deep down, it is the Catholic Church that is suspected of untoward designs and Catholic domination that is feared.

However severe the tensions, however deep the suspicions, that divide Protestant and Catholic and Jew, there are limits beyond which they cannot go. In the last analysis, Protestant and Catholic and Jew stand united through their common anchorage in, and common allegiance to, the American Way of Life. The "unifying" function of education is not annulled because Catholics have their own schools and Jews attempt to inculcate their children with a loyalty to their "people." The same basic values and ideals, the same underlying commitment to the American Way of Life, are promoted by parochial school and public school, by Catholic, Protestant, and Jew, despite the diversity of formal religious creed. After all, are not Protestantism, Catholicism, and Judaism, in their sociological actuality, alike "religions of democracy"? The unity of American life is a unity in multiplicity; it is a unity that is grounded in a "common faith" and is therefore capable of being re-established, despite tension and conflict, on the level of "interfaith."

II

Religion is taken very seriously in present-day America, in a way that would have amazed and chagrined the "advanced" thinkers of half a century ago, who were so sure that the ancient superstition was bound to disappear very shortly in the face of the steady advance of science and reason. Religion has not disappeared; it is probably more pervasive today, and in many ways more influential, than it has been for generations. The only question is: What kind of religion is it? What is its content? What is it that Americans *believe in* when they are religious?

"The 'unknown God' of Americans seems to be faith itself." What Americans believe in when they are religious is, as we have already had occasion to see, religion itself. Of course, religious Americans speak of God and Christ, but what they seem to regard as really redemptive is primarily religion, the "positive" attitude of *believing*. It is this faith in faith, this religion that makes religion its own object, that is the outstanding characteristic of contemporary American religiosity.

As one surveys the contemporary scene, it appears that the "results" Americans want to get out of faith are primarily "peace of mind," happiness, and success in worldly achievement. Religion is valued too as a means of cultural enrichment.

Prosperity, success, and advancement in business are the obvious ends for which religion, or rather the religious attitude of "believing," is held to be useful. There is ordinarily no criticism of the ends themselves in terms of the ultimate loyalties of a God-centered faith, nor is there much concern about what the religion or the faith is all about, since it is not the content of the belief but the attitude of believing that is felt to be operative.

The burden of this criticism of American religion from the point of view of Jewish-Christian faith is that contemporary religion is so naively, so innocently *man-centered*. Not God, but man – man in his individual and corporate being – is the beginning and end of the spiritual system of much of present-day American religiosity. In this kind of religion there is no sense of transcendence, no sense of the nothingness of man and his works before a holy God; in this kind of religion the values of life, and life itself, are not submitted to Almighty God to judge, to shatter, and to reconstruct; on the contrary, life, and the values of life, are given an ultimate sanction by being identified with the divine. In this kind of religion it is not man who serves God, but God who is mobilized and made to serve man and his purposes – whether these purposes be economic prosperity, free enterprise, social reform, democracy, happiness, security, or "peace of mind." God is conceived as man's "omnipotent servant," faith as a sure-fire device to get what we want. The American is a religious man, and in many cases personally humble and conscientious. But religion as he understands it is not something that makes for humility of the uneasy conscience: it is something that reassures him about the essential rightness of everything American, his nation, his culture, and himself; something that validates his goals and his ideals instead of calling them into question; something that enhances his self-regard instead of challenging it; something that feeds his self-sufficiency instead of shattering it; something that offers him salvation on easy terms instead of demanding repentance and a "broken heart." Because it does all these things, his religion, however sincere and well-meant, is ultimately vitiated by a strong and pervasive idolatrous element.

III

Returning from a five-month visit to the United States, Bishop Eivind Berggrav, the eminent Norwegian Lutheran churchman, reported his impressions of religious life in America. He not only defended American churches against the charge of "materialism" and "activism," so often leveled against them by European observers; he also testified that "American Christianity is real, true, and personal." He found the American churches in a "period of youthful vigor," representing "a family rather than an individual Christianity," in which the congregation was a true "organism of fellowship." While he foresaw a future period of "crisis" for the American churches, he confessed himself much impressed by them and their genuine vitality.

Similar testimonies may be noted in the comments of other European churchmen, Catholic as well as Protestant. With all their criticism of American religion, they find in American religious life a vigor and a closeness to the people, a pervasive sense of the importance of religion, that is most impressive.

Yet this is the same American religion that, seen from another angle, we have found to be so empty and contentless, so conformist, so utilitarian, so sentimental, so individualistic, and so self-righteous. Each judgment has its validity and is necessary to correct and supplement the other. Both may be summed up by saying that Americans are "at one and the same time, one of the most religious and most secular of nations."

The secularism characteristic of the American mind is implicit and is not felt to be at all inconsistent with the most sincere attachment to religion. It is, nevertheless, real and pervasive, and in this sense Oscar Handlin is certainly right in saying that

America is growing more secularist, at the very time when in another sense, in the sense of affiliation and identification and of the importance attributed to religion, America is becoming increasingly more religious.

87 FLANNERY O'CONNOR

"Novelist and Believer" (1963)

Being a novelist and not a philosopher or theologian, I shall have to enter this discussion at a much lower level and proceed along a much narrower course than that held up to us here as desirable. It has been suggested that for the purposes of this symposium, we conceive religion broadly as an expression of man's ultimate concern rather than identify it with institutional Judaism or Christianity or with "going to church."

I see the utility of this. It's an attempt to enlarge your ideas of what religion is and of how the religious need may be expressed in the art of our time; but there is always the danger that in trying to enlarge the ideas of students, we will evaporate them instead, and I think nothing in this world lends itself to quick vaporization so much as the religious concern. As a novelist, the major part of my task is to make everything, even an ultimate concern, as solid, as concrete, as specific as possible. The novelist begins his work where human knowledge begins – with the senses; he works through the limitations of matter, and unless he is writing fantasy, he has to stay within the concrete possibilities of his culture. He is bound by his particular past and by those institutions and traditions that this past has left to his society. The Judaeo-Christian tradition has formed us in the west; we are bound to it by ties which may often be invisible, but which are there nevertheless. It has formed the shape of our secularism; it has formed even the shape of modern atheism. For my part, I shall have to remain well within the Judaeo-Christian tradition. I shall have to speak, without apology, of the Church, even when the Church is absent; of Christ, even when Christ is not recognized.

If one spoke as a scientist, I believe it would be possible to disregard large parts of the personality and speak simply as a scientist, but when one speaks as a novelist, he must speak as he writes – with the whole personality. Many contend that the job of the novelist is to show us how man feels, and they say that this is an operation in which his own commitments intrude not at all. The novelist, we are told, is looking for a symbol to express feeling, and whether he be Jew or Christian or Buddhist or whatever makes no difference to the aptness of the symbol. Pain is pain, joy is joy, love is love, and these human emotions are stronger than any mere religious belief; they are what they are and the novelist shows them as they are. This is all well and good so far as it goes, but it just does not go as far as the novel goes. Great fiction involves the whole range of human judgment; it is not simply an imitation of feeling. The good novelist not only finds a symbol for feeling, he finds a symbol and a way of lodging it which tells the intelligent reader whether this feeling is adequate or inadequate, whether it is moral or immoral, whether it is good or evil. And his theology, even in its most remote reaches, will have a direct bearing on this.

It makes a great difference to the look of a novel whether its author believes that the world came late into being and continues to come by a creative act of God, or whether he believes that the world and ourselves are the product of a cosmic accident. It makes a great difference to his novel whether he believes that we are created in God's image, or whether he believes we create God in our own. It makes a great difference whether he believes that our wills are free, or bound like those of the other animals.

St. Augustine wrote that the things of the world pour forth from God in a double way: intellectually into the minds of the angels and physically into the world of things. To the person who believes this – as the western world did up until a few centuries ago – this physical, sensible world is good because it proceeds from a divine source. The artist usually knows this by instinct; his senses, which are used to penetrating the concrete, tell him so. When Conrad said that his aim as an artist was to render the highest possible justice to the visible universe, he was speaking with the novelist's surest instinct. The artist penetrates the concrete world in order to find at its depths the image of its source, the image of ultimate reality. This in no way hinders his perception of evil but rather sharpens it, for only when the natural world is seen as good does evil become intelligible as a destructive force and a necessary result of our freedom.

For the last few centuries we have lived in a world which has been increasingly convinced that the reaches of reality end very close to the surface, that there is no ultimate divine source, that the things of the world do not pour forth from God in a double way, or at all. For nearly two centuries the popular spirit of each succeeding generation has tended more and more to the view that the mysteries of life will eventually fall before the mind of man. Many modern novelists have been more concerned with the processes of consciousness than with the objective world outside the mind. In twentieth-century fiction it increasingly happens that a meaningless, absurd world impinges upon the sacred consciousness of author or character; author and character seldom now go out to explore and penetrate a world in which the sacred is reflected.

Nevertheless, the novelist always has to create a world and a believable one. The virtues of art, like the virtues of faith, are such that they reach beyond the limitations of the intellect, beyond any mere theory that a writer may entertain. If the novelist is doing what as an artist he is bound to do, he will inevitably suggest that image of ultimate reality as it can be glimpsed in some aspect of the human situation. In this sense, art reveals, and the theologian has learned that he can't ignore it. In many universities, you will find departments of theology vigorously courting departments of English. The theologian is interested specifically in the modern novel because there he sees reflected the man of our time, the unbeliever, who is nevertheless grappling in a desperate and usually honest way with intense problems of the spirit.

We live, in an unbelieving age but one which is markedly and lopsidedly spiritual. There is one type of modern man who recognizes spirit in himself but who fails to recognize a being outside himself whom he can adore as Creator and Lord; consequently he has become his own ultimate concern. He says with Swinburne, "Glory to man in the highest, for he is the master of things," or with Steinbeck, "In the end was the word and the word was with men." For him, man has his own natural spirit of courage and dignity and pride and must consider it a point of honor to be satisfied with this.

There is another type of modern man who recognizes a divine being not himself, but who does not believe that this being can be known anagogically or defined dogmatically or received sacramentally. Spirit and matter are separated for him. Man wanders about, caught in a maze of guilt he can't identify, trying to reach a God he can't approach, a God powerless to approach him.

And there is another type of modern man who can neither believe nor contain himself in unbelief and who searches desperately, feeling about in all experience for the lost God.

At its best our age is an age of searchers and discoverers, and at its worst, an age that has domesticated despair and learned to live with it happily. The fiction which celebrates this last state will be the least likely to transcend its limitations, for when the religious need is banished successfully, it usually atrophies, even in the novelist. The sense of mystery vanishes. A kind of reverse evolution takes place, and the whole range of feeling is dulled.

The searchers are another matter. Pascal wrote in his notebook, "If I had not known you, I would not have found you." These unbelieving searchers have their effect even upon those of us who do believe. We begin to examine our own religious notions, to sound them for genuineness, to purify them in the heat of our unbelieving neighbor's anguish. What Christian novelist could compare his concern to Camus'? We have to look in much of the fiction of our time for a kind of sub-religion which expresses its ultimate concern in images that have not yet broken through to show any recognition of a God who has revealed himself. As great as much of this fiction is, as much as it reveals a wholehearted effort to find the only true ultimate concern, as much as in many cases it represents religious values of a high order, I do not believe that it can adequately represent in fiction the central religious experience. That, after all, concerns a relationship with a supreme being recognized through faith. It is the experience of an encounter, of a kind of knowledge which affects the believer's every action. It is Pascal's experience after his conversion and not before.

What I say here would be much more in line with the spirit of our times if I could speak to you about the experience of such novelists as Hemingway and Kafka and Gide and Camus, but all my own experience has been that of the writer who believes, again in Pascal's words, in the "God of Abraham, Isaac, and Jacob and not of the philosophers and scholars." This is an unlimited God and one who has revealed himself specifically. It is one who became man and rose, from the dead. It is one who confounds the senses and the sensibilities, one known early on as a stumbling block. There is no way to gloss over this specification or to make it more acceptable to modern thought. This God is the object of ultimate concern and he has a name.

The problem of the novelist who wishes to write about a man's encounter with this God is how he shall make the experience – which is both natural and supernatural – understandable, and credible, to his reader. In any age this would be a problem, but in our own, it is a well-nigh insurmountable one. Today's audience is one in which religious feeling has become, if not atrophied, at least vaporous and sentimental. When Emerson decided, in 1832, that he could no longer celebrate the Lord's Supper unless the bread and wine were removed, an important step in the vaporization of religion in America was taken, and the spirit of that step has continued apace. When the physical fact is separated from the spiritual reality, the dissolution of belief is eventually inevitable.

The novelist doesn't write to express himself, he doesn't write simply to render a vision he believes true, rather he renders his vision so that it can be transferred, as nearly whole as possible, to his reader. You can safely ignore the reader's taste, but you can't ignore his nature, you can't ignore his limited patience. Your problem is going to be difficult in direct proportion as your beliefs depart from his.

When I write a novel in which the central action is a baptism, I am very well aware that for a majority of my readers, baptism is a meaningless rite, and so in my novel I have to see that this baptism carries enough awe and mystery to jar the reader into some kind of emotional recognition of its significance. To this end I have to bend the whole novel – its language, its structure, its action. I have to make the reader feel in his bones if nowhere else, that something is going on here that counts. Distortion in this case is an instrument; exaggeration has a purpose, and the whole structure of the story or novel has been made what it is because of belief. This is not the kind of distortion that destroys; it is the kind that reveals, or should reveal.

Students often have the idea that the process at work here is one which hinders honesty. They think that inevitably the writer, instead of seeing what is, will see only what he believes. It is perfectly possible, of course, that this will happen. Ever since there have been such things as novels, the world has been flooded with bad fiction for which the religious impulse has been responsible. The sorry religious novel comes about when the writer supposes that because of his belief, he is somehow dispensed from the obligation to penetrate concrete reality. He will think that the eyes of the Church or of the Bible *or of* his particular theology have already done the seeing for him, and that his business is to rearrange this essential vision into satisfying patterns, getting himself as little dirty in the process as possible. His feeling about this may have been made more definite by one of those Manichean-type theologies which sees the natural world as unworthy of penetration. But the real novelist, the one with an instinct for what he is about, knows that he cannot approach the infinite directly, that he must penetrate the natural human world as it is. The more sacramental his theology, the more encouragement he will get from it to do just that.

The supernatural is an embarrassment today even to many of the churches. The naturalistic bias has so well saturated our society that the reader doesn't realize that he has to shift his sights to read fiction which treats of an encounter with God. Let me leave the novelist and talk for a moment about his reader.

This reader has first to get rid of a purely sociological point of view. In the thirties we passed through a period in American letters when social criticism and social realism were considered by many to be the most important aspects of fiction. We still suffer with a hangover from that period. I launched a character, Hazel Motes, whose presiding passion was to rid himself of a conviction that Jesus had redeemed him. Southern degeneracy never entered my head, but Hazel said "I seen" and "I taken" and he was from East Tennessee, and so the general reader's explanation for him was that he must represent some social problem peculiar to that part of the benighted South.

Ten years, however, have made some difference in our attitude toward fiction. The sociological tendency has abated in that particular form and survived in another just as bad. This is the notion that the fiction writer is after the typical. I don't know how many letters I have received telling me that the South is not at all the way I depict it; some tell me that Protestantism in the South is not at all the way I portray it, that a Southern Protestant would never be concerned, as Hazel Motes is, with penitential practices. Of course, as a novelist I've never wanted to characterize the typical South or typical Protestantism. The South and the religion found there are extremely fluid and offer enough variety to give the novelist the widest range of possibilities imaginable, for the novelist is bound by the reasonable possibilities, not the probabilities, of his culture.

There is an even worse bias than these two, and that is the clinical bias, the prejudice that sees everything strange as a case study in the abnormal. Freud brought to light many truths, but his psychology is not an adequate instrument for understanding the religious encounter or the fiction that describes it. Any psychological or cultural or economic determination may be useful up to a point; indeed, such facts can't be ignored, but the novelist will be interested in them only as he is able to go through them to give us a sense of something beyond them. The more we learn about ourselves, the deeper into the unknown we push the frontiers of fiction.

I have observed that most of the best religious fiction of our time is most shocking precisely to those readers who claim to have an intense interest in finding more "spiritual purpose" – as they like to put it – in modern novels than they can at present detect in them. Today's reader, if he believes in grace at all, sees it as something which can be separated from nature and served to him raw as Instant Uplift. This reader's favorite word is compassion. I don't wish to defame the word. There is a better sense in which it can be used but seldom is – the sense of being in travail with and for creation in its subjection to vanity.

This is a sense which implies a recognition of sin; this is a suffering-with, but one which blunts no edges and makes no excuses. When infused into novels, it is often forbidding. Our age doesn't go for it.

I have said a great deal about the religious sense that the modern audience lacks, and by way of objection to this, you may point out to me that there is a real return of intellectuals in our time to an interest in and a respect for religion. I believe that this is true. What this interest in religion will result in for the future remains to be seen. It may, together with the new spirit of ecumenism that we see everywhere around us, herald a new religious age, or it may simply be that religion will suffer the ultimate degradation and become, for a little time, fashionable. Whatever it means for the future, I don't believe that our present society is one whose basic beliefs are religious, except in the South. In any case, you can't have effective allegory in times when people are swept this way and that by momentary convictions, because everyone will read it differently. You can't indicate moral values when morality changes with what is being done, because there is no accepted basis of judgment. And you cannot show the operation of grace when grace is cut off from nature or when the very possibility of grace is denied, because no one will have the least idea of what you are about.

The serious writer has always taken the flaw in human nature for his starting point, usually the flaw in an otherwise admirable character. Drama usually bases itself on the bedrock of original sin, whether the writer thinks in theological terms or not. Then, too, any character in a serious novel is supposed to carry a burden of meaning larger than himself. The novelist doesn't write about people in a vacuum; he writes about people in a world where something is obviously lacking, where there is the general mystery of incompleteness and the particular tragedy of our own times to be demonstrated, and the novelist tries to give you, within the form of the book, a total experience of human nature at any time. For this reason the greatest dramas naturally involve the salvation or loss of the soul. Where there is no belief in the soul, there is very little drama. The Christian novelist is distinguished from his pagan colleagues by recognizing sin as sin. According to his heritage he sees it not as sickness or an accident of environment, but as a responsible choice of offense against God which involves his eternal future. Either one is serious about salvation or one is not. And it is well to realize that the maximum amount of seriousness admits the maximum amount of comedy. Only if we are secure in our beliefs can we see the comical side of the universe. One reason a great deal of our contemporary fiction is humorless is because so many of these writers are relativists and have to be continually justifying the actions of their characters on a sliding scale of values.

Our salvation is a drama played out with the devil, a devil who is not simply generalized evil, but an evil intelligence determined on its own supremacy. I think that if writers with a religious view of the world excel these days in the depiction of evil, it is because they have to make its nature unmistakable to their particular audience.

The novelist and the believer, when they are not the same man, yet have many traits in common – a distrust of the abstract, a respect for boundaries, a desire to penetrate the surface of reality and to find in each thing the spirit which makes it itself and holds the world together. But I don't believe that we shall have great religious fiction until we have again that happy combination of believing artist and believing society. Until that time, the novelist will have to do the best he can in travail with the world he has. He may find in the end that instead of reflecting the image at the heart of things, he has only reflected our broken condition and, through it, the face of the devil we are possessed by. This is a modest achievement, but perhaps a necessary one.

88 MARTIN LUTHER KING, JR.

"Letter from Birmingham Jail" (1963)

April 16, 1963

While confined here in the Birmingham city jail, I came across your recent statement calling my present activities "unwise and untimely." Seldom do I pause to answer criticism of my work and ideas. If I sought to answer all the criticisms that cross my desk, my secretaries would have little time for anything other than such correspondence in the course of the day, and I would have no time for constructive work. But since I feel that you are men of genuine good will and that your criticisms are sincerely set forth, I want to try to answer your statements in what I hope will be patient and reasonable terms.

I think I should indicate why I am here in Birmingham, since you have been influenced by the view which argues against "outsiders coming in." I have the honor of serving as president of the Southern Christian Leadership Conference, an organization operating in every southern state, with headquarters in Atlanta, Georgia. We have some eighty-five affiliated organizations across the South, and one of them is the Alabama Christian Movement for Human Rights. Frequently we share staff, educational and financial resources with our affiliates. Several months ago the affiliate here in Birmingham asked us to be on call to engage in a nonviolent direct-action program if such were deemed necessary. We readily consented, and when the hour came we lived up to our promise. So I, along with several members of my staff, am here because I was invited here. I am here because I have organizational ties here.

But more basically, I am in Birmingham because injustice is here. Just as the prophets of the eighth century B.C. left their villages and carried their "thus saith the Lord" far beyond the boundaries of their home towns, and just as the Apostle Paul left his village of Tarsus and carried the gospel of Jesus Christ to the far corners of the Greco-Roman world, so am I compelled to carry the gospel of freedom beyond my own home town. Like Paul, I must constantly respond to the Macedonian call for aid.

Moreover, I am cognizant of the interrelatedness of all communities and states. I cannot sit idly by in Atlanta and not be concerned about what happens in Birmingham. Injustice anywhere is a threat to justice everywhere. We are caught in an inescapable network of mutuality, tied in a single garment of destiny. Whatever affects one directly, affects all indirectly. Never again can we afford to live with the narrow, provincial "outside agitator" idea. Anyone who lives inside the United States can never be considered an outsider anywhere within its bounds.

You deplore the demonstrations taking place in Birmingham. But your statement, I am sorry to say, fails to express a similar concern for the conditions that brought about the demonstrations. I am sure that none of you would want to rest content with the superficial kind of social analysis that deals merely with effects and does not grapple with underlying causes. It is unfortunate that demonstrations are taking place in Birmingham, but it is even more unfortunate that the city's white power structure left the Negro community with no alternative.

In any nonviolent campaign there are four basic steps: collection of the facts to determine whether injustices exist; negotiation; self-purification; and direct action. We have gone through all these steps in Birmingham. There can be no gainsaying the fact that racial injustice engulfs this community. Birmingham is probably the most thoroughly segregated city in the United States. Its ugly record of brutality is widely known. Negroes have experienced grossly unjust treatment in the courts. There have been more unsolved bombings of Negro homes and churches in Birmingham than in any other city in the nation. These are the hard, brutal facts of the case. On the basis of these conditions, Negro leaders sought to negotiate with the city fathers. But the latter consistently refused to engage in good-faith negotiation.

Then, last September, came the opportunity to talk with leaders of Birmingham's economic community. In the course of the negotiations, certain promises were made by the merchants – for example, to remove the stores' humiliating racial signs. On the basis of these promises, the Reverend Fred Shuttlesworth and the leaders of the Alabama Christian Movement for Human Rights agreed to a moratorium on all demonstrations. As the weeks and months went by, we realized that we were the victims of a broken promise. A few signs, briefly removed, returned; the others remained.

As in so many past experiences, our hopes had been blasted, and the shadow of deep disappointment settled upon us. We had no alternative except to prepare for direct action, whereby we would present our very bodies as a means of laying our case before the conscience of the local and the national community. . . .

You may well ask: "Why direct action? Why sit-ins, marches and so forth? Isn't negotiation a better path?" You are quite right in calling for negotiation. Indeed, this is the very purpose of direct action. Nonviolent direct action seeks to create such a crisis and foster such a tension that a community which has constantly refused to negotiate is forced to confront the issue. It seeks so to dramatize the issue that it can no longer be ignored. My citing the creation of tension as part of the work of the nonviolent-resister may sound rather shocking. But I must confess that I am not afraid of the word "tension." I have earnestly opposed violent tension, but there is a type of constructive, nonviolent tension which is necessary for growth. Just as Socrates felt that it was necessary to create a tension in the mind so that individuals could rise from the bondage of myths and half-truths to the unfettered realm of creative analysis and objective appraisal, we must see the need for nonviolent gadflies to create the kind of tension in society that will help men rise from the dark depths of prejudice and racism to the majestic heights of understanding and brotherhood.

The purpose of our direct-action program is to create a situation so crisis-packed that it will inevitably open the door to negotiation. I therefore concur with you in your call for negotiation. Too long has our beloved South land been bogged down in a tragic effort to live in monologue rather than dialogue.

One of the basic points in your statement is that the action that I and my associates have taken in Birmingham is untimely. Some have asked: "Why didn't you give the new city administration time to act?" The only answer that I can give to this query is that the new Birmingham administration must be prodded about as much as the outgoing one, before it will act. We are sadly mistaken if we feel that the election of Albert Boutwell as mayor will bring the millennium to Birmingham. While Mr. Boutwell is a much more gentle person than Mr. Connor, they are both segregationists, dedicated to maintenance of the status quo. I have hope that Mr. Boutwell will be reasonable enough to see the futility of massive resistance to desegregation. But he will not see this without pressure from devotees of civil rights. My friends, I must say to you that we have not made a single gain in civil rights without determined legal and nonviolent pressure. Lamentably, it is an historical fact that privileged groups seldom give up their privileges voluntarily. Individuals may see the moral light and voluntarily give up their unjust posture; but, as Reinhold Niebuhr has reminded us, groups tend to be more immoral than individuals.

We know through painful experience that freedom is never voluntarily given by the oppressor; it must be demanded by the oppressed. Frankly, I have yet to engage in a direct-action campaign that was "well timed" in the view of those who have not suffered unduly from the disease of segregation. For years now I have heard the word "Wait!" It rings in the ear of every Negro with piercing familiarity. This "Wait" has almost always meant "Never." We must come to see, with one of our distinguished jurists, that "justice too long delayed is justice denied."

We have waited for more than 340 years for our constitutional and God-given rights. The nations of Asia and Africa are moving with jetlike speed toward gaining political independence, but we still creep at horse-and-buggy pace toward gaining a cup of coffee at a lunch counter. Perhaps it is easy for those who have never felt the stinging dart of segregation to say, "Wait." But when you have seen vicious mobs lynch your mothers and fathers at will and drown your sisters and brothers at whim; when you have seen hate-filled policemen curse, kick and even kill your black brothers and sisters; when you see the vast majority of your twenty million Negro brothers smothering in an airtight cage of poverty in the midst of an affluent society; when you suddenly find your tongue twisted and your speech stammering as you seek to explain to your six-year-old daughter why she can't go to the public amusement park that has just been advertised on television, and see tears welling up in her eyes when she is told that Funtown is closed to colored children, and see ominous clouds of inferiority beginning to form in her little mental sky, and see her beginning to distort her personality by developing an unconscious bitterness toward white people; when you have to concoct an answer for a five-year-old son who is asking: "Daddy, why do white people treat colored people so mean?"; when you take a cross-county drive and find it necessary to sleep night after night in the uncomfortable corners of your automobile because no motel will accept you; when you are humiliated day in and day out by nagging signs reading "white" and "colored"; when your first name becomes "nigger," your middle name becomes "boy" (however old you are) and your last name becomes "John," and your wife and mother are never given the respected title "Mrs."; when you are harried by day and haunted by night by the fact that you are a Negro, living constantly at tipoe stance, never quite knowing what to expect next, and are plagued with inner fears and outer resentments; when you are forever fighting a degenerating sense of "nobodiness" then you will understand why we find it difficult to wait. There comes a time when the cup of endurance runs over, and men are no longer willing to be plunged into the abyss of despair. I hope, sirs, you can understand our legitimate and unavoidable impatience.

You express a great deal of anxiety over our willingness to break laws. This is certainly a legitimate concern. Since we so diligently urge people to obey the Supreme Court's decision of 1954 outlawing segregation in the public schools, at first glance it may seem rather paradoxical for us consciously to break laws. One may well ask: "How can you advocate breaking some laws and obeying others?" The answer lies in the fact that there are two types of laws: just and unjust. I would be the first to advocate obeying just laws. One has not only a legal but a moral responsibility to obey just laws. Conversely, one has a moral responsibility to disobey unjust laws. I would agree with St. Augustine that "an unjust law is no law at all."

Now, what is the difference between the two? How does one determine whether a law is just or unjust? A just law is a man-made code that squares with the moral law or the law of God. An unjust law is a code that is out of harmony with the moral law. To put it in the terms of St. Thomas Aquinas: An unjust law is a human law that is not rooted in eternal law and natural law. Any law that uplifts human personality is just. Any law that degrades human personality is unjust. All segregation statutes are unjust because segregation distorts the soul and damages the personality. It gives the segregator a false sense of superiority and the segregated a false sense of inferiority.

Segregation, to use the terminology of the Jewish philosopher Martin Buber, substitutes an "I-it" relationship for an "I-thou" relationship and ends up relegating persons to the status of things. Hence segregation is not only politically, economically and sociologically unsound, it is morally wrong and awful. Paul Tillich said that sin is separation. Is not segregation an existential expression of man's tragic separation, his awful estrangement, his terrible sinfulness? Thus it is that I can urge men to obey the 1954 decision of the Supreme Court, for it is morally right; and I can urge them to disobey segregation ordinances, for they are morally wrong.

Let us consider a more concrete example of just and unjust laws. An unjust law is a code that a numerical or power majority group compels a minority group to obey but does not make binding on itself. This is difference made legal. By the same token, a just law is a code that a majority compels a minority to follow and that it is willing to follow itself. This is sameness made legal.

Let me give another explanation. A law is unjust if it is inflicted on a minority that, as a result of being denied the right to vote, had no part in enacting or devising the law. Who can say that the legislature of Alabama which set up that state's segregation laws was democratically elected? Throughout Alabama all sorts of devious methods are used to prevent Negroes from becoming registered voters, and there are some counties in which, even though Negroes constitute a majority of the population, not a single Negro is registered. Can any law enacted under such circumstances be considered democratically structured?

Sometimes a law is just on its face and unjust in its application. For instance, I have been arrested on a charge of parading without a permit. Now, there is nothing wrong in having an ordinance which requires a permit for a parade. But such an ordinance becomes unjust when it is used to maintain segregation and to deny citizens the First Amendment privilege of peaceful assembly and protest.

I hope you are able to see the distinction I am trying to point out. In no sense do I advocate evading or defying the law, as would the rabid segregationist. That would lead to anarchy. One who breaks an unjust law must do so openly, lovingly, and with a willingness to accept the penalty. I submit that an individual who breaks a law that conscience tells him is unjust and who willingly accepts the penalty of imprisonment in order to arouse the conscience of the community over its injustice, is in reality expressing the highest respect for law.

Of course, there is nothing new about this kind of civil disobedience. It was evidenced sublimely in the refusal of Shadrach, Meshach and Abednego to obey the laws of Nebuchadnezzar, on the ground that a higher moral law was at stake. It was practiced superbly by the early Christians, who were willing to face hungry lions and the excruciating pain of chopping blocks rather than submit to certain unjust laws of the Roman Empire. To a degree, academic freedom is a reality today because Socrates practiced civil disobedience. In our own nation, the Boston Tea Party represented a massive act of civil disobedience. . . .

I must make two honest confessions to you, my Christian and Jewish brothers. First, I must confess that over the past few years I have been gravely disappointed with the white moderate. I have almost reached the regrettable conclusion that the Negro's great stumbling block in his stride toward freedom is not the White Citizen's Councilor or the Ku Klux Klanner, but the white moderate, who is more devoted to "order" than to justice; who prefers a negative peace which is the absence of tension to a positive peace which is the presence of justice; who constantly says: "I agree with you in the goal you seek, but I cannot agree with your methods of direct action"; who paternalistically believes he can set the timetable for another man's freedom; who lives by a mythical concept of time and who constantly advises the Negro to wait for a "more convenient season." Shallow understanding from people of good will is more frustrating than absolute misunderstanding from people of ill will. Lukewarm acceptance is much more bewildering than outright rejection.

I had hoped that the white moderate would understand that law and order exist for the purpose of establishing justice and that when they fail in this purpose they become the dangerously structured dams that block the flow of social progress. I had hoped that the white moderate would understand that the present tension in the South is a necessary phase of the transition from an obnoxious negative peace, in which the Negro passively accepted his unjust plight, to a substantive and positive peace, in which all men will respect the dignity and worth of human personality. Actually, we who engage in nonviolent direct action are not the creators of tension. We merely bring to the surface the hidden tension that is already alive. We bring it out in the open, where it can be seen and dealt with. Like a boil that can never be cured so long as it is covered up but must be opened with all its ugliness to the natural medicines of air and light, injustice must be exposed, with all the tension its exposure creates, to the light of human conscience and the air of national opinion before it can be cured.

In your statement you assert that our actions, even though peaceful, must be condemned because they precipitate violence. But is this a logical assertion? Isn't this like condemning a robbed man because his possession of money precipitated the evil act of robbery? Isn't this like condemning Socrates because his unswerving commitment to truth and his philosophical inquiries precipitated the act by the misguided populace in which they made him drink hemlock? Isn't this like condemning Jesus because his unique God-consciousness and never-ceasing devotion to God's will precipitated the evil act of crucifixion? We must come to see that, as the federal courts have consistently affirmed, it is wrong to urge an individual to cease his efforts to gain his basic constitutional rights because the quest may precipitate violence. Society must protect the robbed and punish the robber.

I had also hoped that the white moderate would reject the myth concerning time in relation to the struggle for freedom. I have just received a letter from a white brother in Texas. He writes: "All Christians know that the colored people will receive equal rights eventually, but it is possible that you are in too great a religious hurry. It has taken Christianity almost two thousand years to accomplish what it has. The teachings of Christ take time to come to earth." Such an attitude stems from a tragic misconception of time, from the strangely rational notion that there is something in the very flow of time that will inevitably cure all ills. Actually, time itself is neutral; it can be used either destructively or constructively. More and more I feel that the people of ill will have used time much more effectively than have the people of good will. We will have to repent in this generation not merely for the hateful words and actions of the bad people but for the appalling silence of the good people. Human progress never rolls in on wheels of inevitability; it comes through the tireless efforts of men willing to be co-workers with God, and without this hard work, time itself becomes an ally of the forces of social stagnation. We must use time creatively, in the knowledge that the time is always ripe to do right. Now is the time to make real the promise of democracy and transform our pending national elegy into a creative psalm of brotherhood. Now is the time to lift our national policy from the quicksand of racial injustice to the solid rock of human dignity.

[margin note: repetition again]

You speak of our activity in Birmingham as extreme. At first I was rather disappointed that fellow clergymen would see my nonviolent efforts as those of an extremist. I began thinking about the fact that we stand in the middle of two opposing forces in the Negro community. One is a force of complacency, made up in part of Negroes who, as a result of long years of oppression, are so drained of self-respect and a sense of "somebodiness" that they have adjusted to segregation; and in part of a few middle class Negroes who, because of a degree of academic and economic security and because in some ways they profit by segregation, have become insensitive to the problems of the masses. The other force is one of bitterness and hatred, and it comes perilously close to advocating violence. It is expressed in the various black nationalist groups that are springing up across the nation, the largest and best-known being Elijah Muhammad's Muslim movement. Nourished by the Negro's frustration over the continued existence of racial discrimination, this movement is made up of people who have lost faith in America, who have absolutely repudiated Christianity, and who have concluded that the white man is an incorrigible "devil."

I have tried to stand between these two forces, saying that we need emulate neither the "do-nothingism" of the complacent nor the hatred and despair of the black nationalist. For there is the more excellent way of love and nonviolent protest. I am grateful to God that, through the influence of the Negro church, the way of nonviolence became an integral part of our struggle.

If this philosophy had not emerged, by now many streets of the South would, I am convinced, be flowing with blood. And I am further convinced that if our white brothers dismiss as "rabble-rousers" and "outside agitators" those of us who employ nonviolent direct action, and if they refuse to support our nonviolent efforts, millions of Negroes will, out of frustration and despair, seek solace and security in black-nationalist ideologies, a development that would inevitably lead to a frightening racial nightmare.

Oppressed people cannot remain oppressed forever. The yearning for freedom eventually manifests itself, and that is what has happened to the American Negro. Something within has reminded him of his birthright of freedom, and something without has reminded him that it can be gained. Consciously or unconsciously, he has been caught up by the Zeitgeist, and with his black brothers of Africa and his brown and yellow brothers of Asia, South America and the Caribbean, the United States Negro is moving with a sense of great urgency toward the promised land of racial justice. If one recognizes this vital urge that has engulfed the Negro community, one should readily understand why public demonstrations are taking place. The Negro has many pent-up resentments and latent frustrations, and he must release them. So let him march; let him make prayer pilgrimages to the city hall; let him go on freedom rides – and try to understand why he must do so. If his repressed emotions are not released in nonviolent ways, they will seek expression through violence; this is not a threat but a fact of history. So I have not said to my people: "Get rid of your discontent." Rather, I have tried to say that this normal and healthy discontent can be channeled into the creative outlet of nonviolent direct action. And now this approach is being termed extremist.

But though I was initially disappointed at being categorized as an extremist, as I continued to think about the matter I gradually gained a measure of satisfaction from the label. Was not Jesus an extremist for love: "Love your enemies, bless them that curse you, do good to them that hate you, and pray for them which despitefully use you, and persecute you." Was not Amos an extremist for justice: "Let justice roll down like waters and righteousness like an ever-flowing stream." Was not Paul an extremist for the Christian gospel: "I bear in my body the marks of the Lord Jesus." Was not Martin Luther an extremist: "Here I stand; I cannot do otherwise, so help me God." And John Bunyan: "I will stay in jail to the end of my days before I make a butchery of my conscience." And Abraham Lincoln: "This nation cannot survive half slave and half free." And Thomas Jefferson: "We hold these truths to be self-evident, that all men are created equal . . ." So the question is not whether we will be extremists, but what kind of extremists we will be. Will we be extremists for hate or for love? Will we be extremist for the preservation of injustice or for the extension of justice? In that dramatic scene on Calvary's hill three men were crucified. We must never forget that all three were crucified for the same crime – the crime of extremism. Two were extremists for immorality, and thus fell below their environment. The other, Jesus Christ, was an extremist for love, truth and goodness, and thereby rose above his environment. Perhaps the South, the nation and the world are in dire need of creative extremists. . . .

I have been so greatly disappointed with the white church and its leadership. Of course, there are some notable exceptions . . . . But despite these notable exceptions, I must honestly reiterate that I have been disappointed with the church. I do not say this as one of those negative critics who can always find something wrong with the church. I say this as a minister of the gospel, who loves the church; who was nurtured in its bosom; who has been sustained by its spiritual blessings and who will remain true to it as long as the cord of life shall lengthen.

When I was suddenly catapulted into the leadership of the bus protest in Montgomery, Alabama, a few years ago, I felt we would be supported by the white church, felt that the white ministers, priests and rabbis of the South would be among our strongest allies. Instead, some have been outright opponents, refusing to understand the freedom movement and misrepresenting its leaders; all too many others have been more cautious than courageous and have remained silent behind the anesthetizing security of stained-glass windows.

In spite of my shattered dreams, I came to Birmingham with the hope that the white religious leadership of this community would see the justice of our cause and, with deep moral concern, would serve as the channel through which our just grievances could reach the power structure. I had hoped that each of you would understand. But again I have been disappointed.

I have heard numerous southern religious leaders admonish their worshipers to comply with a desegregation decision because it is the law, but I have longed to hear white ministers declare: "Follow this decree because integration is morally right and because the Negro is your brother." In the midst of blatant injustices inflicted upon the Negro, I have watched white churchmen stand on the sideline and mouth pious irrelevancies and sanctimonious trivialities. In the midst of a mighty struggle to rid our nation of racial and economic injustice, I have heard many ministers say: "Those are social issues, with which the gospel has no real concern." And I have watched many churches commit themselves to a completely other worldly religion which makes a strange, un-Biblical distinction between body and soul, between the sacred and the secular.

I have traveled the length and breadth of Alabama, Mississippi and all the other southern states. On sweltering summer days and crisp autumn mornings I have looked at the South's beautiful churches with their lofty spires pointing heavenward. I have beheld the impressive outlines of her massive religious-education buildings. Over and over I have found myself asking: "What kind of people worship here? Who is their God? Where were their voices when the lips of Governor Barnett dripped with words of interposition and nullification? Where were they when Governor Wallace gave a clarion call for defiance and hatred? Where were their voices of support when bruised and weary Negro men and women decided to rise from the dark dungeons of complacency to the bright hills of creative protest?"

Yes, these questions are still in my mind. In deep disappointment I have wept over the laxity of the church. But be assured that my tears have been tears of love. There can be no deep disappointment where there is not deep love. Yes, I love the church. How could I do otherwise? I am in the rather unique position of being the son, the grandson and the great-grandson of preachers. Yes, I see the church as the body of Christ. But, oh! How we have blemished and scarred that body through social neglect and through fear of being nonconformists.

There was a time when the church was very powerful, in the time when the early Christians rejoiced at being deemed worthy to suffer for what they believed. In those days the church was not merely a thermometer that recorded the ideas and principles of popular opinion; it was a thermostat that transformed the mores of society. Whenever the early Christians entered a town, the people in power became disturbed and immediately sought to convict the Christians for being "disturbers of the peace" and "outside agitators." But the Christians pressed on, in the conviction that they were "a colony of heaven," called to obey God rather than man. Small in number, they were big in commitment. They were too God intoxicated to be "astronomically intimidated." By their effort and example they brought an end to such ancient evils as infanticide and gladiatorial contests.

Things are different now. So often the contemporary church is a weak, ineffectual voice with an uncertain sound. So often it is an archdefender of the status quo. Far from being disturbed by the presence of the church, the power structure of the average community is consoled by the church's silent and often even vocal sanction of things as they are.

But the judgment of God is upon the church as never before. If today's church does not recapture the sacrificial spirit of the early church, it will lose its authenticity, forfeit the loyalty of millions, and be dismissed as an irrelevant social club with no meaning for the twentieth century. Every day I meet young people whose disappointment with the church has turned into outright disgust.

Perhaps I have once again been too optimistic. Is organized religion too inextricably bound to the status quo to save our nation and the world? Perhaps I must turn my faith to the inner spiritual church, the church within the church, as the true ekklesia and the hope of the world. But again I am thankful to God that some noble souls from the ranks of organized religion have broken loose from the paralyzing chains of conformity and joined us as active partners in the struggle for freedom. They have left their secure congregations and walked the streets of Albany, Georgia, with us. They have gone down the highways of the South on tortuous rides for freedom. Yes, they have gone to jail with us. Some have been dismissed from their churches, have lost the support of their bishops and fellow ministers. But they have acted in the faith that right defeated is stronger than evil triumphant. Their witness has been the spiritual salt that has preserved the true meaning of the gospel in these troubled times. They have carved a tunnel of hope through the dark mountain of disappointment.

I hope the church as a whole will meet the challenge of this decisive hour. But even if the church does not come to the aid of justice, I have no despair about the future. I have no fear about the outcome of our struggle in Birmingham, even if our motives are at present misunderstood. We will reach the goal of freedom in Birmingham, and all over the nation, because the goal of America is freedom. Abused and scorned though we may be, our destiny is tied up with America's destiny. Before the pilgrims landed at Plymouth, we were here. Before the pen of Jefferson etched the majestic words of the Declaration of Independence across the pages of history, we were here. For more than two centuries our forebears labored in this country without wages; they made cotton king; they built the homes of their masters while suffering gross injustice and shameful humiliation – and yet out of a bottomless vitality they continued to thrive and develop. If the inexpressible cruelties of slavery could not stop us, the opposition we now face will surely fail. We will win our freedom because the sacred heritage of our nation and the eternal will of God are embodied in our echoing demands.

Before closing I feel impelled to mention one other point in your statement that has troubled me profoundly. You warmly commended the Birmingham police force for keeping "order" and "preventing violence." I doubt that you would have so warmly commended the police force if you had seen its dogs sinking their teeth into unarmed, nonviolent Negroes. I doubt that you would so quickly commend the policemen if you were to observe their ugly and inhumane treatment of Negroes here in the city jail; if you were to watch them push and curse old Negro women and young Negro girls; if you were to see them slap and kick old Negro men and young boys; if you were to observe them, as they did on two occasions, refuse to give us food because we wanted to sing our grace together. I cannot join you in your praise of the Birmingham police department.

It is true that the police have exercised a degree of discipline in handling the demonstrators. In this sense they have conducted themselves rather "nonviolently" in public. But for what purpose? To preserve the evil system of segregation. Over the past few years I have consistently preached that nonviolence demands that the means we use must be as pure as the ends we seek. I have tried to make clear that it is wrong to use immoral means to attain moral ends. But now I must affirm that it is just as wrong, or perhaps even more so, to use moral means to preserve immoral ends. Perhaps Mr. Connor and his policemen have been rather nonviolent in public, as was Chief Pritchett in Albany, Georgia but they have used the moral means of nonviolence to maintain the immoral end of racial injustice. As T. S. Eliot has said: "The last temptation is the greatest treason: To do the right deed for the wrong reason."

I wish you had commended the Negro sit-inners and demonstrators of Birmingham for their sublime courage, their willingness to suffer and their amazing discipline in the midst of great provocation. One day the South will recognize its real heroes. They will be the James Merediths, with the noble sense of purpose that enables them to face jeering, and hostile mobs, and with the agonizing loneliness that characterizes the life of the pioneer. They will be old, oppressed, battered Negro women, symbolized in a seventy-two-year-old woman in Montgomery, Alabama, who rose up with a sense of dignity and with her people decided not to ride segregated buses, and who responded with ungrammatical profundity to one who inquired about her weariness: "My feets is tired, but my soul is at rest." They will be the young high school and college students, the young ministers of the gospel and a host of their elders, courageously and nonviolently sitting in at lunch counters and willingly going to jail for conscience' sake. One day the South will know that when these disinherited children of God sat down at lunch counters, they were in reality standing up for what is best in the American dream and for the most sacred values in our Judaeo-Christian heritage, thereby bringing our nation back to those great wells of democracy which were dug deep by the founding fathers in their formulation of the Constitution and the Declaration of Independence.

Never before have I written so long a letter. I'm afraid it is much too long to take your precious time. I can assure you that it would have been much shorter if I had been writing from a comfortable desk, but what else can one do when he is alone in a narrow jail cell, other than write long letters, think long thoughts and pray long prayers?

If I have said anything in this letter that overstates the truth and indicates an unreasonable impatience, I beg you to forgive me. If I have said anything that understates the truth and indicates my having a patience that allows me to settle for anything less than brotherhood, I beg God to forgive me.

I hope this letter finds you strong in the faith. I also hope that circumstances will soon make it possible for me to meet each of you, not as an integrationist or a civil rights leader but as a fellow clergyman and a Christian brother. Let us all hope that the dark clouds of racial prejudice will soon pass away and the deep fog of misunderstanding will be lifted from our fear-drenched communities, and in some not too distant tomorrow the radiant stars of love and brotherhood will shine over our great nation with all their scintillating beauty.

Yours for the cause of Peace and Brotherhood,
Martin Luther King, Jr.

89 BILLY GRAHAM

"The Unfinished Dream" (1970)

The Bible says in First Peter 2:17: "Honor all men. Fear God. Honor the king." And the king referred to was the Roman emperor. Since our nation is a republic and not a monarchy, this Scripture could read, "Honor the nation."

Today, in the capital of the United States, thousands of us have come together to honor America on her 194th birthday.

We stand here today within the shadow of three great monuments.

That great shaft over there honors George Washington, who led the revolution that obtained our freedom.

Not far away is the memorial to Thomas Jefferson, father of the Declaration of Independence, which proclaimed the rights of free men and began the greatest experiment in freedom the world has ever known.

Behind us is the memorial honoring Abraham Lincoln, who helped preserve the unity of this country by his courage, faith, and perseverance and who gave black men hope that they, too, would become first-class citizens.

We can listen to no better voices than these men who gave us the dream that has become America. These men represent thousands who worked, prayed, suffered, and died to give us this nation.

We are not here today only to honor America; we are come as citizens to renew our dedication and allegiance to the principles and institutions that made her great. Lately our institutions have been under attack: the Supreme Court, the Congress, the presidency, the flag, the home, the educational system, and even the church – but we are here to say with loud voices that in spite of their faults and failures we believe in these institutions!

Let the world know today that the vast majority of us still proudly sing: "My country, 'tis of thee, sweet land of liberty." America needs to sing again! America needs to celebrate again! America needs to wave the flag again! This flag belongs to all Americans – black and white, rich and poor, liberal and conservative, Republican and Democrat.

I think there is too much discouragement, despair, and negativism in the nation today. On every hand critics tell us what is wrong with America, where we have failed, and why we are hated. We have listened and watched while a relatively small extremist element, both to the left and to the right in our society, has knocked our courts, desecrated our flag, disrupted our educational system, laughed at our religious heritage, and threatened to burn down our cities – and is now threatening to assassinate our leaders.

The overwhelming majority of concerned Americans – white and black, hawks and doves, parents and students, Republicans and Democrats – who hate violence have stood by and viewed all of this with mounting alarm and concern. Today we call upon all Americans to stop this polarization before it is too late – and let's proudly gather around the flag and all that it stands for.

Many people have asked me why I, as a citizen of heaven and a Christian minister, join in honoring any secular state. Jesus said, "Render unto Caesar the things that are

Caesar's." The Apostle Paul proudly boasted of being a Roman citizen. The Bible says "Honor the nation." As a Christian, or as a Jew, or as an atheist, each of us has a responsibility to an America that has always stood for liberty, protection, and opportunity.

There are many reasons why we honor America today.

First, we honor America because she has opened her heart and her doors to the distressed and the persecuted of the world. Millions have crossed our threshold into the fresh air of freedom. I believe that the Bible teaches that God blesses a nation which carries out the words of Jesus, "For I was hungered, and ye gave me meat: I was thirsty, and ye gave me drink: I was a stranger, and ye took me in."

Secondly, we honor America because she has been the most generous nation in history. We have shared our wealth and faith with a world in need. When a disaster occurs any place in the world, America is there with help. In famine, in earthquakes, in floods, in stresses of every kind, we pour out millions of dollars every year, even if we have to borrow the money and go in debt.

Thirdly, we honor America because she has never hidden her problems and debts. With our freedom of the press and open communications system, we don't sweep our sins under the rug. If poverty exists, if racial tension exists, if riots occur, the whole world knows about it. Instead of an Iron Curtain we have a picture window. "The whole world watches" – sometimes critically and sometimes with admiration, but nobody can accuse America of trying to hide her problems.

Fourthly, we honor America because she is honestly recognizing and is courageously trying to solve her social problems. In order to fulfill the ultimate problem, much remains to be done – but even our critics abroad are saying, "America is trying." The men who penned the Declaration of Independence were moved by a magnificent dream. This dream amazed the world 194 years ago. And this dream is rooted in a book we call the Bible. It proclaims freedoms that most people of the world thought were impossible. We are still striving to achieve for all men equally those freedoms bought at such a high price. From the beginning, the dream of freedom and equal opportunity has been a beacon to oppressed peoples all over the world.

Let those who claim they want to improve the nation by destroying it join all of us in a new unity and a new dedication by peaceful means to make these dreams come true.

Fifthly, we honor America because she defends the right of her citizens to dissent. Dissent is impossible in many countries of the world, whereas constructive dissent is the hallmark of our freedom in America. But when dissent takes violent forms and has no moral purpose, it is no longer dissent but anarchy. We will listen respectfully to those who dissent in accordance with constitutional principles, but we strongly reject violence and the erosion of any of our liberties under the guise of a dissent that promises everything but delivers only chaos. As General Eisenhower once wrote: "We must never confuse honest dissent with disloyal subversion."

Sixthly, we honor America because there is woven into the warp and woof of our nation faith in God. The ethical and moral principles of the Judeo-Christian faith and the God of that tradition are found throughout the Declaration of Independence. Most presidents of the United States have declared their faith in God and have encouraged us to read the Bible. I am encouraged to believe that Americans at this hour are striving to retain their spiritual identity despite the inroads of materialism and the rising tide of permissiveness.

On the front page of a Chicago newspaper some time ago there appeared a picture of Betsy Ross sewing the first American flag. Over the picture was the caption, "Time to check our stitches." Let's check the stitches of racism that still persist in our country. Let's check the stitches of poverty that bind some of our countrymen. Let's check the stitches of foreign policy to be sure that our objectives and goals are in keeping with the American dream. Let's check the stitches of pollution brought on by technology. Let's check the stitches of a moral permissiveness that could lead us to decadence. Let's even check the stitches of freedom to see if our freedom in America has become licence. A liberal British writer recently said, "You Americans have become too free until you are no longer free."

I'm asking all Americans today, especially our young people, to pursue this vision under God, to work for freedom and for peace. It will not be easy. The journey will be hard. The day will be long. And the obstacles will be many.

But I remember today a word spoken by Sir Winston Churchill, whose courage and faith and persistence carried his nation through the darkest days of World War II. The headmaster of Harrow, the famous prep school that Churchill had attended as a boy, asked Mr Churchill to address the students. The headmaster told the young people to bring their pencils and their notebooks to record what Britain's greatest man of the century would say. The moment they waited for came. The old man stood to his feet and spoke these words: "Never give in! Never give in! Never! Never!"

I say to you today, "Pursue the vision, reach the goal, fulfill the American dream – and as you move to do it, never give in! Never give in! Never! Never! Never! Never!"

90 RICHARD RODRIGUEZ

"Credo" (1981)

The steps of the church defined the eternal square where children played and adults talked after dinner. He remembers the way the church building was at the center of town life. She remembers the way one could hear the bell throughout the day, telling time. And the way the town completely closed down for certain feastdays. He remembers that the church spire was the first thing he'd see walking back into town. Both my parents have tried to describe something of what it was like for them to have grown up Catholic in small Mexican towns. They remember towns where everyone was a Catholic.

With their move to America, my mother and father left behind that Mexican Church to find themselves (she praying in whispered Spanish) in an Irish-American parish. In a way, they found themselves at ease in such a church. My parents had much in common with the Irish-born priests and nuns. Like my parents, the priests remembered what it was like to have been Catholic in villages and cities where everyone else was a Catholic. In their American classrooms, the nuns worked very hard to approximate that other place, that earlier kind of religious experience. For a time they succeeded. For a time I too enjoyed a Catholicism something like that enjoyed a generation before me by my parents.

I grew up a Catholic at home and at school, in private and in public. My mother and father were deeply pious *católicos*; all my relatives were Catholics. At home, there were holy pictures on a wall of nearly every room, and a crucifix hung over my bed. My first twelve years as a student were spent in Catholic schools where I could look up to the front of the room and see a crucifix hanging over the clock . . . .

When we were eleven years old, the nuns would warn us about the dangers of mixed marriage (between a Catholic and a non-Catholic). And we heard a priest say that it was a mortal sin to read newspaper accounts of a Billy Graham sermon. But the ghetto Catholic Church, so defensive, so fearful of contact with non-Catholics, was already outdated when I entered the classroom. My classmates and I were destined to live in a world very different from that which the nuns remembered in Ireland or my parents remembered in Mexico. We were destined to live on unhallowed ground, beyond the gated city of God . . . .

It was to be in college, at Stanford, that my religious faith would seem to me suddenly pared. I would remain a Catholic, but a Catholic defined by a non-Catholic world. This is how I think of myself now. I remember my early Catholic schooling and recall an experience of religion very different from anything I have known since. Never since have I felt so much at home in the Church, so easy at mass. My grammar school years especially were the years when the great Church doors opened to enclose me, filling my day as I was certain the Church filled all time. Living in a community of shared faith, I enjoyed much more than mere social reenforcement of religious belief. Experienced continuously in public and private, Catholicism shaped my whole day. It framed my experience of eating and sleeping and washing; it named the season and the hour . . . .

I was *un católico* before I was a Catholic. That is, I acquired my earliest sense of the Church – and my membership in it – through my parents' Mexican Catholicism. It was in Spanish that I first learned to pray. I recited family prayers – not from any book. And in those years when we felt alienated from *los gringos*, my family went across town every week to the wooden church of Our Lady of Guadalupe, which was decorated with yellow Christmas tree lights all year long.

Very early, however, the *gringo* church in our neighborhood began to superimpose itself on our family life. The first English-speaking dinner guest at our house was a priest from Sacred Heart Church. I was about four years old at the time, so I retain only random details with which to remember the evening. But the visit was too important an event for me to forget. I remember how my mother dressed her four children in outfits it had taken her weeks to sew. I wore a white shirt and blue woolen shorts. (It was the first time I had been dressed up for a stranger.) I remember hearing the priest's English laughter. . . . He left a large picture of a sad-eyed Christ, exposing his punctured heart. (A caption below records the date of his visit and the imprimatur of Francis Cardinal Spellman.) That picture survives. Hanging prominently over the radio or, later, the television set in the front room, it has retained a position of prominence in all the houses my parents have lived in since. It has been one of the few permanent fixtures in the environment of my life. Visitors to our house doubtlessly noticed it when they entered the door – saw it immediately as the sign we were Catholics. But I saw the picture too often to pay it much heed.

I saw a picture of the Sacred Heart in the grammar school classroom I entered two years after the priest's visit. The picture drew an important continuity between home and the classroom. When all else was different for me (as a scholarship boy) between the two worlds of my life, the Church provided an essential link. During my first months in school, I remember being struck by the fact that – although they worshipped in English – the nuns and my classmates shared my family's religion. The *gringos* were, in some way, like me, *católicos*. Gradually, however, with my assimilation in the schoolroom, I began to think of myself and my family as Catholics. The distinction blurred. At home and in class I heard about sin and Christ and Satan and the consoling presence of Mary the Virgin. It became one Catholic faith for me.

Only now do I trouble to notice what intricate differences separated home Catholicism from classroom Catholicism. In school, religious instruction stressed that man was a sinner. Influenced, I suspect, by a bleak melancholic strain in Irish Catholicism, the nuns portrayed God as a judge . . . .

Unlike others who have described their Catholic schooling, I do not remember the nuns or the priests to have been obsessed with sexual sins. Perhaps that says more about me or my Mexican Catholicism than it says about what actually went on in the classroom. I remember, in any case, that I would sometimes hear with irony warnings about the sins of the flesh. When we were in eighth grade the priest told us how dangerous it was to look at our naked bodies, even while taking a bath – and I noticed that he made the remark directly under a near-naked figure of Christ on the cross.

The Church, in fact, excited more sexual wonderment than it repressed. I regarded with awe the "wedding ring" on a nun's finger, her black "wedding veil" – symbols of marriage to God. I would study pictures of martyrs – white-robed virgins fallen in death and the young, almost smiling, St. Sebastian, transfigured in pain. At Easter high mass I was dizzied by the mucous perfume of white flowers at the celebration of rebirth. At such moments, the Church touched alive some very private sexual excitement; it pronounced my sexuality important . . . .

In contrast to the Catholicism of school, the Mexican Catholicism of home was less concerned with man the sinner than with man the supplicant. God the Father was not so much a stern judge as One with the power to change our lives. My family turned to God not in guilt so much as in need. We prayed for favors and at desperate times. I prayed for help in finding a quarter I had lost on my way home. I prayed with my family at times of illness and when my father was temporarily out of a job. And when there was death in the family, we prayed.

I remember my family's religion, and I hear the whispering voices of women. For although men in my family went to church, women prayed most audibly. Whether by man or woman, however, God the Father was rarely addressed directly. There were intermediaries to carry one's petition to Him. My mother had her group of Mexican and South American saints and near-saints (persons moving toward canonization). She favored a black Brazilian priest who, she claimed, was especially efficacious. Above all mediators there was Mary, *Santa Maria*, the Mother. Whereas at school the primary mediator was Christ, at home that role was assumed by the Mexican Virgin, *Nuestra Señora de Guadalupe*, the focus of devotion and pride for

Mexican Catholics. The Mexican Mary "honored our people," my mother would say. "She could have appeared to anyone in the whole world, but she appeared to a Mexican." Someone like us. And she appeared, I could see from her picture, as a young Indian maiden – dark just like me.

On her feastday in early December my family would go to the Mexican church for a predawn high mass. The celebration would begin in the cold dark with a blare of trumpets imitating the cries of a cock. The Virgin's wavering statue on the shoulders of men would lead a procession into the warm yellow church. Often an usher would roughly separate me from my parents and pull me into a line of young children. (My mother nodded calmly when I looked back.) Sometimes alone, sometimes with my brother and sisters, I would find myself near the altar amid two or three hundred children, many of them dressed like Mexican cowboys and cowgirls.

Sitting on the floor it was easier to see the congregation than the altar. So, as the mass progressed, my eye would wander through the crowd. Invariably, my attention settled on old women – mysterious supplicants in black – bent deep, their hands clasped tight to hold steady the attention of the Mexican Virgin, who was pictured high over the altar, astride a black moon.

The *gringo* Catholic church, a block from our house, was a very different place. In the *gringo* church Mary's statue was relegated to a side altar, imaged there as a serene white lady who matter-of-factly squashed the Genesis serpent with her bare feet. (Very early I knew that I was supposed to believe that the shy Mexican Mary was the same as this European Mary triumphant.) In the *gringo* church the floors were made not of squeaky wood but of marble. And there was not the devotional clutter of so many pictures and statues and candle racks. "It doesn't feel like a church," my mother complained. But as it became our regular church, I grew to love its elegant simplicity: the formal march of its eight black pillars toward the altar; the Easter-egg-shaped sanctuary that arched high over the tabernacle; and the dim pink light suffused throughout on summer afternoons when I came in not to pray but to marvel at the cool calm.

The holy darkness of church never frightened me. It was never nighttime darkness. Religion at school and at church was never nighttime religion like religion at home. Catholicism at home was shaped by the sounds of the "family rosary": tired voices repeating the syllables of the Hail Mary; our fingers inching forward on beads toward the point of beginning; my knees aching; the coming of sleep.

Religion at home was a religion of bedtime. Prayers before sleeping spoke of death coming during the night. It was then a religion of shadows. The last thing I'd see before closing my eyes would be the cheap statue of Mary aglow next to my bed.

But the dark at the foot of my bed billowed with malevolent shapes. Those nights when I'd shudder awake from a nightmare, I'd remember my grandmother's instruction to make a sign of the cross in the direction of my window. (That way Satan would find his way barred.) Sitting up in bed, I'd aim the sign of the cross against the dim rectangle of light. Quickly, then, I'd say the Prayer to My Guardian Angel, which would enable me to fall back to sleep.

10

EDUCATION

Introduction   300

 91 *Robert Coram*   303
     FROM "The Necessity of Compulsory Primary Education" (1791)

 92 *John Dewey*   305
     "My Pedagogic Creed" (1897)

 93 *Booker T. Washington*   308
     "A Harder Task Than Making Bricks Without Straw" (1901)

 94 *Mary Antin*   312
     FROM *The Promised Land* (1912)

 95 *US Supreme Court*   315
     The 1954 Supreme Court Decision on Segregation

 96 *US Congressmen*   317
     "Protest from the South" (1956)

 97 *Jonathan Kozol*   318
     FROM *Death at an Early Age: The Destruction of the Hearts and
     Minds of Negro Children in the Boston Public Schools* (1967)

 98 *Studs Terkel*   322
     FROM "Public School Teacher: Rose Hoffman" (1972)

 99 *Elizabeth Loza Newby*   324
     FROM "An Impossible Dream" (1977)

100 *Allan Bloom*   327
     "The Closing of the American Mind" (1987)

Figure 10 Students watching African American students escorted. A few weeks after the desegregation of Little Rock's Central High School, only six of the nine African American students are escorted into the school, the other three reporting in sick, October 16, 1957 © Bettmann/CORBIS

INTRODUCTION

In the course of their history Americans have displayed a strong faith in education as a means of climbing the social ladder and as an important tool for transmitting American common values to the people. Earlier than in Europe Americans sensed the importance of education as a means of social mobility.

In text 91 Robert Coram, a Delaware newspaper editor, argues that the best way of alleviating poverty is through education. Writing after the American Revolution, Coram is concerned with the challenges facing America after its newly won independence, and he makes a strong case for free elementary compulsory education.

Horace Mann was the most influential American philosopher of education during the 1900s (see Mann's *Lectures and Annual Reports on Education*, 1867), but John Dewey remains the most famous American philosopher and educational theorist. Over the years Dewey developed and reformulated his ideas of education, stressing throughout (as in text 92, "My Pedagogic Creed") the importance of a philosophy of experience and its relation to education. Dewey also argued that skills taught in schools should not be put to selfish use but applied to what he called "a common and shared life" (*The New Era in Home and School*, 1934).

Booker T. Washington was a true revolutionary in the education of African American students. At a time when black people suffered severe setbacks in the South, Washington started and directed his Tuskegee Institute (founded in 1881) in Alabama. Beginning in a simple shanty, it is now (since 1985) the Tuskegee University. In Washington's school vocational training was just as important as the teaching of scientific theory. To Washington education was a means to certify himself as a free individual, as well as a way to prepare others for leadership in the black communities. In a sense he was a strong advocate of Dewey's program of learning by doing, as text 93, a chapter from his autobiography *Up From Slavery*, will show.

During the time of mass immigration to the United States, the public school became the prime institution of assimilation. To Mary Antin, a young Jewish immigrant from Russia, whose father had immigrated alone two years before he sent for the rest of his family, the elementary school was the main instrument for bringing her into the melting pot she so strongly aspired to. In her story about her immigrant father taking her to school in Massachusetts and her first school years there she is full of praise for the American educational system. To her education was the best initiation into American life (text 94).

One of the headaches of American education has been the unequal opportunities offered to white and black children, primarily owing to the policy of placing blacks and whites in separate schools. The decision of the Supreme Court in 1896, *Plessy* v. *Ferguson*, approved segregation of the races as being in accordance with the fourteenth amendment (see also the introduction to chapter 13, p. 407 below). The principle of "separate but equal" helped to justify *de jure* segregation in schools and hit in particular black children in poor school districts. The "separate but equal" doctrine was not challenged by the Supreme Court until 1954 (text 95), when the Court in its famous decision *Brown* v. *Board of Education of Topeka* declared the policy of "separate but equal" as unconstitutional and banned segregation in public schools. The specific case concerned Oliver Brown's application for his 8-year-old daughter to be allowed to go to a white school in Topeka, Kansas. This was the first major breakthrough after World War II for the blacks in their fight for equality within the school system.

The Supreme Court decision was opposed primarily by southern states, and in 1956 ninety-six congressmen from the South came out against the decision (text 96). In the following years school desegregation efforts were often met with strong resistance from southern authorities, and on several occasions the Federal government had to resort to the National Guard to enforce the law and sustain order.

By the late 1960s, however, some blacks had lost faith in integration as a means of achieving equal educational opportunities, and many blacks urged a new form of segregation and separation in educational matters.

Although there is *de jure* equality of educational opportunities in the United States today, no observer of the American system can fail to notice that the *de facto* situation is far from satisfying. The now classic text from 1967 by Jonathan Kozol points out some of the inadequacies of the ghetto school as observed by a teacher (text 97). Kozol taught in the Boston public schools until he was fired. Controversy arose over his use of a poem by Langston Hughes in his fourth grade classroom. The poem, "Ballad of the Landlord," is free of profanity and obscenity: it concerns the conflict between a black tenant and a white landlord. In a newer study of children in American classrooms entitled *Savage Inequalities* (1991), Kozol reiterates his theme.

In text 99 by Elizabeth Loza Newby the problem of education is not so much with the school as with her own ethnic background. She describes a probably typical dilemma for many immigrant women in the United States, forced to choose between the protection of the family and the chances to get higher education.

Public concern about the lack of quality in American education has been pervasive in the 1980s and early 1990s. In 1983 the US Department of Education issued *A Nation at Risk*, a blunt alarm that captured the attention of the public troubled by the deterioration of the schools. A focus on quality and student achievement has since then become a respectable enterprise, even though the reform movement of the 1980s did not achieve its aim of substantially improving education in the United States. A recent comparison of 13-year-old American and foreign students by the Educational Testing Service ranked Americans last in mathematics and near the bottom in science.

Professor Allan Bloom's book *The Closing of the American Mind* (1987), from which a chapter is included as text 100, attributes the social/political crisis of twentieth-century America to an intellectual crisis, a crisis in the educational system. In 1989 the National Governors' Association issued a set of educational objectives that ultimately became the national goals for education and evolved into *America 2000*, an education strategy unveiled in April 1991 by President Bush (the elder). One part of *America 2000* has particularly touched a nerve with educators: the development of national standards and voluntary examinations in five core subjects: English, history, mathematics, science, and geography. Arguments against a national curriculum come from educational pluralists who fear intellectual homogenization and Orwellian thought control.

Although aspects of the educational system are in disarray, American education is, from another perspective, quite successful. Studs Terkel's interview with Rose Hoffman (text 98) brings us into the classroom. Hoffman shows how the day-to-day educational challenges at the primary level are meaningful and rewarding for a dedicated teacher.

Probably no country can match the excellence and the scholarship of the top American universities, and top students around the world choose US graduate schools to learn science and engineering. Combined with this intellectual quality is the creation of a comprehensive system of higher education. The percentage of young students in high school and college in the United States is unrivalled in the world.

A more recent Education Act, *The No Child Left Behind Act* (2001), is based on a system of test scores. Schools have to test their students each year in reading and mathematics, and it is the state departments of education which decide whether the schools are performing adequately, i.e. if enough students are reaching an appropriate level of competence. Punitive measures are taken to rehabilitate schools that do not perform as well as expected, creating an atmosphere of test-driven instruction. Whether this will improve the quality of teaching is a matter of intense dispute.

Questions and Topics

1 Discuss to what extent Coram's idea of alleviating poverty through education is a viable idea. To what extent is the educational policy of the Federal government today governed by this idea?

2 Try to formulate the basic principles of John Dewey's pedagogical philosophy. Are his ideas outdated or valid in today's schools?

3 The American school system was regarded as the chief promoter of assimilation. Use the excerpt from Antin's book and Newby's essay to discuss how schools helped to shape waves of immigrant children.
4 The Supreme Court decision of 1954 declared the policy of "separate but equal" unconstitutional. To what extent has this decision changed the educational climate in the United States?
5 Reading the interview with Rose Hoffman, we may be led to think that a dedicated teacher can conquer all the problems of an insufficient system. How does she manage?

Suggestions for further reading

Boone, Richard G., *Education in the United States: Its History from the Earliest Settlements* (Bristol: Thoemmes Press, 1999).
Kozol, Jonathan, *Savage Inequalities* (New York: HarperCollins, 1991).
Moses, Michele S., *Embracing Race: Why We Need Race-Conscious Educational Policy* (New York: Teacher College Press, 2002).
Sowell, T., *Inside American Education: The Decline, the Deception, the Dogmas* (New York: Macmillan, 1993).
Spring, Joel, *The American School 1642–2004* (New York: Longman, 2004).

91 ROBERT CORAM

FROM *"The Necessity of Compulsory Primary Education" (1791)*

Society should then furnish the people with means of subsistence, and those means should be an inherent quality in the nature of the government, universal, permanent, and uniform, because their natural means were so. The means I allude to are the means of acquiring knowledge, as it is by the knowledge of some art or science that man is to provide for subsistence in civil society. These means of acquiring knowledge, as I said before, should be an inherent quality in the nature of the government: that is, the education of children should be provided for in the constitution of every state.

By education, I mean instruction in arts as well as sciences. Education, then, ought to be secured by government to every class of citizens, to every child in the state. The citizens should be instructed in sciences by public schools, and in arts by laws enacted for that purpose, by which parents and others, having authority over children, should be compelled to bind them out to certain trades or professions, that they may be enabled to support themselves with becoming independency when they shall arrive to years of maturity.

Education should not be left to the caprice or negligence of parents, to chance, or confined to the children of wealthy citizens; it is a shame, a scandal to civilized society, that part only of the citizens should be sent to colleges and universities to learn to cheat the rest of their liberties. Are ye aware, legislators, that in making knowledge necessary to the subsistence of your subjects, ye are in duty bound to secure to them the means of acquiring it? Else what is the bond of society but a rope of sand, incapable of supporting its own weight? A heterogeneous jumble of contradiction and absurdity, from which the subject knows not how to extricate himself, but often falls a victim to his natural wants or to cruel and inexorable laws – starves or is hanged. . . .

We despise thieves, not caring to reflect that human nature is always the same; that when it is a man's interest to be a thief he becomes one, but when it is his interest to support a good character he becomes an honest man; that even thieves are honest among each other, because it is their interest to be so. We seldom hear of a man in independent circumstances being indicted for petit felony: the man would be an idiot indeed who would stake a fair character for a few shillings which he did not need, but the greatest part of those indicted for petit felonies are men who have no characters to lose, that is – no substance, which the world always takes for good character.

If a man has no fortune and through poverty or neglect of his parents he has had no education and learned no trade, in such a forlorn situation, which demands our charity and our tears, the equitable and humane laws of England spurn him from their protection, under the harsh term of a vagrant or a vagabond, and he is cruelly ordered to be whipped out of the county. . . .

We have already demonstrated that government should furnish the subject with some substitute in lieu of his natural means of subsistence, which he gave up to government when he submitted to exclusive property in lands. An education is also necessary in order that the subject may know the obligations he is under to government.

The following observations of a celebrated English historian are very applicable: "Every law," says Mrs. Macaulay in her *History of England* [1763], "relating to public or private property and in particular penal statutes ought to be rendered so clear and plain and promulgated in such a manner to the public as to give a full information of its nature and extent to every citizen. Ignorance of laws, if not wilful, is a just excuse for their transgression, and if the care of government does not extend to the proper education of the subject and to their proper information on the nature of moral turpitude and legal crimes and to the encouragement of virtue, with what face of justice can they punish delinquency? But if on the contrary, the citizens, by the oppression of heavy taxes, are rendered incapable, by the utmost exertion of honest industry, of bringing up or providing for a numerous family, if every encouragement is given to licentiousness for the purpose of amusing and debasing the minds of the people or for raising a revenue on the vices of the subject, is punishment in this case better than legal murder? Or, to use a strong yet adequate expression, is it better than infernal tyranny?

"Two regulations are essential to the continuance of republican governments: 1. Such a distribution of lands and such principles of descent and alienation as shall give every citizen a power of acquiring what his industry merits. 2. Such a system of education as gives every citizen an opportunity of acquiring knowledge and fitting himself for places of trust. These are fundamental articles, the *sine qua non* of the existence of the American republics.

"Hence the absurdity of our copying the manners and adopting the institutions of monarchies. In several states we find laws passed establishing provisions for colleges and academies where people of property may educate their sons, but no provision is made for instructing the poorer rank of people even in reading and writing. Yet in these same states every citizen who is worth a few shillings annually is entitled to vote for legislators. This appears to me a most glaring solecism in government. The constitutions are *republican* and the laws of education are *monarchical*. The *former* extend civil rights to every honest industrious man, the *latter* deprive a large proportion of the citizens of a most valuable privilege.

"In our American republics, where government is in the hands of the people, knowledge should be universally diffused by means of public schools. Of such consequence is it to society that the people who make laws should be well informed that I conceive no legislature can be justified in neglecting proper establishments for this purpose.

"Such a general system of education is neither impracticable nor difficult, and excepting the formation of a federal government that shall be efficient and permanent, it demands the first attention of American patriots. Until such a system shall be adopted and pursued, until the statesman and divine shall unite their efforts in *forming* the human mind, rather than in lopping its excrescences after it has been neglected, until legislators discover that the only way to make good citizens and subjects is to nourish them from infancy, and until parents shall be convinced that the *worst* of men are not the proper teachers to make the *best*, mankind cannot know to what degree of perfection society and government may be carried. America affords the fairest opportunities for making the experiment and opens the most encouraging prospect of success." Suffer me then, Americans, to arrest, to command your attention to this important subject. To make mankind better is a duty which every man owes to his posterity, to his country, and to his God; and remember, my friends, there is but one way to effect this important purpose – which is – by incorporating education with government. – *This is the rock on which you must build your political salvation!*

92 JOHN DEWEY

"My Pedagogic Creed" (1897)

ARTICLE I. WHAT EDUCATION IS.

I believe that all education proceeds by the participation of the individual in the social consciousness of the race. This process begins unconsciously almost at birth, and is continually shaping the individual's powers, saturating his consciousness, forming his habits, training his ideas, and arousing his feelings and emotions. Through this unconscious education the individual gradually comes to share in the intellectual and moral resources which humanity has succeeded in getting together. He becomes an inheritor of the funded capital of civilization. The most formal and technical education in the world cannot safely depart from this general process. It can only organize it; or differentiate it in some particular direction.

I believe that the only true education comes through the stimulation of the child's powers by the demands of the social situations in which he finds himself. Through these demands he is stimulated to act as a member of a unity, to emerge from his original narrowness of action and feeling and to conceive of himself from the standpoint of the welfare of the group to which he belongs. Through the responses which others make to his own activities he comes to know what these mean in social terms. The value which they have is reflected back into them. For instance, through the response which is made to the child's instinctive babblings the child comes to know what those babblings mean; they are transformed into articulate language and thus the child is introduced into the consolidated wealth of ideas and emotions which are now summed up in language.

I believe that this educational process has two sides – one psychological and one sociological; and that neither can be subordinated to the other or neglected without evil results following. Of these two sides, the psychological is the basis. The child's own instincts and powers furnish the material and give the starting point for all education. Save as the efforts of the educator connect with some activity which the child is carrying on on his own initiative independent of the educator, education becomes reduced to a pressure from without. It may, indeed, give certain external results but cannot truly be called educative. Without insight into the psychological structure and activities of the individual, the educative process will, therefore, be haphazard and arbitrary. If it chances to coincide with the child's activity it will get a leverage; if it does not, it will result in friction, or disintegration, or arrest of the child's nature.

I believe that knowledge of social conditions, of the present state of civilization, is necessary in order properly to interpret that child's powers. The child has his own instincts and tendencies, but we do not know what these mean until we can translate them into their social equivalents. We must be able to carry them back into a social past and see them as the inheritance of previous race activities. We must also be able to project them into the future to see what their outcome and end will be. In the illustration just used, it is the ability to see in the child's babblings the promise and potency of a future social intercourse and conversation which enables one to deal in the proper way with that instinct.

I believe that the psychological and social sides are organically related and that education cannot be regarded as a compromise between the two, or a superimposition of one upon the other. We are told that the psychological definition of education is barren and formal – that it gives us only the idea of a development of all the mental powers without giving us any idea of the use to which these powers are put. On the other hand, it is urged that the social definition of education, as getting adjusted to civilization, makes of it a forced and external process, and results in subordinating the freedom of the individual to a preconceived social and political status.

I believe each of these objections is true when urged against one side isolated from the other. In order to know what a power really is we must know what its end, use, or function is; and this we cannot know save as we conceive of the individual as active in social relationships. But, on the other hand, the only possible adjustment which we can give to the child under existing conditions, is that which arises through putting him in complete possession of all his powers. With the advent of democracy and modern industrial conditions, it is impossible to foretell definitely just what civilization will be twenty years from now. Hence it is impossible to prepare the child for any precise set of conditions. To prepare him for the future life means to give him command of himself; it means so to train him that he will have the full and ready use of all his capacities; that his eye and ear and hand may be tools ready to command, that his judgment may be capable of grasping the conditions under which it has to work, and the executive forces be trained to act economically and efficiently. It is impossible to reach this sort of adjustment save as constant regard is had to the individual's own powers, tastes, and interests – say, that is, as education is continually converted into psychological terms.

In sum, I believe that the individual who is to be educated is a social individual and that society is an organic union of individuals. If we eliminate the social factor from the child we are left only with an abstraction; if we eliminate the individual factor from society, we are left only with an inert and lifeless mass. Education, therefore, must begin with a psychological insight into the child's capacities, interests, and habits. It must be controlled at every point by reference to these same considerations. These powers, interests, and habits must be continually interpreted – we must know what they mean. They must be translated into terms of their social equivalents – into terms of what they are capable of in the way of social service.

ARTICLE II. WHAT THE SCHOOL IS.

I believe that the school is primarily a social institution. Education being a social process, the school is simply that form of community life in which all those agencies are concentrated that will be most effective in bringing the child to share in the inherited resources of the race, and to use his own powers for social ends.

I believe that education, therefore, is a process of living and not a preparation for future living.

I believe that the school must represent present life – life as real and vital to the child as that which he carries on in the home, in the neighborhood, or on the play-ground.

I believe that education which does not occur through forms of life, or that are worth living for their own sake, is always a poor substitute for the genuine reality and tends to cramp and to deaden.

I believe that the school, as an institution, should simplify existing social life; should reduce it, as it were, to an embryonic form. Existing life is so complex that the child cannot be brought into contact with it without either confusion or distraction; he is either overwhelmed by the multiplicity of activities which are going on, so that he loses his own power of orderly reaction, or he is so stimulated by these various activities that his powers are prematurely called into play and he becomes either unduly specialized or else disintegrated.

I believe that, as such simplified social life, the school life should grow gradually out of the home life; that it should take up and continue the activities with which the child is already familiar in the home.

I believe that it should exhibit these activities to the child, and reproduce them in such ways that the child will gradually learn the meaning of them, and be capable of playing his own part in relation to them.

I believe that this is a psychological necessity, because it is the only way of securing continuity in the child's growth, the only way of giving a back-ground of past experience to the new ideas given in school.

I believe it is also a social necessity because the home is the form of social life in which the child has been nurtured and in connection with which he has had his moral training. It is the business of the school to deepen and extend his sense of the values bound up in his home life.

I believe that much of present education fails because it neglects this fundamental principle of the school as a form of community life. It conceives the school as a place where certain information is to be given, where certain lessons are to be learned, or where certain habits are to be formed. The value of these is conceived as lying largely in the remote future; the child must do these things for the sake of something else he is to do; they are mere preparation. As a result they do not become a part of the life experience of the child and so are not truly educative.

I believe that the moral education centers about this conception of the school as a mode of social life, that the best and deepest moral training is precisely that which one gets through having to enter into proper relations with others in a unity of work and thought. The present educational systems, so far as they destroy or neglect this unity, render it difficult or impossible to get any genuine, regular moral training.

I believe that the child should be stimulated and controlled in his work through the life of the community.

I believe that under existing conditions far too much of the stimulus and control proceeds from the teacher, because of neglect of the idea of the school as a form of social life.

I believe that the teacher's place and work in the school is to be interpreted from this same basis. The teacher is not in the school to impose certain ideas or to form certain habits in the child, but is there as a member of the community to select the influences which shall affect the child and to assist him in properly responding to these influences.

I believe that the discipline of the school should proceed from the life of the school as a whole and not directly from the teacher.

I believe that the teacher's business is simply to determine on the basis of larger experience and riper wisdom, how the discipline of life shall come to the child.

I believe that all questions of the grading of the child and his promotion should be determined by reference to the same standard. Examinations are of use only so far as they test the child's fitness for social life and reveal the place in which he can be of the most service and where he can receive the most help.

93 BOOKER T. WASHINGTON

"A Harder Task Than Making Bricks Without Straw" (1901)

From the very beginning, at Tuskegee, I was determined to have the students do not only the agricultural and domestic work, but to have them erect their own buildings. My plan was to have them, while performing this service, taught the latest and best methods of labor, so that the school would not only get the benefit of their efforts, but the students themselves would be taught to see not only utility in labor, but beauty and dignity, would be taught, in fact, how to lift labor up from mere drudgery and toil, and would learn to love work for its own sake. My plan was not to teach them to work in the old way, but to show them how to make the forces of nature – air, water, steam, electricity, horse-power – assist them in their labor.

At first many advised against the experiment of having the buildings erected by the labor of the students, but I was determined to stick to it. I told those who doubted the wisdom of the plan that I knew that our first buildings would not be so comfortable or so complete in their finish as buildings erected by the experienced hands of outside workmen, but that in the teaching of civilization, self-help, and self-reliance, the erection of the buildings by the students themselves would more than compensate for any lack of comfort or fine finish.

I further told those who doubted the wisdom of this plan, that the majority of our students came to us in poverty, from the cabins of the cotton, sugar, and rice plantations of the South, and that while I knew it would please the students very much to place them at once in finely constructed buildings, I felt that it would be following out a more natural process of development to teach them how to construct their own buildings. Mistakes I knew would be made, but these mistakes would teach us valuable lessons for the future.

During the now nineteen years' existence of the Tuskegee school, the plan of having the buildings erected by student labor has been adhered to. In this time forty buildings, counting small and large, have been built, and all except four are almost wholly the product of student labor. As an additional result, hundreds of men are now scattered throughout the South who received their knowledge of mechanics while being taught how to erect these buildings. Skill and knowledge are now handed down from one set of students to another in this way, until at the present time a building of any description or size can be constructed wholly by our instructors and students, from the drawing of the plans to the putting in of electric fixtures without going off the grounds for a single workman.

Not a few times, when a new student has been led into the temptation of marring the looks of some building by leadpencil marks or by the cuts of a jack-knife, I have heard an old student remind him: "Don't do that. That is our building. I helped put it up."

In the early days of the school I think my most trying experience was in the matter of brickmaking. As soon as we got the farm work reasonably well started, we directed our next efforts toward the industry of making bricks. We needed these for the use in connection with the erection of our new buildings, but there was also another reason for establishing this industry. There was no brickyard in the town, and in addition to our own needs there was a demand for bricks in the general market . . .

In the first place the work was hard and dirty, and it was difficult to get the students to help. When it came to brickmaking, their distaste for manual labor in connection with book education became especially manifest. It was not a pleasant task for one to stand in the mud-pit for hours, with the mud up to his knees. More than one man became disgusted and left the school . . .

The making of these bricks taught me an important lesson in regard to the relations of the two races in the South. Many white people who had had no contact with the school, and perhaps no sympathy with it, came to us to buy bricks because they found out that ours were good bricks. They discovered that we were supplying a real want in the community. The making of these bricks caused many of the white residents of the neighborhood to begin to feel that the education of the Negro was not making him worthless, but that in educating our students we were adding something to the wealth and comfort of the community. As the people of the neighborhood came to us to buy bricks, we got acquainted with them; they traded with us and we with them. Our business interests became intermingled. We had something which they wanted; they had something which we wanted. This, in a large measure, helped to lay the foundation of the pleasant relations that have continued to exist between us and the white people in that section, and which now extend throughout the South . . .

My experience is that there is always something in human nature which always makes an individual recognize and reward merit, no matter under what color of skin merit is found. I have found, too, that it is the visible, the tangible, that goes a long way to softening prejudices. The actual sight of a first-class house that a Negro has built is ten times more potent than pages of discussion about a house that he ought to build, or perhaps could build.

The same principle of industrial education has been carried out in the building of our wagons, carts, and buggies, from the first. We now own and use on our farm and about the school dozens of these vehicles, and every one of them has been built by the hands of the students. Aside from this, we help supply the local market with these vehicles. The supplying of them to the people in the community has had the same effect as the supplying of bricks, and the man who learns at Tuskegee to build and repair wagons and carts is regarded as a benefactor by both races in the community where he goes. The people with whom he lives and works are going to think twice before they part with such a man.

The individual who can do something that the world wants done will, in the end, make his way regardless of his race. One man may go into a community prepared to supply the people there with an analysis of Greek sentences. The community may not at that time be prepared for, or feel the need of, Greek analysis, but it may feel its need of bricks and houses and wagons. If the man can supply the need of those, then, it will eventually lead to a demand for the first product, and with the demand will come the ability to appreciate it and to profit by it.

About the time that we succeeded in burning our first kiln of bricks we began facing in an emphasized form the objection of the students to being taught to work. By this time it had gotten to be pretty well advertised throughout the state that every student who came to Tuskegee, no matter what his financial ability might be, must learn some industry. Quite a number of letters came from parents protesting against their children engaging in labor while they were in the school. Others parents came to the school to protest in person. Most of the new students brought a written or a verbal request from their parents to the effect that they wanted their children taught nothing but books. The more books, the larger they were, and the longer the titles printed upon them, the better pleased the students and their parents seemed to be.

I gave little heed to those protests, except that I lost no opportunity to go into as many parts of the state as I could, for the purpose of speaking to the parents, and showing them the value of industrial education. Besides, I talked to the students constantly on the subject. Notwithstanding the unpopularity of industrial work, the school continued to increase in numbers to such an extent that by the middle of the second year there was an attendance of about one hundred and fifty, representing almost all parts of the state of Alabama, and including a few from other states . . .

As soon as our first building was near enough to completion so that we could occupy a portion of it – which was near the middle of the second year of the school – we opened a boarding department. Students had begun coming from quite a distance, and in such increasing numbers that we felt more and more that we were merely skimming over the surface, in that we were not getting hold of the students in their home life.

We had nothing but the students and their appetites with which to begin a boarding department. No provision had been made in the new building for a kitchen and dining room; but we discovered that by digging out a large amount of earth from under the building we could make a partially lighted basement room that could be used for a kitchen and dining room. Again I called on the students to volunteer for work, this time to assist in digging out the basement. This they did, and in a few weeks we had a place to cook and eat in, although it was very rough and uncomfortable. Any one seeing the place now would never believe that it was once used for a dining room.

The most serious problem, though, was to get the boarding department started off in the running order, with nothing to do with in the way of furniture, and with no money with which to buy anything. The merchants in the town would let us have what food we wanted on credit. In fact, in those earlier years I was constantly embarrassed because people seemed to have more faith in me than I had in myself. It was pretty hard to cook, however, without stoves, and awkward to eat without dishes. At first the cooking was done out-of-doors, in the old-fashioned, primitive style, in pots and skillets placed over a fire. Some of the carpenters' benches that had been used in the construction of the building were utilized for tables. As for dishes, there were too few to make it worth while to spend time in describing them.

No one connected with the boarding department seemed to have any idea that meals must be served at certain fixed and regular hours, and this was a source of great worry. Everything was so out of joint and so inconvenient that I feel safe in saying that for the first two weeks something was wrong at every meal. Either the meat was not done or had been burnt, or the salt had been left out of the bread, or the tea had been forgotten.

Early one morning I was standing near the dining-room door listening to the complaints of the students. The complaints that morning were especially emphatic and numerous, because the whole breakfast had been a failure. One of the girls who had failed to get any breakfast came out and went to the well to draw some water to drink to take the place of the breakfast which she had not been able to get. When she reached the well, she found that the rope was broken and that she could get no water. She turned from the well and said, in the most discouraged tone, not knowing that I was where I could hear her, "We can't even get water to drink at this school." I think no one remark ever came so near discouraging me as that one . . .

But gradually, by patience and hard work, we brought order out of chaos, just as will be true of any problem if we stick to it with patience and earnest effort.

As I look back now over the part of our struggle, I am glad that we had it. I am glad that we endured all those discomforts and inconveniences. I am glad that our students had to dig out the place for their kitchen and dining room. I am glad that our first boarding-place was in that dismal, ill-lighted, and damp basement. Had we started in a fine, attractive, convenient room, I fear we would have "lost our heads" and become "stuck up." It means a great deal, I think, to start off on a foundation which one has made for one's self.

When our old students return to Tuskegee now [1901], as they often do, and go into our large beautiful, well-ventilated, and well-lighted dining room, and see tempting, well-cooked food – largely grown by the students themselves – and see tables, neat tablecloths and napkins, and vases of flowers upon the tables, and hear singing birds, and note that each meal is served exactly upon the minute, with no disorder, and with almost no complaint coming from the hundreds that now fill our dining room, they, too, often say to me that they are glad we started out as we did, and built ourselves up year by year, by slow and natural process of growth.

94 MARY ANTIN

FROM *The Promised Land (1912)*

Education was free. That subject my father had written about repeatedly, as comprising his chief hopes for us children, the essence of American opportunity, the treasure that no thief could touch, not even misfortune or poverty. It was the one thing that he was able to promise us when he sent for us; surer, safer than bread or shelter. . . .

The apex of my civic pride and personal contentment was reached on the bright September morning when I entered the public school. That day I must always remember, even if I live to be so old that I cannot tell my name. To most people their first day at school is a memorable occasion. In my case the importance of the day was a hundred times magnified, on account of the years I had waited, the road I had come, and the conscious ambitions I entertained. . . .

Father himself conducted us to school. He would not have delegated that mission to the president of the United States. He had awaited the day with impatience equal to mine, and the visions he saw as he hurried us over the sun-flecked pavements transcended all my dreams. Almost his first act on landing on American soil, three years before, had been his application for naturalization. He had taken the remaining steps in the process with eager promptness, and at the earliest moment allowed by the law, he became a citizen of the United States. It is true that he had left home in search of bread for his hungry family, but he went blessing the necessity that drove him to America. The boasted freedom of the New World meant to him far more than the right to reside, travel, and work wherever he pleased; it meant the freedom to speak his thoughts, to throw off the shackles of superstition, to test his own fate, unhindered by political and religious tyranny. He was only a young man when he landed – thirty-two; and most of his life he had been held in leading-strings. He was hungry for his untasted manhood.

Three years passed in sordid struggle and disappointment. . . . He had very little opportunity to prosecute his education, which, in truth, had never begun. His struggle for a bare living left him no time to take advantage of the public evening school, but he lost nothing of what was to be learned through reading, through attendance at public meetings, through exercising the rights of citizenship. Even here he was hindered by a natural inability to acquire the English language. In time, indeed, he learned to read, to follow a conversation or lecture; but he never learned to write correctly, and his pronunciation remains extremely foreign to this day.

If education, culture, the higher life were shining things to be worshipped from afar, he had still a means left whereby he could draw one step nearer to them. He could send his children to school, to learn all those things that he knew by fame to be desirable. The common school, at least, perhaps high school; for one or two, perhaps even college! His children should be students, should fill his house with books and intellectual company; and thus he would walk by proxy in the Elysian Fields of liberal learning. As for the children themselves, he knew no surer way to their advancement and happiness.

So it was with a heart full of longing and hope that my father led us to school on that first day. He took long strides in his eagerness, the rest of us running and hopping to keep up.

At last the four of us stood around the teacher's desk; and my father, in his impossible English, gave us over in her charge, with some broken word of his hopes for us that his swelling heart could no longer contain. I venture to say that Miss Nixon [the teacher] was struck by something uncommon in the group we made, something outside of Semitic features and the abashed manner of the alien. My little sister was as pretty as a doll, with her clear pink-and-white face, short golden curls, and eyes like blue violets when you caught them looking up. My brother might have been a girl, too, with his cherubic contours of face, rich red color, glossy black hair, and fine eyebrows. Whatever secret fears were in his heart, remembering his former teachers [in Russia], who had taught with the rod, he stood up straight and uncringing before the American teacher, his cap respectfully doffed. Next to him stood a starved-looking girl with eyes ready to pop out, and short dark curls that would not have made much of a wig for a Jewish bride.

All three children carried themselves rather better than the common run of "green" pupils that were brought to Miss Nixon. But the figure that challenged attention to the group was the tall, straight father, with his earnest face and fine forehead, nervous hands eloquent in gesture, and a voice full of feeling. This foreigner, who brought his children to school as is it was an act of consecration, who regarded the teacher of the primer class with reverence, who spoke of visions, like a man inspired, in a common schoolroom, was not like other aliens, who brought their children in dull obedience to the law; was not like the native fathers, who brought their unmanageable boys, glad to be relieved of their care. I think Miss Nixon guessed what my father's best English could not convey. I think she divined that by the simple act of delivering our school certificates to her he took possession of America. . . .

It is not worth while to refer to voluminous school statistics to see how many "green" pupils entered school last September, not knowing the days of the week in English, who next February will be declaiming patriotic verses in honor of George Washington or Abraham Lincoln, with a foreign accent, indeed, but with plenty of enthusiasm. It is enough to know that this hundred-fold miracle is common to the schools in every part of the United States where immigrants are received. And if I was one of Chelsea's [in Massachusetts] hundred in 1894, it was only to be expected, since I was one of the older of the "green" children, and had had a start in my irregular schooling in Russia, and was carried along by a tremendous desire to learn, and had my family to cheer me on.

I was a bit too large for my little chair and desk in the baby class, but in my mind, of course, was too mature by six or seven years for the work. So as soon as I could understand what the teacher said in class, I was advanced to second grade. This was within a week after Miss Nixon took me in hand. But I do not mean to give my dear teacher all the credit for my rapid progress, nor even half the credit. I shall divide it with her on behalf of my race and my family. I was Jew enough to have an aptitude for language in general, and to bend my mind earnestly to my task; I was Antin enough to read each lesson with my heart, which gave me an inkling of what was coming next, and so carried me along by leaps and bounds. . . .

If I was eager and diligent, my teachers did not sleep. As fast as my knowledge of English allowed, they advanced me from grade to grade, without reference to the usual schedule of promotions. My father was right, when he often said, in discussing my prospects, that ability would be promptly recognized in the public schools. . . .

About the middle of the year I was promoted to the grammar school. Then it was that I walked on air. For I said to myself that I was a *student* now, in earnest, not merely a school-girl learning to spell and cipher. I was going to learn out-of-the-way things, things that had to do with ordinary life – things to know. When I walked home afterwards, with the great big geography book under my arm, it seemed to me that the earth was conscious of my step. Sometimes I carried home half the books in my desk, not because I should need them, but because I loved to hold them; and also because I loved to be seen carrying books. It was a badge of scholarship, and I was proud of it. I remember the days in Vitebsk when I used to watch my cousin Hirshel start for school in the morning, every thread of his student's uniform, every worn copybook in his satchel, glorified in my envious eyes. And now I was myself as he: aye, greater than he; for I knew English, and I could write poetry.

The public school has done its best for us foreigners, and for the country, when it has made us into good Americans. I am glad it is mine to tell how the miracle was wrought in one case. You should be glad to hear of it, you born Americans; for it is the story of the growth of your country; of the flocking of your brothers and sisters from the far ends of the earth to the flag you love; of the recruiting of your armies of workers, thinkers, and leaders. And you will be glad to hear of it, my comrades in adoption; for it is a rehearsal of your own experience, the thrill and wonder of which your own hearts have felt.

How long would you say, wise reader, it takes to make an American? By the middle of my second year in school I had reached the sixth grade. When, after the Christmas holidays, we began to study the life of Washington, running through a summary of the Revolution, and the early days of the Republic, it seemed to me that all my reading and study had been idle until then. The reader, the arithmetic, the song book, that had fascinated me until now, became suddenly sober exercise books, tools wherewith to hew a way to the source of inspiration. When the teacher read to us out of a big book with many bookmarks in it, I sat rigid with attention in my little chair, my hands tightly clasped on the edge of my desk; and I painfully held my breath, to prevent sighs of disappointment escaping, as I saw the teacher skip the parts between the bookmarks. When the class read, and it became my turn, my voice shook and the book trembled in my hands. I could not pronounce the name of George Washington without a pause. Never had I prayed, never had I chanted the songs of David, never had I called upon the Most Holy, in such utter reverence and worship as I repeated the simple sentences of my child's story of the patriot. I gazed with adoration at the portraits of George and Martha Washington, till I could see them with my eyes shut. And whereas formerly my self-consciousness had bordered on conceit, and I thought myself an uncommon person, parading my schoolbooks through the streets, and swelling with pride when a teacher detained me in conversation, now I grew humble all at once, seeing how insignificant I was beside the Great.

As I read about the noble boy who would not tell a lie to save himself from punishment, I was for the first time truly repentant of my sins.

95 US SUPREME COURT

The 1954 Supreme Court Decision on Segregation

In the first cases in this Court construing the Fourteenth Amendment, decided shortly after its adoption, the Court interpreted it as proscribing all state-imposed discriminations against the Negro race. The doctrine of "separate but equal" did not make its appearance in this Court until 1896 in the case of *Plessy* v. *Ferguson*, *supra*, involving not education but transportation. American courts have since labored with the doctrine for over half a century. In this Court, there have been six cases involving the "separate but equal" doctrine in the field of public education.

In none of these cases was it necessary to re-examine the doctrine to grant relief to the Negro plaintiff: And in *Sweatt* v. *Painter*, *supra*, the Court expressly reserved decision on the question whether *Plessy* v. *Ferguson* should be held inapplicable to public education.

In the instant cases, that question is directly presented. Here, unlike *Sweatt* v. *Painter*, there are findings below that the Negro and white schools involved have been equalized, or are being equalized, with respect to buildings, curricula, qualifications and salaries of teachers, and other "tangible" factors. Our decision, therefore, cannot turn on merely a comparison of these tangible factors in the Negro and white schools involved in each of the cases. We must look instead to the effect of segregation itself on public education.

In approaching this problem, we cannot turn the clock back to 1868 when the Amendment was adopted, or even to 1896 when *Plessy* v. *Ferguson* was written. We must consider public education in the light of its full development and its present place in American life throughout the Nation. Only in this way can it be determined if segregation in public schools deprives these plaintiffs of the equal protection of the laws.

Today, education is perhaps the most important function of state and local governments. Compulsory school attendance laws and the great expenditures for education both demonstrate our recognition of the importance of education to our democratic society. It is required in the performance of our most basic public responsibilities, even service in the armed forces. It is the very foundation of good citizenship. Today it is a principal instrument in awakening the child to cultural values, in preparing him for later professional training, and in helping him to adjust normally to his environment. In these days, it is doubtful that any child may reasonably be expected to succeed in life if he is denied the opportunity of an education. Such an opportunity, where the state has undertaken to provide it, is a right which must be made available to all on equal terms.

We come then to the question presented: Does segregation of children in public schools solely on the basis of race, even though the physical facilities and other "tangible" factors may be equal, deprive the children of the minority group of equal educational opportunities? We believe that it does.

In *Sweatt* v. *Painter, supra*, in finding that a segregated law school for Negroes could not provide them equal educational opportunities, this Court relied in large part on "those equalities which are incapable of objective measurement but which make for greatness in a law school". In *McLaurin* v. *Oklahoma State Regents, supra*, the Court, in requiring that a Negro admitted to a white graduate school be treated like all other students, again resorted to intangible considerations: ". . . his ability to study, to engage in discussions and exchange views with other students, and, in general, to learn his profession". Such considerations apply with added force to children in grade and high schools. To separate them from others of similar age and qualifications solely because of their race generates a feeling of inferiority as to their status in the community that may affect their hearts and minds in a way unlikely ever to be undone. The effect of this separation on their educational opportunities was well stated by a finding in the Kansas case by a court which nevertheless felt compelled to rule against the Negro plaintiffs:

> Segregation of white and colored children in public schools has a detrimental effect upon the colored children. The impact is greater when it has the sanction of the law; for the policy of separating the races is usually interpreted as denoting the inferiority of the negro group. A sense of inferiority affects the motivation of a child to learn. Segregation with the sanction of law, therefore has a tendency to [retard] the educational and mental development of negro children and to deprive them of some of the benefits they would receive in a racial[ly] integrated school system.

Whatever may have been the extent of psychological knowledge at the time of *Plessy* v. *Ferguson*, this finding is amply supported by modern authority. Any language in *Plessy* v. *Ferguson* contrary to this finding is rejected. We conclude that in the field of public education the doctrine of "separate but equal" has no place. Separate educational facilities are inherently unequal. Therefore, we hold that the plaintiffs and others similarly situated for whom the actions have been brought are, by reason of the segregation complained of, deprived of the equal protection of the laws guaranteed by the Fourteenth Amendment.

96 US CONGRESSMEN

"Protest from the South" (1956)

We regard the decision of the Supreme Court in the school cases as clear abuse of judicial power. It climaxes a trend in the Federal judiciary undertaking to legislate, in derogation of the authority of Congress, and to encroach upon the reserved rights of the states and the people.

The original Constitution does not mention education. Neither does the Fourteenth Amendment nor any other amendment. The debates preceding the submission of the Fourteenth Amendment clearly show that there was no intent that it should affect the systems of education maintained by the states.

The very Congress which proposed the amendment subsequently provided for segregated schools in the District of Columbia.

When the amendment was adopted in 1868, there were thirty-seven states of the Union. Every one of the twenty-six states that had any substantial racial differences among its people either approved the operation of segregated schools already in existence or subsequently established such schools by action of the same law-making body which considered the Fourteenth Amendment.

As admitted by the Supreme Court in the public school case (*Brown* v. *Board of Education*), the doctrine of separate but equal schools "apparently originated in *Roberts* v. *City of Boston* (1849), upholding school segregation against attack as being violative of a state constitutional guarantee of equality." This constitutional doctrine began in the North – not in the South – and it was followed not only in Massachusetts but in Connecticut, New York, Illinois, Indiana, Michigan, Minnesota, New Jersey, Ohio, Pennsylvania and other northern states until they, exercising their rights as states through the constitutional processes of local self-government, changed their school systems.

In the case of *Plessy* v. *Ferguson* in 1896 the Supreme Court expressly declared that under the Fourteenth Amendment no person was denied any of his rights if the states provided separate but equal public facilities. This decision has been followed in many other cases. It is notable that the Supreme Court, speaking through Chief Justice Taft, a former President of the United States, unanimously declared in 1927 in *Lum* v. *Rice* that the "separate but equal" principle is ". . . within the discretion of the state in regulating its public schools and does not conflict with the Fourteenth Amendment."

This interpretation, restated time and again, became a part of the life of the people of many of the states and confirmed their habits, customs, traditions and way of life. It is founded on elemental humanity and common sense, for parents should not be deprived by Government of the right to direct the lives and education of their own children.

Though there has been no constitutional amendment or act of Congress changing this established legal principle almost a century old, the Supreme Court of the United States, with no legal basis for such action, undertook to exercise their naked judicial power and substituted their personal political and social ideas for the established law of the land.

This unwarranted exercise of power by the court, contrary to the Constitution, is creating chaos and confusion in the states principally affected. It is destroying the amicable relations between the white and Negro races that have been created through ninety years of patient effort by the good people of both races. It has planted hatred and suspicion where there has been heretofore friendship and understanding.

Without regard to the consent of the governed, outside agitators are threatening immediate and revolutionary changes in our public school systems. If done, this is certain to destroy the system of public education in some of the states.

With the gravest concern for the explosive and dangerous condition created by this decision and inflamed by outside meddlers:

We reaffirm our reliance on the Constitution as the fundamental law of the land.

We decry the Supreme Court's encroachments on rights reserved to the states and to the people, contrary to established law and to the Constitution.

We commend the motives of those states which have declared the intention to resist forced integration by any lawful means.

We appeal to the states and people who are not directly affected by these decisions to consider the constitutional principles involved against the time when they too, on issues vital to them, may be the victims of judicial encroachment.

Even though we constitute a minority in the present Congress, we have full faith that a majority of the American people believe in the dual system of government which has enabled us to achieve our greatness and will in time demand that the reserved rights of the states and of the people be made secure against judicial usurpation.

We pledge ourselves to use all lawful means to bring about a reversal of this decision which is contrary to the Constitution and to prevent the use of force in its implementation.

In this trying period, as we all seek to right this wrong, we appeal to our people not to be provoked by the agitators and troublemakers invading our states and to scrupulously refrain from disorder and lawless acts.

97 JONATHAN KOZOL

FROM *Death at an Early Age: The Destruction of the Hearts and Minds of Negro Children in the Boston Public Schools (1967)*

Perhaps a reader would like to know what it is like to go into a new classroom in the same way that I did and to see before you suddenly, and in terms you cannot avoid recognizing, the dreadful consequences of a year's wastage of real lives.

You walk into a narrow and old wood-smelling classroom and you see before you 35 curious, cautious and untrusting children, aged eight to thirteen, of whom about two-thirds are Negro. Three of the children are designated to you as special students. Thirty per cent of the class is reading at the Second Grade level in a year and in a month in which they should be reading at the height of Fourth Grade performance or at the beginning of the Fifth. Seven children out of the class are up to par. Ten substitutes or teacher changes. Or twelve changes. Or eight. Or eleven. Nobody seems to know how many teachers they have had. Seven of their lifetime records are missing:

symptomatic and emblematic at once of the chaos that has been with them all year long. Many more lives than just seven have already been wasted but the seven missing records become an embittering symbol of the lives behind them which, equally, have been lost or mislaid. (You have to spend the first three nights staying up until dawn trying to reconstruct these records out of notes and scraps.) On the first math test you give, the class average comes out to 36. The children tell you with embarrassment that it has been like that since fall.

You check around the classroom. Of forty desks, five have tops with no hinges. You lift a desk-top to fetch a paper and you find that the top has fallen off. There are three windows. One cannot be opened. A sign on it written in the messy scribble of a hurried teacher or some custodial person warns you: DO NOT UNLOCK THIS WINDOW IT IS BROKEN. The general look of the room is as of a bleak-light photograph of a mental hospital. Above the one poor blackboard, gray rather than really black, and hard to write on, hangs from one tack, lopsided, a motto attributed to Benjamin Franklin: "*Well begun is half done.*" Everything, or almost everything like that, seems a mockery of itself.

Into this grim scenario, drawing on your own pleasures and memories, you do what you can to bring some kind of life. You bring in some cheerful and colorful paintings by Joan Miro and Paul Klee. While the paintings by Miro do not arouse much interest, the ones by Klee become an instantaneous success. One picture in particular, a watercolor titled "Bird Garden," catches the fascination of the entire class. You slip it out of the book and tack it up on the wall beside the doorway and it creates a traffic jam every time the children have to file in or file out. You discuss with your students some of the reasons why Klee may have painted the way he did and you talk about the things that can be accomplished in a painting which could not be accomplished in a photograph. None of this seems to be above the children's heads. Despite this, you are advised flatly by the Art Teacher that your naïveté has gotten the best of you and that the children cannot possibly appreciate this. Klee is too difficult. Children will not enjoy it. You are unable to escape the idea that the Art Teacher means herself instead.

For poetry, in place of the recommended memory gems, going back again into your own college days, you make up your mind to introduce a poem of William Butler Yeats. It is about a lake isle called Innisfree, about birds that have the funny name of "linnets" and about a "bee-loud glade". The children do not all go crazy about it but a number of them seem to like it as much as you do and you tell them how once, three years before, you were living in England and you helped a man in the country to make his home from wattles and clay. The children become intrigued. They pay good attention and many of them grow more curious about the poem than they appeared at first. Here again, however, you are advised by older teachers that you are making a mistake: Yeats is too difficult for children. They can't enjoy it, won't appreciate it, wouldn't like it. You are aiming way above their heads . . . Another idea comes to mind and you decide to try out an easy and rather well-known and not very complicated poem of Robert Frost. The poem is called "Stopping By Woods on a Snowy Evening." This time, your supervisor happens to drop in from the School Department. He looks over the mimeograph, agrees with you that it's a nice poem, then points out to you – tolerantly, but strictly – that you have made another mistake. "Stopping By

Woods" is scheduled for Sixth Grade. It is not "a Fourth Grade poem," and it is not to be read or looked at during the Fourth Grade. Bewildered as you are by what appears to be a kind of idiocy, you still feel reproved and criticized and muted and set back and you feel that you have been caught in the commission of a serious mistake.

On a series of other occasions, the situation is repeated. The children are offered something new and something lively. They respond to it energetically and they are attentive and their attention does not waver. For the first time in a long while perhaps there is actually some real excitement and some growing and some thinking going on within that small room. In each case, however, you are advised sooner or later that you are making a mistake. Your mistake, in fact, is to have impinged upon the standardized condescension on which the entire administration of the school is based. To hand Paul Klee's pictures to the children in this classroom, and particularly in a twenty-dollar volume, constitutes a threat to this school system. It is not different from sending a little girl from the Negro ghetto into an art class near Harvard Yard. Transcending the field of familiarity of the administration, you are endangering its authority and casting a blow at its confidence. The way the threat is handled is by a continual and standardized underrating of children. They can't do it, couldn't do it, wouldn't like it, don't deserve it . . . In such a manner, many children are tragically and unjustifiably held back from a great many of the good things that they might come to like or admire and are pinned down instead to books the teacher knows and to easy tastes that she can handle. This included, above all, of course the kind of material that is contained in the Course of Study.

Try to imagine, for a child, how great the gap between the outside world and the world conveyed within this kind of school must seem: A little girl, maybe Negro, comes in from a street that is lined with car-carcasses. Old purple Hudsons and one-wheel-missing Cadillacs represent her horizon and mark the edges of her dreams. In the kitchen of her house roaches creep and large rats crawl. On the way to school a wino totters. Some teenage white boys slow down their car to insult her, and speed on. At school, she stands frozen for fifteen minutes in a yard of cracked cement that overlooks a hillside on which trash has been unloaded and at the bottom of which the New York, New Haven and Hartford Railroad rumbles past. In the basement, she sits upon broken or splintery seats in filthy toilets and she is yelled at in the halls. Upstairs, when something has been stolen, she is told that she is the one who stole it and is called a liar and forced abjectly to apologize before a teacher who has not the slightest idea in the world of who the culprit really was. The same teacher, behind the child's back, ponders audibly with imagined compassion: "What can you do with this kind of material? How can you begin to teach this kind of child?"

Gradually going crazy, the child is sent after two years of misery to a pupil adjustment counselor who arranges for her to have some tests and considers the entire situation and discusses it with the teacher and finally files a long report. She is, some months later, put onto a waiting-list some place for once-a-week therapy but another year passes before she has gotten anywhere near to the front of a long line. By now she is fourteen, has lost whatever innocence she still had in the back seat of the old Cadillac and, within two additional years, she will be ready and eager for dropping out of school.

Once at school, when she was eight or nine, she drew a picture of a rich-looking lady in an evening gown with a handsome man bowing before her but she was told by an insensate and wild-eyed teacher that what she had done was junk and garbage and the picture was torn up and thrown away before her eyes. The rock and roll music that she hears on the Negro station is considered "primitive" by her teachers but she prefers its insistent rhythms to the dreary monotony of school. Once, in Fourth Grade, she got excited at school about some writing she had never heard about before. A handsome green book, brand new, was held up before her and then put into her hands. Out of this book her teacher read a poem. The poem was about a Negro – a woman who was a maid in the house of a white person – and she liked it. It remained in her memory. Somehow without meaning to, she found that she had done the impossible for her: she had memorized that poem. Perhaps, horribly, in the heart of her already she was aware that it was telling about her future: fifty dollars a week to scrub floors and bathe little white babies in the suburbs after an hour's street-car ride. The poem made her want to cry. The white lady, the lady for whom the maid was working, told the maid she loved her. But the maid in the poem wasn't going to tell any lies in return. She knew she didn't feel any love for the white lady and she told the lady so. The poem was shocking to her, but it seemed bitter, strong and true. Another poem in the same green book was about a little boy on a merry-go-round. She laughed with the class at the question he asked about a Jim Crow section on a merry-go-round, but she also was old enough to know that it was not a funny poem really and it made her, valuably, sad. She wanted to know how she could get hold of that poem, and maybe that whole book. The poems were moving to her . . .

This child was in my class. Details are changed somewhat but it is essentially one child. The girl was one of the three unplaced special students in that Fourth Grade room. She was not an easy girl to teach and it was hard even to keep her at her seat on many mornings, but I do not remember that there was any difficulty at all in gaining and holding onto her attention on the day that I brought in that green book of Langston Hughes.

Of all the poems of Langston Hughes that I read to my Fourth Graders, the one that the children liked most was a poem that has the title "Ballad of the Landlord" . . . This poem may not satisfy the taste of every critic, and I am not making any claims to immortality for a poem just because I happen to like it a great deal. But the reason this poem did have so much value and meaning for me and, I believe, for many of my students, is that it not only seems moving in an obvious and immediate human way but that it *finds* its emotion in something ordinary. It is a poem which really does allow both heroism and pathos to poor people, sees strength in awkwardness and attributes to a poor person standing on the stoop of his slum house every bit as much significance as William Wordsworth saw in daffodils, waterfalls and clouds. At the request of the children later on I mimeographed that poem and, although nobody in the classroom was asked to do this, several of the children took it home and memorized it on their own. I did not assign it for memory, because I do not think that memorizing a poem has any special value. Some of the children just came in and asked if they could recite it. Before long, almost every child in the room had asked to have a turn.

All of the poems that you read to Negro children obviously are not going to be by or about Negro people. Nor would anyone expect that all poems which are read to a class of poor children ought to be grim or gloomy or heart-breaking or sad. But when, among works of many different authors, you do have the will to read children a poem by a man so highly renowned as Langston Hughes, then I think it is important not to try to pick a poem that is innocuous, being like any other poet's kind of poem, but I think you ought to choose a poem that is genuinely representative and then try to make it real to the children in front of you in a way that I tried. I also think it ought to be taken seriously by a teacher when a group of young children come in to him one morning to announce that they have liked something so much that they have memorized it voluntarily. It surprised me and impressed me when that happened. It was all I needed to know to confirm for me the value of reading that poem and the value of reading many other poems to children which will build upon, and not attempt to break down, the most important observations and very deepest foundations of their lives.

98 STUDS TERKEL

FROM *"Public School Teacher: Rose Hoffman"* (1972)

I'm a teacher. It's a profession I loved and still love. It's been my ambition since I was eight years old. I have been teaching since 1937. Dedication was the thing in my day. I adored teaching. I used to think that teachers had golden toilets. (Laughs.) They didn't do anything we common people did.

She teaches third grade at a school in a changing neighborhood. It is her second school in thirty-three years. She has been at this one for twenty years. "I have a self-contained group. You keep them all day."

Oh, I have seen a great change since January 6, 1937. (Laughs.) It was the Depression, and there was something so wonderful about these dedicated people. The teachers, the children, we were all in the same position. We worked our way out of it, worked hard. I was called a Jewish Polack. (Laughs.) My husband tells me I wash floors on my knees like a Polack. (Laughs.) I was assigned to a fourth grade class. The students were Polish primarily. We had two colored families, but they were sweet. We had a smattering of ethnic groups in those times – people who worked themselves out of the Depression by hard work.

I was the teacher and they were my students. They weren't my equal. I loved them. There isn't one child that had me that can't say they didn't respect me. But I wasn't on an intimate basis. I don't want to know what's happened in the family, if there's a divorce, a broken home. I don't look at the record and find out how many divorces in the family. I'm not a doctor. I don't believe you should study the family's background. I'm not interested in the gory details. I don't care if their father had twenty wives, if their mother is sleeping around. It's none of my business.

A little girl in my class tells me, "My mom's getting married. She's marrying a hippie. I don't like him." I don't want to hear it. It is not my nature to pry.

I have eight-year-olds. Thirty-one in the class and there's about twenty-three Spanish. I have maybe two Appalachians. The twenty-three Puerto Ricans are getting some type of help. The two little Appalachians, they never have the special attention these other children get. Their names aren't Spanish. My heart breaks for them. . . .

I've always been a strong disciplinarian, but I don't give these kids assignments over their head. They know exactly what they do. Habit. This is very boring, very monotonous, but habit is a great thing for these children. I don't tell them the reason for things. I give them the rote method, how to do it. After that, reasoning comes. Each one has to go to the board and show me that they really know. Because I don't trust the papers. They cheat and copy. I don't know how they do it. I walk up and down and watch them. I tell you, it's a way of life. (Laughs.)

At nine o'clock, as soon as the children come in, we have a salute to the flag. I'm watching them. We sing "My Country 'Tis of Thee." And then we sing a parody I found of "My Country 'Tis of Thee."

> To serve my country is to banish selfishness
> And bring world peace
> I love every girl and boy
> New friendships I'll enjoy
> The Golden Rule employ
> Till wars shall cease.

And then we sing "The Star-Spangled Banner." I watch them. It's a dignified exercise. These children love the idea of habit. Something schmaltzy, something wonderful.

I start with arithmetic. I have tables-fun on the board – multiplication. Everything has to be fun, fun, fun, play, play, play. You don't say tables, you say tables-fun. Everything to motivate. See how fast they can do it. It's a catchy thing. When they're doing it, I mark the papers. I'm very fast. God has been good to me. While I'm doing that, I take attendance. That is a must. All this happens before nine fifteen, nine twenty. . . .

Then I have a penmanship lesson on the board. There it is in my beautiful handwriting. I had a Palmer Method diploma. On Mondays I write beautifully, "If we go to an assembly, we do not whistle or talk, because good manners are important. If our manners are good, you'll be very happy and make everyone happy, too." On Friday we give them a test. They adore it. Habit, they love habit. . . .

They drink their milk. I have to take them to toilet recess. I have to watch them. No one goes unless they're supervised. We watch them outside. If there's too much monkey business, I have to go in and stop them. When they raise their hands in class, I let them go, even if they're lying. I tell them "If you're lying and get in trouble, you won't be able to go again." So I hope they tell me the truth every once in a while.

About eleven o'clock I give them an English workbook. I pass the free lunch tickets out about a quarter to twelve. Sometime during the day I give them stretching exercises. Sideways, then up and down, and we put our hands on our hips and heads up and so on. I'm good at it. I'm better than the kids.

I have reading groups. One is advanced, one is the middle, and one is the lowest. At a quarter to two we have our spelling – two words a day. Six words a week, really. If I did any more, it's lost. I tried other ways, they did everything wrong. I didn't scold them. I researched my soul. What am I doing wrong? I found out two words a day is just right. Spelling is a big deal. We break the words. We give them sentences. I try to make it last till two o'clock. Fifteen, twenty minutes, that's their attention span. Some days it's great. Some days I can't get them to do anything.

I take them to the toilet again because they're getting restless. Again you watch them. From a quarter after to about two thirty we read together. I give them music, too. That's up to me, up to my throat. They love music. I have it two, three times a week. At two thirty, if they're good, I give them art. I make beautiful Valentines. We show them how to decorate it. And that's the day. . . .

I don't take any work home with me. With these children, you show them their mistakes immediately. Otherwise they forget. When I'm home, I forget about school, absolutely, absolutely, absolutely. I have never thought of being a principal. I have fulfilled my goal.

As for retirement, yes and no. I'm not sixty-five yet. (Laughs.) I'm not tired. It's no effort for me. My day goes fast, especially when I go out the night before and have a wonderful time. I'm the original La Dolce Vita. If I have a good time, I can do anything. I can even come home at two, three in the morning and get up and go to work. I must have something on the outside to stimulate me.

There are some children I love. Some have looks and brains and personality. I try not to play favorites. I give each one a chance to be monitor. I tell them I'm their school mother. When I scold them, it doesn't mean I hate them. I love them, that's why I scold them. I say to them, "Doesn't your mother scold you?" . . .

There is one little girl who stands out in my mind in all the years I've been teaching. She has become tall and lovely. Pam. She was not too bright, but she was sweet. She was never any trouble. She was special. I see her every once in a while. She's a checker at Treasure Island (a supermarket in the community). She gives no trouble today, either. She has the same smile for everyone.

99 ELIZABETH LOZA NEWBY

FROM *"An Impossible Dream"* (1977)

As I grew up in both the American and Mexican cultures, I was able to pick up the English language easily. Though Spanish was spoken at home and I was comfortable using Spanish with my family and friends, I knew that if I were to escape from the migrant life, I was going to have to master English. Since I viewed education as the most important thing in my life, I knew that I had to be able to speak and comprehend the language that was used at school. With the help of some very special teachers and an understanding mother, I was able to break the cycle that has imprisoned so many of my people.

At the end of my sophomore year in high school my father decided that my education should be terminated. He thought that school filled me with too many foolish ideas, such as going to college; and besides, school was too worldly. My mother, on the other hand, always encouraged me to continue my education and was happy that I stayed, but she hardly ever opposed Dad's wishes. He was the ruler of the home, and he made sure that we knew that. He did not see the need for me to continue my education: He had arranged a marriage for me when I was a child and schooling was not necessary for me to be a wife and mother. I had known of this arrangement for a long time, for my parents had talked of it incessantly after my fifteenth birthday. Of course, this marriage arrangement custom was and is very old and is hardly ever practiced anymore. But since my father was very "old country" he saw nothing wrong with this ancient custom.

The young man whose wife I was supposed to become was about twenty-eight years old. He came from a very old French and Spanish family of our native home in Mexico. The first time I saw him was on a rainy spring afternoon when I arrived home from school. As I opened the door to our home, I was greeted by five smiling brown faces. . . . The five people in the room were my mother and father, Pablo Rodriguez (the man I was to marry), and his mother and father. The Rodriguezes had traveled all the way from Mexico City to meet me and to take me back with them so that I could marry Pablo.

I was almost sixteen years old. I had had enough education and had developed enough determination to oppose my parents' wishes. . . . I immediately let my negative feelings concerning this arranged marriage be known to all in the room. . . . I was determined not to be forced into a marriage I did not desire just for the sake of tradition. Consequently, I objected and refused to marry the chosen young man.

This action brought shame and disgrace to my father and it was not to be forgotten. . . .

It is easy to see how difficult it was for me to get my father's permission to continue my education after what had occurred.

My dear mother settled him down, and the next day she assured me that I would be allowed to finish school. She said that my father had been reluctant to give his permission; but late that evening, following a convincing argument by my mother he had consented. She also said that she was counting on me not to disappoint her. I hugged her and told her not to worry. We then began to make plans for the completion of my last year in high school, sharing a mood of great happiness.

The last year of high school went by quickly. The work load was tremendous; the pressures were great; and my work at home was heavy. Often I stayed up late studying and got up early to do my chores before I left for school. Such was my routine, day in and day out. Mother did all she could to lighten my load, but I knew she couldn't do more. Besides, I did not want her to overwork. . . .

I took one day at a time; and finally, at the end of the year, I received my high school diploma. Tears were flowing from my eyes as I walked down the center aisle in the school gymnasium and proudly accepted my diploma from the school principal. It was a joyous occasion, and I can still remember the proud expression on my mother's face as she snapped one picture after another with a camera she had borrowed from a neighbor. . . .

It was a grand day of celebration; but even though it was a day to remember and the most exciting event that had ever happened to me up to that time, a more profound life-changing event was about to occur.

Late one afternoon, within a week following my graduation from high school, Mother greeted me at the door . . . holding a letter that was addressed to me from the school principal. She anxiously handed me the letter and asked me to open it immediately. I was nervous and scared as I ripped open the envelope, expecting to read the crushing news that there had been a mixup in their records and that, for some reason, they were rescinding my diploma. As I read the letter I discovered that I could not have been further from the truth. The note said that I was the recipient of a one-thousand-dollar scholarship for college.

The feeling that I experienced at that moment is indescribable. This was an impossible dream come true – an answer to prayer. At last I was being given the opportunity to escape from my dreary migrant existence.

While most of my classmates were destined to go to institutions of higher learning, I considered myself fortunate just to complete high school. My sense of accomplishment, which my mother shared, is beyond expression in words. For Mother it was a wonderful experience to see one of her children graduate from high school, let alone have an opportunity to continue study in college. We were both ecstatic! . . .

Mom and I decided to select an institution near relatives, where I could get help in obtaining employment or perhaps even stay with them while in college. After much consideration we decided on a college in southern Texas, where we had many relatives. We sent for an application and entrance papers and made all the arrangements.

We knew it was going to be difficult to tell Dad; but at this point I felt that I was in so much trouble with Dad from our previous problems that one more defiant act on my part would not make me any less endearing. . . .

He was furious! He was, in fact, so upset that he could hardly speak. The first thing he said was: "I knew I should never have let you go to school this last year. I have been too free with you, and all I have received in return is disgrace!" All this was beyond me, for I failed to see how going to college could be rebellious or disgraceful; and I pointed this out to him. Nevertheless, he continued his tirade and gave me the longest lecture I had ever heard on the evils of college and the terrible nature of career women. It seemed as though he would never finish. Mom and I sat in grave silence until his tirade ended. At this point we tried to tell him about the advantages of higher education and how I would be under the careful eye of relatives while I was in college. This argument did not help, and he stormed out the door while we stood there helpless. . . . He could not understand why I could not accept the traditional life-style of the typical Mexican migrant girl. I know that he loved me, but he just could not understand the changing times and felt threatened by higher education. . . . Dad did not speak to me for the rest of the week. The following Sunday, the day before I was supposed to leave, he finally approached me. . . . He said, "I have given this matter much thought, and I have only one thing to say; so listen carefully for you will have to live with the decision you make. Once we terminate this conversation we shall never speak of it again." By this time my stomach was in knots, and I knew somehow this decision was going to hurt. Then, in the very brief statement he made next, my world came crashing down all around me, leaving me drained and speechless. He continued: "I have decided that you can give up all these foolish ideas about college and have the love and protection of your family, or you can go ahead with your foolish plans to enter college. But the minute you walk out our door, consider it closed to you forever."

I was numb. I couldn't believe what I was hearing. . . .

After Dad had left, Mom came in to comfort me. She placed her hands on my shoulders and said, "Elizabeth I know this is a difficult decision you have to make, but I want you to think about this: Don't let emotion and 'old country' traditions hinder your future. You *are* and *always will be* my daughter. Your father can never take that away from me. I want you to go and take advantage of this wonderful opportunity. Make us all proud. Your father is slow to change, but give him time and pray for him. Please go with my blessing."

With great reluctance I left home that last Monday of August 1966. It was the most difficult decision I had ever had to make, for I knew full well the consequences of being disowned. That day was a turning point in my life in that my family ties and relationships could never be the same again – I had lost my father forever. I was frightened and lonely as I boarded the bus for college, and my heart was heavy for Mom and the family. I knew that life would never be as it had so long been. Mine was a tearful and sad departure. I cried most of the way to Texas, thinking about the family which I had lost. . . .

100 ALLAN BLOOM

"The Closing of the American Mind" (1987)

I have begun to wonder whether the experience of the greatest texts from early childhood is not a prerequisite for a concern throughout life for them and for lesser but important literature. The soul's longing, its intolerable irritation under the constraints of the conditional and limited, may very well require encouragement at the outset. At all events, whatever the cause, our students have lost the practice of and the taste for reading. They have not learned how to read, nor do they have the expectation of delight or improvement from reading. They are "authentic," as against the immediately preceding university generations, in having few cultural pretensions and in refusing hypocritical ritual bows to high culture.

When I first noticed the decline in reading during the late sixties, I began asking my large introductory classes, and any other group of younger students to which I spoke, what books really count for them. Most are silent, puzzled by the question. The notion of books as companions is foreign to them. Justice Black with his tattered copy of the Constitution in his pocket at all times is not an example that would mean much to them. There is no printed word to which they look for counsel, inspiration or joy. Sometimes one student will say "the Bible." (He learned it at home, and his Biblical studies are not usually continued at the university.) There is always a girl who mentions Ayn Rand's *The Fountainhead*, a book, although hardly literature, which, with its sub-Nietzschean assertiveness, excites somewhat eccentric youngsters to a new way of life. A few students mention recent books that struck them and supported their distinction of human types. It is a complex set of experiences that enables one to say so simply, "He is a Scrooge." Without literature, no such observations are possible and the fine art of comparison is lost. The psychological obtuseness of our students is appalling, because they have only pop psychology to tell them what people are like, and the range of their motives. As the awareness that we owed almost exclusively to literary genius falters, people become more alike, for want of knowing they can be otherwise. What poor substitutes for real diversity are the wild rainbows of dyed hair and other external differences that tell the observer nothing about what is inside.

Lack of education simply results in students' seeking for enlightenment wherever it is readily available, without being able to distinguish between the sublime and trash, insight and propaganda. For the most part students turn to the movies, ready prey to interested moralisms such as the depictions of Gandhi or Thomas More – largely designed to further passing political movements and to appeal to simplistic needs for greatness – or to insinuating flattery of their secret aspirations and vices, giving them a sense of significance. *Kramer vs. Kramer* may be up-to-date about divorces and sex roles, but anyone who does not have *Anna Karenina* or *The Red and the Black* as part of his viewing equipment cannot sense what might be lacking, or the difference between an honest presentation and an exercise in consciousness-raising, trashy sentimentality and elevated sentiment. As films have emancipated themselves from the literary tyranny under which they suffered and which gave them a bad conscience, the ones with serious pretensions have become intolerably ignorant and manipulative. The distance from the contemporary and its high seriousness that students most need in order not to indulge their petty desires and to discover what is most serious about themselves cannot be found in the cinema, which now only knows the present. Thus, the failure to read good books both enfeebles the vision and strengthens our most fatal tendency – the belief that the here and now is all there is.

The only way to counteract this tendency is to intervene most vigorously in the education of those few who come to the university with a strong urge for *un je ne sais quoi*, who fear that they may fail to discover it, and that the cultivation of their minds is required for the success of their quest. We are long past the age when a whole tradition could be stored up in all students, to be fruitfully used later by some. Only those who are willing to take risks and are ready to believe the implausible are now fit for a bookish adventure. The desire must come from within. People do what they want, and now the most needful things appear so implausible to them that it is hopeless to attempt universal reform. Teachers of writing in state universities, among the noblest and most despised laborers in the academy, have told me that they cannot teach writing to students who do not read, and that it is practically impossible to get them to read, let alone like it. This is where high schools have failed most, filled with teachers who are products of the sixties and reflecting the pallor of university-level humanities. The old teachers who loved Shakespeare or Austen or Donne, and whose only reward for teaching was the perpetuation of their taste, have all but disappeared.

The latest enemy of the vitality of classic texts is feminism. The struggles against elitism and racism in the sixties and seventies had little direct effect on students' relations to books. The democratization of the university helped dismantle its structure and caused it to lose its focus. But the activists had no special quarrel with the classic texts, and they were even a bit infected by their Frankfurt School masters' habit of parading their intimacy with high culture. Radicals had at an earlier stage of egalitarianism already dealt with the monarchic, aristocratic and antidemocratic character of most literary classics by no longer paying attention to their manifest political content. Literary criticism concentrated on the private, the intimate, the feelings, thoughts and relations of individuals, while reducing to the status of a literary convention of the past the fact that the heroes of many classic works were soldiers and statesmen engaged in ruling and faced with political problems. Shakespeare, as he has been read for most of this century, does not constitute a threat to egalitarian right thinking. And as for racism, it just did not play a role in the classic literature, at least in the forms in which we are concerned about it today, and no great work of literature is ordinarily considered racist.

But *all* literature up to today is sexist. The Muses never sang to the poets about liberated women. It's the same old *chanson* from the Bible and Homer through Joyce and Proust. And this is particularly grave for literature, since the love interest was most of what remained in the classics after politics was purged in the academy, and was also what drew students to reading them. These books appealed to eros while educating it. So activism has been directed against the content of books. The latest translation of Biblical text – sponsored by the National Council of the Churches of Christ – suppresses gender references to God, so that future generations will not have to grapple with the fact that God was once a sexist. But this technique has only limited applicability. Another tactic is to expunge the most offensive authors – for example, Rousseau – from the education of the young or to include feminist responses in college courses, pointing out the distorting prejudices, and using the books only as evidence of the misunderstanding of woman's nature and the history of injustice to it. Moreover, the great female characters can be used as examples of the various ways women have coped with their enslavement to the sexual role. But never, never, must a student be attracted to those old ways and take them as models for him or herself. However, all this effort is wasted. Students cannot imagine that the old literature could teach them anything about the relations they want to have or will be permitted to have. So they are indifferent.

Having heard over a period of years the same kinds of responses to my question about favorite books, I began to ask students who their heroes are. Again, there is usually silence, and most frequently nothing follows. Why should anyone have heroes? One should be oneself and not form oneself in an alien mold. Here positive ideology supports them: their lack of hero-worship is a sign of maturity. They posit their own values. They have turned into a channel first established in the *Republic* by Socrates, who liberated himself from Achilles, and picked up in earnest by Rousseau in *Emile*. Following on Rousseau, Tolstoy depicts Prince Andrei in *War and Peace*, who was educated in Plutarch and is alienated from himself by his admiration for Napoleon. But we tend to forget that Andrei is a very noble man indeed and that his heroic longings give him a splendor of soul that dwarfs the petty, vain, self-regarding concerns of the bourgeoisie that surrounds him. Only a combination of natural sentiment and unity with the spirit of Russia and its history can, for Tolstoy, produce human beings superior to Andrei, and even they are only ambiguously superior. But in America we have only the bourgeoisie, and the love of the heroic is one of the few counterpoises available to us. In us the contempt for the heroic is only an extension of the perversion of the democratic principle that denies greatness and wants everyone to feel comfortable in his skin without having to suffer unpleasant comparisons. Students have not the slightest notion of what an achievement it is to free oneself from public guidance and find resources for guidance within oneself. From what source within themselves would they draw the goals they think they set for themselves? Liberation from the heroic only means that they have no resource whatsoever against conformity to the current "role models." They are constantly thinking of themselves in terms of fixed standards that they did not make. Instead of being overwhelmed by Cyrus, Thesus, Moses or Romulus, they unconsciously act out the roles of the doctors, lawyers, businessmen or TV personalities around them. One can only pity young people without admirations they can respect or avow, who are artificially restrained from the enthusiasm for great virtue.

In encouraging this deformity, democratic relativism joins a branch of conservatism that is impressed by the dangerous political consequences of idealism. These conservatives want young people to know that this tawdry old world cannot respond to their demands for perfection. In the choice between the somewhat arbitrarily distinguished realism and idealism, a sensible person would want to be both, or neither. But, momentarily accepting a distinction I reject, idealism as it is commonly conceived should have primacy in an education, for man is a being who must take his orientation by his possible perfection. To attempt to suppress this most natural of all inclinations because of possible abuses is, almost literally, to throw out the baby with the bath. Utopianism is, as Plato taught us at the outset, the fire with which we must play because it is the only way we can find out what we are. We need to criticize false understandings of Utopia, but the easy way out provided by realism is deadly. As it now stands, students have powerful images of what a perfect body is and pursue it incessantly. But deprived of literary guidance, they no longer have any image of a perfect soul, and hence do not long to have one. They do not even imagine that there is such a thing.

Following on what I learned from this second question, I began asking a third: Who do you think is evil? To this one there is an immediate response: Hitler. (Stalin is hardly mentioned.) After him, who else? Up until a couple of years ago, a few students said Nixon, but he has been forgotten and at the same time is being rehabilitated. And there it stops. They have no idea of evil; they doubt its existence. Hitler is just another abstraction, an item to fill up an empty category. Although they live in a world in which the most terrible deeds are being performed and they see brutal crime in the streets, they turn aside. Perhaps they believe that evil deeds are performed by persons who, if they got the proper therapy, would not do them again – that there are evil deeds, not evil people. There is no *Inferno* in this comedy. Thus, the most common student view lacks an awareness of the depths as well as the heights, and hence lacks gravity.

11

LANGUAGE AND THE MEDIA

Introduction		333
101	*Noah Webster* FROM "The Reforming of Spelling" (1789)	336
102	*New York Herald* Review of *Uncle Tom's Cabin* (1853)	339
103	*Helen Keller* "Everything has a Name" (1903)	341
104	*Wilfred Funk and Norman Lewis* "Thirty Days to a More Powerful Vocabulary" (1942)	343
105	*William Labov* "The Non-Standard Vernacular of the Negro Community" (1967)	345
106	*Bob Woodward and Carl Bernstein* "GOP Security Aide Among 5 Arrested in Bugging Affair" (1972)	350
107	*Neil Postman* FROM "The Age of Show Business" (1985)	353
108	*Garrison Keillor* "Forebears" (1985)	356
109	*Amy Tan* "Mother Tongue" (1990)	359
110	*William Branigin* "The Checkpoint Killing" (2003)	363

A Golden Girl from Somewhere

When the Spring is on the mountain and the day is at the door—a golden girl from somewhere stands wondering, expectant, on the world's far edge.

Somewhere beyond that unfathomable sky—beyond the purple hills—lie laughter and joy and smooth delight.

Lithe and splendid, touched with a happy craving that will not be denied, she is going to the place where fairy tales come true.

May she choose the Playboy for her companion to the end of the traveled road—then a wonderful horse on up the slope with Spring to the desolate lone of outer space.

JORDAN

JORDAN MOTOR CAR COMPANY Inc., Cleveland, Ohio

Figure 11 Advertisement for Jordan motor cars, *Saturday Evening Post* 196,
March 29, 1924

INTRODUCTION

Not all students of English know the man behind the endless series of Webster's dictionaries. Noah Webster (1758–1843) argued for an American version of the English language, with a tone, diction, and a pronunciation of its own, independent of British English. To him, the project of setting up an American language was part of the national spirit of the late eighteenth century and the early Romantic age, when it was commonly stated that every nation was supposed to have its own language. Webster's life project of writing *The American Dictionary of the English Language* was not concluded until he was 70 years old in 1828, but this dictionary has since become an American classic. He also helped to found the first daily newspaper in New York, and promoted a copyright law to ensure writers their legal rights across the nation. His proposals for a spelling reform (see text 101) did not meet with much success, but it is interesting to see how Webster linked his ideas of language development to the national movement and the idea of a strong federal government.

Perhaps the most remarkable story of language acquisition in the United States is that of Helen Keller (1880–1968). Her story of how she, against all possible odds, discovered the power of words, and how language gradually opened up a door for her, is an American miracle story known all over the world (text 103). She was born in a small town in Alabama, where her father edited the local paper. Having lost her sight and her hearing before she was two years old, Helen was considered to be a lost case, without a chance to communicate with the outside world. Her parents, however, contacted Alexander Graham Bell, the inventor of the telephone, whose deep concern for deaf children finally brought Helen into the hands of Anne Sullivan, a truly patient language teacher. Helen was able to earn a BA from Radcliffe College in 1904, the first deaf blind person to achieve such a degree. As the story of her life became a version of the American success story, her support of the left in politics was largely overlooked, but she has remained a role model to generations. Movies and plays were constructed on the story of her life.

Immigration meant the use of languages other than American English, at least for a short period of time and in small pockets of immigrant communities throughout the United States. As immigrant clusters developed into ethnic groups, the language changed from immigrant parents to children born and raised in the United States. The sound and style of language developed from the flavor of the immigrant's mother tongue to the standard American English of the child. This transfer is well described by Amy Tan, a second-generation Chinese-American author (text 109). Her reflections on the language of her mother shed light on the language and assimilation of non-English-speaking newcomers to the United States. During the time of mass immigration, prior to the 1920s, cultures in languages other than English persisted in many parts of the United States. Polish was spoken and written in Chicago, Italian in New York, Scandinavian languages in several pockets of the Midwest, and in San Francisco Chinese was used as American language.

The melting-pot philosophy, however, turned the use of several American languages into an almost exclusive use of English. Particularly after several immigration restriction laws were passed in the 1920s, languages other than English came under enormous pressure. Over the last decades the flow of new immigrants

from Latin American countries has made Spanish the most powerful second lan-
guage in the United States, and has triggered attempts in several states to make
English the only official language in the country. In her essay Amy Tan assesses the
English of her Chinese-speaking mother. Her bilingualism shows that immigrant
groups have added, and continue to add, a linguistic richness of tone to American
English.

No American has changed the way we think of language and grammar more than
Noam Chomsky (1928–), who also for years has been an active political essayist on
the left. His work on generative grammar has influenced the teaching of language
all over the world. But for the study of American English in a cultural context,
William Labov (1927–), for many years professor of linguistics at the University
of Pennsylvania, may be said to be of equal importance. In his pioneer studies of
the African-American vernacular in American cities during the 1960s and 1970s,
he consistently argued that the variety of English spoken in the ghettos should not be
regarded as substandard (text 105).

In popular culture the use of proper language has been celebrated as a road to
certain financial success. Funk and Lewis's essay (text 104) is a typical American
guideline to success through the use of language. Their views on the values of life, of
language, and of society are totally different from Labov's.

In the United States, the popularity of Webster's dictionary and spellers increased
as general literacy became common. The advent of the penny paper during the first
half of the nineteenth century added a new segment of the American population to
the newspaper audience, making the newspapers the true mass media of the century.
Aided by the rapid development in communication, the cheap newspaper became an
important source of news and cultural information in the United States. The number
of American newspapers, including the mercantile dailies and the political papers in
addition to the penny papers, was 1200 in 1833 (three times as many as in England
or France), growing to about 3000 by 1860. In text 102 a review (1853) of the theatre
version of *Uncle Tom's Cabin* from the *New York Herald* shows how art criticism in a
newspaper reflected the political mood of the pre-Civil War epoch, and how
newspapers were not always proposing changes to the status quo.

An item in the *Washington Post* of June 19, 1972, however, turned out to be of massive
political consequence, launching the process that toppled a president from power.
Woodward and Bernstein's piece (text 106) uses the style of short paragraphs so
characteristic of newspaper essays. Read in retrospect, the one-line paragraph stating
that "The White House did not comment" reads like a warning of things to come.
President Nixon was forced not only to answer, but to resign, at the end of a process
started, in a sense, by this rather insignificant newspaper article. So when Vice-
president Gerald Ford took over in 1974, and Americans could buy T-shirts with his
picture above the words: "I got my job through the *Washington Post*", that was more
than just a joke.

In his preface to a very influential study of American media, entitled *Understanding
Media: The Extensions of Man* (1964), Marshall McLuhan argued in the very first
sentence that "the medium is the message." The press, he says (in his chapter 21), "is
a group confessional form that provides communal participation." Read in this
context, American journalists who write from theatres of war abroad may invite the

reader into a very special and personal situation which is, however, intended for general participation. William Brangin's report from the war in Iraq (see text 110) has the intensity and style of Hemingway's prose, but is reporting real events. As an American reporter, Branigin was with the American infantry division when they fired on a Land Rover filled with Iraqi civilians, yet his report is not like the first official American view of the episode.

In his above-mentioned study of the media, media theorist McLuhan argues that television is "the most recent and spectacular electric extension of our central nervous system", and has "affected the totality of our lives." Nowhere is this truer than in the United States where the mass production and use of television began. Neil Postman, one of the most renowned media analysts on the American scene, critically examines the role of television in American society (text 107) and concludes that TV is a medium for entertainment only, not for serious discourse, reflection, or education.

American TV has been accused of breeding violence and producing hollow soap operas, but it is sometimes also praised for excellent documentaries, social reports, and quality programs. During the first Gulf War in 1991 the American television company Cable News Network (CNN), owned by Ted Turner, established a new kind of global information system which served not only the general public but also the political leaders involved in the war. Incredibly, both the US Defense Secretary and the Chairman of the Joint Chiefs of Staff reportedly referred to CNN as their best source of information on the effect of the first Baghdad bombing. CNN seems thus to have fulfilled the dream of McLuhan, who envisioned a "global village" where citizens gathered around the electronic hearth. CNN's coverage of the war drew sharp criticism from various quarters, however, notably for its glorification of the supposedly clean, high-tech warfare and its glossing over the human sufferings involved.

Perhaps no one in contemporary American culture has managed to return the radio to an educational, non-commercial, yet popular media as has Garrison Keillor (1942–). The radio, argues McLuhan, "affects most people intimately . . . offering a world of unspoken communication between writer-speaker and the listener." In his "Prairie Home Companion" radio programs, Keillor reports from his imaginary, small-town Minnesota to the entire nation. One such program, "Forebears" (text 108), was also included as a chapter in his novel *Lake Wobegon Days*.

Questions and Topics

1 How does Webster argue for a national language, and why was this notion so important at the time?

2 How does Labov define American "non-standard Negro English", and how do you think Funk and Lewis would have reacted to his arguments?

3 How does Amy Tan construct her idea of an American mother tongue, and how important is language in the experience of first- and second-generation American immigrants?

4 Discuss the political role of newspaper reports with reference to the two pieces from the *Washington Post* (1972 and 2003).

5 Why have Garrison Keillor's radio programs become so popular, not only in the Midwest, but in the entire nation?

Suggestions for further reading

Haugen, Einar, *The Norwegian Language in America: A Study in Bilingual Behavior* (Philadelphia, Pa.: University of Philadelphia Press, 1953).

Keillor, Garrison, *Lake Wobegon Days* (New York: Viking, 1985).

Kerr, Elizabeth M. and Ralph M. Aderman, *Aspects of American English* (New York: Harcourt, Brace, Jovanovich [1963], 1971).

Labov, William, *Language in the Inner City: Studies in the Black English Vernacular* (Oxford: Blackwell, 1977).

McLuhan, Marshall, *Understanding Media: The Extensions of Man*, Introduction by Lewis H. Lapham (London: Routledge, [1964], 2001).

101 NOAH WEBSTER

FROM *"The Reforming of Spelling"* (1789)

It has been observed by all writers on the English language, that the orthography or spelling of words is very irregular; the same letters often representing different sounds, and the same sounds often expressed by different letters. For this irregularity, two principal causes may be assigned:

1. The changes to which the pronunciation of a language is liable, from the progress of science and civilization.

2. The mixture of different languages, occasioned by revolutions in England, or by a predilection of the learned, for words of foreign growth and ancient origin.
. . .

The question now occurs: ought the Americans to retain these faults which produce innumerable inconveniences in the acquisition and use of the language, or ought they at once reform these abuses, and introduce order and regularity into the orthography of the AMERICAN TONGUE?

Let us consider this subject with some attention.

Several attempts were formerly made in England to rectify the orthography of the language. But I apprehend their schemes failed of success, rather on account of their intrinsic difficulties than on account of any necessary impracticability of a reform. It was proposed, in most of these schemes, not merely to throw out superfluous and silent letters, but to introduce a number of new characters. Any attempt on such a plan must undoubtedly prove unsuccessful. It is not to be expected that an orthography, perfectly regular and simple, such as would be formed by a "Synod of Grammarians on principles of science," will ever be substituted for that confused mode of spelling which is now established. But it is apprehended that great improvements may be made, and an orthography almost regular, or such as shall obviate most of the present difficulties which occur in learning our language, may be introduced and established with little trouble and opposition.

The principal alterations necessary to render our orthography sufficiently regular and easy, are these:

1. The omission of all superfluous or silent letters; as *a* in *bread*. Thus *bread, head, give, breast, built, meant, realm, friend*, would be spelt *bred, hed, giv, brest, bilt, ment, relm, frend*. Would this alteration produce any inconvenience, any embarrassment or expense? By no means. On the other hand, it would lessen the trouble of writing, and much more, of learning the language; it would reduce the true pronunciation to a certainty; and while it would assist foreigners and our own children in acquiring the language, it would render the pronunciation uniform, in different parts of the country, and almost prevent the possibility of changes.

2. A substitution of a character that has a certain definite sound for one that is more vague and indeterminate. Thus by putting *ee* instead of *ea* or *ie*, the words *mean, near, speak, grieve, zeal*, would become *meen, neer, speek, greev, zeel*. This alteration would not occasion a moment's trouble; at the same time it would prevent a doubt respecting the pronunciation; whereas the *ea* and *ie* having different sounds, may give a learner much difficulty. Thus *greef* should be substituted for *grief*; *kee* for *key*; *beleev* for *believe*; *laf* for *laugh*; *dawter* for *daughter*; *plow* for *plough*; *tuf* for *tough*; *proov* for *prove*; *blud* for *blood*; and *draft* for *draught*. In this manner *ch* in Greek derivatives should be changed into *k*; for the English *ch* has a soft sound, as in *cherish*; but *k* always a hard sound. Therefore *character, chorus, cholic, architecture*, should be written *karacter, korus, kolic, arkitecture*; and were they thus written, no person could mistake their true pronunciation.

Thus *ch* in French derivatives should be changed into *sh*; *machine, chaise, chevalier*, should be written *masheen, chaze, shevaleer*; and *pique, tour, oblique*, should be written *peek, toor, obleek*.

3. A trifling alteration in a character or the addition of a point would distinguish different sounds, with the substitution of a new character. Thus a very small stroke across *th* would distinguish its two sounds. A point over a vowel, in this manner, *a*, or *o*, or *i*, might answer all the purposes of different letters. And for the dipthong *ow*, let the two letters be united by a small stroke, or both engraven on the same piece of metal, with the left hand line of the *w* united to the *o*.

These, with a few other inconsiderable alterations, would answer every purpose, and render the orthography sufficiently correct and regular.

The advantages to be derived from these alterations are numerous, great and permanent.

1. The simplicity of the orthography would facilitate the learning of the language. It is now the work of years for children to learn to spell; and after all, the business is rarely accomplished. A few men, who are bred to some business that requires constant exercise in writing, finally learn to spell most words without hesitation; but most people remain, all their lives, imperfect masters of spelling, and liable to make mistakes, whenever they take up a pen to write a short note. Nay, many people, even of education and fashion, never attempt to write a letter, without frequently consulting a dictionary.

But with the proposed orthography, a child would learn to spell, without trouble, in a very short time, and the orthography being very regular, he would ever afterwards find it difficult to make a mistake. It would, in that case, be as difficult to spell *wrong* as it is now to spell *right*.

Besides this advantage, foreigners would be able to acquire the pronunciation of English, which is now so difficult and embarrassing that they are either wholly discouraged on the first attempt, or obliged, after many years' labor, to rest contented with an imperfect knowledge of the subject.

2. A correct orthography would render the pronunciation of the language as uniform as the spelling in books. A general uniformity thro the United States would be the event of such a reformation as I am here recommending. All persons, of every rank, would speak with some degree of precision and uniformity. Such a uniformity in these states is very desirable; it would remove prejudice, and conciliate mutual affection and respect.

3. Such a reform would diminish the number of letters about one sixteenth or eighteenth. This would save a page in eighteen; and a saving of an eighteenth in the expense of books, is an advantage that should not be overlooked.

4. But a capital advantage of this reform in these states would be, that it would make a difference between the English orthography and the American. This will startle those who have not attended to the subject; but I am confident that such an event is an object of vast political consequence. For the alteration, however small, would encourage the publication of books in our own country. It would render it, in some measure, necessary that all books should be printed in America. The English would never copy our orthography for their own use; and consequently the same impressions of books would not answer for both countries. The inhabitants of the present generation would read the English impressions; but posterity, being taught a different spelling, would prefer the American orthography.

Besides this, *a national language* is a band of *national union*. Every engine should be employed to render the people of this country *national*; to call their attachments home to their own country; and to inspire them with the pride of national character. However they may boast of independence, and the freedom of their government, yet their *opinions* are not sufficiently independent; an astonishing respect for the arts and literature of their parent country, and a blind imitation of its manners, are still prevalent among the Americans. Thus an habitual respect for another country, deserved indeed and once laudable, turns their attention from their own interests, and prevents their respecting themselves. . . .

Sensible I am how much easier it is to propose improvements than to *introduce* them. Everything *new* starts the idea of difficulty; and yet it is often mere novelty that excites the appearance; for on a slight examination of the proposal, the difficulty vanishes. When we firmly *believe* a scheme to be practicable, the work is *half* accomplished. We are more frequently deterred by fear from making an attack than repulsed in the encounter.

Habit also is opposed to changes; for it renders even our errors dear to us. Having surmounted all difficulties in childhood, we forget the labor, the fatigue, and the perplexity we suffered in the attempt, and imagine the progress of our studies to have been smooth and easy. What seems intrinsically right is so merely thro habit.

Indolence is another obstacle to improvements. The most arduous task a reformer has to execute, is to make people *think*; to rouse them from that lethargy which, like the mantle of sleep, covers them in repose and contentment.

But America is in a situation the most favorable for great reformations; and the present time is, in a singular degree, auspicious. The minds of men in this country have been awakened. New scenes have been, for many years, presenting new occasions for exertion; unexpected distresses have called forth the powers of invention; and the application of new expedients has demanded every possible exercise of wisdom and talents. Attention is roused; the mind expanded; and the intellectual faculties invigorated. Here men are prepared to receive improvements, which would be rejected by nations whose habits have not been shaken by similar events.

Now is the time, and *this* the country, in which we may expect success, in attempting changes favorable to language, science and government. Delay, in the plan here proposed, may be fatal; under a tranquil general government, the minds of men may again sink into indolence; a national acquiescence in error will follow; and posterity be doomed to struggle with difficulties, which time and accident will perpetually multiply.

Let us then seize the present moment, and establish a *national language*, as well as a national government. Let us remember that there is a certain respect due to the opinions of other nations. As an independent people, our reputation abroad demands that in all things we should be federal; be *national*; for if we do not respect *ourselves*, we may be assured that *other nations* will not respect us. In short, let it be impressed upon the mind of every American that to neglect the means of commanding respect abroad is treason against the character and dignity of a brave independent people.

102 *NEW YORK HERALD*

Review of Uncle Tom's Cabin (1853)

Mrs. Harriet Beecher Stowe's novel of *Uncle Tom's Cabin* has been dramatized at the National Theatre, and, being something of a novelty, it draws crowded houses nightly.

The practice of dramatizing a popular novel, as soon as it takes a run, has become very common. In many instances, and particularly with regard to the highly dramatic and graphic novels of Dickens, these new plays have been very successful, giving pleasure and satisfaction to the public, and putting money into the pockets of the chuckling manager. But in the presentation of *Uncle Tom's Cabin* upon the boards of a popular theatre, we apprehend the manager has committed a serious and mischievous blunder, the tendencies of which he did not comprehend, or did not care to consider, but in relation to which we have a word or two of friendly counsel to submit.

The novel of *Uncle Tom's Cabin* is at present our nine days' literary wonder. It has sold by thousands, and ten, and hundreds of thousands – not, however, on account of any surpassing or wonderful literary merits which it may be supposed to possess, but because of the widely extended sympathy, in all the North, with the pernicious abolition sympathies and "higher law" moral of this ingenious and cunningly devised abolition fable. The *furore* which it has thus created, has brought out quite a number of catchpenny imitators, *pro* and *con*, desirous of filling their sails while yet the breeze is blowing, though it does appear to us to be the meanest kind of stealing of a lady's thunder. This is, indeed, a new epoch and a new field of abolition authorship – a new field of fiction, humbug and deception, for a more extended agitation of the slavery question – than any that has heretofore imperiled the peace and safety of the Union.

The success of *Uncle Tom's Cabin* as a novel has naturally suggested its success upon the stage; but the fact has been overlooked, that any such representation must be an insult to the South – an exaggerated mockery of Southern institutions – and calculated, more than any other expedient of agitation, to poison the minds of our youth with the pestilent principles of abolitionism. The play, as performed at the National, is a crude and aggravated affair, following the general plot of the story, except in the closing scene, where, instead of allowing Tom to die under the cruel treatment of his new master in Louisiana, he is brought back to a reunion with Wilmot and his wife – returned runaways – all of whom, with Uncle Tom and Aunt Chloe, are set free, with the privilege of remaining upon the old plantation. The incidents of the piece are thus set forth in the "small bill":–

PROGRAMME

ACT 1 – Exterior of Uncle Tom's Cabin on Shelbey's Plantation; Negro Celebration. Chorus, "Nigga in de Cornfield"; Kentucky Breakdown Dance; Innocence Protected; Slave Dealers on hand. Chorus, "Come then to the Feast"; the Mother's Appeal; Capture of Morna; Interior of Uncle Tom's Cabin; Midnight Escape; Tom driven from his Cabin; Search of the Traders; Miraculous Escape of Morna and her Child. Offering Prayer; the Negro's Hope; Affecting Tableau.

ACT 2 – Family Excitement; Dark Threatenings; Ohio River Frozen over; Snow Storm; Flight of Morna and her Child; Pursuit of the Traders; Desperate Resolve and Escape of Morna on Flowing Ice; Mountain Torrent and Ravine; Cave of Crazy Mag; Chase of Edward; Maniac's Protection; Desperate Encounter of Edward and Traders on the Bridge; Fall of Springer down the Roaring Torrent; Negro Chorus, "We Darkies Hoe the Corn"; Meeting of Edward and Morna; Escape over Mountain Rocks.

ACT 3 – Roadside Inn; Advertisement Extraordinary; the Slave Auctioneer; Rencontre between Edward and Slave Dealers; Interposition of Crazy Mag; Arrival from the West Indies; Singular Discovery. Mountain Dell; Recognition of the Lost Mother; Repentance and Remorse; Return of Tom; the Log Cabin in its Pride; Freedom of Edward and Morna &c.

In the progress of these varied scenes, we have the most extravagant exhibitions of the imaginary horrors of Southern slavery. The negro traders, with their long whips, cut and slash their poor slaves about the stage for mere pastime, and a gang of poor wretches, handcuffed to a chain which holds them all in marching order, two by two, are thrashed like cattle to quicken their pace. Uncle Tom is scourged by the trader, who has bought him, for "whining" at his bad luck. A reward is posted up, offering four hundred dollars for the runaway, Edward Wilmot, (who, as well as his wife, is nearly white,) the reward to be paid upon "his recovery, or upon proof that he has been killed." But Wilmot shoots down his pursuers in real Christian style, as fast as they come, and after many marvellous escapes, and many fine ranting abolition speeches, (generally preceding his dead shots,) he is liberated as we have described.

This play, and these scenes, are nightly received at one of our most popular theatres with repeated rounds of applause. True, the audience appears to be pleased with the novelty, without being troubled about the moral of the story, which is mischievous in the extreme.

The institution of Southern slavery is recognized and protected by the federal constitution, upon which this Union was established, and which holds it together. But for the compromises on the slavery question, we should have no constitution and no Union – and would, perhaps, have been at this day, in the condition of the South American republics, divided into several military despotisms, constantly warring with each other, and each within itself. The Fugitive Slave law only carries out one of the plain provisions of the constitution. When a Southern slave escapes to us, we are in honor bound to return him to his master. And yet, here in this city – which owes its wealth, population, power, and prosperity, to the Union and the constitution, and this same institution of slavery, to a greater degree than any other city in the Union – here we have nightly represented, at a popular theatre, the most exaggerated enormities of Southern slavery, playing directly into the hands of the abolitionists and abolition kidnappers of slaves, and doing their work for them. What will our Southern friends think of all our professions of respect for their delicate social institution of slavery, when they find that even our amusements are overdrawn caricatures exhibiting our hatred against it and against them? Is this consistent with good faith, or honor, or the every day obligations of hospitality? No, it is not. It is a sad blunder; for when our stage shall become the deliberate agent in the cause of abolitionism, with the sanction of the public, and their approbation, the peace and harmony of this Union will soon be ended.

We would, from all these considerations, advise all concerned to drop the play of *Uncle Tom's Cabin* at once and for ever. The thing is in bad taste – is not according to good faith to the constitution, or consistent with either of the two Baltimore platforms; and is calculated, if persisted in, to become a firebrand of the most dangerous character to the peace of the whole country.

103 HELEN KELLER

"Everything Has a Name" (1903)

The most important day I remember in all my life is the one on which my teacher, Anne Mansfield Sullivan, came to me. I am filled with wonder when I consider the immeasurable contrast between the two lives which it connects. It was the third of March, 1887, three months before I was seven years old.

On the afternoon of that eventful day, I stood on the porch, dumb, expectant. I guessed vaguely from my mother's signs and from the hurrying to and fro in the house that something unusual was about to happen, so I went to the door and waited on the steps. The afternoon sun penetrated the mass of honeysuckle that covered the porch, and fell on my upturned face. My fingers lingered almost unconsciously on the familiar leaves and blossoms which had just come forth to greet the sweet southern spring. I did not know what the future held of marvel or surprise for me. Anger and bitterness had preyed upon me continually for weeks and a deep languor had succeeded this passionate struggle.

Have you ever been at sea in a dense fog, when it seemed as if a tangible white darkness shut you in, and the great ship, tense and anxious, groped her way toward the shore with plummet and sounding-line, and you waited with beating heart for something to happen? I was like that ship before my education began, only I was without compass or sounding-line, and had no way of knowing how near the harbour was. "Light! give me light!" was the wordless cry of my soul, and the light of love shone on me in that very hour.

I felt approaching footsteps. I stretched out my hand as I supposed to my mother. Some one took it, and I was caught up and held close in the arms of her who had come to reveal all things to me, and, more than all things else, to love me.

The morning after my teacher came she led me into her room and gave me a doll. The little blind children at the Perkins Institution had sent it and Laura Bridgman had dressed it; but I did not know this until afterward. When I had played with it a little while, Miss Sullivan slowly spelled into my hand the word "d-o-l-l." I was at once interested in this finger play and tried to imitate it. When I finally succeeded in making the letters correctly I was flushed with childish pleasure and pride. Running downstairs to my mother I held up my hand and made the letters for doll. I did not know that I was spelling a word or even that words existed; I was simply making my fingers go in monkey-like imitation. In the days that followed I learned to spell in this uncomprehending way a great many words, among them *pin, hat, cup* and a few verbs like *sit, stand* and *walk*. But my teacher had been with me several weeks before I understood that everything has a name.

One day, while I was playing with my new doll, Miss Sullivan put my big rag doll into my lap also, spelled "d-o-l-l" and tried to make me understand that "d-o-l-l" applied to both. Earlier in the day we had had a tussle over the words "m-u-g" and "w-a-t-e-r." Miss Sullivan had tried to impress it upon me that "m-u-g" is *mug* and that "w-a-t-e-r" is *water*, but I persisted in confounding the two. In despair she had dropped the subject for the time, only to renew it at the first oppor-tunity. I became impatient at her repeated attempts and, seizing the new doll, I dashed it upon the floor. I was keenly delighted when I felt the fragments of the broken doll at my feet. Neither sorrow nor regret followed my passionate outburst. I had not loved the doll. In the still, dark world in which I lived there was no strong sentiment or tenderness. I felt my teacher sweep the fragments to one side of the hearth, and I had a sense of satisfaction that the cause of my discomfort was removed. She brought me my hat, and I knew I was going out into the warm sunshine. This thought, if a wordless sensation may be called a thought, made me hop and skip with pleasure.

We walked down the path to the well-house, attracted by the fragrance of the honeysuckle with which it was covered. Some one was drawing water and my teacher placed my hand under the spout. As the cool stream gushed over one hand she spelled into the other the word *water*, first slowly, then rapidly. I stood still, my whole attention fixed upon the motions of her fingers. Suddenly I felt a misty consciousness as of something forgotten – a thrill of returning thought; and somehow the mystery of language was revealed to me. I knew then that "w-a-t-e-r" meant the wonderful cool something that was flowing over my hand. That living word awakened my soul, gave it light, hope, joy, set it free! There were barriers still, it is true, but barriers that could in time be swept away.

I left the well-house eager to learn. Everything had a name, and each name gave birth to a new thought. As we returned to the house every object which I touched seemed to quiver with life. That was because I saw everything with the strange, new sight that had come to me. On entering the door I remembered the doll I had broken. I felt my way to the hearth and picked up the pieces. I tried vainly to put them together. Then my eyes filled with tears; for I realized what I had done, and for the first time I felt repentance and sorrow.

I learned a great many new words that day. I do not remember what they all were; but I do know that *mother, father, sister, teacher* were among them – words that were to make the world blossom for me, "like Aaron's rod, with flowers." It would have been difficult to find a happier child than I was as I lay in my crib at the close of that eventful day and lived over the joys it had brought me, and for the first time longed for a new day to come.

104 WILFRED FUNK AND NORMAN LEWIS

"Thirty Days to a More Powerful Vocabulary" (1942)

FIRST DAY: GIVE US 15 MINUTES A DAY

Your boss has a bigger vocabulary than you have.

That's one good reason why he's your boss.

This discovery has been made in the word laboratories of the world. Not by theoretical English professors, but by practical, hard-headed scholars who have been searching for the secrets of success.

After a host of experiments and years of testing they have found out:

That if your vocabulary is limited your chances of success are limited.

That one of the easiest and quickest ways to get ahead is by consciously building up your knowledge of words.

That the vocabulary of the average person almost stops growing by the middle twenties.

And that from then on it is necessary to have an intelligent plan if progress is to be made. No haphazard hit-or-miss methods will do.

It has long since been satisfactorily established that a high executive does not have a large vocabulary merely because of the opportunities of his position. That would be putting the cart before the horse. Quite the reverse is true. His skill in words was a tremendous help in getting him his job.

Dr. Johnson O'Connor of the Human Engineering Laboratory of Boston and of the Stevens Institute of Technology in Hoboken, New Jersey, gave a vocabulary test to 100 young men who were studying to be industrial executives.

Five years later those who had passed in the upper ten per cent *all*, without exception, had executive positions, *while not a single young man of the lower twenty-five per cent had become an executive.*

You see, there are certain factors in success that can be measured as scientifically as the contents of a test-tube, and it has been discovered that the most common characteristic of outstanding success is "an extensive knowledge of the exact meaning of English words."

The extent of your vocabulary indicates the degree of your intelligence. Your brain power will increase as you learn to know more words. Here's the proof.

Two classes in a high school were selected for an experiment. Their ages and their environment were the same. Each class represented an identical cross-section of the community. One, the control class, took the normal courses. The other class was given special vocabulary training. At the end of the period the marks of the latter class surpassed those of the control group, not only in English, but in every subject, including mathematics and the sciences.

Similarly it has been found by Professor Lewis M. Terman, of Stanford University, that a vocabulary test is as accurate a measure of intelligence as any three units of the standard and accepted Stanford-Binet I.Q. tests.

The study of words is not merely something that has to do with literature. Words are your tools of thought. *You can't even think at all without them.* Try it. If you are planning to go down town this afternoon you will find that you are saying to yourself: "I think I will go down town this afternoon." You can't make such a simple decision as this without using words.

Without words you could make no decisions and form no judgments whatsoever. A pianist may have the most beautiful tunes in his head, but if he had only five keys on his piano he would never get more than a fraction of these tunes out.

Your words are *your* keys for *your* thoughts. And the more words you have at your command the deeper, clearer and more accurate will be your thinking.

A command of English will not only improve the processes of your mind. It will give you assurance; build your self-confidence; lend color to your personality; increase your popularity. Your words are your personality. Your vocabulary is you.

Your words are all that we, your friends, have to know and judge you by. You have no other medium for telling us your thoughts – for convincing us, persuading us, giving us orders.

Words are explosive. Phrases are packed with TNT. A simple word can destroy a friendship, land a large order. The proper phrases in the mouths of clerks have quadrupled the sales of a department store. The wrong words used by a campaign orator have lost an election. For instance, on one occasion the four unfortunate words, "Rum, Romanism and Rebellion" used in a Republican campaign speech threw the Catholic vote and the presidential victory to Grover Cleveland. Wars are won by words. Soldiers fight for a phrase. "Make the world safe for Democracy." "All out for England." "V for Victory." The "Remember the Maine" of Spanish war days has now been changed to "Remember Pearl Harbor."

Words have changed the direction of history. Words can also change the direction of your life. They have often raised a man from mediocrity to success.

If you consciously increase your vocabulary you will unconsciously raise yourself to a more important station in life, and the new and higher position you have won will, in turn, give you a better opportunity for further enriching your vocabulary. It is a beautiful and successful cycle.

It is because of this intimate connection between words and life itself that we have organized this small volume in a new way. We have not given you mere lists of unrelated words to learn. We have grouped the words around various departments of your life.

This book is planned to enlist your active cooperation. The authors wish you to read it with a pencil in your hand, for you will often be asked to make certain notations, to write answers to particular questions. The more you use your pencil, the more deeply you will become involved, and the deeper your involvement the more this book will help you. We shall occasionally ask you to use your voice as well as your pencil – to say things out loud. You see, we really want you to keep up a running conversation with us.

It's fun. And it's so easy. And we've made it like a game. We have filled these pages with a collection of devices that we hope will be stimulating. Here are things to challenge you and your friends. Try these tests on your acquaintances. They will enjoy them and it may encourage them to wider explorations in this exciting field of speech. There are entertaining verbal calisthenics here, colorful facts about language, and many excursions among the words that keep our speech the rich, flexible, lively means of communication that it is.

Come to this book every day. Put the volume by your bedside, if you like. A short time spent on these pages before you turn the lights out each night is better than an irregular hour now and then. If you can find the time to learn only two or three words a day – we will still promise you that at the end of thirty days you will have found a new interest. Give us *fifteen minutes a day*, and we will guarantee, at the end of a month, when you have turned over the last page of this book, that your words and your reading and your conversation and your life will all have a new and deeper meaning for you.

For words can make you great!

105 WILLIAM LABOV

"The Non-Standard Vernacular of the Negro Community" (1967)

Before we approach any of the theoretical or practical problems connected with the language of the urban ghettos, it is necessary to arrive at some kind of *modus vivendi* with the term "Negro dialect." A great many people, including educators, speak of "Negro dialect," and a great many others object and even deny the existence of such a form. Furthermore, there is considerable resistance within the school systems to any mention of the particular characteristics of Negro students or Negro speech.

First, it is obvious to anyone that there is no one speech form, and no linguistic markers, that are common to all Negro people. There is no racial, genetic or physiological feature involved here. There is a culturally inherited pattern which has been transmitted to the centers of most Northern cities by migrants from the South, the great majority of whom happen to be Negroes. Most of the forms heard in the Northern ghettos are also used by some white Southerners. However, it is also a fact that the Negro residents of Northern cities are the chief representives of these Southern regional traits for white Northerners. These traits have lost their geographical significance for most Northerners, and taken on the social significance of identification with the Negro ethnic group.

Not all Southern features survive in the Northern ghettos. A selected set of them are common, while others tend to disappear; the most extraordinary fact is that in city after city the end result is quite similar. The speech of Negro children in Philadelphia, New York, Chicago, or Los Angeles is cast in much the same mold: the differences that do appear can be traced to differences in the surrounding dialect of the white community.

We are currently engaged in a study of the structural and functional differences between the non-standard English of the urban vernacular, and the standard English of the schoolroom. In several publications, we have provided some preliminary information on the principal structural conflicts involved here, and some of the immediate consequences for the teaching of reading. Though I will not attempt to summarize this data here, it will be useful to think of these alternations under four general headings:

[1] There are a number of systematic differences in the sound pattern which have little grammatical significance. There is an asymmetrical neutralization of /th/ and /f/ in final position, for example, so that *Ruth* is merged with *roof*.

[2] A much more important set of phonological differences intersect grammatical features: along this phonological-grammatical intersection lie the most important problems for teachers of speech and reading. The simplification of consonant clusters operates so that *muss* and *must* are homonyms, but also *miss* and *missed*. The phonological process which eliminates final and preconsonantal *r* and *l* is deeply involved with the grammatical problems of the copula and the future respectively. We have dealt with this topic more than any other in our previous publications.

[3] A fairly obvious set of morphological differences might be singled out: plurals such as *mens*, *teeths* or metathesized forms such as *aks* for "ask." Although these forms are quite resistant to alternation with the standard forms, they do not belong to a highly organized system in equilibrium which challenges linguistic analysis.

[4] There are many syntactic rules by which non-standard Negro English differs from standard English. Some, like the optional deletion of the copula in *He with us*, are commonplace and are easily converted to the standard form by speakers. But many other syntactic differences are governed by deep-seated and abstract rules. Embedded yes-no questions such as *I asked Alvin if he knew* appear as *I asked Alvin did he know*. In this case we are dealing with two alternate realizations of an underlying "Question" element: the use of *if* with declarative order, as opposed to no *if* with the inverted order of auxiliary and subject. This non-standard form is surprisingly regular and resistant to conversion to the standard form. The comparative produces a wealth of complex forms very different from standard English: *He runs the same fast as Jim can run*. But, as interesting and complex as such syntactic rules may be, they cannot be

considered as important as the items described under [2], which will undoubtedly draw the major share of pedagogical attention for some time to come.

At this point it may be proper to ask just how deep-seated and extensive are the differences between the non-standard and standard forms we are considering. There are various viewpoints on this subject: some scholars believe that the underlying phrase structures and semantics of non-standard Negro English are quite different, and reflect the influence of an hypothesized earlier Creole grammar. Others believe that this English dialect, like all other dialects of English, is fundamentally identical with standard English, and differs only in relatively superficial respects. One way to look at this argument is to ask whether differences in surface structure (the order of words and the forms they assume) are greater or less than the differences in the most abstract generative rules.

It is not important that we attempt to resolve this issue here. Our own research is concerned more with discriminating the relative depth or abstractness of the rules which govern various forms, and it may be useful to indicate the results of one investigation we have recently conducted into the ability of Negro boys, 10 to 14 years old, to imitate sentences. These trials are conducted as "memory tests," in which groups of Negro boys that we know well are given very strong motivation to try to repeat back sentences exactly. Such tests have been carried out before with young children 3 to 6 years old, but no one has studied imitation or "shadowing" of older children across a dialect boundary. We find that some boys are relatively good at repeating sentences, even very long ones, while a good many others find great difficulty with standard sentences and do better in reproducing the non-standard sentences. The greatest interest for us lies in the differential ability of children with different rules. If we consider the copula, for example, in sentences like *Larry is older than George* and *George is a friend of mine*, we observe very little difficulty in the preservation of the *is*. In our first trials, 21 out of 22 such copulas were given back to us in the standard form. But if we consider the problem of negative concord, which produces such sentences as *Nobody never know nothing about no game today*, we find a different situation. In about half of the cases, the sentences were repeated back with nonstandard negative concord. *Nobody ever said that* becomes *Nobody never said that*; and one can re-emphasize the standard form insistently with little change in the repetitions produced by the boys. Similarly, sentences such as *He asked if I could go to the game today* are repeated instantly without hesitation as *He asked could I go to the game today*. Such results indicate that the deletion of the copula is a relatively superficial rule which occurs relatively late in the grammar and alternates easily with the undeleted form, while the other cases are more fundamental differences in the compulsory rules of the transformational component of the grammar.

We can draw a further set of conclusions from the results of this work. Consider for a moment what is implied about the competence of the speaker who repeats instantly *He asked could I go . . .* when we say *He asked if I could go. . . .* His sentence may be considered a mistake, for which he is penalized in the testing procedure. But what kind of a mistake? It is the correct vernacular form corresponding to the standard form: it means the same thing as the standard form. To produce this non-standard sentence the listener must first *understand* the standard form, automatically convert this into an abstract representation, then produce his own form by a complex series of rules ultimately appearing as *He asked could I go. . . .* We cannot explain this response by imagining that the listener is trying to remember individual words, or failing to match one word to another in the right sequence. This phenomenon is a convincing demonstration of the abstract character of the language mechanism involved, and it also indicates that the structure of Negro non-standard English is quite complex. For many rules, there are two perceptual routes but only one production route. The teacher's task here will be to supply the practice in producing sentences by rules which are already well established in the perceptive apparatus.

We may wish to turn our attention now to the important and complex question of the relative *evaluation* of the two forms of English being considered here. Our studies of language within the speech community indicate that the evolution of language is strongly influenced by sets of social values consciously or unconsciously attributed to linguistic forms by the adult members of the community. So far, each of the studies that we have carried out indicate that there is greater agreement on the normative side than in speech performance, and the Negro community is no exception. Our subjective reaction tests show extraordinary uniformity in the unconscious evaluation of the non-standard forms by all sections of the Negro community, middle class and working class, of Northern or Southern origin.

With the rise of strong nationalist feelings in the Negro community, some observers have thought that separate linguistic norms would appear, and that the non-standard vernacular of the urban ghettos would be treated more positively by the leaders of the Negro community. In actual fact, this has not been so, and there is little reason to think that it will be the case in the future. The norms of correct speech are the same for the Negro community as for the white community; although various groups may move in different directions in their informal, spontaneous and intimate styles, they converge in their attitude on the appropriate forms for school, and public language. Suggestions have been received that reading primers be prepared in the vernacular, to accelerate the process of learning to read in the early grades. The results of our investigations throw considerable doubt on the acceptability of such a program. The Negro adults we have interviewed would agree almost unanimously that their children should be taught standard English in school, and any other policy would probably meet with strong opposition.

This unanimity is a characteristic of the *adult* community; we obtain no such uniform pattern from teen-agers. When we consider that a child learns his basic syntax from 18 to 36 months, and by eight years old has settled most of the fine points of phonology and morphology, it is surprising to discover how late in life he acquires the adult pattern in the evaluation of language. Children learn early, of course, that there is careful and casual style, and they are perfectly able to recognize the teacher's special style – but the wider social significance of dialect differences seems to be hidden from them to a surprising extent. Clearly one approach to facilitating the learning of standard English is to accelerate the acquisition of evaluative norms. At the age of 25, almost everyone comes to realize the import of language stratification, but by then, of course, it is difficult to change patterns of language production.

Our subjective reaction tests determine the unconscious evaluation of individual variables within the dialect pattern. The first evaluation scales that were devised allowed the listener to place the speaker along a scale of job suitability: what was the highest job that a person could hold speaking as he did? In our work in Harlem, we have added to this scale others which register converse attitudes: If the speaker was in a street fight, how likely would he be to win? or how likely is it that the speaker become a friend of yours? As we expected, complementary sets of values are attributed to most non-standard forms. To the extent that the use of a certain form, such as fricative *th* in *this thing*, raises a speaker on the job scale, it lowers him on the scale of toughness or masculinity. These opposing values are equally strong in all social groups: we find that the middle-class adults are most consistent in attributing both sets to a given group of speakers.

We have long been aware of the fact that the non-standard forms are supported by the values of group identity and opposition to middle-class norms which are strong among working-class people. The recent results of our subjective reaction tests suggest that the school system may actually be supporting this opposition or even inculcating it. The adolescent boy knows that there is no correlation in fact between toughness and the use of non-standard English: he knows a great many bad fighters who have perfect command of the vernacular, and many good fighters who do fairly well with school language. But the teacher is not as keenly aware of the limitations of her stereotypes; I think it quite possible that while she attempts to teach the middle-class values of good English, she is simultaneously conveying the notion that good English is inconsistent with toughness and masculinity which is highly valued by adolescent boys. Teaching programs should be carefully examined by men raised in the community who can help detect and eliminate the association of standard English with effeminacy, gentility, and overcultivation. It seems to be true that a perfect command of standard English weakens one's grasp of the vernacular: I have met no one who excelled in both forms. But I think it is important to minimize the loss, and particularly to minimize the opposition of middle-class and working-class values which has come to cluster about the language issue in such a stereotyped manner.

A great deal of our current research is concentrated upon the *functional* conflict between standard and non-standard English. It is too early to make any strong statements in this direction, although we believe that the most important educational applications will stem from an understanding of differences in the use of language. It is worth pointing out that most language testing which takes place within the schools gives a very poor indication of the over-all verbal skills of the children being tested. In an adult-dominated environment – the school, the home, or the recreation center – many children have learned elaborate defensive techniques which involve a minimum of verbal response. Monosyllabic answers, repressed speech, special intonation contours are all characteristic of such face-to-face testing situations. As a result, a great deal of public funds are being spent on programs designed to supply verbal stimulus to "non-verbal" children. The notion of cultural deprivation here is surely faulty: it is based on a mythology that has arisen about children who receive very little verbal stimulus, seldom hear complete sentences – children who are in fact supposed to be culturally empty vehicles.

In our research, we frequently encounter children who behave in a face-to-face encounter with adults as if they were "non-verbal." But when we utilize our knowledge of the social forces which control language behavior, and stimulate speech with more sophisticated techniques, the non-verbal child disappears.

These children have an extremely rich verbal culture; they are proficient at a wide range of verbal skills, even though many of these skills are unacceptable within the school program. The problem, of course, is to teach a different set of verbal skills, used for different purposes; but the teacher should be absolutely clear on the fact that she is opposing one verbal culture with another. If the task were only to fill a cultural vacuum, it would be much easier than it actually turns out to be.

In conclusion, I might suggest one implication of our studies of language use which might have value within the school system. Intelligence and verbal skill within the culture of the street is prized just as highly as it is within the school: but the use of such skills is more often to manipulate and control other people than to convey information to them. Of course it is the school's task to emphasize the value of language in cognitive purposes. But in order to motivate adolescent and pre-adolescent children to learn standard English, it would be wise to emphasize its value for handling social situations, avoiding conflict (or provoking conflict when desired), for influencing and controlling other people. This is the use for which verbal *skills* are already prized in the vernacular culture, and it seems to be good strategy to take advantage of the values that are already present, even while one is modifying them and teaching new ones. Long before the child has learned the full range of middle-class educational values, he must make a good start in mastering the fundamental rules of standard English. Any strategy which gives him strong motivation for reading and writing in standard English should be followed; we are all familiar with the fact that success or failure in these fundamental skills is an important determinant of success or failure in the school program as a whole.

106 BOB WOODWARD AND CARL BERNSTEIN

"GOP Security Aide Among 5 Arrested in Bugging Affair" (1972)

One of the five men arrested early Saturday in the attempt to bug the Democratic National Committee headquarters is the salaried security coordinator for President Nixon's reelection committee.

The suspect, former CIA employee James W. McCord Jr., 53, also holds a separate contract to provide security services to the Republican National Committee, GOP national chairman Bob Dole said yesterday.

Former Attorney General John N. Mitchell, head of the Committee for the Re-Election of the President, said yesterday McCord was employed to help install that committee's own security system.

In a statement issued in Los Angeles, Mitchell said McCord and the other four men arrested at Democratic headquarters Saturday "were not operating either in our behalf or with our consent" in the alleged bugging attempt.

Dole issued a similar statement, adding that "we deplore action of this kind in or out of politics." An aide to Dole said he was unsure at this time exactly what security services McCord was hired to perform by the National Committee.

Police sources said last night that they were seeking a sixth man in connection with the attempted bugging. The sources would give no other details.

Other sources close to the investigation said yesterday that there still was no explanation as to why the five suspects might have attempted to bug Democratic headquarters in the Watergate at 2600 Virginia Ave., NW, or if they were working for other individuals or organizations.

"We're baffled at this point . . . the mystery deepens," a high Democratic party source said.

Democratic National Committee Chairman Lawrence F. O'Brien said the "bugging incident . . . raised the ugliest questions about the integrity of the political process that I have encountered in a quarter century."

"No mere statement of innocence by Mr. Nixon's campaign manager will dispel these questions."

The Democratic presidential candidates were not available for comment yesterday.

O'Brien, in his statement, called on Attorney General Richard G. Kleindienst to order an immediate, "searching professional investigation" of the entire matter by the FBI.

A spokesman for Kleindienst said yesterday, "The FBI is already investigating. . . . Their investigative report will be turned over to the criminal division for appropriate action."

The White House did not comment.

McCord, 53, retired from the Central Intelligence Agency in 1970 after 19 years of service and established his own "security consulting firm," McCord Associates, at 414 Hungerford Drive, Rockville. He lives at 7 Winder Ct., Rockville.

McCord is an active Baptist and colonel in the Air Force Reserve, according to neighbors and friends.

In addition to McCord, the other four suspects, all Miami residents, have been identified as: Frank Sturgis (also known as Frank Florini), an American who served in Fidel Castro's revolutionary army and later trained a guerrilla force of anti-Castro exiles; Eugenio R. Martinez, a real estate agent and notary public who is active in anti-Castro activities in Miami; Virgilio R. Gonzales, a locksmith; and Bernard L. Barker, a native of Havana said by exiles to have worked on and off for the CIA since the Bay of Pigs invasion in 1961.

All five suspects gave the police false names after being arrested Saturday. McCord also told his attorney that his name is Edward Martin, the attorney said.

Sources in Miami said yesterday that at least one of the suspects – Sturgis – was attempting to organize Cubans in Miami to demonstrate at the Democratic National Convention there next month.

The five suspects, well-dressed, wearing rubber surgical gloves and unarmed, were arrested about 2:30 a.m. Saturday when they were surprised by Metropolitan police inside the 29-office suite of the Democratic headquarters on the sixth floor of the Watergate.

The suspects had extensive photographic equipment and some electronic surveillance instruments capable of intercepting both regular conversation and telephone communication.

Police also said that two ceiling panels near party chairman O'Brien's office had been removed in such a way as to make it possible to slip in a bugging device.

McCord was being held in D.C. jail on $30,000 bond yesterday. The other four were being held there on $50,000 bond. All are charged with attempted burglary and attempted interception of telephone and other conversations.

McCord was hired as "security coordinator" of the Committee for the Re-election of the President on Jan. 1, according to Powell Moore, the Nixon committee's director of press and information.

Moore said McCord's contract called for a "take-home" salary of $1,200 per month and that the ex-CIA employee was assigned an office in the committee's headquarters at 1701 Pennsylvania Ave., N.W.

Within the last one or two weeks, Moore said, McCord made a trip to Miami beach – where both the Republican and Democratic National Conventions will be held. The purpose of the trip, Moore said, was "to establish security at the hotel where the Nixon Committee will be staying."

In addition to McCord's monthly salary, he and his firm were paid a total of $2,836 by the Nixon Committee for the purchase and rental of television and other security equipment, according to Moore.

Moore said that he did not know exactly who on the committee staff hired McCord, adding that it "definitely wasn't John Mitchell." According to Moore, McCord has never worked in any previous Nixon election campaigns "because he didn't leave the CIA until two years ago, so it would have been impossible." As of late yesterday, Moore said, McCord was still on the Re-Election Committee payroll.

In his statement from Los Angeles, former Attorney General Mitchell said he was "surprised and dismayed" at reports of McCord's arrest.

"The person involved is the proprietor of a private security agency who was employed by our committee months ago to assist with the installation of our security system," said Mitchell. "He has, as we understand it, a number of business clients and interests and we have no knowledge of these relationships."

Referring to the alleged attempt to bug the opposition's headquarters, Mitchell said: "There is no place in our campaign, or in the electoral process, for this type of activity and we will not permit it nor condone it."

About two hours after Mitchell issued his statement, GOP National Chairman Dole said, "I understand that Jim McCord . . . is the owner of the firm with which the Republican National Committee contracts for security services . . . if our understanding of the facts is accurate," added Dole, "we will of course discontinue our relationship with the firm."

Tom Wilck, deputy chairman of communications for the GOP National Committee, said late yesterday that Republican officials still were checking to find out when McCord was hired, how much he was paid and exactly what his responsibilities were.

McCord lives with his wife in a two-story $45,000 house in Rockville.

After being contacted by The Washington Post yesterday, Harlan A. Westrell, who said he was a friend of McCord's, gave the following background on McCord: He is from Texas, where he and his wife graduated from Baylor University. They have three children, a son who is in his third year at the Air Force Academy, and two daughters.

The McCords have been active in the First Baptist Church of Washington.

Other neighbors said that McCord is a colonel in the Air Force Reserve, and also has taught courses in security at Montgomery Community College. This could not be confirmed yesterday.

McCord's previous employment by the CIA was confirmed by the intelligence agency, but a spokesman there said further data about McCord was not available yesterday.

In Miami, Washington Post Staff Writer Kirk Schartenberg reported that two of the other suspects – Sturgis and Barker – are well known among Cuban exiles there. Both are known to have had extensive contracts with the Central Intelligence Agency, exile sources reported, and Barker was closely associated with Frank Bender, the CIA operative who recruited many members of Brigade 2506, the Bay of Pigs invasion force.

Barker, 55, and Sturgis, 37, reportedly showed up uninvited at a Cuban exile meeting in May and claimed to represent an anticommunist organization of refugees from "captive nations." The purpose of the meeting, at which both men reportedly spoke, was to plan a Miami demonstration in support of President Nixon's decision to mine the harbor of Haiphong.

Barker, a native of Havana who lived both in the U.S. and Cuba during his youth, is a U.S. Army veteran who was imprisoned in a German POW camp during the World War II. He later served in the Cuban Buro de Investigationes – secret police – under Fidel Castro and fled to Miami in 1959. He reportedly was one of the principal leaders of the Cuban Revolutionary Council, the exile organization established with CIA help to organize the Bay of Pigs Invasion.

Sturgis, an American soldier of fortune who joined Castro in the hills of Oriente Province in 1958, left Cuba in 1959 with his close friend, Pedro Diaz Lanz, then chief of the Cuban air force. Diaz Lanz, once active in Cuban exile activities in Miami, more recently has been reported involved in such right-wing movements as the John Birch Society and the Rev. Billy James Hargis' Christian Crusade.

Sturgis, more commonly known as Frank Florini, lost his American citizenship in 1960 for serving in a foreign military force – Castro's army – but, with the aid of then-Florida Sen. George Smathers, regained it.

Contributing to this story were Washington Post Staff Writers E.J. Bachinski, Bill Gold, Claudia Levy, Kirk Scharfenberg, J.Y. Smith and Martin Weil.

107 NEIL POSTMAN

FROM *"The Age of Show Business"* (1985)

A dedicated graduate student I know returned to his small apartment the night before a major examination only to discover that his solitary lamp was broken beyond repair. After a whiff of panic, he was able to restore both his equanimity and his chances for a satisfactory grade by turning on the television set, turning off the sound, and with his back to the set, using its light to read important passages on which he was to be tested. This is one use of television – as a source of illuminating the printed page.

But the television screen is more than a light source. It is also a smooth, nearly flat surface on which the printed word may be displayed. We have all stayed at hotels in which the TV set has had a special channel for describing the day's events in letters rolled endlessly across the screen. This is another use of television – as an electronic bulletin board.

Many television sets are also large and sturdy enough to bear the weight of a small library. The top of an old-fashioned RCA console can handle as many as thirty books, and I know one woman who has securely placed her entire collection of Dickens, Flaubert, and Turgenev on the top of a 21-inch Westinghouse. Here is still another use of television – as bookcase.

I bring forward these quixotic uses of television to ridicule the hope harbored by some that television can be used to support the literate tradition. Such a hope represents exactly what Marshall McLuhan used to call "rear-view mirror" thinking: the assumption that a new medium is merely an extension or amplification of an older one: that an automobile, for example, is only a fast horse, or an electric light a powerful candle. To make such a mistake in the matter at hand is to misconstrue entirely how television redefines the meaning of public discourse. Television does not extend or amplify literate culture. It attacks it. If television is a continuation of anything, it is of a tradition begun by the telegraph and photograph in the mid-nineteenth century, not by the printing press in the fifteenth.

What is television? What kinds of conversations does it permit? What are the intellectual tendencies it encourages? What sort of culture does it produce?

To approach these questions with a minimum of confusion, I must begin by making a distinction between a technology and a medium. We might say that a technology is to a medium as the brain to the mind. Like the brain, a technology is a physical apparatus. Like the mind, a medium is a use to which a physical apparatus is put. A technology becomes a medium as it employs a particular symbolic code, as it finds its place in a particular social setting, as it insinuates itself into economic and political contexts. A technology, in other words, is merely a machine. A medium is the social and intellectual environment a machine creates.

Of course, like the brain itself, every technology has an inherent bias. It has within its physical form a predisposition toward being used in certain ways and not others. Only those who know nothing of the history of technology believe that a technology is entirely neutral. There is an old joke that mocks that naive belief. Thomas Edison, it goes, would have revealed his discovery of the electric light much sooner than he did except for the fact that every time he turned it on, he held it to his mouth and said, "Hello? Hello?"

Not very likely. Each technology has an agenda of its own. It is, as I have suggested, a metaphor waiting to unfold. The printing press, for example, had clear bias toward being used as a linguistic medium. It is *conceivable* to use it exclusively for the reproduction of pictures. And, one imagines, the Roman Catholic Church would not have objected to its being so used in the sixteenth century. Had that been the case, the Protestant Reformation might not have occurred, for as Luther contended, with the word of God on every family's kitchen table, Christians do not require the papacy to interpret it for them. But in fact there never was much chance that the press would be used solely, or even very much for the duplication of icons. From its beginning in the fifteenth century, the press was perceived as an extraordinary opportunity for the display and mass distribution of written language. Everything about its technical possibilities led in that direction. One might even say it was invented for that purpose.

The technology of television has a bias, as well. It is conceivable to use television as a lamp, a surface for texts, a bookcase, even as radio. But it has not been so used and will not be so used, at least in America. Thus, in answering the question, What is television?, we must understand as a first point that we are not talking about television as a technology but television as a medium. There are many places in the world where television, though the same technology as it is in America, is an entirely different medium from that which we know. I refer to places where the majority of people do not have television sets, and those who do have only one; where only one station is available; where television does not operate around the clock; where most programs have as their purpose the direct furtherance of government ideology and policy; where commercials are unknown, and "talking heads" are the principal image; where television is mostly used as if it were radio. For these reasons and more television will not have the same meaning or power as it does in America, which is to say, it is possible for a technology to be used so that its potentialities are prevented from developing and its social consequences kept to a minimum.

But in America, this has not been the case. Television has found in liberal democracy and a relatively free market economy a nurturing climate in which its full potentialities as a technology of images could be exploited. One result of this has been that American television programs are in demand all over the world. The total estimate of U.S. television program exports is approximately 100,000 to 200,000 hours, equally divided among Latin America, Asia and Europe. Over the years, programs like "Gunsmoke," "Bonanza," "Mission: Impossible," "Star Trek," "Kojak," and more recently, "Dallas" and "Dynasty" have been as popular in England, Japan, Israel and Norway as in Omaha Nebraska. I have heard (but not verified) that some years ago the Lapps postponed for several days their annual and, one supposes, essential migratory journey so that they could find out who shot J.R. [in "Dallas". All of this has occurred simultaneously with the decline of America's moral and political prestige, worldwide. American television programs are in demand not because America is loved, but because American television is loved.

We need not be detained too long in figuring out why. In watching American television, one is reminded of George Bernard Shaw's remark on his first seeing the glittering neon signs on Broadway and 42nd Street at night. It must be beautiful, he said, if you cannot read. American television is, indeed, a beautiful spectacle, a visual delight, pouring forth thousands of images on any given day. The average length of a shot on network television is only 3.5 seconds, so that the eye never rests, always has something new to see. Moreover, television offers viewers a variety of subject matter, requires minimal skills to comprehend it, and is largely aimed at emotional gratification. Even commercials, which some regard as an annoyance, are exquisitely crafted, always pleasing to the eye and accompanied by exciting music. There is no question but that the best photography in the world is presently seen on television commercials. American television, in other words, is devoted entirely to supplying its audience with entertainment.

Of course, to say that television is entertaining is merely banal. Such a fact is hardly threatening to a culture, not even worth writing a book about. It may even be a reason for rejoicing. Life, as we like to say, is not a highway strewn with flowers. The sight of a few blossoms here and there may make our journey a trifle more endurable. The Lapps undoubtedly thought so. We may surmise that the ninety million Americans who watch television every night also think so. But what I am claiming here is not that television is entertaining but that it has made entertainment itself the natural format for the representation of all experience. Our television set keeps us in constant communion with the world, but it does so with a face whose smiling countenance is unalterable. The problem is not that television presents us with entertaining subject matter but that all subject matter is presented as entertaining, which is another issue altogether.

To say it still another way: Entertainment is the supra-ideology of all discourse on television. No matter what is depicted or from what point of view, the overarching presumption is that it is there for our amusement and pleasure. That is why even on news shows which provide us daily with fragments of tragedy and barbarism, we are urged by the newscasters to "join them tomorrow." What for? One would think that several minutes of murder and mayhem would suffice as material for a month of sleepless nights. We accept the newscasters' invitation because we know that the "news" is not to be taken seriously, that it is all in fun, so to say. Everything about a news show tells us this – the good looks and amiability of the cast, their pleasant banter, the exciting music that opens and closes the show, the vivid film footage, the attractive commercials – all these and more suggest that what we have just seen is no cause for weeping. A news show, to put it plainly, is a format for entertainment, not for education, reflection or catharsis. And we must not judge too harshly those who have framed it in this way. They are not assembling the news to be read, or broadcasting it to be heard. They are televising the news to be seen. They must follow where their medium leads. There is no conspiracy here, no lack of intelligence, only a straight-forward recognition that "good television" has little to do with what is "good" about exposition or other forms of verbal communication but everything to do with what the pictorial images look like. . . .

108 GARRISON KEILLOR

FROM *"Forebears" (1985)*

The first Norwegians emigrated from Stavanger on the west coast, later ones from Telemark and Hallingdal, and almost none came from Christiania (Oslo). They were country folk who were squeezed by virtue of living in a small country with large mountains that left only so much land to farm, not nearly enough. Crops were poor, and then one fall, the fishing boats returned to Stavanger, riding high in the water. The herring had disappeared.

The people went straight to church and prayed God to send them an answer. No herring! It was as if the sun had vanished.

They were honest and proud people who had always worked hard, and poverty was no shame to them – a comical trait to the sophisticates of Oslo who flocked to the popular operetta *Stavanger! O Ja!*, in which the westerners were portrayed as dolts who played fiddles and ate lutefisk and talked funny and who felt flush if they had a krone in their pocket – but this calamity shook them to the innermost for, without fish, they were faced with death by starvation.

They were certain of one thing, though: they would not migrate to the city, as others had done. Years of fervent preaching had taught them that Oslo was a sinkhole of Swedish depravity and Danish corruption, where honest people quickly descended to atheism and indolence and a taste for worldly display. They had seen young men depart for Oslo with a promise to remain pure on their lips, only to return a few years later, decked out in silken European waistcoats and feathered hats and prissy satin slippers, talking with the fashionable Oslovian stammer, the sophisticated Oslovian lisp, and making fun of their own families, not with the hearty Stavanger laugh (hor-hor) but with the despicable Oslovian nose-laugh (hhn-hhn).

To maintain their honest rural way of life, they decided they must leave the homeland, and America loomed large in their imagination as a country with plenty of country in which to settle and prosper and hold to all they kept closest to their hearts. Some friends had gone to America already and sent back glowing letters that were posted in the churches and copied and passed from hand to hand.

My dear Christian [wrote Gunder Muus, in Wisconsin, to his Stavanger cousin in 1867], you will scarcely believe my good fortune in the six short months I have been in America. I was warmly received in New York from whence I travelled by train to Chicago and thence to here in Muskego where I found a fine situation with a merchant. He is from Norway as are most citizens here, so one feels quite at home instantly but without the deprivation and worry. The air is sweet, the land is good, timber is plentiful, and the fishing is excellent. In the lake near town, two Sundays ago, I caught ten pounds of fish in only an hour – real fighters, both of them, but I hooked them, using only worms for bait, and hauled them onto the shore after an exhilarating duel. This is quite ordinary here. Everyone catches fish! Not like back home where the few good spots are reserved for landowners. Perhaps someday you yourself will come to America, and then I promise you a good time at the lake.

The next year, Muus had relocated in Goodhue County, Minnesota, where he settled down to try his hand at farming, but fishing was uppermost in his mind.

My dear Christian, I have many thoughts of home, most of them sad and full of longing, but when I feel most dissatisfied and lonely, I can always improve my disposition with a few hours on Lake Roscoe or the Zumbrota River. Truly America is a great country where a poor Norwegian immigrant can drop his humble line and bring in great fish. Only string do I use and a hook! No aristocratic contraption for me! And yet with a little patience and industry and some cunning, the ordinary man can lure five-pound fish, as many as he likes, where others much wealthier may not get a single nibble. Thus do we prosper here, and I pray that you will soon be here with us, cousin, and enjoy the bounty of America.

Muus lost all in the Panic of 1873 and had to move to Minneapolis and take a job as a stockboy in a grocery store, a terrible disappointment for him.

My dear Christian, so much has happened since last I wrote and none of it good, but why burden you with my endless troubles? I have a bed and a roof over my head and three meals a day, so I should not complain. God will look after us.

I pray daily that He will show me the way out of this noisy, filthy, disease-ridden city full of scoundrels and liars and thieves – a city of men who want to get rich any way they can as soon as possible – a city on a great river which they have filled with poisons and excrement so that no fish can be taken from it. There are lakes nearby, but on Sunday I am too tired to walk so far, and when I have gone I found them crowded with ignorant people who spend a fortune on a pole and then stand and beat the water with it! They fling the line to and fro until it is tangled around their necks and meanwhile they curse and drink whiskey and drop garbage on the ground and talk disgusting talk. This is no place for a decent man. I am saving my money toward the day when I can go north, where they say the lakes are pure and bountiful and uninhabited. When I reach there, I will write again.

Muus saved $165 in four months by refraining from all entertainment, and the following September he rode the train north to St. Cloud, where he continued on foot, looking for a good lake where Norwegian was spoken. He walked through a pouring rain, carrying his rucksack under his thin coat, singing hymns to give himself strength, and felt weak when he reached the settlement of New Munich two days later, and collapsed on the street, feverish and out of his mind, and was treated there for consumption by a Mrs. Hoppe who decided the poor man was dying and put him on a wagon for Lake Wobegon, where, at least, he could expire among his countrymen. The wagoner, approaching the town, saw no life in his passenger, lying under the canvas, and dumped him in a ditch, knowing what a lot of trouble a person has when he drives into a town with a dead man, and there Muus awoke a few hours later. His fever was gone, and the sun shone down on him. He heard water lapping. He crawled out of the ditch and saw he was thirty feet from the shore of a fine lake. Out on the water, a man sat motionless on a log raft, holding one end of a line. Muus felt as weak as a baby and his throat was parched, so he was surprised at the strength of his voice as it hollered out of him: "How are they biting?"

"Pretty good," the man yelled back.

"Is there room for two?"

"Are you a fisherman?"

"Yes."

"Then there is room." And he poled the raft to shore, helped the formerly dying man onto the raft, and the two of them spent several hours pulling a good string of sunfish and crappies out of the still water among the weeds and water lilies. The man was Magnus Olesen, and he and Muus did not exchange three words all afternoon. In fact, it wasn't until dark that Magnus got around to asking if Muus was ill, and by that time, he was not.

He was the first Norwegian bachelor farmer in Lake Wobegon. He farmed three acres north of the lake, only enough to keep him stocked with beans and tobacco, and his real occupation was fishing, which he did every day except Sundays.

Jonson Ingqvist drove a black Buick touring car with leather upholstery though his home was only two blocks from the bank, and he kept a lake home on Sunfish Bay a quarter-mile from home, and he was said to own fourteen suits, all of them blue. In 1908, he went to Minneapolis for the big Hallingdal picnic, having promised his mother he'd look up her old friends and tell them she was sick and hadn't long but knew she would see them in Heaven. He wore a white linen suit, a white shirt, a straw hat, and a gold stickpin, and on his hip he carried a silver flask of brandy. He knew he would need it, spending a day with his countrymen. He walked from his hotel to the Milwaukee Depot and when he boarded the train to Minnehaha Park, his heart sank, it was as if he had lost everything he had worked for and been thrown back into a former life. The car was packed, so was the next one, with families carrying boxes and baskets that smelled of fried pork and meatballs. The people smelled of lye soap. They were as excited as if it were a train to Niagara Falls and all jabbering in a language he only knew how to be polite in. The park was less than five miles away, but Jonson wished the train had a first-class car where he could sit and talk to men in English.

The picnickers rushed off the train at Minnehaha station and made a beeline for the pavilion to claim a good table. He strolled across the bridge over the creek and had a look at the Falls and hiked along the creek to the Mississippi and back, and by then, the speeches had begun, the worst part of the ordeal. One gasbag after another climbed up on the platform, struck a pose, and launched into a hymn to Norwegian virtue that would have made angels blush, but, judging from the applause, was received by the crowd as no more than their due – grocers, millhands, streetcar conductors, journeymen carpenters, all turned their faces toward the sun of Norwegianness, even the ones in back who couldn't hear a single word of it – and after an hour, Jonson walked away and into the bushes and drew out the flask. "She will see you in heaven," he mumbled.

109 AMY TAN

"Mother Tongue" (1990)

I am not a scholar of English or literature. I cannot give you much more than personal opinions on the English language and its variations in this country or others.

I am a writer. And by that definition, I am someone who has always loved language. I am fascinated by language in daily life. I spend a great deal of my time thinking about the power of language – the way it can evoke an emotion, a visual image; a complex idea, or a simple truth. Language is the tool of my trade. And I use them all – all the Englishes I grew up with.

Recently, I was made keenly aware of the different Englishes I do use. I was giving a talk to a large group of people, the same talk I had already given to half a dozen other groups. The nature of the talk was about my writing, my life, and my book, *The Joy Luck Club*. The talk was going along well enough, until I remembered one major difference that made the whole talk sound wrong. My mother was in the room. And it was perhaps the first time she had heard me give a lengthy speech, using the kind of English I have never used with her. I was saying things like "The intersection of memory upon imagination" and "There is an aspect of my fiction that relates to thus-and-thus" – a speech filled with carefully wrought grammatical phrases, burdened, it suddenly seemed to me, with nominalized forms, past perfect tenses, conditional phrases, all the forms of standard English that I had learned in school and through books, the forms of English I did not use at home with my mother.

Just last week, I was walking down the street with my mother, and I again found myself conscious of the English I was using, the English I do use with her. We were talking about the price of new and used furniture and I heard myself saying this: "Not waste money – that way." My husband was with us as well, and he didn't notice any switch in my English. And then I realized why. It's because over the twenty years we've been together I've often used that same kind of English with him, and sometimes he even uses it with me. It has become our language of intimacy, a different sort of English that relates to family talk, the language I grew up with.

So you'll have some idea of what this family talk I heard sounds like, I'll quote what my mother said during a recent conversation which I videotaped and then transcribed. During this conversation, my mother was talking about a political gangster in Shanghai who had the same last name as her family's, Du, and how the gangster in his early years wanted to be adopted by her family, which was rich by comparison. Later, the gangster became more powerful, far richer than my mother's family, and one day showed up at my mother's wedding to pay his respects. Here's what she said in part:

> "Du Yusong having business like fruit stand. Like off the street kind. He is Du like Du Zong – but not Tsung-ming Island people. The local people call putong, the river east side, he belong to that side local people. That man want to ask Du Zong father take him in like become own family. Du Zong father wasn't look down on him, but didn't take seriously, until that man big like become a mafia. Now important person, very hard to inviting him. Chinese way, came only to show respect, don't stay for dinner. Respect for making big celebration, he shows up. Mean gives lots of respect. Chinese custom. Chinese social life that way. If too important won't have to stay too long. He come to my wedding. I didn't see, I heard it. I gone to boy's side, they have YMCA dinner. Chinese age I was nineteen."

You should know that my mother's expressive command of English belies how much she actually understands. She reads the Forbes report, listens to *Wall Street Week*, converses daily with her stockbroker, reads all of Shirley MacLaine's books. with ease – all kinds of things I can't begin to understand. Yet some of my friends tell me they understand 50 percent of what my mother says. Some say they understand 80 to 90 percent. Some say they understand none of it, as if she were speaking pure Chinese. But to me, my mother's English is perfectly clear, perfectly natural. It's my mother tongue. Her language, as I hear it, is vivid, direct, full of observation and imagery. That was the language that helped shape the way I saw things, expressed things, made sense of the world.

Lately, I've been giving more thought to the kind of English my mother speaks. Like others, I have described it to people as 'broken' or 'fractured' English. But I wince when I say that. It has always bothered me that I can think of no other way to describe it other than 'broken', as if it were damaged and needed to be fixed, as if it lacked a certain wholeness and soundness. I've heard other terms used, 'limited English', for example. But they seem just as bad, as if everything is limited, including people's perceptions of the limited English speaker.

I know this for a fact, because when I was growing up, my mother's 'limited' English limited my perception of her. I was ashamed of her English. I believed that her English reflected the quality of what she had to say. That is, because she expressed them imperfectly her thoughts were imperfect. And I had plenty of empirical evidence to support me: the fact that people in department stores, at banks, and at restaurants did not take her seriously, did not give her good service, pretended not to understand her, or even acted as if they did not hear her.

My mother has long realized the limitations of her English as well. When I was fifteen, she used to have me call people on the phone to pretend I was she. In this guise, I was forced to ask for information or even to complain and yell at people who had been rude to her. One time it was a call to her stockbroker in New York. She had cashed out her small portfolio and it just so happened we were going to go to New York the next week, our very first trip outside California. I had to get on the phone and say in an adolescent voice that was not very convincing, "This is Mrs. Tan."

And my mother was standing in the back whispering loudly, "Why he don't send me check, already two weeks late. So mad he lie to me, losing me money."

And then I said in perfect English, "Yes, I'm getting rather concerned. You had agreed to send the check two weeks ago, but it hasn't arrived."

Then she began to talk more loudly. "What he want, I come to New York tell him front of his boss, *you* cheating me?" And I was trying to calm her down, make her be quiet, while telling the stockbroker, "I can't tolerate any more excuses. If I don't receive the check immediately, I am going to have to speak to *your* manager when I'm in New York next week." And sure enough, the following week there we were in front of this astonished stockbroker, and I was sitting there red-faced and quiet, and my mother, the real Mrs. Tan, was shouting at his boss in her impeccable broken English.

We used a similar routine just five days ago, for a situation that was far less humorous. My mother had gone to the hospital for an appointment, to find out about a benign brain tumor a CAT scan had revealed a month ago. She said she had spoken very good English, her best English, no mistakes. Still, she said, the hospital did not apologize when they said they had lost the CAT scan and she had come for nothing. She said they did not seem to have any sympathy when she told them she was anxious to know the exact diagnosis, since her husband and son had both died of brain tumors. She said they would not give her any more information until the next time and she would have to make another appointment for that. So she said she would not leave until the doctor called her daughter. She wouldn't budge. And when the doctor finally called her daughter, me, who spoke in perfect English – lo and behold – we had assurances the CAT scan would be found, promises that a conference call on Monday would be held, and apologies for any suffering my mother had gone through for a most regrettable mistake.

I think my mother's English almost had an effect on limiting my possibilities in life as well. Sociologists and linguists probably will tell you that a person's developing language skills are more influenced by peers. But I do think that the language spoken in the family, especially in immigrant families which are more insular, plays a large role in shaping the language of the child. And I believe that it affected my results on achievement tests, IQ tests, and the SAT. While my English skills were never judged as poor, compared to math, English could not be considered my strong suit. In grade school I did moderately well, getting perhaps B's, sometimes B-pluses, in English and scoring perhaps in the sixtieth or seventieth percentile on achievement tests. But those scores were not good enough to override the opinion that my true abilities lay in math and science, because in those areas I achieved A's and scored in the ninetieth percentile or higher.

This was understandable. Math is precise; there is only one correct answer. Whereas, for me at least, the answers on English tests were always a judgment call, a matter of opinion and personal experience. These tests were constructed around items like fill-in-the-blank sentence completion, such as "Even though Tom was _, Mary thought he was _" And the correct answer always seemed to be the most bland combinations of thoughts, for example, "Even though Tom was shy, Mary thought he was charming," with the grammatical structure "even though" eliciting the correct answer to some sort of semantic opposites, so you wouldn't get answers like, "Even though Tom was foolish, Mary thought he was ridiculous." Well, according to my mother, there were very few limitations as to what Tom could have been and what Mary might have thought of him. So I never did well on tests like that.

The same was true with word analogies, pairs of words in which you were supposed to find some sort of logical, semantic relationship – for example, "*Sunset* is to *nightfall* as_ is to _ ." And here you would be presented with a list of four possible pairs, one of which showed the same kind of relationship: *red* is to *stoplight*, *bus* is to *arrival*, *chills* is to *fever*, *yawn* is to *boring*. Well, I could never think that way. I knew what the tests were asking, but I could not block out of my mind the images already created by the first pair, "*sunset* is to *nightfall*" – and I would see a burst of colors against a darkening sky, the moon rising, the lowering of a curtain of stars. And all the other pairs of words – red, bus, stoplight, boring – just threw up a mass of confusing images, making it impossible for me to sort out something as logical as saying: "A sunset precedes nightfall" is the same as "a chill precedes a fever". The only way I would have gotten that answer right would have been to imagine an associative situation, for example, my being disobedient and staying out past sunset, catching a chill at night, which turns into feverish pneumonia as punishment, which indeed did happen to me.

I have been thinking about all this lately, about my mother's English, about achievement tests. Because lately I've been asked, as a writer, why there are not more Asian Americans represented in American literature. Why are there few Asian Americans enrolled in creative writing programs? Why do so many Chinese students go into engineering? Well, these are broad sociological questions I can't begin to answer. But I have noticed in surveys – in fact, just last week – that Asian students, as a whole, always do significantly better on math achievement tests than in English. And this makes me think that there are other Asian-American students whose English spoken in the home might also be described as 'broken' or 'limited'. And perhaps they also have teachers who are steering them away from writing and into math and science, which is what happened to me.

Fortunately, I happen to be rebellious in nature and enjoy the challenge of disproving assumptions made about me. I became an English major my first year in college, after being enrolled as pre-med. I started writing nonfiction as a freelancer the week after I was told by my former boss that writing was my worst skill and I should hone my talents toward account management.

But it wasn't until 1985 that I finally began to write fiction. And at first I wrote using what I thought to be wittily crafted sentences, sentences that would finally prove I had mastery over the English language. Here's an example from the first draft of a story that later made its way into *The Joy Luck Club*, but without this line: "That was my mental quandary in its nascent state." A terrible line, which I can barely pronounce.

Fortunately, for reasons I won't get into today, I later decided I should envision a reader for the stories I would write. And the reader I decided upon was my mother, because these were stories about mothers. So with this reader in mind – and in fact she did read my early drafts – I began to write stories using all the Englishes I grew up with: the English I spoke to my mother, which for lack of a better term might be described as 'simple': the English she used with me, which for lack of a better term might be described as 'broken'; my translation of her Chinese, which could certainly be described as 'watered down'; and what I imagined to be her translation of her Chinese if she could speak in perfect English, her internal language, and for that I sought to preserve the essence, but neither an English nor a Chinese structure. I wanted to capture what language ability tests can never reveal: her intent, her passion, her imagery, the rhythms of her speech, and the nature of her thoughts.

Apart from what any critic had to say about my writing, I knew I had succeeded where it counted when my mother finished reading my book and gave me her verdict: "So easy to read."

110 WILLIAM BRANIGIN

"The Checkpoint Killing" (2003)

I covered the first Gulf War. I figured this time around I would try not to repeat the mistakes I made then. In the Gulf War, I started out in what they called a CUCV – basically a Chew Blazer painted tan, essentially an SUV. I was in that with a public affairs officer (PAO). We were going across the desert trying to keep up with tracked vehicles. It was horrendous for a few reasons. One was trying to go fast over the desert in a vehicle that bounced around like crazy. But the real problem was that we just had no idea what was going on as the cavalry division made its famous left hook. We had no radio communications in that vehicle and we traveled at night. Of course we could not see anything anyway. Later on I transferred to a medical track. It just made a world of difference. Not only was the ride a lot smoother, but I could put on a radio headset and hear what was going on. I could hear commanders giving orders. In those situations, it's much more important what you can hear than what you can see. A lot of time you'd drive all through the night and there was nothing to see anyway. And even in the daytime, all you could see was a huge cloud of dust. That was the main lesson I took from the Gulf War. You had to be on the net – the network of military communications.

This war I spent most of my time in an M88, an armored recovery vehicle. It's a fifty-six-ton monster. The only thing heavier is an Abrams tank. Its purpose is to pull tanks and other armored vehicles out of the mud when they get stuck. It can tow a tank. There are four hatches and three crew members. I sat in back, and could pop up any time out of my own hatch whenever I wanted to and see what was going on. I also had a CVC helmet with a radio headset. I could not only hear what was going on, but could also speak to the three guys on my vehicle, and even to the company commander, as long as it was an appropriate time to break in.

A couple of days were spent pulling tanks and Bradleys out of marshes. One day, we spent nine hours in one marsh, and got stuck three times. It really felt like I was wasting my time. Fortunately, this was during a pause and not much was going on anyway. Still, it was frustrating. The M88 certainly had its advantages. The major tradeoff was having to be with that vehicle when it was doing mundane things.

It was pretty uncomfortable being inside the M88. But I knew from experience it could be worse. There was a box in the back that was like a plastic footlocker that I sat on. When I wanted to see what was going on, I would open the hatch and stand on that. I would try to take precautions but see as much as I could. The important thing was the headset, and I had that on most of the time. A lot of times, I would have to write my stories sitting on that box while we were moving. With an eight-hour time difference, there were many times I was up until 1:00 to 2:00 A.M. filing. I had an iridium satellite phone with an antenna attachment that consisted of a wire with a magnet on the end. I would open the hatch and stick the antenna magnet outside, usually on top of the 50-caliber machine gun, which was the highest point on the vehicle. That worked pretty well. Sometimes I would plug my computer into an inverter that was hooked up to one of the vehicle's batteries, but I couldn't do this all the time, especially when the engine was not running. So I had to be very aware of the battery power of my computer. Sometimes I would write out my story longhand and then type it on my computer to save power. At the end of some days, I was so tired that I was falling asleep at the keyboard. Having no lights at night was also a problem. I often had to read my notes and type by the light of my computer screen, and even that had to be blocked because we were under blackout conditions. The crew would complain from time to time that they could see light coming up out of the hatch from the computer screen.

The M88's ride was fairly smooth. Not like it is in a vehicle with tires. The M88 has tracks like a tank. The only thing smoother that I rode in was an Abrams. The trouble was that dust covered everything. It would get into the computer, an IBM ThinkPad. I had a shaving brush that I would constantly use to wipe dust off my computer keyboard and screen. I really worried that the dust would cause the computer to conk out on me.

I didn't want to spend the war only watching tanks being pulled out of a ditch. In fact, there was this one occasion where the battalion was moving forward and the M88 I was on was ordered to haul some piece of equipment back to the maintenance point. Which meant that we would be way behind. Earlier, I'd written a story quoting the guy who gave that order, and he was very happy with the story. His relatives saw it and knew he was okay. So, when this was happening, I told him that if the M88 has to go back, I really have to get off it and get on something that is going forward. So he changed his mind and let us go ahead. By then the battalion was pretty well split up. We were scattered.

One day, there was a small group which included the M88, a couple of other tracked vehicles, and an M 113 medical track. We were in a position under some trees off the highway southwest of Karbala, near a farmhouse. The area was very rural. I was sitting in the vehicle listening on my CVC to the company commander communicate with his platoon. The company was holding Highway 9 and controlling this intersection of a road that goes to the east at the same level basically as the town of Hilla, but it doesn't lead to Hilla. This one platoon was on the road that comes from the east and then deadends into a T-junction on Highway 9. It was from that direction that this vehicle came. It was a paved road, not dirt, but it was a rural area, and the commander saw this vehicle coming. He started to become very alarmed. Two days before, there had been a suicide car bombing and four soldiers of the First Brigade had been killed. That happened south of where we were, in a place we had come from, but the commanders were still spooked by this. It was the same division. The word had gone out to be wary of suicide bombers. For that reason, my battalion was not going to go anywhere near a vehicle or let any vehicles come near them. So this vehicle was approaching fairly fast, from what I understand. The platoon that was out there was apparently not paying attention, was not ready for it. The commander's voice became louder and louder until he was shouting, "Fire a warning shot!" He ordered them to fire a 7.62 round from the Bradley's machine gun. He yelled, "Fire into the engine block." I was about a mile away in the M88, listening and writing notes. Then he was shouting: "Stop fucking around!" Finally he shouted, "Stop him, Red One, stop him!" Red One was the code name for the platoon leader. He shouted that at the top of his voice. Then the Bradley opened up with its 25-millimeter cannon. It sounded like five or six rounds in rapid succession. That just destroyed the vehicle. Then the commander said what I later reported: "You just fucking killed a family because you didn't fire a warning shot soon enough!"

I had tried to keep up and write it all down as best I could. I was writing by hand in my notebook. The commander was really angry. At about this time, the medical track with us sped off to go to the scene. I regretted that I wasn't aware it would immediately leave, and it didn't occur to me to jump out and say "Wait a minute. Can I go with you?" I just couldn't tell the vehicle I was in, the M88, to go somewhere. It is a big tracked vehicle, and it had orders to stay put. I was probably a mile away. I could see the scene on the highway when I popped up. After a while, a crowd gathered on the highway.

The military commanders all said from day one that they understood embedding was going to be for better or for worse. I attended the first media boot camp held in several different places, mostly with the Marines at Quantico. Everybody had said they realized we would have to tell the truth and that there was gonna be stuff they didn't like. Later, I was able to interview the medics and get a clearer picture of what happened. The regret I have was not being able to get to that scene. But my main concern was the conversations back and forth on the radio. A few days afterward, we drove by the scene. The vehicle was still there by the side of the road. It was an old Land Rover and it very unfortunately fit the profile of a suicide bomb vehicle. Apparently these old SUVs were what was being used by suicide bombers.

I later talked to doctors and an Arabic interpreter who had talked to the survivors. They said that they were on their way to Najaf but it was never really clear why. It wasn't clear whether they were fleeing someplace, or just that they were on their way to see relatives in Najaf.

At the time, the officers said the division was going to investigate it. In the end, no disciplinary action was taken. It was judged to be an unfortunate accident. Nothing ever happened to the platoon leader, and he stayed in his position. In fact, the following day, in sort of a bizarre atonement, a family came up to the checkpoint position. It was an Iraqi farmer and his wife and a son who was about ten years old. They had a daughter about three years old who was having a lot of difficulty breathing. They said she was dying and asked if the soldiers could help. This platoon leader's Bradley ended up being the one that took them to the American medical aid station where they saved the girl's life. She had pneumonia.

I talked to the platoon leader the next day briefly. He claimed that he had fired a warning shot. He said the vehicle was coming in at a high speed. He said it had not behaved the way all the others had when they approached and saw the Americans. The other vehicles would then just turn around. But the real dilemma here was that they didn't have any warning signs out or concertina wire across the road. On the one hand, that sort of thing is really necessary to prevent civilians from injury in that exact situation. On the other hand, there was still a war going on, and you do not want to advertise your presence.

Well, I felt sorry for everybody, for the family, for the survivors. It was just a terrible tragedy. One woman had lost her two children who were sitting on her lap. There were fifteen to sixteen people crammed into this vehicle. The adults had children on their laps. Which is why all the children died and some of the adults survived. That was really tragic. I also felt sorry for this platoon and the platoon leader, who was a twenty-three-year-old lieutenant and very earnest. It's also a terrible burden for him to bear.

Personally, I've seen things like this happen before. I'm sure I would have been affected more viscerally if I had seen the bodies. But just listening to it like that, I was a bit removed from it. So it didn't have as strong an impact on me as it might have otherwise.

The Pentagon was giving a much different version than what I reported for the Washington Post. So my editors asked me to provide some more details and to basically work it into my story the next day, to report on the aftermath and confirm exactly what happened. The Pentagon was saying there were seven dead, out of thirteen people in the vehicle. I went back and checked again. It was actually ten dead on the spot. Another passenger was evacuated with critical injuries, and he died later at an American field hospital. That brought the toll to eleven. A medic had given the surviving family members ten body bags. Apparently the Pentagon's initial lower figures came from the platoon leader before they removed the bodies from the vehicles. One mistake I made: It was a Land Rover. I initially understood it to be a Land Cruiser, a Toyota. So that was a mistake I had to correct the next day.

The assistant managing editor for foreign news, Phil Bennett, said he thought it was a very important story and was done well. It was some time later in Baghdad that my colleague, Peter Baker, told me he had written a piece for the American Journalism

Review in which he cited my reporting as an example that being embedded didn't mean "in bed." The only comment I got from the battalion commander was, "I read your story." That was all he said. I said, "Well, you know, it was real unfortunate that the shooting happened." He just left it at that.

12

FOREIGN AFFAIRS

Introduction		370
111	*George Washington* FROM Farewell Address (1796)	374
112	*James Monroe* FROM "The Monroe Doctrine" (1823)	376
113	*Charles A. Beard* FROM "A Foreign Policy for America" (1940)	378
114	*Harry Truman* "The Truman Doctrine" (1947)	381
115	*George C. Marshall* "The Marshall Plan" (1947)	384
116	*Joseph McCarthy* FROM "The Wheeling Speech" (1950)	386
117	*Lyndon B. Johnson* "American Policy in Viet-Nam" (1965)	391
118	*George Bush* "The Launch of Attack on Iraq" (1991)	393
119	*E. L. Doctorow* Open Letter to the President (1991)	395
120	*George W. Bush* The State of the Union Address (January 29, 2002)	397

Figure 12 United Flight 175 impacting Two World Trade Center, September 11, 2001
© Sean Adair/Reuters/CORBIS

INTRODUCTION

The Constitution gives the President a prominent role in conducting relations with foreign nations, although in a sometimes difficult partnership with Congress.

Text 111, George Washington's "Farewell Address" (1796), partly drafted for the president by Alexander Hamilton, is probably best known for its unambiguous advice on US relations with foreign powers, emphasizing the importance of neutrality and warning against "permanent alliances with any portion of the foreign world." Washington's style of writing reveals that this was not a public speech, but a letter to the public, published in a newspaper. Readers should note that at the time Washington published his address, the United States was not a strong nation, and was bound by an alliance with France (1778). Federalists, like Washington and Hamilton, however, would have liked to strengthen ties with Great Britain.

In the years that followed, the United States was in conflict with both France (1798–99) and England (1812–14). This reminded the Americans of the potential European threat to their newly won independence. In what was later known as the Monroe Doctrine President James Monroe in his annual address to Congress in 1823 emphasized the separateness of the old and the new worlds, maintaining that America

370

and Europe must lead separate existences (see text 112). Worked out essentially by Secretary of State John Quincy Adams, the Doctrine stated the non-interventionist intentions of the United States in Europe and in the "existing colonies or dependencies in the Western Hemisphere." Perhaps even more significantly, the United States proclaimed that it would tolerate no interference on the part of European powers in the newly independent Latin American countries (they were not asked if they desired such protection). It is worth noting, however, that the United States was no superpower at the time, and the Monroe Doctrine thus did not for the time being cause great concern among the European powers. Monroe's address became more important as the United States developed into a world power.

As the United States developed into a major nation in the last part of the nineteenth century the fear of foreign invasion or intervention waned and the United States started – despite opposition at home – to show imperialist tendencies, notably in the annexation of Cuba, Puerto Rico and the Philippine Islands (in 1898) after a brief, hectic war with Spain. President Theodore Roosevelt (1901–09) fitted perfectly into the imperialist mood around the turn of the century. In 1904 he formulated his Roosevelt Corollary, which went beyond the Monroe Doctrine by justifying US intervention in the western hemisphere. The next decade witnessed a series of US interventions in line with the Roosevelt Corollary.

Despite the more active US role in foreign affairs in the first part of the twentieth century, the United States stayed out of World War I for three years. The Monroe Doctrine's principle of staying out of Europe was entrenched in the hearts and minds of most Americans. Germany's aggressive warfare was, however, gradually viewed as a danger not only to Europe but to mankind as a whole, and in April 1917 the United States declared war on Germany.

The US departure from isolationism helped to end the war, but did not create a climate of international cooperation as expected. President Wilson's grand design for the future with the establishment of the League of Nations collapsed at home, and very soon Europe was again on the brink of disaster. In the 1920s and 1930s isolationism again became the dominating mood in the United States, and even after the rise of Hitler and Mussolini opposition at home against US involvement in Europe's troubles was strong. The renowned historian Charles A. Beard was perhaps the person who most persuasively argued for the US isolationist stance and represented a serious threat to Roosevelt's internationalist position. In text 113 Beard argues for what he terms Continental Americanism, an isolationist view which had solid support among both Democrats and Republicans. As a matter of fact, the isolationist view was so influential that President Franklin D. Roosevelt was unable to convince Congress to join forces with the allied troops until Japan attacked Pearl Harbor, Hawaii, in 1941.

World War II brought an end to American isolationism. It was no longer possible for the biggest superpower on earth to pretend it could exist in "splendid isolation." The challenges of war had ended, only to be succeeded by the serious tensions of the Cold War, where American foreign policy very soon focused on the goal of containing communism. It was George F. Kennan, in his famous article "The Sources of Soviet Conduct" (July 1947),[1] who introduced the word "containment" into American foreign policy and called for firm resistance to Soviet expansionism. Kennan concluded that "it is clear that the United States cannot expect in the foreseeable future to enjoy political intimacy with the Soviet regime. It must continue to regard the Soviet Union as a rival, not a partner, in the political arena." In his address to a joint session of the Congress of March 12, 1947, President Truman officially proclaimed the American post-war policy toward the Soviet Union. The speech, included here as text 114, meant, in Truman's view, "a turning point in American foreign policy, clearly establishing that wherever aggression, direct or indirect, was a threat to peace, the security of America was also in danger."

The Marshall Plan (proclaimed in June 1947) conveyed a more positive expression of American foreign policy through massive aid to Europe (see text 115). The rationale behind the Marshall Plan was, however, a logical follow-up to Truman's goal for American foreign policy: to assist the free world against communism.

On the domestic scene the Cold War unfortunately spread a sense of unease and anxiety and resulted in a massive witch hunt on radicals and so-called communists in the beginning of the 1950s. Giving his name to the period (McCarthyism), Senator Joseph R. McCarthy was renowned for his blatant demagogic attacks on radicals and moderates alike (well documented in his notorious speech to the Women's Club of Wheeling, West Virginia, reprinted here as text 116), blaming them (even the President was attacked) for treacherous activities and undermining the American system of government.

The most dangerous confrontation between the United States and the Soviet Union in the post-war period occurred in 1962 during the Cuba crisis. President Kennedy's tough and provocative response to the Soviet missile build-up on Cuba signaled that the world was close to a nuclear catastrophe. In Vietnam, the United States had to pay the costs of containment that no policymaker in Washington had dreamed of. Lyndon B. Johnson's speech in April 1965 (see text 117) reveals the logic behind the so-called domino theory, which stated that if South Vietnam was taken by the communists, each of the other Southeast Asian nations in its turn would become communist under the domination of communist China. The domino theory in particular and US involvement in Vietnam in general came under increasingly severe attack both at home and internationally. The anti-war movement, supported by popular songwriters such as Bob Dylan and Joan Baez, was a major factor in Johnson's decision not to run for the White House in 1968 and was certainly one of the reasons for America's withdrawal from Vietnam under Nixon.

Primarily because of the withdrawal from Indo-China, the United States thought from the mid-1970s that there was relatively little it could accomplish by force of arms. Even though Ronald Reagan's tough Cold War rhetoric in the 1980s differed sharply from Jimmy Carter's foreign policy approach in the late 1970s, the real confrontations with the USSR did not materialize. On the contrary, Reagan's actual policy, despite talk of containment, became gradually more conciliatory towards the USSR. With the disintegration of both the USSR and communist eastern Europe during the late 1980s and the early 1990s, the ideological basis of both the Cold War and the policy of containment in Europe suddenly evaporated. In other parts of the world, notably the Third World, the confrontational posture of US foreign policy has been maintained, first during the Reagan years through low-intensity warfare, and then (under George Bush) through direct confrontation during the Gulf War in 1991.

INTRODUCTION

In his statement from the White House on the launch of an attack on Iraq (see text 118), President Bush (the first) explains the rationale for acting now and not waiting any longer, insisting that the sole goal of the attack is the liberation of Kuwait, not the conquest of Iraq. E. L. Doctorow's passionate plea for nonmilitary action against Iraq (text 119), published just before Bush's announcement, recalls sentiments from the Vietnam years, even though Doctorow represented a minority opinion at the time.

On September 11, 2001 three hijacked jetplanes hit the World Trade Center in New York and the Pentagon outside Washington. More than 3000 people were killed. President George W. Bush addressed the nation after the attack and vowed to "find those responsible and bring them to justice." In his State of the Union address four months later (text 120), September 11 figures prominently. Here the President warns that the United States will prevent regimes that "sponsor terror from threatening America and our friends and allies with weapons of mass destruction." Bush goes on to identify specific nations which according to him constitute "an axis of evil." In 2003 the United States and the multinational "Coalition of the Willing" invaded Iraq and deposed Saddam Hussein. The rationale behind the invasion was the claim that Hussein was in possession of weapons of mass destruction and had links with al Qaeda, the Muslim militant group behind 9/11. None of these claims has proved to be true. At the time of writing in 2007, the war is still continuing, and President Bush is being criticized heavily, both at home and abroad, for the quagmire into which the war in Iraq has developed. Whether the general unpopularity of the war in Iraq will eventually mean a shift in US foreign military policy remains to be seen, but will depend on factors like further developments in Iraq, the conflict over Iran's nuclear program, and the outcome of the presidential elections in 2008.

1 George E. Kennan, "The Sources of Soviet Conduct," *Foreign Affairs*, vol. 25, July 1947, pp. 571f.

Questions and Topics

1 Explain why George Washington stressed the importance of US neutrality in his "Farewell Address."
2 What are the differences between the Monroe Doctrine and the principles laid down in Washington's "Farewell Address" and the Truman Doctrine?
3 Discuss whether the Marshall Plan was an act of solidarity or self-interest.
4 Compare the first President Bush's reasons for attacking Iraq with his son's rationale for the war in Iraq.
5 What does President George W. Bush mean by the the term "axis of evil"? Discuss how far this label indicates that President Bush regards the war on terror as a war of civilizations.

Suggestions for further reading

Ambrose, Stephen E., *Rise to Globalism: American Foreign Policy, 1938–1980* (New York: Penguin, 1980).

Eisenstadt, Michael and Eric Mathewson, eds., *US Policy in Post-Saddam Iraq* (Washington, DC: Washington Institute of Near East Policy, 2003).

Foot, Rosemary, *Human Rights and the Counter-Terrorism in America's Asia Policy* (London: International Institute for Strategic Studies, 2004).

Iriye, Akira, *From Nationalism to Internationalism: US Foreign Policy to 1914* (London: Routledge & Kegan Paul, 1977).

Shannon, Vaughn P., *Balancing Act: US Foreign Policy and the Arab–Israeli Conflict* (Aldershot: Ashgate, 2003).

111 GEORGE WASHINGTON

FROM *Farewell Address (1796)*

Friends and Fellow Citizens:

The period for a new election of a citizen, to administer the executive government of the United States, being not far distant, and the time actually arrived, when your thoughts must be employed in designating the person who is to be clothed with that important trust, it appears to me proper, especially as it may conduce a more distinct expression of the public voice, that I should now aprize you of the resolution I have formed, to decline being considered among the number of those, out of whom a choice is to be made. . . .

In looking forward to the moment, which is intended to terminate the career of my public life, my feelings do not permit me to suspend the deep acknowledgment of that debt of gratitude, which I owe to my beloved country for the many honors it has conferred upon me; still more for the steadfast confidence with which it has supported me; and for the opportunities I have thence enjoyed of manifesting my inviolable attachment, by services faithful and reserving, though in usefulness unequal to my zeal. . . .

The name AMERICAN, which belongs to you, in your national capacity, must always exalt the just pride of Patriotism, more than any appellation derived from local discriminations. With slight shades of difference, you have the same religion, manners, habits, and political principles. You have in a comon cause fought and triumphed together; and joint efforts, of common dangers, sufferings, and successes. . . .

Observe good faith and justice toward all Nations. Cultivate peace and harmony with all. Religion and Morality enjoin this conduct. And can it be that good policy does not equally enjoin it? It will be worthy of a free, enlightened, and at no distant period a great nation to give to mankind the magnanimous and too novel example of a people always guided by an exalted justice and benevolence. Who can doubt that in the course of time and things the fruits of such a plan would richly repay any temporary advantages which might be lost by a steady adherence to it? Can it be that Providence has not connected the permanent felicity of a Nation with its Virtue? The experiment, at least, is recommended by every sentiment which ennobles human nature. Alas! is it rendered impossible by its vices?

In the execution of such a plan nothing is more essential than that permanent, inveterate antipathies against particular nations and passionate attachments for others should be excluded, and that in place of them just and amicable feelings toward all should be cultivated. The Nation which indulges toward another an habitual hatred or an habitual fondness is in some degree a slave. It is a slave to its animosity or to its affection, either of which is sufficient to lead it astray from its duty and its interest. Antipathy in one nation against another disposes each more readily to offer insult and injury, to lay hold of slight causes of umbrage, and to be haughty and intractable when accidental or trifling occasions of dispute occur.

Hence frequent collisions, obstinate, envenomed, and bloody contests. The Nation prompted by ill will and resentment sometimes impels to war the government contrary to the best calculations of policy. The government sometimes participates in the national propensity, and adopts through passion what reason would reject. At other times it makes the animosity of the nation subservient to projects of hostility, instigated by pride, ambition, and other sinister and pernicious motives. The peace often, sometimes perhaps the liberty, of nations has been the victim.

So, likewise, a passionate attachment of one nation for another produces a variety of evils. Sympathy for the favorite nation, facilitating the illusion of an imaginary common interest in cases where no real common interest exists, and infusing into one the enmities of the other, betrays the former into a participation in the quarrels and wars of the latter without adequate inducement or justification. It leads also to concessions to the favorite nation of privileges denied to others, which is apt doubly to injure the nation making the concessions by unnecessarily parting with what ought to have been retained, and by exciting jealousy, ill will, and a disposition to retaliate in the parties from whom equal privileges are withheld; and it gives to ambitious, corrupted, or deluded citizens (who devote themselves to the favorite nation) facility to betray or sacrifice the interests of their own country without odium, sometimes even with popularity, gilding with the appearances of a virtuous sense of obligation, a commendable deference for public opinion, or a laudable zeal for public good the base or foolish compliances of ambition, corruption, or infatuation. . . .

The great rule of conduct for us in regard to foreign nations is, in extending our commercial relations to have with them as little *political* connection as possible. So far as we have already formed engagements let them be fulfilled with perfect good faith. Here let us stop.

Europe has a set of primary interests which to us have none or a very remote relation. Hence she must be engaged in frequent controversies, the causes of which are essentially foreign to our concerns. Hence, therefore, it must be unwise in us to implicate ourselves by artificial ties in the ordinary vicissitudes of her politics or the ordinary combinations and collisions of her friendships or enmities.

Our detached and distant situation invites and enables us to pursue a different course. If we remain one people, under an efficient government, the period is not far off when we may defy material injury from external annoyance; when we may take such an attitude as will cause the neutrality we may at any time resolve upon to be scrupulously respected; when belligerent nations, under the impossibility of making acquisitions upon us, will not lightly hazard the giving us provocation; when we may choose peace or war, as our interest, guided by justice, shall counsel.

Why forgo the advantages of so peculiar a situation? Why quit our own to stand upon foreign ground? Why, by interweaving our destiny with that of any part of Europe, entangle our peace and prosperity in the toils of European ambition, rivalship, interest, humor, or caprice?

It is our true policy to steer clear of permanent alliances with any portion of the foreign world, so far, I mean, as we are now at liberty to do it; for let me not be understood as capable of patronizing infidelity to existing engagements. I hold the maxim no less applicable to public than to private affairs that honesty is always the best policy. I repeat, therefore, let those engagements be observed in their genuine sense. But in my opinion it is unnecessary and would be unwise to extend them.

Taking care always to keep ourselves by suitable establishments on a respectable defensive posture, we may safely trust to temporary alliances for extraordinary emergencies.

Harmony, liberal intercourse with all nations are recommended by policy, humanity, and interest. But even our commercial policy should hold an equal and impartial hand, neither seeking nor granting exclusive favors or preferences; consulting the natural course of things; diffusing and diversifying by gentle means the streams of commerce, but forcing nothing; establishing with powers so disposed, in order to give trade a stable course, to define the rights of our merchants, and to enable the Government to support them, conventional rules of intercourse, the best that present circumstances and mutual opinion will permit, but temporary and liable to be from time to time abandoned or varied as experience and circumstances shall dictate; constantly keeping in view that it is folly in one nation to look for disinterested favors from another; that it must pay with a portion of its independence for whatever it may accept under that character; that by such acceptance it may place itself in the condition of having given equivalents for nominal favors, and yet of being reproached with ingratitude for not giving more. There can be no greater error than to expect or calculate upon real favors from nation to nation. It is an illusion which experience must cure, which a just pride ought to discard.

In offering to you, my countrymen, these councels of an old and affectionate friend, I dare not hope they will make the strong and lasting impression I could wish; that they will control the usual current of the passions, or prevent our nation from running the course which has hitherto marked the destiny of all nations. But, if I may flatter myself, that they may be productive of some partial benefit, some occasional good; that they may now and then recur to moderate the fury of party spirit, to warn against the mischiefs of foreign intrigue, to guard against the impostures of pretended patriotism; this hope will be a full recompense for the solicitude for your welfare, by which they have been dictated.

112 JAMES MONROE

FROM *"The Monroe Doctrine" (1823)*

Fellow-citizens of the Senate and the house of representatives:
A precise knowledge of our relations with foreign powers as respects our negotiations and transactions with each is thought to be particularly necessary. . . .

At the proposal of the Russian Imperial government, made through the minister of the emperor residing here, full power and instructions have been transmitted to the minister of the United States at St. Petersburg to arrange by amicable negotiation the respective rights and interests of the two nations on the northwest coast of this continent. A similar proposal had been made by His Imperial Majesty to the government of Great Britain, which has likewise been acceded to. The government of the United States has been desirous, by this friendly proceeding, of manifesting the great value which they have invariably attached to the friendship of the emperor and their solicitude to cultivate the best understanding with his government.

In the discussions to which this interest has given rise and in the arrangements by which they may terminate the occasion has been judged proper for asserting, as a principle in which the rights and interests of the United States are involved, that the American continents, by the free and independent condition which they have assumed and maintain, are henceforth not to be considered as subjects for future colonization by any European powers. . . .

It was stated at the commencement of the last session that great effort was then making in Spain and Portugal to improve the condition of the people of those countries and that it appeared to be conducted with extraordinary moderation. It need scarcely be remarked that the result has been so far very different from what was then anticipated. Of events in that quarter of the globe with which we have so much intercourse and from which we derive our origin, we have always been anxious and interested spectators. The citizens of the United States cherish sentiments the most friendly in favor of the liberty and happiness of their fellowmen on that side of the Atlantic. In the wars of the European powers in matters relating to themselves we have never taken any part, nor does it comport with our policy so to do. It is only when our rights are invaded or seriously menaced that we resent injuries or make preparation for our defense.

With the movements in this hemisphere we are of necessity more immediately connected, and by causes which must be obvious to all enlightened and impartial observers. The political system of the allied powers is essentially different in this respect from that of America. This difference proceeds from that which exists in their respective governments; and to the defense of our own, which has been achieved by the loss of so much blood and treasure, and matured by the wisdom of their most enlightened citizens, and under which we have enjoyed unexampled felicity, this whole nation is devoted. We owe it, therefore, to candor and to the amicable relations existing between the United States and those powers to declare that we should consider any attempt on their part to extend their system to any portion of this hemisphere as dangerous to our peace and safety.

With the existing colonies or dependencies of any European power we have not interfered and shall not interfere. But with the governments who have declared their independence and maintained it, and whose independence we have, on great consideration and on just principles, acknowledged, we could not view any interposition for the purpose of oppressing them, or controlling in any other manner their destiny, by any European power in any other light than as the manifestation of an unfriendly disposition toward the United States. In the war between those new governments and Spain we declared our neutrality at the time of their recognition, and to this we have adhered, and shall continue to adhere, provided no change shall occur which, in the judgment of the competent authorities of this government, shall make a corresponding change on the part of the United States indispensable to their security.

The late events in Spain and Portugal show that Europe is still unsettled. Of this important fact no stronger proof can be adduced than that the allied powers should have thought it proper, on any principle satisfactory to themselves, to have interposed by force in the internal concerns of Spain. To what extent such interposition may be carried, on the same principle, is a question in which all independent powers whose governments differ from theirs are interested, even those most remote, and surely none more so than the United States.

Our policy in regard to Europe, which was adopted at an early stage of the wars which have so long agitated that quarter of the globe, nevertheless remains the same, which is not to interfere in the internal concerns of any of its powers; to consider the government de facto as the legitimate government for us; to cultivate friendly relations with it, and to preserve those relations by a frank, firm, and manly policy, meeting in all instances the just claims of every power, submitting to injuries from none. But in regard to those continents, circumstances are eminently and conspicuously different. It is impossible that the allied powers should extend their political system to any portion of either continent without endangering our peace and happiness; nor can anyone believe that our southern brethren, if left to themselves, would adopt it of their own accord.

It is equally impossible, therefore, that we should behold such interposition in any form with indifference. If we look to the comparative strength and resources of Spain and those new governments, and their distance from each other, it must be obvious that she can never subdue them. It is still the true policy of the United States to leave the parties to themselves, in the hope that other powers will pursue the same course.

113 CHARLES A. BEARD

FROM *"A Foreign Policy for America"* (1940)

The primary foreign policy for the United States may be called for convenience Continental Americanism. The two words imply a concentration of interest on the continental domain and on building here a civilization in many respects peculiar to American life and the potentials of the American heritage. In concrete terms the words mean non-intervention in the controversies and wars of Europe and Asia and resistance to the intrusion of European or Asiatic powers, systems, and imperial ambitions into the western hemisphere. This policy is positive. It is clear-cut. And it was maintained with consistency while the Republic was being founded, democracy extended, and an American civilization developed.

So protected by foreign policy, American civilization stood in marked contrast to the semi-feudal civilizations of Europe, and the country was long regarded as an asylum for the oppressed of all lands. America, it was boasted, offered to toiling masses the example of a nation free from huge conscript armies, staggering debts, and mountainous taxes. For more than a hundred years, while this system lasted, millions of immigrants, fleeing from the wars, oppressions, persecutions, and poverty of Europe, found a haven here; and enlightened Europeans with popular sympathies rejoiced in the fortunes of the United States and in the demonstration of liberty, with all its shortcomings, made on this continent in the presence of the tyrannies of the earth.

No mere adherence to theory or tradition marked the rise and growth of continentalism. The policy was realistically framed with reference to the exigencies of the early Republic and was developed during continuous experience with the vicissitudes of European ambitions, controversies, and wars. When other policies were proposed and departures were made from the established course, continentalism remained a driving force in thought about American foreign policy.

All through the years it was associated with a conception of American civilization. In the beginning the conception was primarily concerned with forms of culture appropriate to the rising Republic; during the middle period of American history it was enlarged and enriched under the influence of democratic vistas; and, despite the spread of industrialism in the later years, its characteristic features were powerful factors in shaping the course of American events. . . .

Until near the close of the nineteenth century, the continental policy of non-interference in the disputes of European nations was followed by the Government of the United States with a consistency which almost amounted to a fixed rule. Washington had formulated it. Monroe had extended and applied it. Seward had restated and re-emphasized it. Qualified by the Monroe doctrine as to European intervention in this hemisphere, it seemed to be settled for all time as the nation celebrated the hundredth anniversary of its independence.

But the promise of undisturbed permanence was illusory, for another conception of foreign policy for America was already on the horizon. That was the conception of imperialism, world power, and active participation in the great conflicts of interests everywhere. . . .

Owing to the over-seas character of imperialist operations, naval bureaucrats, naval supply interests, and armor-plate makers naturally furnished practical considerations, while an intelligentsia was educating the people into espousing and praising the new course. As roving men, cruising around over the oceans, American naval officers had early come into contact with American merchants abroad, engaged in garnering better profits in trade than they could expect to reap at home. They saw foreign lands in the Orient and other distant places which, they thought, could be easily seized by the United States and turned into sea bases or trading posts. . . .

In summary, under fine phrases, manufactured for the occasion, pleasing to the popular ear, and gratifying to national vanity, politicians in control of the Government of the United States entangled the country in numerous quarrels in Asia and Europe. They made commitments difficult, if not impossible to cancel. They carried on a campaign of agitation designed to educate the people into the belief that the new course was necessary for the very well-being of the country and at the same time made for international peace and good will. They built up in the State Department a bureaucracy and a tradition absolutely opposed to historic continentalism.

Perhaps unwittingly they prepared the way for the next stage in the development of American foreign policy. From their participation in collective world politics, from the imperialist theory of "doing good to backward peoples," it was but a step to

President Wilson's scheme for permanent and open participation in European and Asiatic affairs in the alleged interest of universal peace and general welfare. . . .

The third foreign policy proposed for the United States is the internationalism which sets *world* peace as the fundamental objective for the Government in the conduct of relations with other countries. Exponents of the policy often claim a monopoly of the American peace movement and generally insist that only by following their methods can the United States obtain the blessings of peace for itself. Thus internationalism is to be distinguished sharply from the policy of keeping peace for the United States within its continental zone of interests and maintaining pacific relations elsewhere, subject to the primacy of security for American civilization and civil liberties.

Internationalism so defined is marked by specific features. It proposes to connect the United States with the European State system by permanent ties, for the accomplishment of its alleged end. It rejects the doctrine of continental independence which was proclaimed in the effort of 1776 to cut America loose from the entanglements associated with its status as a dominion of the British empire. In taking this position, internationalists also make many assumptions respecting the nature of world history and the possibilities of European politics. They assume that permanent world peace is not only desirable but is indivisible and can be obtained by the pursuit of their methods, especially if the United States will associate itself with certain nations supposed to be committed to permanent peace.

According to the internationalist hypothesis, Americans who advocate peace for the United States in the presence of European and Asiatic wars are not peace advocates in the true sense. In the internationalist view, such advocates are not contributing to peace – they are isolationists pursuing a policy which leads to armaments and wars. In internationalist literature, these peace advocates are frequently represented as selfish, cowardly, and immoral persons, who merely wish "to save their own skins," who refuse to recognize the obligations of the United States to other nations suffering not from their own follies but from the neglect of the American people. Hence there arises an apparently irreconcilable contradiction between advocates of permanent world peace and advocates of peace for the American continent and of pacific measures as constant instruments of American foreign policy. . . .

As an outcome of the historical heritage, American foreign policy became a loose intermingling of conflicting elements – continentalism, imperialism, and internationalism. Each of the three programs was supported, more or less, by specific interests and portions of the intelligentsia. At every crisis in world affairs, as the running fire of debate on foreign events continued in the United States, each school maneuvered for possession of the American mind and the direction of policy, through propaganda and the varied use of communication agencies. In the polls of public opinion, the winds of doctrine veered and twisted.

Yet at repeated tests, taken in formal elections and congressional battles, the principal body of that opinion was found consistently on the side of continentalism. Despite temporary victories, politicians who tried to swing the United States off its continental center of gravity toward imperialism or internationalism were never completely successful. . . .

This continentalism did not seek to make a "hermit" nation out of America. From the very beginning under the auspices of the early Republic, it never had embraced that impossible conception. It did not deny the obvious fact that American civilization had made use of its European heritages, was a part of western civilization, and had continuous contacts with Occidental and Oriental cultures. It did not deny the obvious fact that wars in Europe and Asia "affect" or "concern" the United States. . . . It did not mean "indifference" to the sufferings of Europe or China (or India or Ethiopia). In truth, in all history, no people ever poured out treasure more generously in aid of human distresses in every quarter of the globe – distresses springing from wars, famines, revolutions, persecutions, and earthquakes.

With reference to such conflicts and sufferings, continentalism merely meant a recognition of the limited nature of American powers to relieve, restore, and maintain life beyond its own sphere of interest and control – a recognition of the hard fact that the United States, either alone or in any coalition, did not possess the power to force peace on Europe and Asia, to assure the establishment of democratic and pacific governments there, or to provide the social and economic underwriting necessary to the perdurance of such governments.

114 HARRY TRUMAN

"The Truman Doctrine" (1947)

The gravity of the situation which confronts the world today necessitates my appearance before a joint session of the Congress. The foreign policy and the national security of this country are involved.

One aspect of the present situation, which I wish to present to you at this time for your consideration and decision, concerns Greece and Turkey.

The United States has received from the Greek Government an urgent appeal for financial and economic assistance. Preliminary reports from the American Economic Mission now in Greece and reports from the American Ambassador in Greece corroborate the statement of the Greek Government that assistance is imperative if Greece is to survive as a free nation.

I do not believe that the American people and the Congress wish to turn a deaf ear to the appeal of the Greek Government.

Greece is not a rich country. Lack of sufficient natural resources has always forced the Greek people to work hard to make both ends meet. Since 1940, this industrious and peace loving country has suffered invasion, four years of cruel enemy occupation, and bitter internal strife. . . .

The very existence of the Greek state is today threatened by the terrorist activities of several thousand armed men, led by Communists, who defy the Government's authority at a number of points, particularly along the northern boundaries. . . . Meanwhile, the Greek Government is unable to cope with the situation. The Greek army is small and poorly equipped. It needs supplies and equipment if it is to restore the authority of the government throughout Greek territory. Greece must have assistance if it is to become a self-supporting and self-respecting democracy.

The United States must supply this assistance. We have already extended to Greece certain types of relief and economic aid but these are inadequate. There is no other country to which democratic Greece can turn. No other nation is willing and able to provide the necessary support for a democratic Greek Government. The British Government, which has been helping Greece, can give no further financial or economic aid after March 31. Great Britain finds itself under the necessity of reducing or liquidating its commitments in several parts of the world, including Greece.

We have considered how the United Nations might assist in this crisis. But the situation is an urgent one requiring immediate action, and the United Nations and its related organizations are not in a position to extend help of the kind that is required.

It is important to note that the Greek Government has asked for our aid in utilizing effectively the financial and other assistance we may give to Greece, and in improving its public administration. It is of the utmost importance that we supervise the use of any funds made available to Greece; in such a manner that each dollar spent will count toward making Greece self-supporting, and will help to build an economy in which a healthy democracy can flourish.

No government is perfect. One of the chief virtues of a democracy, however, is that its defects are always visible and under democratic processes can be pointed out and corrected. The Government of Greece is not perfect. Nevertheless it represents eighty-five per cent of the members of the Greek Parliament who were chosen in an election last year. Foreign observers, including 692 Americans, considered this election to be a fair expression of the views of the Greek people. . . .

I am fully aware of the broad implications involved if the United States extends assistance to Greece and Turkey, and I shall discuss these implications with you at this time.

One of the primary objectives of the foreign policy of the United States is the creation of conditions in which we and other nations will be able to work out a way of life free from coercion. This was a fundamental issue in the war with Germany and Japan, our victory was won over countries which sought to impose their will, and their way of life, upon other nations.

To ensure the peaceful development of nations, free from coercion, the United States has taken a leading part in establishing the United Nations. The United Nations is designed to make possible lasting freedom and independence for all its members. We shall not realize our objectives, however, unless we are willing to help free peoples to maintain their free institutions and their national integrity against aggressive movements that seek to impose on them totalitarian regimes. This is no more than a frank recognition that totalitarian regimes imposed on free peoples, by direct or indirect aggression, undermine the foundations of international peace and hence the security of the United States.

The peoples of a number of countries of the world have recently had totalitarian regimes forced upon them against their will. The Government of the United States has made frequent protests against coercion and intimidation, in violation of the Yalta Agreement, in Poland, Rumania and Bulgaria. I must also state that in a number of other countries there have been similar developments.

At the present moment in world history nearly every nation must choose between alternative ways of life. The choice is too often not a free one.

One way of life is based upon the will of the majority, and is distinguished by free institutions, representative government, free elections, guarantees of individual liberty, freedom of speech and religion, and freedom from political oppression.

The second way of life is based upon the will of the minority forcibly imposed upon the majority. It relies upon terror and oppression, a controlled press and radio, fixed elections, and the suppression of personal freedoms.

I believe that it must be the policy of the United States to support free peoples who are resisting attempted subjugation by armed minorities or by outside pressures.

I believe that we must assist free peoples to work out their own destinies in their own way.

I believe that our help should be primarily through economic and financial aid which is essential to economic stability and orderly political processes.

The world is not static, and the status quo is not sacred. But we cannot allow changes in the status quo in violation of the Charter of the United Nations by such methods as coercion, or by such subterfuges as political infiltration. In helping free and independent nations to maintain their freedom, the United States will be giving effect to the principles of the Charter of the United Nations.

It is necessary only to glance at a map to realize that the survival and integrity of the Greek nation are of grave importance in a much wider situation. If Greece should fall under the control of an armed minority, the effect upon its neighbor, Turkey, would be immediate and serious. Confusion and disorder might well spread throughout the entire Middle East.

Moreover, the disappearance of Greece as an independent state would have a profound effect upon those countries in Europe whose peoples are struggling against great difficulties to maintain their freedoms and their independence while they repair the damages of war.

It would be an unspeakable tragedy if these countries, which have struggled so long against overwhelming odds, should lose that victory for which they sacrificed so much. Collapse of free institutions and loss of independence would be disastrous not only for them but for the world. Discouragement and possibly failure would quickly be the lot of neighboring peoples striving to maintain their freedom and independence.

Should we fail to aid Greece and Turkey in this fateful hour, the effect will be far-reaching to the West as well as to the East.

We must take immediate and resolute action.

I therefore ask the Congress to provide authority for assistance to Greece and Turkey in the amount of $400,000,000 for the period ending June 30, 1948. In requesting these funds, I have taken into consideration the maximum amount of relief assistance which would be furnished to Greece out of the $350,000,000 which I recently requested that the Congress authorize for the prevention of starvation and suffering in countries devastated by the war.

In addition to funds, I ask the Congress to authorize the detail of American civilian and military personnel to Greece and Turkey, at the request of those countries, to assist in the tasks of reconstruction, and for the purpose of supervising the use of such financial and material assistance as may be furnished. I recommend that authority also be provided for the instruction and training of selected Greek and Turkish personnel.

Finally, I ask that the Congress provide authority which will permit the speediest and most effective use, in terms of needed commodities, supplies, and equipment, of such funds as may be authorized.

If further funds, or further authority, should be needed for purposes indicated in this message, I shall not hesitate to bring the situation before the Congress. On this subject the Executive and Legislative branches of the Government must work together.

This is a serious course upon which we embark.

I would not recommend it except that the alternative is much more serious. The United States contributed $341,000,000,000 toward winning World War II. This is an investment in world freedom and world peace.

The assistance that I am recommending for Greece and Turkey amounts to little more than one tenth of one per cent of this investment. It is only common sense that we should safeguard this investment and make sure that it was not in vain.

The seeds of totalitarian regimes are nurtured by misery and want. They spread and grow in the evil soil of poverty and strife. They reach their full growth when the hope of a people for a better life has died. We must keep that hope alive.

The free peoples of the world look to us for support in maintaining their freedoms.

If we falter in our leadership, we may endanger the peace of the world – and we shall surely endanger the welfare of our own nation.

Great responsibilities have been placed upon us by the swift movement of events. I am confident that the Congress will face these responsibilities squarely.

115 GEORGE C. MARSHALL

"The Marshall Plan" (1947)

I need not tell you gentlemen that the world situation is very serious. That must be apparent to all intelligent people. I think one difficulty is that the problem is one of such enormous complexity that the very mass of facts presented to the public by press and radio make it exceedingly difficult for the man in the street to reach a clear appraisement of the situation. Furthermore, the people of this country are distant from the troubled areas of the earth and it is hard for them to comprehend the plight and consequent reactions of the long-suffering peoples, and the effect of those reactions on their governments in connection with our efforts to promote peace in the world.

In considering the requirements for the rehabilitation of Europe the physical loss of life, the visible destruction of cities, factories, mines, and railroads was correctly estimated, but it has become obvious during recent months that this visible destruction was probably less serious than the dislocation of the entire fabric of European economy. For the past 10 years conditions have been highly abnormal. The feverish preparation for war and the more feverish maintenance of the war effort engulfed all aspects of national economies. Machinery has fallen into disrepair or is entirely obsolete. Under the arbitrary and destructive Nazi rule, virtually every possible enterprise was geared into the German war machine. Long-standing commercial ties, private institutions, banks, insurance companies and shipping companies disappeared through loss of capital, absorption through nationalization or by simple destruction. In many countries, confidence in the local currency has been severely shaken. The breakdown of the business structure of Europe during the war was complete. Recovery has been seriously retarded by the fact that 2 years after the close of hostilities a peace settlement with Germany and Austria has not been agreed upon. But even given a more prompt solution of these difficult problems, the rehabilitation of the economic structure of Europe quite evidently will require a much longer time and greater effort than had been foreseen.

There is a phase of this matter which is both interesting and serious. The farmer has always produced the foodstuffs to exchange with the city dweller for the other necessities of life. This division of labor is the basis of modern civilization. At the present time it is threatened with breakdown. The town and city industries are not producing adequate goods to exchange with the food-producing farmer. Raw materials and fuel are in short supply. Machinery is lacking or worn out. The farmer or the peasant cannot find the goods for sale which he desires to purchase. So the sale of his farm produce for money which he cannot use seems to him an unprofitable transaction. He, therefore, has withdrawn many fields from crop culivation and is using them for grazing. He feeds more grain to stock and finds for himself and his family an ample supply of food, however short he may be on clothing and the other ordinary gadgets of civilization. Meanwhile people in the cities are short of food and fuel. So the governments are forced to use their foreign money and credits to procure these necessities abroad. This process exhausts funds which are urgently needed for reconstruction. Thus a very serious situation is rapidly developing which bodes no good for the world. The modern system of the division of labor upon which the exchange of products is based is in danger of breaking down.

The truth of the matter is that Europe's requirements for the next 3 or 4 years of foreign food and other essential products – principally from America – are so much greater than her present ability to pay that she must have substantial additional help, or face economic, social, and political deterioration of a very grave character.

The remedy lies in breaking the vicious circle and restoring the confidence of the European people in the economic future of their own countries and of Europe as a whole. The manufacturer and the farmer throughout wide areas must be able and willing to exchange their products for currencies the continuing value of which is not open to question.

Aside from the demoralizing effect on the world at large and the possibilities of disturbances arising as a result of the desperation of the people concerned, the consequences to the economy of the United States should be apparent to all. It is logical that the United States should do whatever it is able to do to assist in the return of normal economic health in the world, without which there can be no political stability and no assured peace. Our policy is directed not against any country or doctrine but against hunger, poverty, desperation, and chaos. Its purpose should be the revival of a working economy in the world so as to permit the emergence of political and social conditions in which free institutions can exist. Such assistance, I am convinced, must not be on a piecemeal basis as various crises develop. Any assistance that this Government may render in the future should provide a cure rather than a mere palliative. Any government that is willing to assist in the task of recovery will find full cooperation, I am sure, on the part of the United States Government. Any government which maneuvers to block the recovery of other countries cannot expect help from us. Furthermore, governments, political parties, or groups which seek to perpetuate human misery in order to profit therefrom politically or otherwise will encounter the opposition of the United States.

It is already evident that, before the United States Government can proceed much further in its efforts to alleviate the situation and help start the European world on its way to recovery, there must be some agreement among the countries of Europe as to the requirements of the situation and the part those countries themselves will take in order to give proper effect to whatever action might be undertaken by this Government. It would be neither fitting nor efficacious for this Government to undertake to draw up unilaterally a program designed to place Europe on its feet economically. This is the business of the Europeans. The initiative, I think, must come from Europe. The role of this country should consist of friendly aid in the drafting of a European program and of later support of such a program so far as it may be practical for us to do so. The program should be a joint one, agreed to by a number, if not all European nations.

An essential part of any successful action on the part of the United States is an understanding on the part of the people of America of the character of the problem and the remedies to be applied. Political passion and prejudice should have no part. With foresight, and a willingness on the part of our people to face up to the vast responsibility which history has clearly placed upon our country, the difficulties I have outlined can and will be overcome.

116 JOSEPH McCARTHY

FROM *"The Wheeling Speech" (1950)*

Ladies and gentlemen, tonight as we celebrate the one hundred and forty-first birthday of one of the greatest men in American history, I would like to be able to talk about what a glorious day today is in the history of the world. As we celebrate the birth of this man who with his whole heart and soul hated war, I would like to be able to speak of peace in our time, of war being outlawed, and of worldwide disarmament. These would be truly appropriate things to be able to mention as we celebrate the birthday of Abraham Lincoln.

Five years after a world war has been won, men's hearts should anticipate a long peace, and men's minds should be free from the heavy weight that comes with war. But this is not such a period – for this is not a period of peace. This is a time of the "cold war." This is a time when all the world is split into two vast, increasingly hostile armed camps – a time of a great armaments race.

Today we can almost physically hear the mutterings and rumblings of an invigorated god of war. You can see it, feel it, and hear it all the way from the hills of Indochina, from the shores of Formosa, right over into the very heart of Europe itself.

The one encouraging thing is that the "mad moment" has not yet arrived for the firing of the gun or the exploding of the bomb which will set civilization about the final task of destroying itself. There is still a hope for peace if we finally decide that no longer can we safely blind our eyes and close our ears to those facts which are shaping up more and more clearly. And that is that we are now engaged in a show-down fight – not the usual war between nations for land areas or other material gains, but a war between two diametrically opposed ideologies.

The great difference between our western Christian world and the atheistic Communist world is not political, ladies and gentlemen, it is moral. There are other differences, of course, but those could be reconciled. For instance, the Marxian idea of confiscating the land and factories and running the entire economy as a single enterprise is momentous. Likewise, Lenin's invention of the one-party police state as a way to make Marx's idea work is hardly less momentous.

Stalin's resolute putting across of these two ideas, of course, did much to divide the world. With only those differences, however, the East and the West could most certainly still live in peace.

The real, basic difference, however, lies in the religion of immoralism – invented by Marx, preached feverishly by Lenin, and carried to unimaginable extremes by Stalin. This religion of immoralism, if the Red half of the world wins – and well it may – this religion of immoralism will more deeply wound and damage mankind than any conceivable economic or political system.

Karl Marx dismissed God as a hoax, and Lenin and Stalin have added in clear-cut, unmistakable language their resolve that no nation, no people who believe in a God, can exist side by side with their communistic state.

Karl Marx, for example, expelled people from his Communist Party for mentioning such things as justice, humanity, or morality. He called this soulful ravings and sloppy sentimentality.

While Lincoln was a relatively young man in his late thirties, Karl Marx boasted that the Communist specter was haunting Europe. Since that time, hundreds of millions of people and vast areas of the world have fallen under Communist domination. Today, less than 100 years after Lincoln's death, Stalin brags that this Communist specter is not only haunting the world, but is about to completely subjugate it.

Today we are engaged in a final, all-out battle between communistic atheism and Christianity. The modern champions of communism have selected this as the time. And, ladies and gentlemen, the chips are down – they are truly down.

Lest there be any doubt that the time has been chosen, let us go directly to the leader of communism today – Joseph Stalin. Here is what he said – not back in 1928, not before the war, not during the war – but 2 years after the last war was ended: "To think that the Communist revolution can be carried out peacefully, within the framework of a Christian democracy, means one has either gone out of one's mind and lost all normal understanding, or has grossly and openly repudiated the Communist revolution."

And this is what was said by Lenin in 1919, which was also quoted with approval by Stalin in 1947:

"We are living," said Lenin, "not merely in a state, but in a system of states, and the existence of the Soviet Republic side by side with Christian states for a long time is unthinkable. One or the other must triumph in the end. And before that end supervenes, a series of frightful collisions between the Soviet Republic and the Bourgeois states will be inevitable."

Ladies and gentlemen, can there be anyone here tonight who is so blind as to say that the war is not on? Can there be anyone who fails to realize that the Communist world has said, "The time is now" – that this is the time for the show-down between the democratic Christian world and the Communist atheistic world?

Unless we face this fact, we shall pay the price that must be paid by those who wait too long.

Six years ago, at the time of the first conference to map out the peace – Dumbarton Oaks – there were within the Soviet orbit 180,000,000 people. Lined up on the antitotalitarian side there were in the world at that time roughly 1,625,000,000 people. Today, only 6 years later, there are 800,000,000 people under the absolute domination of Soviet Russia – an increase of over 400 percent. On our side, the figure has shrunk to around 500,000,000. In other words, in less than 6 years the odds have changed from 9 to 1 in our favor to 8 to 5 against us. This indicates the swiftness of the tempo of Communist victories and American defeats in the cold war. As one of our outstanding historical figures once said, "When a great democracy is destroyed, it will not be because of enemies from without, but rather because of enemies from within."

The truth of this statement is becoming terrifyingly clear as we see this country each day losing on every front.

At war's end we were physically the strongest nation on earth and, at least potentially, the most powerful intellectually and morally. Ours could have been the honor of being a beacon in the desert of destruction, a shining living proof that civilization was not yet ready to destroy itself. Unfortunately, we have failed miserably and tragically to arise to the opportunity.

The reason why we find ourselves in a position of impotency is not because our only powerful potential enemy has sent men to invade our shores, but rather because of the traitorous actions of those who have been treated so well by this Nation. It has not been the less fortunate or members of minority groups who have been selling this Nation out, but rather those who have had all the benefits that the wealthiest nation on earth has had to offer – the finest homes, the finest college education, and the finest jobs in Government we can give.

This is glaringly true in the State Department. There the bright young men who are born with silver spoons in their mouths are the ones who have been worst.

Now I know it is very easy for anyone to condemn a particular bureau or department in general terms. Therefore I would like to cite one rather unusual case – the case of a man who has done much to shape our foreign policy.

When Chiang Kai-shek was fighting our war, the State Department had in China a young man named John S. Service. His task, obviously, was not to work for the communization of China. Strangely, however, he sent official reports back to the State Department urging that we torpedo our ally Chiang Kai-shek and stating, in effect, that communism was the best hope of China.

Later, this man – John Service – was picked up by the Federal Bureau of Investigation for turning over to the Communists secret State Department information. Strangely, however, he was never prosecuted. However, Joseph Grew, the Under Secretary of State, who insisted on his prosecution, was forced to resign. Two days after Grew's successor, Dean Acheson, took over as Under Secretary of State, this man – John Service – who had been picked up by the FBI and who had previously urged that communism was the best hope of China, was not only reinstated in the State Department but promoted. And finally, under Acheson, placed in charge of all placements and promotions.

Today, ladies and gentlemen, this man Service is on his way to represent the State Department and Acheson in Calcutta – by far and away the most important listening post in the Far East.

Now, let's see what happens when individuals with Communist connections are forced out of the State Department. Gustave Duran, who was labeled as (I quote) "a notorious international Communist," was made assistant to the Assistant Secretary of State in charge of Latin American affairs. He was taken into the State Department from his job as a lieutenant colonel in the Communist International Brigade. Finally, after intense congressional pressure and criticism, he resigned in 1946 from the State Department – and, ladies and gentlemen, where do you think he is now? He took over a high-salaried job as Chief of Cultural Activities Section in the office of the Assistant Secretary General of the United Nations.

Then there was a Mrs. Mary Jane Kenny, from the Board of Economic Warfare in the State Department, who was named in an FBI report and in a House committee report as a courier for the Communist Party while working for the Government. And where do you think Mrs. Kenny is – she is now an editor in the United Nations Document Bureau.

Another interesting case was that of Julian H. Wadleigh, economist in the Trade Agreements Section of the State Department for 11 years and [sic] was sent to Turkey and Italy and other countries as United States representative. After the statute of limitations had run so he could not be prosecuted for treason, he openly and brazenly not only admitted but proclaimed that he had been a member of the Communist Party . . . that while working for the State Department he stole a vast number of secret documents . . . and furnished these documents to the Russian spy ring of which he was a part.

You will recall last spring there was held in New York what was known as the World Peace Conference – a conference which was labeled by the State Department and Mr. Truman as the sounding board for Communist propaganda and a front for Russia. Dr. Harlow Shapley was the chairman of that conference. Interestingly enough, according to the new release put out by the Department in July, the Secretary of State appointed Shapley on a commission which acts as liaison between UNESCO and the State Department.

This, ladies and gentlemen, gives you somewhat of a picture of the type of individuals who have been helping to shape our foreign policy. In my opinion the State Department, which is one of the most important government departments, is thoroughly infested with Communists.

I have in my hand 57 cases of individuals who would appear to be either card carrying members or certainly loyal to the Communist Party, but who nevertheless are still helping to shape our foreign policy.

One thing to remember in discussing the Communists in our Government is that we are not dealing with spies who get 30 pieces of silver to steal the blueprints of a new weapon. We are dealing with a far more sinister type of activity because it permits the enemy to guide and shape our policy. . . .

This brings us down to the case of one Alger Hiss who is important not as an individual any more, but rather because he is so representative of a group in the State Department. It is unnecessary to go over the sordid events showing how he sold out the Nation which had given him so much. Those are rather fresh in all of our minds.

However, it should be remembered that the facts in regard to his connection with this international Communist spy ring were made known to the then Under Secretary of State Berle 3 days after Hitler and Stalin signed the Russo-German alliance pact. At that time one Whittaker Chambers – who was also part of the spy ring – apparently decided that with Russia on Hitler's side, he could no longer betray our Nation to Russia. He gave Under Secretary of State Berle – and this is all a matter of record – practically all, if not more, of the facts upon which Hiss' conviction was based.

Under Secretary Berle promptly contacted Dean Acheson and received word in return that Acheson (and I quote) "could vouch for Hiss absolutely" – at which time the matter was dropped. And this, you understand, was at a time when Russia was an ally of Germany. This condition existed while Russia and Germany were invading and dismembering Poland, and while the Communist groups here were screaming "warmonger" at the United States for their support of the allied nations.

Again in 1943, the FBI had occasion to investigate the facts surrounding Hiss' contacts with the Russian spy ring. But even after that FBI report was submitted, nothing was done.

Then late in 1948 – on August 5 – when the Un-American Activities Committee called Alger Hiss to give an accounting, President Truman at once issued a Presidential directive ordering all Government agencies to refuse to turn over any information whatsoever in regard to the Communist activities of any Government employee to a congressional committee.

Incidentally, even after Hiss was convicted – it is interesting to note that the President still labeled the exposé of Hiss as a "red herring."

If time permitted, it might be well to go into detail about the fact that Hiss was Roosevelt's chief adviser at Yalta when Roosevelt was admittedly in ill health and tired physically and mentally . . . and when, according to the Secretary of State, Hiss and Gromyko drafted the report on the conference.

According to the then Secretary of State Stettinius, here are some of the things that Hiss helped to decide at Yalta. (1) The establishment of a European High Commission; (2) the treatment of Germany – this you will recall was the conference at which it was decided that we would occupy Berlin with Russia occupying an area completely circling the city, which, as you know, resulted in the Berlin airlift which cost 31 American lives; (3) the Polish question; (4) the relationship between UNRRA and the Soviet Union; (5) the rights of Americans on control commissions of Rumania, Bulgaria, and Hungary; (6) Iran; (7) China – here's where we gave away Manchuria; (8) Turkish Straits question; (9) international trusteeships; (10) Korea.

Of the results of this conference, Arthur Bliss Lane of the State Department had this to say: "As I glanced over the document, I could not believe my eyes. To me, almost every line spoke of a surrender to Stalin."

As you hear this story of high treason, I know that you are saying to yourself, "Well, why doesn't the Congress do something about it?" Actually, ladies and gentlemen, one of the important reasons for the graft, the corruption, the dishonesty, the disloyalty, the treason in high Government positions – one of the most important reasons why this continues is a lack of moral uprising on the part of the 140,000,000 American people. In the light of history, however, this is not hard to explain.

It is the result of an emotional hang-over and a temporary moral lapse which follows every war. It is the apathy to evil which people who have been subjected to the tremendous evils of war feel. As the people of the world see mass murder, the destruction of defenseless and innocent people, and all of the crime and lack of morals which go with war, they become numb and apathetic. It has always been thus after war.

However, the morals of our people have not been destroyed. They still exist. This cloak of numbness and apathy has only needed a spark to rekindle them. Happily, this spark has finally been supplied.

117 LYNDON B. JOHNSON

"American Policy in Viet-Nam" (1965)

Over this war – and all Asia – is another reality: the deepening shadow of Communist China. The rulers in Hanoi are urged on by Peking. This is a regime which has destroyed freedom in Tibet, which has attacked India, and has been condemned by the United Nations for aggression in Korea. It is a nation which is helping the forces of violence in almost every continent. The contest in Viet-Nam is part of a wider pattern of aggressive purposes.

Why are these realities our concern? Why are we in South Viet-Nam?

We are there because we have a promise to keep. Since 1954 every American President has offered support to the people of South Viet-Nam. We have helped to build, and we have helped to defend. Thus, over many years, we have made a national pledge to help South Viet-Nam defend its independence.

And I intend to keep that promise.

To dishonor that pledge, to abandon this small and brave nation to its enemies, and to the terror that must follow, would be an unforgivable wrong.

We are also there to strengthen world order. Around the globe, from Berlin to Thailand, are people whose well-being rests, in part, on the belief that they can count on us if they are attacked. To leave Viet-Nam to its fate would shake the confidence of all these people in the value of an American commitment and in the value of America's word. The result would be increased unrest and instability, and even wider war.

We are also there because there are great stakes in the balance. Let no one think for a moment that retreat from Viet-Nam would bring an end to conflict. The battle would be renewed in one country and then another. The central lesson of our time is that the appetite of aggression is never satisfied. To withdraw from one battlefield means only to prepare for the next. We must say in Southeast Asia – as we did in Europe – in the words of the Bible: "Hitherto shalt thou come, but no further."

There are those who say that all our effort there will be futile – that China's power is such that it is bound to dominate all Southeast Asia. But there is no end to that argument until all of the nations of Asia are swallowed up.

There are those who wonder why we have a responsibility there. Well, we have it there for the same reason that we have a responsibility for the defense of Europe. World War II was fought in both Europe and Asia, and when it ended we found ourselves with continued responsibility for the defense of freedom.

Our objective is the independence of South Viet-Nam and its freedom from attack. We want nothing for ourselves – only that the people of South Viet-Nam be allowed to guide their own country in their own way.

We will do everything necessary to reach that objective. And we will do only what is absolutely necessary.

In recent months attacks on South Viet-Nam were stepped up. Thus, it became necessary for us to increase our response and to make attacks by air. This is not a change of purpose. It is a change in what we believe that purpose requires.

We do this in order to slow down aggression.

We do this to increase the confidence of the brave people of South Viet-Nam who have bravely borne this brutal battle for so many years with so many casualties.

And we do this to convince the leaders of North Viet-Nam – and all who seek to share their conquest – of a very simple fact: We will not be defeated. We will not grow tired.

We will not withdraw, either openly or under the cloak of a meaningless agreement.

We know that air attacks alone will not accomplish all of these purposes. But it is our best and prayerful judgment that they are a necessary part of the surest road to peace.

We hope that peace will come swiftly. But that is in the hands of others besides ourselves. And we must be prepared for a long continued conflict. It will require patience as well as bravery, the will to endure as well as the will to resist.

I wish it were possible to convince others with words of what we now find it necessary to say with guns and planes: armed hostility is futile. Our resources are equal to any challenge. Because we fight for values and we fight for principles, rather than territory or colonies, our patience and our determination are unending.

Once this is clear, then it should also be clear that the only path for reasonable men is the path of peaceful settlement.

Such peace demands an independent South Viet-Nam – securely guaranteed and able to shape its own relationships to all others – free from outside interference – tied to no alliance – a military base for no other country.

These are the essentials of any final settlement.

We will never be second in the search for such a peaceful settlement in Viet-Nam.

There may be many ways to this kind of peace: in discussion or negotiation with the governments concerned; in large groups or in small ones; in the reaffirmation of old agreements or their strengthening with new ones.

We have stated this position over and over again, fifty times and more, to friend and foe alike. And we remain ready, with this purpose, for unconditional discussions.

And until that bright and necessary day of peace we will try to keep conflict from spreading. We have no desire to see thousands die in battle – Asians or Americans. We have no desire to devastate that which the people of North Viet-Nam have built with toil and sacrifice. We will use our power with restraint and with all the wisdom that we can command. But we will use it.

118 GEORGE BUSH

"The Launch of Attack on Iraq" (1991)

Just two hours ago, allied air forces began an attack on military targets in Iraq and Kuwait. These attacks continue as I speak. Ground forces are not engaged. This conflict started August 2nd when the dictator of Iraq invaded a small and helpless neighbor. Kuwait, a member of the Arab League and a member of the United Nations was crushed, its people brutalized.

Five months ago, Saddam Hussein started this cruel war against Kuwait; tonight the battle has been joined. This military action, taken in accord with United Nations resolutions and with the consent of the United States Congress, follows months of constant and virtually endless diplomatic activity on the part of the United Nations, the United States and many, many other countries. Arab leaders sought what became known as an Arab solution, only to conclude that Saddam Hussein was unwilling to leave Kuwait. Others travelled to Baghdad in a variety of efforts to restore peace and justice. Our Secretary of State James Baker held an historic meeting in Geneva only to be totally rebuffed. This past weekend, in a last ditch effort, the Secretary General of the United Nations went to the Middle East with peace in his heart – his second such mission and he came back from Baghdad with no progress at all in getting Saddam Hussein to withdraw from Kuwait. Now, the 28 countries with forces in the Gulf area have exhausted all reasonable efforts to reach a peaceful resolution, have no choice but to drive Saddam from Kuwait by force. We will not fail.

As I report to you, air attacks are underway against military targets in Iraq. We are determined to knock out Saddam Hussein's nuclear bomb potential. We will also destroy his chemical weapons facilities. Much of Saddam's artillery and tanks will be destroyed. Our operations are designed to best protect the lives of all the coalition forces by targeting Saddam's vast military arsenal. Initial reports from General Schwarzkopf are that our operations are proceeding according to plan.

Our objectives are clear. Saddam Hussein's forces will leave Kuwait. The legitimate government of Kuwait will be restored to its rightful place and Kuwait will once again be free.

Iraq will eventually comply with all relevant United Nations resolutions and then when peace is restored, it is our hope that Iraq will live as a peaceful and cooperative member of the family of nations, thus enhancing the security and stability of the Gulf.

Some may ask, "Why act now? Why not wait?" The answer is clear. The world could wait no longer. Sanctions, though having some effect, showed no signs of accomplishing their objective. Sanctions were tried for well over five months and we and our allies concluded that sanctions alone would not force Saddam from Kuwait.

While the world waited Saddam Hussein systematically raped, pillaged and plundered a tiny nation – no threat to his own. He subjected the people of Kuwait to unspeakable atrocities, and among those maimed and murdered – innocent children. While the world waited Saddam sought to add to the chemical weapons arsenal he now possesses an infinitely more dangerous weapon of mass destruction, a nuclear weapon.

And while the world waited, while the world talked peace and withdrawal Saddam Hussein dug in and moved massive forces into Kuwait. While the world waited, while Saddam stalled, more damage was being done to the fragile economies of the Third World, the emerging democracies of Eastern Europe, to the entire world, including to our own economy.

The United States, together with the United Nations, exhausted every means at our disposal to bring this crisis to a peaceful end. However, Saddam clearly felt that by stalling and threatening and defying the United Nations he could weaken the forces arrayed against him.

While the world waited Saddam Hussein met every overture of peace with open contempt. While the world prayed for peace Saddam prepared for war.

I had hoped that when the United States Congress, in historic debate, took its resolute action Saddam would realize he could not prevail and would move out of Kuwait in accord with the United Nations resolutions. He did not do that.

Instead, he remained intransigent, certain that time was on his side. Saddam was warned over and over again to comply with the will of the United Nations – leave Kuwait or be driven out.

Saddam has arrogantly rejected all warnings. Instead, he tried to make this a dispute between Iraq and the United States of America. Well, he failed. Tonight, 28 nations, countries from five continents – Europe and Asia, Africa and the Arab League have forces in the Gulf area standing shoulder-to-shoulder against Saddam Hussein. These countries had hoped the use of force could be avoided. Regrettably, we now believe that only force will make him leave.

Prior to ordering our forces into battle, I instructed our military commanders to take every necessary step to prevail as quickly as possible and with the greatest degree of protection possible for American and allied servicemen and women. I've told the American people before that this will not be another Vietnam. And I repeat this here tonight. Our troops will have the best possible support in the entire world. And they will not be asked to fight with one hand tied behind their back.

I'm hopeful that this fighting will not go on for long and that casualties will be held to an absolute minimum. This is an historic moment. We have in this past year made great progress in ending the long era of conflict and Cold War. We have before us the opportunity to forge for ourselves and for future generations a new world order, a world where the rule of law, not the law of the jungle, governs the conduct of nations. When we are successful, and we will be, we have a real chance at this new world order, an order in which a credible United Nations can use its peacekeeping role to fulfill the promise and vision of the UN's founders.

We have no argument with the people of Iraq. Indeed, for the innocents caught in this conflict, I pray for their safety. Our goal is not the conquest of Iraq. It is the liberation of Kuwait. It is my hope that somehow the Iraqi people can even now convince their dictator that he must lay down his arms, leave Kuwait and let Iraq itself rejoin the family of peace-loving nations.

Thomas Paine wrote many years ago: "These are the times that try men's souls." Those well-known words are so very true today. But even as planes of the multi-national forces attack Iraq, I prefer to think of peace not war. I am convinced not only that we will prevail, but that out of the horror of combat will come the recognition that no nation can stand against a world united, no nation will be permitted to brutally assault its neighbor.

No president can easily commit our sons and daughters to war. They are the nation's finest. Ours is an all-volunteer force, magnificently trained, highly motivated.

The troops know why they're there. And listen to what they say, for they've said it better than any president or prime minister ever could. Listen to Hollywood Huddleston, Marine Lance Corporal. He says, "Let's free these people so we can go home and be free again." And he's right. The terrible crimes and tortures committed by Saddam's henchmen against the innocent people of Kuwait are an affront to mankind and a challenge to the freedom of all.

Listen to one of our great officers out there, Marine Lieutenant General Walter Boomer. He said, "There are things worth fighting for. A world in which brutality and lawlessness are allowed to go unchecked isn't the kind of world we're going to want to live in."

Listen to Master Sargeant J. K. Kendall of the 82nd Airborne. "We're here for more than just the price of a gallon of gas. What we're doing is going to chart the future of the world for the next 100 years. It's better to deal with this guy now than five years from now."

And finally, we should all sit up and listen to Jackie Jones, an Army lieutenant, when she says, "If we let him get away with this, who knows what's going to be next?"

I've called upon Hollywood and Walter and J. K. and Jackie and all their courageous comrades in arms to do what must be done. Tonight America and the world are deeply grateful to them and to their families.

And let me say to everyone listening or watching tonight: When the troops we've sent in finish their work, I'm determined to bring them home as soon as possible. Tonight, as our forces fight, they and their families are in our prayers.

May God bless each and every one of them and the coalition forces at our side in the Gulf, and may He continue to bless our nation, the United States of America.

119 E. L. DOCTOROW

Open Letter to the President (1991)

Dear Mr. President:

When the United Nations voted sanctions against Iraq something quite unusual took place: A world congress made a virtually unanimous moral judgment against the depredations of a rogue state and then implemented its judgment with action. In international concert, troops were sent to guard Saudi Arabia's borders, and military means of interdiction, on the sea and in the air, were established to punish Iraq by economic strangulation. And it was the United States government, your Administration, that was the creative force behind this achievement.

I wonder why you don't understand what a great thing you accomplished.

This U.N. action, the first major cooperative international action since the end of the cold war, was not a mere repetition of previous instances of voted sactions. Old alliances were breached, old animosities discarded. History has given us a moment to recognize and exploit a characterological change in the nature of the world order.

Think of this ad hoc union of nation-states coalescing in the perception of a moral outrage and then taking a powerful noninvasive action to rectify it. There is a moral end – the restitution of what was stolen, the reconstruction of what was destroyed; and there is a moral means to achieve it – the withdrawal of economic fellowship. What makes this action resound is that it comes beneficently in a time of crumbling international real-political structures – when new structures take their being from the course of historical events. Whatever the motives of the allies backing your initiative, and whatever the inducements given them, almost accidentally there is a new united consciousness of nations that can begin to compose the civilized future.

War is an expedient of Saddam Hussein, Mr. President, because he is of the barbarous past. You have the chance to create a future in which, on a smaller and smaller globe, technology races to rectify the damage of earlier technology, and the needs of any one state are becoming the needs of all – air to breathe, water to drink, soil and climate to grow crops, and an unalienated, literate citizenry to advance the civilizations of a democratic planet.

In this light, it becomes tragically regressive to raise troop levels and think only with a military mind. A new period in history brings with it a new sensibility, and what is acceptable in an earlier age is understood as monstrous in our own. As we approach the twenty-first century, it is radiantly apparent that there is now no person on earth who has an inherent moral authority to send other people to their deaths. It is no longer philosophically possible. A chief executive is not a chieftain. Nor can he be a zealot.

There is a rumor going about that even as you've instructed your Secretary of State to visit Baghdad, the Quartermaster Corps of the Army has ordered 80,000 body bags. It was George Washington, in his prescience, who decided that holders of your office would be addressed as *Mr. President*. It was George Washington who decided we would not have kings. You do not rule by divine right. You are not ordained. You are a Mister. Unless you claim celestial lineage, you simply cannot elevate yourself to an ethical justification of a course of military action that may result in 80,000 dead American young men and women. Or 8,000. Or 800. I have not heard you say that our basic survival and identity as a nation are at issue here. It is no longer a chief executive's license to articulate a national interest, other than our basic survival, that requires the death of 80,000 young men and women.

The last time – another age, a distant past – something like that happened is celebrated now in austere solemnity, one might even think in the spirit of penitence, by that dark granite monument that sits with the names of the Vietnam War dead not far from your office. Tell me now to what end those soldiers died. What acute national interest did their deaths serve? We have hospitals full of those permanently maimed and paralyzed from that war. What real-political analysis of former Secretary of State Kissinger, now again urging blitzkrieg as one of the wise men of television, was borne out in the subsequent history of our security and comfort as a nation? Does he now say of the domino theory that he once so shrilly in his wisdom insisted upon that 50,000 of a generation died so that he can make the rounds at black-tie dinners? It is my understanding we have been talking lately to the Vietnamese about getting the remains of our MIAs home. There is something like normal diplomatic intercourse with these terrors of the Asian continent. And north of Vietnam there is still a Communist monolith government in China doing what Communist governments have always done, but as far as I can tell, you look on China now with a passion no more intense than a salesman's affection for a customer.

I wonder if you give yourself in any day the quiet hours of solitude that this situation requires. Do they let you alone? Do they give you time to think? Even to men with ordinary responsibilities, thinking is hard. Are you able to think? Do you make the mistake of assuming that having committed more than 400,000 troops to the desert you must, if your ultimatum is ignored, set them to fighting or *lose face*? I want to know whose face you would be losing. Do you delude yourself that it would not be a kind of criminal behavior to go to war to *save face*? I want to know whose face you would be saving. Nations are not people. Nations do not have faces – they have histories, they have constitutions, but they do not have faces. Perhaps you confuse the nation with yourself and have in mind your own face. But if I were a national leader I would welcome any degree of personal humiliation if it would preserve the life of one 18-year-old solider. I would live content in everlasting disgrace if one paraplegic could get up and walk.

A modern nation's honor is not the honor of a warrior; it is the honor of a father providing for his children, it is the honor of a mother providing for *her* children. Surely that is the true meaning of the otherwise strange internal collapse of the Soviet superstate as well as the overthrow of its satellite governments of Eastern Europe – the universal perception of what, after all, twenty-first-century enlightenment demands.

But if you would still don the helmet, let me suggest that U.N. sanctions and embargo themselves constitute a military action. It is called a siege. As all military leaders from biblical times have understood, the siege is the most cost-effective of all military strategies. Without endangering one's own forces, it brings slow but inevitable doom to the enemy. He lives for a while on his own fat, and then he either surrenders or starves to death. And nothing need be negotiated with him because he is no longer in a position to negotiate.

I look forward with you to the day when Saddam Hussein and everything he represents is buried in the sands of the desert. All we have to do is stand here silently, in our armor, and watch it happen. And go on and see what kind of twenty-first-century world God has given us the opportunity to make.

Yours sincerely,
E. L. Doctorow

120 GEORGE W. BUSH

The State of the Union Address (January 29, 2002)

Thank you very much. Mr. Speaker, Vice President Cheney, members of Congress, distinguished guests, fellow citizens: As we gather tonight, our nation is at war, our economy is in recession, and the civilized world faces unprecedented dangers. Yet the state of our Union has never been stronger. (Applause.)

We last met in an hour of shock and suffering. In four short months, our nation has comforted the victims, begun to rebuild New York and the Pentagon, rallied a great coalition, captured, arrested, and rid the world of thousands of terrorists, destroyed Afghanistan's terrorist training camps, saved a people from starvation, and freed a country from brutal oppression. (Applause.)

The American flag flies again over our embassy in Kabul. Terrorists who once occupied Afghanistan now occupy cells at Guantanamo Bay. (Applause.) And terrorist leaders who urged followers to sacrifice their lives are running for their own. (Applause.)

America and Afghanistan are now allies against terror. We'll be partners in rebuilding that country. And this evening we welcome the distinguished interim leader of a liberated Afghanistan: Chairman Hamid Karzai. (Applause.)

The last time we met in this chamber, the mothers and daughters of Afghanistan were captives in their own homes, forbidden from working or going to school. Today women are free, and are part of Afghanistan's new government. And we welcome the new Minister of Women's Affairs, Doctor Sima Samar. (Applause.)

Our progress is a tribute to the spirit of the Afghan people, to the resolve of our coalition, and to the might of the United States military. (Applause.) When I called our troops into action, I did so with complete confidence in their courage and skill. And tonight, thanks to them, we are winning the war on terror. (Applause.) The men and women of our Armed Forces have delivered a message now clear to every enemy of the United States: Even 7,000 miles away, across oceans and continents, on mountaintops and in caves – you will not escape the justice of this nation. (Applause.)

For many Americans, these four months have brought sorrow, and pain that will never completely go away. Every day a retired firefighter returns to Ground Zero, to feel closer to his two sons who died there. At a memorial in New York, a little boy left his football with a note for his lost father: Dear Daddy, please take this to heaven. I don't want to play football until I can play with you again some day.

Last month, at the grave of her husband, Michael, a CIA officer and Marine who died in Mazur-e-Sharif, Shannon Spann said these words of farewell: "Semper Fi, my love." Shannon is with us tonight. (Applause.)

Shannon, I assure you and all who have lost a loved one that our cause is just, and our country will never forget the debt we owe Michael and all who gave their lives for freedom.

Our cause is just, and it continues. Our discoveries in Afghanistan confirmed our worst fears, and showed us the true scope of the task ahead. We have seen the depth of our enemies' hatred in videos, where they laugh about the loss of innocent life. And the depth of their hatred is equaled by the madness of the destruction they design. We have found diagrams of American nuclear power plants and public water facilities, detailed instructions for making chemical weapons, surveillance maps of American cities, and thorough descriptions of landmarks in America and throughout the world.

What we have found in Afghanistan confirms that, far from ending there, our war against terror is only beginning. Most of the 19 men who hijacked planes on September the 11th were trained in Afghanistan's camps, and so were tens of thousands of others. Thousands of dangerous killers, schooled in the methods of murder, often supported by outlaw regimes, are now spread throughout the world like ticking time bombs, set to go off without warning.

Thanks to the work of our law enforcement officials and coalition partners, hundreds of terrorists have been arrested. Yet, tens of thousands of trained terrorists are still at large. These enemies view the entire world as a battlefield, and we must pursue them wherever they are. (Applause.) So long as training camps operate, so long as nations harbor terrorists, freedom is at risk. And America and our allies must not, and will not, allow it. (Applause.)

Our nation will continue to be steadfast and patient and persistent in the pursuit of two great objectives. First, we will shut down terrorist camps, disrupt terrorist plans, and bring terrorists to justice. And, second, we must prevent the terrorists and regimes who seek chemical, biological or nuclear weapons from threatening the United States and the world. (Applause.)

Our military has put the terror training camps of Afghanistan out of business, yet camps still exist in at least a dozen countries. A terrorist underworld – including groups like Hamas, Hezbollah, Islamic Jihad, Jaish-i-Mohammed – operates in remote jungles and deserts, and hides in the centers of large cities.

While the most visible military action is in Afghanistan, America is acting elsewhere. We now have troops in the Philippines, helping to train that country's armed forces to go after terrorist cells that have executed an American, and still hold hostages. Our soldiers, working with the Bosnian government, seized terrorists who were plotting to bomb our embassy. Our Navy is patrolling the coast of Africa to block the shipment of weapons and the establishment of terrorist camps in Somalia.

My hope is that all nations will heed our call, and eliminate the terrorist parasites who threaten their countries and our own. Many nations are acting forcefully. Pakistan is now cracking down on terror, and I admire the strong leadership of President Musharraf. (Applause.)

But some governments will be timid in the face of terror. And make no mistake about it: If they do not act, America will. (Applause.)

Our second goal is to prevent regimes that sponsor terror from threatening America or our friends and allies with weapons of mass destruction. Some of these regimes have been pretty quiet since September the 11th. But we know their true nature. North Korea is a regime arming with missiles and weapons of mass destruction, while starving its citizens.

Iran aggressively pursues these weapons and exports terror, while an unelected few repress the Iranian people's hope for freedom.

Iraq continues to flaunt its hostility toward America and to support terror. The Iraqi regime has plotted to develop anthrax, and nerve gas, and nuclear weapons for over a decade. This is a regime that has already used poison gas to murder thousands of its own citizens – leaving the bodies of mothers huddled over their dead children. This is a regime that agreed to international inspections – then kicked out the inspectors. This is a regime that has something to hide from the civilized world.

States like these, and their terrorist allies, constitute an axis of evil, arming to threaten the peace of the world. By seeking weapons of mass destruction, these regimes pose a grave and growing danger. They could provide these arms to terrorists, giving them the means to match their hatred. They could attack our allies or attempt to blackmail the United States. In any of these cases, the price of indifference would be catastrophic.

We will work closely with our coalition to deny terrorists and their state sponsors the materials, technology, and expertise to make and deliver weapons of mass destruction. We will develop and deploy effective missile defenses to protect America and our allies from sudden attack. (Applause.) And all nations should know: America will do what is necessary to ensure our nation's security.

We'll be deliberate, yet time is not on our side. I will not wait on events, while dangers gather. I will not stand by, as peril draws closer and closer. The United States of America will not permit the world's most dangerous regimes to threaten us with the world's most destructive weapons. (Applause.)

Our war on terror is well begun, but it is only begun. This campaign may not be finished on our watch – yet it must be and it will be waged on our watch.

We can't stop short. If we stop now – leaving terror camps intact and terror states unchecked – our sense of security would be false and temporary. History has called America and our allies to action, and it is both our responsibility and our privilege to fight freedom's fight. (Applause.)

Our first priority must always be the security of our nation, and that will be reflected in the budget I send to Congress. My budget supports three great goals for America: We will win this war; we'll protect our homeland; and we will revive our economy.

September the 11th brought out the best in America, and the best in this Congress. And I join the American people in applauding your unity and resolve. (Applause.) Now Americans deserve to have this same spirit directed toward addressing problems here at home. I'm a proud member of my party – yet as we act to win the war, protect our people, and create jobs in America, we must act, first and foremost, not as Republicans, not as Democrats, but as Americans. (Applause.)

It costs a lot to fight this war. We have spent more than a billion dollars a month – over $30 million a day – and we must be prepared for future operations. Afghanistan proved that expensive precision weapons defeat the enemy and spare innocent lives, and we need more of them. We need to replace aging aircraft and make our military more agile, to put our troops anywhere in the world quickly and safely. Our men and women in uniform deserve the best weapons, the best equipment, the best training – and they also deserve another pay raise. (Applause.)

My budget includes the largest increase in defense spending in two decades – because while the price of freedom and security is high, it is never too high. Whatever it costs to defend our country, we will pay. (Applause.)

The next priority of my budget is to do everything possible to protect our citizens and strengthen our nation against the ongoing threat of another attack. Time and distance from the events of September the 11th will not make us safer unless we act on its lessons. America is no longer protected by vast oceans. We are protected from attack only by vigorous action abroad, and increased vigilance at home.

My budget nearly doubles funding for a sustained strategy of homeland security, focused on four key areas: bioterrorism, emergency response, airport and border security, and improved intelligence. We will develop vaccines to fight anthrax and other deadly diseases. We'll increase funding to help states and communities train and equip our heroic police and firefighters. (Applause.) We will improve intelligence collection and sharing, expand patrols at our borders, strengthen the security of air travel, and use technology to track the arrivals and departures of visitors to the United States. (Applause.)

Homeland security will make America not only stronger, but, in many ways, better. Knowledge gained from bioterrorism research will improve public health. Stronger police and fire departments will mean safer neighborhoods. Stricter border enforcement will help combat illegal drugs. (Applause.) And as government works to better secure our homeland, America will continue to depend on the eyes and ears of alert citizens.

A few days before Christmas, an airline flight attendant spotted a passenger lighting a match. The crew and passengers quickly subdued the man, who had been trained by al Qaeda and was armed with explosives. The people on that plane were alert and, as a result, likely saved nearly 200 lives. And tonight we welcome and thank flight attendants Hermis Moutardier and Christina Jones. (Applause.)

Once we have funded our national security and our homeland security, the final great priority of my budget is economic security for the American people. (Applause.) To achieve these great national objectives – to win the war, protect the homeland, and revitalize our economy – our budget will run a deficit that will be small and short-term, so long as Congress restrains spending and acts in a fiscally responsible manner. (Applause.) We have clear priorities and we must act at home with the same purpose and resolve we have shown overseas: We'll prevail in the war, and we will defeat this recession. (Applause.) . . .

During these last few months, I've been humbled and privileged to see the true character of this country in a time of testing. Our enemies believed America was weak and materialistic, that we would splinter in fear and selfishness. They were as wrong as they are evil. (Applause.)

The American people have responded magnificently, with courage and compassion, strength and resolve. As I have met the heroes, hugged the families, and looked into the tired faces of rescuers, I have stood in awe of the American people.

And I hope you will join me – I hope you will join me in expressing thanks to one American for the strength and calm and comfort she brings to our nation in crisis, our First Lady, Laura Bush. (Applause.)

None of us would ever wish the evil that was done on September the 11th. Yet after America was attacked, it was as if our entire country looked into a mirror and saw our better selves. We were reminded that we are citizens, with obligations to each other, to our country, and to history. We began to think less of the goods we can accumulate, and more about the good we can do.

For too long our culture has said, "If it feels good, do it." Now America is embracing a new ethic and a new creed: "Let's roll." (Applause.) In the sacrifice of soldiers, the fierce brotherhood of firefighters, and the bravery and generosity of ordinary citizens, we have glimpsed what a new culture of responsibility could look like. We want to be a nation that serves goals larger than self. We've been offered a unique opportunity, and we must not let this moment pass. (Applause.)

My call tonight is for every American to commit at least two years – 4,000 hours over the rest of your lifetime – to the service of your neighbors and your nation. (Applause.) Many are already serving, and I thank you. If you aren't sure how to help, I've got a good place to start. To sustain and extend the best that has emerged in America, I invite you to join the new USA Freedom Corps. The Freedom Corps will focus on three areas of need: responding in case of crisis at home; rebuilding our communities; and extending American compassion throughout the world.

One purpose of the USA Freedom Corps will be homeland security. America needs retired doctors and nurses who can be mobilized in major emergencies; volunteers to help police and fire departments; transportation and utility workers well-trained in spotting danger.

Our country also needs citizens working to rebuild our communities. We need mentors to love children, especially children whose parents are in prison. And we need more talented teachers in troubled schools. USA Freedom Corps will expand and improve the good efforts of AmeriCorps and Senior Corps to recruit more than 200,000 new volunteers.

And America needs citizens to extend the compassion of our country to every part of the world. So we will renew the promise of the Peace Corps, double its volunteers over the next five years – (applause) – and ask it to join a new effort to encourage development and education and opportunity in the Islamic world. (Applause.)

This time of adversity offers a unique moment of opportunity – a moment we must seize to change our culture. Through the gathering momentum of millions of acts of service and decency and kindness, I know we can overcome evil with greater good. (Applause.) And we have a great opportunity during this time of war to lead the world toward the values that will bring lasting peace.

All fathers and mothers, in all societies, want their children to be educated, and live free from poverty and violence. No people on Earth yearn to be oppressed, or aspire to servitude, or eagerly await the midnight knock of the secret police.

If anyone doubts this, let them look to Afghanistan, where the Islamic "street" greeted the fall of tyranny with song and celebration. Let the skeptics look to Islam's own rich history, with its centuries of learning, and tolerance and progress. America will lead by defending liberty and justice because they are right and true and unchanging for all people everywhere. (Applause.)

No nation owns these aspirations, and no nation is exempt from them. We have no intention of imposing our culture. But America will always stand firm for the non-negotiable demands of human dignity: the rule of law; limits on the power of the state; respect for women; private property; free speech; equal justice; and religious tolerance. (Applause.)

America will take the side of brave men and women who advocate these values around the world, including the Islamic world, because we have a greater objective than eliminating threats and containing resentment. We seek a just and peaceful world beyond the war on terror.

In this moment of opportunity, a common danger is erasing old rivalries. America is working with Russia and China and India, in ways we have never before, to achieve peace and prosperity. In every region, free markets and free trade and free societies are proving their power to lift lives. Together with friends and allies from Europe to Asia, and Africa to Latin America, we will demonstrate that the forces of terror cannot stop the momentum of freedom. (Applause.)

The last time I spoke here, I expressed the hope that life would return to normal. In some ways, it has. In others, it never will. Those of us who have lived through these challenging times have been changed by them. We've come to know truths that we will never question: evil is real, and it must be opposed. (Applause.) Beyond all differences of race or creed, we are one country, mourning together and facing danger together. Deep in the American character, there is honor, and it is stronger than cynicism. And many have discovered again that even in tragedy – especially in tragedy – God is near. (Applause.)

In a single instant, we realized that this will be a decisive decade in the history of liberty, that we've been called to a unique role in human events. Rarely has the world faced a choice more clear or consequential.

Our enemies send other people's children on missions of suicide and murder. They embrace tyranny and death as a cause and a creed. We stand for a different choice, made long ago, on the day of our founding. We affirm it again today. We choose freedom and the dignity of every life. (Applause.)

Steadfast in our purpose, we now press on. We have known freedom's price. We have shown freedom's power. And in this great conflict, my fellow Americans, we will see freedom's victory.

Thank you all. May God bless. (Applause.)

13

IDEOLOGY: DOMINANT BELIEFS AND VALUES

Introduction		406
121	*Thomas Jefferson* A Bill for Establishing Religious Freedom in the State of Virginia (1779)	409
122	*Horace Mann* FROM "Report to the Massachusetts Board of Education" (1848)	411
123	*William James* FROM *Pragmatism* (1907)	417
124	*Jane Addams* FROM *Twenty Years at Hull House* (1910)	418
125	*Bruce Barton* FROM "Christ as a Businessman" (1925)	419
126	*Dale Carnegie* FROM *How to Win Friends and Influence People* (1936)	423
127	*Franklin D. Roosevelt* State of the Union Address (January 6, 1941)	424
128	*Dwight D. Eisenhower* "The Military-Industrial Complex" (1961)	430
129	*Studs Terkel* FROM "Jay Slabaugh, 48" (Interview with a Corporate Executive, 1980)	431
130	*Rush H. Limbaugh, III* FROM *See, I Told You So* (1993)	432

Figure 13 Detail of *Peaceable Kingdom* by Edward Hicks © Burstein Collection/CORBIS

INTRODUCTION

In his well-known study *An American Dilemma: The Negro Problem and Modern Democracy* (1944) the Swedish sociologist Gunnar Myrdal speaks of "a *social* ethos, a political creed" that is shared by Americans of all national origins, classes, and faiths and that functions as "the cement in the structure of this great and disparate nation." In Myrdal's words:

> These ideals of the essential dignity of the individual human being, of the fundamental equality of all men, and of certain inalienable rights to freedom, justice, and a fair opportunity represent to the American people the essential meaning of the nation's early struggle for independence. In the clarity and intellectual boldness of the Enlightenment period these tenets were written into the Declaration of Independence, the Preamble of the Constitution, the Bill of Rights and into the constitutions of the several states.[1]

The ideas of the hallowed documents mentioned by Myrdal are still regarded as the ideological foundation of American life and politics. Our reader is referred to chapter 5 for the text of the American Constitution and the central articles of the Bill of Rights (text 41). Since Thomas Jefferson's Declaration of Independence is anthologized in most major collections of American literature, it is not included in this book.

According to the epitaph that Jefferson wrote for his own tombstone, he wanted to be remembered for three things: "Here was buried Thomas Jefferson, author of the Declaration of American Independence, of the statute of Virginia for religious freedom, and father of the University of Virginia." Text 121, on American beliefs and values, is therefore Jefferson's 1779 proposal to the Virginia State Assembly for a bill on religious freedom (it was later amended and adopted as a statute in 1786); it thus precedes the guarantee of religious freedom that was formulated in the first article of the Bill of Rights, added to the American Constitution in 1791. Jefferson returned to the issue several times, particularly in his *Notes on the State of Virginia* (Query XVII: Religion), in which he pointed to the status of "the English Church" in the new nation. His text has assumed a particular pertinence in this day and age when the introduction of prayer in public schools is a repeatedly debated issue.

For nineteenth- and twentieth-century documents that have become part of the canon of texts pertaining to American ideals of freedom and equality, the reader is referred to the 1848 Seneca Falls Declaration of women's rights in chapter 4 (text 32), Lincoln's Emancipation Proclamation of 1863 in chapter 3 (text 24), the fourteenth amendment to the Constitution (1868) in chapter 5 (text 41), John Marshall Harlan's dissent in the Supreme Court case of *Plessy* v. *Ferguson* (1896) in the same chapter (text 46), the 1954 Supreme Court decision in *Brown* v. *Board of Education* excerpted in chapter 10 (text 95), Martin Luther King's speech from 1963 "I Have a Dream" in chapter 3 (text 27), and the Civil Rights Act of 1964 in the same chapter (text 28).

These documents are specifically concerned with civil rights. In this chapter on American ideology, however, we have given space to texts that give voice to basic American ideas and values from other angles and within other contexts. In text 123 (from *Pragmatism*, 1907) William James suggests that theory should not be considered apart from practice and argues that metaphysical issues must be judged in terms of their practical consequences; his was an expression, as it were, of American utilitarianism within the field of philosophy. In the preceding text (122), Horace Mann, Secretary of the Massachusetts Board of Education in the middle of the nineteenth century, sees universal education as the chief practical instrument of freedom and social mobility, "the great equalizer of the conditions of men." That human ideals demand practical action is also the main tenet of text 124, in which the social reformer Jane Addams writes of the philanthropic and humanitarian ideas that had led her to establish Hull House in Chicago in 1889; it was an attempt, as she puts it, to relieve "the overaccumulation at one end of society and the destitution at the other." Hull House was one of the so-called settlement houses founded in several American cities at the end of the nineteenth century to help alleviate the problems of poverty and squalor among the urban lower classes, particularly in immigrant tenement districts.

Within the economic realm, the American dream of freedom is not linked to the philosophy of egalitarianism that we find in religious, constitutional, or legal discourse (the idea that we are all equal in the eyes of God or the law); it is instead linked to the concept of meritocracy, of rising in society according to one's abilities. Three texts in this chapter deal with the meritocratic ideals of American free enterprise, but from very different perspectives. In text 125, an excerpt from a book entitled *The Man Nobody Knows*, Bruce Barton, an advertising executive, sees Christ himself as the very embodiment of "the principles of modern salesmanship," the prototype of the businessman "who picked up twelve men from the bottom ranks of business and forged them into an organization that conquered the world." Already this text from the 1920s seems, however, to signal a shift in values from the production ethos of self-reliance and self-assertion (prevalent in the first three centuries of American history) to the ethos of a consumer culture emphasizing personality and popularity. This trend is even more obvious in the subsequent text (126) excerpted from Dale Carnegie's *How to Win Friends and Influence People* (1936), a book that went through close to a hundred printings in its first three decades of publication. Here success is connected not so much with exertion, aggressiveness, or inner-directed self-assertion as with personal dynamism, winning ways, and other-directed approbation – qualities that have to do with handling people and getting along with superiors in large corporate structures. In text 129, however, excerpted from an interview with a corporate executive in 1980, we are back with a traditional ethos of aggressive individualism where life in general and business in particular are viewed in Darwinist terms of cut-throat competition rather than cooperation; Jay Slabaugh evokes a world in which "[t]ere is never enough of anything," in which you always "go for more," and in which enterprise becomes a question of moving either up or down, of becoming either a success or a failure. Here no middle ground exists, and no-growth is inconceivable.

In the American rhetoric of free enterprise we often find that government and business are viewed in opposition to each other. A great many government programs are, however, designed to promote business and private growth. In text 128 President Dwight D. Eisenhower, a former US military hero, a Republican and also a heroic figure to American business, issued, to many people's surprise, a strong warning at his departure from office against monopoly in the form of a "military-industrial complex" – the close and interdependent relationship between government and the private defense industry.

In text 127, excerpted from Franklin D. Roosevelt's State of the Union Address of 1941, the American discourse of democracy and equality assumes a double relevance: domestically with reference to the right to work and to old-age, sickness, and unemployment benefits, and in terms of foreign policy with reference to four freedoms threatened by tyranny and war in the western world – freedom of speech, freedom of religion, freedom from want, and freedom from fear. The liberal Democratic ideology of social reform and economic redress was of course extended in subsequent decades through Harry Truman's Fair Deal, John F. Kennedy's New Frontier, and Lyndon B. Johnson's Great Society (see Johnson's "The War on Poverty," text 56).

In the last entry (130) Rush H. Limbaugh, prominent spokesman of the ultra-conservative right and famous for his own radio and TV shows in the 1990s, attacks contemporary political liberalism for poisoning American life with its moral relativism and secular humanism. This text can in many ways be said to be representative of the strongly conservative currents in American life and politics over the last twenty years.

1 Gunnar Myrdal, *An American Dilemma: The Negro Problem and Modern Democracy* (New York: Harper and Row, 1962), pp. 3, 4.

Questions and Topics

1 What are Thomas Jefferson's main arguments for the establishment of religious freedom?
2 Discuss how Horace Mann and Jane Addams each in their way want to redress inequalities in the American society of their own time.
3 Dale Carnegie and Jay Slabaugh are both concerned with the idea of succeeding in American business. In what ways do their views differ?
4 Why does Dwight D. Eisenhower find the close relationship between the American military and the defense industry problematic?
5 Franklin D. Roosevelt and Rush Limbaugh seem to define freedom very differently. Discuss some of their differences.

Suggestions for further reading

Bellah, Robert N., Richard Madsen, William M. Sullivan, Ann Swidler, and Steven M. Tipton, *Habits of the Heart: Individualism and Commitment in American Life* (Berkeley: University of California Press, 1985).

Bloom, A., *The Closing of the American Mind* (Harmondsworth: Penguin, 1988).

Kammen, M., *People of Paradox: An Inquiry Concerning the Origins of American Civilization* (Ithaca, NY: Cornell University Press, 1990).

Lerner, Max, *America as a Civilization*, 2 vols (New York: Simon and Schuster, 1957).

Parrington, Vernon L., *Main Currents in American Thought*, 2 vols (New York: Harcourt, Brace & World, [1927], 1954).

Wilkinson, R., *The Pursuit of American Character* (New York: Harper & Row, 1988).

121 THOMAS JEFFERSON

A Bill for Establishing Religious Freedom in the State of Virginia (1779)

SECTION I. Well aware that the opinions and belief of men depend not on their own will, but follow involuntarily the evidence proposed to their minds; that Almighty God hath created the mind free, and manifested his supreme will that free it shall remain by making it altogether insusceptible of restraint; that all attempts to influence it by temporal punishments, or burthens, or by civil incapacitations, tend only to beget habits of hypocrisy and meanness, and are a departure from the plan of the holy author of our religion, who being lord both of body and mind, yet chose not to propagate it by coercions on either, as was in his Almighty power to do, but to exalt it by its influence on reason alone; that the impious presumption of legislators and rulers, civil as well as ecclesiastical, who, being themselves but fallible and uninspired men, have assumed dominion over the faith of others, setting up their own opinions and modes of thinking as the only true and infallible, and as such endeavoring to impose them on others, hath established and maintained false religions over the greatest part of the world and through all time: That to compel a man to furnish contributions of money for the propagation of opinions which he disbelieves and abhors, is sinful and tyrannical; that even the forcing him to support this or that teacher of his own religious persuasion, is depriving him of the comfortable liberty of giving his contributions to the particular pastor whose morals he would make his pattern, and whose powers he feels most persuasive to righteousness; and is withdrawing from the ministry those temporary rewards, which proceeding from an approbation of their personal conduct, are an additional incitement to earnest and unremitting labours for the instruction of mankind; that our civil rights have no dependence on our religious opinions, any more than our opinions in physics or geometry; that therefore the proscribing any citizen as unworthy the public confidence by laying upon him an incapacity of being alled to offices of trust and emolument, unless he profess or renounce this or that religious opinion, is depriving him injuriously of those privileges and advantages to which, in common with his fellow citizens, he has a natural right; that it tends also to corrupt the principles of that very religion it is meant to encourage, by bribing, with a monopoly of worldly honours and emoluments, those who will externally profess and conform to it; that though indeed these are criminals who do not withstand such temptation, yet neither are those innocent who lay the bait in their way; that the opinions of men are not the object of civil government, nor under its jurisdiction; that to suffer the civil magistrate to intrude his powers into the field of opinion and to restrain the profession or propagation of principles on supposition of their ill tendency is a dangerous fallacy, which at once destroys all religious liberty, because he being of course judge of that tendency will make his opinions the rule of judgment, and approve or condemn the sentiments of others only as they shall square with or differ from his own; that it is time enough for the rightful purposes of civil government for its officers to interfere when principles break out into overt acts against peace and good order; and finally, that truth is great and will prevail if left to herself; that she is the proper and sufficient antagonist to error, and has nothing to fear from the conflict unless by human interposition disarmed of her natural weapons, free argument and debate; errors ceasing to be dangerous when it is permitted freely to contradict them.

SECTION II. We the General Assembly of Virginia do enact that no man shall be compelled to frequent or support any religious worship, place, or ministry whatsoever, nor shall be enforced, restrained, molested, or burthened in his body or goods, nor shall otherwise suffer, on account of his religious opinions or belief; but that all men shall be free to profess, and by argument to maintain, their opinions in matters of religion, and that the same shall in no wise diminish, enlarge, or affect their civil capacities.

SECTION III. And though we well know that this Assembly, elected by the people for the ordinary purposes of legislation only, have no power to restrain the acts of succeeding Assemblies, constituted with powers equal to our own, and that therefore to declare this act irrevocable would be of no effect in law; yet we are free to declare, and do declare, that the rights hereby asserted are of the natural rights of mankind, and that if any act shall be hereafter passed to repeal the present or to narrow its operation, such act will be an infringement of natural right.

122 HORACE MANN

FROM *"Report to the Massachusetts Board of Education" (1848)*

Poverty is a public as well as a private evil. There is no physical law necessitating its existence. The earth contains abundant resources for ten times – doubtless for twenty times – its present inhabitants. Cold, hunger, and nakedness are not, like death, an inevitable lot. There are many single States in this Union which could supply an abundance of edible products for the inhabitants of the thirty States that compose it. There are single States capable of raising a sufficient quantity of cotton to clothe the whole nation; and there are other States having sufficient factories and machinery to manufacture it. The coal-fields of Pennsylvania are sufficiently abundant to keep every house in the land at the temperature of sixty-five degrees for centuries to come. Were there to be a competition, on the one hand, to supply wool for every conceivable fabric, and, on the other, to wear out these fabrics as fast as possible, the single State of New York would beat the whole country. There is, indeed, no assignable limit to the capacities of the earth for producing whatever is necessary for the sustenance, comfort, and improvement of the race. Indigence, therefore, and the miseries and degradations incident to indigence, seem to be no part of the eternal ordinances of Heaven. The bounty of God is not brought into question or suspicion by its existence; for man who suffers it might have avoided it. Even the wealth which the world now has on hand is more than sufficient to supply all the rational wants of every individual in it. Privations and sufferings exist, not from the smallness of its sum, but from the inequality of its distribution. Poverty is set over against profusion. In some, all healthy appetite is cloyed and sickened by repletion; while in others, the stomach seems to be a supernumerary organ in the system; or, like the human eye or human lungs before birth, is waiting to be transferred to some other region, where its functions may come into use. One gorgeous palace absorbs all the labor and expense that might have made a thousand hovels comfortable. That one man may ride in carriages of Oriental luxury, hundreds of other men are turned into beasts of burden. To supply a superfluous wardrobe for the gratification of one man's pride, a thousand women and children shiver with cold; and, for every flash of the diamonds that royalty wears, there is a tear of distress in the poor man's dwelling. Not one Lazarus, but a hundred, sit at the gate of Dives. Tantalus is no fiction. The ancient one might have been fabulous; but the modern ones are terrible realities. Millions are perishing in the midst of superfluities.

According to the European theory, men are divided into classes, – some toil to earn, others seize and enjoy. According to the Massachusetts theory, all are to have an equal chance for earning, and equal security in the enjoyment of what they earn. The latter tends to equality of condition; the former, to the grossest inequalities. Tried by any Christian standard of morals, or even by any of the better sort of heathen standards, can any one hesitate, for a moment, in declaring which of the two will produce the greater amount of human welfare, and which, therefore, is the more comfortable to the divine will? The European theory is blind to what constitutes the highest glory as well as the highest duty of a State. Its advocates and admirers are forgetful of that which should be their highest ambition, and proud of that which constitutes their shame. How can any one possessed of the attributes of humanity look with satisfaction upon the splendid treasures, the golden regalia, deposited in the Tower of London or in Windsor Palace, each "an India in itself," while thousands around are dying of starvation, or have been made criminals by the combined forces of temptation and neglect? . . .

Our ambition as a State should trace itself to a different origin, and propose to itself a different object. Its flame should be lighted at the skies. Its radiance and its warmth should reach the darkest and the coldest abodes of men. It should seek the solution of such problems as these: To what extent can competence displace pauperism? How nearly can we free ourselves from the low-minded and the vicious, not by their expatriation, but by their elevation? To what extent can the resources and powers of Nature be converted into human welfare, the peaceful arts of life be advanced, and the vast treasures of human talent and genius be developed? How much of suffering, in all its forms, can be relieved? or, what is better than relief, how much can be prevented? Cannot the classes of crimes be lessened, and the number of criminals in each class be diminished? Our exemplars, both for public and for private imitation, should be the parables of the lost sheep and of the lost piece of silver. When we have spread competence through all the abodes of poverty, when we have substituted knowledge for ignorance in the minds of the whole people, when we have reformed the vicious and reclaimed the criminal, then may we invite all neighboring nations to behold the spectacle, and say to them, in the conscious elation of virtue, "Rejoice with me, for I have found that which is lost." Until that day shall arrive, our duties will not be wholly fulfilled, and our ambition will have new honors to win. . . .

I suppose it to be the universal sentiment of all those who mingle any ingredient of benevolence with their notions on political economy, that vast and overshadowing private fortunes are among the greatest dangers to which the happiness of the people in a republic can be subjected. Such fortunes would create a feudalism of a new kind, but one more oppressive and unrelenting than that of the Middle Ages. The feudal lords in England and on the Continent never held their retainers in a more abject condition of servitude than the great majority of foreign manufacturers and capitalists hold their operatives and laborers at the present day. The means employed are different; but the similarity in results is striking. What force did then, money does now. The villein of the Middle Ages had no spot of earth on which he could live, unless one were granted to him by his lord. The operative or laborer of the present day has no employment, and therefore no bread, unless the capitalist will accept his services. The vassal had no shelter but such as his master provided for him. Not one in five thousand of English operatives or farm-laborers is able to build or own even a hovel; and therefore they must accept such shelter as capital offers them. The baron prescribed his own terms to his retainers: those terms were peremptory, and the serf must submit or perish. The British manufacturer or farmer prescribes the rate of wages he will give to his work-people; he reduces these wages under whatever pretext he pleases; and they, too, have no alternative but submission or starvation. In some respects, indeed, the condition of the modern dependant is more forlorn than that of the corresponding serf class in former times. Some attributes of the patriarchal relation did spring up between the lord and his lieges to soften the harsh relations subsisting between them. Hence came some oversight of the condition of children, some relief in sickness, some protection and support in the decrepitude of age. But only in instances comparatively few have kindly offices smoothed the rugged relation between British capital and British labor. The children of the work-people are abandoned to their fate; and notwithstanding the privations they suffer, and the dangers they threaten, no power in the realm has yet been able to secure them an education; and when the adult laborer is prostrated by sickness, or eventually worn out by toil and age, the poor-house, which has all along been his destination, becomes his destiny.

Now, two or three things will doubtless be admitted to be true, beyond all controversy, in regard to Massachusetts. By its industrial condition, and its business operations, it is exposed, far beyond any other State in the Union, to the fatal extremes of overgrown wealth and desperate poverty. Its population is far more dense than that of any other State. It is four or five times more dense than the average of all the other States taken together; and density of population has always been one of the proximate causes of social inequality. According to population and territorial extent, there is far more capital in Massachusetts – capital which is movable, and instantaneously available – than in any other State in the Union; and probably both these qualifications respecting population and territory could be omitted without endangering the truth of the assertion. It has been recently stated in a very respectable public journal, on the authority of a writer conversant with the subject, that from the last of June, 1846, to the first of August, 1848, the amount of money invested by the citizens of Massachusetts "in manufacturing cities, railroads, and other improvements," is "fifty-seven millions of dollars, of which more than fifty has been paid in and expended." The dividends to be received by citizens of Massachusetts from June, 1848, to April, 1849, are estimated by the same writer at ten millions, and the annual increase of capital a "little short of twenty-two millions." If this be so, are we not in danger of neutralizing and domesticating among ourselves those hideous evils which are always engendered between capital and labor, when all the capital is in the hands of one class, and all the labor is thrown upon another?

Now, surely nothing but universal education can counterwork this tendency to the domination of capital and the servility of labor. If one class possesses all the wealth and the education, while the residue of society is ignorant and poor, it matters not by what name the relation between them may be called: the latter, in fact and in truth, will be the servile dependants and subjects of the former. But, if education be equably diffused, it will draw property after it by the strongest of all attractions; for such a thing never did happen, and never can happen, as that an intelligent and practical body of men should be permanently poor. Property and labor in different classes are essentially antagonistic; but property and labor in the same class are essentially fraternal. The people of Massachusetts have, in some degree, appreciated the truth, that the unexampled prosperity of the State – its comfort, its competence, its general intelligence and virtue – is attributable to the education, more or less perfect, which all its people have received: but are they sensible of a fact equally important; namely, that it is to this same education that two-thirds of the people are indebted for not being to-day the vassals of as severe a tyranny, in the form of capital, as the lower classes of Europe are bound to in the form of brute force?

Education, then, beyond all other devices of human origin, is the great equalizer of the conditions of men, – the balance-wheel of the social machinery. I do not here mean that it so elevates the moral nature as to make men disdain and abhor the oppression of their fellow-men. This idea pertains to another of its attributes: But I mean that it gives each man the independence and the means by which he can resist the selfishness of other men. It does better than to disarm the poor of their hostility towards the rich: it prevents being poor. Agrarianism is the revenge of poverty against wealth. The wanton destruction of the property of others – the burning of hay-ricks and corn-ricks, the demolition of machinery because it supersedes hand-labor, the sprinkling of vitriol on rich dresses – is only agrarianism run mad. Education prevents both the revenge and the madness. On the other hand, a fellow-feeling for one's class or caste is the common instinct of hearts not wholly sunk in selfish regards for person or for family. The spread of education, by enlarging the cultivated class or caste, will open a wider area over which the social feelings will expand; and, if this education should be universal and complete, it would do more than all things else to obliterate distinctions in society.

The main idea set forth in the creeds of some political reformers, or revolutionizers, is, that some people are poor *because* others are rich. This idea supposes a fixed amount of property in the community, which by fraud or force, or arbitrary law, is unequally divided among men; and the problem presented for solution is, how to transfer a portion of this property from those who are supposed to have too much to those who feel and know that they have too little. At this point, both their theory and their expectation of reform stop. But the beneficent power of education would not be exhausted, even though it should peaceably abolish all the miseries that spring from the co-existence, side by side, of enormous wealth and squalid want. It has a higher function. Beyond the power of diffusing old wealth, it has the prerogative of creating new. It is a thousand times more lucrative than fraud, and adds a thousand-fold more to a nation's resources than the most successful conquests. Knaves and robbers can obtain only what was before possessed by others. But education creates or develops new treasures, – treasures not before possessed or dreamed of by any one. . . .

It is a remarkable fact, that human progress, even in regard to the worldly interests of the race, did not begin with those improvements which are most closely allied to material prosperity. One would have supposed, beforehand, that improvements would commence with the near rather than with the remote. Yet mankind had made great advances in astronomy, in geometry, and other mathematical sciences; in the writing of history, in oratory, and in poetry: it is supposed by many to have reached the highest point of yet attained perfection in painting and in sculpture, and in those kinds of architecture which may be called regal or religious, centuries before the great mechanical discoveries and inventions which now bless the world were brought to light. And the question has often forced itself upon reflecting minds, why there was this preposterousness, this inversion of what would appear to be the natural order of progress. Why was it, for instance, that men should have learned the courses of the stars, and the revolutions of the planets, before they found out how to make a good wagon-wheel? Why was it that they built the Parthenon and the Colosseum before they knew how to construct a comfortable, healthful dwelling-house? Why did they construct the Roman aqueducts before they constructed a saw-mill? Or why did they achieve the noblest models in eloquence, in poetry, and in the drama, before they invented movable types? I think we have now arrived at a point where we can unriddle this enigma. *The labor of the world has been performed by ignorant men*, by classes doomed to ignorance from sire to son, by the bondmen and bond-women of the Jews; by the helots of Sparta, by the captives who passed under the Roman yoke, and by the villeins and serfs and slaves of more modern times. The masters – the aristocratic or patrician orders – not only disdained labor for themselves and their children, which was one fatal mistake; but they supposed that knowledge was of no use to a laborer, which was a mistake stil more fatal. Hence, ignorance, for almost six thousand years, has gone on plying its animal muscles, and dropping its bloody sweat, and never discovered any way, nor dreamed that there was any way, by which it might accomplish many times more work with many times less labor. And yet nothing is more true than that an ignorant man will toil all his life long, moving to and fro within an inch of some great discovery, and will never see it. All the elements of a great discovery may fall into his hands, or be thrust into his face; but his eyes will be too blind to behold it. . . .

If a savage will learn how to swim, he can fasten a dozen pounds' weight to his back, and transport it across a narrow river or other body of water of moderate width. If he will invent an axe, or other instrument, by which to cut down a tree, he can use the tree for a float, and one of its limbs for a paddle, and can thus transport many times the former weight many times the former distance. Hollowing out this log, he will increase what may be called its tonnage, or rather its *poundage*; and, by sharpening its ends, it will cleave the water both more easily and more swiftly. Fastening several trees together, he makes a raft, and thus increases the buoyant power of his embryo water-craft. Turning up the ends of small poles, or using knees of timber instead of straight pieces, and grooving them together, or filling up the interstices between them in some other way, so as to make them water-tight, he brings his rude raft literally into *ship-shape*. Improving upon hull below and rigging above, he makes a proud merchantman, to be wafted by the winds from continent to continent. But even this does not content the adventurous naval architect. He frames iron arms for his ship; and, for oars, affixes iron wheels, capable of swift revolution, and stronger than the strong sea. Into iron-walled cavities in her bosom he puts iron organs of massive structure and strength, and of cohesion insoluble by fire. Within these he kindles a small volcano; and then, like a sentient and rational existence, this wonderful creation of his hands cleaves oceans, breasts tides, defies tempests, and bears its living and jubilant freight around the globe. Now, take away intelligence from the ship-builder, and the steamship – that miracle of human art – falls back into a floating log; the log itself is lost; and the savage swimmer, bearing his dozen pounds on his back, alone remains.

And so it is, not in one department only, but in the whole circle of human labors. The annihilation of the sun would no more certainly be followed by darkness than the extinction of human intelligence would plunge the race at once into the weakness and helplessness of barbarism. To have created such beings as we are, and to have placed them in this world without the light of the sun, would be no more cruel than for a government to suffer its laboring classes to grow up without knowledge.

In this fact, then, we find a solution of the problem that so long embarrassed inquirers. The reason why the mechanical and useful arts, those arts which have done so much to civilize mankind, and which have given comforts and luxuries to the common laborer of the present day, such as kings and queens could not command three centuries ago, – the reason why these arts made no progress, and until recently, indeed, can hardly be said to have had any thing more than a beginning, is, that the labor of the world was performed by ignorant men. As soon as some degree of intelligence dawned upon the workman, then a corresponding degree of improvement in his work followed. At first, this intelligence was confined to a very small number, and therefore improvements were few; and they followed each other only after long intervals. They uniformly began in the nations and among the classes where there was most intelligence. The middle classes of England, and the people of Holland and Scotland, have done a hundred times more than all the Eastern hemisphere besides. What single improvement in art, or discovery in science, has ever originated in Spain, or throughout the vast empire of the Russias? But just in proportion as intelligence – that is, education – has quickened and stimulated a greater and a greater number of minds, just in the same proportion have inventions and discoveries increased in their wonderfulness, and in the rapidity of their succession. The progression has been rather geometrical than arithmetical. By the laws of Nature, it must be so. If, among ten well-educated children, the chance is that at least one of them will originate some new and useful processes in the arts, or will discover some new scientific principle, or some new application of one, then, among a hundred such well-educated children, there is a moral certainty that there will be more than ten such originators or dis-coverers of new utilities; for the action of the mind is like the action of fire. One billet of wood will hardly burn alone, though dry as suns and north-west winds can make it, and though placed in the range of a current of air; ten such billets will burn well together; but a hundred will create a heat fifty times as intense as ten, will make a current of air to fan their own flame, and consume even greenness itself.

For the creation of wealth, then, – for the existence of a wealthy people and a wealthy nation, – intelligence is the grand condition. The number of improvers will increase as the intellectual constituency, if I may so call it, increases. In former times, and in most parts of the world even at the present day, not one man in a million has ever had such a development of mind as made it possible for him to become a contributor to art or science. Let this development precede, and contributions, numberless, and of inestimable value, will be sure to follow. That political economy, therefore, which busies itself about capital and labor, supply and demand, interest and rents, favorable balances of trade, but leaves out of account the element of a widespread mental development, is nought but stupendous folly. The greatest of all the arts in political economy is to change a consumer into a producer; and the next greatest is to increase the producer's producing power, an end to be directly attained by increasing his intelligence. For mere delving, an ignorant man is but little better than a swine, whom he so much resembles in his appetites, and surpasses in his powers of mischief.

123 WILLIAM JAMES

FROM *Pragmatism (1907)*

The pragmatic method is primarily a method of settling metaphysical disputes that otherwise might be interminable. Is the world one or many? – fated or free? – material or spiritual? – here are notions either of which may or may not hold good of the world; and disputes over such notions are unending. The pragmatic method in such cases is to try to interpret each notion by tracing its respective practical consequences. What difference would it practically make to any one if this notion rather than that notion were true? If no practical difference whatever can be traced, then the alternatives mean practically the same thing, and all dispute is idle. Whenever a dispute is serious, we ought to be able to show some practical difference that must follow from one side or the other's being right.

A glance at the history of the idea will show you still better what pragmatism means. The term is derived from the same Greek word πραγμα, meaning action, from which our words "practice" and "practical" come. It was first introduced into philosophy by Mr. Charles Peirce in 1878. In an article entitled "How to Make Our Ideas Clear," in the "Popular Science Monthly" for January of that year, Mr. Peirce, after pointing out that our beliefs are really rules for action, said that, to develop a thought's meaning, we need only determine what conduct it is fitted to produce: that conduct is for us its sole significance. And the tangible fact at the root of all our thought-distinctions, however subtle, is that there is no one of them so fine as to consist in anything but a possible difference of practice. To attain perfect clearness in our thoughts of an object, then, we need only consider what conceivable effects of a practical kind the object may involve – what sensations we are to expect from it, and what reactions we must prepare. . . .

It is astonishing to see how many philosophical disputes collapse into insignificance the moment you subject them to this simple test of tracing a concrete consequence. There can *be* no difference anywhere that doesn't *make* a difference elsewhere – no difference in abstract truth that doesn't express itself in a difference in concrete fact and in conduct consequent upon that fact, imposed on somebody, somehow, somewhere, and somewhen. The whole function of philosophy ought to be to find out what definite difference it will make to you and me, at definite instants of our life, if this world-formula or that world-formula be the true one. . . .

Pragmatism represents a perfectly familiar attitude in philosophy, the empiricist attitude, but it represents it, as it seems to me, both in a more radical and in a less objectionable form than it has ever yet assumed. A pragmatist turns his back resolutely and once for all upon a lot of inveterate habits dear to professional philosophers. He turns away from abstraction and insufficiency, from verbal solutions, from bad *a priori* reasons, from fixed principles, closed systems, and pretended absolutes and origins. He turns towards concreteness and adequacy, towards facts, towards action and towards power. That means the empiricist temper regnant and the rationalist temper sincerely given up. It means the open air and possibilities of nature, as against dogma, artificiality, and the pretence of finality in truth.

At the same time it does not stand for any special results. It is a method only. But the general triumph of that method would mean an enormous change in what I called in my last lecture the "temperament" of philosophy. Teachers of the ultra-rationalistic type would be frozen out, much as the courtier type is frozen out in republics, as the ultramontane type of priest is frozen out in protestant lands. Science and metaphysics would come much nearer together, would in fact work absolutely hand in hand. . . .

Theories thus become instruments, not answers to enigmas, in which we can rest. We don't lie back upon them, we move forward, and, on occasion, make nature over again by their aid. Pragmatism unstiffens all our theories, limbers them up and sets each one at work. Being nothing essentially new, it harmonizes with many ancient philosophic tendencies. It agrees with nominalism for instance, in always appealing to particulars; with utilitarianism in emphasizing practical aspects; with positivism in its disdain for verbal solutions, useless questions and metaphysical abstractions.

124 JANE ADDAMS

FROM *Twenty Years at Hull House (1910)*

The Ethical Culture Societies held a summer school at Plymouth, Massachusetts, in 1892, to which they invited several people representing the then new Settlement movement, that they might discuss with others the general theme of Philanthropy and Social Progress.

I venture to produce here parts of a lecture I delivered in Plymouth, both because I have found it impossible to formulate with the same freshness those early motives and strivings, and because, when published with other papers given that summer, it was received by the Settlement people themselves as a satisfactory statement . . .:

In a thousand voices singing the Hallelujah Chorus in Handel's "Messiah," it is possible to distinguish the leading voices, but the differences of training and cultivation between them and the voices of the chorus, are lost in the unity of purpose and in the fact that they are all human voices lifted by a high motive. This is a weak illustration of what a Settlement attempts to do. It aims, in a measure, to develop whatever of social life its neighborhood may afford, to focus and give form to that life, to bring to bear upon it the results of cultivation and training; but it receives in exchange for the music of isolated voices the volume and strength of the chorus. It is quite impossible for me to say in what proportion or degree the subjective necessity which led to the opening of Hull-House combined the three trends: first, the desire to interpret democracy in social terms; secondly, the impulse beating at the very source of our lives, urging us to aid in the race progress; and, thirdly, the Christian movement toward humanitarianism. It is difficult to analyze a living thing; the analysis is at best imperfect. Many more motives may blend with the three trends; possibly the desire for a new form of social success due to the nicety of imagination, which refuses worldly pleasures unmixed with the joys of self-sacrifice; possibly a love of approbation, so vast that it is not content with the treble clapping of delicate hands, but wishes also to hear the bass notes from toughened palms, may mingle with these.

The Settlement, then, is an experimental effort to aid in the solution of the social and industrial problems which are engendered by the modern conditions of life in a great city. It insists that these problems are not confined to any one portion of a city. It is an attempt to relieve, at the same time, the over-accumulation at one end of society and the destitution at the other; but it assumes that this overaccumulation and destitution is most sorely felt in the things that pertain to social and educational advantages. From its very nature it can stand for no political or social propaganda. It must, in a sense, give the warm welcome of an inn to all such propaganda, if perchance one of them be found an angel. The one thing to be dreaded in the Settlement is that it lose its flexibility, its power of quick adaptation, its readiness to change its methods as its environment may demand. It must be open to conviction and must have a deep and abiding sense of tolerance. It must be hospitable and ready for experiment. It should demand from its residents a scientific patience in the accumulation of facts and the steady holding of their sympathies as one of the best instruments for that accumulation. It must be grounded in a philosophy whose foundation is on the solidarity of the human race, a philosophy which will not waver when the race happens to be represented by a drunken woman or an idiot boy. Its residents must be emptied of all conceit of opinion and all self-assertion, and ready to arouse and interpret the public opinion of their neighborhood. They must be content to live quietly side by side with their neighbors, until they grow into a sense of relationship and mutual interests. Their neighbors are held apart by differences of race and language which the residents can more easily overcome. They are bound to see the needs of their neighborhood as a whole, to furnish data for legislation, and to use their influence to secure it. In short, residents are pledged to devote themselves to the duties of good citizenhip and to the arousing of the social energies which too largely lie dormant in every neighborhood given over to industrialism. They are bound to regard the entire life of their city as organic, to make an effort to unify it, and to protest against its over-differentiation.

It is always easy to make all philosophy point one particular moral and all history adorn one particular tale; but I may be forgiven the reminder that the best speculative philosophy sets forth the solidarity of the human race; that the highest moralists have taught that without the advance and improvement of the whole, no man can hope for any lasting improvement in his own moral or material individual condition; and that the subjective necessity for Social Settlements is therefore identical with that necessity, which urges us on toward social and individual salvation.

125 BRUCE BARTON

FROM *"Christ as a Businessman"* (1925)

The little boy's body sat bolt upright in the rough wooden chair, but his mind was very busy.

This was his weekly hour of revolt.

The kindly lady who could never seem to find her glasses would have been terribly shocked if she had known what was going on inside the little boy's mind.

"You must love Jesus," she said every Sunday, "and God."

The little boy did not say anything. He was afraid to say anything; he was almost afraid that something would happen to him because of the things he thought.

Love God! Who was always picking on people for having a good time, and sending little boys to hell because they couldn't do better in a world which he had made so hard! Why didn't God take some one his own size?

Love Jesus! The little boy looked up at the picture which hung on the Sunday-school wall. It showed a pale young man with flabby forearms and a sad expression. The young man had red whiskers.

Then the little boy looked across to the other wall. There was Daniel, good old Daniel, standing off the lions. The little boy liked Daniel. He liked David, too, with the trusty sling that landed a stone square on the forehead of Goliath. And Moses, with his rod and his big brass snake. They were winners – those three. He wondered if David could whip Jeffries. Samson could! Say, that would have been a fight!

But Jesus! Jesus was the "lamb of God." The little boy did not know what that meant, but it sounded like Mary's little lamb. Something for girls – sissified. Jesus was also "meek and lowly," a "man of sorrow and acquainted with grief." He went around for three years telling people not to do things.

Sunday was Jesus' day; it was wrong to feel comfortable or laugh on Sunday.

The little boy was glad when the superintendent thumped the bell and announced: "We will now sing the closing hymn." One more bad hour was over. For one more week the little boy had got rid of Jesus.

Years went by and the boy grew up and became a business man. He began to wonder about Jesus.

He said to himself "Only strong magnetic men inspire great enthusiasm and build great organizations. Yet Jesus built the greatest organization of all. It is extraordinary."

The more sermons the man heard and the more books he read the more mystified he became.

One day he decided to wipe his mind clean of books and sermons. He said, "I will read what the men who knew Jesus personally said about him. I will read about him as though he were a new historical character, about whom I had never heard anything at all."

The man was amazed.

A physical weakling! Where did they get that idea? Jesus pushed a plane and swung an adze; he was a successful carpenter. He slept outdoors and spent his days walking around his favorite lake. His muscles were so strong that when he drove the money-changers out, nobody dared to oppose him!

A kill joy! He was the most popular dinner guest in Jerusalem! The criticism which proper people made was that he spent too much time with publicans and sinners (very good fellows, on the whole, the man thought) and enjoyed society too much. They called him a "wine bibber and a gluttonous man."

A failure! He picked up twelve men from the bottom ranks of business and forged them into an organization that conquered the world. When the man had finished his reading he exclaimed, "This is a man nobody knows."

"Some day," said he, "some one will write a book about Jesus. Every business man will read it and send it to his partners and his salesmen. For it will tell the story of the founder of modern business."

So the man waited for some one to write the book, but no one did. Instead, more books were published about the "lamb of God" who was weak and unhappy and glad to die.

The man became impatient. One day he said, "I believe I will try to write that book, myself."

And he did. . . .

HIS METHOD

Many leaders have dared to lay out ambitious programs, but this is the most daring of all:

"Go ye into all the world," Jesus said, "and preach the gospel to *the whole creation*."

Consider the sublime audacity of that command. To carry Roman civilization across the then known world had cost millions of lives and billions in treasure. To create any sort of reception for a new idea or product to-day involves a vast machinery of propaganda and expense. Jesus had no funds and no machinery. His organization was a tiny group of uneducated men, one of whom had already abandoned the cause as hopeless, deserting to the enemy. He had come proclaiming a Kingdom and was to end upon a cross; yet he dared to talk of conquering all creation. What was the source of his faith in that handful of followers? By what methods had he trained them? What had they learned from him of the secrets of influencing men?

We speak of the law of "supply and demand," but the words have got turned around. With anything which is not a basic necessity the supply always precedes the demand. Elias Howe invented the sewing machine, but it nearly rusted away before American women could be persuaded to use it. With their sewing finished so quickly what would they ever do with their spare time? Howe had vision, and had made his vision come true; but he could not sell! So his biographer paints a tragic picture – the man who had done more than any other in his generation to lighten the labor of women is forced to attend the funeral of the woman he loved in a borrowed suit of clothes! . . .

What were his methods of training? How did he meet prospective believers? How did he deal with objections? By what sort of strategy did he interest and persuade? . . .

He was making the journey back from Jerusalem after his spectacular triumph in cleansing the Temple, when he came to Jacob's Well, and being tired, sat down. His disciples had stopped behind at one of the villages to purchase food, so he was alone. The well furnished the water-supply for the neighboring city of the Samaritans, and after a little time a woman came out to it, carrying her pitcher on her shoulder. Between her people, the Samaritans, and his people, the Jews, there was a feud of centuries. To be touched by even the shadow of a Samaritan was defilement according to the strict code of the Pharisees; to speak to one was a crime. The woman made no concealment of her resentment at finding him there. Almost any remark from his lips would have kindled her anger. She would at least have turned away in scorn; she might have summoned her relatives and driven him off

An impossible situation, you will admit. How could he meet it? How give his message to one who was forbidden by everything holy to listen? The incident is very revealing: there are times when any word is the wrong word; when only silence can prevail. Jesus knew well his precious secret. As the woman drew closer he made no move to indicate that he was conscious of her approach. His gaze was on the ground. When he spoke it was quietly, musingly, as if to himself.

"If you knew who I am," he said, "you would not need to come out here for water. I would give you living water."

The woman stopped short, her interest challenged in spite of herself; she set down the pitcher and looked at the stranger. It was a burning hot day; the well was far from the city; she was heated and tired. What did he mean by such a remark? She started to speak, checked herself and burst out impulsively, her curiosity overleaping her caution:

"What are you talking about? Do you mean to say you are greater than our father Jacob who gave us this well? Have you some magic that will save us this long walk in the sun?"

Dramatic, isn't it – a single sentence achieving triumph, arousing interest and creating desire. With sure instinct he followed up his initial advantage. He began to talk to her in terms of her own life, her ambitions, her hopes, knowing so well that each of us is interested first of all and most of all in himself. When the disciples came up a few minutes later they found an unbelievable sight – a Samaritan listening with rapt attention to the teaching of a Jew . . .

Surely no one will consider us lacking in reverence if we say that every one of the "principles of modern salesmanship" on which business men so much pride themselves, is brilliantly exemplified in Jesus' talk and work. The first of these and perhaps the most important is the necessity for "putting yourself in step with your prospect." . . .

THE FOUNDER OF MODERN BUSINESS

When Jesus was twelve years old his father and mother took him to the Feast at Jerusalem.

It was the big national vacation; even peasant families saved their pennies and looked forward to it through the year. Towns like Nazareth were emptied of their inhabitants except for the few old folks who were left behind to look after the very young ones. Crowds of cheerful pilgrims filled the highways, laughing their way across the hills and under the stars at night.

In such a mass of folk it was not surprising that a boy of twelve should be lost. When Mary and Joseph missed him on the homeward trip, they took it calmly and began a search among the relatives.

The inquiry produced no result. Some remembered having seen him in the Temple, but no one had seen him since. . . .

Mary stepped forward and grasped his arm.

"Son, why hast thou thus dealt with us?" she demanded. "Behold thy father and I have sought thee sorrowing."

"How is it that ye sought me?" he asked. "Wist ye not that I must be about my father's *business*?" . . .

What interests us most in this one recorded incident of his boyhood is the fact that for the first time he defined the purpose of his career. He did not say, "Wist ye not that I must practise preaching?" or "Wist ye not that I must get ready to meet the arguments of men like these?" The language was quite different, and well worth remembering. "Wist ye not that I must be about my father's *business*?" he said. He thought of his life as *business*. What did he mean by business? To what extent are the principles by which he conducted his business applicable to ours? And if he were among us again, in our highly competitive world, would his business philosophy work?

126 DALE CARNEGIE

FROM *How to Win Friends and Influence People (1936)*

Actions speak louder than words, and a smile says, "I like you. You make me happy. I am glad to see you."

That is why dogs make such a hit. They are so glad to see us that they almost jump out of their skins. So, naturally, we are glad to see them. An insincere grin? No. That doesn't fool anybody. We know it is mechanical and we resent it. I am talking about a real smile, a heart-warming smile, a smile that comes from within, the kind of a smile that will bring a good price in the market place.

The employment manager of a large New York department store told me he would rather hire a sales girl who hadn't finished grade school, if she had a lovely smile, than hire a doctor of philosophy with a sober face. . . .

You don't feel like smiling? Then what? Two things. First, force yourself to smile. If you are alone, force yourself to whistle or hum a tune or sing. Act as if you were already happy, and that will tend to make you happy. Here is the way the late Professor William James of Harvard put it:

"Action seems to follow feeling, but really action and feeling go together, and by regulating the action, which is under the more direct control of the will, we can indirectly regulate the feeling, which is not.

"Thus the sovereign voluntary path to cheerfulness, if our cheerfulness be lost, is to sit up cheerfully and to act and speak as if cheerfulness were already there. . . ."

Everybody in the world is seeking happiness – and there is one sure way to find it. That is by controlling your thoughts. Happiness doesn't depend on outward conditions. It depends on inner conditions.

It isn't what you have or who you are or where you are or what you are doing that makes you happy or unhappy. It is what you think about it. For example, two people may be in the same place, doing the same thing; both may have about an equal amount of money and prestige – and yet one may be miserable and the other happy. Why? Because of a different mental attitude. I saw just as many happy faces among the Chinese coolies sweating and toiling in the devastating heat of China for seven cents a day as I see on Park Avenue.

"Nothing is good or bad," said Shakespeare, "but thinking makes it so."

Abe Lincoln once remarked that "most folks are about as happy as they make up their minds to be." He was right. . . .

Franklin Bettger, former third baseman for the St. Louis Cardinals, and now one of the most successful insurance men in America, told me that he figured out years ago that a man with a smile is always welcome. So, before entering a man's office, he always pauses for an instant and thinks of the many things he has to be thankful for, works up a great big honest-to-goodness smile, and then enters the room with the smile just vanishing from his face.

This simple technique, he believes, has had much to do with his extraordinary success in selling insurance. . . .

IN A NUTSHELL

Six Ways to Make People Like You

RULE 1: Become genuinely interested in other people.

RULE 2: Smile.

RULE 3: Remember that a man's name is to him the sweetest and most important sound in any language.

RULE 4: Be a good listener. Encourage others to talk about themselves.

RULE 5: Talk in terms of the other man's interest.

RULE 6: Make the other person feel important – and do it sincerely.

127 FRANKLIN D. ROOSEVELT

State of the Union Address (January 6, 1941)

Mr. President, Mr. Speaker, Members of the Seventy-seventh Congress:

I address you, the Members of the Seventy-seventh Congress, at a moment unprecedented in the history of the Union. I use the word "unprecedented," because at no previous time has American security been as seriously threatened from without as it is today.

Since the permanent formation of our Government under the Constitution, in 1789, most of the periods of crisis in our history have related to our domestic affairs. Fortunately, only one of these – the four-year War Between the States – ever threatened our national unity. Today, thank God, one hundred and thirty million Americans, in forty-eight States, have forgotten points of the compass in our national unity.

It is true that prior to 1914 the United States often had been disturbed by events in other Continents. We had even engaged in two wars with European nations and in a number of undeclared wars in the West Indies, in the Mediterranean and in the Pacific for the maintenance of American rights and for the principles of peaceful commerce. But in no case had a serious threat been raised against our national safety or our continued independence.

What I seek to convey is the historic truth that the United States as a nation has at all times maintained clear, definite opposition to any attempt to lock us in behind an ancient Chinese wall while the procession of civilization went past. Today, thinking of our children and of their children, we oppose enforced isolation for ourselves or for any other part of the Americas.

That determination of ours, extending over all these years, was proved, for example, during the quarter century of wars following the French Revolution. While the Napoleonic struggles did threaten interests of the United States because of the French foothold in the West Indies and in Louisiana, and while we engaged in the War of 1812 to vindicate our right to peaceful trade, it is nevertheless clear that neither France nor Great Britain, nor any other nation, was aiming at domination of the whole world.

In like fashion from 1815 to 1914 – ninety-nine years – no single war in Europe or in Asia constituted a real threat against our future or against the future of any other American nation.

Except in the Maximilian interlude in Mexico, no foreign power sought to establish itself in this Hemisphere; and the strength of the British fleet in the Atlantic has been a friendly strength. It is still a friendly strength.

Even when the World War broke out in 1914, it seemed to contain only small threat of danger to our own American future. But, as time went on, the American people began to visualize what the downfall of democratic nations might mean to our own democracy.

We need not overemphasize imperfections in the Peace of Versailles. We need not harp on failure of the democracies to deal with problems of world reconstruction. We should remember that the Peace of 1919 was far less unjust than the kind of "pacification" which began even before Munich, and which is being carried on under the new order of tyranny that seeks to spread over every continent today. The American people have unalterably set their faces against that tyranny.

Every realist knows that the democratic way of life is at this moment being directly assailed in every part of the world – assailed either by arms, or by secret spreading of poisonous propaganda by those who seek to destroy unity and promote discord in nations that are still at peace.

During sixteen long months this assault has blotted out the whole pattern of democratic life in an appalling number of independent nations, great and small. The assailants are still on the march, threatening other nations, great and small.

Therefore, as your President, performing my constitutional duty to "give to the Congress information of the state of the Union," I find it, unhappily, necessary to report that the future and the safety of our country and of our democracy are overwhelmingly involved in events far beyond our borders.

Armed defense of democratic existence is now being gallantly waged in four continents. If that defense fails, all the population and all the resources of Europe, Asia, Africa and Australasia will be dominated by the conquerors. Let us remember that the total of those populations and their resources in those four continents greatly exceeds the sum total of the population and the resources of the whole of the Western Hemisphere – many times over.

In times like these it is immature – and incidentally, untrue – for anybody to brag that an unprepared America, single-handed, and with one hand tied behind its back, can hold off the whole world.

No realistic American can expect from a dictator's peace international generosity, or return of true independence, or world disarmament, or freedom of expression, or freedom of religion – or even good business.

Such a peace would bring no security for us or for our neighbors. "Those, who would give up essential liberty to purchase a little temporary safety, deserve neither liberty nor safety."

As a nation, we may take pride in the fact that we are soft-hearted; but we cannot afford to be soft-headed.

We must always be wary of those who with sounding brass and a tinkling cymbal preach the "ism" of appeasement.

We must especially beware of that small group of selfish men who would clip the wings of the American eagle in order to feather their own nests.

I have recently pointed out how quickly the tempo of modern warfare could bring into our very midst the physical attack which we must eventually expect if the dictator nations win this war.

There is much loose talk of our immunity from immediate and direct invasion from across the seas. Obviously, as long as the British Navy retains its power, no such danger exists. Even if there were no British Navy, it is not probable that any enemy would be stupid enough to attack us by landing troops in the United States from across thousands of miles of ocean, until it had acquired strategic bases from which to operate.

But we learn much from the lessons of the past years in Europe – particularly the lesson of Norway, whose essential seaports were captured by treachery and surprise built up over a series of years.

The first phase of the invasion of this Hemisphere would not be the landing of regular troops. The necessary strategic points would be occupied by secret agents and their dupes – and great numbers of them are already here, and in Latin America.

As long as the aggressor nations maintain the offensive, they – not we – will choose the time and the place and the method of their attack.

That is why the future of all the American Republics is today in serious danger.

That is why this Annual Message to the Congress is unique in our history.

That is why every member of the Executive Branch of the Government and every member of the Congress faces great responsibility and great accountability.

The need of the moment is that our actions and our policy should be devoted primarily – almost exclusively – to meeting this foreign peril. For all our domestic problems are now a part of the great emergency.

Just as our national policy in internal affairs has been based upon a decent respect for the rights and the dignity of all our fellow men within our gates, so our national policy in foreign affairs has been based on a decent respect for the rights and dignity of all nations, large and small. And the justice of morality must and will win in the end.

Our national policy is this:

First, by an impressive expression of the public will and without regard to partisanship, we are committed to all-inclusive national defense.

Second, by an impressive expression of the public will and without regard to partisanship, we are committed to full support of all those resolute peoples, everywhere, who are resisting aggression and are thereby keeping war away from our Hemisphere. By this support, we express our determination that the democratic cause shall prevail; and we strengthen the defense and the security of our own nation.

Third, by an impressive expression of the public will and without regard to partisanship, we are committed to the proposition that principles of morality and considerations for our own security will never permit us to acquiesce in a peace dictated by aggressors and sponsored by appeasers. We know that enduring peace cannot be bought at the cost of other people's freedom.

In the recent national election there was no substantial difference between the two great parties in respect to that national policy. No issue was fought out on this line before the American electorate. Today it is abundantly evident that American citizens everywhere are demanding and supporting speedy and complete action in recognition of obvious danger.

Therefore, the immediate need is a swift and driving increase in our armament production.

Leaders of industry and labor have responded to our summons. Goals of speed have been set. In some cases these goals are being reached ahead of time; in some cases we are on schedule; in other cases there are slight but not serious delays; and in some cases – and I am sorry to say very important cases – we are all concerned by the slowness of the accomplishment of our plans.

The Army and Navy, however, have made substantial progress during the past year. Actual experience is improving and speeding up our methods of production with every passing day. And today's best is not good enough for tomorrow.

I am not satisfied with the progress thus far made. The men in charge of the program represent the best in training, in ability, and in patriotism. They are not satisfied with the progress thus far made. None of us will be satisfied until the job is done.

No matter whether the original goal was set too high or too low, our objective is quicker and better results. To give you two illustrations:

We are behind schedule in turning out finished airplanes; we are working day and night to solve the innumerable problems and to catch up.

We are ahead of schedule in building warships but we are working to get even further ahead of that schedule.

To change a whole nation from a basis of peacetime production of implements of peace to a basis of wartime production of implements of war is no small task. And the greatest difficulty comes at the beginning of the program, when new tools, new plant facilities, new assembly lines, and new ship ways must first be constructed before the actual materiel begins to flow steadily and speedily from them.

The Congress, of course, must rightly keep itself informed at all times of the progress of the program. However, there is certain information, as the Congress itself will readily recognize, which, in the interests of our own security and those of the nations that we are supporting, must of needs be kept in confidence.

New circumstances are constantly begetting new needs for our safety. I shall ask this Congress for greatly increased new appropriations and authorizations to carry on what we have begun.

I also ask this Congress for authority and for funds sufficient to manufacture additional munitions and war supplies of many kinds, to be turned over to those nations which are now in actual war with aggressor nations.

Our most useful and immediate role is to act as an arsenal for them as well as for ourselves. They do not need manpower, but they do need billions of dollars worth of the weapons of defense.

The time is near when they will not be able to pay for them all in ready cash. We cannot, and we will not, tell them that they must surrender, merely because of present inability to pay for the weapons which we know they must have.

I do not recommend that we make them a loan of dollars with which to pay for these weapons – a loan to be repaid in dollars.

I recommend that we make it possible for those nations to continue to obtain war materials in the United States, fitting their orders into our own program. Nearly all their materiel would, if the time ever came, be useful for our own defense.

Taking counsel of expert military and naval authorities, considering what is best for our own security, we are free to decide how much should be kept here and how much should be sent abroad to our friends who by their determined and heroic resistance are giving us time in which to make ready our own defense.

For what we send abroad, we shall be repaid within a reasonable time following the close of hostilities, in similar materials, or, at our option, in other goods of many kinds, which they can produce and which we need.

Let us say to the democracies: "We Americans are vitally concerned in your defense of freedom. We are putting forth our energies, our resources and our organizing powers to give you the strength to regain and maintain a free world. We shall send you, in ever-increasing numbers, ships, planes, tanks, guns. This is our purpose and our pledge."

In fulfillment of this purpose we will not be intimidated by the threats of dictators that they will regard as a breach of international law or as an act of war our aid to the democracies which dare to resist their aggression. Such aid is not an act of war, even if a dictator should unilaterally proclaim it so to be.

When the dictators, if the dictators, are ready to make war upon us, they will not wait for an act of war on our part. They did not wait for Norway or Belgium or the Netherlands to commit an act of war.

Their only interest is in a new one-way international law, which lacks mutuality in its observance, and, therefore, becomes an instrument of oppression.

The happiness of future generations of Americans may well depend upon how effective and how immediate we can make our aid felt. No one can tell the exact character of the emergency situations that we may be called upon to meet. The Nation's hands must not be tied when the Nation's life is in danger.

We must all prepare to make the sacrifices that the emergency – almost as serious as war itself – demands. Whatever stands in the way of speed and efficiency in defense preparations must give way to the national need.

A free nation has the right to expect full cooperation from all groups. A free nation has the right to look to the leaders of business, of labor, and of agriculture to take the lead in stimulating effort, not among other groups but within their own groups.

The best way of dealing with the few slackers or trouble makers in our midst is, first, to shame them by patriotic example, and, if that fails, to use the sovereignty of Government to save Government.

As men do not live by bread alone, they do not fight by armaments alone. Those who man our defenses, and those behind them who build our defenses, must have the stamina and the courage which come from unshakable belief in the manner of life which they are defending. The mighty action that we are calling for cannot be based on a disregard of all things worth fighting for.

The Nation takes great satisfaction and much strength from the things which have been done to make its people conscious of their individual stake in the preservation of democratic life in America. Those things have toughened the fibre of our people, have renewed their faith and strengthened their devotion to the institutions we make ready to protect.

Certainly this is no time for any of us to stop thinking about the social and economic problems which are the root cause of the social revolution which is today a supreme factor in the world.

For there is nothing mysterious about the foundations of a healthy and strong democracy. The basic things expected by our people of their political and economic systems are simple. They are:

Equality of opportunity for youth and for others.

Jobs for those who can work.

Security for those who need it.

The ending of special privilege for the few.

The preservation of civil liberties for all.

The enjoyment of the fruits of scientific progress in a wider and constantly rising standard of living.

These are the simple, basic things that must never be lost sight of in the turmoil and unbelievable complexity of our modern world. The inner and abiding strength of our economic and political systems is dependent upon the degree to which they fulfill these expectations.

Many subjects connected with our social economy call for immediate improvement. As examples:

We should bring more citizens under the coverage of old-age pensions and unemployment insurance.

We should widen the opportunities for adequate medical care.

We should plan a better system by which persons deserving or needing gainful employment may obtain it.

I have called for personal sacrifice. I am assured of the willingness of almost all Americans to respond to that call.

A part of the sacrifice means the payment of more money in taxes. In my Budget Message I shall recommend that a greater portion of this great defense program be paid for from taxation than we are paying today. No person should try, or be allowed, to get rich out of this program; and the principle of tax payments in accordance with ability to pay should be constantly before our eyes to guide our legislation.

If the Congress maintains these principles, the voters, putting patriotism ahead of pocketbooks, will give you their applause.

In the future days, which we seek to make secure, we look forward to a world founded upon four essential human freedoms.

The first is freedom of speech and expression – everywhere in the world.

The second is freedom of every person to worship God in his own way – everywhere in the world.

The third is freedom from want – which, translated into world terms, means economic understandings which will secure to every nation a healthy peacetime life for its inhabitants – everywhere in the world.

The fourth is freedom from fear – which, translated into world terms, means a world-wide reduction of armaments to such a point and in such a thorough fashion that no nation will be in a position to commit an act of physical aggression against any neighbor – anywhere in the world.

That is no vision of a distant millennium. It is a definite basis for a kind of world attainable in our own time and generation. That kind of world is the very antithesis of the so-called new order of tyranny which the dictators seek to create with the crash of a bomb.

To that new order we oppose the greater conception – the moral order. A good society is able to face schemes of world domination and foreign revolutions alike without fear.

Since the beginning of our American history, we have been engaged in change – in a perpetual peaceful revolution – a revolution which goes on steadily, quietly adjusting itself to changing conditions – without the concentration camp or the quicklime in the ditch. The world order which we seek is the cooperation of free countries, working together in a friendly, civilized society.

This nation has placed its destiny in the hands and heads and hearts of its millions of free men and women; and its faith in freedom under the guidance of God. Freedom means the supremacy of human rights everywhere. Our support goes to those who struggle to gain those rights or keep them. Our strength is our unity of purpose. To that high concept there can be no end save victory.

128 DWIGHT D. EISENHOWER

"The Military-Industrial Complex" (1961)

A vital element in keeping the peace is our military establishment. Our arms must be mighty, ready for instant action, so that no potential aggressor may be tempted to risk his own destruction.

Our military organization today bears little relation to that known by any of my predecessors in peacetime, or indeed by the fighting men of World War II or Korea.

Until the latest of our world conflicts, the United States had no armaments industry. American makers of plowshares could, with time and as required, make swords as well. But now we can no longer risk emergency improvisation of national defense; we have been compelled to create a permanent armaments industry of vast proportions.

Added to this, three and a half million men and women are directly engaged in the defense establishment. We annually spend on military security more than the net income of all United States corporations.

This conjunction of an immense military establishment and a large arms industry is new in the American experience. The total influence – economic, political, even spiritual – is felt in every city, every state house, every office of the federal government.

We recognize the imperative need for this development. Yet we must not fail to comprehend its grave implications. Our toil, resources and livelihood are all involved; so is the very structure of our society.

In the councils of government, we must guard against the acquisition of unwarranted influence, whether sought or unsought, by the military-industrial complex. The potential for the disastrous rise of misplaced power exists and will persist.

We must never let the weight of this combination endanger our liberties or democratic processes. We should take nothing for granted. Only an alert and knowledgeable citizenry can compel the proper meshing of the huge industrial and military machinery of defense with our peaceful methods and goals, so that security and liberty may prosper together.

Akin to, and largely responsible for the sweeping changes in our industrial-military posture, has been the technological revolution during the recent decades. In this revolution, research has become central; it also becomes more formalized, complex and costly. A steadily increasing share is conducted for, by or at the direction of, the federal government.

The solitary inventor, tinkering in his shop, has been overshadowed by task forces of scientists in laboratories and testing fields. In the same fashion, the free university, historically the fountainhead of free ideas and scientific discovery, has experienced a revolution in the conduct of research. Partly because of the huge costs involved, a government contract becomes virtually a substitute for intellectual curiosity. For every old blackboard there are now hundreds of new electronic computers.

The prospect of domination of the nation's scholars by federal employment, project allocations and the power of money is ever present – and is gravely to be regarded. Yet, in holding scientific research and discovery in respect, as we should, we must also be alert to the equal and opposite danger that public policy could itself become the captive of a scientific-technological elite.

It is the task of statesmanship to mold, to balance and to integrate these and other forces, new and old, within the principles of our democratic system – ever aiming toward the supreme goals of our free society.

129 STUDS TERKEL

from *"Jay Slabaugh, 48" (Interview with a Corporate Executive, 1980)*

I sometimes think of myself as a hired gun. I come into a company and correct the problem, then go on to another company. . . .

You must be aggressive. I've always had the feeling that if you don't go up, you go down. Nothing ever stays the same. You get better and bigger, or you go the other way.

My feeling is everybody in business is against you. Everybody in the world is against you. Your people are against you because they want more money for less hours than you can afford to pay them. Your suppliers are against you because they want more money for the product than you can afford to give them. Your customers are against you because they want your product for less money than you can afford to sell it. The city is against you because they want to tax you more. The federal government is against you because they want to control you more. The parent company is against you because they want to take more cash out of your operation and don't want to put the cash investment into it. When anybody gets in the way of your being a vital, growing force in the economy, they're hurting themselves and everybody around them.

Let's face it. If we don't grow and get more profit, there isn't more money for raises, there aren't promotions for people. If you don't grow, you don't buy more products from your suppliers. You don't have new machines, so you don't give more and better products to your customers. There's not more income for the government to tax. I can make a case of hurting God because there isn't more money for the collection plate. (Laughs.)

The American Dream is to be better off than you are. How much money is "enough money"? "Enough money" is always a little bit more than you have. There's never enough of anything. This is why people go on. If there was enough, everybody would stop. You always go for the brass ring that's always out there about a hundred yards farther. It's like a mirage in the desert: it always stays about a hundred yards ahead of you.

If I had more, if the company had more, I could accomplish much more. I could do more good for the economy. You must go for more – for faster, for better. If you're not getting better and faster, you're getting worse.

(Reflectively) Growth – better – faster. I guess that's my one big vice. I feel a very heavy sense of compulsion, a sense of urgency. When I get in a car, I also feel it. I drive much too fast. I'm always moving.

130 RUSH H. LIMBAUGH, III

FROM *See, I Told You So (1993)*

You hold in your hot little hands, my friends, America's next great publishing milestone. Soon, *See, I Told You So* will eclipse all publishing records known in the English-speaking world – most of which, by the way, were set by my first tome, *The Way Things Ought to Be*.

But this book was never supposed to be. In fact, the conventional wisdom was that after the 1992 election, I was just going to fade away into obscurity – a relic of a Republican era of greed and selfishness. They said there would be no room for me in the Age of Compassion that would assuredly be dawning come January 20, 1993.

Well, once again, the "experts" were wrong. Dead wrong. Not only did the Rush Limbaugh radio program soar to new, previously uncharted heights in the annals of Marconi's invention, but my television show also became the nation's hottest new late-night program. *The Limbaugh Letter*, my stellar journal of opinion, became what is arguably the most successful start-up publication in history. . . .

Our country is inherently evil. The whole idea of America is corrupt. The history of this nation is strewn with examples of oppression and genocide. The story of the United States is cultural imperialism – how a bunch of repressed white men imposed their will and values on peaceful indigenous people, black slaves from Africa, and women.

No, don't worry. Rush has not become a commie-lib. The paragraph above, though, does summarize what is being taught today about American history on the average college or university campus. Why? What makes the education establishment so hostile to America? Because, in the last twenty-five years, a relatively small, angry group of anti-American radicals have bullied their way into power positions in academia. And while they preach about the evils of "cultural imperialism," they themselves are, ironically, the ultimate practitioners of it.

The indoctrination taking place today in American academia is disingenuously disguised as "multiculturalism" by its academic purveyors. A more accurate description would be "politically motivated historical and cultural distortion." It is a primitive type of historical revisionism. . . .

Let's start at the beginning with America's first important dead white male – Christopher Columbus. The politically correct view of old Chris today is that the Italian explorer did not actually discover America, because people were already living here. And, more important, he brought nothing to the peaceful New World "paradise" but oppression, disease, brutality, and genocide.

First of all, let me state something unequivocally: *Columbus really did discover America.* By making that claim, I am obviously not suggesting that no human being had set foot on the continent before 1492. But there can be no denying that Columbus was the person who brought America to the attention of the technologically advanced, civilized world and paved the way for the expansion of Western civilization (what a horrifying thought). . . .

This brings us to our Founding Fathers – the geniuses who crafted the Declaration of Independence and the U.S. Constitution. These were men who shook up the entire world by proclaiming the idea that people had certain God-given freedoms and rights and that the government's only raison d'être was to protect those freedoms and rights from both internal and external forces. That simple yet brilliant insight has been all but lost today in liberalism's relentless march toward bigger, more powerful, more intrusive government.

Don't believe the conventional wisdom of our day that claims these men were anything but orthodox, Bible-believing Christians. They were. And they were quite adamant in stating that the Constitution – as brilliant a document as it is – would work only in the context of a moral society.

"Our Constitution was made for a moral and religious people," stated second president John Adams. "It is wholly inadequate for the governance of any other."

George Washington, the father of our country, was of like mind. He said: "Of all the dispositions and habits that lead to political prosperity, religion and morality are indispensable supports."

James Madison, primary author of the Constitution, agreed: "We have staked the whole future of the American civilization, not upon the power of government, far from it. We have staked the future . . . upon the capacity of each and all of us to govern ourselves, to control ourselves, to sustain ourselves, according to the Ten Command-ments of God.". . .

You can't fully appreciate how screwed up modern liberalism is without contrasting its vision (or lack thereof) with the broad view of our nation's founders. Americans throughout history – from the earliest settlers to the generation that fought World War

II – have always understood and accepted sacrifice. They intuitively knew there were things worth dying for.

The early pioneers tamed a wilderness. Nothing was handed to them. And they sought only freedom and a better life for their children. Today, government is taking away our freedom and mortgaging with debt the future lives of our children. But not to worry. Government is more than willing to provide you with food stamps, welfare payments, unemployment benefits, day care, socialized medicine, free condoms, subsidized abortions – you name it. Can't you see how the vision has been turned upside down?

The founders knew they were bestowing upon us only an ingenious political system of checks and balances, limited government, and a legacy of human and civil rights. It would be up to future generations to make it all work. But it would only work, they warned (reread the quotes from Adams, Washington, and Madison . . .), if the society was girded on a bedrock of solid values and Judeo-Christian principles.

Where and how did we lose our moorings? With such a great start, why did we allow liberalism, moral relativism, and secular humanism to poison our nation's soul? And what can we do to recapture the original American spirit of freedom and individualism?

American Civilization

An introduction

4th edition

David Mauk and John Oakland

Thoroughly revised, this fourth edition of a hugely successful text provides students of American studies with the perfect background and introductory information on contemporary American life.

Brought up to date with new illustrations and case studies, the book examines the second Gulf War, the War on Terror and the 2004 Presidential election.

Like its three excellent predecessors, this new edition covers all the central dimensions of American society from geography and the environment, government and politics to religion, education, media and the arts.

American Civilization:

- covers all core American studies topics at introductory level
- contains essential historical background for American studies students at the start of the twenty-first century
- analyzes gender, class and race, and America's cosmopolitan population
- includes photos, case studies, questions and terms for discussion, and suggests websites for further research.

This text enables all students of American studies to lay solid and sound foundations in their degree course studies.

ISBN: 978–0–415–35830–9 (hbk)
ISBN: 978–0–415–35831–6 (pbk)

Available at all good bookshops
For ordering and further information please visit:
www.routledge.com

American Cultural Studies

An introduction to American culture

2nd edition

Neil Campbell and Alasdair Kean

This update of *American Cultural Studies* takes into account the developments of the last seven years, providing an introduction to the central themes in modern American culture and exploring how these themes can be interpreted.

Campbell and Kean discuss the various aspects of American cultural life such as religion, gender and sexuality, regionalism, and updates and revisions include:

- a new introduction engaging with current debates in the field
- an all-new chapter on foreign policy
- thorough discussion of globalization and Americanization
- new case studies
- updated further-reading lists.

A refreshing and contemporary update of a staple text in American studies.

ISBN: 978–0–415–34665–8 (hbk)
ISBN: 978–0–415–34666–5 (pbk)

Available at all good bookshops
For ordering and further information please visit:
www.routledge.com

The Routledge Atlas of American History

5th edition

Martin Gilbert

This new edition of *The Routledge Atlas of American History* presents a series of 157 clear and detailed maps, accompanied by informative captions, facts and figures. Updated with additional maps and text and including significant recent events, the complete history of America is unravelled through vivid representations of all the significant landmarks, including:

- politics – from the annexation of Texas to the battle for black voting rights and the results of the 2004 Presidential election
- military events – from the War of Independence and America's standing in two world wars to the conflicts in Korea, Vietnam and the Gulf, includes new maps covering the war in Iraq, the American campaign in Afghanistan and the War on Terror
- social history – from the abolition of slavery to the growth of female emancipation
- transport – from nineteenth-century railroads and canals to recent ventures into space
- economics – from early farming and industry to the state of America today.

The history of North America from early settlement to the present day is presented to students and enthusiasts of the subject in this fundamental reference book.

ISBN: 978–0–415–35902–3 (hbk)
ISBN: 978–0–415–35903–0 (pbk)

Available at all good bookshops
For ordering and further information please visit:
www.routledge.com